THE RESTORATION
OF ROME

Also by Peter Heather

THE FALL OF THE ROMAN EMPIRE

EMPIRES AND BARBARIANS

PETER HEATHER

THE RESTORATION
OF ROME

Barbarian Popes & Imperial Pretenders

MACMILLAN

First published 2013 by Macmillan
an imprint of Pan Macmillan, a division of Macmillan Publishers Limited
Pan Macmillan, 20 New Wharf Road, London N1 9RR
Basingstoke and Oxford
Associated companies throughout the world
www.panmacmillan.com

ISBN 978-0-230-70015-4

1 3 5 7 9 8 6 4 2

A CIP catalogue record for this book is available from the British Library.

Maps artwork by ML Design
Typeset by SetSystems Ltd, Saffron Walden, Essex
Printed and bound by CPI Group (UK) Ltd, Croydon, CR0 4YY

FOR ANITA HOLM SAWYER

CONTENTS

List of Illustrations ix

List of Maps and Figures xi

PROLOGUE *xiii*

PART ONE

'A COPY OF THE ONLY EMPIRE'

1. GENS PURPURA
3

2. A PHILOSOPHER IN PURPLE
52

PART TWO

'THE CONQUEROR OF MANY NATIONS'

3. 'BY THE AUTHORITY OF GOD'
105

4. SAILING TO BYZANTIUM
154

PART THREE

THE FATHER OF EUROPE

5. CHRISTMAS DAY, 800
207

6. 'THE CENTRE CANNOT HOLD'
248

PART FOUR

SECOND COMING

7. CHARLES THE GREAT AND LEO THE POPE
299
8. *HABEMUS PAPAM*: PAPAL LIFT-OFF
349

EPILOGUE: THE GODFATHER (PART 3) 405

NOTES 415

PRIMARY SOURCES 439

BIBLIOGRAPHY 441

ACKNOWLEDGEMENTS 457

INDEX 459

List of Illustrations

1. Mosaic of Theoderic from St Apollinare Nuovo in Ravenna. (Bridgeman)
2. Eagle brooches from the Apahida treasure. (Bridgeman)
3. Coin of the Emperor Zeno. (Bridgeman)
4. The Walls of Constantinople. (Bridgeman)
5. The Emperor Anastasius portrayed in ivory. (AKG)
6. Mosaic of Theoderic's Palace from St Apollinare Nuovo. (AKG)
7. Theoderic's mausoleum, following Roman imperial models, at Ravenna. (AKG)
8. Theoderic on the Senigallia Medallion. (Bridgeman)
9. Baptism of Christ from the so-called Arian Bapistry in Ravenna. (Bridgeman)
10. Justinian and his court in the famous mosaic from the Church of San Vitale in Ravenna. (Bridgeman)
11. Theodora as portrayed in San Vitale. (Bridgeman)
12. Justinian's great church of Hagia Sofia in Istanbul. (Bridgeman)
13. The Harbour of Carthage, capital of the Vandals' North African kingdom. (Bridgeman)
14. The *Corpus Iuris Civilis*. (Bridgeman)
15. The Iron Crown of Lombardy. (Bridgeman)
16. Charlemagne's reliquary from Aachen. (Bridgeman)
17. A copy of Pope Leo's famous mosaic, portraying both Charlemagne and the Pope as subordinate to St Peter. (AKG)
18. The coronation of Louis the Pious. (AKG)
19. Charles the Bald. (AKG)
20. Charles the Bald's Gospel Book of Joshua. (AKG)
21. Carolingian minuscule. (Bridgeman)
22. The Plan of St Gall. (© Stiftsbibliothek, St Gall)
23. The trial of Pope Formosus. (Bridgeman)
24. Leo IX: the greatest of the barbarian Popes and the Patriarch of Constantinople. (Alamy)

25. The death of Leo IX. (Alamy)
26. The Emperor Henry IV and Countess Matilda. (Bridgeman)
27. Gratian's *Decretum*. (Bridgeman)
28. Old St Peter's, Rome. (Bridgeman)
29. Pope Innocent III. (Bridgeman)

List of Maps and Figures

1. Amal Genealogy 10

2. 5th Century Constantinople 16

3. Theoderic's Goths in the East Roman Balkans 31

4. Theoderic's Western Empire c. 511 57

5. Justiniana Prima/Caricingrad 106

6. East Rome and Persia in the 6th Century 130

7. The Ceremonial Centre of Constantinople 134

8. The Conquest of North Africa 148

9. The Conquest of Italy 161

10. The Rise of the Avars 182

11. The Rise of the Franks 210

12. The Rise of the Carolingians 220

13. Italy in the 8th Century 233

14. Carolingian Divisions of the 9th Century with a 6th Century comparison 264–5

15. Major Autonomous Political Units of Latin Christendom in c. 1000 284

16. Carolingian intellectual centres 347

PROLOGUE

On or about 4 September 476, a senior officer of the Roman army of Italy called Odovacar arrested and executed the uncle of the reigning Western emperor Romulus, known as 'Augustulus': the little Augustus. Seven days before, Odovacar had done the same with Romulus' father. The emperor himself was only a child and his father and uncle had been running the empire. Now in charge, Odovacar proved reasonably merciful. Romulus was despatched to live out his days on an estate in Campania. More significantly for the course of European history, Odovacar also induced the Senate of Rome to send an embassy to the East Roman emperor Zeno in Constantinople. This declared that:

> there was no need of a divided rule and that one, shared emperor
> was sufficient for both [Eastern and Western imperial] territories.

It was soon followed by a further embassy which took to Constantinople the imperial vestments of the West, including the imperial cloak and diadem which it was treason for anyone but the emperor to wear. Although he maintained the fiction of Zeno's imperial sovereignty, Odovacar had not the slightest intention in practice of allowing Constantinople to interfere in the affairs of the Italian-based state that he now ran. Odovacar's two embassies brought to an end an imperial tradition based on Rome which stretched back nearly 750 years.[1]

But Odovacar's deposition of Romulus Augustulus was no more than a *coup de grâce*. The western half of the Roman Empire had been killed off progressively over the three previous political generations, as a remarkable revolution in the balance of strategic power worked itself out across the broader European land mass. Apart from some very early successes, such as the capture of Sicily in the third century BC, the bulk of the Roman Empire had been acquired in the two centuries either side of the birth of Christ. This was an era when non-Mediterranean Europe was subdivided into three broad geographical regions – west and south, north-central, and north and east – each home to human societies which were operating at strikingly different levels of development. Levels of food production, population density, economic complexity, settlement size and scales of political organization: all of these were much higher in La Tene Europe to the west and south, and fell off substantially as you moved east and north through the other two zones. During this crucial 200 years of empire-building, Rome's Mediterranean heartlands provided sufficient economic and demographic resources, combined with a formidable military organization, to conquer all of the European land mass which was worth conquering. In practice, only the west and south offered post-conquest receipts and sufficient spoils of war to justify large-scale campaigning, and it was on its far borders that the legions' hobnails came to a halt.

Human ambition being what it is, though, efforts were also made to subdue parts of the central zone, largely dominated by Germanic-speaking populations, and it is often thought that Arminius' great victory over a Roman army in the Teutoburg Forest in AD 9 put a stop to the process. Reality is more prosaic. Further Roman campaigns destroyed Arminius subsequently, and it was really the logic of an imperial cost-benefit equation which meant that Rome eventually allowed its frontier to coagulate on the river Rhine and not push it on further to the east. At the start of the first millennium, the north-central zone was not worth the costs of conquest, while outer Europe, the third zone to the north and east, never even figured on the imperial radar.

Over the next 400 years, however – above all because of the kick-start provided by interaction with the Roman Empire to everything from economics to political and cultural patterns – an accelerating process of development transformed patterns of life in this central zone. By the mid-fourth century AD, agricultural production had intensified, population densities increased massively, and economic patterns acquired previously unknown complexity. The military capacity of the region as a whole had also grown markedly – not least through the adoption of Roman weaponry – and its political structures had become much more robust. It remained impossible to build large, enduring states within the region because economic and administrative substructures could still not support complex political superstructures, so that Rome, broadly speaking, retained overall strategic control. Nonetheless, by the fourth century AD, the empire was having to run its frontier security by a careful mix of stick and carrot to manage a series of reasonably durable medium-sized client states who now occupied every inch of space beyond the frontier. The old order in the central zone – one of small, sparsely distributed tribal societies – had long gone. These clients may not have threatened the empire's overall existence, but they certainly possessed sufficient political and military capacity to formulate their own medium- to long-term political agendas. And when conditions were in their favour – usually when Rome was at war with Persia – they could even fend off the most intrusive aspects of Roman imperial domination, which took the form of incessant demands for military manpower, foodstuffs, raw materials and, occasionally, even the demand that Christian missionaries be allowed to operate freely. Even if the transformed north-central zone remained too divided politically to pose an overall threat, much of the original demographic and economic advantage – the edge which had allowed Rome's European empire to come into existence half a millennium before – had been undermined by these revolutionary processes of development which had unfolded in between.[2]

My father was an explosives expert, who spent much of his life among dangerous substances. A fundamental safety principle he picked up early on in his training was that wherever human activity created a flammable atmosphere, 'God – i.e. some accident or another – would provide the spark'. In other words, safety had to focus on preventing the build-up of flammable conditions, since trying to guard against sparks was utterly hopeless. In the case of European history, the fundamental transformation of the old north-central zone created a potentially highly flammable political situation – at least as regards the long-term future of Roman imperialism – and the spark eventually came along in the form of the Huns. Exploding on to the fringes of Europe in two stages in the final quarter of the fourth century, the Huns pushed two large mixed blocks of old Roman clients from the transformed north-central region (together with some other groups from much further away) on to imperial territory in two distinct clusters: the first in AD 375–80, and the second a quarter of a century later in 405–10. The first of these moments coincided with the Huns' occupation of lands immediately north of the Black Sea, and the second, in all probability, with their further penetration westwards on to the great Hungarian Plain. In the face of (natural) Roman hostility which saw large numbers of those caught up in the movements either killed or reduced to slavery, the survivors of both immigrant blocks (and many of the original participants had fallen en route) had, by the end of the 410s, reorganized themselves into two new composite groupings on West Roman soil, which were larger and more coherent than anything that had existed on the other side of the frontier in the fourth century: the Visigothic and Vandal–Alan coalitions. Each was composed of at least three major, previously independent, sources of military manpower, and both had evolved more centralized leadership structures to match. They had become larger to survive in the face of Roman counter-attack, and the greater wealth of the Roman world, compared to that beyond the frontier, made it possible for new dynasties to mobilize sufficient resources to maintain themselves in power.

But while the immigrants' initial motivations focused primarily on escaping Hunnic predation, they always had it in mind to benefit from Roman wealth too, and their arrival on imperial soil materially damaged the empire's capacity to survive. Fundamentally, the empire functioned by taxing agricultural production to fund its professional army and other governmental structures. When these new immigrant coalitions forced the Western Empire to recognize their occupation of parts of its territories, this reduced the empire's revenues significantly, and, by direct extension, the size of the armies it could support. And other outsiders not directly threatened by the Huns, such as Anglo-Saxon intruders into southern Britain, were quick to take advantage of the military and political retrenchment that these losses of revenue enforced. Particularly once the Vandal–Alan coalition had captured the Western Empire's richest North African provinces in 439, the Western Empire found itself caught in a vicious circle. Lower troop numbers meant more losses of territory both to the original groups of outsiders (Visigoths and Vandal–Alans), and to new ones (like the Franks), whom the empire's declining military capacity encouraged to come to the party.

Odovacar's coup administered the last rites in this saga of imperial unravelling. He was part of a final set of refugees from the old north-central zone who found their way on to Roman soil as a result of the infighting which followed the collapse of Attila's Hunnic Empire in central Europe in the later 450s and 460s. A prince of the Sciri and son of one of Attila's chief henchmen, he was forced to relocate to Italy when his group's independent position was destroyed. And the military discontent he exploited to mount his *coup d'état* was caused by a shortage of funds within Italy to pay the soldiers he led in revolt. This shortage was a direct result of the loss of tax revenues from the provinces as they progressively fell under the control of outside intruders: the process which forms the central narrative spine of West Roman history in the fifth century. The flow of funds to support the Roman army of Italy progressively dwindled and Odovacar was there to benefit from the resulting unrest. The spark supplied by the Huns set off a strategic explosion which pushed enough of the military manpower of transformed north-central Europe on to Roman soil to undermine the Western Empire's control of its territorial base.[3]

New rulers at the head of politically reasonably coherent bodies of military manpower, which had within living memory originated from beyond the imperial frontier, were now masters of the bulk of the old Roman west. Alongside Odovacar, Anglo-Saxon kings controlled most of central and southern Britain, their Frankish counterparts ran northern and eastern Gaul, Visigothic monarchs controlled south-western Gaul and Spain, Burgundian dynasts the Rhone valley, and the richest lands of Roman North Africa were in the hands of the Vandalic Hasding dynasty (Figure 4). Groups from the old north-central zone of Europe as it had stood at the birth of Christ thus generated a huge revolution on Roman soil, replacing the old monolithic empire with a series of successor states.

An equally profound – if much less documented – revolution then followed in the central zone itself in the century or so after 476, bringing Slavic-speaking groups from the old third zone to the north and east into prominence across much of central and Eastern Europe. This related story cannot be reconstructed in detail, although enough indications survive to make it clear that the creation of Slavic Europe was the aggregate result of a range of complex, diverse and long-drawn-out processes, rather than a sudden revolution. What it does make crystal clear, however, is that the dismantling of the Western Roman Empire has to be seen as part of a total recalibration of prevailing Europe-wide balances of strategic power, equivalent to the kinds of processes working themselves out in our own time, as the regional and global political consequences of the massive expansion of Near Eastern, Asian and some southern economies slowly make themselves clear.[4]

But, in the midst of all this restructuring, the Roman concept of empire not only lived on, but proved remarkably durable. After an astonishing half a millennium of existence (and the British Empire at its maximum extent lasted, by comparison, less than a century), this is perhaps not so surprising. The West Roman imperial superstate may have gone, but in many (though not all) parts of its old territories, Roman provincial populations had survived the eclipse of empire with their social, economic, legal and cultural structures intact. Within these groups, Roman ideas and even some administrative institutions were alive and kicking. Nor, in fact, were the outsiders who had destroyed the empire implacably hostile to all things Roman. Many were its old frontier clients, and they had not mounted their individual takeovers of parcels of Roman territory under the banner of an ideological crusade against imperialism. They had long been used to operating within an overarching Roman framework, and the new leaderships of the successor states in particular could see much that was useful to them in the structures of Roman government, society and culture, as they set about creating a new order from the chaos of collapse.

Picking up the story from Odovacar's fateful embassy which handed over the Western imperial vestments to Constantinople, this sequel to the *Fall of the Roman Empire* tells the story of three great imperial pretenders who attempted to revive the Roman inheritance in Western Europe: Theoderic, Justinian and Charlemagne. Each was astonishingly successful. Coming from entirely dissimilar backgrounds and operating with different power bases constructed in completely diverse contexts, they each managed to put back together enough of the old Roman West to stake a plausible claim to the Western imperial title.

But even as they played out their extraordinary careers, the broader patterns of human life across the European land mass continued to move away from the three-speed pattern which had characterized it at the birth of Christ. As successful as each of these pretenders was in their own right, therefore, circumstances in the second half of the first millennium AD increasingly militated against the possibility of sustaining a durable imperial structure on the kind of scale that the old Western Empire had managed for most of the previous 500 years. In the end, a restoration of stable imperial power on a truly Roman scale proved possible only when fresh blood, from a part of Europe that the old Romans deemed utterly barbaric, used some of the Roman imperial toolkit to generate an entirely new kind of empire. By reinventing the papacy in the eleventh century, Europe's barbarians found the means to establish a new Roman Empire which has so far lasted a thousand years.

PART ONE

'A COPY OF THE ONLY EMPIRE'

1

GENS PURPURA

IN 507 OR THEREABOUTS, the ruler of Italy, Theoderic the Goth, wrote to the Eastern Roman emperor Anastasius in Constantinople:

> You are the fairest ornament of all realms; you are the healthful defence of the whole world, to which all other rulers rightfully look up with reverence, because they know that there is in you something which is unlike all others: we above all, who by Divine help learned in your Republic [Constantinople: Theoderic had spent ten years in the city as a child] the art of governing Romans with equity. Our royalty is an imitation of yours, modelled on your good purpose, a copy of the only Empire; and in so far as we follow you do we excel all other nations.

This is an extraordinary letter. To Romans of any era Theoderic could only have been viewed as a barbarian. Yet here we have a Gothic king claiming to be copying Roman ideals. Naturally enough, it's as famous as it is extraordinary, and has often been cited as evidence of Rome's continuing psychological dominance, a generation after there had last been a Western emperor enthroned in the purple.

But on closer inspection, it demonstrates a great deal more than that. Like many diplomatic letters produced in almost any era of human history, it is written in a kind of code, carefully transmitting its full meaning via a set of conventions equally well understood by both the original parties to the correspondence. In this case, the key is provided by the long-standing ideological claims that sustained the self-understanding of the Roman imperial state. Roman ideologies claimed that the empire's existence was so closely interwoven into the beneficent deity's plans for bringing humankind to its fullest possible potential that it was actually providential divine power which had first brought it into existence, and supported it subsequently. An extension of an idea set that had first been rigorously articulated for the self-aggrandizing and thoroughly non-Christian successors of Alexander the

Great (and is hence often labelled Hellenistic kingship), it had required remarkably little alteration when the emperor Constantine declared his allegiance to Christianity. The claim to divine support for a divinely ordained mission remained constant: the divinity providing said support was just re-identified as the Christian God, and the purpose of the mission was recalibrated to one of spreading the Christian Gospel.

Read against this ideology, Theoderic's remarks become significantly less deferential. The critical phrase is 'Divine help' (*auxilio divino*). By employing it, the Goth made it clear to Anastasius that, in his own view of course (no one knows what the Eastern emperor thought when this was read out to him, although I could hazard a pretty good guess), Theoderic's capacity to govern Italy as a fully fledged Roman ruler was the product not of chance or even of his own personal capacities honed by ten years' observation of Romanness in action in Constantinople (although these played a part), but most fundamentally of God's direct intervention. The central plank of Roman state ideology was the claim that the empire existed because it was key to the divine plan for humankind. Theoderic's parallel claim that the divinity underpinned his own capacity to govern in a properly Roman manner amounted to a statement that he himself, together with the realm he governed, were just as legitimately 'Roman' – i.e. divinely ordained – as the Eastern Empire itself. As set up in this letter, Theoderic's Romanness was not indirectly acquired from the Eastern Empire, but directly from God. Who was this Gothic upstart making these extraordinary claims, and how much substance was there in this assertion of his own Romanness?[1]

GETICA

The first image to survive of the young Theoderic is that of a seven- or eight-year-old boy being sent as a hostage to the great capital city of the Eastern Roman Empire: Constantinople. The year was 461 or thereabouts, and, young as he was, Theoderic had an important role to play. His uncle had just forged a new diplomatic agreement with the then Eastern emperor Leo, as a result of which he was awarded foreign aid – or a subsidy, call it what you will – to the tune of 300 pounds weight of gold a year. The young Theoderic was sent to Constantinople in return as the physical embodiment of one of the agreement's security clauses. All this was routine. Since time immemorial, Rome had demanded high-status hostages to ensure that treaties would be complied with.[2]

The image comes from the Gothic History or *Getica* of a certain Jordanes, composed in Constantinople around the year 550, and this text has played a central role in modern understandings of who the child actually was. Later in life, when securely enthroned in Italy, Theoderic liked to state (particularly to foreign potentates) that he belonged to a uniquely purple (i.e. imperial) dynasty: a *gens purpura*. His own legitimacy flowed from the fact that members of his family had ruled unchallenged over the Goths for seventeen generations by the time power reached his grandson and successor Athalaric in the 520s. Jordanes *Getica* has long been taken to provide crucial narrative support for this statement, its text including not only a full genealogy of Theoderic's Amal family (Figure 1), but also a panoply of stories about some of its more distinguished individual members.[3]

Before swallowing this vision whole, however, it is important to look more closely at its sources. One of its main ones, as Jordanes states in his preface and a broader comparison with the author's other surviving writings confirms, was a now lost Gothic history written by the Roman senator Cassiodorus, whom we will meet again in the next chapter. Jordanes tells us that he only had access to Cassiodorus' History for three days, but the really important point here is that Cassiodorus was an insider at Theoderic's court and composed his history while serving the king. What this does, of course, is effectively undermine any claim that Jordanes provides independent confirmation of the unique royal status of the Amal family, since both Theoderic's claims and the *Getica*'s historical support ultimately derive from the same context: Theoderic's own court.[4] Once this is recognized and you go digging around a little further in the sources, it becomes possible quite quickly to shed rather more light on the real family history of the young Theoderic the Amal, whose horse plodded into Constantinople in the early 460s. He was certainly from a fairly grand family, otherwise he would not have been sent to Constantinople as a hostage in the first place. But that grandeur was both more recent and of a more limited degree than Theoderic would later pretend.

His father was the middle in age of three brothers – Valamer, Thiudimer and Vidimer in order of birth – who emerge in reasonably reliable sources as the leaders by the later 450s of a sizeable group of Goths which had been subordinate previously, and for a number of decades, to the Hunnic Empire of Attila, whose career of terror in the 440s had stretched from the walls of Constantinople to the outskirts of Paris. The traditional view of the Amal family – stemming directly from the kind of information that Theoderic was prone to give out in Italy – is that it had ruled one half of the overall Gothic 'people' – the Ostrogoths or 'Eastern' Goths – since at least the middle of the third century AD. The other half are conventionally called Visigoths ('Western' Goths) and have been seen as having a largely separate history from their Amal-dominated cousins, again from the third century. But all this is a fantasy directly generated by Theoderic's own propaganda. The grandeur of the Amal dynasty, prior to the phenomenal successes of Theoderic's own lifetime, was much more limited than the visions modern commentators have conjured into existence on the back of the king's later pretensions.

For one thing, the Goths left in central and Eastern Europe by the 463 were far from united. Aside from those Goths led by Theoderic's father and two uncles, settled somewhere in the old Roman province of Pannonia around what is now Lake Balaton in modern Hungary, there was another large group of allied Goths living by agreement on East Roman territory in Thrace, a moderately large third group still under Hunnic domination (where we find them as late as 467) and two more separate – if seemingly smaller – Gothic groups in the Crimea and on the eastern shores of the Sea of Azov. Numbers are not exact, of course, but, at most, the Amal family can have led no more than roughly a quarter of all the Goths of central and Eastern Europe that we know about as Hunnic power collapsed. And this makes no allowance for the perfectly real possibility that there might have been other Gothic groups of whom we know absolutely nothing.[5]

Equally important, the unchallenged rule of the Amal brothers over even the Pannonian Goths was a recent creation. A snippet of misunderstood narrative in the *Getica* catches pretended Amal grandeur with its hands in the historical till. What this passage describes is not, as it thinks, some of the successes of a Hunnic conqueror of the Goths (whom it labels Valamver), but actually the early career of Theoderic's uncle, Valamer himself. And the picture is electric. Far from being the latest in a long line of kings exercising unchallenged dominion over half of all Goths, it shows Valamer elbowing himself to the head of a pack of other Gothic warband leaders. He starts by personally killing a certain Vinitharius and marrying the victim's granddaughter, Vadamerca. At the same time, a rival line comprising a father (Hunimund), two brothers (Thorismund and Gensemund) and a grandson (Thorismund's son Beremund) was steadily eliminated. After various deaths in the older generation, Gensemund chose to accept the inevitable and resigned himself to Valamer's authority, while Beremund decided to take his personal following westwards and remove himself from the competition. The prominence of Valamer and his brothers by the late 450s, even over the Pannonian Goths, was the result of hard-fought struggles with multiple rivals among them, all probably fought out since Attila's death in 453, since the latter's management techniques did not generally tolerate overmighty rulers among his subject peoples.[6]

What this material does, in fact, is turn the Amal dynasty into a pretty familiar fifth-century story. To be the unchallenged leader of a large group of warriors required strong levers of power. There are many possible variations in detail, but this always meant an interlinked mixture of stick and carrot: enough brute force to keep potential rivals from chancing their arms against you, combined with a plentiful flow of ready cash to keep enough foot soldiers and middle-rank leaders happy, actually to generate that brute force. But both, and particularly the cash, tended to be in relatively short supply in the non-complex economies characteristic of the world beyond Rome's European frontiers before the arrival of the Huns. Pre-AD 400, for instance, all you tend to find in non-Roman archaeological contexts is a modest amount of silver and almost no gold at all. Not that there was no gold around; it was just too valuable to be buried with the dead or for anyone to lose with any regularity.

Non-Roman, largely agricultural economies also produced only small annual surpluses which could support only relatively limited numbers of specialist non-farmers. As a result, both professional full-time warriors and the cash with which to buy their services were far from abundant, and it was only in highly unusual circumstances (mostly involving access to Roman funds by fair means or foul) that kings beyond the frontier could assemble enough military might to dominate larger geographical spaces. Small-scale kingships, run essentially by warband leaders, were the natural order of the day, not great imperial dynasties; and larger hegemonies tended to be highly temporary, limited to the lifetime of particularly effective leaders.

The rise and fall of Attila's Hunnic Empire altered this situation in two fundamental ways. First, there was an explosion of gold in the non-Roman world beyond the frontier, in particular in the Huns' Middle Danubian heartlands. Moveable Roman wealth was the central object of Hunnic campaigning, whether taken as booty, or in the form of annual subsidies which increased with every Hunnic victory to a maximum of 2,000 pounds in weight per annum. Not only is all this clear in the texts but it is also reflected in the archaeology, where the new wealth of the Hunnic era shows up in a large number of gold-rich burials. As Hunnic hegemony began to collapse in the mid-450s, therefore, there was now enough wealth knocking around both to generate intense competition between the rival warband leaders – like Theoderic's uncle and his rivals – who had formed the empire's second-tier leadership, and to sustain in the short term the larger political structures that their conflicts tended to create.

Second, even after the wheels came off in the mid-450s, the overall effect of the Hunnic period – the combined product of Attila's victories and the greater concentration of military manpower he had assembled to win them – was to shift the longer-term strategic balance of power on the Danube frontier away from the Roman Empire. The imperial authorities of East and West were now having to deal with larger numbers of bigger, more militarily effective neighbouring forces. This meant that the new powers which formed around figures such as Valamer in the 450s were able in their own right (or wrong!) to retain access to Roman wealth by a combination of moving on to parcels of former Roman territory which still had more developed economies than anything beyond the frontier, and setting up political relations with the Roman state which involved the payment of subsidies. As Hunnic power receded – and it did so astonishingly quickly in the decade after Attila's death – and the Hunnic brake on political centralization among subject groups such as the Goths was removed, new and militarily effective groupings quickly formed among the Huns' former subjects. Apart from squabbling with one another, they started casting covetous eyes over bits of former particularly West Roman territory, and on potential particularly East Roman subsidies.

Valamer followed both elements of this recipe for success to the letter. Soon after the elimination of his immediate Gothic rivals, we find him both in possession of part of the old West Roman province of Pannonia, and pushing hard for foreign aid from Constantinople. The young Theoderic trotted towards Constantinople precisely as one of the sureties for the deal which sent 300 pounds of gold per annum in Valamer's direction in return – a quantity of regular cash which came in extremely handy when you had to convince warriors that you deserved their loyalty. The archaeological evidence makes it entirely clear, in fact, how Valamer and his peers used this wealth to win political support. The remains of post-Hunnic central Europe throw up a mixture of Roman imports, not least wine amphorae, and some extremely rich personal ornamentation for both males and females. Parties and bling provided an excellent recipe for stamping your power on a potential following. The correlation between non-Roman dynasts moving actually on to (or at least closer into) Roman territory, and their being able to use Roman wealth to build up their power by attracting a much larger body of military support than had previously been possible, had been and remained an extremely strong one as the Western Empire collapsed in the fifth century.[7]

We find it operating, for instance, among the Vandals and Visigoths who founded successor states to Rome respectively in North Africa and southern Gaul and Spain in the first half of the fifth century. Both started out as loose alliances of separate groups with their own independent leaderships, and became centralized under a single leader only on Roman soil. In the case of these groups, it was not only that the positive possibilities opened up by the greater wealth of the Roman world facilitated a centralization of power, but also the fact that their unity grew at a time when the West Roman state was still powerful enough actually to threaten to destroy them. The historical detail preserved by our sources makes it clear that the negative impulse provided by a still very vital Roman threat played a major role in making the originally independent groups, of which both were composed, willing to overturn their long-standing traditions of separation and create the political relationships on which the new groupings were based.

In many ways the closest parallel to the Amals' story, however, is provided by the Frankish Merovingian dynasty, whose power, like that of Theoderic's family, was substantially a post-Roman phenomenon, not brokered by any effective imperial threat. In this case, the history

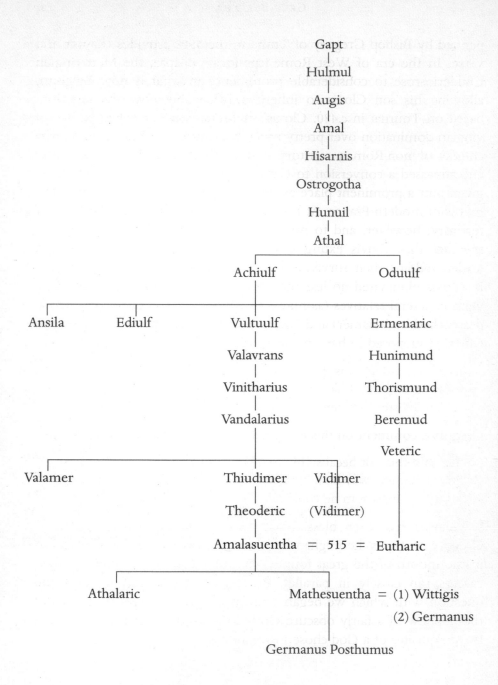

Amal Genealogy

penned by Bishop Gregory of Tours in the 590s provides chapter and verse. In the era of West Roman political collapse, the Merovingian Childeric rose to considerable prominence in what is now Belgium, allowing his son Clovis to inherit a reasonably powerful kingdom based on Tournai in *c*.480. Clovis' subsequent career extended Merovingian domination over pretty much the entirety of France, and large chunks of non-Roman territory east of the Rhine. It also famously encompassed a conversion to Catholicism, both of which points have given him a prominent place as 'founder of the nation' in the political myths of modern France. At least as important as his conquests of new territory, however, and to my mind perhaps even key to them, was the fact that Clovis extinguished a whole series of rival warband leaders, adding their surviving followers to his own. As Gregory tells it, Clovis eliminated no less than seven rivals. At least some of these were collateral relatives (as may also have been true of some of those despatched by Valamer) and Gregory closes the chapters with a speech Clovis is supposed to have made at a Frankish assembly:

> How sad a thing it is that I live among strangers like some solitary pilgrim, and that I have none of my own relations left to help me when disaster threatens!

Gregory's comment on this is typical of his own dark sense of humour:

> He said this not because he grieved for their deaths, but because in his cunning way he hoped to find some relative still in the land of the living whom he could kill.

If Valamer had been blessed with a historian of similar stature to Gregory of Tours, he might well have found something similar to put in the mouth of the great founder of Amal power. Certainly the two careers ran closely in parallel. But all of this merely restates the question with which we began with much greater urgency. How did the nephew of a fairly obscure Gothic warband leader come to affect the perquisites of a God-chosen Roman emperor?[8]

CONSTANTINOPLE

What the young Gothic hostage thought of his new surroundings and how much anxiety he felt are not recorded, but, by 463, what had been the small and relatively undistinguished – if certainly ancient – Greek city of Byzantium on the Bosphorus had been transformed into a mighty imperial capital. That process was less than 150 years old, initiated in the 320s – after some umming and erring – by the same Constantine who had turned the official religion of the empire towards Christianity. At one point, feeling in a classical turn of mind, and no doubt influenced by the old Roman claim that their city had been founded by the fleeing remnants of Troy's destruction, the emperor had considered rebuilding the topless towers of Ilium. The sources also record that at another point Constantine boldly declared that 'Serdica [Sofia, capital of modern Bulgaria] is my Rome'. But that proved another false start, and his choice finally fell on Byzantium, sited on a peninsula strategically placed to control the crossing of the Hellespont, from Europe to Asia, and equipped with abundant sheltered waters for large fleets to lie at anchor, both in the Bosphorus itself and particularly in the Golden Horn that snakes up its eastern shoreline.

In the first generation, Constantine's decision looked far from momentous. Many structures were half-built at the time of the emperor's death in 337, he had trouble persuading the richer landowners of the Eastern Empire to relocate to his new capital, and a fundamental problem with the water supply remained to be resolved. Like many peninsulas around the rim of the Mediterranean, it was a struggle to concentrate enough water to supply all the needs of even Byzantium's few thousand inhabitants in the 320s, let alone the larger masses of all social classes who flocked to an imperial capital, with all the job opportunities, free food distributions, and extravagant entertainments that could be anticipated. And, in fact, many Roman emperors over the years had turned their favourite cities into new capitals which lasted maybe a generation or two at best before whim or new circumstances led to a further political and administrative relocation.

Constantinople proved the exception. Two key political developments under Constantine's son Constantius II located political power much more permanently within its new walls. First, the new emperor created there an imperial senate for the eastern half of the Roman Empire, which was designed to match the grandeur of its Roman counterpart. This time, there were sufficient inducements on offer and a cross-section of the richer landowners of the eastern Mediterranean duly trotted off to new houses, duties and honours beside the Bosphorus. Henceforth, the Senate of Constantinople became the prime political audience for imperial policy: the men to whom imperial policies had to be sold and justified, and whose continued importance in the home provinces from which they came made their support for imperial initiatives a *sine qua non* for their successful implementation. Second, the fourth century in general saw a steady expansion in the size of the empire's central bureaucratic offices. This operated equally in east and west, but, in the eastern half of the empire, all the new offices were located securely in Constantinople, bringing a further reinforcement of important personnel and functions to the city. Between them, these two developments made it impossible for effective central power ever to be exercised from anywhere else in the eastern Mediterranean. And once central power was so firmly committed to the site, the will was automatically there too, both to resolve all its logistic difficulties and provide the new capital with an appropriate range of amenities. By the time Theoderic came to Constantinople, therefore, a bog standard small-to-medium Greek city had emerged from its chrysalis as an astonishing metropolitan butterfly.[9]

Coming from the north-west, along the main military road through the Balkans, the young Goth entered the city by the Charisius Gate. This was the most northerly of the main gates through the Theodosian landwalls which guarded the city. Rarely has any city been so well guarded. The first obstacle to be crossed was a moat twenty metres wide and another ten in depth; this was succeeded – beyond a further twenty metres of flat killing ground – by the outer wall which was two metres thick at its base and eight and a half metres high, studded by a grand total of ninety-six towers, placed at fifty-five-metre intervals. There then followed another twenty-metre terrace before you came finally to the full might of the main wall: five metres thick and twelve metres high, reinforced with another ninety-six towers placed in between those of the outer wall, and these a full twenty metres from foot to battlement. Constructed in the years around AD 410, and still substantially visible in modern Istanbul, they were so strong that they protected the landward approaches to the city until cannon finally blew open the breach in which, according to some stories, the last Byzantine emperor, Constantine XI, fell fighting on 23 May 1453.[10]

Theoderic had no cannon, and neither did anyone else in the fifth century, so to his eight-year-old eyes, the city's fortifications can only have transmitted an impression of overwhelming power. He would have known that they had proved more than strong enough to ward off Attila the Hun less than twenty years before. The line of the walls – for excellent military reasons – was set on high ground, which reached maximum elevation towards the north, where Theoderic had entered. Once through the gate and archway, the whole imperial metropolis was laid out before him.

The immediate effect can only have been shock. Theoderic had just ridden in from the Middle Danubian plain, west of the Carpathians in modern Hungary, where he had spent his early years. In the high Roman period, this was a heavily defended frontier region which had seen much imperial investment and great prosperity in the first four centuries AD. Legionary bases studded the line of the river, and, around the soldiers' spending power, real Roman towns had grown up, while the agricultural potential of the hinterland was exploited by retired legionaries, new settlers from Italy, and native populations turning themselves into fully paid up Romans. As multiple excavations have emphasized, the region at its height boasted walled cities, temples, then cathedrals as Christianity took over, theatres and amphitheatres, aqueducts, road systems, statues, town councils, inscriptions and villas in glorious abundance. But that was before the crisis years of West Roman collapse, and aside from a handful of massively fortified – perhaps originally imperial – villas which the new rulers of this landscape adapted to their own purposes, by the mid-fifth century the rest had fallen into decay. There was still a substantial population, and some of it inhabited the old sites, but no one was preserving any of the old cultural forms, so stonework and statues were turning rapidly to rubble, togas had been put away for good, and most of the villas had long since been destroyed.[11]

The contrast between the debris of old Roman provincial prosperity and the full-on metropolitan imperial splendour of mid-fifth-century Constantinople could not have been greater. The first thing to assault his senses was the sheer scale of the city. Chronologically, the Theodosian Walls were the city's third set. The old Greek city of Byzantium possessed the first set; these enclosed a roughly rectangular area at the end of the peninsula of about two kilometres by one and a half (Figure 2). The walls added by Constantine in the 320s more than trebled the enclosed area, and then those of the emperor Theodosius more than doubled it again. Not all of the enclosed area was built up – there were extensive market gardens and parks, especially between the Theodosian and Constantinian walls – but a standard late Roman town of maybe 10,000 inhabitants had probably already become, by 463, the largest city of the Mediterranean, with a population estimated at over half a million.

Huge logistical problems had been solved along the way. Part of the solution to one of the most pressing came into Theoderic's view immediately on his left as he rode away from the gate. The area between the Theodosian and Constantinian walls was home to the city's three enormous open-air reservoirs, one of which – that of Aetius – lay beside Theoderic's road. Their remains can still be seen (at least at the time of writing), each home to temporary-looking housing and a couple of football fields. These man-made lakes were supplemented by over a hundred smaller underground cisterns with a total storage capacity between them of over a million cubic metres. But that was only part of the water story. To keep these storage tanks filled, over 250 kilometres of aqueduct snaked away from the city, fanning out to the north and west to ensnare the rainfall of the Thracian hills. As with water, the mechanics of the solution to the problem of food were literally in front of Theoderic's eyes: front left lay the two small harbours of the old Greek city, but straight ahead he could see the two new massive ones built by the emperors Julian and Theodosius to receive the grain fleets whose periodic deliveries, especially from Egypt, fed the city. Each of the harbours was lined with massive granaries where the food was stored.

Whether the thoughts of an eight-year-old Goth from the ruins of provincial Pannonia would have turned to the logistic problems of feeding and watering 500,000 people must, I guess, be slightly doubtful. More probably, his eyes were captured by the city's astonishing range of pristine monuments which dwarfed any of the wrecks he'd seen back home or en route. First in view was Constantine's Church of the Holy Apostles, imperial burial place and home to the skulls of

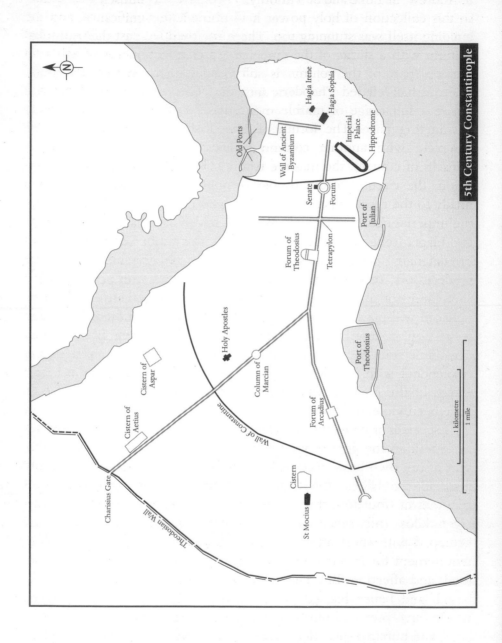

5th Century Constantinople

St Andrew, St Luke and St Timothy. Theoderic was himself a Christian, so this collection of holy power held immediate significance, and the building itself was stunning too. The route then led past the triumphal column with a statue of the emperor Marcian, conqueror of Attila on the top (part of the column is still visible), then on to the Capitol. There a half-left led Theoderic into the ceremonial heart of the city where a full range of marble monuments succeeded one another at bewildering pace. The forum of Theodosius (now Beyazit Square), complete with another column and triumphal statue (Theodosius himself, of course), the massive triumphal arch complex of the Tetra-pylon, the circular forum proper complete with Senate house, then finally to the great imperial centre of hippodrome, palace buildings and the imperial churches of Holy Wisdom and Holy Peace: Hagia Sophia and Hagia Irene. These were not, in 463, the famous domed churches of that name which can still be seen in modern Istanbul, but their predecessors: rectangular, classic basilica churches with gently pitched roofs and not a dome in sight. The story of how these came to be replaced will play a major role in Chapter 3, but for now it is enough to recognize how overwhelming this all must have been. When Theoderic rode through the Charisius Gate, the city was in its pomp, resplendent with marble facades, bronze roofs and gilded statues. The extent of the contrast with everything he had ever known can only have been violently disorienting.[12]

Especially if you have had children, it is only natural to think about Theoderic in the light of youngsters known to you. A quick consultation of my own boys' records tells me that the average eight-year-old male in the UK at the turn of the millennium stood about 128 centimetres (four foot three inches) high and weighed around twenty-eight kilos (fifty-seven pounds). Most eight-year-olds also come equipped with short attention spans, abundant energy and a built-in requirement for frequent inputs (in smallish quantities) of stimulation, food, and affection. But Theoderic was a prince of (reasonably) royal blood, and hence blessed (or otherwise) with an upbringing which would have prepared him better than most for the emotional depriv-ation and public display demanded by his new life in Constantinople.

He was the oldest male child yet produced by the three brothers, which is why presumably he was sent to guarantee the treaty. Valamer does not seem to have had any male children (the amateur psychologist might wonder if the fact that he had killed his wife's grandfather may have had something to do with that), but, even if he had, this would not have prevented Theoderic being brought up from the outset as a potential leader. At this point, the leadership of the Pannonian Goths was still being shared, as between Valamer and his brothers. There was no primogeniture, and any male child was a potential leader of the future. Moreover, the job description was both so specific and so dangerous that you needed plenty of alternatives to hand in case of either early death or the possibility that the character of any particular individual failed to match the task. Not only did you have to sit on a horse in the front of the battle line at crunchtime, but you had also more generally to inspire a large number of alpha males with sufficient confidence to follow you enthusiastically into battle in the first place. This requires not only physical strength and personal bravery, but also that infectious charisma which comes from self-confidence, matched too with enough brainpower to know which battles to fight – and which not – and how exactly to wage them.

Succession in these kinds of contexts rarely runs simply from father to eldest son. Historians have often criticized the contemporary Merovingians for failing to develop primogeniture, since the dynasty's succession history is broadly one of repeated infighting. But this is to miss the point. You can only have primogeniture when the personal characteristics of the son don't matter so much; that is, when leadership is not so personal and charismatic. The troops will not be willing to be led into battle either by a poet, for instance, or – not more than once, at least – by an idiotic macho man who may be big and charismatic, but will also throw their lives away in hopeless fights against ridiculous odds. The best analogy to early medieval succession I know of is provided by *The Godfather*, where the chief aides and independent second-rank leaders like Tom Hagen, Luca Brasi and Peter Clemenza carefully evaluate the qualities of Vito Corleone's different sons. Worth thinking about particularly carefully, I think, are the better and worse sides of the oldest of the three:

> Sonny Corleone had strength, he had courage. He was generous and his heart was as big as his organ. Yet he did not have his father's humility, but instead a quick, hot temper that led him into errors of judgment. Though he was a great help in his father's business, there were many who doubted that he would become the heir to it.[13]

In the end, the much quieter but smarter and equally brave third son proves infinitely superior to his charismatic but rash eldest brother, while the middle son lacks the qualities ever to rank as a contender. Leading a warband, large or small, was a heavy responsibility, and potential heirs were always being watched.

The qualities of Theoderic's home life are unlikely to have been much conducive to sentimentality, therefore, even in an eight-year-old. We know that he had brothers and sisters, although whether they had been born by 463 is unclear. More likely than not, however, they were the products of various unions. Even semi-royal warband leaders based their unions as much on political necessity as affection or desire, and often formed various simultaneous unions – by both marriage and concubinage – as circumstance dictated. Sometimes, things didn't go quite as planned. Reputedly the Gepid princess Rosamund murdered her husband, the Lombard king Alboin, for too much boasting that he'd turned her defeated father's skull into a drinking cup. Whether Vadamerca harboured inklings of revenge towards Valamer is unrecorded, but, even where royal family life was not so fraught, tensions between wives, mistresses, and their natural ambitions for their various children, made the experience of growing up in a fifth-century, even moderately royal family a million miles away from the norms and hopes of a modern nuclear family. And that's without taking into account tensions between the three brothers. Valamer, Thiudimer and Vidimer may have agreed to share power in their own lifetime, but that doesn't mean they remotely agreed on what was to happen next (anyone who has inherited something jointly from parents and then has to contemplate the next generation will, I think, recognize the experience). Jordanes records that Theoderic's father did not want Valamer to use him as the hostage, and that has the ring of truth about it. The older brother may well have wanted his nephew out of the way in Constantinople, so that he couldn't do anything to establish the ties of respect with the second-rank leadership which would make him the natural heir for the next generation, and maybe also in the hope that he could have sons of his own in the meantime.[14]

Some of these thoughts may be wide of the mark, but their general trajectory is certainly correct. It was no ordinary eight-year-old who rode through the Charisius Gate. He must have been anxious and alarmed, but his upbringing had ensured that he was uncommonly hardened. What exactly he did for the next ten years in Constantinople is not recorded, but from many other examples of hostages at Roman imperial courts over the preceding centuries, we have a very good idea of the kind of programme on offer. For while Theoderic was certainly there to guarantee that Valamer's Goths would respect the new treaty, and the threat was real enough that he might be executed if they did not, the line of thought behind the Romans' hostage reflex was much more ambitious. To state it succinctly, the Romans aimed to get inside the heads of royal hostages to make them pliable and useful in the longer term. They hoped to engender a mixture of genuine respect for the wonders of Roman civilization and a well-informed awe of Roman imperial power that, having eventually returned home, the ex-hostage would influence the foreign policy of his group in directions that served Rome's interests.

Although certainly watched, but surrounded by some of his own retinue, he would have undergone at least part of the standard education programme for an upper-class Roman (as alluded to in the letter to Anastasius). The longer-term plan, after all, was to shape his opinions, and what better way to implant Roman values than by a Roman education. He would also have been free to move about at court and in the city, attending circuses, theatres, and Church too, since Constantinople still had a distinct non-Nicene Church community at this point. He may even have been attached to the Roman army for the odd operation or two as he grew older. All in all, although there was that faint shadow hanging over him – he really was a hostage after all – he was given every opportunity to learn about everything Roman, with the hope that this would make him a reliable partner if and when he succeeded to the throne back home.[15] But whatever the precise details of the educational programme unloaded in Theoderic's direction, it spectacularly failed to work. Within five years of his return to Pannonia, and still only in his early twenties, he came back to the walls of Constantinople: this time at the head of an army of 10,000 men. How did this happen, and what had gone wrong with his education?

SINGIDUNUM

No strategy works every time. Human beings can always respond in one of two extreme ways to any stimulus – complete acceptance or complete rejection – and most will probably fall somewhere in between, picking up some of the ideas thrown in their direction but rejecting others. In the case of Theoderic the Amal, the evidence suggests that we are dealing with a fascinatingly complex reaction: an individual who appreciated the full weight of imperial power, and the many advantages of Roman ideas and administrative structures. At the same time, he was not remotely intimidated by what he observed, calculating instead how carefully selected elements of *Romanitas* might be turned to advantage. All this has to be deduced – Theoderic's private diaries do not exist – but the message screams out loud and clear from his subsequent career.

Why exactly Theoderic returned home at the age of eighteen is unclear. He was obviously pretty full grown, but in Roman law, you came of majority age only at twenty-five and we don't know what Gothic custom might have been. There are two basic possibilities: either the return date was written into the original treaty, or it was generated by more immediate circumstances. If the latter, two lines of thought suggest themselves. First, by the early 470s Valamer was dead, killed in one of the competitive struggles for hegemony that litter the post-Attilan history of the Middle Danube region. Not only did this make Theoderic's father Thiudimer now the pre-eminent leader of the Pannonian Goths, but it also made Theoderic, as his father's eldest son, potentially a very immediate heir, since Valamer seems still not to have produced any male children. The imperative here to secure the boy's return is obvious.

But Valamer's death may have occurred as early as the mid-460s, which would deny it much of a role as the trigger behind Theoderic's return, and, by the early 470s, momentous events were also afoot within Constantinople. For the previous twenty years, the great king-maker had been Aspar, a general and patrician. His non-Roman Alanic origins made it impossible for him – in his own view too, it seems – to take the throne himself, but the emperors Marcian (probably 450–7) and Leo I (457 onwards) were his candidates and his pre-eminence within Constantinople was unchallenged. He also enjoyed particularly close ties to the large group of Thracian Goths who formed much of the Eastern Empire's Balkan military establishment and provided him with the martial clout he needed, not least in the form of garrison troops in the capital, to face down any would-be rivals.

Until, that is, the emperor Leo started to scheme for independence and used the leaders of recently recruited Isaurian troops from mountainous regions of the Taurus (modern Turkey) as a counterweight to Aspar's power. Major recruiting drives had begun in this region in the 440s, when the empire needed to expand its forces to fend off Attila, and, by the 460s, the political consequences of this move were becoming apparent. The most prominent of the Isaurians, Zeno (Greek *xenon*, 'stranger', 'guest', as in 'xenophobia': 'hatred of guests'), first emerges in the disgracing of Aspar's son Ardaburius in 466, and then moved swiftly up the military hierarchies, making the requisite contacts as he went. By 471, emperor and Isaurian were ready to strike. Reportedly urged on by Zeno, Leo had Aspar cut down in the palace, earning the sobriquet Macelles 'the Butcher'. The move also prompted an immediate uprising among the Thracian Goths, which can't have come as any surprise. Like many in similar circumstances, before and since, however, Leo also found out that relying on someone else to rescue you from unwanted dependence is not such a good strategy. Zeno had married Leo's daughter Ariadne, and their son, Leo II, was heir to the throne, so one *éminence grise* replaced another. Whether the butcher slept more happily at night, history doesn't record.[16]

It was in the midst of all this mayhem that Theoderic left Constantinople, just possibly because of it in some way, and, even if not, what had originally been two separate sequences of events quickly became inextricably entwined as a result of what our Gothic tyro chose to do next. On his return to Pannonia, Theoderic's most immediate need was to establish some legitimacy as the son of his father and potential leader of the group. Not surprisingly, we quickly find him leading a plundering expedition against some Sarmatians who were occupying territory close to the old Roman city of Singidunum (modern Belgrade). The Sarmatians had once been fierce but in late antiquity they had evolved into everyone's favourite whipping boy. In similar circumstances, in the autumn following the Romans' shocking defeat at Hadrianople, the very-soon-to-be Emperor Theodosius I picked on the Sarmatians to show that God was on his side. Nearly a hundred years later, Theoderic chose the same victims. According to Jordanes, here likely enough following Cassiodorus again, he mounted his expedition without his father's knowledge, but I don't believe a word of it. After such a long gap, and with so much at stake now that Valamer was dead without male offspring, father and son had a joint interest in establishing Theoderic's credibility. The point was duly made by the Sarmatians' 'slaves and treasure' with which he returned.[17]

Not only were the Sarmatians suitably supine, but Singidunum was itself a significant choice. For the newly returned Theoderic had, much more ambitiously, convinced his father that the political upheavals generated by the murder of Aspar offered an unmissable opportunity, which the Pannonian Goths set about grabbing with both hands. As with most really 'big' decisions, the evidence suggests that a range of motivations were in play. For one thing, his sojourn in Constantinople must have rammed home for Theoderic the limitations of the Goths' current situation in Pannonia. Here they were locked into an intra-regional struggle for dominance with a whole series of other highly militarized groups which had emerged in the region from the wreck of Attila's war machine: Rugi, Suevi, Sciri, Gepids, Alans, not to mention the poor old Sarmatians and contingents of actual Huns under various of Attila's sons. Attila's trick had been to unite all of these – just about – and point them in a Roman direction, extracting very large amounts of gold bullion and other forms of wealth, which show up, as we've seen, so dramatically in the Hunnic-period archaeology of the region. But, if it didn't stop, the flow of new wealth into the area quickly subsided once the groups were no longer acting together. The new intra-regional conflicts which replaced long-distance wealth-extraction expeditions on to Roman soil thus quickly became struggles over less and less (not least as the existing wealth was buried with the dead), but remained equally nasty. It was in one round of these battles that Valamer had fallen:

> [He] rode on his horse before the line to encourage his men, the horse was wounded and fell, overthrowing its rider. Valamer was quickly pierced by his enemies' spears and slain.[18]

The fact that his followers are said to have extracted great revenge would have been of little comfort to the king who had just died so unpleasantly. The prospect of continuing the endless struggle for mastery in the Middle Danube, a fight for control of a declining stock of assets, with an eventual nasty death a likely outcome, did not strike the returning Theoderic as a fantastic career path. Constantinople had opened his eyes to a much bigger world.

In particular, the revolt of the Thracian Goths provided the leadership of the Pannonian Goths with real reason to think that an exciting opportunity might be up for grabs. To understand its nature, it is necessary to understand the highly privileged position occupied by the Thracian Goths within the East Roman polity. Barbarian soldiers per se were not any kind of oddity within Roman armies of any era. From Augustus onwards, at least half the imperial military establishment had been composed of non-citizens. In the late Roman era, however, a new type of agreement came to be made, whereby non-Roman contingents were allowed to settle on Roman soil and placed permanently on the army roster under their own leaderships, retaining a considerable degree of legal and political (and hence possibly too cultural) autonomy. This stood in marked contrast to earlier periods, when barbarian soldiers permanently in the Roman army always served under Roman officers, or contingents under their own leaderships were temporary reinforcements for particular campaigns drafted in from client kingdoms beyond the frontier. There is much argument about when the new kind of arrangement – which created groups known to the Romans as *foederati* (often rendered into English as 'federates', though the term is bandied about far too loosely) first came into existence. And although the new arrangements probably evolved in stages, an excellent case can be made that they were first deployed in their full form precisely for the Thracian Goths. They originated as a group of Hunnic subjects extracted from their overlords' domination by Roman military action in Pannonia in the 420s, and resettled in Thrace. For the Romans, the gain was twofold: Hunnic military manpower was substantially reduced, and their own consequently increased. For the Goths, all too aggressive Hunnic overlordship was replaced by a privileged position within the East Roman state.

By the time Theoderic was observing it at first hand in the 460s, this relationship was into its second and third generations, and the advantages to the Thracian Goths were obvious. For one thing, the pay wasn't at all bad. Where Valamer had been able to extract 300 pounds of gold per annum from Constantinople in the treaty which had sent his nephew to the Eastern court, the leader of the Thracian Goths received seven times that amount per year as payment for his followers' services. The Thracian Goths were also extremely well connected at court. By the early 470s, their paramount leader was also called Theoderic: an astonishing, not to say confusing, coincidence you might say, except that in Gothic the name means 'King of the People' so it's a likely enough name to give to any self-respecting princeling. In this case the Thracian Theoderic comes equipped with a nickname – Strabo 'the Squinter' – which can be used to avoid confusion. Strabo, we know, was the nephew of Aspar's wife, so a marriage alliance tied the Thracian leadership closely to the great patrician. They also had strong ties to a range of other top court functionaries, and supplied at least part of the city's garrison. Nor, unlike their Pannonian counterparts, did they have to spend their time fighting off the attentions of Suevi, Sciri and others in a futile competition over a declining stock of old Hunnic assets in the Middle Danube, occupying instead good settlement areas on the Thracian Plain, with recognized land rights which supplemented their yearly pay.[19]

This happy situation was rudely interrupted by Leo's penchant for Isaurians and the murder of their patron. You can entirely see why they went into revolt. As was usually the case in late Roman politics, the crash of so dominant a figure as Aspar generated a period of great political instability, and the Thracian leadership must have calculated that their revolt would help undermine the Isaurian position and offer them a path back to the good old days. What they had failed to notice is that the young Gothic prince from Pannonia had taken full stock of their privileges, and detected in the Thracian uprising a massive opportunity for self-advancement. This is why the decision to prove his mettle against the Sarmatians of Singidunum had a wider significance. For Singidunum, which Theoderic refused to return to imperial control, was a key crossroads, whose control opened up major routes south into the East Roman Balkans (Figure 3). Theoderic had returned to Pannonia with the daring plan that he and his father should move their joint enterprise lock, stock and two smoking barrels right on to East Roman soil, offering themselves as direct replacements for the revolting Thracians. Probably in late summer 472, the Pannonian Goths gathered themselves up and hit the road south. Constantinopolitan politics, tricky enough at the best of times, were about to get a lot more complicated.

This decision was not undertaken lightly. The sheer logistics were staggering enough. Theoderic and Thiudimer controlled between them in excess of 10,000 warriors, but it wasn't just an armed body of men which hit the road. Nineteenth-century nationalists, reviewing the action of the fourth to the sixth centuries, saw in groups like the Pannonian Goths ancestral 'peoples' for the nations of modern Europe. As a result, German nationalists in particular usually threw a little wishful thinking into the mix about what they saw as their own nation's particular moral virtues, and came up with a vision of free and equal, culturally homogeneous groups of men, women and children, closed to outsiders, moving off complete with farming equipment, animals and folk dances: miniature ancestral nations on the march, some of which survived the trek to found kingdoms which lasted, and some of which did not.

In the last two scholarly generations, there has been a great deal of necessary revision to this hopelessly romantic picture. This has generated some consensus, but also points of continuing dispute. Consensus, I think, exists in two areas. First, that the warrior groups were not composed of equals. Contemporary narrative sources show us that there were at least two hierarchically ranked status groups among just the warriors, and the point is confirmed by more or less contemporary legal materials, which describe armed free and semi-free classes and note that there were unarmed slaves besides (what the law codes can't give you is any sense of what proportion of the groups' total populations belong to each of the status groups). Second – and this reflects a sea change in the way in which the group affiliations of individual human beings have come to be understood more generally in the post-war period – everyone would agree that it was entirely possible for individuals to change their group identity in the course of their own lifetime. As a result, the old vision of these groups as mini, ancestral, culturally homogeneous proto-nations just won't hold water.

Two further issues, though, remain highly contentious. First, does the fact that some individuals demonstrably changed their affiliations mean that the larger entities we meet in the narrative sources (like the Pannonian Goths) had no real group identity at all? A negative answer would mean that they were never more than loose and shifting agglomerations of disparate warriors. Second, and it is in fact closely related, were these groups constituted solely for military action, or were the warriors part of a broader society which engaged in farming and other activities besides?

It is extremely difficult to get a sense of where consensus might be falling when you're a participant in an ongoing debate, as I am in this one. The jury is still out, but, for what it's worth, let me state my views on these issues, because the line you adopt on this absolutely dictates what you envisage to have set out from Hungary in 472 to follow the old Roman roads south into the Balkans. Taking them in reverse order: once in the Roman Balkans, the negotiating positions of both the Pannonian Goths' own leadership, and of the imperial representatives sent to treat with them, explicitly assumed that any resolution of their relations would involve finding the Goths a block of farming land on Roman soil, which the Goths would exploit themselves. They were, in other words, farmers as well as fighters. This does make good general sense. Specialist warriors numbering 10,000–plus can only exist in a relatively developed economic context, when enough surplus wealth is being produced by non-fighting farming populations to feed, clothe and arm them. Non-Roman agricultural economies look nothing like this productive, and we know that non-Roman kings of the fourth and fifth centuries maintained specialist warrior retinues only of a few hundred, not several thousand men.

Nor does it follow, just because some individuals can be seen changing allegiance, that the groups they were moving between had no real solidity at all. What matters here are the rules and norms regulating the entry and subsequent behaviour of individuals on the move. Is membership open to all, do new members enjoy full rights within the group, and does membership involve responsibilities as well as privileges? Here the fact that the groups demonstrably contained higher and lower grades of warrior – not to mention slaves – makes it clear that membership was by no means a matter of unrestricted personal choice, unless we are thinking, of course, that many thousands of individuals across fifth-century Europe simply wanted to be slaves. I would argue, therefore, that the higher-status warrior elites within each group, at least, did have a strong sense of group *political* identity (whether they also had the same folk costumes and folk dances as nineteenth-century nationalists imagined, I have no idea), though, like any identity, even that could change in the right circumstances. But, at the same time, the lower-status warriors and even more the slaves had much less of a stake in their group's existence, so that the strength of individual affiliation to the group's identity fell off dramatically as you moved down the social scale.[20]

Either way, your response to these debates forms your view of what the Pannonian Goths looked like on the road. We know that the group contained many non-combatants and a wagon train at least 2,000 strong. For self-styled revisionists, who see them as essentially a free-form warrior group, this is just the normal baggage train that attended most pre-modern armies, where you would find many women, wives and prostitutes, together with children, cooks, barbers, entertainers and God knows who else. In my view, however, the fact that surrounding economic structures (and this is an important difference between the fifth century and pre-modern or even high medieval Europe) could not support large numbers of specialist warriors, the diplomatic emphasis on the need to find farmland, and the fact that higher-level group membership was not remotely open to all-comers, brings a different model to mind. Rather than an early modern army going off to war with its baggage train, to my mind the Pannonian Goths would have looked much more like one of the Boer wagon trains rumbling off on the great trek north away from British imperial rule: a collection of farmer-fighters and their families, together with all their accoutrements. In this model, the group would consist of higher numbers of non-combatants, with a more 'normal' age distribution among them, and faced a much greater need to take with them everything associated with farming as well as weaponry and substantial food supplies.

But if sheer logistics meant that any decision to move anywhere could not be taken lightly, there's no doubt that in this instance everything really turned on the politics. The higher-status warriors had to be convinced that the potential opportunities presented by Constantinopolitan chaos were sufficiently promising to make such an enormous effort worth their while. Again, the general context came to Thiudimer's and Theoderic's assistance. It is a demonstrated fact that population groups with an established history of migration are more ready than more settled peers, even if that history has skipped a generation or two, to use further movement as a strategy for self-advancement, and at least the warrior elites – the key group who needed to be convinced – had a long-established history of migration.

They were descended from Gothic populations who had made – perhaps in several shorter stages – one long trek from the shores of the Baltic to the Black Sea in the third and earlier fourth centuries, and another from east of the Carpathian Mountains to Middle Danubian Hungary in the late fourth and fifth. As such, they will have been easier to persuade that hitting the road again was worthwhile.[21]

At least, some of them were. For all the potential positives, Theoderic had convinced his father to take what was certainly a massive gamble. While the Western Empire was fast running out of money and hence soldiers in the early 470s, caught in a fierce downdraught that was about to extinguish its final embers, its eastern counterpart was alive and kicking. Attila had been faced down, there was peace with Persia, and Constantinople's flow of tax revenues from its eastern provinces – the lifeblood of its armies – was fully intact. Moving into its territories as uninvited guests, therefore, even if you were claiming to be there to help, was always likely to generate substantial nastiness, and no one with any brains at all within the group can have had the slightest doubt that this would be the case. Not surprisingly, the decision to move caused a split – and a highly significant one – within the group.

Late fourth- and fifth-century sources record several moments when different non-Roman groups similar in type to the Pannonian Goths faced comparable decisions about whether to move on or stay put. In all cases, a mixture of positive and negative motives applied (in this instance, respectively the greater riches potentially available on East Roman soil on the one hand, and the declining profits of the violent competition for pre-eminence in the Middle Danube on the other), though the balance between them varied. The earlier Gothic Tervingi and Greuthungi who had crossed the Danube in 376, for instance, were, like the Pannonian Goths, attracted by the potential wealth of Roman economic structures, but Hunnic violence is what made them move in the first place. In every case where we have any detailed evidence, and whatever the precise mix of motivations, such treks caused political splits in the groups undertaking them. This reflects the degree of stress involved in major migrations, even for populations with an established migration reflex. It also naturally took the form of one influential body among the leadership arguing for the move, and another arguing against it. In the case of the Pannonian Goths, Jordanes preserves the following:

> As the spoil taken from one and another of the neighbouring tribes diminished, the Goths began to lack food and clothing, and peace became distasteful to men for whom war had long furnished the necessaries of life. So all the Goths approached their king Thiudimer and, with great outcry, begged him to lead forth his army in whatsoever direction he might wish. He summoned his brother [Vithimer] and, after casting lots, bade him go into the land of Italy . . . saying that he himself as the mightier would go east against a mightier Empire.

This is another moment when Jordanes is at least partly reproducing the kind of sanitized version of the Gothic past that Cassiodorus had generated at Theoderic's court in Italy. Not only does the casting of lots partly camouflage the deeply predatory intent with which the Gothic leadership was contemplating the move east, but it also attempts to hide the clear division among them. The third of the brothers, Vithimer, clearly was not happy to follow Thiudimer on to East Roman soil, and Thiudimer, I feel great confidence in claiming, was happy enough to use the issue to cut him out of the group.

Theoderic's return to Pannonia as an adult male had reopened that perennial can of worms which was succession. So far, the three Amal brothers had shared power and, when the eldest died, pre-eminence had passed to the next in age. In Theoderic's own generation, however, no such arrangements would apply, even though he had at least one brother, Theodimund. To my mind, it is as clear as daylight that Thiudimer used the argument over the move into the Balkans to present the second-rank leaders with his solution to the current succession dilemma: his eldest son, fresh from Constantinople and a nice win over the Sarmatians, was to be preferred to his younger brother. No doubt opinion was canvassed and prepared before the crunch moment, since Thiudimer couldn't afford to lose too much of his military manpower with a predatory intrusion into the East Roman Balkans in mind, but the gambit worked. Vidimer (like Beremund before him in the previous generation) departed for the West to leave Theoderic unchallenged, and clearly took only a small number of followers with him (probably just his own family – for he did have a son: another reason why Thiudimer and Theoderic wanted him gone – and a personal retinue of warriors numbering no more than a few hundred) since the refugees do not figure again as an independent unit

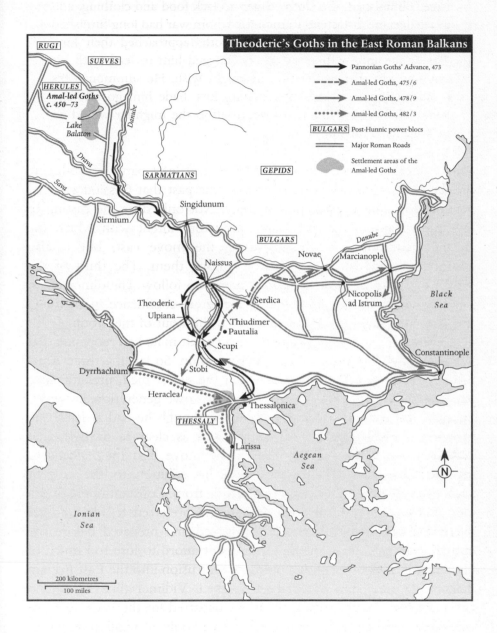

Theoderic's Goths in the East Roman Balkans

Legend:
- → Pannonian Goths' Advance, 473
- ⇢ Amal-led Goths, 475/6
- → Amal-led Goths, 478/9
- ⇢ Amal-led Goths, 482/3
- **BULGARS** Post-Hunnic power-blocs
- Major Roman Roads
- Settlement areas of the Amal-led Goths

Labels on map:

RUGI

SUEVES

HERULES
Amal-led Goths
c. 450–73

Lake Balaton

Danube

Drava

Sava

SARMATIANS

GEPIDS

Singidunum

Sirmium

BULGARS

Naissus

Novae

Danube

Marcianople

Theoderic

Serdica

Nicopolis ad Istrum

Black Sea

Ulpiana

Thiudimer
● Pautalia

Scupi

Constantinople

Dyrrhachium

Stobi

Heraclea

THESSALY

Thessalonica

Larissa

Aegean Sea

Ionian Sea

200 kilometres
100 miles

N

and had to attach themselves to the service of the Visigothic king Euric in Gaul.[22] This completed the dramatic revolution initiated by Theoderic's return from Constantinople: succession resolved, the Pannonian Goths prepared to move down the Roman road systems into the Balkans laid open for them by Theoderic's capture of Singidunum.

EPIDAMNUS

Getting 10,000-plus warriors, together with their familial and personal dependants, farming equipment, animals and as many personal items as could be fitted into their many thousand wagons, all moving in the same direction at the same time was a massive feat of organization. The congestion on the roads will have been extraordinary. One of the most haunting historical facts that I've ever come across is that the wagon train hauling the Confederate wounded home after Gettysburg took a full twenty-four hours to pass any given spot. The Gothic wagon train working its way south through the Balkans in 472 can have been no shorter, though it was much less a cavalcade of misery. The problem facing Thiudimer and Theoderic was that, with such a monster at their heels, movement was confined to the main roads, and there was really only one major route available. The mountainous terrain of the Balkans still, in fact, confines travel to a few highways; in this case the Axius/Vardar valley is the crucial route. For part of its length, there were two alternatives, and Jordanes records explicitly that both were utilized. After taking the city of Naissus (modern Nis), Thiudimer headed directly south, while Theoderic led his forces round to Ulpiana via Castrum Herculius (Figure 3). Both had the same destination, however: Thessalonica, capital of the Roman Balkans, and seat of the prefecture of Illyricum, responsible for everything west of the Succi Pass. There they were confronted by the patrician Hilarianus who had been sent to meet them with such forces as he could muster, and the negotiations began. The Goths' strategy was straightforward. Pose a threat to Thessalonica, offer to negotiate rather than fight, and see what the empire would put on the table.

At this point, Jordanes' narrative of Balkans events gives out rather abruptly and cuts with wonderful dexterity to a happy scene where emperor and Gothic leader agree, after a few years of happy coexistence, that the latter would move on to Italy, because all this peace and harmony was making his followers a little bored.[23] Whether this was because Cassiodorus skipped over what happened next out of embarrassment (not impossible) or whether Jordanes' notes, like those of many a student in the middle of an essay crisis, became rather scrappy at this point as his three days ran out, is unclear.

Thankfully, East Roman sources take up the story and a beautifully complex one it turns out to be. Jordanes omits a full sixteen years of political cut and thrust, which was the real backdrop to the Goths' eventual departure for *la bella Italia*. The father-and-son team's bold gambit set up a struggle for power with their Thracian rivals which not only reverberated through the Balkans but spilled over with even greater toxicity into the imperial palace at Constantinople.

The list of active political protagonists for these years is a lengthy one, but getting them straight at the start helps explain why it proved so difficult to resolve the dilemma posed by the Pannonian Goths' arrival on East Roman soil. Out in the Balkans itself, first of all, there were two groups of Goths: the parvenus from Pannonia and the long-established Thracian *foederati*, presently in revolt but accustomed to a privileged, inside role. Whoever was in power in Constantinople, there were funds (or maybe the necessary political will) available only to pay one of these groups the much higher rate of annual subsidy becoming to fully fledged Roman allied soldiery, rather than the three-ha'pence farthing customarily dished out in foreign aid. Thus only one of the two Gothic groups could be made fully part of a ruling coalition at any one time (or so the authorities in Constantinople liked to claim): and, in fact, the interests of the two groups' leaderships were so much at odds that even if you had managed to pay them both, they probably would still have fought.[24]

Inside Constantinople, we have, at the beginning at least, the emperor Leo and various members of the imperial family, engaging, as you would expect, in the normal kinds of struggle either for the imperial throne itself, or, as appropriate to their own eminence, for the various positions of power around it. These tussles were played out in front of a traditional (and occasionally itself participatory) audience of court bureaucracy and imperial senate, and the higher echelons of the regular army general staff. This entirely normal cast of

Constantinopolitan characters was supplemented, however, in the 470s by leading officers among the new Isaurian forces which had been originally recruited to help fight Attila. And by the early 470s, they really had risen a long way. The most prominent among them, Zeno, had married the emperor Leo's daughter Ariadne, and they already had a son (born in 467) who carried the uncompromisingly significant name of his grandfather, whom he was clearly destined to succeed. Zeno's startling climb up the greasy pole, you will remember, had also directly generated the fall of Aspar and the rebellion of the Gothic *foederati*, so that Isaurians and Thracian Goths were in some ways natural political enemies that any ruling coalition would again find difficult to combine. But, here again, there is a complication: Zeno was only the most prominent of several Isaurian leaders, each of whom led their own men and were potentially their own bosses. Zeno could not simply or naturally command the allegiance of other Isaurian generals such as Illus, therefore, but had to win it. Two groups of Goths, and at least two groups of Isaurians, combined in exciting ways with the normal cast of the long-running Constantinopolitan political soap opera to make the years after 473 compulsive viewing.

By the end of the year, an initial compromise had been negotiated. The patrician Hilarianus diverted the Pannonian Goths away from Thessalonica, and granted them billets in a series of small agricultural towns in the canton of Euboia to the west of the city (Figure 3). But in gathering an army to face Thiudimer and Theoderic in the western Balkans, Leo was forced to remove troops from the eastern Balkans, giving the other Theoderic, Strabo, a free hand. His forces ranged freely among the cities of the Via Egnatia, burning the suburbs of Philippi and laying siege to Arcadiopolis, all to apply political pressure on the emperor. Leo quickly had enough. The Thracian Goths were returned to favour, with Strabo being appointed to the most important position on the imperial general staff – *magister militum praesentalis* to be precise – and annual payment of 2,000 pounds of gold restored to his following in the appointment's wake.

The initial effect of the arrival of the Pannonians, paradoxically, had been to make it imperative for the emperor to do a deal with the Thracians. But this was a holding action, not a solution with any long-term viability. For one thing, the Amal-led Goths had achieved none of the benefits for which they had trekked south: the massive annual gold payment to the Thracian Goths agreed by the emperor Leo precluded anything similar to themselves. Equally important, both Gothic leaderships were now locked in a potential death struggle, and they knew it. The agreement between Theoderic Strabo and the emperor is summarized for us in considerable detail by an East Roman historian called Malchus of Philadelphia. It included the fascinating stipulations that:

> [Theoderic Strabo] should be 'sole ruler' of the Goths, and that the emperor should not give admission to anyone who wished to cross into his territory.

Strabo was clearly feeling the pressure. He did not want Thiudimer and Theoderic moving on to his patch and claiming either his honours or – potentially – attracting away the Gothic rank and file from whom he derived his power. And this, it is important to realize, was a distinct possibility. Although some very close confidants were too committed to one dynasty or another to do so, the motto of much of the warrior manpower of these Gothic (and other non-Roman) groups loose on Roman soil in the late fourth and fifth centuries was clearly 'this spear's for hire'. Clovis not only eliminated his rivals, but he also expanded his own power at the same time by adding most of their warbands to his own, and this was no isolated occurrence. In the years after 473, Gothic manpower was indeed to move backwards and forwards between the two leaderships, and, in securing the emperor's backing for his own pre-eminence as Gothic leader, Strabo was merely getting his retaliation in first.[25]

If the compromise of 473 could never have lasted long, the deaths in quick succession of three main protagonists ensured perhaps its extremely swift demise. The first two occurred in Constantinople. On 18 January 474, aged seventy-three, the emperor Leo passed away, to be succeeded by his grandson via Zeno, the younger Leo. Leo II was crowned on the same day that his grandfather died. The evident haste is itself a sign that urgent agendas were afoot, and less than a month later, on 9 February, the young emperor crowned his father joint Augustus. Zeno, it seemed, had completed the ascent from Isaurian warlord to divinely chosen emperor of the Romans: an astonishing career progression and one of the most bizarre legacies of Attila to the Roman world.

But before the end of the year, the young Leo died (of natural causes: 474 being a very bad year for Leos) leaving Zeno in sole occupation of the throne. The Isaurian might have faced competition for control of his son in any case, but Leo's death deprived Zeno of his cloak of imperial legitimacy – his son, after all, was the offspring of an imperial princess – and the plotting thickened. In particular, Leo I's widow, Verina, had a brother called Basiliscus, and these two were much better placed than Zeno to win support from the traditional movers and shakers within Constantinople. Theoderic Strabo, Zeno's natural enemy, was only too willing to join in, as was one of the other major Isaurian power brokers, the general Illus. Sensing that power was slipping through his fingers, Zeno crept out of the city in the first month of the new year, and Basiliscus became emperor, crowned on 9 January 475.

A very Constantinopolitan coup had achieved the desired effect, but the outcome was far from normal. Most deposed emperors met a quick end, unless they retained the loyalty of a large portion of the field army and its commanders, which Zeno did not. But as an Isaurian chieftain, Zeno had other resources at his disposal, and because he had clearly got some notice of the plot and left the city early, he made a successful dash for Isauria, taking refuge in one of the mountain fortresses at the heart of his domain.

Illus was duly sent to Isauria to mount a siege: set one Isaurian to catch another. We don't know exactly where Zeno's fortress was situated, but extensive fieldwork in the Taurus Mountains has uncovered the kind of structure we need to be thinking of. If you have in mind high walls on top of a bare mountainous crag, dominating a narrow but agriculturally productive valley below, you're in the right ballpark. Well supplied by cisterns with water, and with lots of hidden ways of getting food inside at odd moments, these mountain fastnesses were essentially impregnable, and could only be taken by starvation or betrayal. Illus' own headquarters, for instance, withstood a four-year siege in the 480s.[26] Happily ensconced in the purple as he was, therefore, Basiliscus would still have been uneasy in the spring of 475, knowing that Zeno remained at large and that bringing him to heel would be no easy matter. Unease turned to concern as soon as news reached him of what was happening simultaneously out in the western Balkans.

When exactly it happened we don't know, but soon after the former Pannonian Goths were established in Macedonia, Thiudimer, the third of our major protagonists, bit the dust. He need only have been in his mid-forties, but his foresight in cutting out his younger brother Vidimer from the group was rewarded. With no challenger in sight, kingship duly passed to Theoderic, still only in his early twenties. This was a problem for Basiliscus, because Theoderic was not content to stand still. Sensing renewed opportunity in all the mayhem, he made contact with Zeno, pledging his Goths' support in return for an imperial generalship and all the financial and other privileges that Leo had restored to Strabo and the Thracian Goths in 473. Everything was packed up in the wagons once again, and the whole group set off from their Balkans backwater towards the business end of events: the Thracian Plain much closer to Constantinople, and the enormous challenge posed by their Gothic rivals. Again, the young king's daring is striking, although this move was really only a continuation of the same gamble that had brought everyone south from Pannonia; and, in a very real sense, Theoderic had no choice but to keep rolling the dice. To be stuck in political no-man's-land out in Euboia was not a long-term option, if warrior manpower was not to start shifting to his rival.

Back in Constantinople, Theoderic's mobilization, combined with an extraordinary stroke of chance – the kind of thing that really does make you think of Fates out there having fun – derailed Basiliscus' regime. Theoderic's move from Euboia was directed precisely at the Thracian Goths. Its effect was to keep Strabo and his men, the most definitively anti-Zeno force available to Basiliscus, occupied in the summer of 476, at the crunch moment when a revivified Zeno was advancing on Constantinople. This advance was itself the result of that stroke of luck, which at first cannot have seemed so. By spring 476, Illus had been cooling his heels below Zeno's fortress gates for over a year, when he happened to capture Zeno's brother Longinus. This should have been a further setback for the deposed emperor, you might think, but, in a world of personalized politics, the effect was electric. Having Zeno's brother Longinus at his disposal actually gave Illus leverage on the former emperor, security that Zeno would keep any bargain they might make. Perhaps they had already been negoti-ating, we don't know, but Longinus was the vital guarantee that Illus required. He promptly switched sides back to Zeno, and the two Isaurians marched their combined forces back towards Constantinople.

By this stage, concern was turning to alarm, and Basiliscus sent his last remaining field forces to confront them, led by his nephew Armatus: a safe enough choice, you would have thought. But Basiliscus had children, including sons, whereas Zeno, after the death of Leo II, had not. Zeno thus offered Armatus all the usual court honours, and then tossed in the clincher: he would make Armatus' son (also called Basiliscus) Caesar: effectively heir to the throne. Armatus bit, changed sides as well, and suddenly Basiliscus had no armed forces at all. His regime had melted away as the key players each saw more to be extracted from Zeno's restoration and Theoderic the Amal kept the Thracian Goths occupied.

As a textbook case study in human nastiness and the vanity of ambition this could hardly be bettered, and events soon generated an appropriate denouement. Basiliscus and his family sought sanctuary in a church, and were lured out when Zeno promised not to execute them. He exiled them instead to Limnae in Cappadocia where, true to his word, they were not executed. Instead, he had them walled up in a dry cistern and left to die. As for Zeno, he regained the throne in August 476, just in time to receive the embassy from Odovacar, new ruler of Italy, which handed over the imperial vestments of the deposed Romulus Augustulus in that striking gesture with which we began (page xiii). After so many centuries, the western half of the Roman Empire had ceased to exist. How and why the young Theoderic would play a starring role in the first attempt to restore it, stems directly from what the emperor Zeno did next.[27]

Although Zeno had returned to power, or at least its semblance, after eighteen months of exile, his situation was in fact far from satisfactory. For one thing, he now owed a great deal – altogether too much – to a series of kingmakers, especially Armatus and Illus, who had swapped sides for their own reasons at the crucial moments. Then there was the Gothic problem. The Thracian Goths had been prevented from keeping Basiliscus on the throne, but Strabo's power remained intact. Some things were easily resolved. No one, it seems, much cared for Armatus. An arrogant dandy who liked to dress up as Achilles and parade in the Hippodrome, his betrayal of his uncle Basiliscus left him pretty fair game. Zeno duly had him murdered by one of his own protégés, a certain Onoulphus who was actually the brother of Odovacar, the ruler of Italy, but who had decided to pursue a career in Constantinopolitan circles rather than follow his brother west. Both were originally princes of the Sciri but they had been forced to follow new pathways when the

Sciri had suffered a massive defeat at the hands of the Pannonian Goths in the 460s, though this was also the battle in which Valamer was killed (a point that will not be without significance in what follows). Armatus' son was spared but ordained a priest, and no one else seems to have batted an eyelid. Zeno's preference for direct action will need to be borne in mind, however, when trying to understand the behaviour of his various political opponents over the next decade.

The Thracian Goths posed a more substantial problem. The numbers preserved in our sources (pretty good ones by early medieval standards) indicate that they could field somewhat more than 10,000 warriors. As part of one deal, Strabo was granted rations and pay for 13,000 men: a good indication of the size of his command. The figures we have for Theoderic the Amal's following suggest that it too was of about this size, and the general narrative outline confirms the point: neither group, by itself, was able decisively to confront the other. And therein lay Zeno's problem. Theoderic originally promised to attack the Thracian Goths, but in the end, undertook no more than a little skirmishing in 476 and 477, while asking Zeno for imperial assistance. The emperor dithered and even thought of trying to do a deal with Strabo instead, not least because the latter had attracted some deserters from the Pannonian Goths.[28] If this sounds odd, it should be remembered that Theoderic was not yet the all-victorious ruler of Italy, but a young leader who had risked his men in a major gamble. And some of the latter, at least, had clearly come to think that Strabo was the better bet.

In the end, Zeno stuck by his young ally, and over the winter of 477–8 an agreement was reached for the next campaigning season that:

> Theoderic should move his own force, which was concentrated around Marcianople, and bring it closer in. When he reached the gates of the Haemus range, the master of the soldiers of Thrace would come to him with 2,000 cavalry and 10,000 infantry. When he had crossed the Haemus range, another force of 20,000 infantry and 6,000 infantry would meet him . . . near to Hadrianople.

Still more soldiers were to be available from the garrison forces of cities on the Thracian Plain, but surely they wouldn't be needed. Since Strabo had around – perhaps a bit over – 10,000 men, as did Theoderic himself, the plan was to mobilize close to 50,000 men against him: a four-to-one advantage. This was more than sufficient to crush the Thracian Goths once and for all (Figure 3).[29]

The result, however, was not remotely what Theoderic had in mind. Eighteen months later, he found himself back in the western Balkans, outside the great Roman port of Epidamnus (modern Durres in Albania), deep in discussions with an imperial ambassador. The Goth had three specific complaints about what had actually happened in the campaigning season of 478, compared to what had been planned:

> First, you promised that the general of Thrace would immediately join me with his forces. He never appeared. Then you promised that Claudius, the paymaster of the Gothic soldiery, would come with the mercenaries' pay. I never saw him. Third, you gave me guides who left the easier way towards the enemy and led me aside over a steep path with sheer cliffs on both sides. Here, since I was naturally travelling with the cavalry, wagons and all the army's baggage, I was not far from complete destruction with all my force, had the enemy suddenly attacked.[30]

In fact, the route down which he was guided, as we know from Malchus' narrative, led Theoderic's forces straight into the arms (in both senses of the word) of Strabo and the Thracian Goths. This was no accident. Zeno had been negotiating with Strabo in the winter of 477–8 before he decided – apparently – to solve his Gothic problem by helping Theoderic win, so he knew precisely where the Thracian Goths were encamped. Rather than implementing what had been agreed, Zeno's real intention, in 478, was to manipulate the two Gothic groups into the set-piece confrontation they'd been avoiding since 476. He did indeed mobilize the armies mentioned in the agreement with Theoderic, but kept them back: presumably to mop up whatever remained of both groups' military manpower after the two Theoderics had fought each other to a standstill. Having removed Armatus from the scene, our Isaurian emperor was trying to simplify the political chess game still further, by organizing the dramatic removal of both Gothic pieces from the board in one fell swoop.

In the event, Zeno's cunning plan was derailed by two further developments, one beyond his control, the other of his own making. First, the Goths refused to fight. Malchus gives us a highly rhetorical scene where Theoderic Strabo has to persuade his younger namesake to recognize the emperor's treachery:

Having summoned you and having announced that they would
come and campaign along with you, [the Romans] are not here
nor did they meet you at the gates [of the Haemus Mountains] as
they promised. They have left you alone to be destroyed most
disgracefully and to pay to the people whom you have betrayed a
just penalty for your rashness.

I really doubt, bereft as he was of reinforcements and pay, and brought
down an odd route which just happened to lead him straight to Strabo,
that Theoderic needed anyone to point out to him that he'd been
betrayed. Malchus also has Strabo spell out Zeno's real intentions:

While remaining at peace, [the Romans] wish the Goths to wear
each other down. Whichever of us falls, they will be the winners
with none of the effort, and whichever of us destroys the other
side will enjoy a Cadmean victory, as they say, since he will be
left in diminished numbers to face Roman treachery.

Again, I doubt either that Theoderic needed any assistance in grasping
the point, or that Strabo would have seen a reference to Cadmus (the
founder of Thebes who was left with only five warriors, born from the
dragon's teeth, after they fought themselves to a standstill) as a likely
clincher for his argument, but there is a smell of greater authenticity
about how Malchus closes the scene. In his account, it is Theoderic's
Pannonian followers who force him not to fight; they realize exactly
how much they are likely to lose as a result of any confrontation, and
threaten to vote with their feet (as some of their compatriots had
already done) should their young leader attempt to fight.[31] The result
was a Gothic non-aggression pact. Each was allowed to extract from
Constantinople whatever deal they might, but they would not fight
one another.

Since the Goths weren't stupid, Zeno must have always calculated
that this was a possible outcome, and his mobilized armies were there
to step in and retrieve matters if necessary. Or they should have been.
In fact, they weren't, because Illus had left Constantinople in high
dudgeon and the central field armies – as always this means their
officers – were in such an uproar that they had to be sent back to
winter quarters. Again, the Gothic problem and events in Constantinople intertwined. Zeno seems to have been a bit too greedy in 478,
looking to orchestrate a *Godfather*-like finale where all the obstacles to

his power were removed simultaneously. Illus, you will remember, had been a key figure in putting Zeno back on the throne in 476, but did so only because he held leverage over him in the form of the emperor's hostage brother. This was not a situation that Zeno was going to leave unresolved for long: not, at least, if he could help it. True to form, he had a first go at assassinating Illus in 477, which the Isaurian not only survived but chose to profit from, extracting extra honours from Zeno, including the consulship for 478, as the price for his continued participation in the regime. Early in 478, however, there was a second attempt. Again Illus survived, but this time, in the aftermath, he took the perpetrator with him to Isauria to help him with his inquiries. The dispute made the central field army unreliable, and it was this development which really brought the Gothic chickens home to roost.

Once the two Theoderics had worked out what was actually going on and decided not to fight – a process that must have taken all of two nanoseconds – the younger of them advanced towards Constantinople. Betrayed and disgusted, with a following that was becoming deeply unruly given the failure – so far – of the great gamble to pay off (literally, if the reported complaints about the non-appearance of the Gothic paymaster are to be believed, and which I see no reason to doubt), the younger Theoderic was badly in need of success. Some of his following had defected to Strabo the year before, and their overall loyalty was based on his uncle's personal prowess, not an ancient unbroken tradition of royalty. In 478 the Eastern Empire, at least in the person of Zeno, had responded with a decided negative to the – entirely uninvited and thoroughly self-interested – offer of support enacted by the Pannonian Goths' trek south five years before, and everyone was trying to work out what to do. Zeno had two hostile Gothic groups at large in the vicinity of his capital, and no reliable army. Since Strabo was a bit less angry about it all than his younger rival, the emperor decided to do a deal with him, offering a blank cheque, which the Thracian leader duly filled out. The senior general-ship in the empire became his, and gold and rations flowed out of Constantinople northwards to his followers.

This bought Zeno some time while Theoderic cooled off, but the poor provincial populations of the Balkans had to pay a stiff price for it. From his time as a hostage, the Goth knew that its walls made Constantinople impregnable, so he made a slow retreat westwards along the 1,120 kilometres of one of the greatest of ancient imperial highways: the Via Egnatia, first constructed in the second century BC to link a chain of Roman colonies stretching from the Adriatic to the Bosphorus. To keep his followers happy with booty, to vent his spleen, and to force Zeno to make him an offer – in almost equal quantities – major towns en route were sacked; the archaeology of both Philippi and Stobi bear the scars. He then decided to make a dash with his more mobile forces for the highly defensible and strategic port of Epidamnus, which he seized by subterfuge in the summer of 479. And there, Malchus tells us, his plan was to wait and see what would happen next.[32]

It was also at a small strongpoint just outside the city that he met the imperial ambassador to voice his complaints about the campaigning season of 478. Having got all that off his chest, and feeling confident behind the city walls, he also put a series of proposals to the no doubt discomfited ambassador. Should everything else be resolved between them, he would be willing to place his non-combatants in a city of Zeno's choice, hand over his mother and sister as hostages, and campaign with 6,000 of his men wherever the emperor chose. His first idea, not surprisingly, was that:

> With these and the Illyrian troops and whatever others the emperor should send, he would destroy all the Goths in Thrace, on condition that, if he did this, he would become general in place of [Strabo] and be received in the City to live as a citizen in the Roman manner.

Alternatively:

> He was willing, if the emperor commanded it, to go to Dalmatia and restore Nepos.

Julius Nepos was the last Western Roman emperor recognized by Leo in Constantinople. Commander of the West Roman forces in Dalmatia, he had landed at Portus (one of Rome's two seaports, further down the Tiber to the sea) on 19 June 474 to overthrow the pretender Glycerius, being proclaimed emperor there in his place on the same day, and again in Rome a few days later. He had been overthrown in turn by the Italian army commander Orestes, whose son Romulus, know as Augustulus, is commonly designated the last Western emperor, and upon whose deposition in 476 Odovacar had sent the imperial vestments to Constantinople.

Restoring Nepos, therefore, would involve marching upon Italy and Rome itself.[33] How serious Theoderic was in making this offer in 479 is very unclear; I suppose he more expected some kind of renewed alliance against Strabo. But his offer was to prove prophetic: within a decade, Theoderic's wagon train would head back north out of the Balkans, its destination not a return to Pannonia, but to Italy itself. The circumstances which generated this outcome would have been unforeseeable to Theoderic as he left his meeting with Zeno's ambassador at the back end of summer 479.

RAVENNA

Getting Theoderic from Epidamnus to Ravenna is a harder task than getting him from Singidunum to Epidamnus, because we run out of extracts from the extraordinarily detailed history of Malchus of Philadelphia, quite likely because the history itself came to an end. There is enough in other sources to tell the story in outline, not least because of the insight that Malchus' material provides into long-term negotiating positions, rivalries and motivations. The available material still leaves open – or half-open – one major issue of interpretation, as we shall see in a moment, but I guess that's not such bad going when the events happened over 1,500 years ago.

By autumn 479, matters had reached stalemate. Zeno had concluded a deal that was massively advantageous to the Thracian Goths – because he had no choice – while Theoderic had seized a strategic asset. What Theoderic didn't know as he discussed matters with Zeno's ambassador, however, was that his slow-moving baggage train had been ambushed as it trundled towards Epidamnus, resulting in the capture of 2,000 wagons, 5,000 prisoners and a mass of booty. This was enough of a success for Zeno to think that a sufficient military advantage might yet be achieved over the Amal's forces to enable him to dictate the terms of a lasting settlement, and perhaps even the Goths' retreat from Roman territory.[34] Sadly, we never hear what actually happened to the wagon train and prisoners, or what Theoderic tried to do when he heard of their loss. There probably was not a great deal he could do in the immediate aftermath, but his more or less complete loss of initiative was to be reversed as the political soap opera continued to deliver its twists and turns in Constantinople.

The fact that Zeno and Strabo had done a deal could not hide the fact that they did not trust each other more than two and a half centimetres, for the very simple reason that their longer-term interests were diametrically opposed. When a new plot unfolded against Zeno late in 479, therefore, Strabo backed it. As usual, a minor royal was at the heart of it: this time a certain Marcian, who was a grandson of that Marcian who had preceded Leo I on the eastern throne, and who was married to Leontia, a younger daughter of Leo (hence he was also Zeno's brother-in-law). When the plot broke, Strabo advanced quickly towards the city to put the Thracian Goths' weight behind the coup, but it was suppressed too quickly, leaving Strabo stranded. When challenged by Zeno's envoys, he claimed to have been coming to Zeno's rescue. You have to admire the Goth's *cojones*, but no one believed him, and the agreement of 478 quickly unravelled. Zeno hired some Bulgars from beyond the frontier to keep Strabo busy during the campaigning season of 480, but, in 481, Strabo was free to move, presumably because most of Zeno's available troops were in the western Balkans where a military option was still being pursued against the other Theoderic, whose base remained at Epidamnus.

Strabo's move was bold and irrevocable. Mobilizing all his forces, he advanced again on Constantinople: this time determined to storm it. The first assault fell on the main gates of the city, but was beaten off by Illus' troops. The Theodosian Walls had proved themselves once again fit for purpose. Strabo then renewed operations from Sycae on the other side of the Golden Horn, but still got nowhere. He finally moved to near Hestiae and Sosthenium, small harbour towns beside the Bosphorus, in an attempt to move his forces over to Asia Minor, but the imperial navy frustrated this stratagem as well.

As this final manoeuvre makes clear, Strabo had by this time given up entirely on the idea of coming to any kind of agreement with Zeno. Since the last coup's failure, he had been giving asylum to two of Marcian's brothers, and his plan was probably to put one of these on the imperial throne. Indeed, whether he ever really thought he could take the city by storm must be doubtful. Malchus stresses Strabo's close links to important circles at court – as befits the leader of military forces who had been integral to the empire's armies for two generations – and I suspect the plan was that the Goths' advance would stimulate a major coup within the walls. When that failed, the projected move to Asia Minor was surely not about assaulting the city from another (even more difficult) direction, but designed to stimulate a broader revolt against Zeno in the heartlands of the Eastern Empire, to isolate him and force his eventual overthrow.

Zeno, however, had Illus' forces to secure the city, and the imperial navy to frustrate Strabo's grander designs, leaving the Gothic leader uncertain what to do next. Eventually he decided to move his forces westwards along the Via Egnatia, perhaps hoping to concoct a new plan involving his younger namesake who was still holed up at the other end of it. What that plan might have been is unclear, because one of history's great 'ouch' moments intervened: 'while mounting his horse early one morning, it threw him on to an upright spear standing at the side of his tent'. So passed Theoderic Strabo.

Reflecting Amal propaganda, Jordanes dismisses him with barely a sentence, implying that, because he was not a member of the Amal dynasty, he was of negligible significance. This is manifestly untrue. Where Theoderic the Amal, perhaps because of his inexperience, was busy signing up for one after another of Zeno's questionable deals between 475 and 478 (what a second-hand-car salesman that emperor would have made), Strabo had kept a cool eye on the longer term and successfully attracted away some of his Gothic rival's supporters. With just a little more luck, it could easily have been Strabo who emerged triumphant from the clash of the two Theoderics, since both before and after (as we shall see in Chapter 3) these Goths were open to leaders from outside the Amal family, just so long as they were effective. That, of course, was fated not to happen, and, instead, his untimely death presented our Amal gambler with a whole new set of opportunities.[35]

Succession among the Thracian Goths passed initially to Strabo's son Recitach, ruling jointly with two of his uncles. The resemblance here to the power-sharing arrangement of the Amal family in the generation before Theoderic is striking. And, like those arrangements, the agreement underlying it fell apart – only with more speed and greater nastiness. Quickly, Recitach had his two uncles murdered to assume sole power: once again, this makes the point that family ties work differently among the very powerful, where relations are always as much potential rivals as allies. This clearly stretched loyalties among those crucial second-rank leaders, whose choices always play such a critical role in the success of any reign. All right, Recitach was Strabo's son, and Strabo had been a first-rate leader; but was Recitach of the same calibre?

Outside events soon conspired to suggest not. Strabo's great if ultimately doomed campaign of 481 had only been possible in the absence of any imperial field forces from the vicinity of Constantinople. Zeno responded by withdrawing the forces who had been facing Theoderic in the West, which in turn meant that he had to switch from a military to a diplomatic option in his dealings with the Pannonian Goths. And what a price Theoderic extracted, his argumentative ardour fuelled no doubt by the emperor's previous betrayals. Under the terms of a new agreement in 482–3, his forces were resettled in the eastern Balkans, in Dacia Ripensis and Lower Moesia, while Theoderic himself was appointed senior imperial general, with the elevated levels of remuneration for his forces that this implied. After a decade of intermittent movement and fighting, the great gamble had paid off.

What's more, Theoderic was appointed consul designate for the year 484: the announcement of which was made sometime in 483. The consulship was by this point in imperial history not an office, but the supreme honour within the imperial gift, conferring a type of immortality since Romans named the years after the consuls, and was customarily held only by emperors and their closest associates. No individual who owed his political prominence to the fact that he was in command of a non-Roman military force had ever received such an honour before. Clearly Zeno had been forced to find something entirely beyond the norm to pay off Theoderic for the double-dealing of 478. The balance had shifted. All the momentum was now behind Theoderic the Amal and he was not a man to waste it. Late in 483 or early in 484, but certainly after the agreement which so favoured him had come into force, Theoderic had Recitach murdered on his way from a bath to a feast in a district of Constantinople known as Bonophatianae.

And this is where we have to face a critical gap in the sources. No one tells us what the bulk of the second-rank leaders among the Thracian Goths did next. A handful did nothing. A few of the senior officers of the East Roman military in the next generation are referred to as Goths who did not follow Theoderic to Italy. On the other hand, the Thracian Gothic *foederati* completely disappear from the pages of East Roman history at this point, in what is much more than a mere argument from silence. The Balkans military was the focus of a major revolt against Zeno's successor Anastasius in the next generation, for instance, which receives detailed coverage in our surviving sources. There is not the slightest sniff that the Thracian Goths, such a major feature of the 470s, still existed there as a coherent unit. Since it is also apparent that Theoderic led out of the Balkans far more than the 10,000 or so warriors he had led into it – the best estimate is 20,000-plus – there is no doubt where the smart money lies. On the elimination of Recitach, most of the second-rank leaders among the Thracian Goths switched their allegiance over to Theoderic, reversing the move made by some of the Amal's followers in 477–8. (Indeed, this had probably all been carefully pre-negotiated before the Bonophatianae hit.) At the beginning of 484, Theoderic was triumphant. Assured of immortality by the consulship, he had secured a huge flow of cash for his followers and eliminated another set of rival Gothic dynasts.[36]

According to our sources, Zeno was not only in on the plan, but pushed it. The gain for him was twofold. For one thing, it simplified the political scene enormously. Instead of two Gothic leaderships, one of which would always be out of favour and therefore hostile, there was now only one. Equally important, he had his eyes on a larger prize. The biggest pain in Zeno's neck was actually Illus. Illus had kept him in power at crucial moments, bringing Isaurian troops to the capital both to suppress Marcian's coup in 479 and to fight Strabo's Goths at the walls of the city in 480. But Illus also had Zeno's brother as a hostage which gave him unacceptable leverage, and Zeno was always looking for a chance to eliminate him. In 481, he had tried assassination for a third time, which cost Illus part of an ear, and Zeno an arm and a leg. To restore good relations afterwards, the emperor had been forced to grant Illus a more or less free hand in part of the empire's richest eastern lands. Illus set up base in Antioch, second city of the empire, and ruled from there virtually an independent fiefdom. This was not a situation that Zeno could tolerate in the long term, and solving the Gothic problem by promoting Theoderic to such heights prepared for the final showdown. All his available forces – including large numbers of Theoderic's Goths – could now be concentrated against his great Isaurian rival. At the same time as Recitach was being eliminated, therefore, Zeno broke with Illus by notionally dismissing him from his official posts and setting in motion a trial of strength. Perhaps Theoderic's Goths swayed the military balance, but it was all over pretty quickly. Both sides mobilized everything they could, yet when the two armies met near Antioch in September 484, Illus was decisively defeated. He fled to his mountain fortress in Isauria, much as Zeno had done in 475, and proved equally hard to dislodge. He plotted away for four years, but, in the end found no way back into Constantinople. Finally, the fortress was betrayed and Illus taken and executed, but already by autumn 484 Illus had been effectively eliminated from Constantinopolitan politics.[37]

And then there were two. The minor royals had been steadily eliminated: all the likely contenders from among the old Emperor Leo's in-laws had made their moves and paid the price. Zeno's main Isaurian rival had been cut down, and the Thracian Goths had lost their coherence as an independent political force. The only cloud left on Zeno's horizon in late 484 was Theoderic the Amal: consul, imperial general and, above all, commander of an independent force – now numbering upwards of 20,000 men – which owed its primary allegiance to him and not to the emperor. Given Zeno's track record of tolerating political pluralism, this was not a situation that was ever likely to last. Even though the Goth was not a serious contender for the Eastern throne himself (being even less of an insider than Aspar), he might back someone else who was. The final reckoning was not long in coming. Initial whisperings started even during the Illus campaign, causing Theoderic to return to Constantinople, though the force he had sent continued to fight. Once Illus was safely bottled up and the army returned, however, Theoderic moved into open rebellion in 485.

It is reported that, in doing so, the Goth had in mind the fate of Armatus: made general for life by Zeno in 476 but quickly assassinated. This makes perfect sense, but Theoderic might just as well have been thinking of Basiliscus or Illus besides. When it came to sharing power or making promises, Zeno could not be trusted: any more, of course, than could Theoderic from Zeno's point of view. By 487, the endgame had been reached. Theoderic advanced towards Constantinople, causing considerable damage in some of the wealthy suburbs outside its walls, but, more importantly, cutting part of the aqueduct system. From his time in the city, the Goth knew exactly how dependent its half a million inhabitants were upon the flow of collected rainfall from the hills of Thrace. But Theoderic was not intent on actually taking the city. Nor, unlike Strabo six years before, does he seem to have had in mind his own candidate for the imperial throne. His aim was to pressure Zeno into a final solution of their grievances that both sides could actually believe in. That, however, was the problem. Zeno had spent the last decade and a bit fighting off the influence of over-mighty subjects, and Theoderic was yet another, especially after the incorporation of most of the Thracian Goths into his following.

We have no detailed account of the negotiations which followed outside the city, nor even a sense of how long they took. But eventually – or maybe quickly – both sides recognized the impossibility of real coexistence and agreed that the departure of the Goths for Italy would be the ideal solution to their problems. Later Western sources stemming from Theoderic's court in Italy stress his initiative in the decision and ignore Zeno, as you might expect. That doesn't mean they are necessarily wrong, though, even if their Constantinopolitan counterparts take precisely the opposite view. Theoderic's thoughts had turned towards Italy as long ago as 479 at that meeting outside Epidamnus, and, however seriously he meant it at that point, the idea had conceivably been bubbling away in the back of his mind ever since. Either way, both sides were soon to adopt it, and, after a year's break which again emphasizes the logistical nightmares such moves entailed, the Gothic wagon train rumbled north-west out of the East Roman Balkans in autumn 488: its eyes firmly on the prize of rich new lands in Italy.[38]

Others had different ideas. One major battle against the Gepids and a series of skirmishes with various Sarmatians had to be fought before the Goths even reached the frontiers of Italy, and Italy, of course, was not waiting with open arms. Since 476 it had been ruled by Odovacar, and he was not about to resign, even supposing that Theoderic would have let him. Odovacar's paychest was presumably behind the Gepids' and Sarmatians' attempts to erode Theoderic's will and strength en route. But Theoderic fought his way past these obstacles, leading a forced river crossing of what is now the Vuka (close to the site of the horrible massacre of 1991) himself, to bring his wagon trains in due course into Italy by the Vipava valley, the main route through the Julian Alps, connecting the Friulian lowlands with what is now central Slovenia. At Pons Isontii, Odovacar's army was waiting but it was driven back into Italy proper after a major defeat on

28 August 489. Theoderic beat him again on 30 September close to the city of Verona, and that appeared to be that. Odovacar fled to Ravenna, which had become an imperial and then post-Roman capital in the fifth century because its marshes made it impregnable, and its port invulnerable to sieges.

In fact, there were a few twists and turns to go. One of Odovacar's generals (called Tufa) swapped sides to Theoderic early on, but then did so again before the end of 489. And, likewise, a force of Rugi who had joined Theoderic after the destruction of their Austrian kingdom by Odovacar in 487, were nonetheless sufficiently attracted by the latter's promises – for a time – to switch allegiance too. In the winter of 489–90, therefore, Theoderic was himself forced into a fortified redoubt: the city of Pavia. But in summer 490, Theoderic won a third major battle on 11 August, where the road from Lodi to Cremona crosses the river Adda, and over the next two years tightened the noose around Odovacar's neck. Tufa's force was eliminated, the Rugi returned to the fold, and, in August 492, Theoderic began a sea blockade of Ravenna from nearby Rimini. Matters dragged on because Ravenna was so hard to capture, until negotiations finally opened on 25 February 493. On 5 March, Theoderic entered the city having agreed to share power. But the Goth had not spent most of his life in and around Constantinople for nothing. Ten days later, at a banquet:

> Theoderic himself rushed forward and struck him with a sword on the collarbone . . . The fatal blow cut through Odovacar's body as far as the hip, and it is said that Theoderic exclaimed, 'There clearly wasn't a bone in the wretched man's body.'

On the same day, Odovacar's key supporters and their families were rounded up and massacred. The roll of the dice which had begun a full twenty years before had finally paid off.[39] Many thousands of kilometres, a host of minor engagements and several major battles later, the land of Italy was his to rule: and all the result of the Gothic unification his manoeuvring had eventually achieved. But Theoderic had learned a great deal more in Constantinople than how to make agreements in bad faith. With Italy's resources at his back, its new king, still not yet in his forties, set about unleashing a still grander range of ambition even than he'd shown so far. A first attempt to restore the Western Empire was under way.

2

A PHILOSOPHER IN PURPLE

THE RECEIVED IMAGE of Theoderic's rule in Italy stands in almost complete contrast to the bold, highly calculating gambler we have just met, capable of slicing an opponent in half over the brandy and cigars. Not long after his death, Cassiodorus, one of the chief officers of his later years, penned the following portrait:

> When he had laid aside the cares of the State, he would seek through your conversation the opinions of wise men of old, that by his own deeds he might make himself equal to the ancients. Into the courses of the stars, into the gulfs of the sea, into the marvels of springing fountains, this most acute questioner enquired, so that by his diligent investigations into the nature of things he seemed to be a philosopher wearing the purple.[1]

Not so much the violent warband leader, then, as a wise seeker after the most profound truths of nature: an image reinforced by many of the remaining letters of the collection in which this one is preserved. These purport to show his government in action. And in them, in impeccable if slightly baroque late Roman Latin, we find Theoderic busy rooting out corruption, dispensing top-notch justice, building walls and aqueducts, and even supporting the educational pillars of classical culture, often while offering up a little classical homily on the side. The same dedication to wisdom is also apparent in foreign affairs. Here he famously concocted a series of marriage alliances with all of the major peer realms within his orbit (the major kingdoms of the Visigoths, Burgundians, Vandals and Franks, along with some smaller ones: Figure 4), and then endeavoured to keep the peace when a major conflict broke out between two of them, the Visigoths and the Franks in the middle of the first decade of the sixth century.

Look beneath the surface, however, and the contrast between the man of violent, occasionally explosive action who kept Constantinople on the run for a decade and a half, and the purple-clad philosopher who ran Italy, quickly subsides.

CASSIODORUS

Behind every ruler who has gone down in history as a good thing, you will find at least one excellent spin doctor, and Theoderic is no exception. Not only did Cassiodorus write a Gothic History, whose account of the king's youth – in the reworked version of Jordanes – occupied us in the previous chapter, but he also first wrote and then – crucially – collected a body of official letters from his time as senior official of the Gothic kings of Italy: the *Variae*. This text contains some 468 letters, edicts, and model letters (*formulae*) divided among twelve books, and it is the fundamental source for the wise and pacific Theoderic we have just encountered: the lofty philosopher aiming to hold together a Roman west which was otherwise falling into barbarism and violence. It is also a source which requires extremely careful handling.

For although at first glance it doesn't look like one, it is in fact a peculiar (in both the popular and the original senses of the word) example of political autobiography. Many of the collected texts are letters written in the name of different Gothic rulers of the Italian kingdom: the majority for Theoderic himself, but a fair number too for the different successors which followed between his own death in 526 and Cassiodorus' final departure from office in or around 538/9. But Cassiodorus assures his readers in two Prefaces that he really did draft the original letters, and that he was also responsible for selecting and ordering those that we find included. The *Variae* collection does not represent, in other words, every letter that Cassiodorus had ever written for each of the Gothic rulers he served, but a careful selection.

And herein lies the problem. Political autobiography is one of the most slippery of all genres. The combination of self-aggrandizement and self-justification makes it almost proverbially unreliable for historians, and Cassiodorus is no exception, despite offering us the usual prefatory rubbish that he only put pen to paper because his friends had urged him to undertake this task for the public good. The element of self-aggrandizement comes through in the *Variae* loud and clear, not least in the quotation at the head of this chapter, which is taken from a letter Cassiodorus penned to announce his own appointment to high office. In other words, Cassiodorus himself is the interlocutor who spent long evenings instructing Theoderic on everything from philosophy to astronomy. This is substantially hogwash. The image proved an attractive one for commentators of earlier historical generations, who found something comforting in the idea of a Gothic barbarian desiring instruction in classical knowledge, but Cassiodorus was demonstrably not that important to Theoderic's regime; at least not until its final years. Having sliced Odovacar in half in early spring 493, Theoderic ruled his Italian kingdom for the next thirty-three years, until his own death on 30 August 526. During all that time, Cassiodorus held the important office of quaestor between 507 and 511, and the top civilian job of praetorian prefect (chief financial and legal officer) from 524 until the king's death. For the vast majority of Theoderic's reign, therefore, Cassiodorus held no position at all, and particularly not in the first decade or so of his rule, when the crucial lines of Theoderic's governance were set. And even if it is probably right to think that Cassiodorus was not simply mouldering on his estates between 511 and 524, we can convincingly populate Theoderic's court with many other Roman advisers besides, some of whom knew at least as much about classical culture as Cassiodorus, if not rather more. Only for the final two years of Theoderic's thirty-three-year reign, then, does the picture Cassiodorus paints for us of their relations look remotely plausible.[2]

Even more important, by the time he was producing the *Variae* collection, Cassiodorus was a man with a great deal to explain. At that point, the Gothic kingdom was coming towards an untimely close at the hands of East Roman armies bent on a full-scale conquest (it is sometimes called a 'reconquest', but Constantinople had never before ruled, or even attempted to rule, Italy). The war began in 536, and, although the last letters in the collection are impossible to date exactly, they certainly belong to the dog days of late 538 or even 539, by which time the writing was firmly on the wall. East Roman forces had complete strategic initiative and were closing in rapidly on Cassiodorus and the last of his Gothic rulers, Wittigis, in the kingdom's final redoubt, Ravenna. Cassiodorus thus produced the collection at a moment when defeat was looking inevitable at the hands of an East Roman army that he himself – as the Gothic regime's chief financial officer – had spent at least three campaigning seasons helping to resist.

Amongst other things, his office was responsible for victualling and army pay, and the letters imply that he was close to royal decision-making at a time when unpleasant policy decisions were having to be taken, not least one to execute some senatorial hostages, as the Gothic regime came under increasing pressure. If the victorious East Roman soldiers had had playing cards marked up with their chief opponents in 539–40, Cassiodorus' face would have been somewhere on one of the picture cards. When Ravenna fell in summer 540, therefore, he was duly hauled off to Constantinople. For Cassiodorus, the *Variae* had an extremely important function to fulfil: they had to justify to the new East Roman rulers of Italy why he had continued to serve Gothic kings despite their arrival on Italian soil.

The potential for distortion in this agenda is enormous, since Cassiodorus, as a rich Italian landowner, had a lot to lose: potentially even his life in the worst-case scenario. Fortunately for us, his strategy in the late 530s was closely aligned – as other sources confirm – with that of Theoderic when the letters were first being drafted. Cassiodorus' central justification for having continued to serve Gothic kings lay in the contention that it was right to do so because he had in fact been serving – entirely in good faith – a Gothic regime which was fundamentally 'Roman' in nature and practice. If, in His infinite wisdom, God eventually decided to give victory to Constantinople, then it was not for humans to dispute His judgement, but no blame – the *Variae* implicitly claimed – should be attached on this account to Cassiodorus himself, as he was and always had been merely a good Roman acting entirely in ways that a good Roman public servant should do. In his desire to present Theoderic's Gothic kingdom as a fundamentally Roman regime, therefore, Cassiodorus' needs as that kingdom collapsed so strongly echoed the king's own propaganda at the height of his power, that there was little need for Cassiodorus to alter much in the contents of the letters.[3]

To understand how first Theoderic himself and then Cassiodorus later could claim that the Gothic regime in Italy was in fact 'Roman', when the Amal dynasty to which he belonged had so palpable and recent an origin beyond the old imperial frontier, it is necessary to explore how Romanness was understood. It was a concept that did not exist in a vacuum. As so often with self-definitions, it required a second party to display the inverse of the qualities claimed by Romans themselves: 'barbarians'. Late Roman state ideologies identified a number of related characteristics which differentiated the two. A central contention was that the population of the Roman Empire (or at least its elite) was made more rational than other human beings by the classical literature in which it was customarily educated. Rationality was defined as the individual's ability to control bodily passions by exercising the intellect. Immersion in classical literature exposed the individual to accumulated examples of men behaving well and badly, which, if properly digested, enabled the body to be controlled. Barbarians, by contrast, were prey to their passions, totally unable to steer a sensible course, and particularly given to gratifying the desires of the flesh. For society as a whole, the greater rationality of its individual members meant that Romans were also prepared to subordinate immediate gratification to the rule of written law: the guarantee of an ordered society. Thus for Romans the overwhelming superiority of imperial society – encapsulated, in the late imperial period by the word *civilitas* (roughly 'civilization') – came to be symbolized as the rule of written law.

Christianity gave this sense of superiority a further dimension. Graeco-Roman natural philosophy identified an underlying order in the cosmos, whose structure reflected, throughout, one divine, organizing principle which had shaped it from primeval chaos. Thus in a view descending from Pythagoras and Ptolemy, distances from earth to the planets mirrored harmonic ratios and exact proportionality. The Christian Roman Empire, following the strong lead of pagan Emperors, claimed that there was a political dimension to this cosmological order. No earthly ruler could hold power unless the Divinity so ordered. This idea was developed still further to support the claim that the Roman Empire was the particular agent of divine power for perfecting humanity. Thus Eusebius of Caesarea argued that it was no accident that Christ should have been born in the reign of Augustus. It was part of the Divine Plan that the founders of Christianity and the Roman Empire had coexisted. More generally Christian emperors arrogated to themselves the role of Christ's vicegerent on earth. Imperial ceremonial echoed the majesty of heaven, and an aura of Christian sacrality surrounded the imperial person and his officers. A proper classical education thus led the individual to appreciate the benefits of the Roman way of life, and its historical importance within the divine scheme of things.[4]

Theoderic's regime seized upon this vision of *Romanitas* in its

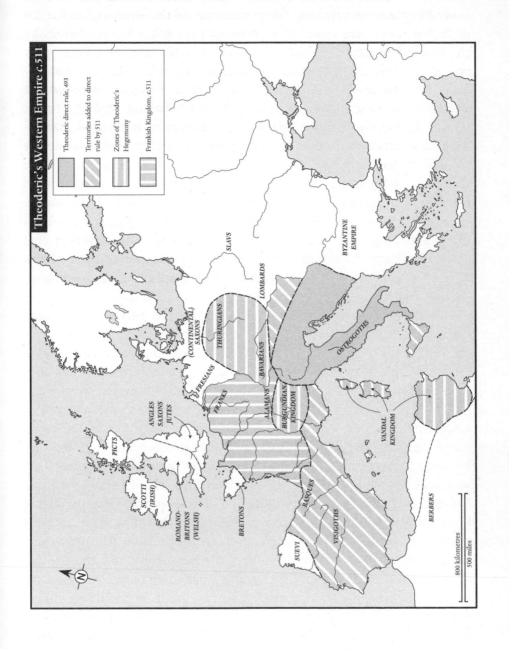

Theoderic's Western Empire c.511

Theoderic direct rule, 493

Territories added to direct rule by 511

Zones of Theoderic's Hegemony

Frankish Kingdom, c.511

PICTS

SCOTTI (IRISH)

ANGLES SAXONS JUTES

ROMANO-BRITONS (WELSH)

BRETONS

FRANKS

FRESIANS

(CONTINENTAL) SAXONS

THURINGIANS

SLAVS

LOMBARDS

BAVARIANS

ALAMANS

BURGUNDIAN KINGDOM

OSTROGOTHS

BYZANTINE EMPIRE

SUEVI

BASQUES

VISIGOTHS

VANDAL KINGDOM

BERBERS

N

800 kilometres

500 miles

entirety, not least the claim to be part of a divinely inspired world order. We have already seen him make this central claim in the letter to Anastasius (page 3), and it is in many of the other *Variae* besides. There is, fortunately, plenty of external confirmation that this self-presentation was Theoderic's own, and not some construction of Cassiodorus' desperate imagination as the East Roman noose tightened around his neck in Ravenna. Above all, we have the mosaics of St Apollinare Nuovo in Ravenna, which originally portrayed Theoderic enthroned in majesty, surrounded by his court in the new palace he had built there. Opposite him was displayed Christ Pantocrator – the 'Ruler of All' – and the majesty of heaven. The greater authority (heaven) was thus shown directly sustaining the lesser (Theoderic). Theoderic's Italian palaces (that of Ravenna is best known, but two others were built at Pavia and Verona) seem to have imitated the architectural pattern of the imperial palace in Constantinople. Theoderic, of course, knew it well, from his ten years as a hostage, and he not only built 'imperial' palaces, but also deployed in them the imperial cult of the sacred ruler. Great public occasions such as his staged triumphal entry into Rome in the year 500 – absolutely modelled on the old imperial ceremony of the *adventus* – were designed to proclaim, after the Constantinopolitan pattern, the sanctity and divinely inspired nature of his rule.[5]

This is a particularly striking element of Theoderic's self-presentation because he was not – at least according to the majority of his Italo-Roman subjects – an Orthodox Christian. That is, he did not adhere to the definition of the Christian Trinity laid down at the Council of Nicaea in 325, which asserted the complete equality of Father and Son. Like many Goths, Theoderic belonged to a brand of Christianity which has gone down in the textbooks as 'Arianism': so-called after a priest of the city of Alexandria who flourished in the 320s and 330s. We don't really know what Arius thought, since only fragments of his works survive as quoted by his victorious opponents, and they tend to cite, usually out of context, only the things they think are most damaging. What we can say is that Theoderic's branch of Christianity was fully Roman in origin (it was not some kind of barbarian oddity) and did not descend in any meaningful way from the teachings of Arius (whatever they may have been). It actually represented a strand of traditional pre-Nicene Christian belief rooted in the Gospel evidence (where Jesus prays to the Father 'Thy will be done', for instance, which doesn't sound much like an equal relationship when all's said and done) which was itself Orthodoxy at the moment of the first large-scale Gothic conversion to Christianity in the 370s. But whereas the Roman world, having hesitated for two generations, moved decisively towards Nicaea in the 380s, the majority of the Goths and other barbarians who came into contact with Christianity retained the older faith, preferring to define the Son as 'like' the Father, rather than, as Nicaea would have it, stating that both were of 'the same substance'.

Given that he was ruling Italy, the land of the papacy and defender-in-chief of Nicene Orthodoxy, you might think that Theoderic's claim to have been appointed by God should have been a touch divisive. Not so. For the vast majority of his reign, Theoderic and the Catholic establishment treated one another with the greatest respect. On his great ceremonial *adventus* into Rome in 500, for instance, Theoderic greeted the Pope 'as if he were St Peter himself'. The compliment was duly returned. The king's good offices were sought by the Church of Rome itself when it was divided down the middle by a disputed papal succession: the so-called Laurentian schism, named after Laurentius, one of the participants (along with Pope Symmachus) and the eventual loser, destined to go down in history therefore as an antipope. It used to be argued that Theoderic's handling of the dispute was deeply partisan (and echoes of that view are still there, I note, in the relevant Wikipedia article), but the best and most recent scholarly study of the dispute (from which extensive documentation survives) has come to the conclusion that the king went out of his way to operate even-handedly and according to established procedures, and to do his best to bring about a speedy and conciliatory resolution. The dispute still took eight years to work its way to a conclusion, but it remains a striking testimony to the level of de facto recognition given by the Catholic Church to Theoderic's legitimacy.

A similar recognition was granted him in formal Church assemblies. The official minutes of a Roman synod of March 499 survive and make fascinating reading. At its opening, the assembled churchmen jumped to their feet and shouted, 'Hear us Christ. Long live Theoderic.' They repeated it thirty times. Such acclamations were a standard part of imperial ceremonial, but the churchmen made not the slightest mention of the emperor Anastasius. Many individual churchmen were also ready to serve Theoderic, both actively and ideologically. A Catholic deacon called Ennodius pronounced a public panegyric before the king in 507, for instance, which explained how God had brought Theoderic to Italy to subdue the demon-possessed Odovacar.[6] Notwithstanding his own particular creed, Theoderic thus claimed divine inspiration for his rule, acted accordingly in all Church matters, and received an appropriate response from the leading churchmen of his domains.

The propaganda and public acts of his regime also showed great awareness of the other essential elements of *Romanitas*. Theoderic was particularly aware of the ideological importance of written law, and of being seen to further individual human rationality via an education in the classics. Ennodius' panegyric further observed that *ius* and *civilitas* presided in Theoderic's palace, *ius* designating the fundamentals of Roman law, *civilitas*, as we have seen, the state of higher civilization that written law generated. Closely related to this was the concept of true freedom (*libertas*) of the individual, which could be attained only by those who obeyed this law. Many of the letters written for Theoderic by Cassiodorus demanded respect for Roman law, cited it, reflected upon fundamental correctness, or referred to the enduring *civilitas* that the king maintained.[7] Education, too, received its due. Ennodius' panegyric again stressed the importance of the classical education Theoderic had received in Constantinople. In his letter to Anastasius, Theoderic claimed, as we have seen, that it was precisely this education which had taught him to govern Romans properly. A number of the *Variae* underline the attention he devoted to it, or perhaps – better – wanted to be seen devoting to it. He proclaimed education to be the key to morality. Through it, the individual learns self-control, without which obedience to Roman law is impossible. Likewise, the individual who lacks self-control cannot be trusted to govern others. For the maintainance of good social order – *civilitas* – education had to function properly, and not for nothing did Theoderic's family like to be seen subsidizing the pay of grammarians.[8]

A whole battery of means was deployed, then, to get over the message that Theoderic's regime was 'Roman' in that most fundamental of ideological senses: it was in tune with God's plans for humankind. Panegyrics, official letters, coinage (some of Theoderic's coins proclaimed *invicta Roma*), visual representations and buildings were all used to sustain this claim and its supporting pillars: reverence for Roman law and classical education. The fullest and clearest expression of all this is to be found in the *Variae*, but the ideas which surface in it are found elsewhere, and the tone of the regime was set before Cassiodorus ever took office. The pen portrait which showed Cassiodorus helpfully instructing Theoderic on their evenings off was also written after the king was safely dead. Cassiodorus' pretensions need to be put to one side; there is not the slightest doubt that his regime's determinedly self-Romanizing agenda was set by Theoderic himself.[9] Why did a Gothic warlord from the Amal dynasty go to so much trouble to present himself as thoroughly Roman?

THE IMPORTANCE OF BEING ROMAN

It has sometimes been ascribed to sentiment: a profound respect for all things imperial. But this doesn't do justice to the obvious calculation with which Theoderic framed the public statements of his Italian regime. Nor does it fit with the Theoderic we met in the Balkans, who had always been ready, when necessary, to confront the Eastern Empire head on, and whose desire for a closer relationship with Constantinople was so profoundly self-interested. A little more thought provides a much more satisfactory answer. Theoderic's determined *Romanitas* was a highly intelligent – and frankly pushy – strategy with some very practical applications.

Appropriating the ideologies of Roman rule clothed Theoderic's seizure of power in Italy within a verbal and ceremonial language which his Roman subjects – especially the most important among them – could immediately understand, and set the public stance of his regime on an extremely reassuring footing. This made it easier for them to respond positively to the regime that he set about building in Italy, with distinct benefits to both sides. Take, for instance, Catholic churchmen. That Theoderic claimed to have been appointed by God and then behaved as such – in showing, for instance, almost exaggerated respect for the Bishop of Rome – allowed churchmen explicitly to accept his claim in their conciliar prayers and behave respectfully in return. This allowed churchmen to retain all the advantages they had built up under a century and a half of Christian imperial rule – a long list of lands, revenues, rights and consequent influence – and even press for new ones. Theoderic thus gained extra legitimacy from the churchmen's approval and even some influence over this powerful institution, although in big things, such as the election of popes, he was careful to be seen acting in even-handed fashion. The dangers of not participating in such a dance routine of mutual courtship are illustrated by contemporary Vandal Africa, whose rulers belonged to the same brand of Christianity as Theoderic, but where State and Church locked horns in combat. The result there was periodic bouts of Vandal persecution. In their worst moments, these plunged the kingdom virtually into civil war, particularly in the year 484, and generated some substantial losses of buildings and revenues, not to mention prestige and influence, for the Catholic Church in substantial parts of the kingdom. And not only did this conflict generally make it difficult for Vandal kings to maintain good relations with Catholic churchmen, it also poisoned relations with some of their richer Roman subjects, who were largely Catholic by this date as well. So everybody lost.[10]

Theoderic's self-presentation also carefully homed in on the other main route into the hearts of both the ecclesiastical and secular Roman elites of his new Italian domains. The secular elite comprised a block of families, relatively few in number, who controlled the reservoirs of financial power in the kingdom. Both they and indeed the various institutions of the Catholic Church derived their pre-eminence first and foremost from the lands that they owned. This provided the wealth which also allowed them to dominate local politics and administration. Indeed, under the empire, it was their willingness to raise and pay over to the state taxes derived from the agricultural activities of their own estates and from those of their tenants and social inferiors that had sustained the whole imperial edifice. A militarily dominant ruler can always try to compel payment, but taxation is a political issue, and successful taxation usually requires a strong element of consent. In the Roman case, the state bought it from the landowning elite partly through the patronage it pushed in their direction in the form of offices, but more fundamentally through its legal system. Because it was relatively small and owned so much, the Roman landowning elite was potentially highly vulnerable to attack from the many who were much less fortunate. And when all the bullshit about rational, divinely inspired social order is put to one side, Roman law was all about defining and protecting property rights, so that the state-generated and state-supported legal system was the basic prop of the established elite's social dominance. This indeed was the basic quid pro quo which made them willing to raise and pay over taxation in return.

Here too, Theoderic was right on the money, in that a key aspect of his determined *Romanitas* took the form of a basic commitment to the continuation of Roman law. At heart, this amounted to an explicit guarantee to the old Roman elites of Italy (not to mention richer churchmen) that their landed fortunes had a future in the new political era. The old bargain would be respected by the new management. This was again far more than mere inertia on Theoderic's part. During his struggle with Odovacar, he at one point threatened to cancel the testamentary powers of all those Roman landowners who had not actively supported him. Those affected would have lost the right to leave their landed fortunes to the heirs of their choice, and hence would have faced effective dispossession. Eventually, Theoderic gave way in the face of an embassy led by Bishop Epiphanius of Milan, and landowner palpitations could subside.[11] I doubt that Theoderic ever meant to implement the policy, at least not in full, but the threat was a salutary reminder of what the new king might do if he so chose. Making and then withdrawing the threat made it crystal clear to the Roman landowners of Italy that active participation in the governmental structures of the new regime was an enormously good idea.

It also helped Theoderic negotiate the immense public relations problem that could not be avoided at the start of his reign. There was one thing straightforwardly not Roman about Italy's new ruler: the army he had brought with him from the Balkans. Some of it, particularly the former Thracian Goths, had been on a Roman imperial payroll, and for a long time, but in revolt even the Thracian *foederati* had not behaved like a normal Roman army, and the Pannonian Goths, Rugi and assorted others that Theoderic brought with him besides, all had recent non-Roman origins. By 493, some of this force had been fighting with him for twenty years. In the interim, they had marched thousands of kilometres, fought numerous small-scale engagements, and survived some major battles, both before and after crossing into Italy. Throughout, Theoderic had not simply been able to assume his followers' loyalty, but had had to earn it. It had been a struggle for him to retain the loyalty even of some of his original Pannonian Goths immediately after his father's death, he had won over the bulk of the Thracian Goths in the mid-480s, and the same problem had shown up in Italy, where the Rugi cheerfully swapped sides according to their perception of where the best offer was likely to come from. And now, after all that effort, his army had won a rollover jackpot in the form of Italy and all its wealth. This astonishing success merely posed the old loyalty problem in a new form. Having just, by feat of arms and endurance, put their man in total control of an extremely rich kingdom, his followers were naturally expecting full and proper rewards.

This represented a problem of potentially huge dimensions. The act of rewarding was not something Theoderic could afford to skimp on. The lives of early medieval rulers who failed to reward their followers in line with those followers' expectations tended to be brief and not a little painful. And wealth really only took one basic form in the ancient and early medieval worlds: land and the income that could be generated from it. Hence the problem. There was so much else that would work so beautifully if the Italo-Roman landowning elite, secular and ecclesiastical, could be kept onside, but his warriors needed compensation, and where was Theoderic going to find the wherewithal if not from the landed portfolios of Italy's established elites?

Left to their own devices, matters could have got massively out of hand. Historians are so used to the fact that the rewarding process in Italy had another outcome that they tend not even to recognize the potential for disaster. It certainly existed. Domesday Book vividly illustrates what could happen when the land-grabbing activities of a victorious army ran unchecked. Within twenty years of the Battle of Hastings, incoming Norman barons and their henchmen had replaced Anglo-Saxon landowners across almost the entirety of the English kingdom. And not only was Theoderic's Gothic army bigger than William's, but elsewhere in the post-Roman West other regional bodies of Roman landowners were already set, by the 490s, on trajectories towards terminal extinction at the hands of militarized intruders (again, notably, in the British Isles).[12]

How Theoderic's regime solved its problem gets virtually no coverage in the *Variae*, partly because the job had long been completed by 507 when Cassiodorus held his first official post, and as a result we know precious little about the detail of what went on. The main outlines of the settlement can, however, just about be pieced together. The two things Cassiodorus does tell us are both significant. First, Theoderic appointed a Roman frontman to help him find the solution:

one Petrus Marcellinus Felix Liberius, usually known as Liberius. He was from an old Roman landowning and senatorial family, and about as blue-blooded as it was possible to be. He had also begun his public career under Odovacar and won brownie points by refusing to jump ship to Theoderic until his former employer lay in a heap (actually two separate heaps if our source can be believed) on that dining-room floor in Ravenna. At that point, Liberius swapped over to Theoderic's employ and, for his pains, was made praetorian prefect and given overall responsibility for settling the army into the Italian countryside. Second, Cassiodorus tells that the solution he came up with suitably enriched the Gothic army while the Romans felt 'scarcely any loss'. The same formulation reoccurs in a letter to Liberius himself written by the deacon Ennodius – who spent his time hanging around the fringes of Theoderic's court in search of various favours – so it was obviously the official line of the regime.[13]

Official lines in totalitarian regimes – even ancient ones – do not necessarily bear much relationship to reality, however, so what exactly do we know about how Liberius proceeded? His task was further defined and in part complicated by strategic imperatives, because Theoderic could not afford to disperse his armed followers, the basis of his military strength, in penny packets right across the Italian landscape. When East Roman forces invaded Italy in the later 530s, they found concentrated clusters of Goths in the north-east and north-west, around Ravenna and the coastal region to its south, and either side of the main routes through the Apennines from Ravenna to Rome. Such a distribution makes perfect sense, covering all the main likely avenues of land attack from the north, East Roman sea attack in the east, and the crucial avenue of power between the kingdom's two major political centres.[14]

Areas outside the settlement clusters were the easiest to deal with. A third of the normal tax revenues from these unaffected districts (called with the Latin bureaucrat's usual imaginative inventiveness *tertiae*: 'thirds') was earmarked for the army's further support, and used to provide the regular cash supplements – called donatives – which were handed out periodically to qualified men of military age. In addition, East Roman sources insist that land grants were found, and this does also make good sense. There have been some highly vocal attempts in recent years to deny that physical land changed hands in the 490s, but these all depend on an argument from silence: the fact that Roman landowners did not complain about being dispossessed. But all of our contemporary Italian sources from Theoderic's reign are official ones, where you could not expect to find such complaints, although, as we have seen, even the official line – dutifully echoed in both Cassiodorus and Ennodius – did not say that there had been *no* loss to Romans: just that it hadn't been very large. If even official sources were willing to make that much of an admission, there is no good reason not to accept what the sources report; title deeds were indeed changing hands in the mid-490s.

How exactly Liberius and his team found the necessary assets, in the particular places where elements of the army were to be settled, varied from place to place. For one thing, subgroups of different sizes from Theoderic's overall army were being settled in the different localities, and, as we saw in the last chapter, some of these groups had a reasonably complex pre-existing social structure. There were two statuses of warrior and unarmed slaves besides. Plausibly, each of the warrior classes qualified for a different kind of landed allotment, maybe also in legal terms as well as in quantity; it seems unlikely that slaves would have received anything for themselves. What Liberius would always have known, however, was how much land (measured in terms of the annual income it generated, not by physical extent) was available in each locality, and who owned it. The late Roman state maintained detailed registers of precisely this information for tax purposes, and we know that this bureaucratic structure survived into the reign of Odovacar. All the necessary basic data would have been available to Liberius, then, and it was at that point that his political skills came in: being inventive in how to balance Gothic gains and Roman losses to maximize the satisfaction of both.

The details of his various micro-solutions are entirely beyond recovery, but the kinds of options available to him can be reconstructed. In some places, the job may not have been that difficult. Odovacar had gone through a similar process at the start of his reign in 476 because, as more and more provinces had dropped out of the imperial orbit, the available tax revenues were by then insufficient to support the old imperial field army of Italy in the manner to which it was accustomed, which is precisely why it was ready to revolt. Some of Odovacar's forces were re-employed by Theoderic but others were not; where not, their possessions provided a politically cost-free stock of assets. Another low-cost stock of land, in political terms, came in the form of publicly owned assets belonging to towns and public corporations of one kind or another (bath houses, guilds, etc.). When Roman administrators (exactly like Liberius and his team) had had to find lands elsewhere in North Africa for Roman landowners displaced by the Vandal conquest of its central provinces in the 450s, it was precisely to these kinds of asset that they turned. I also strongly suspect, but couldn't prove, that any private landowners who did lose some of their lands were compensated by tax reductions on the parts of their estates that they retained, minimizing the impact on their actual annual incomes. The nitty-gritty, in other words, would have been complex and varied as Liberius' administrators – I'm sure he did policy decisions, not the detail – set about matching army subgroup to particular locality. It must also have been time-consuming.[15]

But, eventually, the task was complete, and when Liberius duly retired from his prefecture in the year 500 (and perhaps this did mark the end of the settlement process) the boss' pleasure was evident. Liberius was given an entirely honorific but rare and highly prestigious title: patrician. As far as we can see, he thoroughly deserved it. Roman landowners remained alive and kicking, and an unjust settlement process was never raised as a criticism of the regime, even when the East Romans looked to discredit it in the 530s (as we shall see in the next chapter). Theoderic's army seems to have been happy enough as well. The king did have to execute the odd notable from time to time subsequently, but there is no sign of any large-scale revolts, which there would have been if expectations had not generally been met. Indeed, there is so little about the Gothic army in the *Variae*, that it has become part of one recent line of argument that Theoderic's original followers were all so happy with what they received, that the original army essentially melted away into the Italian landscape from the later 490s, content to make olive oil and tread the grapes. You don't have to believe that Theoderic's army was largely Gothic in its culture to find that a highly unconvincing picture.

For one thing, when you do go looking for it, vignettes of army management subsequent to the settlement process can be found in individual letters of Cassiodorus' collection. We see Theoderic, and sometimes his successors too, calling subgroups from particular localities in to receive their donatives (making it clear that a register of qualified individuals was being kept, as it would have to be, for the system to work), making special arrangements to protect one of his former soldiers who had passed the age of active service and had fallen on hard times, and even approving the leader which one subgroup had elected as *prior* – literally 'first man' – of the Goths of their locality.[16] There may, of course, originally have been much more. Pulling out from the files letters dealing with the Gothic army was not to Cassiodorus' purpose as the kingdom came crashing down around his ears. Be that as it may, there is, fortunately, a stronger block of evidence for the continued importance and existence of Theoderic's army after the 490s. For while his self-proclaimed *Romanitas* certainly had a role in foreign affairs too, as well as in making Roman landowners feel better about life, the universe and everything, the army continued to play a massive role in the subsequent fortunes of Theoderic's regime after the initial conquest of Italy. It was these activities which gave real substance to the Goth's most grandiose claims.

THE 2,000TH YEAR OF GOTHIC HISTORY

No complete narrative can be reconstructed of Theoderic's reign in Italy. Quite how much was originally in Cassiodorus' lost Gothic History is difficult to say. Produced in the early 520s in the king's final years, it ran to twelve books and was certainly triumphalist in tone. But we don't know how long each book was, and Jordanes chose not to include much of what it had to say about the activities of Theoderic's adult lifetime. As we saw in the last chapter, the *Getica* goes into some detail about Theoderic's return from Constantinople and the events leading up to the advance on Thessalonica in 473, but runs over the next fifty-three years in a patchy narrative, sporting only very few highlights. This is then followed by an equally sparse summary of events after Theoderic's death (which could not have come from Cassiodorus' original), terminating with the surrender of Wittigis in the year 540.

In recording this capitulation, which took Cassiodorus to Constantinople and whose approach had set him to work on the *Variae*, Jordanes makes the following observation:

> And thus a famous kingdom and most valiant race, which had
> long held sway, was at last overcome in almost its two thousand
> and thirtieth year.[17]

2,030 is an extremely odd number, and it really can only be an
extrapolation from a note about a supposed 2,000th anniversary of the
start of the Gothic kingdom. Subtracting 'almost' thirty from 540 puts
us in the ballpark region of $c.510$, and hence certainly within the
timeframe of Cassiodorus' now lost history. I'm extremely confident,
in fact, that Jordanes found this supposed anniversary in Cassiodorus'
work, not least because Cassiodorus had established form in the field
of chronological computation by the time he wrote his history, having
just previously produced a world chronicle which ran down to 519. It
is no stretch, therefore, to detect his fertile brain behind the invention
of such a grand anniversary for the Goths. Just as important, when
you go back to what can be reconstructed of Theoderic's reign, there
is also really only one possible candidate for this most august of
anniversaries. To understand why, it is necessary, once again, to get
behind the double dose of image-making we are faced with in the
Variae: Theoderic's original pretensions to *Romanitas* as further intensified by Cassiodorus' considerable need to cover his rear end as the
wheels were finally falling off the Gothic wagons in the late 530s.

I'm not a believer in the supposed Scandinavian origins of the
Goths (an idea that, again, is found in the *Getica* and may also have
been in Cassiodorus' History), but the image of Theoderic's foreign
policy which emerges from an initial reading of the *Variae* does make
him look like a Norwegian peace mission on speed. As we have already
seen, he was addicted to diplomatic marriage alliances. He himself
married Clovis' sister; he was also armed with many and varied female
relatives of his own – and was not afraid to use them. Sundry of these
were duly married off therefore to kings or princes of the Visigoths,
Burgundians and Vandals. What could be more conducive to international peace than spreading a web of Amalocentric domestic harmony across the households of post-Roman Europe?

Then there's his record on the big international relations issue of
his day: not the Middle East in this era, but Gaul. When Romulus
Augustulus was deposed in 476, Gaul was divided not into three parts
as Caesar found it, but four. The dominant power was the Visigothic
kingdom which held everything from the Loire valley southwards

except for the upper and middle Rhone which formed the core of the Burgundian kingdom, although the Visigoths again controlled what is now the French Riviera where the river reaches the Mediterranean. The very north-east of Gaul was under Frankish rule while everywhere from Soissons westwards was in the hands of local more or less Roman forces of one kind or another (Figure 4).

By the time Theoderic came into his pomp a couple of decades later, a huge increase in Frankish power was busy altering this situation. This had its roots, as we saw, in a process similar to that which had brought Theoderic's dynasty to the fore. In the case of the Franks, it was the father-and-son team of Childeric and Clovis, above all the son, who united many previously independent warbands to create an unprecedentedly large power base (page 11), which, by the first decade of the sixth century, was busy redrawing the map of the post-Roman West and Gaul in particular. At this point, the various Roman groups of the north-west had long been conquered, and Frankish pressure was building on both the Visigothic and Burgundian kingdoms to the south. Clovis also had his eyes on the Alamanni, north-eastern neighbours of the Burgundians. It all came to a head around the year 505, when Clovis first smashed Alammanic indepen-dence and then closed in for the kill on the Visigoths, forcing the Burgundians to become his junior partners in crime. In 507, there duly followed the famous battle of Vouille when a Visigothic army was shredded and their king, Alaric II, killed, and when, according to French national myth, the boundaries of modern France first more or less came into being: divided Gaul had morphed into united Francia.[18]

From the year of the battle, the *Variae* preserve a series of letters which show Theoderic, to the great credit of his historical reputation, magnificently failing to preserve peace in his time. The smell of conflict may have been in the air, but the Amal was not deterred. To his brother-in-law Alaric II, king of the Visigoths, he penned the following:

> Do not let some blind resentment carry you away. Self-restraint is foresighted, and a preserver of tribes; rage, though, often precipi-tates a crisis; and only when justice can no longer find a place with one's opponent, is it then useful to appeal to arms.[19]

Gundobad of the Burgundians, caught in the middle, received a mixture of homily and appeal:

For it befits such mighty kings [Clovis and Alaric] not to seek out regrettable quarrels among themselves, with the result of injuring us too, by their own mischances. Therefore, let your fraternity labour, with my assistance, to restore their concord.[20]

And the mighty Clovis?:

What might you yourself think of me, if you knew I had ignored your dispute? Let there be no war, in which one of you will be defeated and come to grief ... I have decided to send ... my envoys to Your Excellency; and I have also sent my letters, by them, to your brother and my son Alaric, that no foreigner's ill-will may in any way sow quarrels between you. Rather, you should remain at peace, and terminate what quarrels there are by the mediation of your friends ... You should trust one whom you know to rejoice in your advantage, for it is certain that a man who directs another into dangerous courses can be no honest counsellor.[21]

It may all have been for nothing in the end, but the Theoderic of the *Variae* cannot be faulted, sending his letters and peace envoys shuttling around the courts of the post-Roman West in a desperate effort to stave off the impending showdown. Indeed, put it all together with the extraordinary letter to Anastasius with which we began, and an almost irresistibly seductive portrait emerges. Thus Theoderic has gone down in history as the former Roman hostage who was so marked by Roman values during ten years at Constantinople that he spent the remainder of his career trying to keep order among the bunch of unruly barbarians who'd taken over the rest of the Roman West.

But here, once more, we're dealing with what was originally Theoderic's self-presentation of his policies and their motivations. And if modern political history teaches us nothing else, it emphasizes again and again that you should never accept the self-presentation of any political leader without first giving it a thorough kicking. Equally important, we're only dealing with a small selection of Theoderic's letters: those which Cassiodorus thought would portray his record of service for the king and his successors in the best possible light. So two reasons already to be careful, and, as we saw in the previous chapter, the younger Theoderic was always a lot more interested in pursuing Roman cash than Roman values. Hence it should come as no great surprise to find that, looked at in the round, the evidence for the great Gallic crisis demonstrates that Theoderic's foreign policies at this point were not nearly so pacific as an initial perusal of the *Variae* suggests.

Cue the letter to Anastasius again. We've already seen one level of subversion within it: the idea that Theoderic's power and overall *Romanitas* came directly from God, rather than merely from his time in Constantinople, making him just as legitimately 'Roman' in the proper sense of the word as the Eastern emperor, and superior, again like the emperor, to any other ruler. Having made these initial points, the letter continues:

> We have thought fit therefore to send . . . ambassadors to your most serene Piety, that Peace, which has been broken, through a variety of causes, may, by the removal of all matters of dispute be firmly restored between us. For we think you will not suffer that any discord should remain between two Republics [the Eastern and Western Roman states] which are declared to have ever formed one body under their ancient princes, and which ought not to be joined by a mere sentiment of love, but actively to aid one another with all their powers. Let there be always one will, one purpose in the Roman Kingdom. Therefore, while greeting you with our respectful salutations, we humbly beg that you will not remove from us the high honour of your Mildness' affection, which we have a right to hope for if it were never granted to any others.[22]

The second half of the letter thus glides seamlessly into what is effectively a demand note. Because Theoderic runs the only other authentically Roman state in the world, then Constantinople should be in peaceful and harmonious alliance with him. The Goth's *Romanitas* has turned into an effective rhetorical stick with which to beat away at the emperor to end all quarrels.

Behind the velvet glove, Theoderic's iron fist is not so well hidden, and the evidence makes it clear that this was no isolated moment, but, in fact, the general rule in his relations with Constantinople. Much scholarly ink, for instance, has been expended in trying to work out the exact nature of the agreement that had sent Theoderic to Italy in 488/9. This reflects a basic disagreement in the sources which falls, as we saw, exactly where you would expect it. Eastern sources stress the emperor Zeno's initiative and that Theoderic was to rule in Italy as a thoroughly dependent subordinate. Western sources, many of them stemming directly or indirectly from Theoderic's court, emphasize Theoderic's initiative and independence. As with many diplomatic agreements designed to solve an immediate crisis – as this one was; remember thousands of armed Goths were sitting outside Constantinople – it cannot be pinned down precisely because its whole point was to fudge in the short term the different agendas of the two main participants in the hope that, in the longer term, and having experienced peace in the interim, neither party would want to return to war. But if it was already a fudge from the outset, then, having successfully inserted himself into power in Italy, Theoderic set about renegotiating its terms with determination.

We know that a first embassy went back to Zeno as early as 491, a second followed to Anastasius following Zeno's death in 492, but full agreement only came in 497 or 498 when a third embassy won concessions from Constantinople which included sending royal clothing and palace ornaments to Ravenna.

What went on in Italy took matters a great deal further than that. On ceremonial occasions, which as we have noted always involved the ritual shouting of acclamations, not only was Theoderic's name shouted rather than (or possibly before) that of the eastern emperor, but his statues were also placed in the position of honour, with those of the emperor relegated to the left-hand side. It was nice that they were there at all, of course, but the emperor expected his to be on the right. Theoderic furthermore won or merely arrogated to himself the right to grant the major honours of the Roman state – nomination to the consulship, the rank of patrician, and to membership of the Senate – and took full legal authority over both Roman notables and dignitaries of the Catholic Church.[23]

We don't know how much of this Anastasius explicitly signed up to in 498 and how much Theoderic simply did off his own bat. But the emperor clearly agreed to quite a lot of it, since the vestments were sent and Theoderic's consular nominees were recognized in the East. And we can also be absolutely sure of two other points of enormous importance. First, it hadn't all been granted freely. Theoderic extracted it with the same type of aggressive diplomacy we find not so well hidden beneath the surface of the letter to Anastasius at the head of the *Variae* collection. Second, the mixture of diplomatic concessions from Constantinople and self-asserted expropriations on

Theoderic's own part added up to one thing, and one thing only: from 498 onwards, Theoderic was ruling with all the rights and perquisites of a Western emperor, clothed in some of the appropriate vestments, and living in a palace which was not only styled on that of Constantinople, but decorated as such. As he stated in the letter to Anastasius, Theoderic had clearly learned how to rule as a Roman in Constantinople, but to rule as a fellow emperor, and not as a subordinate. And looked at again, it rapidly becomes clear that Theoderic's whole foreign policy, not just his relations with Constantinople, was run on exactly the same premise, even when he was apparently engaged in shuttle diplomacy.

The first foreign power to feel the weight of Theoderic's might was Vandal Africa. In the time of Odovacar, the Vandals had maintained partial control over Sicily and extracted protection money not to attack it further. As early as 491, Theoderic's armies defeated a Vandal force there which was trying to take advantage of his war against Odovacar. This led to the Vandals abandoning their claims to any Sicilian cash, and, in about 500, there followed a marriage alliance between the two kingdoms. A handsome dowry went to the Vandal king Thrasamund along with his new bride, Theoderic's sister Amalafrida, but the Ostrogothic princess was accompanied to the wedding by a military force of reportedly 5,000 men, some of whom stayed on afterwards. This was not a meeting of equals. About ten years later, Thrasamund was caught out by Theoderic actively supporting one of his enemies. A very 'disappointed' Gothic king wrote to his brother-in-law:

> We are sure that you cannot have taken counsel in this matter with your wife, who would neither have liked to see her brother injured, nor the fair fame of her husband tarnished by such doubtful intrigues. We send you . . . our ambassadors who will speak to you further on this matter.

Thrasamund's response prompted a second surviving letter:

> You have shown, most prudent of Kings, that wise men know how to amend their faults, instead of persisting in them with that obstinacy which is the characteristic of brutes. In the noblest and most truly kinglike manner you have humbled yourself to confess

your fault ... We thank you and praise you, and accept your
purgation of yourself from this offence with all our heart. As for
the presents ... we accept them with our minds, but not with
our hands. Let them return to your Treasury that it may be seen
that it was simply love of justice, not desire of gain, which
prompted our complaints.[24]

The exchange beautifully illustrates the nature of relations between
Italy and North Africa at this point. Having been told to jump,
Thrasamund asked how high, and immediately tried to buy his way
back into Theoderic's good books. But the Goth was having none of
it. In the language of gift-giving, sending back a present, whatever the
words used, was always a calculated insult. Theoderic was warning
Thrasamund that the Vandal kingdom was still on probation.

Theoderic's next recorded expansionary move came in 504–5 when
he increased the boundaries of his kingdom in the Middle Danubian
region. He had inherited from Odovacar parts of Dalmatia and the
province of Savia. A well-directed campaign against the Gepids of
Trasericus (whose father had been killed trying to stop Theoderic's
advance into Italy at the back end of 488) then allowed him to add to
this the old Roman province of Pannonia II along with its main city,
the ex-imperial capital of Sirmium. Again, Theoderic did not baulk
from conflict with Constantinople. Anastasius did not view the Goth's
waxing strength with untarnished joy, and intervened with a force,
consisting mostly of Bulgar mercenaries but led by an imperial general.
This too Theoderic defeated.[25] Even after the conquest of Italy, then,
Theoderic's record is not remotely that of a peacemaker. Aggressive
towards Constantinople, dominant over the Vandals, expansionary in
the Middle Danube, though the narrative sources are fragmentary and
brief they are more than enough to demonstrate that the Gothic
leopard did not change its spots just because it had shifted its centre of
operations and started to employ first-class Roman spin doctors. This
track record also gives the lie to the idea that Theoderic's army had
simply melted away into the Italian landscape. Nor, looked at closely,
does the dossier of letters relating to the Gallic crisis of 506–7 suggest
that Theoderic was quite so fixated upon peace as is often thought.

Alaric II, king of the Visigoths, was certainly Theoderic's main ally.
The Visigothic kingdom had supplied some extra military muscle at a
crucial point in the war against Odovacar, and there's nothing in any

of the surviving material to suggest that Theoderic was anything other than serious in his support of the Visigothic kingdom. On closer inspection, however, the letters to both Gundobad and Clovis are much less emollient in total than more isolated sentences suggest. The king of the Burgundians had a warning shot fired across his bows:

> If our kinsmen go bloodily to war while we allow it, our malice will be to blame. From me you hold every pledge of high affection; the two of us are united; if you do anything wrong on your own account, you sin gravely by causing me sorrow.

And, in fact, Theoderic's general tone to Gundobad throughout the *Variae* is haughty and patronizing. Even the ostensibly friendly gift of two time pieces (a sun dial and a water clock) could be made the occasion of a pointed assertion of superiority:

> Possess in your native country what you once saw in the city of Rome ... Under your rule, let Burgundy learn to scrutinise devices of the highest ingenuity, and to praise the inventions of the ancients ... Let it distinguish the parts of the day by their inventions; let it fix the hours with precision. The order of life becomes confused if this separation is not truly known. Indeed, it is the habit of beasts to feel the hours by their bellies' hunger, and to be unsure of something obviously granted for human purposes.

Classical cultural ideologies, you will recall, considered that it was rationality that distinguished the truly human from men still living in ignorance like beasts. Even when giving presents, Theoderic used the occasion to offer a cultural leg up, and emphasize that the Burgundians were still lumbering about like animals. There were more than enough educated Romans still at Gundobad's court, notably Bishop Avitus of Vienne, for this calculated insult to be fully understood.[26]

The Burgundians were not just being urged to use their good offices to help maintain the peace, but Theoderic was also more or less ordering them not to deviate from his line by siding with Clovis. As for Clovis, well, he was too powerful to be bossed around like Gundobad, but not too grand to avoid a telling-off:

> The holy laws of kinship [the marriage ties he had with the rulers of both the Franks and the Visigoths] have purposed to take root among monarchs for this reason: that their tranquil spirit may

bring the peace which peoples long for ... In view of all this, I am astonished that your spirit has been so roused by trivial causes that you mean to engage in a most grim conflict.

This was followed by a warning:

Your courage should not become an unforeseen disaster for your country, since the jealousy of kings over light causes is a great matter, and a heavy catastrophe for their peoples.

What catastrophe was Clovis facing? On one level, potential defeat at the hands of the Visigoths, since the outcome of war is often not straightforward, but also the threat that Theoderic would himself intervene. Indeed, Theoderic was not remotely averse to warning off Clovis, having done so a year or so earlier when the latter was threatening to pursue some of the defeated Alamanni on to Italian soil:

Accept the advice of one long experienced in such affairs: those wars of mine have turned out well which were carried through with moderation at the end. For it is the man who knows how to exercise restraint in all things that is habitually the victor ... Submit gently, then, to my guiding spirit ... So you will be seen to gratify my requests, and you will have no anxiety over what you know affects me.[27]

More tactful than the handling of Gundobad, certainly, but the message is clear nonetheless. It would be a good idea for Clovis to exercise restraint or Theoderic will become involved, and, being a man of restraint himself, he's never yet lost a war ...

There's not enough in the subtexts of these letters to convict Theoderic actually of stirring up the crisis; he does seem to have been genuinely trying to ward it off. On the other hand, his authoritarian and patronizing missives to both Clovis and Gundobad were far from conciliatory in tone, and cannot have been well received. If he was not fomenting war, therefore, neither was he desperately trying to avoid it. Just as much, he was pointing out to the aggressors the likely consequences should he be forced to join in.

And, as matters turned out, the prime beneficiary of the crisis proved to be Theoderic himself. This is usually missed because Clovis' dynasty and the Franks in general were destined for historical greatness, as we shall see later in this book. But even from the fragmentary narrative available to us, the extent of Theoderic's gains emerges in glorious Technicolor. Not that everything went according to plan. In 507, Theoderic was prevented from coming to Alaric's assistance by an East Roman seaborne raid on the Adriatic shore of Italy. This, indeed, brings out the full and final layer of meaning in that famous letter to Anastasius. Fed up with Theoderic's aggressive renegotiating of his agreements, not to mention the defeat of their army of Bulgar mercenaries, the authorities in Constantinople had signed up to an alliance with Clovis and kept the Goth busy while their ally defeated the Visigoths. But Clovis' victory over Alaric, stunning as it was, was not the end of the story. In 508, Theoderic's forces, free now from the Constantinopolitan threat, surged out of Italy and over the Alps. Both Frankish and Burgundian forces (Gundobad had not heeded the warnings) were driven back, although the Franks did gain and retain control over much of Aquitaine. And there was still more to come.

Defeat at Vouille left the Visigothic kingdom in disarray. Power passed in the first instance to Alaric's son Gesalic, the product of a union prior to the king's marriage to Theoderic's daughter. Having driven off the invaders and secured the new and reduced frontiers, Theoderic was finally ready to act. In 511, his commanders drove Gesalic out of the kingdom (it was Thrasamund's support for the fugitive which led to that letter exchange which generated the fit of abject Vandal grovelling we have already met). It is sometimes said that Theoderic mounted this *coup d'état* in favour of his daughter's son by Alaric II: Amalaric by name. There is, however, not the slightest evidence of this. Rather, Theoderic proceeded to rule both Gothic kingdoms – his own in Italy and its Visigothic peer in southern Gaul and Spain – as an entirely unitary state. The Visigothic royal treasury was shipped to Ravenna and Theoderic took control of the registers recording the lists of Visigothic military manpower. The one relevant letter Cassiodorus included in his collection (there is only one because Cassiodorus left office precisely in 511) also shows problems of governmental administration in the Visigothic kingdom being dealt with centrally from Ravenna.[28]

There's little doubt, therefore, that 511 was the *annus mirabilis* picked out by Cassiodorus for the 2,000th anniversary of the Gothic kingdom. By dint of his military power, Theoderic had now come into direct control of Italy, Mediterranean Gaul, most of Spain, the Dalmatian coast, and a goodly chunk of the Middle Danubian region south of the river. He was also exercising, though Thrasamund clearly resented it, hegemony over the Vandal kingdom, and possibly also over the Burgundians too, by the time his intervention came to an end. In short, by the end of 511, the son of a moderately important Gothic warband leader was directing the affairs – one way or another – of somewhere between a third and a half of the old Western Empire, and his dominance of the post-Roman West was beyond challenge. What better year to identify with a massive – if entirely notional – anniversary for the emergence of Gothic power?

SEMPER AUGUSTUS

Despite Theoderic's astounding success, he continued to hold back about one quarter of a step from claiming the title of West Roman emperor explicitly, although his cards were firmly on the table. The extent of his domains, the imperial ceremonial he adopted, his rhetorical pretensions as the font of rationality and classical learning in the western Mediterranean, all proclaimed the Goth's own vision of his status as straightforwardly Roman and imperial. Why he hesitated to take that extra quarter step is a fascinating question, but I suspect Theoderic was showing his customary ability to recognize when prudence was better than valour. For one thing, making his claim still more explicit could only have worsened relations with Constantinople. Already in 507–8, Anastasius had shown himself happy to fish in troubled waters if it could help cut Theoderic down to size, and that was before the Spanish *coup de main*. Were Theoderic to have styled himself emperor, that hostility would only deepen, threatening some of the diplomatic concessions he had already invested so much effort into extracting, not least the right to have his nominees for the consulship – that dignity so beloved of the Italian elite – recognized in the East.

I do wonder, too, whether he might not have risked alienating opinion among his leading Gothic henchmen. Equating the year 511 with a notional 2,000th anniversary of the Gothic kingdom was a significant choice. According to all the standard calculations, the history of Rome began with the foundation of the city in 753 BC, an understanding encapsulated in massive celebrations of its 1,000th anniversary by the emperor Philip in AD 248. Simple maths will tell you that equating 511 with the Goths' 2,000th anniversary amounted to a claim that the Gothic realm was older than Rome itself. This suggests that Cassiodorus – and Theoderic too – may have had to factor into their calculations the opinions of some within Theoderic's immediate following who were not signed up to a vision of the total superiority of all things Roman, and for whom *Emperor* Theoderic would have been unpalatable.

But this well-placed regard for some of the more acute sensibilities of the key constituencies with whom he had to operate still left no one in the slightest doubt about the extent of Theoderic's actual power, and the claim being made about its nature. Certainly not Catholic churchmen. Victory in 508 and the coup of 511 had brought substantial new territories in southern Gaul under Theoderic's control, including the see of Arles and its highly prominent leader, Bishop Caesarius. Soon after 511, the bishop made a trip to Italy. According to his *Life*, this was involuntary, prompted by suspicions that his loyalty was questionable. I rather suspect that the author (one of Caesarius' deacons writing shortly after the bishop's death) didn't want his Catholic hero to be remembered as cosying up too closely with an Arian Goth. But even the *Life* doesn't try to hide that, as soon as they met, Arian quasi-emperor and Catholic bishop hit it off like wildfire. Theoderic instantly recognized Caesarius' holiness, and, loading him with gifts, sent him on to Rome for the Pope to give him the pallium – a plain strip of cloth – which recognized Caesarius' status as papal vicar and the most senior prelate of southern Gaul. This status then provided the bishop with the launching pad for what is his great claim to ecclesiastical fame: a series of reforming Church councils in the 520s, which formalized many standard practices of early medieval Christianity. The extra point which is not so often noticed is exactly how much in tune with Theoderic's plans Caesarius' activities actually were. The pallium gave Caesarius a notional reach that extended beyond the boundary of his own see to all those that fell within his metropolitan jurisdiction, including many of the sees which were now part of the Burgundian kingdom. Theoderic, likewise, claimed a kind of hegemony over the Burgundians, and it was a further assertion of Gothic dominance over the Burgundian kingdom in the early 520s (to

which we will return in a moment) which would later make sure that
the bishops of these sees would actually attend Caesarius' meetings.[29]

If Roman – and Catholic – churchmen courted Theoderic as
though he were an emperor, the Goth did nothing to discourage them,
and all the signs were being read by members of the secular Roman
elite as well. The hints could not, indeed, have been more brazen, or,
indeed, golden. A unique object to survive from Theoderic's reign is
the so-called Senigallia medallion, a solid gold coin bearing a represen-
tation of the king (Plate 8). The reverse inscription describes him as
'conqueror of peoples', so it was perhaps issued precisely to celebrate
the great triumphs which culminated in 511. But issuing gold coins
was an imperial monopoly, which was generally respected in the
former Roman west, at least down to the later sixth century. The fact
that Theoderic ignored this nicety of protocol is yet another occasion
of his non-imperial mask slipping slightly, and no one was remotely
fooled by the pretence. In so many ways, aside from his actual power,
Theoderic deliberately allowed those who so wished, to see him as the
first in a new line of Western emperors, and many were happy to do
so. When one of his leading Roman senatorial subjects, a certain
Caecina Mavortius Basilius Decius, chose, in a particularly famous
inscription, to hail Theoderic as *semper Augustus* (forever Augustus),
that most imperial of titles, he was merely stating out loud what
everyone was supposed to think.[30]

Amidst all the success of 511, however, there remained two clouds
on the Goth's horizon. First, the East Roman Empire was hardly
reconciled to Theoderic's new-found grandeur. It had already been
hostile in 508; it takes no guesswork to imagine how Anastasius and
his advisers felt about Theoderic pretty much doubling his power base
by adding in Spain and southern Gaul and the military manpower
of the Visigothic kingdom. The other problem was an internal one.
By 511, Theoderic was fast approaching sixty and had no sons, his
marriage with Clovis' sister Audefleda having produced just the one
known daughter: Amalasuentha. This posed the problem of succession
in a highly acute form. Although we know with hindsight that
Theoderic would actually live for another fifteen years, sixty was
already old for a medieval ruler. No one has ever had the patience to
calculate average age at death for all medieval rulers, but males of
Charlemagne's dynasty averaged around fifty years, and this probably
gives us a reasonable guide. The Goth's great Western rival Clovis

himself died in 511 (which would surely have concentrated minds in Italy on the succession issue, although I'm confident they would not have needed concentrating), and he cannot have been much above fifty. And while female succession was not absolutely impossible, it was certainly difficult. The main element in the job description was controlling a potentially unruly gang of armed followers, who would not be easily reconciled to female rule. By 511, Theoderic could conceivably have dropped dead at any moment and there was not a plausible heir in sight.

Uncertain succession, moreover, was the mother of all internal political problems in the ancient and medieval worlds, with the capacity to generate more internal strife for a body politic than every other issue combined. Why this was so is straightforward. To start with, it encouraged every even vaguely plausible contender to come out of the woodwork: collateral male relatives, strong generals married to junior female members of the dynasty, everybody with any ambition and half a claim. The result could only be division and contention within the leadership group of the kingdom. Worse, the different candidates needed to court supporters. One obvious body of support would be those not doing so well under the current regime, since the disgruntled are always relatively easy to rally to the flag of future change. But that kind of recruiting drive only served to unsettle those who were already doing well, since they needed a candidate for continuity, to guarantee that, when the old man finally kicked it, they would not lose their current privileges. And this takes no account, of course, of those who were doing quite well currently, but thought that they might do a bit better: such being the nature of human aspiration. Insecure succession in other words – like US presidential elections at the end of a second presidential term, or in a year when the economy's bad – encouraged multiple, mutually condemnatory candidacies and a huge jockeying for position which had the potential to turn all existing political alliances on their head. If, at the end of 511, Constantinople's continued hostility was far from desirable, Theoderic's lack of an heir was potentially disastrous. As it turned out, events in the East were to give Theoderic the opportunity to resolve both matters before the end of the decade.

By 515 at the latest, Theoderic clearly abandoned all hope of having a son of his own, but found another means to vest succession in his own direct line. To that end he married Amalasuentha to a

certain Eutharic, or Flavius Eutharic Cilliga to give him his kennel
name. This was both a canny and fascinating choice. In the Amal
genealogy transmitted by Jordanes' *Getica*, but originating certainly in
Cassiodorus' Gothic History, Eutharic is presented as a collateral
relative: the grandson of Beremund the son of Hunimund who gave
up the struggle against Valamer's inexorable rise to power and fled
west to the Visigothic kingdom, probably sometime in the late 450s
(Figure 1 and above, page 7). There is no independent confirmation of
this relationship outside the *Getica*, but while it's completely unclear
whether Beremund was himself originally related to Valamer as the
genealogy suggests (although, as we saw, Clovis' industrious elimination of collateral male relatives might make a good parallel) it seems
likely enough that Eutharic was indeed Beremund's grandson. That is
probably too close a relationship to have attempted to lie about in
prominent political circles where ancestry tended to be a known
quantity. Theoderic thus chose for his daughter's consort and his own
heir an individual who could reasonably claim some residual loyalty
from among the core of military supporters in his following who
derived from the original Pannonian Goths. At the same time, Eutharic
was important in his own right as a noble from the Visigothic kingdom,
and came to Ravenna from Spain for the marriage. To my mind, there
is not the slightest doubt, therefore, that Theoderic intended the happy
couple to inherit from him both his Italian and his Hispanic and
southern Gallic territories; in other words that the newly united Gothic
kingdom should continue on after his death. The point here, of course,
is that Eutharic had strong pre-existing ties to the Visigothic nobility,
and could be reasonably counted on to help stabilize that part of the
realm. One more or less contemporary source also describes him as
'an excessively rough man', which was entirely to the point when the
job description involved controlling several thousand members of a
Gothic warrior elite dispersed in a geographic arc from the Adriatic
coast of Italy to the Mediterranean coast of eastern Spain.[31]

The hostility of Constantinople was defused by a more convoluted
route. When Theoderic came to power, much of the Eastern Church,
and particularly the patriarchate of Constantinople, was, from a Roman
point of view, in a state of schism. Apart from Attila and the Hunnic
Empire, the middle years of the fifth century had also been difficult in
theological terms. Everyone accepted that man and God were combined somehow in the person of Jesus, but exactly how was not so

clear. One Patriarch of Constantinople, Nestorius (428–31, when he was deposed), had argued that it was absurd to suppose that the Almighty God element in Christ could have died by crucifixion and argued therefore that only the human was involved at this point. Other Eastern churchmen, however, particularly Patriarch Cyril of Alexandria, thought that the mystery of salvation absolutely required God to die on the Cross, so the result was a vitriolic dispute which spanned the generations, leading the emperor Marcian to attempt to resolve it by calling a council of the entire Church (an ecumenical council) at Chalcedon, just across the Bosphorus from Constantinople, in 451. The then Pope, Leo I, didn't attend but he sent his delegates and contributed a major doctrinal statement: the *Tome of Leo*. As a result, papal prestige was inextricably linked to the theological outcomes of the council which helpfully declared Christ to be both man and God, constructed 'in two natures'.

Except that it wasn't helpful at all. It did enough to rule out the most extreme version of Nestorius' line of argument, but, for many of Cyril's latter-day supporters, had come up with a definition of faith which was hazy enough to allow some dodgy, overly Nestorian thinkers still to sign up to it. So dispute did not go away after 451, but reoriented itself around a debate on Chalcedon itself. By 482, the Emperor Zeno had had enough of the bickering and pressured his then Patriarch of Constantinople, Acacius, to issue a compromise document – the *Henotikon* (literally 'Act of Union') – to try to get everyone to shut up about the word nature, and get on with the rest of Christianity. But this involved stepping back to some extent from what had been said at Chalcedon, and the papacy was having none of it. Exchanges of letters and mutual recriminations followed, with the result that Pope Felix and Acacius excommunicated each other in 484, inaugurating the so-called Acacian schism (Christian schisms are universally named from the Orthodox – i.e. winning – point of view: that is, after the name of whoever lost and whose fault therefore the whole damn thing is held to be).[32]

Such are the tortuous paths of international diplomacy that the eventual resolution of this schism provided Theoderic with the mechanism he needed for overturning East Roman hostility. The schism was acutely embarrassing for the Eastern Empire. No one could doubt the prestige of the Roman see, with its connections to St Peter and St Paul, so for the Patriarch of Constantinople, head Church of the divinely appointed emperor's dominions, to be labelled by it as mistaken on matters of faith was a substantial PR problem. Not surprisingly, any likely opportunity was taken up with explorations to find a resolution, a particularly busy period following the change of papal regime on the death of Pope Symmachus in July 514. Multiple embassies and letter exchanges led nowhere, however, and it was regime change in Constantinople which eventually provided the right moment. On 9 July 518 Anastasius passed away. He had no sons and had either been unwilling – or, more likely, unable – to mobilize sufficient political support behind one of his several nephews (who will reappear in the next chapter). Succession passed instead to a fairly elderly, rather distinguished-looking guards officer by the name of Justin.

Opportunity came knocking thereby at Theoderic's door because one of the areas in which the new regime chose to put clear blue water between itself and its predecessor was by bringing the embarrassing schism to an end. Normal Roman imperial ideologies still held sway, so a properly divinely appointed emperor might be expected to act decisively to create unity in matters of religion. It was also a good idea from an East Roman perspective since much of its Balkans military had been in revolt since 514 under the command of its general Vitalian, one of whose complaints against Anastasius was precisely his rejection of Chalcedon. Once Justin and his advisers had decided to include Vitalian in their regime and end the revolt, then they were pretty much also committed to reinstating the full authority of Chalcedon.

Events moved fast. Justin wrote to Pope Hormisdas for the first time on 1 August 518, announcing his succession. A further letter was despatched with an imperial legate on 7 September, asking the Pope to send back to him envoys who were ready to negotiate peace, and a letter from the new emperor's nephew, Justinian, asking if the Pope would even like to come to Constantinople. The legate didn't reach Rome until 20 December, but in January 519 the papal mission was on its way. It was met ten miles outside the city by a high-ranking imperial delegation, including the general Vitalian, on 25 March, which was the Monday of Holy Week in that year. Just three days later, Patriarch John of Constantinople signed up to the letters from Rome, and poor old Acacius was erased from the diptychs, the official listings of true-believing patriarchs regularly prayed for and to in the liturgical practice of the Church.[33]

All well and good, but what has any of this to do with Theoderic? Not a lot, you could be forgiven for thinking, and, in fact, one line of scholarship has long seen the ending of schism as marking an ominous turn in the history of Theoderic's kingdom. When he came to power, the fact of schism kept the Church of Rome and all the good – especially senatorial landowning – Catholics of Italy isolated from their natural peers in the Eastern Empire. Once the schism was resolved, nothing stood in the way of these men cosying up to Constantinople, and the peace and harmony of the Arian Theoderic's relations with them – and hence the political and administrative workings of his kingdom – were bound to suffer. Sounds plausible in the abstract, but it's not in tune with how things went. The alert reader will have noticed that Justin's legate took rather a long time to get to Rome. Having left Constantinople on 7 September, he got there only on 20 December. This is because he had spent a great deal of time at Theoderic's court at Ravenna on the way. The Pope, likewise, consulted carefully with the Goth before sending back his own embassy which presided over the great Constantinopolitan climbdown in Holy Week 519. In other words, Theoderic was entirely in on the deal, and so good and so close were his relations with Rome, that the Pope had not moved a muscle without his approval, repeating a pattern already seen, in fact, in the papal response to the peace offers of the ageing Anastasius.

Not only did Theoderic not see any threat in the termination of the schism, therefore, but he actually made it happen. Indeed, with the brilliant opportunism that we have by now come to know and love – or at least recognize – he turned the situation to absolute maximum advantage. For what happened at court in Ravenna in autumn 518 was the construction of the deal to end all deals. In return for his good offices in bringing the schism to an end, Theoderic extracted formal East Roman recognition of his choice of heir, Amalasuentha's husband Eutharic, a union which had already been blessed with its own son and future heir for the next generation: Athalaric. Recognition came in two forms. First, Eutharic was adopted as the emperor Justin's son-at-arms, which involved sending formal gifts of weaponry in a diplomatic protocol which was being used very widely by the empire in the sixth century as an act of recognition. Even more dramatically, Justin agreed to serve as joint consul with Eutharic for the year 519. They officially took up this dignity on New Year's Day 519, so that the arrangement was negotiated at the latest in the previous autumn.

For the new emperor to agree to share the consulship with Theoderic's chosen heir was about as big a statement of friendship as you can possibly imagine.

Theoderic's cup was overflowing: East Roman hostility and succession issues erased simultaneously. There had been more than a few rocky moments along the way, but Theoderic's reborn Western Empire looked set for prosperity into its next generation, based now not only on brute force and self-assertion but also on official Constantinopolitan recognition. 1 January 519 was a red-letter day for the new Western Empire, and to celebrate Cassiodorus had a first stab at history, producing his (still surviving) *Chronicle*, which presented world and salvation history as culminating in Eutharic's consulship.[34]

By the time of Theoderic's eventual death on 30 August 526, however, these joyous and costly celebrations were a distant and bitter memory. At this point, the Catholic Church was minus one pope. John I returned to Italy in May 526 after an embassy to Constantinople which the official papal biography writes up as an overwhelming success. Theoderic clearly didn't think so, since he threw him in jail immediately, where the Pope soon died. He was joining in jail – metaphorically, that is – two leading members of the Roman Senate, Symmachus and his much more famous son-in-law Boethius, both of whom had been accused of treason, imprisoned, and then finally executed in 525 and 524 respectively. And to cap it all, the ruler who had enjoyed such excellent relations with the Catholic Church throughout his reign was reputedly on the cusp of launching a major persecution – according to one source – when death intervened. After more than thirty years of group-hugging with Italian landowners and the Roman Church, long-cherished relationships had come crashing down. The change was so inexplicable to one anonymous Italian chronicler, writing within a couple of decades of Theoderic's death, that he could only conclude that Theoderic had literally gone to the Devil.[35] What on earth – or, maybe, in hell – had gone wrong?

DEATH IN RAVENNA

The narrative silence on Theoderic's last years, apart from our Italian chronicler, is pretty much deafening, but some scholars have felt confident that they know what went wrong. In particular, one of the giants of post-war classical studies, Arnaldo Momigliano, produced a wonderfully crafted and highly influential paper, which started life as a lecture to the British Academy in the later 1950s. In this he argued that the root cause of the disasters of Theoderic's final years lay in the fact that, all appearances to the contrary notwithstanding, the Goth's original charm offensive had never really worked. In his view, you could identify a profound divide in the overall Italo-Roman landowning elite, between the much less grand – more or less gentry level – bureaucratic functionaries (like our old friend Cassiodorus), who happily signed up to the new regime, and the real old-time Roman senatorial aristocracy, who were never convinced. Men such as Symmachus and Boethius would always have preferred to be part of the Roman Empire, and when, in the 520s, they were caught in treasonable correspondence with Constantinople, this was but the last act in a long-running saga of political failure.

It's an emotionally satisfying story, and features Roman grandees acting as you might think they ought to have done: rejecting barbarian rule, no matter how many imperial vestments it borrowed, and holding on to Roman ideals. I suspect, too, that much closer to World War Two, its story of an established bureaucracy collaborating happily with conquering outsiders carried an extra resonance.[36] But emotionally pleasing (and as beautifully written) as it is, the picture really doesn't work very well when confronted with all the evidence.

One huge problem is the career trajectory of Boethius. Just before he wound up in jail, the scholar-cum-politician enjoyed a period of enormous success in Theoderic's service. Both his father-in-law Symmachus and he himself seem to have been actively if peripherally involved in the ending of the Acacian schism, which was, as we have just seen, positively desired by Theoderic. There should thus have been no problem in this as far as Theoderic was concerned, and this is exactly what our evidence indicates. For in 522, or thereabouts (the lack of narrative sources makes the chronology just a little fuzzy), Boethius left his study and assumed one of the most important administrative positions in the entire system: the post of *magister officiorum* (master of offices). It's hard to overstate the importance of this job, since its holder was responsible for overseeing much of the rest of the bureaucracy, and for many of the day-to-day operations of the court, such as scheduling legal hearings, introducing foreign ambassadors, as well as being generally a constant presence at the ruler's side. If that were not mark of favour enough, both of Boethius' infant sons were made joint consuls for the year 522. The consulship was the single greatest public service gong available in the late Roman world, and no one had ever seen both of their children hold it at the same time before. And since Theoderic and Constantinople each usually nominated one consul, this also means that the emperor Justin's positive approval was part of the story.[37]

Not much of an aristocratic/bureaucratic divide here, then, nor the slightest trace of an ideological problem. And when you go looking for it, our scanty information throws up much more of a track record of positive engagement with Theoderic's regime on the part of the high aristocracy than Momigliano's evocative picture suggested. For one thing, he did not say very much about our old friend Liberius, responsible for finding suitable financial compensation for the incoming army at the beginning of the reign. The blood in Liberius' veins was blue enough to be virtually purple, but he co-operated more than happily with Italy's new rulers. Equally important, there were a number of different forms of participation. It had not been at all de rigueur, or indeed usual, for members of the old elite families of Italy to pursue active careers in government and administration, even when Italy had still formed part of the Western Empire. Some did, but it was really a matter of how ambitious a particular individual actually was. Basically, they were all so damn rich that they didn't need to be politically active unless they really wanted to. But that did not mean that they were not prominent in public life more generally. The old senatorial ideology of leisure – *otium* – meant freedom from office-holding and the daily grind, but it did not mean sitting around the house all day peeling grapes. Senators were expected to be active in cultural terms, editing the old classics, writing commentaries on them, and discussing them; not to mention occasionally adding their own compositions to the pile. They were also, by dint of their wealth and connections, much in demand as patrons for a wide range of communities right across Italy, and that is all without even mentioning the Senate itself. As a body of extremely rich men, it was a public body of and in itself, even if it had none of the formal powers of some of its counterparts in modern democracies. Just being a senator made you a public figure, therefore, and brought you into direct contact with your ruler on a whole series of levels.[38]

Judged against this broader definition of what positive participation might look like, Boethius and his father-in-law were both publicly active figures in Theoderic's kingdom long before the 520s. Much of the evidence comes from Cassiodorus' *Variae*, so it is limited in time to the brief period that Cassiodorus was in office before Boethius' fall, that is 506/7–11, but that really makes it only the more impressive. During those few years, Boethius was charged with finding diplomatic gifts on two separate occasions for foreign rulers (Clovis himself, no less, and Gundobad of the Burgundians: the famous clocks), and in making the second of these requests Theoderic showed extensive, detailed knowledge of Boethius' scholastic activities (of course, Theoderic hadn't read the books, but he could be bothered to detail one of his functionaries to do the necessary research). Symmachus brought actions in the Senate, was one of five senators appointed to advise in the trial of some senators accused of magical practices, and himself tried a case of parricide. All of these involved Symmachus in extensive contacts with Theoderic, who also reimbursed him for expenses he had taken on in repair works to the Theatre of Pompey in Rome, so he was clearly *persona grata* at court at this point. Indeed, we know from a manuscript annotation that he also conducted some of his own cultural studies actually in Ravenna. The note is undated, and might have been in the time of Odovacar rather than Theoderic, but the odds are on the latter, and what it anyway underlines is that Momigliano's absolute distinction between the aristocracy and the bureaucracy, between Rome and Ravenna, was much too clearly drawn.[39]

Top bureaucrats were aristocrats in origin or became new ones by virtue of the wealth and distinction they acquired from holding office, sometimes marrying off their children – as has happened at all times and in all places – to the offspring of those with older distinctions, but lesser means. Aristocrats were also just as – if not more – likely to fight with other aristocrats as with bureaucrats, since their fellow aristos were their usual competitors for the utmost heights of power and privilege. And, in this context, it is certainly worth noting that some of their fellow aristocrats (not just Momigliano's bureaucratic functionaries) were happy both to conduct the trials which condemned Boethius and Symmachus in the 520s, and to continue to work with Gothic rule in the aftermath of their fall. The two were condemned by their fellow senators, and men such as Liberius did not forsake their Gothic allegiance because of their fall.

In short, neither the activities of Boethius and Symmachus, nor what we can reconstruct about the general context provide real support for Momigliano's view of the working of Italian politics. Nor is there any sign either of his crucial extra ingredient. Momigliano assumed that Boethius was caught in treasonable correspondence with Constantinople which was encouraging an East Roman intervention to restore direct imperial rule in Italy. His thinking was influenced here by the fact that Justin's successor Justinian would order an invasion of Italy just over a decade after Theoderic's death. But, as we will explore in the next chapter, conditions in Constantinople were entirely different by the mid-530s compared to the 520s, and, at that earlier date, a military intervention was simply not on the cards. As recently as 519, Justin had gone so far as to recognize Theoderic's choice of heir, and an East Roman chronicle written in the early 520s by a functionary with court connections, who can be taken to be echoing the official line of the regime, was happy to condemn Anastasius' attacks on Italy in 508 as a 'piratical assault upon fellow Romans'.[40] The construction of a consistently dissident aristocracy trying to engineer an East Roman military intervention just doesn't hold up. The fall of Boethius does not look so much like the final act in a long-running saga of aristocratic resistance, but the sudden falling out of the ruler and one of the great men who had been circling around his court throughout the reign.

What caused this catastrophic breakdown in relations? It cannot have been something that affected all or even many of the Italo-Roman aristocracy, since most of the usual suspects carried on working for Theoderic afterwards. And some even benefited from it: particularly Cassiodorus, who became *magister officiorum* immediately after Boethius' disgrace. From Boethius himself, we have the famous *Consolation of Philosophy* penned while he was in prison, but all he says there is that the charges were false and that he was really imprisoned because the upright form of government which philosophy compelled him to bring to his tenure of office had made him enemies at what was in fact a highly corrupt court. But he doesn't say what the charges actually were, and, on the whole, the *Consolation* leaves us none the wiser as to what had brought Theoderic and his so recently best friend, the *magister officiorum* Boethius, to loggerheads.[41]

If you step back from the detail and the furore surrounding Theoderic's last years, however, there is really only one issue that could possibly have caused this amount of chaos: succession. Theoderic thought he had it nailed when he married off Amalasuentha to Eutharic, and especially when the marriage quickly produced an heir apparent in the person of Athalaric. But here the king's own vigorous longevity proved counterproductive, since, now pretty much into his seventieth year, Theoderic outlived his chosen heir. True to narrative form – or the lack of it for Theoderic's kingdom – we don't know exactly when Eutharic expired, but it was somewhere in and around 522 or 523. Immediately, of course, all bets were off, and the whole can of succession worms flew open. Athalaric was born in 516 or 518, so was at most seven years old, and there were manifestly sharp differences of opinion over whether a minor could conceivably inherit Theoderic's mantle.

Theoderic eventually decided that he could. We don't know how long it took him to come to this decision, but the sources make it clear that he did. It was also precisely at this moment, during Cassiodorus' tenure of the post of *magister officiorum*, that all the nonsense we encountered in the previous chapter about the Amals being a unique *gens purpura* started to appear at every available opportunity in the letters he had to compose for his master. Dynastic continuity was the main card to be played in Athalaric's favour, and Theoderic threw it in at every opportunity as he sensed mortality catching up with him. But even Theoderic's undoubted prestige was not enough to guarantee a smooth succession for his chosen heir, when that chosen heir lacked the wherewithal to fulfil the basic job description of effective war leader.

We also don't know whether Theoderic himself considered other possibilities before throwing all his weight behind Athalaric, but others certainly did. Perhaps the most obvious alternative was Theoderic's nephew Theodahad. He was an Amal of majority age, and he received a very large pay-off at the beginning of Athalaric's reign because he had been 'obedient'. The smart money is on this 'obedience' having taken the form of Theodahad not putting himself forward as a candidate at the moment of Theoderic's death when there was certainly unrest around. Cassiodorus tells us, for instance, that Liguria – home to one of the main Gothic settlement clusters – saw serious disturbances on Athalaric's succession: conceivably agitation in favour of a different candidate. Others had looked elsewhere. A senior noble called Tuluin who had already distinguished himself on the battlefield, likewise received major rewards for supporting Athalaric's succession, including the titular honour of patrician, the first Italian Goth to receive this title, which had been borne in the past by such luminaries as Aetius, who had laboured so long and hard to hold the Western Empire together in the 430s and 440s. Tuluin also received a letter explicitly comparing him to a great Gothic hero of the past, that Gensemund, the son of Hunimund, who had chosen to support the three Amal brothers as they built up their power base rather than continue the fight – that his brother Thorismund and nephew Bere-mund pursued in different ways – to remain independent lords in their own right (page 7). Tuluin had obviously done something similar; that is, not press his own claim and, again, the *Variae* make it clear that a non-Amal heir was at one point considered.[42]

In Spain, too, the consequences of Eutharic's death started to reveal themselves. One reason for choosing Eutharic was that, as a Visigothic noble in origin, he could help keep together the vast realm that Theoderic gathered into his hands by ousting Gesalic. But Alaric II had another son, Amalaric, this one Theoderic's own grandson via his daughter Theodegotho. So peripheral was this grandson to Theo-deric's succession plans that he sent one of his henchmen, a certain Theudis, to Spain explicitly to make sure that no one used Amalaric to stir up trouble. After Eutharic's death, however, Theudis started to see things differently. He had himself made an excellent match in Spain, a Roman heiress of great wealth, and used her money to maintain a private army of a few thousand men. In the uncertain conditions created by Eutharic's exit, Theudis now acted increasingly indepen-dently, absolutely refusing several summonses to Ravenna. Instead of keeping guard over Amalaric, he now actively championed his cause, positioning himself as the *éminence grise* behind a potential throne, and eventually got his way. After Theoderic's death, Italy and the Visigothic kingdom were repartitioned, with Amalaric inheriting the latter. But this was a deal done after Theoderic's demise, not one that he had sanctioned. Our main East Roman source, the historian Procopius, is quite explicit that the split was something agreed between Athalaric and Amalaric (for which, read their supporters) after Theoderic's death, not something that the old king wanted. And, for his part, Theudis was not disobeying orders out of some devotion to his young charge, but for his own gain. On Amalaric's death, he would himself inherit the Visigothic throne, and hold it for an impressive seventeen years.[43]

In short, Eutharic's death landed Theoderic in a position analogous to that of the classic lame-duck president. Aged more or less seventy, and absolutely in the latter days of his final term in office, Theoderic was struggling to make anybody listen to him any more. All the major players at court were busy calculating who might make a decent successor, while all those worried about losing their current gains were looking to offer support to someone who would reassure them, and those who had not done so well were hunting for someone to reverse their current misfortunes. Further away in Spain, Theudis would never have dared to grab power so blatantly had Theoderic's court not been in such disarray, and he was not the only outsider to smell an opportunity. In 522, the Burgundian king Sigismund executed his son and ex-heir Sergeric. Sergeric was Sigismund's son by Theoderic's daughter Ostrogotha who had just died, and part of this story was an attempt to throw off Theoderic's hegemonic influence. In 523, likewise, after the death of King Thrasamund, the new Vandal king Hilderic killed the Gothic military retinue which had stayed in North Africa with Theoderic's other daughter Amalafrida, and had her arrested. She eventually died in detention. In both cases, timely deaths at home were part of the story, but so too was the death of Eutharic and the paralysis at Theoderic's court. Nothing could offer his unwilling satellites a better opportunity to throw off his hegemony, and they happily took it.

One of them was successful, the other not. A fleet was being readied for a punishment expedition to the Vandal kingdom in the summer of 526, reportedly, but, on Theoderic's own death, it never sailed, so that Hilderic never had to face the music. The Burgundians were not so fortunate. Power passed to Sigismund's brother Godomar, who held on to his throne in the face of both Frankish and Gothic interventions, but Tuluin added further lustre to his potential candidacy by detaching more territory in Provence from Burgundian rule and adding it to Theoderic's domains, so the old king at least had the satisfaction of seeing the uppity Burgundians get some kind of come-uppance.[44]

If all this were not enough, the smell of the old order's blood in the water attracted one other, still larger shark to the last rites of Theoderic's regime: Constantinople. Both the Burgundians and the Vandals looked to reinforce their new assertions of independence from Ravenna by making alliances with the Eastern Empire. These were granted, most happily. At much the same time, Justin's regime began to persecute non-Nicene Christians – of the same persuasion as Theoderic and his Goths – living within its borders, having tolerated these communities for well over a century. Theoderic saw this as a personal slight and threatened countermeasures against Italian Catholics. This might seem like an overreaction on the old king's part, except for one thing. Justin's regime also refused to grant Theoderic's eventual choice of heir, Athalaric, the same recognition that had been granted his father. We know this because Cassiodorus wrote a letter to the emperor on behalf of his new master shortly after his accession, asking that Athalaric be adopted as son-at-arms, just as his father had been. I have no doubt that Theoderic had asked for this to happen, having made his choice probably fairly swiftly after Eutharic's death and certainly a year or two before his own. This prompts the conclusion that Justin's regime deliberately refused to grant the request of their erstwhile ally, whose good offices had helped heal the Acacian schism. Such a stance can in turn only mean that it was attempting to exacerbate the political unrest paralysing Theoderic's court and giving encouragement to all those wanted to undermine his power. To my mind, this is probably also the problem that led Pope John to breathe his last in one of Theoderic's jails. Clearly, his embassy had failed to negotiate something that Theoderic wanted, despite all the celebrations and applause that the Pope reportedly received in Constantinople. The most likely concession that Theoderic would have wanted at this stage was East Roman recognition for his heir, and this was not forthcoming.[45]

From this perspective, you can understand the old Goth's irritation at the sudden outbreak of religious persecution. Add that to the alliances with the rebellious Vandals and Burgundians, and the non-recognition of his heir, and it is an inescapable conclusion that all the bonhomie of the late 510s meant absolutely nothing. As soon as opportunity presented itself, the duplicitous East Romans returned to type, acting not as allies but to undermine Theoderic's power and prestige in every way they could. Their object in this, I suspect, although it is nowhere recorded, was not to prepare the path for an invasion of Italy. As we shall see in the next chapter, a huge amount of highly contingent water would still have to flow under an equally large number of bridges, over the next decade or so, before Constantinople became seriously interested in annexing Italy to its direct rule. In my view, the East Romans were much more likely seeking to sow enough dissent within the elite political circles of the kingdom to break up Theoderic's Gothic superstate, and detach the Visigothic kingdom from Ravenna's rule. This made perfect sense. No other single act would more weaken whoever came to power in Ravenna after Theoderic's death, and, since the two had only so recently been combined, it was a highly achievable goal.

It was also in precisely this web of deceit, I fear, that Boethius and his father-in-law eventually found themselves ensnared. Boethius is much too evasive in the *Consolation* for us to be absolutely certain why he met such a terrible fate. He did have strong connections in Constantinople, so that, perhaps like Pope John, he fell foul of Justin's determination to stir up as much trouble as possible in the Italian kingdom by refusing to recognize the new choice of heir. Given these connections, you can see that Theoderic might well have expected his *magister officiorum* to be able to deliver the recognition that would have helped secure Athalaric's succession and stabilize the political scene at Ravenna once again. And when that recognition was not forthcoming – a bit like Cardinal Wolsey when he failed to secure that famous divorce – the king's wrath was unrelenting.

This reconstruction, I think, is entirely possible, but there is also a second, more specific alternative. Boethius, you will recall, states that his fall was all to do with Theoderic's regime having rejected philosophy's good teaching on the art of government. That could be code, as others have suggested before. For, of the various potential candidates for the throne after Eutharic's death, Theodahad is known to have had strong interests in Neoplatonic philosophy. We also happen to know that there were reasonably close ties between him and Boethius. The main alternative to the Cardinal Wolsey scenario, therefore, is that Boethius fell because he backed the wrong horse in the intense political manoeuvring which followed Eutharic's death.[46] Either way, it's a safe bet that Boethius got caught up somewhere in the fallout. Succession was the big, chaotic and unresolvable issue of Theoderic's final years, and it was this that surely claimed Boethius' life.

THE ROMAN EMPIRE OF THE GOTHS

Within a few months of Theoderic's death, the imperial aura had quickly and decisively faded away from his former domains. The break-up of the united kingdom of Italy, Gaul and Spain was the fundamental cause, but it was reinforced by the Vandal Hilderic's entirely successful rejection of Ostrogothic overlordship and the Burgundians' partially successful acts of self-assertion. In its heyday after 511, Theoderic really had put together a very decent copy of the only empire, as he proclaimed to be his aim in the famous letter to Anastasius. The territorial extent of his direct rule was enormous, and his hegemony stretched not only over North Africa and the Burgundian kingdom of the Rhone valley, but also, with an ever-increasing degree of looseness, up into central Europe. It is worth stressing this point, because it has so often been missed. The fact that the Franks, as we shall see later in the book, were destined for longer-term historical stardom must not be allowed to hide the fact that, in their own lifetimes, Theoderic's career eclipsed that of Clovis, and that, in the second decade of the sixth century, it was his power that was truly imperial in character. It was his friendship, not that of Clovis, that was sought both by leading Gallic churchmen, such as Caesarius of Arles, and the papacy alike. *Semper Augustus* was not brown-nosing hyperbole but an entirely appropriate title for the greatest ruler of his day.

Several reasons have been identified over the years for the subsequent failure of his imperial project, not least the impacts of the potential religious divide between Arian and Catholic, and a political one caused by the fact that he only ever generated lukewarm acceptance from those ever-important blue-blooded Romans of Rome. The religious divide only became an issue, however, when the regime of Justin and Justinian chose to make it so, by persecuting the old Arian communities of their domains while simultaneously refusing to recognize Theoderic's new choice of heir after the death of Eutharic. After all the rapprochement of the 510s and the joint consulship of 519, I can only conclude that Theoderic was entirely correct to interpret the new Constantinopolitan religious policy as a deliberate diplomatic slight, and entirely reasonable in threatening countermeasures. All the heat went out of the issue, however, when Theoderic's united Gothic realm failed to survive his own demise, and Catholic–Arian relations both within Italy and on the diplomatic front between Ravenna and Constantinople quickly returned to the cheerful old ways of happy coexistence. Caesarius of Arles' greatest days of influence, for instance, came after Theoderic's death, notably with the Council of Orange in 529 under the rule of Athalaric. The fall from grace of Boethius and his father and Symmachus, likewise, do not look, on close inspection, to provide good evidence of a long-standing fault line in the foundations of Theoderic's rule. Their deaths were part of a major crisis, no doubt, but belong to a different story than the one that is normally spun around them: more that of perennial favourite of autocratic ruler falling out with former regime loyalists over a major new issue, than of long-term resistance to a hated tyrant.

The real reason for loss of imperial status was much more prosaic: the inability of Theoderic's chosen successor to hold on to the overwhelming military might represented by a combination of the Gothic armies of both the old Visigothic and Theoderic's new Ostrogothic kingdoms. That this combination failed to survive his death, however, is not really so very surprising. He had only brought the two military capabilities together in 511, so that no long-standing ties and traditions of co-operation, nor even of joint campaigning, knit them together. Even if Eutharic had not predeceased him, therefore, it must be highly doubtful that Theoderic's Gothic Roman Empire could really have replicated itself in the next political generation. And with the renewal of the old Gothic division, Theoderic's successors were in no position to match his level of political pre-eminence in the former Roman West. The descendants of the force he led into Italy in 489 clearly were still much more powerful than the forces of the Burgundian or Vandal kingdoms, and probably too, to judge by events of the first decade of the sixth century, of those of the reinvented Visigothic kingdom. But, especially once his successors had fully integrated Clovis' new conquests east and west of the Rhine, the Franks certainly became at least as powerful. Dividing again the Gothic military of Italy and Spain in this broader strategic context made it impossible for

Theoderic's successors to bestride the old Roman West in his colossal footsteps.

The roots of Theoderic's failure on the imperial stage thus in the end lie in the fragility of his control over those most recent, Visigothic additions to his military power base. But at the same time, it is worth pointing up the countervailing durability of that centrepiece of his life's political project: the combined army that he brought with him to Italy in 489. This is a point which has come rather to be lost in recent scholarly emphases on the all-encompassing fluidity of so-called barbarian group identities in the fifth and sixth centuries, so it is worth taking just a moment to survey the major planks of the case. Certainly, Theoderic's following was no ancient 'people', united by ancient cultural commonalities, and, thus far, I have no issue at all with revisionist approaches to the subject. Theoderic's Ostrogoths were an entirely new formation created out of two major components – the Pannonian Goths and the Thracian Gothic allies – which had had entirely separate histories for at least several generations prior to their unification in the 480s (and in fact potentially for centuries, since their fourth-century ancestors may well have belonged to separate Gothic kingdoms north of the Black Sea). Even this much, however, goes nowhere close to bringing out the full messiness of the army's origins. The Pannonian Goths themselves had only been created in the 450s by Theoderic's uncle from a series of warbands who had been incorporated into the Hunnic Empire of Attila, while the Thracian Goths too may have in fact also been an amalgam of originally smaller groups with various origins, even if it does look as though a resettling of former Hunnic subjects in the 420s from Pannonia to Thrace started the whole enterprise off. And if its two main component parts had messy origins, Theoderic had also recruited plenty of other human flotsam and jetsam from the collapse of Attila's empire by the time he entered Italy. Rugi from the kingdom destroyed by Odovacar formed the biggest group, but Bittigur Huns also turn up in Italy, and others besides.

From these highly ragged beginnings, Theoderic managed to knit the various components together into a highly effective military machine. The tools he had available were mostly Roman in origin, some positive, some negative. On the negative side, Zeno's double-dealing hostility provided all these various recruits with one excellent reason for operating together. If they did not, the emperor was aiming at their mutual destruction. But the empire also provided more positive motivation too, since, operating together, they stood much more chance of extracting a share of Zeno's tax revenues in the form of annual subsidies. And it was this positive side of things which really won out in Italy, where the strength of the united army allowed Theoderic to take such total control of the landscape that he was then able to mobilize Italian wealth, in the form of both land grants and continuing tax flows, to reward his loyal followers. The strength of their loyalty to him, and the overall power that he had welded together, shows up in the extent to which this army allowed Theoderic to dominate at least the western Mediterranean even before the Visigoths were added to his musters.

This was no mean achievement given the massively disparate origins of his army, and, in early medieval terms, the group identity of the army he created was extremely durable. Certainly, not everyone felt the same degree of loyalty to their leader. The Rugi, as we have seen, were quick to change sides during the initial conquest, but they were a *very* recent addition at that point of course, having joined up only in 487/8. Likewise, when East Roman armies moved into Italy in the 530s, in the generation after the king's death, some elements of the Gothic forces surrendered immediately.[47] But in point of fact, only a small minority did so, and, as we shall see in Chapter 4, the vast majority of the descendants of those whom Theoderic had brought to Italy had to be fought to a standstill over twenty-five years of campaigning before the identity of the group was broken down. This identity was not ancient; it had first been created in Theoderic's lifetime. Nonetheless, it was far from ephemeral. The experiences of campaigning together and the bonds of the shared struggle against first Zeno and then Odovacar had a major transformative effect. Then, I suppose above everything else, you put on top of all that the wealth distributions that followed from the conquest of Italy and which gave the original army members and their descendants a common and powerful interest in defending the major new privileges that had come their way. The result was a new group identity certainly, and, for the majority of the army's membership, not remotely an ephemeral one, since it took twenty years of armed struggle to dismantle.

Even if this army was by itself an insufficient power base for asserting empire in the post-Roman world, its essential character does bring into focus exactly why the Roman Empire in Western Europe had ceased to exist by the end of the fifth century. When the empire first came into existence, the largest political structures they encountered in the Germanic-dominated world of the central zone were temporary alliances of military manpower from a large number of separate groupings, put together for highly immediate offensive or defensive purposes. At most, such structures had enough staying power to win a single big victory, like that of Arminius over Varus' legions in the Teutoburg Forest, but that was a very rare phenomenon, and, within a few years of that victory, the victorious alliance had already ceased to exist. Theoderic, by contrast, could create an extremely large force by putting together just two base units – the Pannonian and Thracian Goths – which were already substantial in size: a much simpler type of political problem involving many fewer key decision-makers. Add to that situation a set of common bonds which came from serious and eventually successful joint campaigning, plus a joint interest in maintaining control over the reward set that Theoderic pushed their way after the conquest of Italy, and you can absolutely understand why the vast majority of this force, even in its second and third generation of descent, proved so resilient in the face of the East Roman invasion of Italy.

All the bodies of military manpower which created the successor states to the Western Empire were, like Theoderic's Goths, new formations very much created on the march. But that did not make their group identity any more ephemeral than that of the Italian Goths. All of these groups – such as Visigoths, Vandals, and eventually Franks – went through very similar experiences and all came out much the same way. Forged in the fierce fires of the competition they found on Roman soil originally for survival in the face of Roman counter-attack, but then increasingly – faced with a weakening central empire – for an ever larger slice of the old Roman tax base, the already substantially big base units from which they were born became larger still, and that much more durable. The contrast with Germanic groups of the first centuries BC and AD could not be stronger. Long-term transformation had created the building blocks for really large and lasting military formations capable of carving off slices of Roman territory when they were forced into that vital final process of political unification. And once they started to do that, the central Roman authorities quickly found both tax base and the armies it had supported were fading away. Even the largest Germanic alliance of the period of Roman expansion could never have stood up to Roman imperial power in this way, and the fact that, in the course of the fifth century, several groups of this kind were loose on Roman soil does indeed explain why the central imperial authorities found it impossible any longer to maintain the structural integrity of the empire.[48]

But if the new size and durability of the Germanic groups that could be put together on Roman soil in the fifth century explains the erosion of that military edge which had made empire possible, the new groups were also strong enough, in the main, to fend off each other's attentions. Theoderic's coup of 511 aside, no one successor state in the post-Roman West of the sixth century disposed of a large enough military power base of sufficient resilience to build a state with long-term viability that was truly imperial in scale. Theoderic could browbeat Burgundian and Vandal kingdoms when at the height of his career, and temporarily extend his direct rule over the Visigoths when their kingdom was disrupted by defeat; but neither his kingdom nor that of any of his rivals – all of whom had equally been born in the highly competitive circumstances of the fifth century – had sufficient military strength definitively to absorb enough of their neighbours to build something that really looked like a restoration of Rome over the long term. Not surprisingly, therefore, the second major attempt to re-establish empire in the West had to come from outside the old Western imperial territories entirely. It was rooted, instead, in the East Roman Empire, whose resources dwarfed those of any of the individual Western successor states. That power had always been there, of course, but for two political generations after the defeat of its great Armada of 468, its last serious attempt to maintain the existence of a serious Western empire, Constantinople limited its interventions in the western Mediterranean to carefully targeted diplomatic interference, such as that which so disturbed Theoderic's final years. How and why that came to change leads us straight to the emperor Justinian.

PART TWO

'THE CONQUEROR OF
MANY NATIONS'

3

'BY THE AUTHORITY OF GOD'

MILES FROM BLOODY ANYWHERE, even in specifically Serbian terms, there is a narrow plateau delineated by the step-sided valleys of two small rivers. The plateau is located on neither of the main thoroughfares which have channelled traffic through this part of the Balkans since time immemorial: the Moravia–Vardar corridor, and the passage from ancient Naissus (modern Nis) to Scupi (modern Skopje). These were the two roads that the Pannonian Goths had flooded with their wagons when making that fateful march south into East Roman territory. Some agriculture is possible in the vicinity, but the climate and soil around the plateau have never supported a very dense population.

Despite these drawbacks, the authorities in Constantinople built a brand new and thoroughly monumental city on the top of it in the middle of the sixth century, starting within a decade of Theoderic's death in Ravenna. Excavations are still under way, now in the hands of a combined French and Serbian team, but the findings so far are already extraordinary. The plateau's north-western extremity was occupied by the city's final redoubt, its acropolis, surrounded by a massive rampart made irregular by the terrain and studded with five huge towers and just the one gate (Figure 5). Within, a massive episcopal complex (basilica, baptistery and audience hall) faced an equally monumental seat of secular authority across a colonnaded square. This redoubt was surrounded by another set of walls marking off five hectares or thereabouts of the upper town, which sat comfortably behind two sets of fortified gates. Here, the Romans constructed still more churches, arcaded streets and a huge granary, together with several rich residences and some of the usual paraphernalia of water management in the ancient world, including a water tower, without which it would be impossible ever to have such a concentrated population in this pretty arid part of the world. Outside, the lower town encompassed a further three hectares, and excavations have so

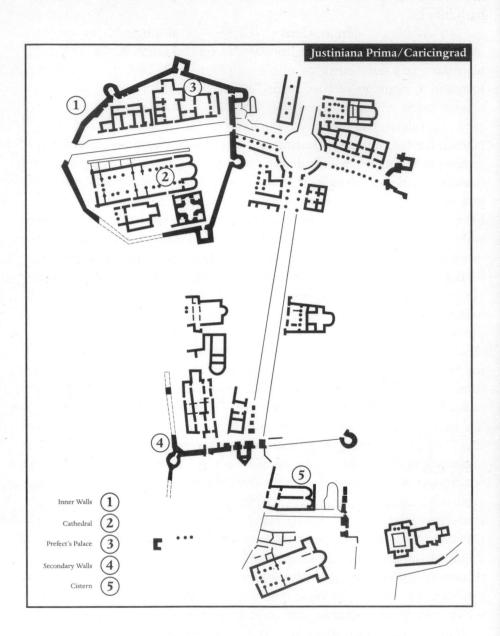

Justiniana Prima/Caricingrad

Inner Walls ①
Cathedral ②
Prefect's Palace ③
Secondary Walls ④
Cistern ⑤

far thrown up still more churches, a huge water tank, and two massive bath blocks.

No economic, administrative, religious or strategic necessity, or even logic, generated this mighty exercise in civil engineering. What it is, in fact, is a monument to one overmighty individual: the emperor Justinian I, nephew of that Justin whose promotion solved the succession crisis which followed the death of Anastasius, and for whose sake Theoderic had brokered the end of the Acacian schism. Our plateau hosted the city of Justiniana Prima – Caricingrad is its modern designation – which was built for no reason other than to commemorate the obscure birthplace – nearby it seems, not actually on the plateau – of one of history's great egos. And not only did a city blossom here from nowhere, but secular and ecclesiastical geography was rearranged around it. A law of 535 declared the emperor's intention to transfer to Justiniana Prima the seat of the prefecture of Illyricum (responsible for governing all the western Balkans and Greece) from the ancient city of Thessalonica, while the city's new bishop was given metropolitan rights to become the senior prelate of the entire northern Balkans.[1]

The remains of Caricingrad make an altogether suitable monument for one of the most extraordinary characters from the entirety of Roman imperial history. Justinian is pretty well known to the general public, but not as well known as he would have been had he lived in the first century AD, say, and he is certainly worth his place alongside the Caligulas, Neros and Claudiuses who have such a hold on the imagination. He came to the throne in 527, when Theoderic's body was barely cold in the ground, and has gone down among historians as one of the most visionary – if perhaps also misguided – Roman emperors ever to have lived. For many, he was the one ruler of Constantinople after 476 who was serious about wanting to restore the might of Rome to the full heights of its ancient glory. He came to the throne, it is often claimed, with a burning desire to reconquer the lost provinces of the Roman West, and then set about doing precisely that, while occupying his more idle moments with a complete reform of the entire corpus of Roman law. But if, at the end of his life, Roman borders had been massively advanced, and a revised text of Roman law produced which was to have a massive influence on medieval and early modern Europe, it is equally a commonplace that, like any proper anti-hero, Justinian's legacy to his successors was a profoundly poisoned chalice. Within two normal lifespans of his death, East Rome was to lose not only the majority of what he conquered, but also most of the rest of its territory besides, and find itself plunged into the deepest of political, economic and even ideological crises as it struggled to cope with direst defeat.

Not the least cause of all the confusion surrounding his reputation is the astonishingly inconsistent picture of Justinian that emerges from the works of the greatest historian of his era: a lawyer from the city of Caesarea, in what is now Israel, by the name of Procopius. His home town was a prosperous port city in the late antique period, much of which is in the process of being opened up in large-scale excavations, not least of the harbour area, where a generation of marine archaeologists now have been enjoying their summers swimming in the warm waters of the eastern Mediterranean. Procopius doesn't give us much specific information about his own background, but he clearly belonged to the gentry landowning class, since his works show that he had enjoyed the extensive education in classical Greek language and literature which was the mark of this class and above in the later empire, and – being entirely private – was affordable only to them. Since he appears in his own writings as an *assessor* – legal adviser – to Justinian's most famous general, Belisarius, he would then appear to have moved on to legal studies, the costs of which again confirm the kind of privileged background from which he came. It was Belisarius, with Procopius in tow, who led first Justinian's conquest of Vandal Africa in 533, and then the initial phases of the war in Italy, whose successes led Cassiodorus to his inexorable date with a Constantinopolitan destiny in the later 530s.

ANEKDOTA

Procopius' pen (probably his voice, since it was normal to dictate) has left us three separate works. By far the longest is a narrative history of Justinian's wars focusing on the years 527 to 552/3, constructed on a generous scale. No one – not even Procopius himself – has ever thought it a perfectly sufficient account of Justinian's reign, and it was written according to the conventions governing this type of history in the late Roman period. This gives it a number of peculiarities. You were not allowed to use any 'modern' vocabulary – officially anything not sanctified by the founding Greek grammarians of the classical period – which meant finding, amongst other matters, alternative ways of describing Christian bishops, priests and monks, since none of these had existed back in fourth- and fifth-century BC Athens. Introductory digressions designed to amuse and show off learning, rather than necessarily to educate, were also de rigueur before you plunged into the central narrative progression. Subject matter, too, was strictly prescribed – no new-fangled Christianity again, for instance, but rather a ruthless focus on military and diplomatic history – and it had become customary if not quite essential for the author to have participated personally in some of the events, both to provide extra interest and a kind of guarantee that his text contained the truth.[2] Procopius' war narrative provides a huge amount of detailed information which no one has ever provided serious reason to doubt. Indeed, so vast is the body of data that, unless you work really hard, there is a tendency for any history of Justinian's reign to consist merely of writing out Procopius in your own words with a little extra comment.

Equally dense, in its own way, is Procopius' second work – normally known in English as *Buildings* – dealing in four lengthy books with the construction works authorized by the emperor. Again, there's lots of information, but also some potentially severe problems. For one thing, Procopius is – at least to modern tastes – excessively adulatory. In this work, the emperor is everything that imperial propaganda suggested that he ought to be. Divinely ordained, he is holy and pious, and his many and varied construction works both ornament and safeguard the empire. Historians have long been concerned about the sheer scale of the alleged activity. Some of it is unproblematic. Book 1 focuses on Constantinople – Istanbul as is – and some of Justinian's structures are still there, not least the great Church of Hagia Sophia, which is pretty much everything Procopius wrote it up to be (even if the dome had to be remodelled later in the reign when the original collapsed in the fierce earthquake of 558). But in Book 3 and especially Book 4, Procopius' originally precise and varied accounts give way to what are essentially lists, and very long lists too, raising doubts that so many structures could ever really have been built. Indeed, historians being the counter-suggestive animals they are, it became something of a trend in the 1980s to argue that much of what Procopius was attributing to Justinian had in fact been built in the reign of his predecessor Anastasius. This was based above all on an argument about the key Persian frontier fortress of Dara (of which more in the next chapter), where Procopius had originally been stationed with Belisarius, and of which he gives a long and highly specific account of what Justinian was supposed to have constructed. For the most part, it came to be claimed, this was just nonsense, and pretty much everything had in fact been built by Anastasius, who certainly started fortifying the site. And if Procopius could be so deeply wrong about somewhere he had actually been, why should we believe a word he has to say about countless other constructions in tracts of territory whose air he had never once breathed?

On balance, thankfully, we need not be quite so pessimistic. Anastasius did build much of what you can still see at Dara if you're minded to go there, but the very specific things Procopius describes Justinian doing are also there, and do look like a secondary phase of construction: some of them, indeed, while now gone, are visible in the old black and white photos taken by Gertrude Bell and others in the late nineteenth and early twentieth centuries. And, more generally, there is a comfortable coincidence between Procopius' account of Caricingrad, and what the archaeologists have been unearthing. In short, substantial exaggeration but not complete fabrication seems to have been the order of Procopius' day in *Buildings*. While Justinian was certainly happy to take the credit for structures finished in his reign, even if started by Anastasius, no one has yet really caught Procopius with his hand in the till, attributing something specifically to Justinian which very definitely either was never there at all, or was equally definitely built by someone else. Nauseatingly sycophantic as the *Buildings* is, its overall point is not completely mendacious. Justinian did build a huge number of buildings and those where Procopius provides specific details probably were very much as recorded.[3]

The key problem with Procopius' account of the reign of Justinian is posed neither by the *Wars* nor the *Buildings*, but by his third and shortest work, the *Anekdota*, or, as it's usually called in English, the *Secret History*. A copy of this text was known to a late tenth-century Byzantine encyclopaedist, but then it disappeared from view until a

solitary manuscript was discovered in the Vatican Library and published at Lyons in 1623. But getting hold of the text in the first place
was only a minor irritant. Much more troublesome are its contents.
For where the *Wars* and even – in a kind of way – the *Buildings* fall
into recognizable genres of ancient literature – classicizing history and
panegyric respectively – so that we know essentially how to read
them, the *Secret History* does not. What it says also lobs the proverbial
cat among the feathered friends in terms of potentially undermining
absolutely everything else Procopius has to say in his other, much
longer works.

The problem posed by the *Secret History* – if problem it be; in fact,
the whole thing is a hugely intriguing and in the end highly entertain-
ing puzzle – comes in several interlocking layers. On the one hand,
the work's preface tells us exactly why Procopius wrote it. We are
in the very early 550s, and he had already written and published all
but the final book of the *Wars*. But, he reports:

> In the case of many of the events described in that previous
> narrative, I was compelled to conceal the causes which led up to
> them. It will therefore be necessary for me to disclose in this
> book, not only those things which have thus far remained
> undivulged, but also the causes of those occurrences which have
> already been described.[4]

Afraid of 'a most cruel death' and of being discovered in flagrante by
the emperor's 'multitudes of spies', Procopius had produced only a
highly sanitized version of the wars of conquest. Now he promises to
tell us the truth, the whole truth, and nothing but the truth.

So far so good, but then you read on and find out exactly what
Procopius' 'truth' consists of. First of all, he trashes his former
employer, the general Belisarius, and his wife Antonina, but the full
weight of fire is withheld for the emperor Justinian himself, and his
wife, the empress Theodora. First Justinian:

> This man was both an evil-doer and easily led into evil, the sort
> of a person whom they call a moral pervert, never of his own
> accord speaking the truth to those with whom he conversed, but
> having a deceitful and crafty intent behind every word and action
> . . . [He] was insincere, crafty, hypocritical, dissembling his anger,
> double-dealing, clever, a perfect artist in acting out an opinion

which he pretended to hold, and even able to produce tears . . . And to sum up the whole matter, he neither had any money himself, nor would he allow anyone else in the world to have it, as though he were not a victim of avarice, but simply consumed by envy of those who possessed money. Consequently he lightly banished wealth from the Roman world and became the creator of poverty for all.[5]

Theodora also left a lot to be desired, if not, it seems, to the imagination:

As soon as she came of age and was at last mature, she joined the women of the stage and straightaway became a prostitute of the sort whom men of ancient times used to call the 'infantry'. For she was neither a flute-player nor a harpist, no, she had not even acquired skill in the dance, but she sold her beauty to those who chanced to come along.

And in Procopius' view it was not just economic necessity which drove Theodora on:

There never was anyone who was such a slave to pleasure in all forms; for many a time she would go to a feast with ten youths or even more, all of exceptional bodily vigour who had great expertise in fornication, and she would lie with all her banquet companions the whole night long, and when they were all too exhausted to go on, she would go to their attendants, perhaps thirty in number, and pair off with each one of them.

She used to complain that nature had not endowed her with still more ways of enjoying sexual pleasure, and that's not even mentioning her famous stage act involving chickens, grains of barley and such private parts as she did have, although, according to Procopius, private is about the last thing they actually were. At the same time, she was massively strong-willed and extremely clever, and by mind and body succeeded in capturing the heart of Justinian, who even had the law changed so that he could marry her.[6]

Together, they made perfect partners in crime. Each was as greedy as the other, and as intolerant of any opposition to their will, so they combined to ruin everyone with whom they came into contact, and by this means the empire as a whole. Nor was this outcome purely the result of human folly. For Justinian's mother confessed at one point:

> When she was about to conceive him, a demon visited her; he was invisible but affected her with a certain impression that he was there with her as a man having intercourse with a woman and then disappeared as in a dream. And some of those who were present with the emperor at very late hours of the night ... asserted that he would rise suddenly from the imperial throne and walk up and down there (indeed he was never accustomed to remain seated for long), and the head of Justinian would disappear suddenly, but the rest of his body seemed to keep making these same long circuits ... And another person said that he stood beside [Justinian], sat and suddenly saw that his face had become like featureless flesh, for neither eyebrows nor eyes were in their proper place.

The identification was finally confirmed by a Holy Man who came to Constantinople for an imperial audience, but couldn't go into the throne room because he saw the Prince of the Demons sitting there instead of the emperor. And it turned out that the Devil had long since come to a pact with Theodora too, that, with him as her lover, she would never again want for money.[7] So there we have it. The real truth about why things happened as they did in Justinian's reign. When *The Exorcist* meets *Deep Throat*, with nothing but avarice in mind, how could the outcome be anything other than disastrous for humankind?

The problem all this poses for the general credibility of Procopius on Justinian is straightforward. When the same author tells you in *Buildings* that on the one hand the emperor was God-appointed, righteous and pretty much infallible – he even received messages from God via a dream as to how to solve a pressing architectural problem in the construction of Hagia Sophia – but on the other that he's an *Omen* prequel, it's not immediately obvious what to think. How are we to reconcile the extraordinary juxtaposition of *Anekdota*'s claims to be revealing the full and final truth about the regime with the pornographic portrayal of Theodora and its entirely diabolical Justinian? To my mind there's a host of clues that Procopius is playing with his readers in *Anekdota* – not that he doesn't mean what he says in vilifying the regime, but in the sense that neither does he expect us to accept its contents as 'truth' in a straightforwardly literal sense. One is the vivid pornography of the Theodora passage. The response of at least 95 per cent of all the students I've taught in the last twenty-five years, especially to all the chickens, has been to laugh (with just a few from very sheltered backgrounds looking a bit shocked). It's always a little dangerous to judge the cultural values of another time and place, but I'm extremely confident here that laughter is precisely the response Procopius was after. This doesn't mean that the portrayal may not have a serious purpose; ridicule is one of the most effective strategies for cutting enemies down to size. And, in Theodora's case, the portrayal does an A1 job of turning her into the exact mirror image of what imperial propaganda demanded that she ought to be. Instead of the modestly virtuous, divinely chosen consort of her emperor, she is a greedy and wilful nympho, with Procopius taking particular delight in all the ironies surrounding her establishment in Constantinople of a home for reformed prostitutes.[8]

The same is also true of the *Anekdota*'s portrayal of Justinian. Instead of a God-chosen emperor, the empire was in fact being run by the Devil's own child. And here too, I'm confident that we're meant to laugh. The headless figure and dissolving face descriptions are both pretty funny and all surrounded by careful verbal formulations if you look closely, that suggest we're not meant to be thinking in terms of literal truth: 'seemed', 'asserted' and 'said' litter the account. The same is even more true of the outrageous cock and bull story with which Procopius surrounds his report of what Justinian actually looked like.

> He was neither tall in stature nor particularly short, but of a medium height, yet not thin but slightly fleshy, and his face was round and not uncomely; for his complexion remained ruddy even after two days of fasting. But that I may describe his appearance as a whole in few words, I would say that he resembled Domitian, son of Vespasian, very closely.

The fact that Procopius could know this, however, was not straightforward. For Domitian was the ultimate bogeyman, the very worst imperial tyrant thrown up in the entirety of Roman imperial history, whose reputation in the ancient world was much worse than Caligula and Nero who are better known to modern audiences. Domitian's reputation was so bad, Procopius tells us, that not only did the populace literally tear his body to pieces, but, after his death, the

Senate ordered the destruction of all his statues. So how did Procopius know that Justinian looked just like Domitian?

> [Domitian's wife], collecting the flesh of Domitian, and putting the pieces accurately together and fitting them one to the other, sewed up the whole body; then, displaying it to the sculptors, she bade them represent in a bronze statue the fate which had befallen her husband . . . [she] set it up in the street leading to the Capitol . . . and it shows both the features and fate of Domitian even to the present.

If you're not laughing yet, I really think you should be. The whole story is total nonsense, and, you'll note, the said statue is located safely far away in Rome when Procopius is writing for an audience in Constantinople, so no one could check. Again, we're in the brilliant world of Procopius' imagination; the whole artifice is just a clever way for him to draw a parallel between Justinian and the worst tyrant in imperial history. What we're dealing with in the *Anekdota*, in other words, is high quality political satire, and there are other late Roman examples where precisely his chosen routes – sexuality and demonization – were used to belittle and hence destroy their targets' credibility.[9]

All this offers us two broad conclusions about the great historian of Justinian's age: one more comforting, the other rather less so. On the one hand, I'm pretty confident that we can know broadly what Procopius thought about the regime of Justinian and its achievements. Like many other East Romans, I suspect, the first victory in North Africa in 533–4 inspired a sense of triumph, which may even have provided the initial impetus to his historical ambitions, since he was profoundly involved in the action as Belisarius' aide. But if so, enthusiasm quickly gave way to profound disenchantment as subsequent and consequent wars dragged on through the 540s, until, by *c.*550 at the absolute latest, he was implacably and consistently hostile towards the regime and all its works: there being no need to see *Buildings* as anything more than a perhaps commissioned panegyric.

Rather less comforting is the image of the clever and playful Procopius which emerges so starkly from *Anekdota*. This might seem paradoxical, but it's not. The more clever the writer, especially an extremely well-informed one like Procopius, then the more difficult it is to escape from the world view that they have so artfully constructed.

With writers in the ancient rhetorical tradition – and history was viewed as a branch of rhetoric – this is a particular problem because they were always encoding into their writings cross-references to the ancient authorities in which both they and their potential audience had been educated. Sometimes these were just verbal reminiscences with no particular meaning, reflecting the fact that particularly apt phrases tended to get memorized and handed on: a bit like the astonishing number of proverbs that are in *Hamlet*, that you pick up from elsewhere long before you've ever seen or read the play. But cross-references could also be used to encode extra layers of meaning, for instance where an author provided one half of a well-known quotation in his text, and when the reader added the other half it twists or even subverts the ostensible meaning of the passage (like a more sophisticated version of the game of adding 'not' to the end of positive statements – 'Justinian was a holy and divinely appointed emperor: not', which is a pretty good summary of *Anekdota*). The trouble with ancient rhetorically trained authors like Procopius is that they spent the best part of a decade in their teens trawling through ancient literature under professional guidance, whereas most of us now do not. Being totally sure that you've garnered every last grain of such an author's meaning is extremely difficult, therefore, and the cleverer your author, the more difficult it is to know. As I write this, the jury, it seems to me, is still considering its verdict on Procopius. That he is a clever and artful writer seems inescapable. But exactly how clever? The case has recently been made that he was actually extremely clever, and constructed a philosophically based critique of Justinian's regime for a group of like-minded analysts in sixth-century Constantinople, rather than merely lampooning out of an overarching sense of disgust. But while this case can certainly be constructed from Procopius' works, it might be adding an unwarranted final level of depth to the author's own intentions, and independent evidence for the existence of the supposed audience is lacking, so the jury is still out.[10]

Fortunately, however, we do have a second body of material to work with. For alongside the wars of conquest explored by Procopius, Justinian's reign possesses arguably even greater significance for its total recodification of Roman law. The legal material is by its very nature more intractable than the standard type of historical narrative produced by Procopius, and hence, despite or perhaps because of its bulk, doesn't get discussed in nearly as much detail. Looked at from the right direction, however, it throws a bright and thankfully non-Procopian shaft of light on to the regime of Justinian: in particular its earliest years.

THE WHOLE BODY OF THE LAW

Justinian's reform of late Roman law would prove to be an epochal moment for much of the European land mass. It wasn't at the time, since none of the former Roman West was then controlled from Constantinople, and some other parts of Europe had never been Roman at all, but the long-term effects of Justinian's project could hardly have been greater. Essentially, it preserved by codification a carefully chosen selection from a thousand years of so of Roman jurisprudence. This was done in such a systematic fashion that the resulting text – the *Corpus Iuris Civilis* or *Body of the Civil Law* – provided an overall model together with numerous individual pieces of legislation for many of the developing legal systems of central and Western Europe from the medieval into the early modern periods. It was precisely thanks to Justinian, therefore, that study of Roman law remained central to many university legal courses until very recently (only being demoted from compulsory to voluntary at Oxford, for instance, in the 1990s). How Justinian's text came to enjoy this astonishingly influential afterlife is a story that is central to the final section of this book, but none of it could have been foretold in the late 520s and early 530s when it was being created. What's important for the moment is the nature and significance of the project at the moment of its creation.

In effect, legal reform quickly became the flagship home affairs project of Justinian's new regime when he took sole power on the death of his uncle Justin on 1 August 527. The project came in several parts, the first of which was announced as early as 13 February 528, just six months after the new emperor's accession. And if, as a Roman ruler, you wanted to make a huge noise about your own fitness to rule, then, in matters internal to the Roman state at least, there was no better task to throw yourself into than legal reform – for two reasons.

First – and we've already seen Theoderic's response to the same point – Roman imperial state ideology had long since identified the existence of written law as the single factor which distinguished the Roman world as a higher order of divinely inspired human society, far superior to that of any known or conceivable neighbour. As Justinian himself put it in *Deo Auctore* (*By the Authority of God*), the order which set in motion the second element of reform on 15 December 530:

> Nothing in any sphere is found so worthy of study as the authority of law, which sets in good order affairs both divine and human and casts out all injustice.[11]

Identifying written law as the key constituent of Roman superiority was a habit which descended directly from classical Greek ruminations on why their society was superior to all-comers. The Greek originals, however, had focused not just on one factor, but on several, which were all mutually reinforcing. In particular, Greek thought had laid great stress on the value of an intense education system (in a descendant of which Procopius was trained) in producing individuals of high moral sensibility, who could see the value of self-control in the face of life's vicissitudes, and were willing, therefore, to subject their individual wills to written rules and regulations. In this system of thought, it wasn't entirely clear whether you had already to be superior as a person before you were willing to accept written law, but the later empire's ideology gradually dropped the other ideas to make law the undisputed centrepiece of Roman superiority, and in all the formal comparisons of civilized Roman and barbarian society (even the highly sophisticated Persians) which appear in our sources from the fifth century onwards, it is the existence of written law that marks out the former as so superior. One Roman author famously has the Visigothic king Athaulf say that he gave up on the idea of replacing the Roman Empire with a Gothic one precisely because his followers couldn't obey written laws. Hence the best option he could come up with was to use Gothic military might to support Rome. Another author – equally famously – reduces a Roman merchant turned highly prosperous Hun to tears at the memory of the overall quality of life that written law could sustain. And, within the post-Roman West as a whole, issuing a written law code, however virtual and impractical, was tantamount to a declaration that your polity belonged to the club of civilized Christian nations.[12]

Why law in particular should have emerged from the cluster of older ideas to play this starring role is not central to this story, but my hunch is that the Christianization of Roman imperial ideology lies behind it. The old Greek ideology of superiority was unashamedly elitist – since the only superior individuals were fully educated ones, and since that education was private and expensive, then by definition only a few (generally male) persons could belong to the elite club of the fully human. But Christianity held that everyone – even women – had souls and could be saved, so that the old Graeco-Roman vision of superiority was far too exclusive. Dropping the rest of the ideological apparatus and concentrating instead on law overcame this problem since law and the social structures it defined gave everybody a place. Some were in positions of greater authority and power, some more humble, but everyone had a position, and this worked much better in the Christian Empire, which, after the Gospel texts, was committed to the central contention that everybody could be saved. Either way, the late imperial focus on written law as the key to Roman superiority meant that there could be no more ambitious move for any regime to make than legal reform.

The second reason for Justinian to have picked on legal reform requires a little more teasing out. It starts from the straightforward observation that reforming Roman law was, by the summer of 527, a job that certainly needed doing. When he came to the throne, the potential sources of legal authority that might be cited in court were too many and too diverse to make it easy to resolve more complex cases. Simply leaving it there, however, and concluding that the new emperor was a far-sighted ruler who introduced sweeping legal reforms for the good of his subjects is an insufficient response to what went on. To see why, we need to kick the subject a little harder.

By the sixth century (and for several centuries previously in fact), there were two main types of legal authority commonly being referred to in imperial law courts: the writings of lawyers more or less officially licensed by past emperors to give authoritative legal opinions (so-called jurisconsults), and rulings of different kinds given directly by emperors, whether in the form of official general edicts or rulings which might originally have related only to one specific case, but which made a point of potentially more general significance. Justinian's reforms came in three tranches, and addressed themselves both to the separate problems posed by each body of material on its own, and the further overarching problem which followed when you tried to use them side by side. Of the three, the third was a piece of cake. This came at the end and took the form of producing a new introductory textbook for law students, which reflected the changes to the law generated by the other elements of the project. It also closely followed, where it could, the pre-existing manual for students, written by the third-century jurist Gaius, including about one half of this earlier work.[13] But if banging out the final textbook was a relatively easy task, the labours which had preceded it had been much more onerous.

Part one of the reform, the element kick-started in February 528, set itself, first, the task of collecting new imperial legislation issued since the last such collection: the *Theodosian Code* of 438. This covered the period from *c*. AD 300 onwards. It then had to combine this new selection from ninety years of imperial legislation with the three other codes of imperial laws which already existed: that of Theodosius and two earlier codes compiled by Hermogenianus and Gregorianus in the 290s. Between them, the latter two provided a selection of imperial law dating back to the 130s. The job was undertaken by a commission of eight senior administrators-cum-politicians of high standing within the regime, and two practising barristers.

Their general working parameters were well set, since they were following models set by both the *Theodosian Code* and intervening initiatives to collect subsequent new legislation:

a) You started by throwing away any laws which pertained only to one particular case, identifying thereby laws of actual or potential general significance (the operative concept here was *generalitas* in the Latin).

b) These chosen laws were then edited, initially by throwing away much of the rhetorically self-justificatory bullshit with which emperors customarily introduced their rulings.

c) Then you separated out the various parts of any law which related to different topics, because emperors often issued composite laws covering several subjects.

d) Finally, you arranged your edited extracts under thematic chapter headings within numbered books, maintaining chronological order within the individual chapters.

This much was pretty straightforward, since the editing approach and even most of the book and chapter titles could follow the pre-existing models of the older codes. A much harder task was to decide what to keep from those three older works, and how to integrate their materials with the selection from new imperial law that the commissioners had just made.

The commission proved itself up to the task, however, and brought home the completed Code in just over a year, the new volume being formally promulgated on 7 April 529. By comparison, it had taken the corresponding *Theodosian Code* commission nine years to complete only the first of these tasks, and it never even tried to produce the combined volume, although, to be fair, new bureaucratic habits of collection and the fact that they had a model to follow had made some aspects of life easier for Justinian's commissioners.[14] Nonetheless, to edit the new laws and integrate all imperial legislation into one book, and within thirteen months from start to finish, showed formidable despatch.

It was this very despatch, I suspect, which encouraged Justinian to set up a second commission in December 530 to tackle the still bigger problem of the jurisconsult writings. *Deo Auctore* set out the principles.

> We therefore command you to read and work upon the books dealing with Roman law, written by those learned men of old to whom the most revered emperors gave authority to compose and interpret the laws [the jurisconsults], so that the whole substance may be extracted from them, all repetition and discrepancy being as far as possible removed, and out of them one single work may be compiled, which will suffice in place of them all ... so that nothing may be capable of being left outside the finished work ... but that in these fifty books the entire ancient law – in a state of confusion for almost fourteen hundreds years, and rectified by us – may be as if defended by a wall and leave nothing outside itself. All legal writers will have equal weight and no superior authority will be reserved for any author, since not all are regarded as either better or worse in all respects, but only some in particular respects.[15]

Chairing the new commission was entrusted to one of the barristers attached to the previous work, Tribonian, who had clearly distinguished himself in that task, and had certainly been doing some preparatory work between the publication of the Code in April 529 and the announcement of the new project in December 530. They already knew by then that the next text would be drawn up in fifty books, and the principles with which they would approach the jurisconsult writings were carefully laid out: no pre-judging, every opinion to be weighed on its merits.

None of this preparatory work took much away from the difficulty of the task. By its own account, the commission had to read legal opinions totalling 2,000 books and 3 million lines. In the end, they reduced this mass to fifty books and 150,000 lines, but that doesn't tell half the story. Not only was there a huge amount of jurisconsult material, but it was deeply intractable. Pretty much the only legal writings we have from the jurisconsults are those which survived the red pens of Tribonian and his fellow commissioners, and their brains imposed an order and logic on this material which clearly had not existed before. The key thing to remember about lawyers is that for the most part they make their living from clients, and clients employ lawyers to win cases. And going to law – especially in non-criminal cases and it was mostly non-criminal, civil law that jurisconsults wrote opinions on – is a costly activity whose purpose is overwhelmingly to protect or achieve some kind of financial gain. Thus, not surprisingly, the chief problem Tribonian's commissioners found in the jurisconsult material was not the amount of it, but the fact that its leading practitioners often disagreed with one another. That they did so is not surprising: many of these disagreements were generated by the need to provide no doubt ingenious arguments for particular clients. Cutting the jurisconsults down to size was not just an editing problem, therefore, but one of intellectual decision-making. Which among the competing opinions on any particular issue would the commission choose to support?

The scale of the problem was vast, as several hundred years of mutually competitive jurisconsult opinion-giving had created the kind of confusion which is the paid lawyer's paradise. Dickens' *Bleak House* with its interminable legal case which eventually ate up the value of the property under dispute is no bad image to have in your head. Roman law was a jungle whose tigers were the lawyers, among whom the best – those most able to adapt jurisconsult opinion and imperial ruling to their clients' needs – could command astronomic fees.[16]

Without this backstory, it is impossible to grasp what a high-risk strategy the second element of Justinian's legal reform actually involved. To work, it had to cut through the Gordian knot of traditional Roman legal authority, and, in so doing, challenge the vested interests who benefited so substantially from the status quo. That the reform was necessary was never in doubt, but the realities of the task had already frightened off Theodosius' legal team, who had quietly dropped this part of their project by the late 430s, and it had not got any easier in the meantime. *Deo Auctore* not only laid out logical working principles, therefore, but nailed the regime's colours to the mast. In December 530, Justinian's regime committed itself to boldly go where no emperor had dared go before.

Nor was legal reform the only high-risk project adopted by Justinian's administration as it took up the reins of power. Never mind hairy European barbarians of one kind or another, East Rome's traditional bête noire, inherited from the Greeks, was Persia. When the new Sasanian dynasty achieved an unprecedented degree of centralized control over what is now Iran and Iraq in the 220s, this heralded two political generations and more of disaster for Rome, involving three massive defeats and a sequence of humiliations, not least the capture and subsequent display of the emperor Valerian, monumentalized in the great rock reliefs close to Naqs-I Rustum. Only after a turbulent fifty-year process of political and administrative reform, which enabled emperors to point a larger share of their realms' assets in the direction they wished, was parity restored on the eastern front in the last decade of the third century. Further conflict had then followed at intervals through most of the fourth century, but, in its final decade and a half and above all then in the fifth century, periodic superpower confrontation gave way to both practical and ideological coexistence. Both empires were facing fierce, especially Steppe nomad enemies on other frontiers, and the Persians suffered their own equivalent of Hadrianople when the shah-in-shah Perozes and his army were massacred by the Hephthalite Huns in 484. It may only have been a myth, but, by the early sixth century, both empires understood this period of relatively good relations as having been heralded by an agreement between the emperor Arcadius and the shah-in-shah Yazdegerd, that the latter would adopt Arcadius' young son Theodosius II in an act designed to smooth the latter's accession in case of Arcadius' early death. The arrangement proved prophetic in that Arcadius died in 408 when Theodosius was only six.[17]

As the nomad threat finally receded for both parties, the early sixth century saw a partial return to the old Cold War patterns of behaviour, with matters of dispute sometimes being resolved by warfare rather than by negotiation (as had happened throughout the fifth century) and both sides looking to stir up trouble for the other in their border marches, particularly at the eastern end of the Black Sea. The goodwill of the fifth century had not completely dissipated, however, and in 522 the then Persian ruler, Cavades, waved a new olive branch in Constantinople's direction. He had a very particular reason for doing so, since he wished to make a younger son, Chosroes, his heir, by-passing the claims of an older son with whom he had had a major falling out. What he did, was hark back to the example of Theodosius II and Yazdegerd, and ask the then reigning emperor Justin to adopt Chosroes in an entirely parallel move. According to the account in Procopius, Justin and Justinian were about to accede to the request when they received some troubling advice from the then chief legal officer, the quaestor Proculus:

> This embassy openly and straight from the very first words means to make this Chosroes, whoever he is, the adopted heir of the Roman Emperor. And I would have you reason thus in this matter: by nature the possessions of fathers are due to their sons and while the laws among all men are always in conflict with each other by reason of their varying nature, in this matter both among the Romans and among all barbarians they are in agreement and harmony with each other, in that they declare sons to be masters of their fathers' inheritance. Take this first resolve if you choose: if you do you must agree to all its consequences.

Thank goodness for Proculus! He rumbled Cavades' cunning plan to make Chosroes ruler of the Roman as well as the Persian Empire, and, after negotiations went backwards and forwards for a while, the request was finally rejected in the summer of 527, by which time Justinian was co-Augustus and already effective co-emperor. Instead of meeting the Persian request in full, the Romans offered to adopt Chosroes as son-at-arms in the fashion they used with the rulers of Western successor states and other so-called 'barbarians'. Offended, Cavades broke off the negotiations and soon invaded Roman territory.[18]

It's a fascinating episode but I've always found it strange that

Proculus' advice has often been taken seriously, sometimes with an appreciative comment on the quality of information available to Procopius: that he could know so much of the secret counsels doing the rounds at court. As soon as you stop to think about it, the whole thing is total nonsense. The way you became emperor in Constantinople, and had done since time immemorial, was to win sufficient backing from a critical mass of the key constituencies: major senatorial landowners, leading bureaucratic administrators, court officials and chief officers of the army, amongst which categories there was anyway considerable overlap. Justin adopting Chosroes would tick none of these boxes and gave the latter not the slightest hope of succeeding to the throne of Constantinople after Justin's death, any more than Yazdegerd adopting Theodosius (if it happened) gave him a claim to the Persian throne.

Without an iota of doubt, rejecting Cavades' diplomatic initiative on the basis of this pretext was deliberately insulting, as was, of course, the offer to treat the heir to the Persian throne like a western barbarian. And this, you will recall, is not the first time that we have observed Justin and Justinian with their hands in the till on matters of succession. At the same time as Cavades' approaches were being first parried and then rejected, the same parties were busy refusing recognition to Theoderic's choice of heir after the death of Eutharic (page 95). It is impossible, in my view, to reach any conclusion from this episode other than that Justinian, in his final rejection of Cavades' approach, was behaving in a deliberately insulting fashion with the hope presumably, as had been the point of the equivalent policy in relation to the Gothic kingdom, of destabilizing the Persian Empire over Chosroes' unconstitutional and disputed succession.

In other words, Justinian opened his reign by adopting a very high-risk strategy in the field of foreign affairs, as well as at home. But, just as was equally true of the legal-reform project, should it be possible to claim a good outcome from the war with Persia that Roman behaviour now made virtually inevitable, the ideological pay-off was potentially huge. Ever since the Persians turned Valerian's pickled pelt into a wine skin in the third century, Persia had been the enemy of ideological choice when it came to claiming victory. Constantius II had ridiculed Julian's victory over the Alamanni at Strasbourg in 357 by saying that, compared to the Persians, half-dressed savages weren't real enemies, and Julian himself had looked to cement his hold on power by

launching a massive and ultimately doomed invasion of Persian territory. For emperors who claimed to be divinely appointed and divinely
supported, the ultimate test of legitimacy was a decent military victory
or two. For how better could the support of the Almighty (who was
indeed almighty) actually show itself, if not through victory on the
battlefield? There was no more prestigious enemy to overcome than
the Persians.[19]

Legal reforms and the quarrel with Persia need to be seen together in
my view when we're trying to understand the opening salvos of
Justinian's reign. In its first few months, the regime took not one high-
stakes gamble, but two: and simultaneously. What this really reflects
is the severe insecurity underlying Justinian's hold on power at this
point. His uncle Justin's promotion to the imperial throne on the death
of the emperor Anastasius was an entirely improvised affair, rather
than a carefully worked out succession commanding widespread consent among the political classes in Constantinople. Anastasius himself
had clearly not felt secure enough in his power to arrange succession
before his death; if he had, presumably he would have picked one of
the three nephews (Hypatius, Pompeius and Probus) who were his
closest relatives. Justin was a prominent officer in the imperial guards,
who, according to our sources, exploited the power vacuum launching
what was in effect a *coup d'état*. Charged with disbursing large sums in
bribes on behalf of another candidate entirely, a certain Theocritus, he
spent the money instead on securing the loyalty of his guards corps,
the excubitors, who then promptly put him in power. And, once
on the throne, Justin busied himself removing any rivals, actual and
potential, who stuck their heads above the parapet; notably that
Theocritus whose funds he had misappropriated, and Vitalianus, the
senior general who had led the Chalcedonian opposition to Anastasius
and who played a large role in the reconciliation with the papacy
which marked the start of the reign, and from which Theoderic
apparently benefited so much (page 86).

During the years which followed these somewhat inauspicious
beginnings, Justinian, by all accounts (not just that of Procopius)
worked tirelessly to gain effective control over the reins of power and
make himself un-bypassable in the short term as the old emperor's
immediate heir. But that did not mean he was securely in power.

Uncle-to-nephew succession was no automatic given in the world of Constantinopolitan politics; it was, after all, precisely what had *not* happened on the death of Anastasius. And, amongst other possible candidates, Anastasius' nephews were still knocking around at court, some of them in very high office, and Roman imperial regimes were always coalitions of the powerful. By the summer of 527, Justinian had worked his way on to the throne, but he was not yet securely in power. Taking on these huge – and risky – projects was all about winning sufficient political capital to turn mere occupation of the throne into the power actually to rule. Success on either front would demonstrate that the practical power of the Divinity was securely underpinning Justinian's throne: that he was a fully legitimate ruler of the Roman world.[20]

Justinian emerges from these first few months of his rule as an imaginative and ambitious chancer, looking to exploit the two main ideological routes open to an East Roman emperor to cement his hold on power. This is a substantially different image to any of the normal range of responses to Procopius' wildly inconsistent pictures of Justinian, but its essential accuracy is confirmed by some of the details of the actual legal reform which followed. A strong element of the short cut was already there, in fact, in the basic project design. The Theodosian version of necessary reform to the Roman legal system, you will recall, envisaged one final *über*-code which would bring together imperial pronouncements and jurisconsult writings into a single seamless garment. Justinian's version was considerably less ambitious, looking to end up instead with two not-quite-so-*über*-codes, one of imperial law, the other of jurisconsult material. This was easier, but left open potential problems of disagreement or – more likely – differences of emphasis between the two bodies of material for the ambitious lawyer to exploit in court. The speed at which Justinian's reforms proceeded is of and in itself also highly indicative. As *Constitutio Tanta*, which confirmed the legal status of the code on 16 December 533, commented, when the task was first announced no one expected it to be completed in less than ten years, and ten years, pretty much, was what it had taken the Theodosian team to produce just their code of imperial pronouncements.[21] Ramming the whole thing through in three years required a whole lot more than mere efficiency, reflecting rather the amount of political will and capital that Justinian's regime was willing to invest in cutting the many legal

Gordian knots with which they were faced. Some evidence of this
process survives.

An essential strategy for sorting out the mess of jurisconsult discord
was the series of so-called 'Fifty Decisions', which resolved by new
legislation a series of thorny old chestnuts within Roman jurisprudence.
The greatest modern scholar of the process reckons that there were
in fact more than fifty, but they were all hammered through between
1 August 530 and 30 April 531 (another indication that preparations
were well in hand before the project was officially announced in December 530). Some of these problems had been around for centuries and
resolving them so quickly wasn't just a question of logical argument
or administrative efficiency, but of making an argument stick in the
face of the vested interests which had preserved the disagreements, no
doubt to their own profit, over preceding generations. Part of the
answer as to how Tribonian and Justinian got them through was
certainly brute force (as we shall see in more detail shortly), but they
also offered a deal to some of the interested parties. In the final
reconstitution of the legal profession in the Eastern Empire, representatives of the legal schools of Constantinople and Beirut, which were,
it seems, the most distinguished, were central to the process. At the
very end of this process, however, two other law schools, Caesarea
and Alexandria, were explicitly suppressed, their teachers being no
longer allowed to take students. This is classic divide and rule. Consent
from the most distinguished part of the legal establishment for the
reform package was won in part by ensuring that they would enjoy a
duopoly over law students, thereby securing higher fee incomes than
had previously come their way.[22]

In short, Justinian's law reform was just as much a political project
as it was a legal one, and a political project which was rushed through
with every possible despatch because its success was deemed essential
to the prestige of the regime. *The Whole Body of the Law*, one of the
prefatory constitutions to the finished work, claimed that 'everything
has now been reformed and arranged', but there were some loose ends
left hanging in order to get the job finished. My favourite final
indication of the fundamental truth of this observation comes in
Constitutio Tanta. The key aims of the second element of the legal
reform was to pare down the jurisconsult material to remove superflu-
ities, repetitions, and, above all, contradictions. On the matter of
repetitions, *Tanta* comments:

> Should it chance that here and there, in so great a collection of legal rules, taken as it is from an immense number of books, some cases of repetition should occur, this no one must be severe upon; it should rather be ascribed first of all to human weakness, which is part of our nature ... It should also be borne in mind that there are some rules of exceeding brevity in which repetition may be admitted to good purpose.

So don't be too hard on us if you do find any repetitions, but, anyway, there aren't many and they are probably there deliberately: as wonderful a piece of fatuous rear-end covering as you're likely to find. Best of all are its comments on contradiction:

> As for any contradiction occurring in this book, none such has any claim to a place in it, nor will any be found, if we consider fully the grounds of diversity; some special differential feature will be discovered, however obscure, which does away with the imputation of inconsistency, puts a different complexion on the matter and keeps it safe from the imputation of discrepancy.[23]

So there are no contradictions in the book, and if you think you've found one, think a little harder and you'll find a way of making it disappear. Orwell's Ministry of Truth could not have done better. Not only was the reform pushed through with massive haste, by means of a political deal with some of the legal establishment, but even the commissioners realized that, in their haste, not everything had been fully resolved.

It is hardly surprising, therefore, that the legal-reform project, in the person of Tribonian, its chief architect, should have become an issue in the political upheavals which marked the early years of Justinian's rule. This was not necessarily a response to the precise details of the Fifty Decisions or any other specific aspect of the commission's legal work, but a general reflection of the fact that the stakes were so high. Because a successful legal reform would have gone a long way to making Justinian untouchable in political terms, it was only natural that those opposed to him more generally would seek to block it. In this purpose, Justinian's opponents were greatly aided by the fact that the emperor's other massive gamble led to disaster.

Cavades responded to Justinian's insulting rebuff with a predictable

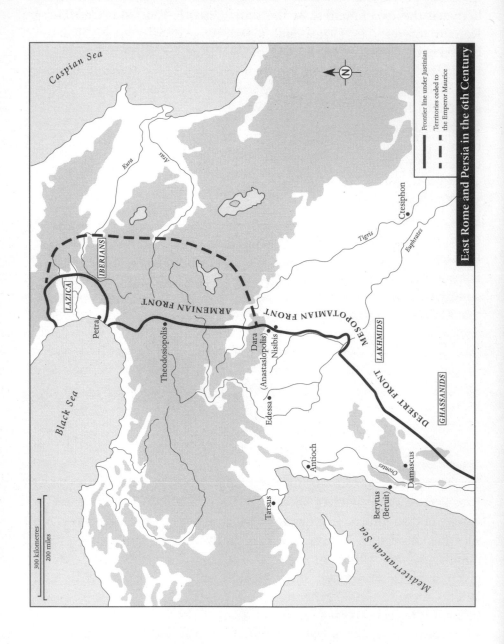

East Rome and Persia in the 6th Century

invasion of Roman territory on the main Mesopotamian frontier between the two empires. At the same time, he started undermining Roman interests in Lazica and Iberia, two of the marginal states between the empires in the Caucasus and at the eastern end of the Black Sea (Figure 6). In 528, two Roman attempts to threaten Nisibis, the main Persian base in Mesopotamia, were defeated and things started to look a little bleak from a Constantinopolitan perspective. Incipient disaster was rescued by a Roman victory in 530 outside Dara, however, Rome's main base, against a Persian force which had come to besiege it. This was won by Belisarius with Procopius now in tow, and the regime celebrated. But the celebrations were precipitate. In 531 the Persians made an unexpected attack on Roman territory and Belisarius suffered a defeat at Callinicum, which was so bad that a committee of inquiry was established to look into the circumstances.[24] By late 531, the storm clouds were gathering over Justinian's rule. Dara aside, the Persian gambit had failed. After Callinicum, Justinian could no longer claim military success against the auld enemy as proof that God was behind his rule. The political vultures were beginning to circle.

NIKA

Their opportunity came from an entirely unpredictable quarter. The East Roman equivalent of soccer – the veritable opium of the masses – was not so much religion as chariot racing. Charioteers were the sporting superstars of the age, commanding massive salaries and popularity, and whose movements between the set teams within a given city – Greens and Blues being the most popular, Reds and Whites the also-rans – generated fanatical responses of despair or joy. In total, the factions, at least in the largest cities of the empire, were something more than supporters' clubs: by the sixth century they had become hierarchical organizations with plenty of muscle who ran particular neighbourhoods with a rod of iron: Manchester United supporters club meets the Mafia, say. These young men liked, Procopius tells us, maximum facial hair, mullets, wide lapels, and plenty of bling. Generally speaking, they worked hand in glove with the more official city authorities. But in a world with more than its fair share of extreme poverty and more or less no police forces, lines of acceptability could be crossed fairly easily, and there was a limit to how much extortion and intimidation could be tolerated, especially within the imperial capital itself. Hence on Sunday 11 January 532, seven members of the two main factions – the Greens and the Blues – were due to be hanged, but then there occurred a fatal blunder. Two ropes broke and a pair of reprieved reprobates – one from each faction – fled for sanctuary in a nearby church.

The next Tuesday was another chariot-racing day and, in line with an ancient tradition of using such occasions to ask for favours by organized, ritual chanting called acclamation, the assembled crowd asked the emperor, who was present in the royal box, to pardon the prisoners. Justinian refused, at which point the Greens and Blues started a massed riot. Using the watchword *nika* – 'victory': a trad- itional battlecry of the Roman army – they stormed the capital's prison, releasing all the inmates. Things were already looking pretty nasty, but then came an extraordinary change of pace. More chariot racing was due for the Wednesday, which the emperor, fearing even worse trouble should he suppress it, allowed to go ahead. The event saw more chanted demands, but this time they were overtly and specifically political. What the crowd wanted now was not merely a pardon for some of its fellow hooligans, but the dismissal of three of Justinian's leading ministers, including Tribonian, who at this point, of course, was still busily throwing most of the chaotic mess that was classical Roman jurisprudence into the wastepapyrus basket.

Now seriously frightened, Justinian dismissed all three, but to no avail. On Thursday, the demands escalated further with the crowd trying to find Probus, one of the nephews of Anastasius, and raise him to the purple in Justinian's place. Probus proved not to be in the city, but the move set off three days of rioting which makes the summer of 2011 in Britain look like a nursery tea party. As violent street fighting and huge fires swept the city, Justinian decided on the Saturday to expel from the palace a series of leading senators who had taken refuge there, including the two other nephews of Anastasius: Hypatius and Pompeius. On Sunday a huge crowd gathered in the Hippodrome, home of the chariot racing and whose royal box was connected to the palace by an enclosed passage. They had come partly out of pure excitement, but also in response to an announcement – following a precedent established by Anastasius at a moment of extreme turmoil in his reign (that time over religious policies) – that Justinian would appear before the crowd to offer apologies and an unconditional amnesty to all the rioters. That may have been the announcement, but it was not what happened. The crowd – or part of it – acclaimed Hypatius as emperor, and he ended up being crowned in the royal box surrounded by the baying crowd; how many of the Hippodrome's 100,000 seats were occupied at this point is unclear.

Justinian had reached the ultimate crunch moment for all dictators facing rebellion: do I run (though it's unclear what the sixth-century equivalents of South Africa or Saudi Arabia were) or do I order the troops to fire? Justinian's first instinct, Procopius reports, was to leave (in the published *Wars*, so it was presumably acceptable to tell the story thus in public in Constantinople by *c*.550). Maybe, as has been true of some modern dictators, he wasn't sure that the troops *would* fire. But Theodora put new fight into him, declaring, again according to Procopius in the *Wars*, in an almost classical turn of phrase, that: 'Purple makes a fine burial shroud.'

In other words, our former actress would rather die than give up the throne. Thus emboldened, the regime deployed its remaining assets. The eunuch Narses, whom we shall meet again in the next chapter, went into the Hippodrome crowd alone, sought out the leaders of the Blues and promised them a huge sum of gold; according to reports, he had some of it with him. He also reminded them that Hypatius, whom they were currently busy crowning, had long supported the Greens. The argument proved sufficient. In the middle of the coronation, the Blues simply left the Hippodrome, leaving the Greens stunned.

Stupefaction turned to panic as the departing Blues were replaced by the regime's most loyal troops, guardsmen and personal retainers from the Persian front led by Belisarius, and Herulian *foederati* from the Balkans led by Mundus: both bodies of troops, you will notice, with no pre-existing ties within Constantinople. The original plan was for Belisarius' men to burst into the Hippodrome through the royal box, but the official palace guard – waiting to see which way the wind would blow – refused to take sides by opening the gate at the end of the passage. Belisarius was forced to work his way round to another entrance and led the charge, at which point, hearing the tumult,

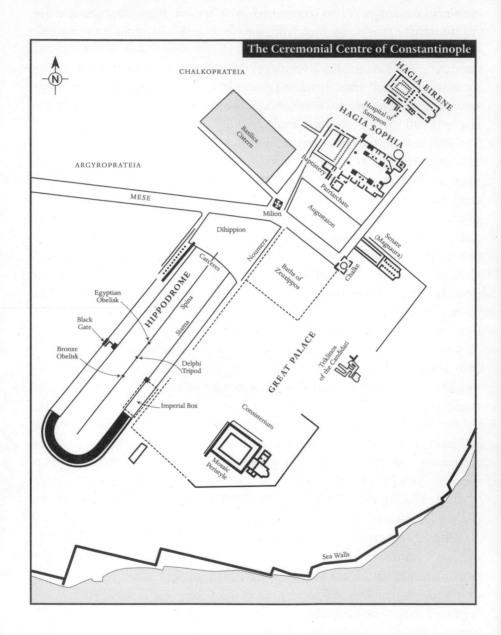

The Ceremonial Centre of Constantinople

Mundus also burst in from the Black gate opposite (Figure 7). The result was carnage. The Greens had their armed thugs, but these were no match for crack imperial troopers, and, amid the slaughter, no one even tried to defend Hypatius and Pompeius who were tamely captured. Held in prison overnight, they claimed to have been acting against their will, but Justinian would have none of it. They were executed on the Monday morning and their bodies thrown into the sea, with all their property confiscated to the imperial treasury.

The regime had held on to power, but a bit like Syria in the early 1980s or now, at astronomic cost to its citizens, and, in this case, not even in a provincial city but the central imperial capital. Two separate contemporaries tell us that around 30,000 people died in a combination of the street fighting and the massacre in the Hippodrome. That is of a similar order of magnitude to Syria in the early 1980s, by all accounts, but you do also have to think about relative scale. The population of Constantinople is generally reckoned to have peaked at half a million from around the middle of the fifth century. So the Nika fighting led to the deaths of something like 5 per cent of the city's population, the equivalent of 400,000 being killed out of the current population of Greater London. The fires also destroyed the great palace church of Hagia Sophia, its smaller neighbour Hagia Irene, the Senate House, many of the palace's outer buildings, and several of the ceremonial arcades at the heart of the city. Again, a London equivalent would be rioting that destroyed the Houses of Parliament, Westminster Abbey and pretty much the entirety of Whitehall down to Horse Guards and Admiralty Arch. It would be almost impossible to overestimate, therefore, the level of dissent and destruction evidenced in the riot.[25]

But, despite the detail of our sources, a number of key questions cannot be answered conclusively. Who exactly lay behind the politicization of the protests as Tuesday's demands for pardons for a couple of thugs, gave way over the next forty-eight hours to demands, first, that Justinian emasculate his regime, and then for an entirely new emperor? What was Justinian's thinking when he threw Anastasius' nephews out of the palace? Was it a mistake that he failed to observe Vito Corleone's famous dictum to keep his friends close, but his enemies even closer? Or was the emperor trying to engineer a showdown by bringing their latent opposition out into the open? And how much should we believe of Procopius' famous scene where Theodora puts the fight back into Justinian? Her famous phrase is a misquotation. The original reads '*Tyranny* makes a fine burial shroud.' So it looks a fair guess that the same Procopius who wrote the *Secret History* reckoned he could bank on a lack of classical education in the higher reaches of the regime and crack a little joke for those in the know at the imperial couple's expense.[26] But the story of the empress' bottle appears in the *Wars*, which was published openly, so presumably it encapsulates a line on the riot that the regime was in a general sense happy to see publicized, at least by *c.*550.

These hard questions are unanswerable, but the presence in the city of the troops of Belisarius and Mundus suggests that the emperor may have been anticipating a need for troops who could not have been suborned by disaffected elements at court. And this may in turn suggest that there was an element of entrapment in his expulsion of Anastasius' nephews from the palace, although this could also be explained as the desire to forestall the possibility an overnight *coup d'état* within the palace walls at the hands of palace guards, whose refusal to open up the passage to the imperial box indicates that they had been approached in some way by the opposition. At the very least, Justinian was sure where responsibility for the politicization of the violence lay, carried forward, no doubt, by the same kind of targeted bribery which Narses used to detach the Blues from the Greens inside the Hippodrome. Not only were Anastasius' unfortunate nephews executed on the Monday, but another eighteen senators were banished from the city and their estates confiscated. There was probably an element of score-settling in this, with the emperor's officials not being overly sparing in the accuracy of their condemnations, but I don't doubt either that Justinian was entirely correct in supposing that, halfway through that dreadful week, conspiracy took over from sheer hooliganism, and directed the latter's violence towards some highly specific political aims.

None of this lifted the air of defeat and disaster that hung over the regime. The deliberate quarrel picked with Persia had led to a series of defeats, of which the latest was serious enough to set off a committee of inquiry, the chief architect of the legal reform and two other leading henchmen had been dismissed, 5 per cent of the capital's population lay dead in its streets, and its ceremonial centre was a smoking ruin. This was not a record which was in any way compatible with the notion that Justinian was God-appointed, ruling with the direct assistance and guidance of the said Divinity. In short, by the end of that terrible Nika week in January 532, the regime had lost pretty much all its political capital, and all obvious consent to its rule. It had held on at spear point, but was teetering on the brink. And it is striking that Justinian didn't even feel strong enough to bring his dismissed ministers back into office.

It is against this background that we need to think about the policy of Western conquest which is considered the leitmotif of the regime in much modern historical writing. According to such views, launching the wars of conquest in the West had always been Justinian's main aim. A Latin-speaking traditionalist from Illyricum, which had formed part of the Western Empire in most of the late Roman period, he was desperate – it is thought – to recover the lost Roman territories. It is, moreover, entirely possible to find statements to this effect in his propaganda:

> We are inspired with the hope that God will grant us rule over the rest of what, subject to the ancient Romans to the limits of both seas, they later lost by their neglect.

The problem, however, is that this, the first known statement to this effect, dates only to the tenth year of his reign, 536, and followed two successful bouts of conquest: the seizure of Africa in 533–4 and an almost bloodless acquisition of Sicily in 535. And the conquest of Africa had itself originally been justified on religious and not political grounds at all:

> That which the omnipotent God has now . . . deemed proper to demonstrate through us exceeds all wonderful acts which have happened in the course of all time – namely that freedom should, through us, in so short a time be received by Africa, which 105 years before was captured by the Vandals who were enemies of both mind and body . . . By what language, therefore, or by what works worthy of God that He deemed it proper that the injuries of the Church should be avenged through me, the least of His servants.

It was only when Justinian was eyeing up further gains in Italy after these two initial successes, and setting his sights on Theoderic's old Gothic kingdom, that we hear a first whisper of any imperative need to reconquer the lost Roman West.[27]

The chronology of Justinian's propaganda has long been recognized, but it has nevertheless been thought that the cunning plan always existed, and that, as soon as an end could be put to troubles on the Persian frontier, the emperor was dead set on regaining the lost Roman territories. In my opinion, every detail we have indicates that this was absolutely not the case. Justinian's regime picked a deliberate quarrel with Persia in 527, when the opportunity was there to reach at least a temporary peaceful accommodation. If Justinian had really wanted to devote himself to the West, he could have dropped the nonsense about the adoption of Chosroes and gone straight for the Western jugular. It is also extremely to the point to realize that the conquest policy emerged only slowly and in highly contingent – i.e. entirely *unpredictable* – circumstances.

The first of the conquests – that of the Vandal kingdom – was triggered by events that were originally internal to North Africa. Unlike Theoderic's Italy (the unfortunate imprisonment of Pope John aside) where Arian rulers and Catholic Nicene churchmen got on famously, the course of inter-sect relations did not run so smoothly south of the Mediterranean. To a very significant degree, this was due to the different circumstances of the founding of the Vandal kingdom. This had been carved out of the living body of a still very vital Western Empire by the Vandal conquest of Carthage in 439, whereas all the other Western successor states emerged both more slowly and more consensually, a generation or so later, as the central Roman state gradually ran out of revenues and the capacity to direct events. And since Catholicism was unambiguously the religion of the empire, Vandal monarchs tended to be highly hostile towards it, deliberately fostering an alternate Christianity among the warriors who had put them in power. The other component here was that the North African Catholic Church had a long history of resisting persecution with might and main, and saw, perhaps, a touch more virtue in courting it than was true elsewhere. But, nonetheless, Vandal aggression was at the heart of the episodes of systematic small-scale and occasionally vicious (especially under Huneric in 484) persecution of Catholic clergy and laity which remained characteristic of the Vandal kingdom even after the Western Empire had ceased to exist.[28]

Breaking with the established mould, a Carthage spring was ushered in by the new king Hilderic who succeeded that Thrasamund whose gifts Theoderic had so unceremoniously returned, when he died on 6 May 523. Hilderic was the son of Huneric of the 484 persecution fame, but, in one of those ironies with which history abounds, his main new policy was to end all persecution and allow the Catholic Church of North Africa to function without impediment, and in particular to hold the first full general council of all its bishops for two generations in Carthage in 525. His religious policy was part of the major realignment of Vandal foreign policy, as we saw in the last chapter, away from the Ostrogothic axis-cum-domination, which had been ushered in by Thrasamund's marriage to Theoderic's sister Amalafrida, and towards Constantinople. In the end, he was lucky. Where the Burgundians suffered Theoderic's wrath for similar uppity behaviour when Tuluin seized extra territory from them in Gaul, the ships at least for the corresponding North African expeditionary force were still at anchor, waiting for the king's final order, when the old Gothic warrior eventually succumbed in summer 526 (page 94).

If Hilderic thus got away with a more than slightly dangerous show of independence at the start of his reign, he eventually ran into problems from another quarter. Within North Africa as a whole, or rather on its fringes, the great political problem was provided by indigenous Moorish groups who grew in size, organization, and effectiveness during the Vandal period of rule. Some of these groups inflicted a major defeat on his armies in the province of Byzacium in 529–30, and this was enough to trigger a *coup d'état* against him led by his royal cousin Gelimer on 19 May 530 (May seems to have been a bit of an unlucky month for sixth-century Vandal kings). Gelimer was a great-grandson of the first Vandal king of North Africa, Geiseric, where as Hilderic was a grandson (by a different branch of the family), and the younger man set about seizing full control of the reins of power. This involved both a clearout of Vandal supporters of Hilderic and a – moderate – reversal of the latter's pro-Catholic policies, although there is no sign that he re-instituted any kind of full-on persecution.[29]

Hilderic had been a loyal ally of Justinian, but when news arrived in Constantinople of his overthrow, the emperor was still fully involved in and hopeful of a good outcome to his Persian war (defeat at Callinicum would only come the following year). He therefore contented himself with a couple of stiff notes to the new king, and another advising Theoderic's grandson Athalaric not to recognize the new king over the water in Carthage. It was only two years later, in fact, in the summer of 532 (and here it's really important not to collapse the chronology) that Justinian began to show the slightest interest in doing anything more than writing the occasional letter. And by this time, two key events had intervened. Nika itself, of course, had come and gone with disastrous consequences for the prestige of Justinian's regime left just about standing among the piles of rubble at the heart of Constantinople. And the downward trend had been entirely confirmed by the terms of the so-called 'Eternal Peace' made with Persia soon after, in the spring of 532, which involved Justinian in large annual indemnities.

By the middle of that year, therefore, Justinian was desperate for some kind of political success, and this put an African adventure seriously on the menu. Even so, the decision to try to rescue the regime via a successful intervention there had not yet been definitely taken. The court was simultaneously exploring other possible avenues for a propaganda coup, initiating discussions which might have healed a current schism within the East Roman Church. A series of 'conversations' had been held in February just after Nika, which made progress but didn't come to any final positive outcome. Interestingly, the kind of religious compromise that would have been required to resolve the schism would have alienated churchmen in the non-Roman western Mediterranean, so that these conversations were pulling Justinian's regime in an opposite direction, to some extent, to the African option. But even after the conversations failed to reach any conclusion, the emperor still hesitated to pull the trigger.[30]

There were very good reasons to hesitate. Since the Vandals had taken Carthage in 439, there had been three serious attempts to recapture the lost provinces from them, and all three had ended in disaster. The essential problem was getting a large enough force across the Mediterranean and safely on to North African soil. The first expedition of 441–2 had been building up a combined expeditionary force from the Eastern and Western empires in Sicily when the first of Attila the Hun's campaigns into the Balkans had forced its abandonment, since the Eastern forces were urgently required at home. The second of 461 had gathered in Spain to make the short crossing over the Straits of Gibraltar, but the Vandals got wind of the operation and destroyed the Roman shipping while it was still in harbour. The third and final attempt had come in 468. Then a huge East Roman armada had set sail from Constantinople but come to grief off North Africa itself, nailed by hostile winds to a rocky shoreline and made a sitting duck for Vandal fireships. The loss of life had been horrendous, and the fleet's failure marked the end of serious attempts to keep the Western Empire afloat, triggering the free-for-all which saw its last assets being swallowed up wholesale by the nearest barbarian power. It also emptied the Eastern treasury to such an extent that it had not recovered by the time of the emperor Leo's death five years later. Even though Justinian was so desperate for a success, and Africa was so tempting a possibility, the odds were not on the face of it inviting.[31]

According to Procopius' account in *Wars*, divine inspiration eventually resolved the dilemma. Justinian was told in a dream to launch the attack. I'm quite prepared to believe that the emperor had a dream as well, but it looks as though another set of contingent events actually prompted Justinian to push the button. Over the autumn/winter of 532–3, two important pieces of news reached Constantinople. First, at the eastern end of the Vandal kingdom, in Tripolitania (modern Libya) a revolt against Gelimer broke out led by a local notable called Pudentius. No Vandals had been settled in this extremity of the Vandal kingdom, so there was no actual – or at least much – fighting to be done to declare independence. Pudentius immediately sent to Constantinople for assistance, asking for Tripolitania to be taken back under direct imperial rule. By itself, this still might not have been enough to arouse imperial interest in a full-on Vandal adventure, but the second piece of news then pushed Africa right up the imperial agenda. For, hot on the heels of the messages from Libya came news of a second revolt from within the Vandal domains. This time, Godas, the governor of the island of Sardinia, Gelimer's northernmost holding, declared independence and, again, wrote to Constantinople asking for imperial support. This message also arrived in autumn/winter 532–3, and was enough to make Justinian commit his forces. With two revolts convulsing Gelimer's kingdom, there was now much more chance of success.[32]

Accordingly, preparations for the Byzantine expeditionary force (BEF) were brought to completion in spring and early summer 533, its huge fleet assembling in the quiet waters of the Bosphorus and the Golden Horn. Its task was to transport to North Africa 10,000 infantry and 5,000 cavalry under the command of Belisarius, 'hero', if that's the right word, of the massacre in the Hippodrome. Leaving Constantinople in mid-June, the fleet made slow and occasionally rocky progress to the eastern coast of Italy and then on to Sicily where it holed up at a deserted spot close to Mount Etna. Two Hunnic soldiers had had to be executed for killing one of their comrades while drunk, and an astonishing 500 men had died from eating infected bread. But if these cannot have seemed anything but ill omens at the time, lady luck was firmly on the side of the expedition and helped it avoid the humiliating fate of its British counterparts of the early part of World War Two, whose regular need for evacuation under intense air bombardment led parts of the Royal Navy – unfairly of course – to construe the real meaning of BEF as 'back every Friday'. Procopius was sent forward to Syracusa and came back with some crucial intelligence. Gelimer, it turned out, was entirely unprepared for an East Roman invasion, and had sent the Vandal fleet and an elite force of 7,000 men off to Sardinia to quell the revolt of Godas. The problem in the past had always been the same. It had manifested itself in different ways in 441, 461 and 468, but the key difficulty was getting your army on to North African soil in the first place. Thanks to Godas, the road to Carthage was now open.[33]

And it was right at that moment, I suspect, in that deserted spot close to Mount Etna, close presumably to the beautiful city of Taormina with its wonderful Greek theatre, that Justinian's Western conquest policy was finally born. For, as Procopius tells us, it was only on hearing that the Vandal fleet was elsewhere, that Belisarius took the decision to head straight for the heart of Gelimer's kingdom. This suggests – and when you think about it, it must have been so – that Belisarius had been sent off from Constantinople with entirely contingent orders. Justinian and his key advisers knew that there was some chaos in the Vandal kingdom, but news travelled so slowly in the ancient world, even around the Mediterranean, that what was known in Constantinople in mid-June 533 was weeks if not months out of date. The same fact also made it impossible for Belisarius, on finding out more, to refer back to Justinian for further orders. In reality, therefore, his orders must have contained several options – from least to most ambitious – depending on what he actually found when he got to Sicily. If the situation looked less promising, the fleet could always sail on to safely to Tripolitania, and by securing that province confirm at least some kind of 'victory' for Justinian's propagandists to do with what they could. As it was, the Vandal cat turned out to be away, and much wider vistas fell open. Set in the twists and turns of the early years of Justinian's reign, Western conquest turns out to have

1. Mosaic of Theoderic from St Apollinare Nuovo in Ravenna. When this was found hidden beneath layers of plaster, art historians interpreted it as Justinian and restored it as such, but St Apollinare was Theoderic's palace church, making it overwhelmingly likely that he is the figure portrayed.

2. Eagle brooches from the Apahida treasure: one example of the vast gold wealth which accumulated in central Europe thanks to Attila's astonishing victories of the 440s. The struggle for its control underlay the competitive process which pulled the Hunnic Empire apart and saw the Pannonian Goths rise to prominence.

3. Coin of the Emperor Zeno (474–491). His unending struggle to hold on to imperial power created the conditions which allowed Theoderic the Amal to create a larger still powerbase at the expense of his Thracian Gothic rivals, and even secure the emperor's approval for his conquest of Italy.

4. The Emperor Anastasius portrayed in ivory.

5. The walls of Constantinople. Built in the early fifth century, they were too powerful for Attila or either of the two Theoderics to breach. In fact they resisted all-comers for a thousand years until the Turks brought their cannon.

6. Mosaic of Theoderic's Palace from St Apollinare Nuovo. Major political figures – with the king presumably in the centre – were originally portrayed between the arches, but removed after Justinian's conquest. One hand can still be seen on a pillar.

8. Theoderic on the Senigallia Medallion. Issuing gold coins was an imperial prerogative; this triumphal portrayal is a clear sign of his claim to quasi-imperial status.

7. Theoderic's mausoleum, following Roman imperial models, at Ravenna. The roof was formed from one stupendous piece of marble.

9. Baptism of Christ, from the so-called Arian Baptistry in Ravenna. Non-Nicene and Nicene Christians cooperated very happily under Theoderic's rule, with the king even being called in to resolve a difficult papal schism.

10. Justinian and his court in the famous mosaic from the church of San Vitale in Ravenna. The church was begun under Theodoric, but the decorative scheme was modified after Belisarius' capture of the city.

11. Theodora as portrayed in the mosaic panel directly opposite that of Justinian in San Vitale. Here she is every inch the divinely chosen empress, the mirror image of her portrayal in Procopius' *Secret History*.

12. Justinian's great church of Hagia Sofia in Istanbul. Whether it would have been constructed had the original not been burned down in the Nika Riot is a moot point.

13. The harbour of Carthage, capital of the Vandals' North African kingdom. Belisarius' total and unexpectedly easy conquest of the kingdom, together with the successful completion of legal reform, re-established Justinian's claim to be a divinely chosen, legitimate emperor in the aftermath of the Nika disaster.

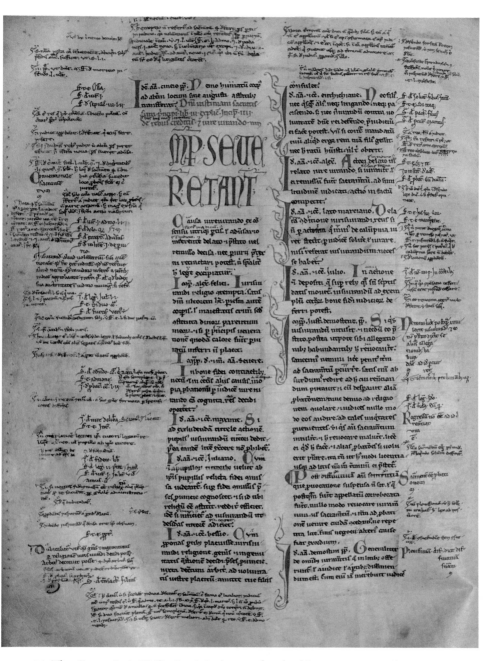

14. The *Corpus Iuris Civilis*: Justinian's great legal achievement was as important to him in ideological terms as his victories in Africa and Italy.

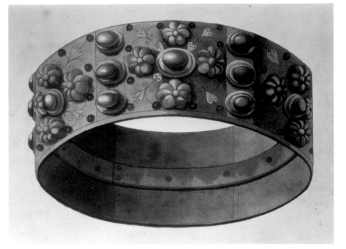

15. A nineteenth-century aquatint showing the Iron Crown of Lombardy. Charlemagne's conquest of his Italian neighbours marked a step-change in ambition, setting him decisively on the road to his imperial coronation.

16. Charlemagne's reliquary from Aachen. His son and grandsons were unable to maintain the legacy of imperial unity which he – in fact by chance – passed on to them on his death in 813.

been not the deep-seated, long-standing plan of a romantic visionary, but another type of phenomenon altogether, one that is much better known to historians: overseas adventurism as the last desperate gamble of a bankrupt regime. Between them, Nika and defeat at the hands of the Persians had put Justinian's regime in deepest jeopardy. As contingent factors unfolded around them, the emperor and his advisers eventually decided – three years later – that avenging their old ally Hilderic offered the best chance of re-establishing the regime, and it was in Belisarius' hands finally to roll the dice of war.

TO AD DECIMUM AND BEYOND

It is impossible to overestimate the importance of the fact that the Vandal fleet was away in Sardinia. Never before had a Roman army – Western, Eastern, or combined – managed actually to land unmolested on the shores of the Vandal kingdom. Belisarius' armada, however, was able to push on south from Sicily in total confidence. After brief stops on the intervening islands of Gozo and Malta, they arrived off the headland of Caput Vada (now Ras Kabudia) opposite the province of Byzacena more or less three months after the fleet had left Constantinople. A fortified disembarkation camp was quickly constructed, food obtained from the surrounding area (with a little calculated punishment of some looters thrown in to reassure local opinion), and, within three days the army began its march on Carthage, capital of the Vandal kingdom (Figure 8). The route took them past Lepcis Minor to Hadrumentum and Grasse where a first skirmish followed with Gelimer's forces. On the fourth day of the march – 13 September – the army arrived at the town of Ad Decimum, so called because it was established at the tenth mile post from Carthage. There battle commenced.

First of all Belisarius' light reconnaissance forces drove in the Vandal advance guard killing its commander, Ammatas, one of Gelimer's brothers. As they followed up against the now retreating enemy, some of the Roman main body reached the same spot to find there Gelimer and the bulk of his army which promptly attacked them and drove them back. Belisarius and the bulk of his cavalry were not far behind, however, and when they rode over the horizon to the rescue they found the Vandal army in the disorder of apparent victory. The general saw his chance and launched an immediate attack which routed the disordered Vandals, inflicting significant casualties. The Romans had won a first major victory, without remotely planning to; the bulk of Belisarius' force, his infantry, had never even left its camp. On 14 September, the army moved up to the outskirts of Carthage but didn't enter, since Belisarius was concerned that Gelimer might spring an ambush. The general also wanted to make sure that his soldiers would not take advantage of nightfall to start looting in the city. But trap was there none, and the next day the Romans entered the city in triumph.[34] Within about a week of their initial landing, Belisarius' soldiers were safely ensconced in the greatest city of North Africa. The contrast between their fate and those of their predecessors of 441, 461 and 468 could not be greater.

There then followed an extended period of quiet. Cautious as ever, and conscious no doubt that the capture of Carthage was already a much greater success than his emperor's minimum requirement from the expedition, Belisarius carefully fortified the city, whose walls the Vandals had allowed to degenerate. Gelimer meanwhile licked his wounds, consolidated his forces, and advanced towards Carthage, but contented himself with a little harassing work. Initially, he was awaiting the return of his fleet and 7,000 reinforcements from the Sardinian campaign, but, even when they returned, he did not want to attack Carthage and become embroiled in the kind of siege warfare in which the Vandals had had no practice for generations. Tactical initiative lay entirely with Belisarius. The final struggle would begin when he chose.

Three months later, the general was ready. His army moved forward in two groups. The advance guard was composed again of the bulk of the cavalry which had triumphed at Ad Decimum under the command of an officer of Armenian origins, John, who had earlier led those screening forces which had killed Gelimer's brother. Not far behind was the main body under Belisarius himself, comprising all the infantry and a small force of 500 cavalry, together with the general's personal guardsmen. In the evening, the advance guard duly found Gelimer and his army at Tricamarum, some twenty miles from Carthage. Things started quietly enough on the next day, but around midday the Vandals came out of their camp in battle array and drew themselves up in formation on one side of a small river. John did the same with forces on the other side, but, before any fighting could begin, Belisarius and the last of the cavalry arrived on the scene, with the infantry following as best they could.

The engagement opened with a series of skirmishes, always initiated by the Romans, until full-scale battle was eventually joined. Belisarius' men had by far the best of it, losing reportedly less than fifty men, where the Vandals lost 800. Eventually the Vandals had had enough and retreated to their camp, but Belisarius wasn't finished. By now, his infantry had arrived and a full-scale assault was prepared for the middle of the afternoon. In the event, it was not required. Gelimer had already fled from the camp in panic, and, when the rest of his forces realized this, they too collapsed into disorder. Organized resistance disappeared and the routed Vandals, many of whom had been accompanied by their women and children, were simply cut down as they ran. But the Vandal camp also contained a huge amount of moveable wealth, so Belisarius' army too lost its coherence as it turned from fighting to looting.[35]

In the end, then, the battle of Tricamarum became extremely messy, but it was no less decisive for that. Gelimer kept running westwards along the coastal cities of his former kingdom. Belisarius paused, to restore discipline among his own men, and to round up all the shattered Vandals that he could, to ensure that they could never be remobilized against him. And, in fact, they never were. Satisfied that matters were in hand, Belisarius then set off after Gelimer, and eventually captured the Vandal royal treasure and a demoralized gaggle of leading Vandals at Hippo Regius. Gelimer himself had fled for safety to some friendly Moors on the inaccessible Mount Papua on the borders of Numidia, where he was safe enough, but could do nothing to prevent Belisarius rounding up all the remaining Vandals in sight. With no assets left for a comeback, Gelimer had had enough by March 534, and negotiated terms of surrender. Within ten months of the landing at Caput Vada, it was all over. That same summer Belisarius returned to Constantinople with Gelimer in tow, and a host of Vandal prisoners. He received, as was his due, every honour that Justinian could find. He was the first non-emperor to be granted a triumphal procession in centuries, and he was made consul-designate, the highest honour in the imperial medal cabinet, for the following year.[36]

The horrors of the Nika riot of January 532 had given way – finally

– to another kind of victory altogether, and Justinian's regime was back in business. God's authority had been displayed. The emperor's virtue was manifest in this extraordinary triumph whose scale and ease no one had foretold, and nothing but nothing could better display the hand of God than a stunning military victory. Except, perhaps, driving through the legal reform. Even while out of office, Tribonian seems to have carried on working, and he was back formally in his post by the autumn of 532. A year later, he was ready to publish, and by then Justinian's forces had already captured Carthage. This half-victory, even before Gelimer's final defeat, was more than enough to give the emperor the final political leverage he required to dare to push through the reform to completion. On 16 December 533, before news of Tricamarum can have reached Constantinople, Justinian confirmed the *Digest* of jurisconsult writings and linked together all his triumphs:

> God has granted us, after Our peace with the Persians, Our triumph over the Vandals, Our taking of the whole of Libya, Our regaining of most famous Carthage, to fulfil the task of restoring the ancient laws – something which none of the Emperors that reigned before Us ever hoped even to conceive, nor would they have thought it humanly possible at all.

God had spoken, and the regime was now safe. Amidst all the plaudits and self-congratulation, Justinian could afford to be magnanimous. The eighteen senators banished after Nika were pardoned, and the estates of Hypatius and Pompeius were returned to their families. The emperor's last desperate gamble had paid off in spades; his position was now untouchable, and everyone knew it.[37]

Not only did the overwhelming contrast between the various kinds of disaster that had attended the Vandal expeditions of the mid-fifth century and the astonishingly swift victory of Belisarius provide irrefutable evidence that Justinian was indeed ruling by the authority of God, but it clearly also set the grey matter whirring at court in Constantinople. Two engagements in three months had been enough to wrap up an entire kingdom which had terrorized much of the Mediterranean world for the bulk of the fifth century. Where had this reversal in prevailing balances of power come from?

In part, it really was as simple as the fact that, this time, the East

Romans were able to land their army intact on North African shores. Maybe the Vandals would have been pretty much as easy to defeat in the fifth century if only the eagles had ever landed? But, in fact, the Vandals had had to fight their way eastwards from Morocco, taking Carthage and the richest lands of the province in 439, only after an eight-year struggle against combined Eastern and Western forces, which doesn't suggest that they were then so incapable of fighting off Roman armies. And, in fact, the key point seems to lie in a major reconfiguration of the nature of East Roman armies which had taken place by the time Belisarius left for North Africa.

Traditionally, Roman armies had relied on the foot soldier. The armies of Caesar and Augustus which had underpinned Roman domination of the entire Mediterranean and much of its hinterland were built around the power of the legions, and legionaries were foot soldiers par excellence. Nearly a third of Belisarius' army, however, was cavalry, and they played the crucial part. (As we saw, at Ad Decimum the Roman infantry never even engaged.) Many of these horsemen, moreover, were cavalry of a particular kind: heavy mounted archers. East Roman armies had developed this new military arm, which combined the hitting power from distance of the Hunnic mounted archers that they had been forced to combat in the mid-fifth century, with the shock and awe at close quarters of the armoured cavalry charge, and the result was a versatile force capable of dominating sixth-century battlefields.

I'm not myself generally a great believer in the broader explanatory power of military technology. God is generally on the side of the big battalions. But just occasionally – and usually only for a short time until the opposition picks up the changes too, or finds an alternative means for dealing with it – new hardware can give one side or the other a temporary edge. In this case, a temporary but sufficient advantage was given by a more flexible adoption of the capacities of the Hunnic mounted archer, and the result was devastating. Procopius' battle narratives for the Vandal campaign leave a huge amount to be desired. He doesn't tell us exactly why it was that the Vandals lost 800 men and the Romans only fifty during the initial skirmishing phase of the battle of Tricamarum, but given that John and the cavalry were continually sallying and then retreating, it's a pretty fair bet that their archery was doing most of the damage. He is much more explicit in at least some of the battles which followed in Italy against the Goths, and

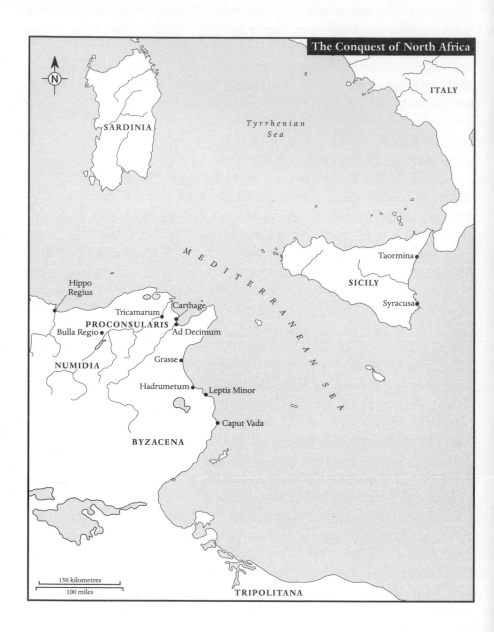

The Conquest of North Africa

there the Goths' consistent problem was getting to grips with an East Roman cavalry arm whose capacity to hurt from a distance gave them a massive tactical advantage. The main focus of this adaptation, which can be dated to the later fifth century, must have been Constantinople's traditional enemy in the east: Persia and all its works. But the Vandal gamble showed how much distance it had also put between Roman armies and those of the Western successor states. And once you know you have a major military advantage, so long as no third party is holding you in check, the temptation to use it, as we've seen in our own times, can become overwhelming.[38]

Again, however, the regime was extremely cautious and still did not rush headlong into a policy of total war in the West. The initial propaganda generated by the Vandal victory heralded it as a triumph over heretics who were oppressing fellow Catholic Christians. It was couched, in other words, in terms entirely specific to the North African situation, and made no threats – explicit or implicit – to other Western powers. Indeed, Belisarius' whole campaign would have been impossible without the logistic licence that Ostrogothic Italy had allowed the Roman fleet within its territorial waters. But Ostrogothic Italy was the next plausible Western target for East Roman armies, and you did not get to win and retain power in sixth-century Constantinople by remaining true to entirely disposable friends, or possibly even by having 'friend' anywhere in your conceptual lexicon.

A pretext for playing silly buggers in Italy was duly provided by that old happy hunting ground: succession. Constantinople had already fished productively there once, of course, after the death of Eutharic, with the active aim of undermining Theoderic's newly united Visigothic and Ostrogothic kingdoms (page 95). Whether they responded more positively to the extant request in the *Variae* to recognize Athalaric after Theoderic's death and the re-separation of Spain from Italy is unclear, but likely enough, since their key goal had already been achieved and relations were good enough by the early 530s for Belisarius' fleet to find the logistic support it needed along the Italian coastline. If you were intent on causing trouble, however, the overarching political situation in most of the successor kingdoms was unstable enough that it could usually be relied upon to deliver the aggressor's dream: internal dissent within your target combined with a propaganda angle to give you the requisite respectability.

Athalaric had only been eight or ten at Theoderic's death, and, in political terms, it was impossible for him at this point to exercise real power in his own right. The new game in Ravenna thus became securing influence over Athalaric through the regency council which now effectively governed the realm. Procopius puts a particular spin on the political struggles which followed, claiming that the boy's mother, Theoderic's daughter Amalasuentha, wished her son to have a more Roman education, whereas the other older Gothic males on the council wanted him to be brought up as a more traditional Goth. I'm confident that this is simplificatory shorthand rather than the full story, but controlling the king's upbringing would certainly have been the key to immediate political power, so it would not be remotely surprising if that were indeed one of the issues around which rival political groupings coalesced.

Eventually, and here Procopius becomes more precise, Amalasuentha found herself locked in a struggle with three leading Gothic nobles, anonymous in the *Wars*, which was so threatening that, at one point, she had a ship loaded with treasure in case she needed to make a swift getaway, with Constantinople as her destination of choice. In the end, she won out, but only just; and at considerable cost. She managed to get the three men appointed to important provincial commands and there had them murdered. Two of the three were probably our old friend Tuluin, who held large estates in Gothic Provence (which would count as a provincial command), and another noble by the name of Osuine, who, at about the right time, was appointed to an important and equally provincial command in Dalmatia. Both then disappear without further trace. Who the third was, I have no idea, and nor does anyone else.

The queen had survived one moment of extreme danger, but it was not her fate to pass safely into a more comfortable future. The true cost of survival became clear when Athalaric passed away on 2 October 534, at the tender age of sixteen or eighteen. The pressures were now such that it was impossible for Amalasuentha to rule by herself so she appointed her cousin Theodahad, Theoderic's nephew, as co-ruler. He, however, had already been a potential candidate for the throne in the 520s, and had his own base of influential support. Amalasuentha's *Godfather* moment of simultaneous assassination had also alienated many supporters of her eliminated rivals, making it easy for Theodahad to mobilize a critical mass of support against her.

Power quickly slipped through her fingers, and nor was there an easy out in Constantinople. Theodahad had her first arrested, and then executed – famously in her bath tub. We don't know the exact date of her murder, but she was certainly dead by April 535.[39]

As news of impending Italian instability filtered across the Adriatic, Justinian could smell the aroma of a new opportunity a mile away, and sent in an agent provocateur, Peter the Patrician, something of a cross between James Bond and Lord Carrington, the former British Foreign Secretary so lovingly described by an American Secretary of State as 'that duplicitous bastard'. From Dara in Mesopotamia, where Belisarius had won the early victory over the Persians, Peter (he was not yet 'the Patrician': that particular gong came after his return from Italy in 539) had studied and practised law and was renowned as a scholar. He was also according to Procopius clever, kindly and persuasive, but that's the good news recorded in *Wars*; *Anekdota* adds the bad news that he was grasping and the greatest thief alive. There is no doubting his cleverness and guile, however, nor the trust in which he was held by his emperor.[40]

Peter was originally sent to Italy before Athalaric had actually passed away, since he was halfway there when he met the messengers announcing the king's death going in the other direction. But Athalaric died of a wasting disease whose effects and likely outcome were apparent substantially before October 534, so there is no reason to doubt that impending Italian instability was the cause of Peter's deployment. That said, the young king's death was an eventuality which his orders did not yet encompass so he had to stay put and await instructions. Such was the speed of communication versus that of actual events, that when he finally made it to Italy armed with orders to make Justinian's support for Amalasuentha explicit, the queen was already dead. This probably wasn't that much of a problem. *Anekdota* claims that he had secret instructions to arrange the queen's murder anyway. If so, this was certainly to destabilize the situation further, and, in the wake of Justinian's declared support for her, provide a repeat of the pretext – support of a deposed and murdered monarch – which had sent Belisarius to North Africa. In the summer of 535, he shuttled back and forth to Constantinople, apparently taking Theodahad's messages that Amalasuentha's murder had not been his idea (having been perpetrated by the relatives of her three murdered rivals) and returning with Justinian's response. In fact, he came back to sow as much dissent as he could in the kingdom which now found itself at the top of the East Roman hit list.

In summer 535, Belisarius and the fleet had been despatched to the West for a second time, this time carrying 4,000 regulars, 3,000 Isaurians, and a few hundred others, along with the general's own guardsmen. His destination was ostensibly Carthage, but he also had contingent orders to test out Gothic control of Sicily and, if it could be easily overturned, to do so. He landed close to Catana which quickly surrendered, and the other cities of the island followed suit and almost entirely without resistance, except at Panormus. Syracusa was the last to open its gates and, by chance, Belisarius entered it in triumph in late December, on the final day of his consulship. Again, Justinian had been cautious: note the carefully contingent nature of Belisarius' orders. But, after the bloodless capture of Sicily, emperor and propaganda finally came out of the closet. At this moment, and for the very first time, the celebration of Sicilian victory committed the regime to a potentially unlimited policy of Western conquest (page 137).

Back in Ravenna, Peter went into overdrive, pressuring Theodahad with tales of the military juggernaut which was heading in his direction. Panicked, Theodahad agreed to surrender the kingdom, contemplating the kind of wealthy retirement that his cousin had had in mind when she'd loaded all that treasure on to her ship. But he was between a rock and a hard place, and when news came around Easter 536 that an East Roman assault on Gothic possessions in Dalmatia had been beaten off, he did a complete volte-face, declaring war and throwing his ambassadorial tormentor in jail.

A year earlier, this kind of Gothic resolve, combined with a military setback, might have made Justinian think again, but, after the bloodless seizure of Sicily – an extremely valuable prize in its own right in the ancient world – the emperor was committed to another roll of the dice. And, in fact, Theodahad had moved too slowly against the Roman mission. Before being sent to jail, where he would languish for three whole years, Peter got off the crucial letter – which Justinian had ordered Belisarius to expect and respond to – summoning the general and his army to Italy.[41]

Imperial war-making in the West was no longer dependent on massively favourable and highly contingent circumstances as it had been when Belisarius was despatched with the first fleet in summer

533. Three years later, the Goths were up in arms and had already won one round. But like the neocons nearly 1,500 years later, Justinian was now confident that he had the military hardware to roll over the Gothic kingdom as quickly as he had the Vandals. The dice of war were being thrown with a vengeance and Constantinople committed itself to recovering every last square inch of Roman territory that it could. By a long and tortuous path, Justinian's regime finally came to the policy option which has distinguished it for historians ever since. Who would the winner be, and would they take it all?

4

SAILING TO BYZANTIUM

As far as Procopius was concerned, but this should come as no great surprise, there were no winners at all.

> To state exactly the number of those who were destroyed by him would never be possible, I think, for anyone whomsoever, or for God. One might more quickly, I think, count all the grains of sand than the vast number whom this Emperor destroyed.

His survey started in North Africa which now (*c.550* when *Anekdota* was composed) 'has been so thoroughly ruined that for the traveller who makes a long journey [there] it is no easy matter . . . to meet a human being'. As to what followed in Italy, 'it has become everywhere even more destitute of men than North Africa'. Nor was the destruction confined to the places Justinian's armies attacked. The Roman Balkans in its entirety

> was overrun practically every year by Huns [meaning Bulgars], Sclaveni and Antae, from the time when Justinian took over the Roman Empire, and they wrought frightful havoc among the inhabitants of that region. For in each invasion more than twenty myriads [one myriad is 10,000] of Romans, I think, were destroyed or enslaved there.

And meanwhile in the East:

> The Persians under Chosroes four times made inroads into the rest of the Roman domain and dismantled the cities, and, as for the people whom they found in the captured cities and in each country district, they slew a part and led some away with them, leaving the land bare of inhabitants wherever they chanced to descend.

And that's not counting – as our author then goes on to list – casualties among the Romans' opponents, and those brought down by acts of misgovernment and natural disaster, all of which can reasonably be blamed on his demonic emperor. In all, Procopius reckons that 'a myriad myriads of myriads' – i.e. $10,000^3$, or a trillion people – died because of Justinian's demonic reign. As a footnote to one of the standard English translations helpfully tells us,

> The 'cube of ten thousand' is not the language of exact computation, and Procopius is trying to make out a strong case against Justinian.[1]

But poetic licence need not mean that the basic point is misplaced, and many have felt that Justinian's reign did exhaust the empire, leaving it easy prey for the various disasters which would follow. So, how strong is the case against Justinian? Three related sets of questions need to be answered here. Were the territories his armies annexed in the West worth the cost of conquest? Did those costs of conquest have substantially bad effects upon the population of the empire he inherited from his uncle? And can subsequent territorial losses in the Balkans and the East be justifiably reckoned as the longer-term consequences of Justinian's policies?

TWILIGHT OF THE GOTHS

In the end, as Procopius' judgements would lead you to expect, Justinian's Gothic war ended up costing far more than the emperor and his advisers were expecting. But, a bit like recent Western deployments to Afghanistan and Iraq, it took some time for this to become apparent. In its initial phases, the Italian war looked comfortingly like a rerun of the North African campaign. It began in earnest in summer 536, when Belisarius landed in the south of Italy proper and besieged Naples which eventually fell after a prolonged struggle. We know that it was in East Roman hands by November. In the meantime, Theodahad, still in Rome, did nothing, presumably hoping to find some kind of negotiated solution to his impasse. But the fall of Naples was too much for his chief supporters who deposed and executed him before the end of the year. Thus perished the last male of the great Theoderic's house to rule the remnants of his empire, and, in his place, the leading Goths promoted Wittigis, who had already established his reputation as a capable military leader. The Goths now had a regime that was as much committed to armed confrontation as that of Justinian. The phony war, which had lasted until the fall of Naples, was over, and battle was set to commence when the arrival of better weather set the grass to grow again in the spring of 537.[2]

Wittigis spent the winter preparing. Leaving Rome in December, he went to Ravenna to gather and equip his forces. He also ceded to the Franks the Gallic territories which Theoderic had won in 508 and Tuluin extended in the 520s, to secure the Goths' northern border and free up military forces which would otherwise have been required there for garrison duties. The need was pressing because his armies had already suffered some losses of manpower. Not only had the Naples garrison been destroyed by Belisarius, but some Goths (nothing like a majority as we shall see) had clearly been impressed by the ease of the Vandals' destruction. Thus a certain Pitzas and half the Goths of Samnium immediately surrendered to Belisarius rather than fight for Wittigis.

By February 537, Wittigis had mobilized his forces, but Belisarius had already moved his relatively limited army into Rome, which he had entered shortly after Wittigis vacated it on 9/10 December. The year 537 was thus spent in a fruitless Gothic siege of the old imperial capital. At this point, Procopius was still attached to his general, and he provides a gripping first-hand narrative, full of Gothic bravery and Roman steadfastness. Basically, Wittigis lacked the numbers or skill to break into the city, and Belisarius, despite a continued tactical advantage in weaponry which showed up every time there was an encounter, lacked the numbers to come out and fight. The blockade was briefly halted in December 537, when the arrival of Roman reinforcements prompted the Goths to make a three-month truce, but, otherwise, the year was marked only by some equally inconsequential fighting on the Balkan front in Dalmatia, where again the Goths failed in a siege, this time of Salona, which the Romans had taken in 535.[3]

The stalemate around Rome was broken early in the New Year. Belisarius' reinforcements consisted mainly of cavalry, and, as soon as he could, the Roman general sent them off to raid Picenum. Picenum, on the far side of the Apennines by the Adriatic, was an area of relatively dense Gothic settlement, and Belisarius' aim was to break up the siege of Rome by threatening the wives and children of the men who had him penned in the city. The stratagem worked. By March 538, enough pressure had been applied for Wittigis to be forced to abandon the siege. The Gothic army retreated north through the Apennines along the Via Flaminia, to cut off and destroy Belisarius' cavalry, which had by this point established itself behind the walls of Rimini having spread maximum destruction further south. As he retreated, Wittigis established a series of strongpoints to guard his rear. The strategically placed city of Auximum was given a garrison of particular quality; other forces were left at Clusium (of Lars Porsena fame), Urviventus, Tudera, Petra, Urbinus, Caesena and Montefertra (Figure 9).

With the siege of Rome over, however, Belisarius' forces now enjoyed complete freedom of movement. Rushing reinforcements to Rimini by an alternative route through the mountains before Wittigis' main body – busy establishing its strongpoints – could arrive, he moved a second force by ship to Genoa. It then marched north to take the surrender of Milan and other cities of Liguria in the north-west. With the main part of his army, Belisarius followed Wittigis north-east into Picenum, where, on the receipt of yet more reinforcements, he began to work his way up the coast towards Ravenna.[4] Again, it would seem, the emperor had been cautious. Despite committing his regime to war, he waited to see how the initial encounters went before putting in the extra troops. Presumably, if Belisarius had fared badly, he had it in mind to do a deal based on some kind of partition of the peninsula, which was one of the permutations which had been discussed with Theodahad during the period of phony war. But, by the end of 538, the emperor could afford to think in grander terms. When winter put an end to mobile operations, Wittigis was drawn up around Rimini, Belisarius was closing in fast behind him, and Gothic control of the north-west was ebbing away.

In 539, Belisarius largely retained the strategic initiative. On the main, Adriatic front, he slowly tightened the noose around Wittigis' army. As the summer progressed, Auximum was captured, along with Fiesole. These successes opened up the road network towards Ravenna, and, in December, Belisarius advanced on the city itself. Wittigis had in the meantime sent his nephew Urais with a counter-expedition to Liguria which recaptured the lost cities and sacked Milan in the process. But this was not enough to return the strategic initiative to the Goths. The Roman threat to the region remained sufficient, for instance, to prevent Urais from leaving the Po valley to defend Fiesole at the crucial moment as Wittigis wanted him to.[5]

By the end of the year, Wittigis' position was rapidly deteriorating. Individual Goths and even whole subgroups were abandoning his cause and looking to come to terms with Belisarius. Because of the well-directed military threat to their families and possessions, in a repeat of the Picenum stratagem, both the Gothic garrisons of the Cottian Alps and the bulk of Urais' mobile force disappeared back to their homes. Increasingly isolated in Ravenna, Wittigis tried diplomacy, negotiating for assistance from the Lombards and Franks to the north, and, more desperately, from the Persian Empire to the east, hoping that a Persian invasion of Syria would undermine Justinian's ability to pursue war simultaneously in Italy.[6] But none of this happened soon enough to erode Belisarius' strategic dominance, and this is precisely the moment that Cassiodorus was scribbling away on the *Variae*, trying desperately to reinsure himself against the political disaster which was looming on his doorstep.

Belisarius, by contrast, was now facing what he expected to be the final problem of the campaign: Ravenna itself. Protected by marshes and walls, it was virtually impregnable, and like Theoderic before him in 493, Belisarius looked to find an alternative way inside its walls. Negotiations began, operating simultaneously on a number of levels, as they had done at the outbreak of the war. Openly, the Goths offered formally to submit to Justinian, and to cede to him large tracts of Italian territory. Under this plan, a truncated Gothic kingdom would have been confined to lands north of the river Po: to Liguria and the Venetias, where the bulk of the Goths had been placed by Theoderic back in the 490s. Justinian might have settled for this at the start of the war, but success and reinforcements meant that he now wanted a grander outcome. At the same time, in secret contacts, the Goths tried to seduce Belisarius away from his loyalty to the emperor, offering him 'rule of the West': a further revival of empire in the West based on a combination of Belisarius' army and Gothic military manpower.

Thinking he had his man, Wittigis opened the gates of Ravenna in May 540, but the Goths had been tricked. As Procopius reports it, they surrendered thinking that Belisarius would indeed declare himself emperor of the West, but, once the Romans were inside the city, nothing happened, and there was nothing that Wittigis could do. He and his chief supporters were detained, and the rest of the Gothic army sent home. With Belisarius' *coup de théâtre*, the war seemed over.[7] And if that had been the end of it, I doubt that historians would have spent much time and energy anxiously debating its costs. Victory over Wittigis had taken longer than the eight months or so required to dispose of Gelimer, and there had been bigger collateral costs: above all the sacking of Naples and Milan. Nevertheless, in spring 540, three campaigning seasons to dispose of the Ostrogothic kingdom which, only a generation before, had provided the backbone of a plausible restoration of the Western Empire, must have seemed like a highly reasonable return on Justinian's investment.

But the bill was still a long way from complete. Far away to the east, Justinian's victories over the Vandals had begun to prompt reflections at the Persian court as to whether and to what extent Roman success in the West was altering the balance of power between the two empires. Their urgency was redoubled in the summer of 539 when, by route unknown, an embassy from Wittigis somehow arrived at the Persian capital Ctesiphon with the following report:

> It is clear that, if he can destroy utterly also the Goths, he will march against the Persians together with us and [the Vandals] whom he has enslaved already, and neither will he respect the name of friendship nor will he be ashamed [to break] the oaths that have been sworn.

The embassy was designed to stir up the Persians and relieve pressure on the Goths, but I'm confident that the Persians were perfectly capable of grasping the point without the assistance of the desperate Gothic king, or even that of the Armenians, who were also, according to Procopius, busy trying to stir up Chosroes with reports of increasing Roman power. Either way, in the spring of 540, Chosroes led his army into Roman Mesopotamia and simply ignored the network of massive fortresses that stood in his way to head straight for Antioch: regional capital of the Roman East and one of greatest cities of the empire. He felt able to do so because enough Roman troops had been stripped away for the North African and Italian wars for him to be confident that his forces would not be attacked from behind if they ventured deep within Roman territory.

The results were devastating. The Persians first took the city of Beroia (modern Aleppo) and then, in June 540, fell upon Antioch. The city was captured in a few days and razed to the ground except for two churches, one inside and one outside the walls, together with a small cluster of houses that were disregarded in the outskirts. Not that there was anyone to live in them. The surviving population was frogmarched off to Persia where a new city, in some way a copy of their old, was built within a day's travel of Ctesiphon. Called 'Khusro's Greater Antioch', it had a bathhouse, a hippodrome, charioteers and musicians. No expense was spared in making it an everlasting monument to the greatest victory a Persian shah-in-shah could ever win.[8] Indirectly, therefore, his Western adventures had cost Justinian the second city of his empire: a devastating hit in itself, but by no means the end of the reckoning.

Back in Italy, the bulk of the Goths had been dispersed by Belisarius' well-conceived military stratagem of attacking their homes, but not actually defeated in battle. Moreover, Belisarius had insufficient troops to occupy in force Gothic heartlands north of the Po. The only Roman unit in the area was a group of Heruli under Vitalius at Treviso. As the extent of Belisarius' trickery became clear, tactical opportunity and military manpower were both available, therefore, for more energetic Gothic leaders to rekindle the fires of war. In the summer of 540, two in particular continued to resist: Urais in Pavia and Ildebadus at Verona. Neither conducted aggressive operations, but both refused to surrender, and they continued to press Belisarius to accept the Western imperium.

Had he been able to move north of the Po in force at this point, the war really could have been over. But all hell having broken out on the eastern front, troops were at a premium, and Justinian (reportedly also worried about reports of the Goths' offers to his general) eventually decided that Belisarius too was needed. Belisarius thus left Ravenna in December 540, taking with him Wittigis and the other leading Goths he had captured, not to mention our old friend Cassiodorus. All hope of seducing the general away from his loyalty to Justinian disappeared, and the Goths needed to try a new tack. Ildebadus rallied his supporters for war. Vitalius and his Heruli tried to nip the revolt in the bud, but were heavily defeated.[9] The second phase of the Gothic war was about to begin in earnest, but, first, the Goths needed to sort out their politics.

Initially, Urais deferred to Ildebadus. But power-sharing proved difficult, and, when the two fell out (reportedly over their wives' competitive dressing), Ildebadus engineered Urais' death. This alienated

The Conquest of Italy

LIGURIA

VENETIA

Milan

Po

VIA AEMILIA

Ravenna

Genoa

ALPES COTTIAE

Cassena

Ariminum (Rimini)

VIA AURELIA

Florentia

Urbinem

Petra Pertusa

Ligurian
Sea

TUSCIA
ET
UMBRIA

Tiber

Auximum (Osimo)

PICENUM

Adriatic Sea

CORSICA

VIA AURELIA

VIA CASSIA

VIA FLAMINIA

ROME

Portus

Ostia

Naples

CALABRIA

Captured by
siege autumn 536

SARDINIA

Tyrrhenian
Sea

BRUTTIUM

Ionian
Sea

MEDITERRANEAN SEA

SICILY

Captured summer 535

Syracuse

200 kilometres

100 miles

N

a significant body of the Goths, who had Ildebadus killed in turn. Goscinny and Uderzo were not wrong in identifying faction and civil war as the Gothic disease. Both Goths were dead by the end of 541. In the meantime, Eraric, latest leader of that contingent of Rugi who had followed Theoderic to Italy in 489 and played both ends against the middle during the struggle against Odovacar, put himself forward as a potential king. His main policy was to negotiate with Constantinople, reviving the idea of partitioning Italy. Then he too was murdered, and power passed to Ildebadus' nephew Totila.[10] In the short term, Totila was committed to more martial options.

His years of success, which lasted through the 540s, had two foundations. First, the war with Persia prevented Justinian from reinforcing his Italian armies. Having learned from the Antioch debacle, Justinian was careful never again to leave the eastern front so exposed. Second, Totila won some quick victories. Militarily, they allowed him to regain the tactical initiative. Politically, they encouraged more of the Goths to throw in their lot with the revolt. Totila was also careful to treat prisoners leniently, with the result that many Roman troops (often contingents of allied barbarians who been hired in for the purpose) eventually joined the Goths, especially when their pay failed to arrive. Totila picked certainly hundreds, and perhaps a few thousand reinforcements in this way. At one point, some Roman slaves also took their place in the Gothic army, but Procopius gives us no idea of how many.[11]

Faced with Totila and renewed revolt, 12,000 imperial troops moved north to besiege Verona, one of the chief centres of resistance, in winter 541–2. In spring, Totila went after them with 5,000 men, and won a resounding victory at Faenza, south of the Po, whence the Roman army had retreated. The key moment in the battle came when 300 of Totila's cavalry crashed into the Roman rear. As Procopius reports it, this victory encouraged enough further Gothic recruits to come forward to swell the ranks of Totila's army to 20,000 men. Quick to capitalize on his success, he then besieged the Roman forces holding the city of Florence, and won a second victory there over a Roman relief force sent to its assistance. Between them, the two battles were enough to push the Roman forces in Italy on to the defensive. They looked to do no more than hold on to the fortified centres they had already taken, while Totila was able to spread his revolt south, taking Benevento, Cumae and eventually Naples in spring 543.[12]

In the next two campaigning seasons, Totila took careful aim at important Roman holdings, including the strategic fortress of Auximum. Its capture cut off land communications between Rome and Ravenna, and prepared the ground for an escalation in Gothic military ambitions. At the end of 545, Totila was ready to mount a siege of Rome itself. He pressed it hard throughout the next year, and the city finally surrendered to him on 17 December 546. Totila had succeeded where Wittigis had failed, but Gothic manpower was being stretched to the limit. During the siege, Totila concluded that he had to hand over the province of Venetia to the Frankish king Theudebert, in order to free still more Goths from garrison duties there.[13]

Alarmed by Totila's successes, and with some stability restored in the East, Justinian sent Belisarius back to Italy in winter 544–5. But no reinforcements went with him, and there was little he could do. His best moment came in April 547, when he reoccupied Rome. Chronically short of manpower, Totila had decided not to hold the city himself and made the serious mistake of failing to neutralize its defences. But Belisarius could not do much more, and he was eventually recalled to Constantinople in 548, while the Gothic military successes kept on coming. Stung by his own mistake, Totila besieged Rome for a second time, from the summer of 549, until it fell to him again the following January, during which time Gothic forces also captured a whole string of other fortresses, including Tarentum and Rimini. Totila also chose this moment to create a raiding fleet, which was placed under the command of Indulf, a deserter from the East Roman army. It was then set loose on Constantinople's possessions. The coast of Dalmatia was ravaged in 549, Sicily taken in 550 and Corfu and Epirus attacked in 551.[14]

Despite these successes, Totila faced an overwhelming problem. The East Roman Empire possessed resources of wealth and manpower far in excess of his own. Like Wittigis before him, he had been forced to cede parts of Theoderic's kingdom to the Franks to free Gothic manpower for his campaigns, and every engagement cost further losses. In the mid-540s, Justinian's resources were still being stretched by war on two fronts, as the war with Chosroes which had started with the sack of Antioch rumbled on, but such a situation could not last indefinitely. In such circumstances, outright Gothic victory was impossible and Totila needed to find a way to bring the war to an end with some kind of Gothic kingdom still intact. Totila's vigorous and strikingly successful pursuit of military options was not about trying to win the war outright, but to make its continuation so costly that Justinian would be willing to offer him a deal. Even at the height of his military successes, therefore, Totila kept offering concessions. Immediately after his second capture of Rome, for instance, Totila sent a third embassy to Justinian, and its tone was highly conciliatory. In it, Totila offered to cede Dalmatia and Sicily to Constantinople, to pay an annual tribute, and to provide military contingents for the Eastern Empire's campaigns.[15] Totila clearly understood that, without face-saving gains, Justinian would never be persuaded to end the war, and it was overwhelmingly in the Goths' interest to persuade him to do so.

Justinian, however, rejected every approach. From the emperor's point of view, I suspect, so much prestige had been invested in the conquest policy that it was extremely difficult to abandon it. By the later 540s, too, stability was returning to the eastern front. No more serious engagements took place on the main Mesopotamian front after a failed Persian siege of Edessa in the summer of 544, while, in the Caucasus, major Roman gains in 549 reversed earlier losses and convinced Chosroes that no further advantage was in the offing. A formal peace treaty would not be agreed until 551, but by the time Totila's third embassy arrived in early 550, it would already have been clear to Justinian that the strategic context would soon allow him to find the necessary forces to finish the Italian job. Totila's approaches were all rejected, and the scene was set for the showdown.

Justinian's preferred strategy was a land expedition through the Balkans into northern Italy: the route taken by Theoderic some sixty years before, and so much easier than trying to transport a large army by sea. Preparations began in 550, when the emperor's cousin Germanus was appointed to command the expedition. Wittigis now dead, Germanus also married Matasuentha, Amalasuentha's daughter, in an attempt to confuse Gothic loyalties. Germanus, however, died in the year of his appointment, and it was not until early 552 that the expedition, now under the command of the eunuch general Narses, was ready to move. But the noose had already been tightening in other ways. In summer 551, an imperial force had utterly destroyed Totila's raiding fleet off Ancona, and Procopius reports the alarm and despondency which greeted news of this setback in the Gothic camp.[16]

By April 552, everything was set, and, with the grass now growing again to sustain his baggage animals, Narses advanced into Italy. Totila attempted to block the route to Ravenna (which remained in East Roman hands), by flooding the land south of Verona. He also sent a force of his best men under its own commander, Teias, independently to harass Narses' operations. The East Roman army, however, advanced methodically along the coast to Ravenna, while a second Roman force landed in Calabria in the south, where it defeated some Goths at Crotone. Having replenished stores at Ravenna, Narses came on in search of battle. Totila eventually confronted him – at the end of June or in early July – on a level plain in the northern Apennines called Busta Gallorum. Totila had gathered most of his available troops, and the central drama of the battle was a charge by the Gothic cavalry, the elite of his army:

> Orders had been given to the entire Gothic army that they should use neither bow nor any other weapon in this battle except their spears.

The idea, presumably, was to overcome at close quarters with shock and awe, but it all proved tragically misconceived:

> For in making their charge against their enemy's centre, the [Gothic cavalry] placed themselves in between the 8,000 [Roman] infantry, and [were] raked by their bowshots from either side.

The charge was broken before it could even come to grips with the Roman line, and its retreat prompted a general rout with the Goths reportedly leaving 6,000 dead on the battlefield, a casualty count which was quickly swelled by the subsequent execution of all prisoners. Totila himself was mortally wounded. In the aftermath of victory, Narses quickly occupied Rome and subdued all the remaining Gothic garrisons in Tuscany. Still the Goths weren't quite beaten. Teias gathered as many of the remaining Goths as he could at Pavia, and, realizing he needed help, made a further alliance with the Franks. Battle was renewed in October 552, far to the south, at Mons Lactarius in Campania. After another fierce fight, Teias died breathing defiance, and most of the remaining Goths negotiated an armistice.[17]

The Italian Goths had been destroyed as a coherent military and political force, but Italy had not yet been secured for Justinian. Narses spent the winter subduing some stubborn but entirely isolated centres of resistance. After Teias' death, three Gothic leaders had continued the struggle. Indulf retreated to Pavia with 1,000 men, Aligern fought on at Cumae, and Ragnaris was holding out in Conza della Campania. Then, early in 553, the last Frankish assistance purchased by Teias, an army consisting largely of Alamanni, finally arrived. Advancing south through Liguria and Aemilia, it won some Gothic support among the scattered remnants of Theoderic's former followers, and one of its leaders, Butilinus, was even offered the Gothic kingship. Narses, however, was ready. In 553, his troops subdued the whole of Tuscany, and, in December, brought Aligern to surrender. Butilinus' expedition itself was eventually defeated in 554, at the battle of Casilinum, as a result of which Ragnaris' followers surrendered in spring 555.

Just the mopping up remained. By 560, imperial control was securely established in Liguria, Histria and most of Venetia. Only eastern Venetia was left unsubdued, and it was this region which witnessed the last flicker of Gothic revolt. In 561, a Gothic count called Widin rebelled in Brescia and called again for Frankish help. The manoeuvre failed.[18] Widin's defeat marked the final extinction of Gothic resistance to Justinian's conquest of Italy, and in November 562 Narses formally reported to Constantinople the capture of Verona and Brixia. Twenty-seven years after the near-bloodless seizure of Sicily, imperial domination had finally been established over the Italian peninsula.

COSTING THE EARTH?

Recovering the contingent, events-led drift of Justinian's regime into a policy of Western expansion is relatively straightforward when the events of his early years, and the exact detail of the orders given to Belisarius, are looked at closely. It is also, thanks to Procopius, reasonably easy to recapture something of the narrative drama of the actual conquests, even if his tendency to disperse events happening simultaneously on different fronts into separate books conceals important linkages. Altogether more difficult, however, is the task of forming a convincing overall judgement on the conquest policy and its effects, in both the short term and longer. The hard statistics – what did the campaigns cost, how much taxation did the conquered territories add to the empire's fiscal base, etc. – are all unavailable.[19] Qualitative judgement rather than statistical analysis has to be the order of the day, but that's perhaps not too surprising given that we're dealing with events of the mid-first millennium.

More fundamentally, however, whose perspective should we adopt when making such judgements? The real problem with a wonderfully Sellar and Yeatman type question like 'Was Justinian's policy of Western expansion a good thing?' (variants of which have been seen on many a university exam paper) is, straightforwardly, 'good' from whose perspective? In the era of nationalism, the state tended to be viewed in Western historiography as broadly – again in the terms of *1066 & All That* – a 'good thing', and developments were usually judged according to how they affected the prosperity or otherwise of centres of political authority. But that is only one possible viewpoint, and it is important to try to do justice to everyone caught up in the tornados of conquest which Justinian unleashed.

For many of the human beings concerned, the experience of war was devastating. Not least, the two wars destroyed the Vandal–Alan and Gothic political elites around which twin successor states in North Africa and Italy had been built. There has been a strong tendency to downplay the reality of these units in some recent literature, on the basis that they were not the unified, culturally coherent peoples imagined by scholars working in the nationalist era. Instead, it is suggested, they were loose groups which could slip in and out of existence at the drop of a hat, in which case, of course, their political destruction need not have occasioned any major loss of life. But while, as we've seen, these entities certainly were not ancient 'peoples', the minimalist view of their historical importance is actually based on only a half-understanding of how group identities work. Yes, some individuals can and do change group identity, and one important ingredient of identity is located primarily in the head: the identity that you consider yourself to hold. But the individual's own assertion of what is inside their head does have to be recognized by the broader group – what's inside your head is a kind of claim which may or may not be recognized by the group you want to be part of – and group rules vary over time and space. Some groups impose relatively tight rules on individuals who want to be or are part of them, and hence have a more solid existence, while others do not. To go from an old vision of complete solidity to a new one of complete fluidity, therefore, is to move from one oversimplification to another.

Both the Vandal–Alans who ended up in North Africa, and the Goths of Theoderic, were demonstrably new alliances, sometimes of culturally very diverse groups (where the Vandals were Germanic-speaking agriculturalists, the Alans were Iranian-speaking nomads) created in the fifth century. But that doesn't mean that these alliances had no real group identity. The Vandal–Alan coalition was forged in the furnace of warfare against the Western Empire. Theoderic's Goths, likewise, were constructed, as we saw in Chapter 1, in the context of a sequence of struggles first against other successors to Attila's empire, and then in the Roman Balkans. Social scientists confirm what intuition would anyway suggest: that conflict, and the need to survive it, is one crucial form of social cement, and these groups had enjoyed that in spades. Their settlements in North Africa and Italy then provided a second. Theoderic's most important political task, once Odovacar was eliminated, was to provide economically for the followers who had put him in power. The Vandal–Alan leader Geiseric had to go through the same process in North Africa in the 440s. In both cases, the distribution of assets identified and rewarded key military supporters by gifts of real estate, which continued to be held by their heirs in return for a liability for military service. Though certainly transformed by the process of settlement, the original groups thus continued to exist as a distinctly rewarded and distinctly liable element of the total population of the two kingdoms. In the Gothic case, we know that cohesion was maintained by clustering the settlements and organizing periodic gatherings subsequently, during which further rewards were handed out.[20]

It is in this transformed, but still distinct, manifestation that we then encounter Vandal–Alans and Goths in the war narratives of Procopius. And if you step back from the intense details of particular military encounters, what you see is the destruction by various methods of these core groups. The Vandal campaign was over so fast that the story is quickly told. But the vast majority of all the Vandal–Alan males had been removed from North Africa by the time that the initial conquest was complete. The process in Italy took longer and gets more fully documented, but its overall shape is clear. Theoderic's following consisted of warriors of two distinct statuses, and the higher group were the key to the coherence of the force he led to Italy. They were not just a small nobility in the later medieval sense of the word, but maybe something like a quarter of the total following, so 5,000 individuals or more. The story of the East Roman conquest is the story of the effective elimination of this group, a few by surrender, but many more by death or deportation. Because of the current penchant for stressing fluidity of identity, this evidence tends not to be discussed, but it is plentiful, coherent and detailed. It also fits in perfectly well with the previous history of the group's initial formation and sub- sequent settlement within the Italian landscape. While certainly not ethnic groups, therefore, there is no reason to dismiss either Vandal– Alans or Goths as entirely will-o'-the-wisp groupings in human terms, and their destruction – entirely literally so in the case of many individuals – can and should be reckoned among the costs of Justinian's conquests.[21]

Then, of course, there is all the collateral damage inflicted on the populations of the conquered territories. You don't have to believe in the fantastical facade erected by Cassiodorus – that the creation of Theoderic's kingdom involved no change whatsoever for his Italo- Roman subjects – to see that a whole political generation of periodic warfare, punctuated with bouts of occasionally intense violence, must have generated huge losses for the population of Italy. Particular sacks – such as those of Naples and Milan early on in the war, or Tiber later on – are vividly described by Procopius. Cassiodorus mentions even in the early years a famine that was probably generated by the disloca- tions of army supply. And through it all runs a sub-theme of warfare centring on cities, and disrupted agricultural production, punctuated by moments of social rupture, such as Totila's desperate arming of Roman slaves towards the final stages of the war. It is impossible to come to any kind of quantitative judgement on the effects of the fighting, but it is quite clear that the archaeology of Italy never looked the same again.

Northern Italy in particular, the area taken over by the Lombards, failed to recover from the dislocating effects of the warfare, in the sense that there is almost no evidence for complex exchange systems, and the admittedly incomplete evidence is suggestive of considerable population decline. No figure can be put on the latter, but what had been a great hub of the late Roman world both declined in demo- graphic terms, and saw its economy move decisively towards only very local exchange.

The pattern in areas that remained under Constantinople's control is rather different. Southern Italy retained commercial pottery industries which sold their wares across reasonably wide areas, which suggests that more general patterns of exchange retained greater complexity. The city of Rome also recovered from its various sieges to become, again, a centre of wealth which imported goods in considerable quantities, very considerable in relative terms by the seventh century. All this was on nothing like the scale of the late Roman period, and it is normally reckoned that the city's population dropped by a factor of ten from a few hundred thousand to just a few tens of thousands. Nonetheless, despite the decline, it has been suggested that southern Italy was probably richer than any other part of the old Roman West in the seventh and early eighth centuries. Whether or how much of this economic decline would have been avoided had Justinian's armies not been set loose in the region is difficult to estimate. Cassiodorus' *Variae* give the impression that everything was running as normal prior to 536, but this is only a facade, and it is certainly true that the same kind of economic simplification we observe in Lombard Italy affected every other region of the post-Roman West as well, once the *pax Romana* was removed. So, I have no doubt that Justinian's wars caused a lot of damage and killed many people unnecessarily in the Italian peninsula, but the chances are that the Italian economy – even under Ostrogothic rule – would have moved more towards the simpler patterns of the early medieval north in any case.[22]

Nor was everything sweetness and light in North Africa, despite the speed of the initial conquest. Like the neocons of our own era, the East Roman authorities found that it was much easier to win battles than to establish functioning governmental structures. One problem had nothing to do with Justinian. Rome's old North African provinces – thanks to the relief rainfall generated by the Atlas Mountains – were marked by the close proximity of desert-fringe and upland nomadic Moorish populations to the much more densely populated and agriculturally rich Roman heartland provinces of eastern Numidia, Proconsularis and Byzacena (Figure 9). There had always been some endemic low-level raiding of the Roman provinces, but, for the most part, nomad–settled relations were 'managed' rather than a source of constant conflict. When the Vandal–Alans took over these key provinces with the capture of Carthage in 439, they inherited the network of established relations with the Moors, and started to use the latter in some of their military adventures across the Mediterranean, not least the famous sack of Rome in 457. By some means or another – my suspicion is by a combination of new arms, new wealth and new ambitions acquired in the course of this involvement – the Moorish world of the African fringes then fell out of its old rhythms under Vandal rule, and, by the 480s, larger political structures were appearing, capable of concentrating enough warriors periodically to defeat Vandal forces. One such defeat, indeed, was a major cause of Gelimer's ability to gather a critical mass of political support against Hilderic.

On Belisarius' overthrow of the Vandal kingdom, the Moorish problem landed at the feet of Justinian's new administrators, and raids both on Numidia and Byzacena were reported as early as 534.[23] The quick victory of 533–4 proved illusory. Teething troubles with the Catholic Church, leftover Vandals and Roman soldiers short of pay, quickly gave way to the main event: confrontation with the Moors, amongst whom the dislocations of Vandal rule had stimulated a new capacity for large-scale predatory ambition towards the wealth of the settled agricultural land which formed the beating heart of the province. This took over a decade to resolve itself, at which point the victories of the new Roman commander John Troglita in 547–8 stabilized the situation again in the medium term. All this was no small problem, even if there is no sign that the resulting conflict inflicted losses on anything like the scale of those suffered by the Italian provincials. Only one city ever changed hands, and the main initial damage to the civilian population would seem to have been through wide-ranging but small-scale raiding. And alongside the political stability that seems to have returned to North Africa both within and beyond the settled fringe from the 540s, the archaeological evidence suggests that the North African provinces saw considerable renewal of economic prosperity, even if it never quite recovered to the old late Roman levels.

The hinterland of Carthage, in particular, seems to have prospered, and the period saw considerable investment in city defences and religious buildings. There was also a modest recovery in the export of fine tablewares and agricultural produce such as wine and olive oil. But North Africa's late Roman prosperity had come from the fact that it was tied into a broader system of west Mediterranean exchange which was actually dependent in a series of ways on the West Roman state, not least because it subsidized transport costs for its own purposes, and none of that came back into existence in the mid-sixth century. Instead of being the booming centre of a Western imperial economy, North Africa was now only a moderately prosperous peripheral zone of an East Roman economy whose crucible was located much further to the east around the Aegean and in the Near East. It exported, therefore, but on a much smaller scale, and the general level of wealth in the region seems to have settled back into a more modest prosperity.[24]

From the viewpoint of those caught up in the fighting – whether Vandal–Alans, Goths, Roman troops, or North African and Italian provincials – Justinian's wars can only be considered a major disaster. The longer-term archaeological evidence does not suggest that they were anything like as devastating as Procopius' death toll would indicate, but, in places, the impact – whether of the war itself in Italy or the longer-term struggle for control in North Africa – was extremely fierce. It does not look as though population levels recovered to pre-war levels in either region, although there was clearly plenty of agricultural activity and some revival in patterns of economic exchange and specialization once peace was finally restored. In addition, of course, we must factor in the effect of East Roman tax collectors. So, in sum, it's hard to make the argument that local provincial populations gained anything at all from being incorporated into the East Roman Empire, except perhaps that a showdown with the Moors was on the cards in North Africa even if Justinian hadn't invaded, and his armies were arguably more capable of protecting the settled agricultural areas than the Vandals would have been.

There were few gains either in the conquest policy from the point of view of the second major grouping affected by it: the taxpayers of the Eastern Empire. Some of them, of course, suffered a similar level of collateral damage to their more unlucky peers in North Africa and Italy. The many thousands of individuals – those who survived the sack – dragged hundreds of kilometres away to live in Chosroes' New Antioch are a case in point, although, outside of 540, specific major damage to the Eastern provincial population seems to have been rare. Much more regularly affected by the unpleasant consequences of conflict were the provincial communities of the Roman Balkans. They were plentifully provided with fortified redoubts. Hundreds are listed in Procopius' *Buildings* (most 'repaired', notice, not built: so they had long existed) and none of the invaders of the Balkans in Justinian's reign was much good at capturing fortified centres. What was a problem, however, was the fact that Justinian regularly drew troops away from the Balkans to fight the Italian campaign. To my mind, it is no surprise, therefore, that the first really damaging Bulgar attack on the Balkans occurred in 539, just after Justinian had found Belisarius the reinforcements he needed to exploit his initial gains in Italy. The fortifications show that the emperor was not entirely without thought for his Balkan subjects, but his need for troops exposed them to much greater danger.[25]

Balkan and certain Eastern communities aside, the main effect of the conquest policy, as experienced by the bulk of the East Roman population, came in the form of increased taxes to defray the costs of the wars and the initial garrisoning of the conquered territories, since any extra income from them certainly took a number of years to come fully on stream. Particular individuals involved in army supply – weaponry, food, wagons, ships and a host of other items – will of course have profited. War is always a hugely profitable time for those involved in supply, since the need is pressing and lucrative contracts can usually be negotiated. Most of the Eastern Empire's population, however, will only have seen the tax bills to pay for those contracts, and little if any profit from their filling. One of the great themes running through *Anekdota*, as we saw in the last chapter, is Justinian's voracity for other people's money, and the text combines rebarbative general condemnations with specific examples of individuals who fell foul of either the emperor's greed or that of his wife.

Victory in Africa not only made Justinian politically untouchable, it also emboldened him to take on his richer taxpayers. The year after Gelimer's humiliation in Constantinople saw no less than nine separate measures going round the regions of the Eastern Empire with the express intention of ratcheting up the overall tax-take by getting more out of the wealthy. And this was before the costs of fighting Goths and Persians simultaneously began to bite in the 540s (although it is noticeable – and the career of Totila expresses the fact – that Justinian never tried to fight two full-on wars at once). While I would not for a moment dispute that tax bills must have gone up under Justinian, this does provide a bit more perspective on the complaints of Procopius. All the individuals he mentions being ruined in *Anekdota* are rich ones, and he himself – as his education demonstrates – was certainly from at least a reasonably wealthy gentry-level landowning family. Justinian's wars did increase tax bills, but did so disproportionately for Procopius' class, and the anger that this generated still burns through the pages he wrote.[26]

There are broadly two types of overtaxation: political and economic. Political overtaxation occurs when a population, or a significant element of it, finds the level of taxation it is facing to be so unfair that it puts huge efforts into protest, avoidance, and evasion. The level at which taxation becomes politically too high is of course subjective. Economic overtaxation, by contrast, is much more based on figures. In an industrial economy, taxing production increases the costs of the goods being produced, and if you increase that cost to a point where buyers stop being interested, production and consequently GDP declines. Economic overtaxation, therefore, is measureable in terms of its negative effects on overall economic output, whereas you might get *political* overtaxation at levels where total output is not actually being lowered. It is here that proper allowance for the differences inherent to an agricultural economy comes in. Without good reason (and who can blame them), peasant farmers do not always maximize their production in practice. Unless they have a functioning market to sell cash crops into, they will tend to work hard enough only to feed their families and pay such dues as they owe, preferring to consume some of their potential surplus in the form of more free time and leisure. In such contexts, increasing taxation can sometimes increase overall production, so the automatic linkage between tax hikes and some kind of lowering of total output that you find in modern industrial economies is not necessarily there. Economic overtaxation of peasants, brutally, shows up when families are not left with enough of their production, no matter how hard they work, to sustain themselves in the longer term. This will usually take the form of chronic but not immediately fatal levels of malnutrition which make the population more prone to disease in general with little or no available food reserves, so that periodic, unavoidable crop failures generate bursts of high mortality. Between them, both phenomena start to lower population levels, which in turn causes marginal land to drop out of production first, and eventually perhaps better grades too. Given this kind of framework for qualitative judgement, did Justinian's conquest policies cause overtaxation in the Eastern Empire's heartlands?

With absolutely certainty, it led to political overtaxation among the landowning classes of the empire. Procopius' diatribe is one indication, but there is a better one. One of the easiest ways for a new regime to gain quick political capital is to reverse – fully or partly – the most unpopular policies of its predecessor. And after Justinian's death, the new regime of his nephew Justin II immediately reversed his uncle's policies – or some of them – on taxing the rich.[27] They had obviously been very unpopular, but this is not necessarily proof that they had done serious harm to the structure of the empire. Political overtaxation does serious damage only when it causes important political constituencies to seek entire alternatives to the prevailing order, and in fact there is little or no sign of that in the reign of Justinian. We don't, for instance, find Roman landowning elites seeking a Persian allegiance instead of their traditional Roman one (although Procopius deliberately presented Justinian as no better than his Persian counterpart) either in the time of Justinian or immediately afterwards, so it is difficult to make the case stick that the emperor's tax hikes had seriously damaged the structure of the empire in the long term. More likely, they just seriously annoyed the already rich.

Deciding whether Justinian overtaxed the east in economic terms is greatly complicated by the fact that his reign was also marked by a massive outbreak of plague, which affected the entire Mediterranean in the 540s. In 541 it migrated up the Red Sea, through Egypt to Alexandria, which was such a busy entrepôt that from there it quickly spread around the rest of the empire and, indeed, beyond: reaching Constantinople by spring 542 and cities in Syria, Palestine and Africa by the end of the year. By 543 it had embraced Armenia, Italy, and Gaul before eventually arriving in the British Isles. The Justinianic plague, as it is known, has taken its place alongside the Black Death and an equivalent outbreak in the later nineteenth century as one of the three great pandemics so far known to have affected human history. But controversy surrounds its every aspect, not least cause. The late 530s saw extreme climatic instability right across the Eurasian land mass and included a veiling event in 536–7, when the sun's rays were partially blocked by heavy particles in the atmosphere and temperatures fell worldwide (this much is documented by ice core samples). The veiling was plausibly caused by a massive volcanic explosion in East Asia (although that is not certain), and the consequent change in climate perhaps caused central African plague-carrying rodents to range more widely than usual into the Red Sea area, and hence kick-start the epidemic. However, it is far from certain that the plague was bubonic (with its associated mutations), since contemporary reports suggest that the outbreak did not behave as bubonic plague should. It spread much faster, for instance, than the well-observed late nineteenth-century pandemic, despite the slower contacts and communications.

There is also massive controversy over its effects. Contemporary accounts demonstrate that it killed in large numbers, seemingly in urban and rural contexts alike. Whether it killed on the scale of the Black Death of the fourteenth century, however, when well over a third of the population in affected areas of Western Europe succumbed, is still being argued about. Those who are keen on seeing the plague as a great crisis have attempted to date some clear archaeological evidence for economic decline in the lands of the Eastern Empire to around AD 550. But, as the most recent comprehensive survey of this evidence concludes, the argument has in general terms been extremely unsuccessful. In fact, both the cities and countryside of the Eastern Empire show every sign of continued prosperity in the late sixth century, and there is no evidence at all of any major economic downturn. As we shall see later in the chapter, there is also a perfectly good, and rather different, explanation, for the evident decline which follows after 600. While the plague was certainly horrible, and killed many people, there is no evidence that it led to any generalized, or structurally serious economic dislocation.[28]

As I hope is clear, though, I have no doubt that Justinian's wars were an entirely ghastly sequence of events for a very large chunk of the Mediterranean population. They certainly generated higher tax demands for the east's population, landowners (for whom I have in general much less sympathy) and peasants alike. Many East Roman, Vandal–Alan, and Gothic soldiers died painful, brutal deaths. And, thanks to a mixture of collateral damage and consequent instability, innocent bystanders among the provincial populations of North Africa and Italy certainly in their tens of thousands – and perhaps more – lost a combination of their goods, longer-term livelihoods, and straightforwardly their lives. All to satisfy the demands of a tyrannical autocrat, who initiated the policy in a desperate attempt to win back lost political capital and then became intoxicated by the savour of apparently easy victory. For so many constituencies, Justinian's wars were an unmitigated disaster and that is perhaps the conclusion that needs stressing more than any other. History has all too often been guilty of favouring the viewpoint of autocratic rulers in describing their glorious victories, when there is so much else that needs to be said.

But what, finally, about Justinian's wars when viewed from that final, more traditional viewpoint: the imperial centre? From that particular perspective, despite everyone else's losses, were the wars in any sense worth it? For Justinian himself – the self-proclaimed conqueror of many nations – there is not the slightest doubt that they were. Victory in North Africa had provided him with the mother of all get-out-of-jail-free cards, and gave him all the political capital he needed to rebuild both his regime's standing and the ceremonial centre of Constantinople in the later 530s and beyond. He survived it all to die in his bed at the grand old age of eighty-three (or thereabouts), leaving behind him a series of monuments that still amaze (Hagia Sophia really is amazing) and with each of his wars brought to – from his point of view – fairly successful outcomes. By 565, Africa had been reasonably quiet for nearly two decades, most of Italy for over a decade, and Sicily for the best part of three. For the Illyrian adventurer who was ready to take ship and fly over that ghastly weekend in January 532, the conquest policy had been extraordinarily successful. But this is the tyrant's own viewpoint. What about the entity he ruled, the Eastern Empire as a whole?

There are, I think, two ways to start thinking about this. One is to look at the conquered provinces. From the central, Constantinopolitan perspective, the key issue is whether they brought in enough revenue for long enough to cover the costs of their initial conquest and subsequent defence. Running quickly around them – and again, of course, we have to adopt a qualitative not quantitative approach – the answer would appear to be mixed. Sicily was undoubtedly worth it. Contrary to its role in the modern Italian polity, in the ancient and indeed medieval worlds, Sicily was a great prize: Henry III of England would virtually bankrupt himself in the thirteenth century trying to get his sticky little paws on it. Justinian, by contrast, picked Sicily up at virtually no cost, and the Eastern Empire held it without trouble down to the 650s when the first Arab raids began, and then at rather greater cost until the ninth century. By this date, the island must have more than paid for itself. The same, I think, is likely to have been true of North Africa. There the costs were higher, and it would seem that a somewhat smaller area was eventually secured for the Eastern imperial taxman than his Western predecessor had enjoyed. It also fell much sooner into Arab hands, with the loss of Carthage in the 690s marking the effective end of East Roman rule. Nonetheless, the bulk of the conquered North African territory had been in East Roman hands for 150 years by this time, which was more than long enough for the costs of conquest to have been repaid. Indeed, in the late sixth and early seventh centuries the Sicilian–North African axis was wealthy enough to provide the power base from which the father-and-son team of Heraclius (on whom more in a moment) would take over the entire empire.

The tricky one is Italy. Surprisingly large parts of Italy remained part of the East Roman Empire for a very long time, and, as we have seen, those that did show many more archaeological signs of economic prosperity than those that did not. A substantial enclave around Ravenna, together with Rome and most of central and southern Italy, were ruled directly from Constantinople until the eighth century. At that point Ravenna was lost, and Rome moved out of direct control, in a story we will need to explore in Chapter 7. The southern part of the peninsula would remain solidly East Roman for another 200 years after that, and isolated communities for a lot longer still. Belisarius' capture of Naples thus inaugurated the best part of half a millennium of East Roman rule in southern Italy, making it hard to conclude that the costs of conquest had not long since been repaid by the tenth century.[29] Much more conspicuous than these lengthy examples of continuous East Roman rule, however, is the very swift loss of much of northern Italy, and two central upland duchies – centred on Benevento and Spoleto – immediately after Justinian's death. In 568, the Lombards swept out of the lands they had held in the Middle Danube region for about three generations, and into a northern Italy, where Narses had only just, as we've seen, extinguished the last flickers of Gothic independence, thus ruining the aged general's retirement. This sudden, devastating loss clearly messed up the cost-benefit analysis being run in Constantinople on the value of Justinian's Italian conquests. For historians, it has also become the starting point of a more general argument, that, whatever their short-term successes, Justinian's conquests generated a more or less fatal case of imperial overstretch. For not only could all of Italy not be held, but within forty years of Justinian's death there began a series of major losses of heartland tax base in the Near and Middle East which changed the nature of the

East Roman state forever. How good is the case that these losses represent the longer-term consequences of Justinianic imperial over-reach?

OF ELEPHANTS AND COUCHES

In 583, several embassies went backwards and forwards from Constantinople to the reigning khagan of the Avar confederation. East Romans and Avars were currently at peace, and, in the course of these contacts, the khagan made a sequence of demands for diplomatic presents from the emperor: an elephant, a golden couch, and eventually a huge sum of cash. These exchanges are reported without comment by the East Roman historian Theophylact Simocatta (charmingly, his surname means 'the one-eyed cat'). The Avars were steppe nomads who had only recently arrived in western Eurasia from the fringes of China, who had never seen an elephant and probably barely heard of them. What was clearly going on with the elephant and the couch is that the Avar khagan and his advisers were, first of all, trying to think of something that the Constantinopolitan authorities could not provide in order graphically to demonstrate the limits of the emperor's power. When the Romans delivered the elephant, the Avars opted for a golden couch as the most impossible diplomatic gift they could think of. When that turned up too, it became an excuse for showing disdain and the preface to an unfeasible demand for cash that they knew would lead to war. The whole rigmarole of asking for elaborate presents and then rejecting them was a diplomatic dance, designed to show Avar superiority and then to generate a break in the current state of peace.[30] Its more surreal elements aside, the story also – eventually – takes us to the heart of why the Eastern Empire found it impossible to hold on to more of the Italian peninsula in the years immediately after Justinian's death.

The Avars did not start to figure in imperial calculations until the final decade of Justinian's reign, by which time the last embers of Gothic resistance were being snuffed out, and John Troglita's campaigns had calmed the situation in North Africa. Their first embassy arrived in Constantinople in 558 and, as reported by the historian Menander Protector, conducted itself with the kind of bluster that was a speciality of nomad powers of the mid-first millennium:

> One Kandikh . . . was chosen to be the first envoy of the Avars, and when he came to the palace he told the emperor of the arrival of the greatest and most powerful of the tribes. The Avars were invincible and could easily crush and destroy all who stood in their path. The emperor should make an alliance with them and enjoy their efficient protection. But they would only be well disposed to the Roman state in exchange for the most valuable gifts, yearly payments and very fertile lands to inhabit.

It is also typical of first-millennium nomads that the reality was rather more prosaic. The smart money is on their having in fact been refugees looking to get out of the way of the Western Turks, who were the really dominant steppe power of the mid-sixth century, and whose star was busily ascending at the moment when the Avars – now on the fringes of the Black Sea – sent Kandikh and their calling card to Constantinople. And getting out of the way of the Western Turks was, in fact, an extremely good idea. Theirs was the first nomad superpower known to history. Attila had been bad enough, but, though he is often compared to the great Mongol conquerors like Genghis and Kublai Khan, his was actually a petty-fogging type of enterprise confined to central and south-eastern Europe. The power of the famous Hsiung-Nu, who so pestered the Qin emperors that they built the Great Wall, was likewise confined to the northern fringes of China. The Western Turks, however, established power on a Mongol-type scale, straddling Eurasia all the way from China to the eastern approaches to Europe.[31]

Something pretty monumental was under way in the world of the steppe, but quite what is unclear, since nomads didn't write much, and neither Western nor Chinese sources have the range to allow us to explore inner-steppe processes in detail. Some scholars have therefore played the environmental card, and, certainly, the veiling event which may have played some role in the plague will also have reduced the amount of fodder available on the steppe in the late 530s. This must have increased inter-nomad competition to some extent, and if the effect were large enough, the consequences would be only too predictable for their more settled neighbours.

But this is not the only possibility. Nomads depend upon their settled agricultural neighbours for huge amounts of essential foodstuffs and other items, which can either be traded for or simply extracted, and the amount of leverage that can be exercised over these neighbours' political structures is often at the heart of any particular nomad group's capacity to build an empire. It is just as likely, therefore, that the unprecedented empire-building of the Western Turks had its roots in changes to the world around the steppe as in changes to the steppe itself (although some combination of the two is possible, if not indeed highly likely). Here the plague might figure of course, but, in the absence of sufficient evidence, it is extremely important not to collapse the range of possibilities too quickly.[32] Fortunately, our concern here is not with the rise of the western Turkish khaganate itself, but with one of its main consequences, the appearance of the Avars in the West, and here the documentation is much more straightforward.

Even if they were refugees, the Avars had sufficient military power to cut like a very hot knife through the strategic butter of central and south-eastern Europe of the mid-sixth century. Prior to 558, the situation was fairly straightforward. The Middle Danubian region west of the Carpathians (roughly modern Hungary and western Romania) was divided between two Germanic-speaking kingdoms: that of the Lombards in the west, and the Gepids further east. The lands north of the Black Sea, likewise, were divided between two Turkish-speaking Bulgar nomadic groupings, the Utigurs and the Cutrigurs. In between, the Transylvanian uplands and some of the lands north of the Danube bend were becoming home to a series of – at this stage – very small-scale Slavic entities: chiefdoms of some kind rather than kingdoms (Figure 10). The latter had come into recorded contact with the defended Danube frontier of the Roman state only from around the 520s, from which point their raiding of Roman territory became an increasing problem.

If, like Justinian, you were playing the great game from your palace at Constantinople, the overall strategy was clear. Play Lombards off against Gepids at one end of your northern frontier, and Utigurs against Cutrigurs at the other, while seeking to minimize the amount of raiding damage that the Slavs might do in the middle. And this, broadly, is what Justinian aimed at for the majority of his reign. But no policy is ever perfect, and, because he withdrew army units from the Balkans to fight in Italy, this certainly led to extra losses in the Balkans. Large Cutrigur raids affected the Roman provinces in both

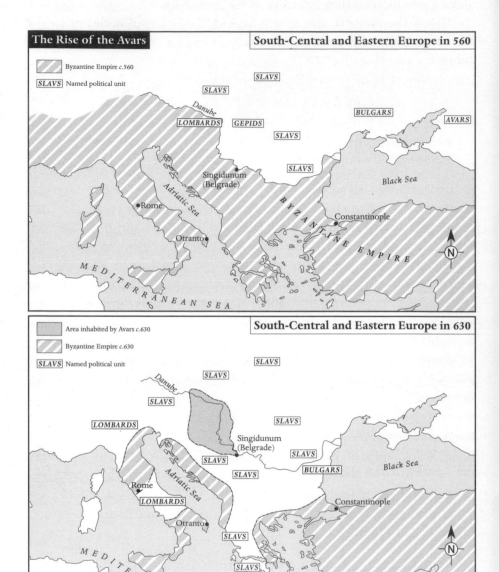

The Rise of the Avars

South-Central and Eastern Europe in 560

- Byzantine Empire *c.560*
- *SLAVS* Named political unit

SLAVS

SLAVS

Danube

LOMBARDS *GEPIDS*

SLAVS

BULGARS

AVARS

SLAVS

Singidunum
(Belgrade)

SLAVS

Black Sea

Rome

Adriatic Sea

B Y Z A N T I N E   E M P I R E

Constantinople

Otranto

M E D I T E R R A N E A N   S E A

N

South-Central and Eastern Europe in 630

- Area inhabited by Avars *c.630*
- Byzantine Empire *c.630*
- *SLAVS* Named political unit

SLAVS

SLAVS

Danube

SLAVS

LOMBARDS

SLAVS

Singidunum
(Belgrade)

SLAVS

SLAVS

Rome

Adriatic Sea

SLAVS

SLAVS

Black Sea

BULGARS

LOMBARDS

Constantinople

Otranto

SLAVS

M E D I T E R R A N E A N   S E A

SLAVS

N

539 and 559, the former enslaving many thousands of prisoners, while Slavic raids increased in intensity in the later 540s.[33]

Given the context, the Avars looked like a useful addition to the mix, and Menander records Justinian's eventual response to that first contact:

> He sent an ambassador Valentinus, one of the imperial bodyguard, and he urged the tribe to make an alliance with the Romans and take up arms against their enemies. This . . . was a very wise move, since whether the Avars prevailed or were defeated, both eventualities would be to the Romans' advantage.[34]

At first, all was sweetness and light. By 562, Avar might extended across the northern shores of the Black Sea, a series of undocumented campaigns having swallowed up both Utigurs and Cutrigurs. This, no doubt, was all entirely according to the imperial plan following the Cutrigurs' second large-scale intrusion into the Roman Balkans in a generation in 559. There was thus no reason not to accord the Avars favoured-ally status and substantial amounts of annual foreign aid (or 'subsidies', depending on your point of view), which they proceeded to enjoy down to Justinian's death in November 565.

At that point, the change of regime brought a decisive change in policy. We've already seen that Justin II attempted to win political capital by reversing his uncle's tax policies, and it was presented as part and parcel of the same policy that he also stopped handing out as much in foreign aid. Thus, when the next Avar embassy trotted into Constantinople to pick up their annual gifts, they got a nasty surprise, the new emperor telling them:

> Never again shall you be loaded at the expense of this empire, and go your way without doing us any service: for from me you shall receive nothing.

According to Menander, this left the ambassadors 'thunderstruck' and extremely hesitant about returning home empty-handed, though they eventually did so.[35]

The ambassadors' response was not mere petty-mindedness. The removal of East Roman foreign aid threatened the whole stability of the Avar confederation. Like the Huns before them, the Avars lacked the capacity, or probably even the desire, to rule subjugated elements of their confederation directly, but operated rather through subordinate princes. This meant that it was easy to add new elements to the confederation, and the whole thing could mushroom quickly. One swift military campaign and a formal submission was all that was required, in essence, for a new subject grouping to be added to the line-up. But the resulting political construction was by the same token fragile, since old patterns of loyalty among subject peoples were not broken down and could easily reassert themselves in bids for independence. Despite the braggart nomad rhetoric recorded in first-millennium sources, all that held their confederations together was the prestige of the dominant leader and his immediate supporters, who were often not that numerous compared to all the subject groupings. And prestige was no more than a combination of exerted or perceived military domination, combined with recycled prestigious gifts. Both were often the products of successful warfare, and both sustained the perception that accepting Avar domination was a much better option than trying to resist it. In 582, they were besieging the important Danubian fortress of Sirmium, and realized that they were not going to win. The Roman commander then received an extraordinary communication from his opposite number, that the Avars were willing to withdraw, but only if the Romans handed over a grand present which the Khagan could use to hide the fact of defeat. Any major loss of prestige might lead to Avar authority being put to the test, at considerable cost in time, effort, and lives, even if it was not in the end overthrown.[36]

The emperor's deliberate slight in 566 would have been only too apparent, leaving the khagan with no choice but to do something both to replace the lost income and to repair the deficit in his prestige. And, in a typically imaginative early medieval policy initiative, the khagan and his advisers decided that the best thing they could do was wage war on somebody. Their choice fell on the Franks, and in the same year they inflicted a major defeat on the easternmost of the Frankish kings, Sigibert, who, afterwards, 'immediately sent to the Avars wheat-flour, vegetables, sheep, and cattle'.[37] It is this increased interest in going west that finally brings us back to Italy.

At the same time as Justin was busy rebuffing the Avars, the latest in a series of spats was breaking out between the Gepids and Lombards. In 566, the Gepids secured some imperial military assistance but then didn't keep their part of the bargain in that they refused to return the city of Sirmium to imperial control. The Romans were not minded to intervene again in 567, therefore, when the Lombards

secured Avar help, at high cost, and with it smashed Gepid independence forever. This is the moment when the Lombard king, Alboin,
reputedly turned the skull of his defeated enemy, Cunimund, into a
drinking cup, but then made the mistake of marrying Cunimund's
daughter Rosamund (page 19).

Early the next year, on 2 April 568 – pretty much as soon as the
grass had started to grow again – the Lombards left the Middle Danube
in a large co-ordinated body, which resembled the cavalcade Theoderic
had led over the same passes ninety years before. At least several tens
of thousands strong, a ragbag of Lombards proper and many others
besides, nobles, freemen and slaves, this human procession fatally
compromised the security of newly conquered East Roman Italy.
Within no time at all Lombard *duces* (you can translate it 'dukes' but
this gives an anachronistic flavour) had taken over most of the cities
of the North Italian Plain, except for an enclave around Ravenna, and
established two separate duchies – Benevento and Spoleto – in the
mountainous uplands of central and southern Italy.

A source written over 200 years later reports that the Lombards
were 'invited' to move into Italy by the very same Narses who had
finished off the Goths, due to a quarrel between himself and Justin's
wife Sophia. Given his past career, and not least that he soon retired
to live quietly in the firmly East Roman city of Rome, this is
completely implausible, and no one believes it. It's no more than one
aspect of the later Lombard claim, highly pertinent in the eighth
century as we shall see in the next chapter, that they had an entirely
legitimate right to establish a kingdom in Italy. Aggressive ambition
presumably had some role to play, since 'pull' as well as 'push' factors
often feature in decisions to migrate. But I have no doubt that the
Lombard leadership was not motivated purely by perceptions of East
Roman weakness. Lombard contingents had been involved in the
Gothic war, after all, and had witnessed at first hand the East Roman
destruction of both the Goths and the large Frankish force which had
come – too late – to the rescue. It cannot have been thinking that
conquering a piece of East Roman territory was going to be a
pushover, therefore, and in making such a disruptive and dangerous
move, it seems clear that, like several late fourth- and early fifth-
century Germanic groups faced with the rise of the Huns, the Lombard
leadership decided – and managed to sell to a large part of their
following – that organized retreat was the best method of dealing with

a rampant enemy. The defeat of Sigibert in 566 followed by the destruction of the Gepids in 567 had rammed home the point that the Avar star was ascending rapidly and that its direction of travel was increasingly westwards. There is a direct causal link between the rise of Avar power in central Europe and the arrival of the Lombards in Justinian's recently conquered province of Italy.[38]

The question of whether Justinian's conquest of Italy was wildly overambitious and destined to lead to imperial overstretch boils down, therefore, to your answers to two slightly more complicated questions. Could East Roman rule in Italy have been consolidated – as it was in North Africa – without the invasion of the Lombards? And, if so, was Justinian fundamentally responsible for the rise of Avar power and its westward shift of focus which prompted the Lombard invasion? The answer to the first question must surely be 'yes'. The assertion of Constantinopolitan rule in Italy certainly generated complaints about imperial taxmen; Justinian had conquered Italy for no one's benefit but his own. At the same time, the tax regime was broadly that which operated in the East itself, and in North Africa, and there is no obvious reason why, lacking any alternative, the population of Italy, greater and lesser, would not have eventually accommodated itself to the norms of East Roman rule, as many parts of central and southern Italy in fact did. And, apart from the sudden Lombard influx, there was no other enemy in sight with the power to overthrow Constantinopolitan rule. At least, Narses' armies had proved more than a match for the various Frankish forces – the only serious competition – that had come to Italy in the 550s to fight over the corpse of Theoderic's kingdom (page 166).

The only way to answer 'yes' to the second question, moreoever, is if you believe the subsidies Justinian handed out in 558 played a critical role in empowering the Avars to make their initial conquests of the Cutrigurs and Utigurs. Otherwise, the remaining stages of Avar expansion were all accomplished without East Roman subsidy, and all the subsequent increases in their power, together with the move west, were arguably more the fault of Justin II, for removing stability payments, than it was of his uncle for handing them out. The build-up of Avar power followed the pattern of the Huns closely, with a virtuous or vicious (depending on your point of view) circle being established, whereby conquests added more subject peoples to increase military capacity, but also still more political strains within the confederation, both of which had an in-built tendency to generate yet further bouts of military expansion. It is just about possible to make the argument that Justinian should have known that the Avars were far too dangerous to use in his traditional games of divide and rule, and should never have given them the original subsidy in 558; but that involves a huge amount of second-guessing and it is not clear that the Roman funds were critical to the Avar conquest of the Bulgars anyway. In other words, it seems much more likely both that the rise of Avar power to such intimidating heights was unforeseeable in 558, and that Justinian's contribution to the process was pretty minimal. And, without the Avar Empire, there is no obvious reason why Constantinople should not have been able to hold on to much or most of the Italian peninsula more or less indefinitely.

All in all, it seems a bit of a stretch to blame the Avars on Justinian, which in turn makes the case for seeing the emperor as strategically reckless much less convincing. The Avars were also responsible, moreover, for major post-Justinianic losses in the Balkans. They looked to secure parts of the north-west for their own purposes, but they also facilitated more general Slavic intrusion into the region. First, Slavic groups wanted to get out of the way of aggressive Avar domination, which was exercised with equal brutality over as many Slavs as the khagan could reach, just as it was over Gepids and Bulgars. The rise of the Avar Empire thus provided a negative stimulus for Slavic intrusions on to Roman territory. At the same time, again echoing the Huns, the Avars periodically mounted major campaigns through the Roman Balkans as part of their remit to demand money with menaces from Constantinople. Especially in the 580s and the 610s, these had the effect of blowing huge holes in the defensive arrangements for the Balkans which Justinian's building campaigns had been designed to complete. This in turn meant that the smaller Slavic groupings, which otherwise the Romans could deal with effectively enough, were able to move on to Roman soil and carve out new territories for themselves.

This was a decisive moment. The Slavicization of large parts of the Balkans, and the definitive loss of the region to Constantinopolitan control, does indeed date back to the decades either side of the year 600, when the Avars made it all possible. So, again, the case for blaming Justinian is not, on reflection, a very good one since the Avars lay at the heart of it all. Indeed, when you stop and really think about how events interconnected in these years, the case against Justinian quickly gets a whole lot weaker still. For while the aggressive Avar campaigns into the Roman Balkans of the 580s led to initial waves of substantial Slavic settlement, the situation was brought substantially back under control by Roman counter-attack in the 590s.[39] It was, in fact, the further Avar campaigns of the 610s that were really critical: generating an uncontrolled Slavicization that was never reversed by further counter-attacks. The reason that there were no further Roman counter-attacks after the 590s has its roots in a second strategic shift of quite colossal historical significance.

THE SEVEN CITIES OF ASIA

In chapters 2 and 3 of the Book of Revelation, the Lord of Hosts dictates letters to the Christian communities of each of seven cities of the Roman province of Asia in what is now western Turkey. They range in size from huge metropolises like Ephesus and Sardis to the smaller Thyatira. The usual pattern is for the church to be named and its prevailing sin identified (for five of the seven). There then follows a warning or challenge and a promise about the benefits of properly faithful behaviour. Each includes the famous, even ominous refrain, 'He who has an ear, let him hear what the Spirit says to the churches.' St John the Divine, particularly when it came to identifying besetting sins, had in mind the Christian communities of his own time, but, if ever these cities needed ominous warnings, it was in the aftermath of Justinian's passing.

Most retained substantial Christian communities down to the forced exchanges of population which followed the Treaty of Lausanne in 1923, but in the eighty or so years after Justinian died, an apocalypse was visited both upon the Christian cities of Roman Asia, and those of its neighbours to the south and east: the heartlands of the East Roman Empire. Syria, Palestine and Egypt fell first to the control of Sasanian Persia and were then swallowed up, shortly afterwards, by the forces of Islam which the Prophet Muhammad had fashioned in the heart of the Arabian desert. The old Christian cities of the conquered regions survived as great conurbations, but Muslim conquest and conversion destined their Christian populations to long-term decline and minority status, in worlds which had once been the beating heart of ancient Christianity. A different kind of apocalypse was visited upon the cities of Asia Minor named in the Book of Revelation. They remained in the hands of the Christian Constantinopolitan authorities, but twentieth-century archaeological investigation has revealed just how profound a shipwreck they had to endure.

Sardis, in particular, declined from great city to fortified military stronghold and perhaps a centre of government, and did so extremely suddenly. Up until the very late sixth century, the city continued to prosper, maintaining its great monuments with gusto. Its commercial life, too, seems to have been as busy as ever, with excavators uncovering a colonnade of shops outside the main bathhouse, which show every sign of vitality. The very wealthiest houses show – perhaps – a little decline in standards, but that's about it. Then all hell broke loose with the Persian sack in 610. Few people were killed it seems, but the refugees did not have time to take their goods with them from the shops, and the city never recovered. On the old main site on the plain, all that excavators have ever found from the seventh century are a few scrappy little clusters of poor houses, and the main centre of activity moved to the nearby fortified hilltop. But this was really only a fortress – made incidentally almost entirely out of reused blocks from the old city – never a centre of population. As a proper city, Sardis ceased to exist: life continued there but only in the form of a garrison and a couple of hamlets. The situation was not quite so bad at nearby Ephesus. Here too, though, straightforward continuity on the old main site was broken. Habitation shifted instead to two new walled enclosures, one a small area – a kilometre square – within the old site, the other marking off a smaller area around what had been the external Church of St John. The population within these two sets of walls was clearly larger and more diverse than that surviving at Sardis, and its economic life remained more diverse; we happen to know, for instance, that a great fair was held there, seemingly on a regular basis. But, even so, this post-600 Ephesus was but a shadow of its former self in size, wealth and grandeur and the archaeological picture from all the late Roman cities of western Asia Minor is very similar.[40]

Once-great cities had been reduced to small garrison posts, or small agricultural market towns, and even Constantinople didn't escape. The

city saw a drastic decline in its population in the seventh century –
perhaps by as much as 90 per cent – and this is when all its grandiose
masonry began to crumble. It still remained a big city in early medieval
terms, but its seventh- and eighth-century manifestation was but a
shadow of its late Roman self. This perfectly reflected the state of
the empire as a whole. By 640, that is within seventy-five years
of Justinian's death, Egypt and the Middle East had fallen to Arab
domination and western Asia Minor had become a battleground.
There's a nice game you can play about the likely effects of these
losses on the tax base of the empire, using figures from the sixteenth-
century Ottoman Empire, which had much the same shape as the
empire of Justinian. These suggest that Muslim conquest of Egypt
and the Middle East, combined with the economic collapse of western
Asia Minor, meant that the emperors of Constantinople would have
lost somewhere between two-thirds and three-quarters of their annual
tax revenues.[41] The micro-apocalypse experienced by the citizens of
Ephesus and Sardis had its counterpart at the macro-level of the
imperial court. This astounding imperial emasculation had its roots in
a collapse of Constantinople's eastern front, and in relations with its
long-time foe and occasional partner, the Persian Empire.

The Persian front was a vast theatre of confrontation which
involved three separate zones of conflict (Figure 6). In the north, the
two empires faced each other in the mountainous region of Caucasia
where fighting tended to take the form of winning and losing control
of the various small valley-based principalities of Armenia, Iberia and –
in the sixth century – Lazica, into which the geography naturally
divided the region's human population. In the south, likewise, wars
tended to be fought through surrogates: Arabs this time, as conventional Roman and Persian armies found it difficult to operate in the
vast sandy underbelly separating their holdings. The geographical
centre, therefore, also tended to be the main theatre of war: Mesopotamia. Here both sides had built up fortresses of huge power since the
third century, manned them with substantial garrisons, and stationed
large field armies to provide support. In this zone, warfare (except in
the highly unusual circumstances of 540: page 160) had long since
bogged down into lengthy sieges of strategically placed strongpoints if
your Empire was in a position to attack, or determined efforts to
disrupt the besieging forces if you were on the defensive.

Justinian's immediate legacy to his imperial successors was peace in all three sectors. There had been bouts of fighting in each between 527 and 532, and again from 540, but the violence in Mesopotamia had quickly reached stalemate, resulting in an armistice there as early as 545. Elsewhere, there seemed to be more to gain and lose, so the fighting went on until 551, when a five-year armistice brought hostilities to a close in the north. This was followed by a general truce in 557 and in 562 by a formal peace agreement which applied everywhere. By Justinian's death, Mesopotamia had been quiet for twenty years, and the Caucasus for a decade and a half.[42]

Two factors kick-started a vicious circle of destabilization – one a perennial feature of Roman–Persian relations, the other entirely new. The old favourite was succession, the arrival on the throne of a new emperor with the usual need to make his mark. Justin II faced the unusually poisonous legacy of his uncle Justinian, the 'conqueror of many nations'. And, in an effort to demonstrate to the balance of factional powers at court that he really was a ruler to be reckoned with, the new emperor was not only very rude, as we have seen, to the Avar ambassadors, but, like the young Justinian before he slid into Western conquests, had a firm eye on establishing his ruling credentials at the expense of Persia. The Persians were the enemy par excellence from a Constantinopolitan perspective, and picking on them as the target of his early ambitions had the additional virtue that Justinian had never scored a major victory over them. The victory speech would be so easy to write. 'Justinian I have surpassed you' was such a seductive prospect.

The problem, of course, was that while they were the target of first choice, the Persians were also a tough nut to crack, as many a Roman emperor had found to his cost. What gave Justin the nerve nonetheless to attempt to define his reign at Persian expense, however, was that second and entirely new factor: the growing power of the Western Turks. By the later 560s (another reason why the Avars were so happy to move on west into the Middle Danube region), western Turkish hegemony had reached the northern fringes of the Aral, Caspian, and even Black Seas, making it a potential factor in Roman–Persian relations, since its armies could now easily intervene in either or both empires by direct attack through the Caucasus. Justin II's strategy focused on mobilizing the Western Turks against the Persians, to which end a succession of embassies and gifts shuttled forth from Constantinople out across the steppe, literally, in this case, going halfway to China. The end result was – from Justin's point of view – apparently satisfactory. A great joint campaign was to be launched by East Roman and western Turkish armies in the year 573. The Romans would assault the Mesopotamian fortress of Nisibis which had been lost to them since the defeat of the emperor Julian 210 years before, while the Turks prevented any Persian response by launching their own attack from the east.

As soon as the grass was growing, the Roman armies rumbled forward towards Nisibis, but the Turks never showed. The result was disaster. The Persian garrison held on in the midst of ferocious fighting, while the undistracted Persians concentrated their forces in a well-placed counter-attack. One division struck into Syria, but Chosroes I (the same Chosroes that Justinian had refused to adopt so long ago) led his main body against the fortress of Dara: jewel in the Roman Mesopotamian crown. After a six-month siege, the Persians forced the walls and sacked the city, enslaving its population. Justin II's great plan had failed utterly. Instead of capturing the Persian flagship, he had ended up losing his own. Distraught, the emperor suffered such a mental and physical collapse that power devolved to a regency council. Why the Turks failed to show is unclear. Some think that it was a cunning plan on their part to set two potential enemies at loggerheads at no cost to themselves. Possibly so, but by the time a new Roman embassy reached them in 576 the old khagan was dead, and it may just be that his passing was behind their non-appearance. Either way, Justin had destabilized relations in the East only to generate a massive Persian victory in Mesopotamia, where it really mattered. His few gains in Caucasia were not the slightest compensation.[43]

For the next decade, war dragged on. The Romans won one spectacular victory on the Mesopotamian front, in 576, capturing the shah's wife, extinguishing the holy flame that he brought on campaign, and even drowning his high priest. This was good enough to keep the regency council in business, and, to be fair, the Romans also kept firm control of their interests in the Caucasus. But the non-stop and highly expensive warfare in Mesopotamia gradually told against them. By the later 580s, the new emperor Maurice was running out of money and militarily hit the wall. In 588, the unpaid garrison of the important frontier city of Martyropolis simply handed their fortress over to the Persians, and much of the imperial field army, stationed near Edessa, rebelled on the news that they were facing a 25 per cent pay cut. Even when their general paraded the famous Mandylion in front of them, an image of Christ 'not made by human hands' and one of the holiest relics of Christendom (it was once thought that it was the Turin Shroud in an earlier incarnation), they were not impressed. They were so unimpressed, in fact, that they pelted it with rocks, and Maurice was forced to reverse his pay cuts and find the necessary savings elsewhere.

Just as the Roman train was approaching the buffers, an escape route appeared in the form of another disputed succession among the Persians. In 589, one of the leading Persian generals Bahram rebelled against the new shah, Hormisdas IV. Bahram had won so many victories, including a decisive one over the Turks in 588, that the shah was sufficiently threatened to want to cut him down to size. He chose to do so, after a reverse against Roman forces in the Caucasus, by sending him women's clothing. In the ensuing mayhem, Hormisdas was deposed and murdered, Bahram seized power, and Hormisdas' son and chosen heir, Chosroes II, fled to Constantinople to ask for Maurice's support, offering a huge advance to the Roman position in the Caucasus in return. Bahram's counter-offer held up the prospect of Persia giving back not only Dara and Martyropolis, but also even Nisibis if support came his way. Maurice eventually opted for Chosroes, because moving the Mespotamian frontier backwards or forwards by two or three fortresses in the end made no fundamental difference. Huge gains in the Caucasus, however, gave the Romans strategic control of the top end of the passes through the Zagros Mountains which led straight to the Persian Empire's economic heartland between the Tigris and the Euphrates (Figure 6): a knife over the Persian jugular.

Maurice's support proved sufficient, and by 591 Chosroes II was established on the throne and the Romans gratefully took most of Armenia when peace was finally declared, nearly two decades after the ill-fated Justin II had sought to play his Turkish trump card. This was all very well in itself, and Constantinopolitan sources duly trumpeted Maurice's triumph. The problem, however, was that the Roman gains were just so big, that they were a further destabilizing factor in themselves. A recent study has labelled this the Eastern Empire's 'Versailles moment'. The treaty gave the Romans such a strategic advantage that any shah was bound to resort again to warfare to redress the balance whenever a suitable opportunity presented itself.[44]

And, as I'm sure has become clear by now, the internal political structures of both empires were sufficiently wobbly, especially when it came to the transfer of political power, that such an opportunity was never likely to be that long in coming.

In this instance, it was a continuation of the strained relations between Maurice and his armed forces which started the ball rolling. With his armies freed from the Persian front by the peace of 591, the emperor set them loose on the Balkans, where they proceeded to overturn some of the Avar successes of the 580s. Maurice's generals insisted, however, that, really to hurt the Avars, it was important to campaign early while the grass was not growing, since this would hamstring the operations of the key cavalry arm of the enemy's forces. As the winter of 602 approached, therefore, the field army was ordered not to return to winter quarters. By November, it had revolted and, under the leadership of an officer by the name of Phocas, was marching on Constantinople. Maurice fled the city on 22 November, but was captured with his family, and Phocas, who was crowned emperor on 24 November, had Maurice executed with four of his five sons three days later. The fifth son, Theodosius, was killed a little later along with many of the former emperor's chief ministers.

Or was he? The head of Theodosius was never displayed in Constantinople, and, only slightly later, an individual claiming to be him turned up in the train of Persian armies who said they were here to avenge the deposed Maurice, benefactor and patron of their reigning shah, Chosroes II. We really don't know if Theodosius escaped or not, but, if he did, Chosroes quickly eliminated him when he ceased to be useful. The result was a new round of cataclysmic warfare between the two great empires of antiquity.[45]

While Roman imperial politics resonated to the sound of coups and rebellions, Chosroes II proceeded, methodically, to roll up virtually the whole of the Eastern Empire. Even the arrival of a new imperial saviour, in the form of Heraclius (and his father) all the way from North Africa via a dashing sea-borne expedition which crashed into Constantinople over its sea walls in October 610, made not the slightest difference. By the end of that year, all the Roman hardpoints on the Mesopotamian front east of the Euphrates had been systematically reduced, laying the path open to grander Persian ambitions. By 607, too, Maurice's Armenian gains in the 591 treaty had been reversed, so everything in the hanging gardens of Babylon was looking pretty rosy.

In 611, Chosroes' chief commander, Shahvaraz, struck deep into Roman Syria, capturing Apamea, Antioch and Emesa. Unlike 540, however, this was no mere raid. The Persians were there to stay.

They also pushed north on to the Anatolian plateau, capturing Caesarea. In the south Damascus soon followed, leading to the loss of all of Palestine including Jerusalem in 614 and the holiest relic of them all: the True Cross reputedly uncovered by Helena, the mother of Constantine. Further north, a scorched-earth policy had been unleashed and in the same year the great city of Ephesus was stormed – bearing out, just a little late, the warnings of Revelation – its centre reduced to ash and rubble.

Chosroes II had the smell of total victory in his nostrils and refused all peace offers from an increasingly desperate Constantinopolitan political establishment, including an extraordinarily abject embassy in 616 ostensibly from the Senate (since the shah refused ever to recognize Heraclius) which offered to accept Chosroes as 'supreme Emperor' and style the Romans as his 'slaves'. A successful invasion of Egypt was duly launched and completed by 621. Sea raids were being mounted concurrently on Cyprus and the island chains of the Aegean, and the attacks continued across Asia Minor, until the nadir was reached in late July 626. At this point, the imperial capital itself faced a Persian army on the other side of the Bosphorus, and the Avar army directly outside the great Theodosian land walls.

An eye-witness description of the siege is preserved in the *Chronicon Paschale*, and makes fascinating reading. The Avar army spent several days demonstrating that it hadn't a hope of smashing through the land walls. Then came crunch time. Some of the subjugated Slavs were highly adept on the water; they'd been famous for their skill with dugout canoes throughout the sixth century, and had been known to make plenty of money out of it when ferrying retreating raiders out of Roman territory. The only possible route into Constantinople was the one Heraclius had taken: water. A vast fleet of canoes was launched therefore with the express orders of fetching Persian reinforcements from the Asian shore. The Romans held their nerve until the encumbered Slavs started to return to the European side, and then the fleet was unleashed, complete with Greek fire. The Slav armada was smashed, and, on viewing the mayhem, other Slavs in the Avar army immediately started legging it for home, requiring the khagan to turn his more loyal forces on them. The siege broke up in disarray. The high tide of Persian conquest had broken on the indomitable rock of Constantinople.

Heraclius himself was not in the city during the siege, so great was his confidence in its defences, but retraining and organizing his field forces further east on the Asian shore. Critically he also managed to negotiate an effective alliance with the Western Turks, that chimera which had led Justin II to war. In 627, a huge Turkish army stormed through the Caucasus into the Persian-dominated kingdom of Iberia. They sacked the regional capital of Tiflis, killing its Persian client king, and handed over to Heraclius 40,000 men for further operations. The emperor went straight for the kill. The combined army force marched over the Zagros Mountains and down the line of the Tigris into the Iranian heartland of the Sasanian Empire, breaking a Persian army just outside Nineveh in December. Rather than taking on the defences of the capital at Ctesiphon, Heraclius employed scorched-earth tactics to batter the economic engine of the Persian Empire. Then he sat back and watched the Persian polity implode. Chosroes II was deposed by a *coup d'état* in early 628, and a sequence of short-lived regimes followed. Eventually Heraclius got the deal he wanted. The Persians withdrew from the conquered Roman provinces, most of whose administration they had not touched, and Heraclius returned to Constantinople with the True Cross.

True, his restored empire had seen better days. Parts of the rich lands of western Asia Minor had been ravaged, and loyalties in Syria, Palestine and Egypt had been muddled by a decade and a half, in some cases, of Persian rule. The situation in the Balkans, likewise, was completely out of hand. With all troops needed on the far side of the Bosphorus, Avars and Slavs had run wild, the settlements of the latter increasing apace. Worst of all, perhaps, the imperial treasury was exhausted. In the depths of crisis, Heraclius had forced through extraordinary measures. Military pay was halved, free bread within the capital ended, the treasuries of the churches emptied of their precious metals. It had been enough, if only just, to pay off the Turks and launch the great counterstrike into Iran. And now Heraclius, armed with the prestige of victory and carrying the True Cross before him as the emblem of God's favour, could set about rebuilding the empire.[46]

Looking at the situation in *c*.630, there was no internal Roman reason why reconstruction should not have been successful. The nightmare of the previous twenty-five years had not involved greater losses for the empire than the depths of the third-century crisis, when, again, large tracts of its eastern provinces fell out of Roman rule. Then, for a decade and a half after the defeat and capture of Valerian, the city of Palmyra had become the centre of a successor state which defeated both Persians and Romans and ran an arc of territory from Egypt through to Asia Minor. And yet the empire had bounced back successfully, restoring its control under Aurelian in the mid-270s, and then refilling its treasuries from the cities' taxation flows. By the mid-fourth century, when sources from these regions had again become plentiful, loyalty to the empire was once more second nature, and the Near East was in the middle of a 300-year patch as Constantinople's heartland.

In principle, there is no reason why a similar rebuilding job could not have been undertaken by Heraclius and his successors. Yes, the Balkans were an additional problem, but they had been in the third century too, and Maurice's campaigns had shown that the Avars could be defeated. And, without the Avars, the Slavs were no worse than raiders; they were not yet capable of facing up to imperial armies in open battle. Nor were the internal religious conflicts within the empire so big a problem as is sometimes imagined. True, debate on the Council of Chalcedon was rumbling on. But if its doctrinal issues were not ultimately solvable, then neither did they threaten the fabric of empire. There is no evidence that religious dissonance had made it easier for the Persians to conquer the Roman Orient, and the quarrel over Chalcedon had shown signs of downgrading itself to minor-irritant status in the later sixth century before the great Persian crisis had broken up the hard-won consistency in imperial policy which had finally emerged on the religious front from the 580s.[47] So Heraclius had every reason for optimism as he marched back to Constantinople. What brought it all to naught was the introduction of a second new factor into the strategic geography of the Near East, one whose impact would massively outweigh that of the Western Turks. For just as Heraclius was beginning to reconstruct his empire from the ashes, an Arab world, newly united by Islam, totally overturned the old certainties of the previous thousand years.

The rise of Islam is another of those extraordinarily influential phenomena which makes the history of western Eurasia in the first millennium still so relevant to the twenty-first century. Along with the end of Rome and the ancient world order of Mediterranean domination, the rise of Christianity, and the integration of the east and north into the European mainstream, the explosion into existence of Islam is the final link in a chain of transformation which separates the medieval and modern worlds from everything that had gone before. And, like those other elements, it's a story of profound complexity. The main historical problem is a lack of early source material from within the Islamic world itself, where no narratives of the life of Muhammad now survive that date from before the ninth century. By this time, Islam had been through two major revolutions: the crisis which generated the split between Sunni and Shia Islam in the seventh century, and the Abbasid revolution of the mid-eighth century. Given his overwhelming importance, the ninth-century narratives understandably give an account of the Prophet's life which legitimizes Islam as it had evolved by that later date, but what relationship any of this may bear to the realities of the early seventh century is less certain.[48]

It is clear, however, that the backstory to the rise of Islam is deeply rooted in superpower conflict between Rome and the Persians. The Arabs of the desert fringe were the critical protagonists of that third, desert frontier zone between the two empires. It was never possible for large conventional armies to operate there, but the desert offered opportunities for raiding at least, and for distracting your opponent's attention from the Armenian and Syrian fronts to the north. Consequently, both sides recruited, paid and armed Arab allies to protect their desert underbellies, and to cause as much trouble as possible for the other side. No one bothered to write a continuous history of these Arab marches of empire, but, if you string together the patchy information available in a surviving sequence of Roman historians, one fact about Arab history from the fourth to the sixth centuries jumps out from the pages. Thanks no doubt to the wealth and weaponry both sides unloaded into the region, the size of the political networks controlled by the empire's Arab allies grew massively in extent, and hence in military power. Whereas, in the fourth and fifth centuries, the Romans operated through a series of Arab allies, by the sixth century both they and the Persians had but one each: the Ghassanids and Lakhmids respectively. And these groups were now so powerful that they had – sometimes at least – their own seat at the negotiating table, and certainly their own agendas. In other words, the Arab world, caught between two superpowers, went through a similar kind of transformation to that which affected the largely Germanic-speaking world on the fringes of the Roman Empire's European frontiers. The kinds of relationship that empires tend to establish with their neighbours has the effect, in the long run, of generating larger and more cohesive political entities in these fringes, and the Arab world was catalysed by the interference of not one, but two empires.[49]

Viewed from this perspective, the non-religious element in the career of Muhammad bears a striking resemblance to that of Attila the Hun. What Attila did was unite against Rome a series of former largely Germanic-speaking frontier clients of the Roman state, who would normally have been just as likely to quarrel among themselves as fight the empire. This created a power-bloc which was large enough to confront the empire directly, and, at its apogee, sometimes even to win. Muhammad's career has close parallels. He united Arab groupings who, over the previous 200 years, had grown accustomed to operating in ever larger and more complex military-political constellations, but which, without Muhammad, don't look at all likely to have reached the climax of unification. Where Muhammad differs so dramatically from Attila is that a powerful new religion was a fundamental element in the political authority he managed to establish, and that religion continued to operate as a unifying force after the death of the confederation's original charismatic leader. After Attila's death, the Hunnic core of his empire consumed itself in civil war, which gave so many of his subjects, like the Pannonian Goths united by Valamer (page 7), the opportunity to re-establish their independence that the Hunnic Empire ceased to exist within a generation. After Muhammad's death, the so-called *Ridda* ('Apostasy') wars saw a large enough core of key supporters retain their religious unity to prevent those who were less committed to the enterprise from breaking away. Instead of rising and falling again with equal speed, as its Hunnic parallel did in central Europe, Muhammad's unification of two empires' Arab clients endured and swiftly conquered virtually the whole of the Roman Orient and, further to the east, all of the Sasanian Empire, and much more besides. The first Islamic Arab armies appeared out of the desert in 633, and, within a generation, a millennium of binary imperial confrontation between the Graeco-Roman Mediterranean and the Persian Near East had been consigned to the dustbin of history.[50]

LEGACY

Adjusting the focus more tightly again, back on to Justinian, one inescapable conclusion emerges. It was the rise of Islam which fundamentally changed the course of East Roman imperial history. Thanks to Muhammad, and the catastrophic losses of imperial heartland to his united Arab soldiery, it proved impossible for Heraclius and his successors to pull off a repeat of the great third-century Roman imperial escape act. These losses confined the East Roman Empire to somewhere between a quarter and a third of its former territorial expanse, and many of its remaining provinces would be regularly fought over in the decades which followed. As the imperial economy collapsed, administration had to be fundamentally recast since still substantial armies had to be maintained more or less on a shoestring, because the Arabs had somehow to be fended off from what was left. The losses even generated religious recalibration because the old imperial ideologies looked increasingly hollow. Claiming to be a unique divinely guided state, destined by the Almighty to bring Christian civilization to the entire globe, lost most of its force after two-thirds of the empire had been conquered by the standard-bearers of a different religion. Fortunately, Judaeo-Christian texts offered another, now more apposite model. From divinely ordained world conquerors, emperors were able to use the Old Testament to morph themselves into the leaders of a Chosen People, riding the Constantinopolitan Ark of salvation through besetting tempests towards final Salvation and Triumph, with apocalypse a recurrently popular genre. This neat sidestep both managed to save face and avoid insulting people's intelligence, since the crushing weight of contemporary reality was overwhelming. In overall terms, the losses of the seventh century demoted what had been an East Roman world power to a Byzantine east Mediterranean regional power, which became, in effect, an unwilling satellite of the Islamic world. All periods of Byzantine expansion subsequent to the seventh century came when the Islamic world was fragmented. Whenever even a largish chunk of the Islamic world was unified, things did not go well in Constantinople.[51]

This sharpens up the line of questioning we need to pursue in relation to Justinian. The real question is whether his conquests so overstretched the empire that they were responsible not just for immediate losses of territory in Italy and the Balkans, but also, in the longer term and above all, for the empire's inability to retain its Eastern heartlands. And in my view, when you take a close look at events subsequent to Justinian's death, it becomes extremely difficult to answer this in the affirmative.

To blame Justinian for the losses of territory in Italy and the Balkans, you have to be able to blame him for the Avar Empire, and we've already seen that this is difficult to do with conviction. The same, it seems to me, is pretty much equally true of the rise of Islam. If you're a true-believing Muslim, there's no case to answer. Muhammad was sent by God, subsequent Islamic conquests were ordained by Him, and anything that Justinian could have said or done was fundamentally irrelevant. But if you're not, pinning the tail of blame on the Justinianic donkey is still far from straightforward. At most, the emperor can be ascribed only a marginal role in the emergence of greater Arab unity. He did promote a new unity among his empire's Arab federates, recognizing the current Ghassanid leader as their overall leader: an entirely unprecedented position. But he did this only reactively and unwillingly. The Persians had already united their federates under one ruler from the Lakhmids, and were able, as a result, to launch a damaging raid through Rome's desert fringes in 529, which was too powerful for any of Constantinople's not-yet-united Arab allies to oppose. For this reason, and this reason only, Justinian created a larger network of allied Arabs in response. Yet that network was itself dismantled again by the emperor Maurice in the 580s, and was not a direct ancestor of the network Muhammad put together in the 620s.[52]

Nor is the line of cause and effect very direct from Justinian to the utter financial exhaustion which made Heraclius' empire of the 630s so ripe for a takeover at the hands of Muhammad's newly united Arabs. The East Roman Empire does show signs of financial strain after Justinian's death, particularly in the reign of the emperor Maurice; but whether that owes more to Justinian or to the cataclysmic head-on conflict with Persia that his successor, Justin II, committed the empire to pursuing, convinced that the Western Turks would come galloping over the horizon at the crucial moment, needs to be thought about extremely carefully. The final half a decade of Justinian's reign was largely peaceful, even on the Persian front, and there is every reason to think that revenues from North Africa and Sicily were by this stage coming substantially on stream. Fighting Persia in Mesopotamia is what really cost the Eastern Empire money, and Justin's actions precipitated eighteen years of full-on conflict there between 573 and the treaty of 591. It is much more likely that this is what put Maurice under so much financial pressure, combined with Justin's wasted payments to the Turks, rather than continued unrequited payouts for the territories Justinian added to the empire from 533.

Nor can the imperial coffers have been much replenished in the twelve-year gap before the outbreak of the next round of Roman–Persian conflict in 603. Throughout that time, Maurice's forces were engaged in rectifying the situation in the Balkans. Fighting the Avars was probably less costly than fighting Persia, but not by much, and whatever financial savings had been made in the 590s were quickly wiped out again after 603, when cataclysmic great-power conflict erupted in the East. Not being a Muslim, I find it difficult to imagine that Muhammad's warriors would have been anything like so success-ful had they not encountered two empires who had just spent twenty-five years fighting each other to a state of bankrupt exhaustion. In other words, the success of the Arab conquest of the Roman East owes far more – in direct terms at least – to the two massive rounds of Roman–Persian conflict which immediately preceded it (and, between them, these were fully active for an extraordinary forty-three out of the fifty-five years between 573 and 628) than it does to Justinian. It was these wars which emptied the imperial treasury and loosened the empire's grip on its Eastern provinces to such an extent that Arab armies were able to roll them over so easily. If Justinian is to be blamed for the loss of the Roman Orient, you have to construct a convincing argument which can hold him *primarily* responsible for ratcheting up Roman–Persian conflict to levels of intensity unseen since the third century.

No doubt some of the blame for this *should* be placed at his door. Justinian's Italian and North African campaigns gave Chosroes I both pretext and opportunity for his successful raid into Roman Syria in 540. But during the rest of the reign, head-on conflict on the key Mesopotamian front occurred only between 540 and 546, and, other-wise, both parties were content with a more limited – and cheaper –

level of engagement on the other two sectors. And, as we have seen, Justinian's final years were distinguished by a general peace on all fronts. The real story of the more or less continuous bouts of head-on confrontation between the two empires between 573 and 628, without which the Arab conquests in the form we know them are patently inconceivable, begins anew, therefore, after Justinian's death. The political decisions of Justin II and Maurice – the one to start world war, the other to enforce a punitive peace – and the appearance of the Western Turks are fundamentally responsible for creating the conditions in which the forces of Islam could conquer the Roman Orient, and not the sporadic and limited spats with Persia which distinguish the reign of Justinian. He might well have fallen into the same hubristic traps as his successors, had he still been in charge in the 570s, but that is another question entirely.

At this point I probably should go explicitly on record, in case the preceding paragraphs make it seem like I'm being too soft on Justinian. By Roman or indeed any standards, Justinian was an autocratic bastard of the worst kind. It worried him not a jot to slaughter his own citizens in huge numbers to keep himself in power, nor to launch speculative attacks on neighbouring states with much the same end in mind, no matter what the collateral damage. He didn't quite kill his own citizens on the scale of a Hitler, a Stalin or a Pol Pot, but the ambition was there, and his reign was as authoritarianly chaotic as any of these. Nor is there any sign that he had the great dreams sometimes ascribed to him, since his regime slipped late into a policy of Western expansion and entirely out of desperation. But, all that said, it is also very difficult to blame him for the subsequent collapse of East Rome into its shadowy Byzantine successor. Yes, his Western conquests aroused some Persian envy, but not enough to propel Chosroes I into anything more than controlled, opportunistic aggression. And, yes, he did create a more unified network of Arab allies on the Roman frontier, but that was not the direct progenitor of Muhammad's military-cum-political-cum-religious alliance network.

While it would make for a much more morally satisfying story to see this entirely horrible emperor bequeathing a poisoned chalice of inevitable collapse to his successors, the argument at best limps along. Avars, Western Turks, Justin II and Maurice, Chosroes II and Muhammad all need to be brought into the story to get anywhere near a convincing understanding of Constantinople's later woes, and their collective contribution to its unfolding are, overall, much greater than that of Justinian. It is one of the most difficult challenges of them all, when writing about a very distant past, to keep a proper sense of chronological perspective. Viewed from the twenty-first century, 565 and 630 seem next door to each other, but they are actually three political generations apart, and no direct line of causation runs from Justinian to the Arab conquests. Justinian did not come to power determined to reconquer the lost Roman West, but neither did he doom Constantinople to strategic demotion.

He was certainly, however, the last ruler of Constantinople to use the resources of his Eastern heartlands to attempt to recreate a Roman Empire in the western Mediterranean and beyond. After 573, East Rome was set for fifty-five years of all-out confrontation on its eastern front, after which no ruler of Constantinople would ever again dispose of a power base large enough to rebuild a Western Empire. With the rise of Islam, the eastern Mediterranean dropped out forever from the list of potential contenders lining up to restore imperial power in the West. Both East and West had now been the bases of failed efforts at Western imperial restoration. The final serious attempt would come from the north.

PART THREE

THE FATHER OF EUROPE

5

CHRISTMAS DAY, 800

ROME: THE MORNING OF 25 DECEMBER in the year of our Lord 800. The Frankish king Charles the Great – Karolus Magnus: Charlemagne – is making a visit to the old imperial capital and enters St Peter's to celebrate Christmas Mass. What happens next is described in the broadly contemporary life of Pope Leo III in the *Liber Pontificalis* (*Book of the Pontiffs*):

> Then with his own hands the venerable bountiful pontiff, crowned [Charles] with a precious crown, and all the faithful Romans, seeing how much he defended and how greatly he loved the holy Roman Church and its vicar, at God's bidding and that of St Peter, key-bearer of the kingdom of heaven, cried aloud with one accord: 'To Charles, pious Augustus, crowned by God, great and pacific Emperor, life and victory.' Three times this was said in front of St Peter's sacred confessio, with the invocation of many saints; and by them all he was established as Emperor of the Romans.

324 years after the deposition of Romulus Augustulus, the lands of the old Roman West had a new emperor, in both name and fact, a figure of such towering beneficence that one of his court poets could style him *Pater Europae*, 'the Father of Europe'. And yet, according to Einhard, Charlemagne's biographer who knew him well, Charlemagne would later say that:

> If he had known in advance of the Pope's plan, he would not have entered the church that day, even though it was a great feast day.[1]

What is the explanation of this extraordinary statement, and how exactly had the Roman Empire come to be reborn in the person of a ruler of the Franks?

A restoration of empire based on a Frankish power base had nearly happened over 200 years earlier, when successive generations of a previous Frankish royal dynasty – the Merovingians – came within a cat's whisker of claiming the imperial title for themselves. Any real understanding of who Charlemagne was, and why the imperial title eventually came to him on Christmas Day 800, requires us to delve (briefly) into this deeper Frankish past. As the alert reader will already be recalling, we have met the Merovingians before, in the person of Clovis who went head to head with the Theoderic the Amal for bragging rights over the former Roman West in the decades either side of the year 500. Theoderic came out on top, but Clovis has long enjoyed the greater historical reputation. This is due not so much to his own achievements, prodigious though these were, as to what happened after his death. Both the rise of his Merovingian dynasty and the reasons why it never quite grasped the imperial torch help bring Charlemagne properly into focus.

LIONS (NO TIGERS) AND BEARS

There are many parallels between the backstory to Theoderic's Amal dynasty and the rise of the Merovingians among the Salian Franks. The main difference is that Attila's Hunnic Empire had little direct part to play in the Frankish story. Attila tried to interfere in the odd Frankish succession dispute, but the Franks were physically beyond his reach, and there is no record that any Frankish groups ever fought for him, or had their leadership structures rearranged at his command.

That aside, the parallels are striking. For one thing, both dynasties emerge into the light of something approximating history at the same moment. The first Merovingian of whom we know anything at all definite is Clovis' father Childeric, who died in c.480 and belonged to the same political generation as Theoderic's father and uncle who first united the Pannonian Goths and steered them into a Constantinopolitan orbit. Childeric, however, did not get quite so far along the road to monarchical authority as Valamer, a relative obscurity which perhaps explains some of the mystery which surrounds him. Apart from having – reputedly – a sea monster for a grandfather, the main puzzle he poses us is that the (highly fragmentary) reports of his activities in the 460s and 470s place him more in central Gaul, participating in events at Orleans, Angers and the mouth of the Loire: bound up in the swiftly changing alliances which mark the last generation of the old Roman West (apart, that is, from a period of exile when his followers got fed up with him seducing their women). But the power base he left his son was centred much further north-east in what is now Belgium, on the old Roman legionary base at Tournai. And this, in the end, is the most securely attested fact of all, since his tomb was uncovered there in the seventeenth century, containing – amongst many other items – a seal ring conveniently inscribed with his name.[2]

Historical records and the contents of the tomb combine to suggest that he was commander of a force powerful enough to be courted, mobilized and rewarded as the last generation of West Roman leadership struggled to hold things together. But then, like most of the other players of this complex game, he eventually realized that it was time to draw a line under things imperial and operate independently, since the Roman centre had ceased to control any assets worth worrying about. We lack a precise chronology for Childeric's moment of truth, but all the other players we know about gave up shortly after 468 when the defeat of Constantinople's great Vandal armada removed all hope of shoring up imperial authority in the West.[3] Within the constellation of figures who started to go it entirely alone at this point, however, Childeric was clearly still only a relatively minor player. Despite the impressive wealth submerged alongside him in Tournai, his son started his political life as only one of several Frankish leaders of similar stature

The pattern, however, was set for decisive change in the lifetime of his son and successor: Clovis. The new king's mother was a princess of the Thuringians called Basina, whom Childeric had met – reputedly – during the involuntary exile brought on by his sex addiction. The later seventh-century chronicler Fredegar (also the source of the sea monster story) records what happened on the night of Clovis' conception. Three times Basina woke up her husband and sent him outside to see what he could see. On the first occasion, he saw lions, unicorns and leopards; then wolves and bears; and the third time lesser beasts like dogs. You can imagine that Childeric may have been befuddled by lack of sleep, as well as slightly irritated at this point, but the queen

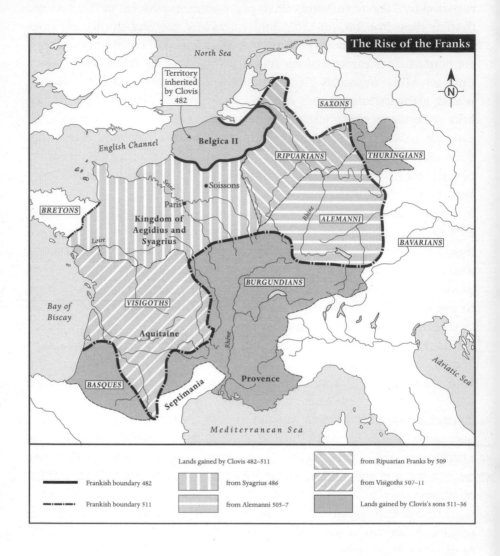

The Rise of the Franks

North Sea

Territory
inherited
by Clovis
482

SAXONS

English Channel

Belgica II

RIPUARIANS

THURINGIANS

Seine

•Soissons

BRETONS

Paris

ALEMANNI

Kingdom of
Aegidius and
Syagrius

Loire

Rhine

BAVARIANS

VISIGOTHS

BURGUNDIANS

Bay of
Biscay

Aquitaine

Rhône

Adriatic Sea

BASQUES

Provence

Septimania

Mediterranean Sea

N

Lands gained by Clovis 482–511

from Ripuarian Franks by 509

Frankish boundary 482

from Syagrius 486

from Visigoths 507–11

Frankish boundary 511

from Alemanni 505–7

Lands gained by Clovis's sons 511–36

helpfully made everything clear. The whole parade, like the vision revealed by Hecate to Macbeth, was an account of what was to come, though this time the line of Childeric's own descendants rather than someone else's. Clovis himself was the lion, of course, and three elements of his career are central to our unfolding story of Frankish Empire. Most obviously, he completed a series of military victories which greatly expanded the territory under his control. First in the firing line was a certain Syagrius, whose defeat is traditionally seen as extending Clovis' territories as far south-west as Paris, or thereabouts. This was followed by other victories which brought the Burgundians of the Rhone valley at least temporarily under Frankish hegemony, and then, in the crisis which would generate Theoderic's finest hour, massive victories over both the Alamanni and the Visigoths. Theoderic eventually imposed some counterbalancing influence over the Burgundians, and forced Clovis back too from Provence and the Mediterranean. Nonetheless, in the course of his maybe thirty-year reign, Clovis expanded his control from an originally pretty restricted corner of Belgium, to take in most of old Roman Gaul and a significant chunk of territory east of the Rhine (Figure 11).

At the same time, paralleling the efforts of Valamer and Theoderic, Clovis eliminated all the rival warband leaders within his sphere. As with much of the chronology of his reign, it is not completely clear when this happened. Our only source, the *Histories* of Gregory of Tours, presents the process as a series of Mafia-like hits organized in part through insiders, but certainly in a rush, at the end of the reign, in the aftermath of his victory over the Visigoths; that is, between 507 and 511. This may or may not be right, but there is no doubt that he effectively eliminated all his major rivals, many or most of whom – with that uplifting care for family we have encountered before among royal dynasties – were his collateral relatives. His sons alone would now inherit their father's much expanded *regnum*.[4]

The third key element of Clovis' career is that he eventually converted to Orthodox, Catholic Christianity. In this case, Gregory of Tours is certainly some way from the truth. He presents the king as going straight from convinced paganism to Catholic Christianity in the middle of the first decade of the sixth century, and winning thereby God's favour for his upcoming campaign against the Visigoths. The latter, like Theoderic, were non-Nicene Christians of the type often mistakenly labelled Arians, so that via this construction Gregory was able to present Clovis in 507 as conducting a victorious Catholic crusade against hated heretics. All very satisfactory to a Catholic churchman, but Gregory was writing three generations after the event, and more contemporary sources suggest a significantly different picture. For one thing, Clovis seems to have declared his Catholic allegiance only after his great victory, and, even more interesting, the context of this declaration was one of intense debate at the Frankish court in which it at one point looked likely that the king might throw his hat into the Arian ring: a dimension of the story which had been entirely suppressed by Gregory's time. In the end, Clovis opted for Catholicism and this too helped set the Franks on the path towards empire.[5] His new, much enlarged Frankish power base combined territories both west and east of the Rhine, a core area in what is now France, Benelux and western Germany that was destined for a long and influential history, even if the exercise of political power within it would be far from smooth.

When Clovis died in 511, the only blot on his almost imperial record was the failure to outface his great Gothic rival. His death occurred precisely in Theoderic's *annus mirabilis*, and news of it can only have added a bit of extra lustre to that creation of the united Gothic kingdom of Italy, Spain and southern Gaul (page 78). Nor was Clovis' Catholicism any trump card. In 511, Theoderic's relations with his Catholic clergy could hardly have been better, except for the fact that their best moment, when he brokered Constantinople's return to the religious fold in the early years of Justinian, was still to come. Prodigious as they were, Clovis' achievements did not rival Theoderic's, and I don't find it surprising that none of the Gallo-Roman aristocrats who had by this stage fallen under Frankish rule felt the same compunction as their Italo-Roman peers to hail their new ruler as *semper Augustus*.

However, as soon as Theoderic's united kingdom broke apart on his death, and even the Italian portion of it was riven with the political struggles first for control of Athalaric and afterwards for the throne itself, Frankish expansion – on hold since 507 – could begin again in earnest. In the early 530s, the Thuringian and Burgundian kingdoms, deprived of the support of an effective Gothic counterweight to Frankish power, were swallowed up, and more was to follow with first Provence and then extensive territories in the northern Alpine foothills being formally ceded to the Franks by Wittigis as he desperately tried to mobilize more troops for the war (above, page 156).

In addition, the sons and grandsons of Clovis – leopards, unicorns, wolves and bears – were busy on their own account east of the Rhine (Figure 11). When Clovis' grandson Theudebert wrote to Justinian in the year 540, he could with justification declare himself 'the ruler of many peoples', including Visigoths, Thuringians, Saxons and Jutes, as well, of course, as the Franks themselves. By the mid-sixth century, Clovis' descendants were close – so close they could almost smell it – to imperial power in the West, in both fact and legal claim. In one ideological dimension, they went even further than Theoderic had dared. It had long been a prerogative of Roman emperors – stretching back into the more distant past when many constituent cities of the empire had issued their own coinages – that they alone could issue gold coins. In the generations after 476, rulers of the successor states essentially respected this prerogative, maintaining only base metal coinages. Theoderic himself minted only the occasional gold medallion (Plate 8). When Merovingian kings started to issue gold denominations regularly, this represented a major break with tradition, and an affront that Procopius noted with disgust. Nonetheless, for all that they were mighty rulers, and praised with many of the epithets that used to be trotted out about emperors, still no one hailed even Clovis' grandsons as truly imperial Augusti, and there is no sign, in the extensive court-based literature of the third quarter of the sixth century, of any conscious project of imperial restoration of the kind undertaken by Theoderic. Although they got close, therefore, no member of the Merovingian dynasty ever quite managed the jump to imperial light-speed.

The reasons they didn't, I think, are straightforward. Extensive as the territories were that fell under Frankish sway in the sixth century, they were only rarely united under a single ruler. As it developed over the sixth century, the Merovingian kingdom came to have five core components – Austrasia, Neustria, Burgundy, Aquitaine and Provence – with differing degrees of hegemony being exercised over satellite territories in Thuringia and Alamannia, Bavaria, Frisia and Saxony (Figure 12). It was standard Merovingian practice even for the core areas of the kingdom to be divided between a ruler's surviving adult sons, whoever the mother, as they were on Clovis' death in 511. Many pages could be written (and have been) detailing the ensuing political struggles – featuring brief periods of unity, lots of potential heirs and nephews, early deaths and straightforward executions – but we don't need to worry about them here. Suffice it to say that any Merovingian pretensions to claim a Western imperial title were materially hampered by the fact that only occasionally was the Frankish kingdom's potentially mighty power base in the hands of just one ruler.[6]

Equally important, the kings of the Franks had to share the former Western imperial airspace with other, entirely legitimate Christian rulers. Especially after their formal conversion from Arianism to Catholic Christianity was declared at the Third Council of Toledo in 589, the Visigothic rulers of Spain and Septimania (an arc of territory in what is now south-eastern France north of the Pyrenees) drenched themselves in a Roman and Christian sacrality, which determinedly echoed that of the emperors in Constantinople. They looked for all the world like perfectly legitimate rulers of a substantial part of the old Western empire. The exact religious status of the Lombards who intruded themselves into northern Italy as Avar power began to entrench itself in the middle Danube region in the late 560s is harder to judge. The sources preserve confused – indeed confusing – indications about whether Lombard rulers were generally Catholic, Arian, or something else. But, at least on occasion, Lombard kings could do a pretty decent impression of respectable Roman-type rulership, not least in 612 when King Agilulf presented Adaloald, his son and chosen heir, to his subjects in the circus at Milan (an old imperial capital) in direct imitation of Roman ceremonial practice. And all this, of course, is to take no account of the fact that, up to the mid-sixth century, the East Roman state – complete with its own 'proper' emperor – remained a highly active force within the Italian peninsula (controlling large swathes of territory around Ravenna, Rome and in the south), not to mention maintaining a thoroughly vital governmental structure over such echt bits of the old Western Empire as North Africa, Sicily, and the Adriatic coast.[7]

At times, the Franks waged major wars against all of these peers, but, in the later sixth century, Frankish intrusions south of both the Alps and the Pyrenees tended to take the more restricted form of raiding, and there were no further serious attempts to increase the amount of former Roman territory under Merovingian control. As a result, no Merovingian was ever dominant – even by a mixture of direct and hegemonic rule – over so large a portion of the Roman West as Theoderic had been in his pomp, and, in general, Frankish imperial credentials lacked sufficient clout to overpower the claims of the other successor states, and indeed of East Rome itself.

If Clovis' sons and grandsons were mighty but not quite imperial, traditional accounts of his seventh- and early eighth-century descend-ants, the lesser beasts of Basina's dream, have been overwhelmingly shaped by historical works produced in the time of the Carolingian dynasty to which Charlemagne belonged. In particular, Einhard, once again writing early in the reign of Charlemagne's son, has left us an irresistible pen portrait of the last Merovingians.

> Nothing was left for the king to do except sit on the throne with his hair long and his beard uncut, satisfied [to hold] the name of king only and pretending to rule . . . he listened to representatives who came from various lands and, as they departed, he seemed to give them decisions of his own, which he had been taught or rather ordered [to pronounce]. Except for the empty name of 'king' and a meagre living allowance which the [mayor of the palace] extended to him as it suited him, he possessed nothing else of his own but one estate with a very small income. On that estate, he had a house and servants who ministered to his needs and obeyed him, but there were few of them. He travelled about on a cart that was pulled by yoked oxen and led . . . by a herdsman . . . In this way he used to go to the palace and so also to the public assembly of his people, which was held annually for the good of the kingdom, and in this manner he also returned home. But it was the [mayor of the palace] who took care of everything, either at home or abroad, that needed to be done and arranged for the administration of the kingdom.

Once the extraordinary history of Gregory of Tours gives out in the mid-590s, no narrative survives with anything like the same scale of circumstantial detail until you reach the Carolingian period, so that there is little with which to challenge Einhard's vivid characterization. In general terms, therefore, historians have often been happy to see later Merovingian kings as lesser beasts, their lack of authority con-demning the Frankish world to disorder, allowing power steadily to coalesce in the hands of second-rank figures: the mayors of the palace. This was the role filled by Charlemagne's ancestors in the north-eastern part of the kingdom, Austrasia (Figure 12), until his father Pippin the Short decided that enough was enough in 751 and made himself king of the Franks instead.[8]

But Einhard was writing in the third political generation after Pippin had become king, and was straightforwardly a Carolingian loyalist. What could be more convenient for the dynasty he served than the idea that the Merovingians had forfeited their right to rule through incapacity? Looked at more closely, as the last generation or two of modern scholarship has done, the sources have yielded a rather different story: one where both the later Merovingians are less useless than Einhard would have us believe and the rise of the Carolingians has become a much more contingent outcome.

Even taking this into account, though, there is not the slightest doubt that representatives of the dynasty ruling between, say, 675 and 700, were essentially occupying a much less powerful political position than their predecessors of a hundred years before. In particular, the interim had seen the rise of well-entrenched groupings of regional nobilities in all the core regions of the Frankish world, through whom any later king had to work, and the power of these nobles insulated many of the localities within those regions from the direct reach of the king. The most vivid picture we have of any of them comes not from Austrasia, but from adjacent Neustria to the west (Figure 12), where a key source, the *Book of Histories of the Franks* (the *Liber Historiae Francorum*), shows us that any Merovingian monarch was expected (not least by the author of the text) to work with and through an interrelated grouping of around half a dozen noble clans. These spent their time marrying and competing with each other for dominance within Neus-tria, which they exercised by holding the position of Neustrian Mayor of the Palace, and then, increasingly, in trying to fight off Carolingian interference.[9] Each of the core regions, in other words, had thrown up their own equivalent of the Carolingian family, and, collectively, these nexuses of nobility greatly reduced the effective power of any king, whatever his personal abilities.

This means that although the ruling dynasty was weakened, the Carolingian replacement of the Merovingians was no simple palace *coup d'état*, where the king's chief minister finally put himself in a position to oust the last member of the old line. What we see, taking the sixth, seventh and eighth centuries together, is a major restructuring of power, in which the Carolingians' seizure of control over the entire Frankish world in the eighth century represented a distinct second stage. In stage one, Charlemagne's ancestors were no more than the winners of a regional, intra-Austrasian competition, and a set of peer rivals were busy winning similar competitions in the other main regions of the Frankish kingdom.

I strongly suspect that if the Carolingians hadn't called time on the increasingly delicate balancing act that was the late Merovingian system, then a rival noble lineage from one of the other core Frankish regions would have done so instead. This does not sound like a recipe for long-term stability, since someone, somewhere was likely to get the idea of reorienting the entire political system around their own authority, if only out of fear that a competitor might do so in their place. A similar sense of instability also shows up on the periphery. Here the sixth-century Merovingians also exercised authority – partly directly, partly by occasional assertions of military hegemony – over a series of satellite areas: Alamannia, Thuringia, Bavaria and even, to a lesser extent, Saxony, which was forced to pay tributes.[10] As the seventh century wore on, these satellite areas all broke away from central control, and this too, as much as the growth of regional noble power, reflects a breaking down of the old system. A sequence of highly contingent events underlay the ability of the Carolingian line to seize total control over Francia, but, by c.700, the Merovingian line was anyway destined for the dustbin of history.

Even if Einhard's characterization of the last Merovingians was satirical, he is at least pointing us in the right direction. The period c.550 to 700 saw a massive net transfer of power from king to regional nobilities, and the result was both overall political instability, and kings who, while remaining important within the system, had lost their capacity to dominate it. This was not the result of dynastic decline that had turned lions into pussycats, and some Merovingian rulers, such as Dagobert I (who died in 639), had not forgotten how to roar; but the later Merovingians were fighting a hopeless cause in the face of structural shifts in the location of power in the Frankish world. By 700, the outer reaches of the Frankish quasi-empire of the sixth century had already fallen out of orbit and the core was fragmenting. How the

Carolingians emerged from this process of central enfeeblement brings us face to face with the career of the first great Charles of the new dynasty: Martel, 'the Hammer'.

THE HAMMER OF THE FRANKS

A centrepiece of any tour of Versailles is the Gallery of Battles. 120 metres long and thirteen wide, it was created out of a series of smaller salons by Louis Philippe in the 1830s. This – almost entirely pacific – king was desperate to show that he belonged to a martial French tradition that had culminated so recently in the career of Napoleon. As I remarked helpfully to a French former penfriend, there's no picture of Waterloo; that aside, the great battles of *l'empereur* are all there.

But the thirty-four major paintings cover a much longer time frame than this. First on the left on the standard tour is a modest 5.42 m by 4.65 m number depicting Charles Martel at the battle of Poitiers (or Tours) traditionally dated to 732, although it might have been 733. This famous battle was fought by Charles as an ally of Eudo, Duke (*dux*) of Aquitaine, who had called Charles in to help him fight off a Muslim army which had penetrated north over the Pyrenees, the old Visigothic kingdom of Spain having been wrapped up by Muslim invaders in the decade or so after their initial victory in 711. After a lengthy stand-off, battle was eventually joined and Charles was victorious, his Muslim opponent Abd ar-Rahman being left dead on the field. Traditionally, this was viewed as the moment when a potential Islamic conquest of the whole of Western Christendom was frustrated, and inspired from Edward Gibbon one of his most famous passages:

> A victorious line of march had been prolonged above a thousand miles from the rock of Gibraltar to the banks of the Loire; the repetition of an equal space would have carried the Saracens to the confines of Poland and the Highlands of Scotland; the Rhine is not more impassable than the Nile or Euphrates, and the Arabian fleet might have sailed without a naval combat into the mouth of

the Thames. Perhaps the interpretation of the Koran would now be taught in the schools of Oxford, and her pulpits might demonstrate to a circumcised people the sanctity and truth of the revelation of Mahomet.

If preserving Christendom was not enough for a day's work, then there was what lay behind Charles' great victory. In traditional narratives of the birth of feudalism, Charles was seen as a prime architect in the emergence of the heavy armoured cavalry which would be such a fundamental feature of the central European middle ages. The downside here was that mailcoats and chargers are both mighty expensive items, so Charles was also remembered as a great nationalizer of Church property, using the wealth of religious institutions to pay for the military forces which had allowed him to fend off Islam.

As so often proves to be the case with traditional views of the past – most of which became entrenched in their national psyches from the later nineteenth century as heightened nationalism and mass education coincided – neither of these twin pillars of Charles' reputation has quite stood up to closer, post-nationalist scrutiny. Abd ar-Rahman was not leading the force of certainly many tens of thousands (and sometimes, amazingly, hundreds of thousands) that he was often credited with, did not suffer catastrophic losses of manpower (although he himself certainly died), and was probably engaged in a little profitable raiding, rather than a determined war of conquest. Whatever else it may have been, Poitiers was no titanic struggle to decide the religious fate of Europe. Nor, sadly, did Charles single-handedly invent feudalism and solve the resulting funding issue. He had a reputation in the century after his death of putting considerable amounts of Church land into lay hands, but this was not a new practice. Many pieces of notionally Church land in the early Middle Ages were held by laymen in semi-permanent tenancies called *precaria*, these laymen often being 'friends' of the religious institution in question, or even relatives of its founder. This went on long before and after Charles, and the big problem with his reputation may be that his victorious career allowed him to grant these tenancies to supporters who had no track record of association with the particular institutions concerned. And while heavy armoured cavalry was in the process of becoming a defining characteristic of Frankish warfare in the eighth century, this seems to have been a steady

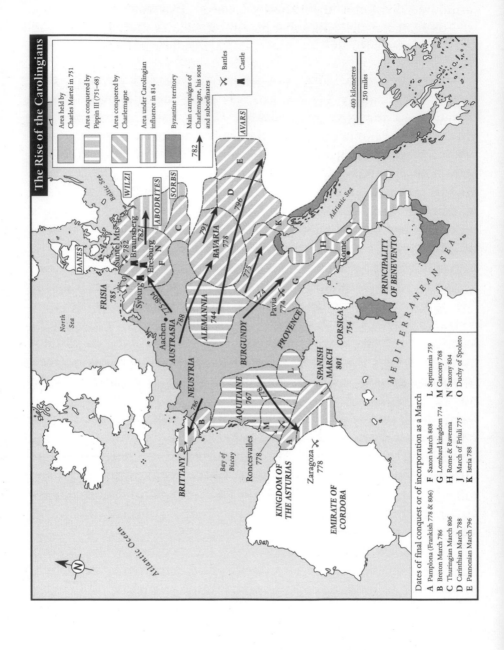

The Rise of the Carolingians

Area held by Charles Martel in 751
Area conquered by Pippin III (751–68)
Area conquered by Charlemagne
Area under Carolingian influence in 814
Byzantine territory
Main campaigns of Charlemagne, his sons and subordinates

782 →

✗ Battles
♜ Castle

400 kilometres
250 miles

Dates of final conquest or of incorporation as a March

A Pamplona (Frankish 778 & 806)
B Breton March 786
C Thuringian March 806
D Carinthian March 788
E Pannonian March 796

F Saxon March 808
G Lombard kingdom 774
H Rome & Ravenna
J March of Friuli 775
K Istria 788

L Septimania 759
M Gascony 768
N Saxony 804
O Duchy of Spoleto

DANES
WILZI
ABODRITES
SORBS
AVARS

Baltic Sea
North Sea
Atlantic Ocean
Bay of Biscay
MEDITERRANEAN SEA
Adriatic Sea

FRISIA 785
AUSTRASIA
NEUSTRIA
BRITTANY
AQUITAINE
BURGUNDY
PROVENCE
ALEMANNIA
BAVARIA
SPANISH MARCH 801
CORSICA 754
PRINCIPALITY OF BENEVENTO
KINGDOM OF THE ASTURIAS
EMIRATE OF CORDOBA

Aachen
Sankt-Mes.
Braunsberg 782
Eresburg 782
Syburg 775–98
772–98

Roncesvalles 778
Zaragoza 778
Pavia 774
Rome

785
786
767
716
744
778
775
774
791
796

N

evolution, not a one-generation revolution like the emergence of the armoured division in the 1930s.[11] But even if we can't hang on to all the trappings of the traditional picture of Charles Martel, there is still no doubt that his career set the Carolingian dynasty decisively on the road to imperial power.

Not that such an outcome looked remotely likely on the death of his father Pippin of Heristal in December 714. This is the first recorded moment when Carolingian skeletons start tumbling out of cupboards, and a nasty round of familial in-fighting plays a major role in the story. The immediate problem was Pippin himself. He had produced two sons with his current wife Plectrude: Drogo and Grimoald. Both, however, predeceased him. Drogo died in 707, and Grimoald just before his father earlier in 714, Grimoald leaving one male heir of his own: Theudoald. But Pippin also had two other adult sons by his concubine Alpaida, Charles (our Charles) and Childebrand. Desperate to protect her grandson's interests, Plectrude had her stepsons, Theudoald's half-uncles, imprisoned, although the redoubtable Charles soon escaped to rally a formidable body of Austrasian supporters.

Although a normal enough kind of intra-familial spat – which would be a regular feature of Carolingian history from now on – the dispute had dire consequences in 714 because Pippin's dominance over the Frankish world had had distinct limitations. As a result, a long list of the aggrieved parties lined up to exploit the political paralysis engendered by the quarrel between Plectrude and her stepson Charles. First in line, not surprisingly, were the Neustrians in the old Frankish heartlands. At the time of Pippin's death, Theudoald was notionally mayor of the palace for Neustria, but Pippin's control there had really only been negative – making sure that no serious rival emerged – and, once death had removed him from the scene, elements of the Neustrian nobility quickly asserted themselves, immediately throwing off any residual allegiance to Theudoald. Beyond the core, the Aquitanians were very ready to use the crisis to assert a greater degree of independence and, as quickly as 715, appear as participants in the action under their own Duke Eudo, as do the Provençales under *dux* Antenor. Even forces from outside the traditional Frankish ring were drawn into the action. Pippin's pre-eminence had always been partly based on successful campaigning beyond Frankish borders. One of his victims had been the Frisians under King Radbod, defeated heavily in 690 and 695. But Radbod remained sufficiently powerful afterwards for

Pippin to marry his son Grimoald to Radbod's daughter, so that Theudoald was Radbod's grandson as well as Pippin's. Radbod, therefore, was ready to weigh in, quite probably with entirely mixed motives in mind, since a decisive reassertion of independence was an attractive goal for him, whether this was achieved by putting a grateful grandson in power, or by defeating Charles and his Austrasian supporters.

In 715, Charles' position was extremely perilous. Many of his father's henchmen had rallied to his standard, but the coalition of his enemies was potentially overwhelming, and the first omens were far from good. Radbod inflicted some kind of defeat on Charles fairly early in 715, but maybe his Austrasian support was not fully mobilized at that point. Certainly, Charles was able to return the favour later in the year and drive Radbod's forces back into Frisia, and that is the last we hear of Radbod in the war, so it was presumably a major victory. The Neustrians, meanwhile, had been far from idle. One Ragenfrid quickly emerged there as mayor of the palace, operating under a Merovingian flag of convenience in the persons first of Dagobert III, and, then, after his death, of Chilperic II. Two substantial but indecisive battles were fought in April 716 and spring 717, by which time Charles had found his own Merovingian, Chlothar IV.

The real showdown came in spring 718 by which time the Aquitanians under Eudo had joined in the struggle to throw over the Austrasian hegemony that Charles now represented. But this time Charles' victory proved decisive, and in its aftermath he was able to stomp right across the Neustrian heartland, capturing the city of Orleans.

Immediate military victory was also turned into lasting political control. In particular, he appointed key supporters to leading positions in the Neustrian heartland, which his father had never done, including his half-nephew Hugh, Drogo's son, who was made abbot of two rich monasteries and five sees including Paris and Rouen. By 720, Charles' position was further consolidated (Chlothar IV having died) when Eudo handed over to him Chilperic II and a substantial quantity of treasure.[12]

Although it had been touch and go, Charles was firmly in control by the early 720s. At that point, the internal Carolingian succession dispute was done and dusted. Drogo's son Hugh received an astonishing pay-off, but he had obviously declared his loyalty to Charles at an early date. Other male descendants of Drogo and Grimoald were less fortunate. Charles didn't have them killed, not even Theudoald, but by 723 they were all safely in custody and there they remained. Moreover, Charles had not only re-established Austrasian hegemony over Neustria, but taken it to a new level. There was now no Neustrian mayor of the palace at all, and Charles was appointing key supporters to rich and influential positions in the Neustrian heartland, a move which had been well beyond his father's political reach. As yet, the old core regions of Burgundy, Provence and Aquitaine (not to mention the satellite duchies) were independent of his control, but much of this would follow before Charles' death in 741.

The details of his subsequent campaigns don't need to delay us, not least since it is impossible to reconstruct them in great detail anyway. But the most plausible outline runs as follows. By the 730s, Charles' effective control had reached Burgundy, where he was now appointing more of his supporters to key positions. Whether this political pre-eminence had required much in the way of actual campaigning, is unclear. Some aristocratic elements within Provence, however, certainly were ready to resist. They had their own duke, one Maurontius, and when Charles started to flex his muscles in their direction, some were ready to fight. Maurontius also negotiated some assistance from his Muslim neighbours, who had taken over, along with the rest of the kingdom, the old Visigothic toehold north of the Pyrenees: the province of Septimania centred on Narbonne. But Charles had allies within Provence too. One of the most interesting documents to survive from this era is the will of the Patrician Abbo (from 739), a major Provençale landowner, who campaigned alongside Charles and received plentiful rewards in return. Of the satellite duchies, the Hammer's domination over Alamannia was pretty much complete by 734, when he expelled the sitting ducal line, and relations with Bavaria – following some initial conflict – were close and amicable, Charles having taken Swanahild, a Bavarian princess, as his second wife in the 720s. Elsewhere, he had asserted his power regularly over the Frisians, who still retained some autonomy, but had made only occasional noises in the direction of the Saxons.[13]

By the time of his death on 22 October 741, Charles' overall achievement was enormous. Of the old core regions of Merovingian Francia, only Aquitaine was beyond his direct control, and his influence over the satellite duchies was considerable. A clear sign of the self-confidence he felt in his later years was that, when his final choice of

Merovingian frontman, Theuderic IV, died in 737, he felt no need to appoint another. For the last four years of his life, Charles ruled Francia in his own name, not as king, but as Duke and Prince of the Franks (*Dux et Princeps Francorum*), and it does seem likely enough that, from the 720s onwards, the Merovingians were finally reduced to the kind of job description set out for them by Einhard. But one important question remains: why was he so successful?

What really needs to be explained, in fact, is how he managed his initial victories. Once he had started to win, then a straightforward logic set in, which meant that one success would generate another. This worked both in Francia and elsewhere in early medieval Europe too, and the reason behind it was simple enough. After the disappearance of the military structures of the old Roman Empire, military forces came to consist in large measure not of full-time professionals, but of landowners accompanied by contingents of their more capable dependants, which probably – for richer landowners at least – included a handful of more or less professional heavies. These landowners had a recognized duty to provide military service, but served much more readily under a leader who was likely to bring victory in his train; that is, one who already had a convincing track record. This was not just because you were less likely to be killed, but also because a victorious leader was expected to reward loyal service with great generosity, both in the form of moveable wealth (as exemplified in the astonishing gold wealth of the seventh-century Staffordshire hoard recently unearthed in England – Plate 00 – and Frankish kings were much richer than their English counterparts), and – for the more prominent – landed estates of one kind or another. Both forms of wealth tended anyway to be much more available to a winner than a loser, since winners were entirely within their rights to confiscate treasure and landed assets from defeated opponents. This is why Charles had negotiated hard with Eudo for the return of both Chilperic and his treasure at the end of the war, and it was precisely the process of rewarding loyal supporters (such as Drogo's son Hugh) with Neustrian assets which generated the Hammer's reputation for being overly liberal with Church property.

From the moment of his decisive victory in 718, Charles' record of success became a massive encouragement to potential new supporters to sign up with him, since he already had plenty to give away. And this same willingness to serve him on the part of further bodies of

militarized landowners (such as the network of Abbo and his supporters in Provence) in turn made it more likely that there would be more
victories and yet more rewards in due course. But for this virtuous
circle to kick in, you do have to win that initial victory, and this is
precisely what our sources fail to explain. It is possible to offer a couple
of observations, however, which must be pretty much along the right
lines. First, it was not really that surprising that most of the militarized
landowners of Austrasia decided to back Charles Martel as Pippin's
heir, rather than his grandson Theudoald. We don't know when
exactly Theudoald was born, but he was only a child, and certainly
not fit to provide the kind of effective military leadership required in
the political crisis unleashed by Pippin's death. Charles was an adult
male of twenty-eight, and a much more plausible candidate. He had
also been playing some kind of public role in his father's entourage for
many years, probably serving on some of the campaigns. He had every
chance to build up working relationships with at least some of his
father's key supporters, and this is presumably why they supported
him rather than his step-nephew.

The choices of these militarized Austrasian landowners also had a
second dimension of importance. Not only did they pick Charles, but
they seem to have served him as a coherent block with a considerable
degree of group loyalty. At least, there is no sign in the sources that
any Austrasians saw a Neustrian leader as potentially a better source
of rewards than their own man. Even in the crisis years of 715 and
716, Charles appears to have been able to count on solid Austrasian
support (although, of course, it was important that he managed not to
suffer any major defeats at this juncture). This has to reflect the
relative political solidity that his father Pippin had built up among
these key supporters during his own lifetime of political success. From
at least the time of his decisive victory over all-comers at the battle of
Tertry in 687 – celebrated in the Carolingian histories of Charlemagne's
time as the start of the dynasty's effective domination of the Frankish
world – Pippin had generated loyalty by handing out rewards aplenty,
obtained both within Francia and by regular campaigns outside it
(whose importance we will look at in the next chapter). It was probably
this broader inheritance of his father's militarily resilient force which
got Charles through the initial testing years.[14]

The only drawback to Charles' reign was that, on his death in
October 741, he left his domains facing a succession which was much

more complicated, in its way, than his own had been some twenty-seven years before. On one level, things were easier. No major Neustrian magnate, or one from anywhere else within the heartlands of Francia for that matter, attempted to use succession as an opportunity to overthrow Carolingian dynastic dominion. And that is a real measure of Charles' political achievement within Francia, because the intra-dynastic quarrel that soon followed was so messy that, had the Hammer's rule not been so securely established, you really would have expected some aristocratic networks from somewhere within a nexus of Neustria, Burgundy or Provence to have at least attempted to reassert their independence.

Within the dynasty itself, however, the fallout from Charles' demise was both spectacular and far-reaching. The Duke and Prince of the Franks left three adult sons by two legitimate marriages: Carloman and Pippin from his marriage to Rotrude (daughter of the Bishop of Trier – best not to ask . . .) and Grifo from his second wife, the Bavarian princess Swanahild. He also had three other sons with his concubine Ruodhaid, who never figured in anyone's political calculations as far as we can see. According to the chronicler Fredegar (actually a continuator adding to the original seventh-century text), Charles decided just before his death, in 740, that his domains should be shared only between the two sons of Rotrude. But this continuation was written later, and there are good indications that Charles had a three-way split in mind, including Grifo in the mix.

Carloman and Pippin, however, didn't hesitate, and the body count begins to rise. They executed poor old Theudoald, the last remaining male descendant of Pippin and Plectrude who had long languished in a kind of protective custody, showing far less compunction than their father. Their half-brother Grifo was imprisoned at more or less the same time, and his mother, Swanahild, packed off to a nunnery. Having cleared out the dynastic undergrowth, they then divided their father's lands between them in 742, before, interestingly, finding themselves a tame Merovingian frontman – the last ever, Childeric III by name – and appointing him king in 743.

It's sometimes thought that this was to forestall any possible political unrest from other, non-Austrasian sections of the Frankish nobility, who might have seen succession as offering a last-ditch opportunity to resist the hitherto seemingly unstoppable rise of the Carolingian line. But there's no other sign of serious internal Frankish unrest, and my own suspicion is that appointing a Merovingian was meant to help keep the peace between two brothers who – to judge by the amount of fraternal amity knocking around within the family – must always have been potential rivals once they had cleared out Grifo and the rest. Whatever the precise driver, the brothers then showed themselves completely ruthless towards outsiders as well. The Aquitanians were determined to hold on to their autonomy, so battle commenced on that front, while attempted resistance on the part of some of the Alamanni led Carloman to call a council of all the nobility of the region to the old fortress of Canstatt in 746. There he assassinated them, liberating their goods and lands for distribution to his own largely Austrasian henchmen.[15]

At this point, matters seemed settled, but this turned out to be only stage one of a two-stage succession process. For in 747, the year after the Canstatt massacre (so it is known), Carloman took the extraordinary decision to withdraw from Frankish politics and head off to Rome for the good of his soul (not, to start with, actually to become a monk). Whether this was linked to Canstatt in some way is unknowable; it has been suggested, for instance, that he might have been filled with remorse. Possibly, but an alternative scenario would be that the massacre and financial redistributions were designed to generate the warmest possible feelings of loyalty towards himself and his line at a moment when he was planning to disappear. For Carloman's plan was that his son Drogo should succeed him, and for any such plan to work, as Plectrude had found to her cost in 715, you needed consent from a critical mass of your warrior aristocracy.

To start with, all seemed well. Carloman trotted off to Rome and there are documents from 747–8 suggesting that Pippin initially ruled equably enough alongside his nephew Drogo; both, at least, held reforming Church councils in 748 (a highly significant point to which we will return in Part IV). But then the pattern of Frankish politics changed forever. With very little fanfare or even explanation in our sources, Pippin suddenly emerges – by himself – as king of the Franks, after a consecration of some kind was held probably in 751 (although it could just about have been 752). For such a massive, game-breaking event as the deposition of the last Merovingian and the crowning of the first Carolingian monarch, you would expect a great deal of historical noise. The fact that it's not there, and that in some places our sources preserve slightly contradictory accounts of what happened, speaks volumes. Pippin's accession to the ranks of royalty involved considerable self-assertion on his part, assertion which was – and this is the potentially embarrassing part – directly at the expense of other close members of his family.

The process began late in 748, when Drogo disappears from the sources. In April of that year, Pippin's wife Betrada had given birth to Pippin's first son, the future Charlemagne, and some have wondered if the birth was a significant moment in the development of Pippin's calculations, giving him an obvious reason to eliminate his nephew from the picture. My own preference would be more along the lines that Pippin couldn't make a move against Drogo until he had first prepared the ground by building up the right kind of contacts with enough of his brother's former key supporters. When push came to shove, would his father's men stand up and fight for Drogo or would they accept Pippin's leadership? It looks as though Pippin did his job extremely well, in fact, for there is no record of any major conflict in 749–50 and I suspect that a real civil war – however embarrassing – would have crept into the historical record. Drogo had enough support, it seems, to stay out of Pippin's clutches, but not enough to resist him on the field of battle, and someone else took the opportunity to muddy the waters still further by helping Grifo to escape from custody as well.

But none of this was enough to prevent Pippin's political band-wagon rumbling towards its final destination. Later sources make great play of the positive reply received to a letter sent by 'the Franks' to the Pope asking whether the man holding real power should hold the royal title, rather than a powerless cipher. But it is unclear that any such letter was ever sent (there are inconsistencies in the accounts), and, as a myth, it was an excellent device for smearing a veneer of divinely ordained legitimacy over Pippin's aggressive self-assertion. Pippin's original coronation in 751/2 was a purely Frankish affair, which may or may not have involved an Old Testament-type anointing. Only subsequently was the Pope brought in to add his blessing. Pope Stephen had his own reasons for travelling to Francia in 753/4, as we shall see in a moment, but, for Pippin, it was all extremely convenient. A second ceremony was arranged for 754, this one certainly involving an anointing, which helped tie up the final loose ends. In 753, with the Pope on the road, Drogo and his never-named younger brother were definitively brought into custody, and Grifo was assassinated. Carloman himself also came back to Francia in the Pope's wake, but was promptly despatched to the monastery where he would die in 755.

Carloman's final journey has generated endless speculation. Was he trying to save his son? There is also a late report that he came as an emissary on behalf of the Lombards. But after Pippin's coronation there was no possible way back for Drogo to a share of power, and I strongly suspect that Carloman's return to Francia was demanded by Pippin as part of the price for the alliance that the Pope was trying to stitch together. For, having got rid of his offspring, Carloman represented the final loose end that Pippin would not want to leave dangling. Perhaps Carloman's return was the price he had to pay to ensure that his son might live out his days in a monastery (as he seems to have done) and not share the fate of the assassinated Grifo. Either way, the papal visit was no more than a bit of useful icing on a fundamentally Frankish cake, and most – or enough – of Carloman's old supporters had clearly accepted their invitations to the ceremony.[16]

With that, the line of Austrasian mayors set the seal on their rise to royal power. Charles Martel blew away the opposition, placing his line on a pedestal far above their former peers in the other core regions of Francia. Pippin's political manoeuvring then helped everyone reach the natural conclusion to his father's career: Carolingians and not Merovingians should now supply the kings of the Franks.

THE DONATION OF CHARLEMAGNE

Like our two previous Western imperial revival acts, the stench of contingency hangs over the events leading up to Christmas Day 800. There is no sign that Pippin entertained even the vaguest of imperial ambitions, and many accidents had to coincide before the thought took shape for his son. But it is true nonetheless that the reasons which made Pope Stephen willing to travel to Francia, to play his walk-on part in the second ceremonial expression of Pippin's acquisition of the mantle of royalty, form the crucial backdrop to Charlemagne's imperial title.

They had their roots in events 2,000 kilometres and more to the east. As we saw in the last chapter, the first round of Muslim conquests in the middle decades of the seventh century robbed the East Roman Empire of its richest Middle and Near Eastern possessions, and demoted it from world to regional power status. But this was not yet the end of its struggles. Conflict with the caliphate intensified again from the 690s and the early 700s, with the imperial capital facing besieging Muslim forces for a full year in 717–18. It survived, but only by the skin of its teeth, and further debilitating losses in Asia Minor followed in the 720s and 730s. The eastern front simply had to be Constantinople's chief priority, and there was no military or economic capacity to spare for the still substantial parts of Italy which had been left in its control in the immediate aftermath of Lombard invasion. As we shall see in more detail in Chapter 7, this both allowed the region around the city of Rome to emerge as an independent state under papal control, which called itself the Republic of St Peter, and encouraged Lombard kings to develop ever more expansionary ambitions within the peninsula.

Initially, the papacy had found that an alliance with the independent Lombard Duke of Spoleto was sufficient to fend off the Lombard monarchy in the north, but by the 740s Pope Zachariah was forced to deal directly with them, negotiating peace (at the cost of some cessation of territory) with King Liutprand (712–44). But as the Byzantine position continued to weaken, by 751 – when Pippin was having himself crowned king – Liutprand's successor Aistulf was marching victoriously into Ravenna and the neighbouring duchy of the Pentapolis (based on five Adriatic coastal cities between Rimini and Ancona: Figure 13). Aistulf's forces were also moving into the Istrian peninsula and had already made a separate peace with the Venetians. His eyes then turned greedily towards Rome.[17]

It was this new strategic situation which set Pope Stephen on the road to Francia in 753. He was happy enough to see Constantinopolitan influence reduced, but had no desire for Byzantine domination to be replaced by that of Lombard monarchs. In his eyes, the Franks were the obvious counterweight to Lombard ambitions, and, because he wanted the Pope's formal blessing for his action, Pippin was ready to play the prescribed role. Ready, that is, up to a point. In both 755 and 756, he led armies across the Alps and besieged the Lombard king in his capital at Pavia. In 755, Aistulf had agreed to hand over to the

Pope control of the territories of the old exarchate and Pentapolis, but, as soon as Pippin left for home, Aistulf went back on his word and launched his own siege of Rome. Pippin therefore returned for a repeat of the same Pavian routine, and a similar outcome. Aistulf agreed to the same deal once again (as did his successor Desiderius in turn in 757), and Pippin returned to Francia where he faced much more pressing issues.

And there, for the remainder of Pippin's reign, the situation rested. Nothing was done to enforce the agreed handover of assets, and the Lombard monarchy was content broadly to leave Rome in peace, so that a new equilibrium had been reached in post-Byzantine northern and central Italy. This suited Pippin and his magnates who were much more interested in their own affairs. The odd campaign against the Saxons aside (such as in 753 and 758), Pippin's focus was for the remainder of his reign firmly set on securing his control of Gaul. From 752 to 759, first of all, a series of ultimately successful campaigns were fought to bring the old Visigothic province of Septimania, now under Muslim management, under his control. Then attention turned to Aquitaine, which had been fully a part of the sixth-century Merovingian kingdom, but where a tenacious ducal house had established an independent position in the early eighth century. From 759, Pippin inexorably ground away at Aquitaine, until, after a series of defeats, the then Duke Waifer (grandson of the Eudo with whom Charles Martel had fought at Poitiers in 732) was assassinated by some of his own men in 768. The struggle was fast approaching its endgame, therefore, when Pippin himself died: unexpectedly, it seems, in September 768. This allowed Waifer's son Hunoald a brief glimmer of hope. Much more important, a new succession saga was about to erupt which would tie the Carolingian line much more firmly to the papacy and eventually generate its claim to the Western imperial throne.[18]

Pippin's death occasioned no challenge whatsoever to the Carolingian line from within Francia, power passing smoothly to his two sons Charles and Carloman. But the familial fraternal tradition ran true to form and, within a year, the two were at loggerheads. After an initial demonstration of solidarity, it was left to Charles to finish off Hunoald of Aquitaine by himself in 769, therefore, while, in the meantime, his mother looked to arrange a marriage alliance between himself and a daughter (probably called Gerperga) of the Lombard king Desiderius. Another of Desiderius' daughters was also married to the Duke of

Bavaria, so this marriage looks as though it was meant to stitch up an alliance network of Charles, the Lombards and the Bavarians, which left out – and hence threatened – Carloman in the middle (Figure 12). The two brothers had the same parents, so it was not just stepmothers like Plectrude, it seems, who played favourites. Later sources present Carloman as peevish, self-pitying and easily flattered, so she may have been moved by clear-headed if rather ruthless analysis of which of her sons was more likely to make the best king (the same kind of analysis which – alongside questions of greed and self-interest – also guided the political choices of key aristocrats), but these characterizations all date long after his death. Nor was Carloman the only one to feel threatened. The marriage negotiations also generated surviving letters from Rome, where Pope Stephen was having kittens at the prospect of a marriage alliance between one of the Frankish kings and the Lombards who still hovered so menacingly over papal territories (and who still had not fulfilled any of the promises laid out in the agreements of the 750s).

Whether – or more likely *when* – fraternal frostiness would have given way to conflict is unclear, because contingency intervened again in the form of Carloman's early death on 4 December 771. Charles took immediate control of his brother's kingdom, and it's perhaps an indication that Carloman was neither loved nor effective that his magnates showed not the slightest inclination to resist. Charles also terminated the marriage negotiations with the Lombards, which makes it pretty evident that the purpose had been an alliance network against his brother, which the latter's death had now rendered redundant.

The consequences were fascinating. In an extraordinary volte-face, Carloman's widow, Gerberga (that's Gerberga with a 'b', not Gerperga with a 'p'), fled for refuge to the Lombard king: so much did she trust Charles with the fate of his nephews and nieces. Desiderius was not only seriously aggrieved by the breaking off of the marriage nego-tiations and hence willing to receive her, but also clearly decided that all bets were off with the Franks and started, once again, to roll up the papal possessions in central Italy which he had previously left alone at Frankish insistence. He was probably also encouraged in this by the death of Pope Stephen in January 772 and the accession of Hadrian I. The first months of any new ruler's reign provide an excellent moment for testing his mettle.

Whether, or how much, Charles would have cared about Desider-ius breaking out of the reservation in other circumstances is unclear,

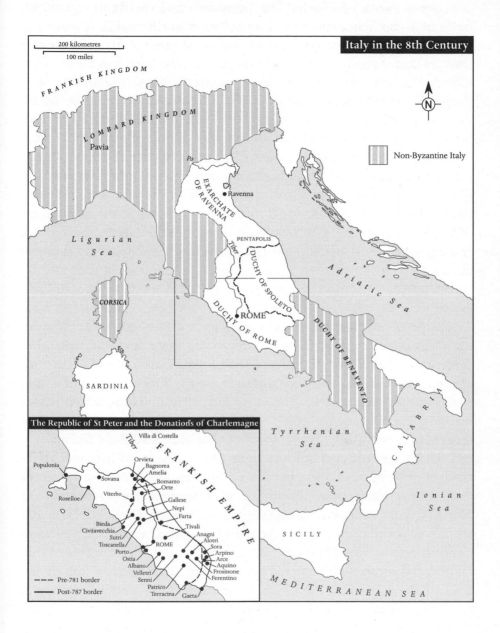

Italy in the 8th Century

FRANKISH KINGDOM

LOMBARD KINGDOM
Pavia

Non-Byzantine Italy

N

Po

EXARCHATE OF RAVENNA
Ravenna

Ligurian Sea

PENTAPOLIS

Tiber

DUCHY OF SPOLETO

DUCHY OF ROME

ROME

Adriatic Sea

CORSICA

DUCHY OF BENEVENTO

SARDINIA

Tyrrhenian Sea

CALABRIA

The Republic of St Peter and the Donations of Charlemagne

Ionian Sea

Tiber

Villa di Costella

FRANKISH EMPIRE

Populonia

Orvieta
Bagnorea
Amelia

Sovana

Bomarzo
Orte

SICILY

Roselloe

Viterbo

Gallese
Nepi
Farta

MEDITERRANEAN SEA

Bieda
Civitavecchia
Sutri
Toscanella
Porto
Ostia
Albano
Velletri
Senni
Patrico
Terracina

Tivali
Anagni
Alotri
ROME
Sora
Arpino
Arce
Aquino
Frosinone
Ferentino

Gaeta

– – – Pre-781 border
—— Post-787 border

but he was pressed by powerful dynastic reasons, and, late in 773, led a large army over the Alps. The Lombard king clearly thought that he was in for a replay of 755 and 756 when Pippin had not had sufficient political confidence to stay away from the Frankish heartland for any length of time. All his predecessor had had to do was hide behind the walls of Pavia, agree to a face-saving treaty, and the Franks would depart with no serious harm done. Charles, however, was confident enough to stay: this again indicates that spreading his authority into his brother's domain had not generated any potentially dangerous political bitterness. The Frankish army besieged Pavia throughout the winter, and Charles made a lengthy visit to Rome. By Easter 774, Desiderius realized that the situation was hopeless and surrendered. He was sent north to become a monk at the monastery of Corbie, while Carloman's children were handed over to their uncle and mysteriously disappear. No one records where those bodies were buried.[19]

At this point, we need to start making an acquaintance with some of the ideas behind one of the most important forgeries of all time: the *Donation of Constantine*. In full and final form, these original ideas and a few more besides would be embodied in a bogus document – the *Constitutum Constantini*, to give it its formal title – which claimed to preserve the text of an official grant of the first Christian Roman emperor, Constantine I. In it, the emperor grants to Pope Sylvester I and his successors, as inheritors of St Peter, dominion not only over the city of Rome, but also over the entire territory of the old Western Empire: everything from Hadrian's Wall to the Atlas Mountains of North Africa. Constantine is making this staggering gift, so the *Donation* tells us, in joyful response to Sylvester's Christian teaching and baptism, and also because the Pope had miraculously cured him of leprosy. The *Constitutum* as we have it would be forged in quite another context, as we shall see in the final chapter, but some of the key ideas incorporated into this later fake were alive and kicking in later eighth-century Rome. They first appear in a letter of 778 which came to Charles from Pope Hadrian I, and which survives because the Franks maintained a file of their papal correspondence, which was later written up and preserved as the *Codex Carolinus*. The letter comes complete with a famous exhortation:

And just as, in the times of the blessed Roman pontiff Sylvester, God's holy, catholic and apostolic Roman Church was raised up and exalted by, and through the bounty of, the most pious Constantine of holy memory, great emperor, who deigned to bestow power in these western regions upon it, so also, in these most happy times in which you and we live, may the holy Church of God, that is of St Peter the apostle – burgeon and exult and continue ever more fully exalted.

So, no prizes for verbal economy, but that was not the point.

The sudden appearance of this idea set was closely related on certainly one and probably two levels to how Charles had responded to the surrender of Desiderius. Highly contingent family matters may originally have brought the Frankish king to Italy, but, having destroyed the current Lombard monarchy to resolve them, Charles took the opportunity to advance his royal status to an unprecedented level. Rather than finding himself a pliant puppet prince from somewhere among the higher Lombard nobility, Charles proceeded to do something which no one had done for several hundred years: declare himself king of the state his forces had just conquered. He did not abolish the concept of the Lombard kingdom, or many of the details of its separate operation, but he added the new title to his existing one, and from the summer of 774 onwards became king of both the Franks and the Lombards. Many of the old officials and nobles would be left in place, but Charles made sure, in the years that followed, that this happened on his terms. In both title and fact, he added the Lombard kingdom to the united Frankish kingdom that he had created by eliminating his brother's line.

In this highly charged context, the story of Constantine's gifts to Sylvester – although some of it at least was several centuries old at this point: the Pope baptizing and curing the emperor are total nonsense but appear in the sixth-century life of Sylvester in the *Liber Pontificalis* – acquired a new and entirely immediate significance. Since the Lombard extinction of Byzantine rule over the exarchate of Ravenna and the cities of the Pentapolis, popes had been anxious not only that Rome might be next on the Lombard shopping list, but also, in more positive vein, to secure their hold on any old papally owned landed estates within these regions that now fell under Lombard rule, and establish a papal right to some of their old public revenues (generated by such devices as taxes, tolls, percentages of legal fines). It was precisely on such matters that Pope Stephen had extracted promises from Pippin in the mid-750s, but Pippin had never delivered much in practice.

Once his son had made himself king of the Lombards, however, the situation looked much more promising. Charles was in total control of the disputed territories, and in a position to make substantial grants. Nothing happened immediately, though, and, as a result, Hadrian's letters from the later 770s are full of references to Charles' need – for the good of both their souls, of course – to fulfil the promises made by his father. In this context, the claim that, back in the fourth century, the emperor Constantine had made such enormous gifts to Pope Sylvester had a straightforward significance. At this point, Hadrian did not have control of the old Western Empire in mind, but something much more prosaic. Having started by referring back to Constantine in such a grandiose manner, Hadrian's letter then got down to real business. Charlemagne is directly equated to the old emperor as 'a new Constantine', and, by dint of the equation, urged to follow the example of his generosity to the Church of St Peter. The Pope here particularly mentioned 'possessions in the Tuscan regions, Spoleto and Benevento, Corsica, and the Sabine patrimony', and sent to the king, along with the letter itself, his representatives armed with the appropriate documentation to prove the Pope's legal rights over these properties in which he was claiming a financial interest.[20]

In the end, all the pressure paid off, although, to be fair, it took Charles several years to consolidate his hold on his new Italian territories, and he may always have been intending to make the grants that he eventually did. Either way, in 781 and again in 787 he made two block grants of financial rights to the papacy, which gave Hadrian much of what he had been asking for since 774. The original texts of these grants do not survive, but we do have the confirmation of them granted by his son Louis the Pious in 819, and they were seriously generous. Charles did not give the papacy full sovereignty over the old Byzantine territories of the exarchate and the Pentapolis, which it looks as though his father Pippin might have promised, but he did grant Hadrian certain new rights in these areas as well as returning to him many individual papal estates dispersed across these lands. In separate grants, he also transferred to the Pope full sovereignty over new blocks of territory on every side of the city of Rome, mostly in

781, but with a supplement in 787 after the conquest of Benevento. The island of Corsica was then thrown in for good measure (Figure 13). All in all, the king guaranteed the papacy a massive increase in its annual revenues.[21]

One thing that is always extremely difficult to judge is the degree of mendacity involved in the creation and transmission of a bogus view of the past. Part of the Constantine and Sylvester story – the baptism and cure – was such an old lie by the time of Pope Hadrian I that he probably just thought it true. Whether this was also true of his letter's extra dimension, that cure and baptism led to a massive transfer of authority to the see of Rome, is impossible to know. In a context where the papacy was having to reconstitute itself in the face of the sudden explosion into Italy of Frankish power, the new connection was so convenient that you do wonder if a papal adviser dreamed it up as Hadrian was busy dictating his letter, four years after the conquest of the Lombards, to provide that extra bit of rhetorical leverage in the face of Charlemagne's so far stubborn refusal to hand over the Pope's share of the spoils. But what survives from papal circles between the sixth and the eighth centuries is so incomplete that even this linkage may have been made long before. Either way, the story of Constantine and Sylvester no doubt helped push things along and, three years later, when the papacy eventually acquired its cut from Charles' great conquest, Hadrian was no doubt duly grateful. There are very good reasons for thinking that, even after the gifts were sealed, some of the other consequences of Charles' success were still of concern to the Pope, however, and that, on a second level, the recast story of Constantine and Sylvester may have been deliberately framed to address these concerns as well.

These concerns had their roots in the unprecedented grandeur of the position that Charles was carving out for himself within Latin Christendom. By the time he had added the Lombard kingdom to his existing domains, the totality now broadly coincided with the territories of the old Western Roman Empire. Lombard Italy and the united Frankish kingdom (which already included all the core territories plus Alamannia, Frisia and Thuringia) put Charles in direct control of a territorial area which was far larger than anything achieved by even the greatest Merovingian of the sixth century, or indeed any Frankish predecessor. Nor was 774 the end of the story. Control of the two independent Lombard duchies of Benevento and Spoleto was duly added to the mix, and an entirely unprovoked intrusion into Bavaria in 787–8 then brought the last of the old satellite duchies under Charles' direct rule. In the meantime, a long and bitter struggle was under way to conquer Saxony and extinguish the paganism which prevailed there. This had begun in earnest in 772, and round one lasted down to the mid-780s including both forced conversions and a massacre of 4,500 opponents in 782. After a brief hiatus, rebellion broke out again in 793, but round two was largely limited to northern Saxony, where it came to an end with a final round of mass deportations in 804. But even this doesn't quite exhaust the list of conquests, since you also need to add a substantial degree of expansion into northern Spain, and the total destruction of the Avar realm between 791 and 796, whose aftermath saw, as Einhard famously reports, a long line of treasure wagons wending its way back to Francia.[22]

After this astonishing career of conquest, and really in fact from the moment of Desiderius' surrender, Charles was indeed Charlemagne: Charles the Great, entirely without rival within Latin Christendom. Constantinople's reach was confined by this point to some scattered territories in southern Italy, and the line of Visigothic monarchs in Spain had been extinguished by Muslim conquest. The fact that Charlemagne wrote some vaguely respectful letters to King Offa of Mercia in the 790s has led some to consider Offa a genuine peer, but this is nonsense. Charlemagne ruled most of Western and central Europe, whereas Offa's reach extended to overlordship of the southern counties of England (Figure 12).[23] There was just no contest.

What concerned the papacy was not the bare fact of Charlemagne's continued successes, two of which – the conquests of the Saxons and Avars – anyway advanced the boundaries of Christendom by extinguishing different brands of paganism. The problem lay in the significance that Charlemagne and his circle of advisers – lay and clerical – might attach to them. As the ruler of more than one separate kingdom, and the unifier of pretty much all of Latin Christian Europe, Charlemagne was so obviously much more than a king that the title 'emperor' was bound to come into view at some point. When precisely it did so for Charlemagne himself is a tricky question. By the 790s, the evidence is explicit that the title of emperor was being discussed in Charlemagne's court circle as the only one appropriate for his new status. Both the specific title of emperor and the more general concept of empire crop up in the writings of court intellectuals at this time, but that doesn't mean that these ideas hadn't been doing the rounds for some time already.

My own hunch would be that the conquest of the Lombards was the real game-changer. Once king and advisers had time to think about that unprecedented achievement in any kind of seriously reflective manner, the word 'empire' would quickly have become unavoidable for an entity which now encompassed more than one kingdom. And even more important than *what* Charlemagne had created, was a related question: *why* had he been able to create it? Given early medieval Christian understandings of historical progression, there was absolutely no choice at all when it came to answering this question. Charlemagne had been able to create his multi-kingdom empire because God had willed it to be so; he was God's agent at work in the world.[24]

Such ideas had long allowed emperors and kings to interfere in ecclesiastical matters when they wanted to, and, again in the 790s, Charlemagne flexed the muscles of his religious authority in a highly significant way. The opportunity was provided – accidentally – by Constantinople. The steady stream of losses it was suffering at the hands of the Muslims in the first half of the eighth century (the same losses which had allowed the Lombards to walk into Ravenna) eventually generated ideological crisis. If Christianity was the right religion and the Eastern emperor God's appointee, why was the empire, supposedly supported by an utterly omnipotent Divinity, losing so many battles to a bunch of non-believers? Based on Old Testament example, where the Children of Israel are regularly chastised for falling into false religious practice, there was an obvious answer: the empire was doing something to offend the Lord, who had sent the Muslims as a warning to bring His people back to the paths of righteousness.

What was much more optional was the answer as to what exactly it was that God was finding so offensive. Under the emperors Leo III and his son Constantine V, the Constantinopolitan establishment formally adopted the view, for reasons that still remain obscure, that the problem was the practice of venerating icons – holy pictures. In Eastern Christianity, it was commonly held that icons captured something of the essence of their subjects, and hence could function as a religious hotline to saint, Mother of God, Jesus, or whoever was portrayed. An icon, in other words, was a type of relic and could be used as a portal – a 'window into Heaven' – to gain access to the intermediary holy power of its subject matter. As far as we can tell, icon veneration had long been part of Eastern Christianity, but from c.700 the idea took hold that icons were in fact 'graven images' as outlawed in the Ten Commandments, and that it was this practice which was making the Almighty so tetchy. Under Leo and Constantine, icons were destroyed and their veneration outlawed, but the doctrine was never accepted in the West, and a succession of popes was happy to condemn the official Constantinopolitan view as heretical. The situation changed again in the later 780s, when a new imperial regime headed by the empress Irene, who had removed and blinded her own son Constantine VI (another example of early medieval royal family love), orchestrated a religious volte-face. A new council was held at Nicaea in 787, and icons – in their full glory as religious powerhouses – came back into fashion. When the news came west, Pope Hadrian declared himself overjoyed and celebrated Constantinople's return to the religious fold.[25]

Charlemagne and his churchmen took a different view. After careful preparations, the king called a major synod at Frankfurt, where a different position from that advocated by Hadrian was hammered out, right under the noses of the Pope's representatives. Religious pictures were perfectly OK, it was agreed, but for instruction only: the Constantinopolitan doctrine of icons as relics of power was rejected. The main target of Charlemagne's self-assertion here was certainly Constantinople rather than Rome. By this date, talk of empire was rumbling around in Charlemagne's circle, and, at least at the beginning, the line used to justify a potential reassertion of empire in the West was that Constantinople's version of it had gone seriously wrong. Religious error was thus an excellent stick to beat the Byzantines with. As the 790s went on, the attack was to be reinforced with the further thought that, given biblical visions of the correct ordering of relations between men and women, then it was clear that a woman – Irene of course – could not possibly legitimately hold the position of God's emperor: the divinely chosen leader of Christendom. This aggressive stance towards Constantinople demonstrates that the talk of empire at Charlemagne's court was no mere game being played by his intellectuals. The fact that so much energy went into arguing that the Byzantine version of empire was illegitimate in God's eyes shows us immediately that Charlemagne himself had his eyes firmly on the imperial prize.[26]

From the papal point of view, all this encompassed one major problem. As Charlemagne's behaviour underlined, the only concept of empire available in the late eighth century carried strong connotations of religious authority, by dint of the idea of divine appointment. And, as we shall see in Chapter 7, the king was already exercising authority in the religious sphere, not only at Frankfurt, but more generally. Charlemagne's imperial pretensions thus meant that the latest heir of St Peter was facing up to a formidable rival for leadership within the Latin, Western Church, and Frankfurt showed that the king had no compunctions about asserting his own religious authority at the expense of that of Rome. This all came into the open in the 790s, but the fundamental early medieval linkage between worldly power and God's will means that the ideas would have been there from the moment Desiderius surrendered. In the years after 774, therefore, for all that the Roman republic had benefited so materially from his grants of 781 and 787, the papacy cannot but have perceived Charlemagne as a threat to its religious authority, and we have good evidence of a natural determination on its part to impose limits on the king's pretensions.

One dimension of ideological response to Charlemagne's challenge is already apparent in the preserved papal letters of the *Codex Carolinus* from the 770s. Where Frankish sources unanimously attribute their king's successes to God, the papal letters attribute them to St Peter's intercession, the payback for Charles' loyalty to Rome. This line of attack was adopted in part, no doubt, to help extract the best possible deal from Charlemagne after the conquest of the Lombards, since the implication was that, should the king not fulfil his promises, St Peter could take victory away again. But it also implicitly limited Charlemagne's part in God's plans by suggesting that the Almighty was not acting directly through Charlemagne but only via the Pope and St Peter. God's central purpose, in other words, was not to put Charlemagne at the head of Western Christendom, but actually to strengthen the Church of Rome.[27]

In this context, the ideas that would eventually be written up in the *Donation of Constantine* have a second dimension of importance, beyond their obvious relevance to papal land-grabbing. Quite explicitly, they also made the case that there was now no justification for having an emperor in the West at all, since Constantine had left dominion over the entire Western Empire to Pope Sylvester when he left for Constantinople. Since Charlemagne had started to look like an emperor as soon as he conquered the Lombard kingdom and soon came to be interested in acquiring the title, and since emperors could by right of divine appointment exercise religious authority on a very large scale, this dimension of the papal argument can hardly be a coincidence. Although the papacy had benefited massively from Charlemagne's victories, it was clearly also, at the same time, doing its level best to keep his successes from getting out of hand. The Constantine and Sylvester story, together with the determined attempt to attribute everything to the intercession of St Peter, show that Charlemagne's successes had quickly set alarm bells ringing in Hadrian's HQ.

We are now, finally, within a whisker of understanding the historical dynamic behind Christmas Day 800. From the moment when he decided to pick a fight over the end of iconoclasm at the absolute latest, and I would suspect considerably earlier, Charlemagne had his eye on the imperial title, with a full understanding of its traditional Roman meaning (one entirely preserved in contemporary Constantinople) as the divinely appointed supreme authority – secular and religious – within Christendom. The papacy had been happy enough to benefit from some of the fruits of his conquests, but did not want any imperial significance to be attached to Charlemagne's career. This leaves us with two final puzzles. Given that the last thing the papacy wanted was to revive the imperial title, why do we find Pope Leo crowning Charlemagne emperor? And why, despite the overwhelming evidence to the contrary, does Einhard maintain that Charlemagne would never have entered St Peter's if he had known what was going to happen?

THE PERILS OF POPE LEO

The answer to the second question is straightforward. The only legitimate emperor, according to all the official definitions of imperial propaganda, was one who was divinely appointed. The trick, of course, was how to be sure that any particular individual was divinely appointed, because theory allowed for the contingency that illegitimate, man-made emperors might insert themselves into the role from time to time.

Generally speaking, two telltale signs were used. First, an emperor who was truly there by divine appointment would be successful, since God was indeed an omnipotent deity. And military victory was usually held up as the sign par excellence of true, God-supported legitimacy. Second, an individual truly chosen by divine will could not help but become emperor, whatever they or anyone else did, because God willed it. By straightforward inversion, overweening ambition was a clear sign that the individual in question was entirely unworthy of the job. Thus the emperor Julian famously muttered 'Purple death has seized me' when appointed Caesar by his cousin the Augustus Constantius II, a Homeric tag that could be used to signal resistance to unwanted promotion. For the same reason, Julian was extremely careful to establish some more or less plausible deniability when his troops later hailed him as Augustus – in a direct challenge to Constantius' authority – when all the indications are that he not only knew that his troops were going to proclaim him, but had in fact had his people organize it. The same trope was also popular in the Christian context where it soon became fashionable for any seriously holy individual to be recorded in his *Life* as having done his damnedest to avoid episcopal office, before finally giving in because there was ultimately no choice.[28] And that was, of course, the perfect mark of true divine appointment: if God willed it, there would, in the end, just be no avoiding it.

Einhard was well read in the classics, modelling his biography of Charlemagne quite substantially on Suetonius and displaying knowledge of a wide variety of other ancient texts besides. He certainly knew plenty, as did many of his fellow intellectuals at court, about how one might set about identifying true divine appointment. In other words, Charlemagne and his advisers knew perfectly well that if they were caught with their hands too obviously in the imperial till, then the presentation of their man as divinely appointed would start to ring hollow. This, then, was Charlemagne's dilemma in the face of a Western imperial tradition that had been broken in the fifth century. As soon as he had definitively smashed the Lombard kingdom, he had fulfilled the criterion of military victory in spades, and the rest of his reign just went on to confirm the fact of God's support, as one territory after another fell into his lap at the point of a sword. But if, by this means, God was making it clear that Charlemagne was chosen to be His emperor, how could that fact finally be proclaimed out loud if neither Charlemagne nor his advisers were allowed to do it themselves?

They were clearly worrying about this at least from the early 790s onwards, and, as we shall see in more detail in the final section of the book, Charlemagne's reform programme was by then showing an industrial level of care for the Church, as also befitted the received job description of the divinely chosen Christian emperor. In other words, Charlemagne not only achieved the kind of battlefield success that screamed the word 'emperor' to anyone who knew their political theory, but his attention to Christian reform (which I'm sure was entirely genuine, lest I sound too cynical) also made the same point under a different heading. When faced with the evidence that Charlemagne and his advisers had their eyes on the imperial title for some years before 800, it has sometimes been objected that, when he actually received the title, his behaviour did not change in any fundamental ways (except that he ceased travelling so far: a fact that is really attributable to his advancing age). That is to miss the point. Charlemagne had been deliberately behaving like an emperor for at least one decade (and quite possibly two) before Christmas Day 800.

The solution to the other, final problem fell obligingly into the imperial lap in the person of Pope Leo III. Leo succeeded Pope Hadrian I in 795 and soon ran into trouble with factions of the Roman nobility hostile to his appointment. Matters came to a head on 25 April 799 when Leo was seized by his opponents and accused of perjury, simony (the selling of ecclesiastical office) and sexual impropriety. The story put about later was that they had attempted to gouge out his eyes and cut out his tongue, and independent sources confirm that he was at least wounded, but Leo was certainly able to see and speak on Christmas Day 800. Papal sources attribute this to miraculous intervention, but you cannot see without eyes and blinding was not that difficult an action to perform, so there's more than a whiff of spin in the air. But Leo was certainly attacked and imprisoned, and only got away by climbing a monastery wall to escape into the protection of one of Charlemagne's representatives in the city. He was then sent north to meet Charlemagne himself at Paderborn later in the same year.

What exactly happened when they met, no source records, and both sides subsequently mounted carefully organized plans of disinformation. But when you realize that Charlemagne clearly wanted the imperial title, whereas Leo would rather have eaten his own liver than see a resurrection of empire in the West, the sequence of events is extremely suggestive. In consultation with his churchmen, Charlemagne declared that no one had the authority to pass judgement on the Pope because he was the *apostolicus*: the direct descendant of St Peter. He then sent Leo back to Rome with enough military force to put down the opposition, and, just over a year later, Charlemagne himself entered the city in November 800. At the start of December, a council was held which reiterated the position that no one had the authority to judge a pope. Nonetheless, on 23 December, supposedly of his own volition, Leo swore a solemn oath that he was innocent of all charges, and two days later proclaimed Charlemagne emperor.[29]

At this point, and in the face of the deafening silence about what was said at Paderborn, I'd like to introduce you to a principle of one of my doctoral supervisors. He is an extremely distinguished ancient historian, who ended up studying the late Roman Empire but with that suspicion of Christianity that is shared by many (though not all) of those who study the classics. He once famously said, 'I may not know much about Christianity, but I do know the smell of rotting fish.' The meeting at Paderborn is a case in point. We will never know how Charlemagne's offer was worded, and who made it (whether it was direct, or whether one of the king's people went for a walk in the woods with one of Leo's). Nor will we ever know if Leo agonized long and hard, or quickly accepted. But there is not an iota of doubt in my soul that, one way or another, Charlemagne effectively said, 'Make me emperor and I'll put you back on the papal throne, no questions asked.'[30]

From Charlemagne's perspective, there could be no better solution. What could be more perfect than getting the Pope to declare out loud what Charlemagne's staggering list of military successes and assiduous care for the Church had been demonstrating for the last twenty years: that he was – without the slightest doubt – God's chosen vessel for the restoration of Christian empire? No one had any doubt that a particular authority attached to the papal see, because its occupants were the descendants of St Peter, even if there was some disagreement about what that authority might mean. So the Pope was a good solution to Charlemagne's problem, and one that was made even neater by the claims laid out in the ideas that would be written up later in the *Donation of Constantine*. Its key claim – that Constantine had given imperial authority in the West to Pope Sylvester when he caught the chariot for Constantinople – had already featured in some of Hadrian's correspondence to Charlemagne. Totally delicious! Who better to proclaim Charlemagne emperor than the latest occupant of the throne to whom imperial power had been left back in the fourth century?

As is always the case with shotgun marriages of the diplomatic kind, both sides quickly publicized their own versions of events. Leo, famously, erected a mosaic in the great hall of the Lateran Palace (at that point papal HQ rather than the Vatican) which depicted Charlemagne and Leo kneeling side by side at the feet of St Peter. The original was destroyed but a copy was made and can now be seen on the exterior of St Peter's (Plate 17). This iconography explicitly denied that Charlemagne had any greater authority than the Pope, and was exactly of a piece with the papal insistence in the letters preserved of the *Codex Carolinus* that Charlemagne's victories came at the behest of St Peter; that is, *not* from God.

Charlemagne's take was rather different. All the Pope had done on Christmas Day 800 was declare the crushingly obvious: God (the main man) not St Peter (his deputy) had chosen Charlemagne for unique imperial authority, because Charlemagne's merits were clearly worth it. Part of the delay between the meeting at Paderborn in the summer of 799, and the coronation which took place over a year later, was to allow time to generate the appropriate level of diplomatic fanfare (although Charlemagne also needed to arrange affairs in the north with a view to his lengthy impending absence). Amongst other exotica, Charlemagne arranged that a deputation from the Patriarch of Jerusalem should just happen to be in Rome when he arrived, to present him with the keys to the city of Jerusalem, the holiest Christian city of them all. When, in due course, he considered the time ripe to pass on the imperial torch, Charlemagne himself performed the ceremony for Louis, his son and heir, entirely by himself, with not even a walk-on part for the Pope, since a sitting God-appointed emperor could certainly, without any imputation of hubris, designate his successor.[31] What happened to this empire, on which Leo's problems had set the final seal, and how Louis and Charlemagne's other successors fared, is the subject of the next chapter.

6

'THE CENTRE CANNOT HOLD'

ON 28 JANUARY 814, at the age of sixty-five (considerable for a Carolingian male, whose lifespans normally weighed in at more like fifty years), the emperor Charlemagne shuffled off his mortal coil. He was also unusually tall. A nineteenth-century estimate put him at about 190 cm, but an X-ray and CT scan of his skeleton performed in 2010 suggested 184 cm. Either result would put him in something like the ninety-ninth percentile for height in his period. Einhard also gives an arresting image of the king in later middle age:

> He had a round head, large and lively eyes, a slightly larger nose than usual, white but still attractive hair, a bright and cheerful expression, a short and fat neck, and he enjoyed good health, except for the fevers that affected him in the last few years of his life. Toward the end, he dragged one leg. Even then, he stubbornly did what he wanted and refused to listen to doctors, indeed he detested them, because they wanted to persuade him to stop eating roast meat, as was his wont, and to be content with boiled meat.[1]

Aside from physical ailments, his latter years had their fair share of other sorrows too, although there was a nasty way in which the most obvious of them greatly simplified the politics of his empire.

As Charlemagne began to age, and even before, the great issue facing his empire was, predictably, succession after the death of its founder. Charlemagne had a first go at settling matters in 806, when a great assembly of Frankish magnates agreed to the arrangements set out in a formal document whose text still survives: the *Divisio Regnorum*. Charlemagne had five wives (just the one at a time), many concubines, and lots of children: the best guesses come in at a round dozen. The settlement of 806, however, focused on three adult male heirs: in order of birth, Charles the Younger, Pippin and Louis. All three were to have access to Italy, but otherwise they were to rule separate realms. Louis had long been established in Aquitaine, Pippin was given much of the old Lombard kingdom in northern Italy, and Charles the largest territories including the old Frankish heartlands in Neustria and Austrasia (Figure 12). No mention was made of the imperial title, but it is usually assumed that it was destined for Charles, because of the evident dominance of his position.

But Pippin of Italy then died in 810 and Charles the Younger in 811, which left Charlemagne with just the one adult son: Louis, destined to be known as Louis the Pious. Succession arrangements were revised accordingly in 813, when Louis was brought to Aachen from Aquitaine, whose designated king he had been since 781 when he was only three. At another great ceremony, Louis was not only named heir to everything, but anointed as emperor. No doubt the old king was saddened by the deaths of his sons, but he was also perfectly well aware of his own, his father's, and his grandfather's successions, where attempted divisions between brothers had generated massive political instability. He may have been able to comfort himself, therefore, with the thought that God, who had obviously created the empire, was now directing affairs in His characteristically mysterious way, to ensure its untroubled replication in the next generation.[2]

Almost exactly seventy-five years later, however, in February 888, the nobility of the western half of the Frankish world chose a non-Carolingian as king: Eudes or Odo. A Carolingian restoration followed in the person of Charles the Simple, great-grandson of Louis the Pious, but Charles was king only of West Francia and never emperor, while by the time of Charles' death in 929 East Francia and Italy had each gone their separate ways under non-Carolingian leadership. For all the success of his own lifetime, Charlemagne's imperial creation came and went within a century, whereas the Roman Empire, by comparison, lasted – depending on what you count – for over 500 years certainly, and maybe 1,000. Even within West Francia, moreover, Carolingian rule was destined not to last out the tenth century, being definitively replaced from 987 by Hugh Capet, grandson of the intrusive Odo's brother Robert, whose line would then rule in an astonishing sequence of uninterrupted father-to-son successions down to 1328. So why did the Carolingian Empire not last longer? As with the overturning of Merovingian rule, we are dealing with a much larger phenomenon than the mere replacement of one dynasty with another. Rather like the mid-to-later seventh century, the mid-to-later ninth century – and indeed afterwards – saw a substantial fragmentation of central control more generally. To understand the swift disappearance of the dynasty's control over large parts of its former empire, it is necessary to get to the heart of how Charlemagne and Louis the Pious governed the enormous territories which God had given them.

THE GODFATHER (PART 1)

Many explanations have been offered for the empire's lack of durability, not least the character of Charlemagne's son and heir: Louis the Pious. Without looking very hard, it's possible to find characterizations of him in the sources as a humourless and unwarlike individual who would have preferred life in a monastery to occupying the most powerful throne of his day. It's then not a difficult step to do a little amateur psychology and come up with variations of the round peg in a square hole. And this is exactly the kind of explanation of which W. B. Yeats, while not thinking remotely of the Carolingians, would have profoundly approved. In his view, the centre couldn't hold because 'the best lack all conviction, while the worst are full of passionate intensity'. But all these characterizations of Louis were post de facto rationalizations, penned by individuals struggling to explain the political troubles that affected his later years, when he was locked in a wrestling match with his three older sons: Lothar, Pippin and Louis the German. These three were Louis' sons with his first wife Irmingard, and in 817 he had publicized a succession settlement for them, the *Ordinatio Imperii*, declaring that he would have no further heirs. By the late 820s, however, he had remarried and had another son, Charles (destined to be known as Charles the Bald, but presumably, aged four, he wasn't yet so), and manoeuvred to include him in the succession. This generated the usual dogfight, which saw Louis generally supported by his younger namesake, but opposed by Lothar and Pippin. In the worst moment, however, all three older sons were united against him, and the emperor was forced into a formal penance and virtual abdication at Soissons in 833. This was followed by a period of monastic confinement until Lothar's overweening ambition led

Louis the German to change sides again, and the emperor – formally rearmed in a ceremony at St Denis in 835 – emerged resplendent. When you add into this picture of a father who, despite everything, could not control his sons, a formal act of public penance that Louis had voluntarily performed in 822 at Attigny to atone for previous sins, then a seductive image of personal insufficiency becomes hard to resist.

Before buying it, however, it's important to see what Louis was actually doing penance *for* in 822. When he came to power in 814, he had no brothers left to fight, but faced a different and equally intractable problem. Since the age of three, his world had been Aquitaine, which he had ruled first in name and then increasingly in fact. He had been to Aachen on only a handful of occasions, and was known to none of the great magnates of the Frankish heartlands, the backbone around which the empire as a whole was constructed. His problem, therefore, was to assert his authority in a world which was used to operating entirely without him. Louis showed both sufficient political acumen to understand the issue, and total ruthlessness in dealing with it. In particular, he swept out of the palace and into a selection of the nearest available monasteries all his many sisters, with whom their father had liked to surround himself, not to mention his concubines, their illegitimate offspring and all the human detritus of Charlemagne's lengthy rule. This was done not quietly but with great fanfare, Louis declaring himself to have rid the palace of countless whores. In parallel propaganda campaigns, he established a model monastery within three miles of the palace to set a determined new tone for his regime, declaring, in 814, that he'd found the running of the empire to be replete with 'oppression' and 'corruption'.

Piety, therefore, was Louis' path to self-assertion and it never stopped him from doing what needed to be done. His eldest brother Charles had not married, but Pippin of Italy had a son, Bernard, who was already seventeen at the time of Charlemagne's death. In true Carolingian style, Louis totally ignored his nephew's claims in the *Ordinatio Imperii* (which simply didn't mention him) and then when he came north of the Alps to negotiate in 817, had Bernard imprisoned and blinded, the unfortunate youth dying two days later from the after-effects. The emperor who did penance in 822 was a thoroughly self-satisfied one who'd taken a firm grip on the reins of power, and could now afford to square things up with both his conscience and the Almighty. Don't be misled by the nickname: Louis the Pious was absolutely as hard a bastard as his father, and it is of a piece with this Louis that the crisis with his older sons was actually caused by him being overly aggressive. The three brothers, it seems, were originally willing (at least for the moment) to tolerate their father's desire to insert their non-hirsute half-sibling into the succession, but Louis wrapped up in this a second process where he sought to humiliate two leading Frankish magnates, counts Hugh of Tours and Matfrid of Orleans, who were close confidants particularly of Lothar, the former Lothar's father-in-law. It was at this point that Lothar smelled a rat and the rebellion began.[3]

As soon as you look at the detail, therefore, Louis the Pious ceases to look very different from his father in the general character of his rule. Charlemagne, as we will explore in much more detail in the next chapter, devoted huge energy to processes of Christian religious reform, and both father and son deployed a calculated mixture of bribery, GBH and Christian piety to achieve their desired ends. And this, broadly speaking, was what the job of early medieval north European ruler required.

Carolingian government was, in its essentials, fairly straight-forward, and did not differ much from what had been inherited from the later Merovingians, although there were many local variations in detail across the wide reaches of the empire. The imperial landscape was divided into numerous local administrative units – *pagi* or counties – of which, it has been calculated, there were in total some 600–700. They varied greatly in size, wealth and importance, but the ability of any Carolingian to rule depended on a range of revenues and services that were levied on their inhabitants by their designated, appointed head, usually a count. Unlike the later Roman Empire, which operated a developed central bureaucracy, comprising 3,000 very senior posts in each half of the empire, together with numerous medium- and lower-level functionaries, its Carolingian successor functioned with almost no central bureaucracy at all, other than a few tens of officials, who often had multiple roles rather than a specialized task.

For an older strand of scholarship, this lack of a central government machine, and of sufficient lay elite literacy to power one, rather than the more personal failings of Louis the Pious, lay at the heart of Carolingian failure. But this myth too has gone the way of all flesh. It is true that bureaucratic methods were a bit rudimentary in Charle-magne's time, but this was more to do with established governmental habits (or the lack of them) rather than a structural problem caused by any basic lack of literacy. Charlemagne and Louis the Pious (and their Merovingian predecessors in fact) issued many orders on paper, and communicated by letter on all manner of subjects. And their magnates were perfectly capable of dealing with what was sent to them. You could always employ a clerical scribe of some kind to pen any reply that might be necessary, and, anyway, old visions of an illiterate lay elite in the early Middle Ages have been overturned. These were Christian men and women, conscious too – whatever their original ethnic background – of a classical heritage where education and civilization were inextricably linked. They certainly learned enough Latin to read their Bibles, therefore, even if, unlike their late Roman predecessors, they were largely learning it at home from their mothers, rather than at school from a professional teacher. As a result, not all of their endings were absolutely correct – thus hastening on the grammatical simplifications which would turn Latin into its various medieval Romance derivatives outside of the Church – and they learned largely passively: to read, that is, rather than to write.[4]

This did generate a massive cultural shift from late Roman norms where the elite had learned to read and to write in a rigid form of classical Latin, to one where the only writing, by and large, was done by clergymen and the secular elite stuck to a little edifying reading. But there is no evidence that any of this seriously hampered the effectiveness of Carolingian rule. Slightly paradoxically, the evidence stacks up in the other direction, since bureaucratic habits waxed stronger in the Carolingian world as actual monarchical power was on the wane, at least in the field of legal affairs.

Roman ideologies focusing on the importance of written law in marking out a higher order of human society were alive, kicking, and thoroughly understood at Charlemagne's court. The overall legal situation within the empire was complicated, however, by the fact that every major region had its own pre-existing law code. Charlemagne was careful to respect these traditions while nonetheless taking every opportunity to appropriate for himself the image of divinely directed imperial legal reformer, after the pattern of Justinian, by reissuing new versions of all the old texts in his imperial name, not least at the first major assembly he held after the coronation, at Lorsch in 802. In fact, the texts were little changed and the whole process was mostly gone through for its propaganda value. At the same time, and particularly after the imperial coronation again, much more practical updating regulations on a whole series of matters – from the moral and religious to the highly pragmatic and immediate – were added to the pile of legally valid regulations operating within the empire. These were often preceded by discussion at the regular assemblies where the ruler met his great men, and, once publicized, were supposed to apply throughout the empire, providing a body of regulations that was supplementary to what was already in the older law codes. If much of this was being put down on paper from 802 onwards, initial Carolingian bureaucratic rustiness shows up in the recording and dissemination of the texts of these new decisions.

Some were recorded on paper as a series of rulings in texts known as capitularies, of which a great many survive from the later years of Charlemagne and the reign of Louis the Pious. But we also know that there were many assemblies and lots of important decisions being taken in the early years of Charlemagne. At that point, however, most of them were not being written down, and, even later in Charlemagne's reign, those decisions that were recorded were not always done so in the same way by all participants at a given assembly. At least, variant texts sometimes survive from the same assembly, so single, authoritative listings of rulings were not always generated.

Not until the middle of the reign of Louis the Pious, moreover, did anyone start systematically to collect the capitularies as a body of material. In the mid-820s, a first attempt was made by Ansegius, abbot of the important monastery of St Wandrille (quite possibly by royal request, though we don't know this), but his efforts show up the limitations of what could be done at that stage, given the weaknesses of past practice. His collection was not able to find all the capitulary texts that have come down to us via alternative routes, and he misattributes some of those that he did find. Up to the 820s, therefore, the empire was only groping towards regularized bureaucratic habits in legal matters. By the time of Louis' son Charles the Bald, these teething troubles had been ironed out. His West Frankish assemblies customarily generated a single, authoritative text of the new decisions, all new sets of rulings were systematically added to the pile of existing capitularies, and it was now commonplace, where appropriate, for new decisions to be cross-referenced to older ones, making all this material so much easier to use.[5]

So, even if it started out a little rusty, Carolingian bureaucracy eventually got the hang of regularized government by paper, and there is no sign that the less intensive patterns of elite lay literacy characteristic of the early Middle Ages were any great hindrance to the process. But the fascinating point is that these bureaucratic habits were reaching their peak in West Francia under Charles the Bald, at precisely the same time as central royal power was beginning to weaken. Indeed, that part of Charlemagne's empire which best maintained traditions of a very powerful central authority into the tenth century (even if not in the hands of a member of the dynasty) was East Francia, and there the written capitulary tradition failed to get off the ground at all. This is not telling us that central government power was *inversely* related to the strength of its bureaucratic structures, I think, merely that these structures did not play any very crucial role in the Carolingian governmental system, in so far as there was one.

Lacking much in the way of a central bureaucracy, the rule of Charlemagne and Louis the Pious relied on the count of the *pagus* as the workhorse of the system, who was responsible almost single-handedly for making it all work. First and perhaps foremost, it was his job to extract any revenues owed to the king. He was sometimes responsible for the income from any royal estates that fell within his jurisdiction, he collected any customs and tolls due from markets or fairs, again passing on to the king his designated share, and he was in addition the chief legal officer charged with presiding over regular courts, and, again, passing on to the king his rightful percentage of any fines levied. To reimburse him for all this effort, the count too was entitled to a percentage of most of the revenues he raised, and might also be temporarily granted – while in post – the annual revenues from a convenient piece of royally owned fisc land.

Counts were also responsible for turning out most of the royal army. Carolingian monarchs maintained in and around their palaces a hard core of what were essentially military professionals: a mixture of hard-bitten lifers and the younger male offspring of some of their leading landowners on temporary attachment. The bulk of Carolingian armies (as of their Merovingian predecessors) consisted not of these professional forces, however, but of local landowners and a designated portion of their dependants. The landowners' obligation to serve was not infinite, and may have been limited to no more than three months in any given year, but, when the royal command came, it was the count's job to mobilize the liable individuals and rendezvous with the king at the stipulated time and place. The contingent also had to be both properly armed and supplied with many of the necessary food-stuffs for the upcoming campaign.

Since counts were themselves, for the most part, from the land-owning community which they led, rather than complete outsiders, Carolingian government was essentially a partnership between ruler and local landowning community more generally, which relied on the count doing his various jobs to make the whole thing work. A certain amount of checking up had to be routine, done partly by the king in person in the areas of the realm where he was customarily to be found. For Charlemagne in his later years and Louis for much of his reign, this generally meant the Frankish heartlands either side of the Rhine in northern Europe. For all the prodigious distances he certainly covered in his life, even the younger Charlemagne had not been a properly itinerant monarch aiming to criss-cross the entirety of his territories in a regular pattern, and many outlying areas of the empire had only ever seen an occasional royal progress. For much of the empire, the checking role was played by *missi*, who, as the system became increasingly regularized under Louis the Pious, generally con-sisted of a pair of high officials: one a cleric, the other a layman.

But even checking had its limits, not least sociopolitical ones, since *missi* were for the most part connected to the same kind of aristocratic-cum-gentry landowner networks as the counts, and the extent to which they were willing to interfere might well depend on pre-existing relationships. The timing of Bishop Wulfad of Bourges' attempt to win control of an estate in Burgundy, for instance, has been plausibly attributed to the fact that one of his kinsmen had recently been appointed *missus* there (although in point of fact his attempt failed). Fundamentally, therefore, effective rule depended on the prevalence of excellent relationships between the king and his counts, and, if relations were not good, there were all kinds of ways that counts could lob a spanner in the royal works without having to go as far as open rebellion. When it came to military service, for instance, all you had to do was just turn up a bit late, or advance to slightly the wrong rendezvous, and that might be enough to derail a campaign.[6]

What really held the empire of Charlemagne together, therefore, were the bonds of personal loyalty and connection that its rulers were able to form with the local landowning elites, who filled the position of count and otherwise dominated their home communities. By

Christmas Day 800, Charlemagne's position was an extremely strong one, and no count was about to step too obviously out of line. But it hadn't always been that way. If his brother had not died so unexpectedly, for instance, so that there had been two Carolingians vying for magnate loyalty over an extended period, then his political situation would have been very different. One recent study, focusing on the realm built by one of Charlemagne's grandsons east of the Rhine, has offered the rule of thumb that it took about ten years on average for a ruler in early medieval (as opposed to Roman) conditions to build up the relationships and bonds of loyalty with local leaders which meant that he was really in charge of his kingdom. Ten years, that is, to identify a body of men from among the landowning magnate class who, if appointed counts, would on the whole serve you loyally and efficiently.

In Charlemagne's case, the early death of his brother coupled with the unexpected scale and ease of his victory over the Lombards probably speeded things up, but the basic political process was the same at the start of every reign, whatever the size of unit concerned. Louis the Pious, for instance, went through exactly the same thing on a smaller scale when he was made sub-king in Aquitaine: hence his problem when suddenly translated to Aachen after his brothers' deaths. What you had to do during these ten years – or five if you were really lucky – was, first, hand out lots of gifts of one kind or another to as many key landowners as possible, which included appointing the right men to all the posts of count within your disposal. This showed not least that you were the generous lord that early medieval ideologies absolutely required. Where we have a good run of charters (documents recording gifts of various kinds) for an early medieval king, they consistently demonstrate that kings had to give away a great deal at the beginning of their reigns, for this is when you recruited the loyal servants who would run the localities in your favour. Louis the Pious, for instance, at the same time as he was sweeping the whores and corruption out of Aachen, made over a hundred donations by charter in the first three years of his reign. This dropped to an average of twelve per year subsequently. If, like Charlemagne, you could work a major victory into these years as well, accompanied by some large-scale expropriations from the losers, then you could accelerate the process accordingly, have lots of extra prestige and a great deal extra to give away.

What you distributed in these years was not just land, although that was the main form of capital wealth in this overwhelmingly agricultural world, so everyone naturally wanted it. But there were lots of other ways of showing favour too: giving individuals the rights to hold a market (and hence collect the tolls), for instance, or your support in a law suit, or you might even arrange a desirable marriage for one of their offspring. With a little imagination, a new king could find countless ways to build up close relations with a functioning network of his landowning magnates.

What you didn't do, however, was just give stuff away willy-nilly. It had to be targeted, which meant you had get to know your magnates well, in order to have a strong sense of the price of their loyalty and of which ones you could really trust with the important post of count. Some might be content with the kind of gift which would just cause another to start plotting against you, and everyone's price would be higher when there was more than one Carolingian to choose from. And some you could never trust, however much you gave them. This kind of information you found out through the cycles of meeting and contact which punctuated the ceremonial year, and, perhaps above all, when out on campaign.

By the time Charlemagne took the throne, it had long been traditional for kings to hold annual assemblies early in the campaigning season (the same assemblies that, later, often generated capitulary texts). This was a great moment not only for reaching decisions on the great matters of the day, but also for gathering information, and mutual exchanges of favour. It was also customary for the assembly to be followed by an actual campaign. In the ninety years from the accession of Charles Martel down to 803/4, a major Frankish army was in the field against foreign foes in all but five: three during 749–51 when Pippin was pulling the strings necessary to have himself crowned, 759 and 790. And when there was no campaign, this was always commented upon in the sources. Campaigning, especially the successful variety which marked Charlemagne's reign, was a great moment for forging the practical bonds of loyalty which would also make it possible for the ruler to win the peace, since they were customarily followed by distributions of whatever booty had come to hand.

Even so, humans being human, you could pretty much guarantee that not every magnate would be equally satisfied, or even satisfied at all. Competing magnates from the same locality were one obvious problem, since if you showed favour to one, the other would be alienated, and sometimes, given the levels of brotherly love around in the upper classes, if you promoted one brother that would make his sibling a lifelong foe. The other thing that had to be done, therefore, especially early in a reign, was root out the malcontents. Tough on rebellion, and even tougher on the causes of rebellion was an excellent Carolingian motto, and no self-respecting king would let the grass grow under his feet on that one. Charlemagne moved heaven and earth – well, crossed the Alps – to remove his brother's family as a potential magnet for the disgruntled. He then brutally put down two subsequent revolts, one by eastern magnates still smarting from their forced incorporation into the Carolingian machine, the other surrounding one of his sons, Pippin the Hunchback, who was being left out of all the succession plans. Pippin himself ended up in a monastery but his supporters were all executed.[7]

Up close and personal, therefore, the Father of Europe celebrated by one of his court poets looks a lot more like the Godfather of Europe. What Charlemagne did, essentially, was share a series of revenues generated in the different localities of his empire on a percentage basis with selected members of the local landowning magnate class. For this to work, the localities had to be run by men the ruler could trust, and he could use a combination of generosity, comradeship and intimidation to make sure that he received his due share. All of this worked beautifully (though still not without some serious hiccups) when there was only one Carolingian around and regular victories were lubricating both the reputation and coffers of the emperor. How the machine started first to misfire and then actually to break apart when those conditions ceased to apply emerges with striking clarity in the era of Charlemagne's grandsons.

'NO SLAUGHTER WAS EVER WORSE'

Hindsight is ever a wonderful thing, but sometimes it's not really necessary. Even at the time, contemporaries were well aware that 25 June 841 marked the day when the struggle for power within

Charlemagne's empire reached an entirely unprecedented level of ferocity. The three surviving sons of Louis the Pious lined up and straightforward, outright battle was joined near the small Belgian village of Fontenoy. No bluffs, no blackmail, no blindings, and no long-term rest cures in monastic establishments: the gloves came off. And the result was a slaughter of Frank upon Frank which could be expressed either prosaically, as it was in the Chronicles, or with a great deal of poetic hand wringing, as in the verses of the otherwise unknown Engelbert who fought there for Lothar, the eldest of the sons:

> No slaughter was ever worse on any field of war;
> The law of Christians was shattered by this shedding of blood,
> Whence the company of hell and the mouth of its three-headed
>   dog rejoice . . .

> Let not that accursed day be counted in the calendar of the year,
> Rather let it be erased from all memory,
> May the sun's rays never fall there, may no dawn ever come to
>   [its] twilight.

Engelbert had fought on the losing side, but even the victors ordered three days of Masses to atone for the horror of inter-Christian civil war, and it wasn't mere sour grapes which prompted our poet's sad reflections. The battle of Fontenoy marked the first in a series of catastrophic Carolingian failures to transmit power efficiently from one generation to the next.

The failure had its roots in the same situation which had led Louis' sons to rebel against him in his own lifetime (page 250). By the time of their father's death on 20 June 840, one of Irmingard's children, Pippin, had died, and this had enabled Louis to make the perhaps as yet still hirsute Charles the Bald king in Aquitaine. The dead Pippin had left a more or less adult son, yet another Pippin, however, so the year up to Fontenoy saw two brothers, a half-brother and a nephew negotiating, feinting and blustering until they backed themselves into a corner by a little village in Belgium, and their warriors paid the price. Or, as Engelbert put it:

> O what grief and wailing! The dead lie there naked,
> While vultures, crows and wolves savagely devour their flesh:
> They shake since they lack graves and their corpses lie there to
>   no end.

Any temptation to blame the whole thing on the sexual incontinence of the father needs to be resisted with the utmost determination.[8]

The three – relatively – peaceful transmissions of power from one sole Carolingian ruler to another sole Carolingian over the 125-year period covered by the reigns of Charles Martel and Louis the Pious (714 to 840) had required an astonishing amount of luck. Charles Martel was able to grab power so easily only because his two half-brothers had died. Pippin's path was eased by his brother's departure for Italy, Charlemagne's by his brother's early death, and Louis' by the convenient deaths of no less than two older brothers. These deaths and departures did not remove all potential causes of dynastic dispute, but they left one individual in each generation with a decisive advantage as measured in the perceptions of the magnates – the equivalents of the aides and second-rank leaders who size up the Godfather's sons so carefully (page 18) – and each had then rammed home that advantage by acting decisively to remove younger collaterals. This longer view of Carolingian dynastic history offers two important perspectives, which should reduce virtually to zero any temptation to lump the blame on Louis the Pious.

First, even without the addition of Charles the follicularly challenged, his three other sons – never mind that they had emerged from the same womb – were a racing certainty to come into conflict at some point: not necessarily on the battlefield, maybe, but certainly a major stand-off of some kind. Charles' addition did not materially add to the problem, as the detail itself shows, since at Fontenoy he and the younger Louis the German lined up together against Lothar. Second, at each stage, the job of dynastic simplification was undertaken only after the death of the previous king, not in his own lifetime, as when Louis the Pious had taken out Bernard of Italy, or when Charlemagne and his father dealt with their brothers' families. Sorting out dynastic complexity, you might say, was the job of each generation when it came to power, not the previous one beforehand, which again extracts Louis from any hook on to which you might feel inclined to hang him.

There were excellent reasons why this had to be so. To start with, death is always an unexpected guest. This is true enough now, but was even more so in the early Middle Ages. A king could not go about pruning his heirs, not only because he – presumably – loved his children (even if they didn't love each other) but also because you never knew who was going to survive. In 806, Charlemagne had three adult sons, but, by the time of his death less than eight years later, he was down to one. And if more than one heir posed problems, having none at all was the ultimate nightmare (as we shall see in a moment). You might control your daughters' marriages, since you wouldn't want multiple grandchildren with a half-decent claim to the throne. The smart money is that Charlemagne had this in mind, as much as his own love for them, when he wouldn't let his daughters marry and leave his court (page 251). But it was foolish to go around killing sons. Equally important, what fundamentally mattered in succession disputes were the magnates' perceptions of the candidates' abilities and characteristics, as it was the magnates' choices of allegiance which actually decided how things would turn out. Not enough of either of the two Carlomans' magnates were ready to fight off the ambitions of Pippin and Charlemagne in defence of their former kings' offspring in 748–9 and 771–2, so power passed quickly and relatively peacefully to one Carolingian alone. In that sense, Louis did his job perfectly well. He made sure that he passed on a decent stock of adult male heirs to the next generation, and it was then up to them to sort out what would happen next.

At this point, the dynasty's luck ran out, so that instead of coming down to just the one well-established adult male heir, who could clear out all the collaterals fairly easily, the 840s saw two very well-established rulers in the persons of Lothar and Louis the German, and a third pretty-well-established one in Charles the Bald. Indeed, it was probably the fact that Charles could exploit the political no-man's-land offered up by the head-to-head between his two half-brothers which allowed him to survive long enough to take a firm grip on the Aquitanian power base which his father had provided for him only two years before his own death. As a result, and Fontenoy notwithstanding, no one could achieve a decisive advantage, so the provisional split left by the father was confirmed by treaty at Verdun in 843 (Figure 14). Lothar retained the imperial title with which his father had endowed him back in 817, and was a touch richer than his brothers, but all three took firm possession of extensive realms. The younger Pippin, son of the dead Pippin, remained in Bordeaux, and his struggle with Charles the Bald carried on for a while, but, by 848, it was clear that his half-uncle was the man more likely to. Magnate support therefore eroded away. By 851/2, Pippin was enjoying full board and lodging at the monastery of Saint-Médard at Soissons, and although he would escape again, and even team up with some Vikings in the 860s, he was never able to attract enough magnate support to make himself a viable rival for Charles the Bald.[9]

We don't need to immerse ourselves – fortunately – in all the complex details of what happened next. In some ways, the brothers exhibited entirely contradictory behavioural traits. On the one hand, there was a huge emphasis in their public statements on an ideology of fraternal love: the importance of sharing nicely. Nor was it all bullshit. They held an astonishing seventy fraternal summit meetings, some of which even generated agreed joint policies. At the same time, they kept a very firm eye on the main chance and proceeded to exploit any opportunity that came their way to achieve a material advantage over their brothers. There were endless small- to medium-sized wars, therefore, such as the moment in 854 when Louis the German sent his second son, Louis the Younger, to Aquitaine in the hope of undermining his half-brother's control there.

This particular round of conflict further solidified matters since it ended with both Charles and Louis expelling magnates from their kingdoms whom they felt were overly inclined to support the other side.

The issue which really stirred things up, however, was the fate of the emperor Lothar's middle kingdom. Lothar died first, on 29 September 855, long before Louis and Charles. He was succeeded by his three sons but one of them soon died without heirs, and his lands were split between the remaining two: Lothar II and Louis II of Italy. The problem here was that Lothar II had no male heirs by his wife Teutberga, so wanted to divorce her and marry the concubine with whom he had already had a son. Seeing an opportunity, Louis the German and Charles the Bald opposed the divorce tooth and nail (although Louis II was more amenable). When Lothar II died in 869, the matter was unresolved and a further fraternal summit at Mersen in 870 led to the uncles dividing up most of the territory while paying off Louis II with a moderate cut (Figure 14).

For all of these adventures, it was necessary to bid for magnate support, whether to ensure that your own landowners were solidly on side, to attempt to seduce over the loyalties of those in your half-brother's kingdom, or to appeal to the rudderless: those left over after a king died without issue. Similar processes of repeated appeal were

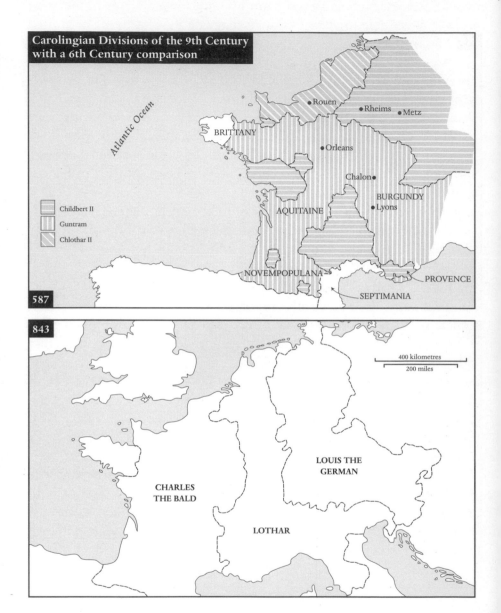

Carolingian Divisions of the 9th Century with a 6th Century comparison

587

Atlantic Ocean

• Rouen
• Rheims
• Metz

BRITTANY

• Orleans

Chalon •

BURGUNDY
• Lyons

AQUITAINE

Childbert II
Guntram
Chlothar II

NOVEMPOPULANA
SEPTIMANIA
PROVENCE

843

400 kilometres
200 miles

CHARLES
THE BALD

LOUIS THE
GERMAN

LOTHAR

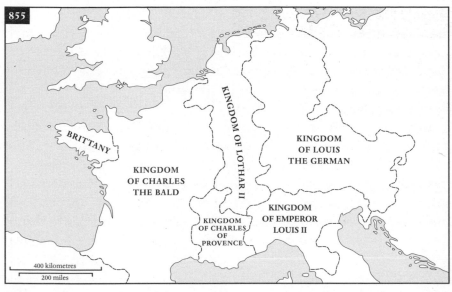

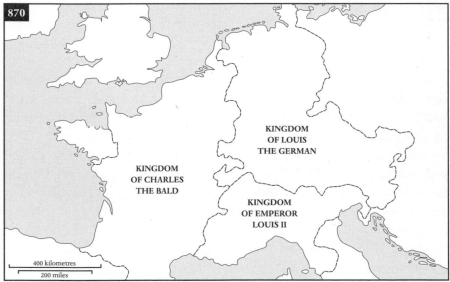

also necessary when, over time, a second dimension of political activity came into play as the children of Louis the German and Charles the Bald themselves came of age. Charles the Bald had six sons with two wives, of whom two made it to a politically active adulthood: Louis the Stammerer and Carloman. Louis had three in this category: Carloman (again), Louis the Younger and Charles the Fat. As true Carolingians, these princes expected a share of power while the fathers were still alive, and were entirely prepared to rebel either if they received nothing, or if what they did get failed to match their expectations. They could usually find some landowner support amongst those who were not doing as well as others in the current configuration of their fathers' regime, and, of course, any member of this next generation had a living half-uncle, who was always ready to stir up a little manure for his half-brother. So Louis the German supported the rebellions of Charles the Bald's sons, particularly that of Carloman, who refused to accept the clerical destiny his father had mapped out for him and pushed the point to such an extent in the early 870s that his father had him blinded and confined to a monastery (although he subsequently escaped again and lived out his days in his half-uncle's kingdom). Charles, likewise, had been happy to get his retaliation in first, when the other Carloman led the way against Louis the German in the early 860s and his brothers followed suit.[10]

While Charles and Louis, having weathered the early storms of vulnerability, were themselves pretty much immoveable from c.850 onwards, the course of Frankish politics was thus rarely stable, both for inner dynastic reasons, and also because Viking invasion was adding an interesting extra dimension to life at the top. Paradoxically, a third and critical dose of instability was provided by the kings' very longevity. This was all very well while they lived, but the problem came after their deaths: that of Louis the German on 28 August 876 aged seventy, closely followed by Charles the Bald on 6 October 877 at the age of fifty-four. It has long been noticed that the passing of these two old warhorses was followed by a clutch of rapid deaths among Carolingian males: no less than seven more in just five years from 879, beginning with Charles the Bald's chosen heir, Louis the Stammerer. The dead included all three sons of Louis the German, and here their father's longevity was the prime culprit. On average, Carolingian males who survived childhood made it to fifty or thereabouts. Louis made it to seventy, so that, at the time of this death, his sons were already forty-six, forty-one and thirty-seven. That they should have died soon after him is thus not so surprising.

And Charles the Bald, too, was at fault, though in a different way. Presumably having learned from his own and his brothers' behaviour, he looked to smooth the path for his one chosen son and heir, Louis the Stammerer, physically and somewhat brutally removing potential alternatives from among his own offspring, such as the blinded Carloman. But as Charlemagne's example showed, you could never be sure that one heir was enough, since if the average age was fifty, this means about half would die younger. Sure enough, Charles' strategy misfired. Instead of letting each generation look after itself, his attempts at assistance for Louis the Stammerer just left things in a mess when Louis himself died in 879 at the age of thirty-three. The Stammerer had two teenage boys, but they both died without male heirs shortly afterwards: another Louis in 882, and another Carloman at the end of 884.

By the mid-880s, therefore, the dynasty was rapidly running out of heirs, which generated a final brief moment of imperial unity, when Louis the German's youngest son Charles the Fat captured the allegiance of a critical mass of magnates from both his father's and his half-uncle's old realms. I was tempted to call this section *German, Bald, and Fat* in his honour, but decided this might be just a little flippant. Born in 839, Charles was already in his forties by the time he gained recognition in West Francia in 884, and his best days were behind him. Whether this contributed to his celebrated failure to break the grip of a large force of Vikings around Paris in 886 is unclear, but it certainly had a major impact on what happened next. As his grip in West Francia began visibly to weaken, the illegitimate son of his brother Carloman, Arnulf of Carinthia, launched a *coup d'état* against him in the autumn of 887. Charles suffered a stroke before he could respond, and from early in 888, Louis the German's old kingdom was in the hands of an illegitimate grandson.[11]

The really significant development, however, was what happened at this point in West Francia. OK, so Arnulf wasn't fully legitimate, but he was a Carolingian, and had the advantage of being a strapping twenty-seven-year-old with – hopefully – another two good decades of political life left in him. The West Frankish magnates, however, chose an entirely different path, electing one of their own number as king instead, an aristocratic landowner by the name of Odo. Nor was this the first moment that some West Frankish aristocrats had opted for a non-Carolingian. On the death of Louis the Stammerer in 879, one group of bishops and nobles from the regions around the rivers Rhone and Saône met in synod at Mantaille and elected as their king Boso of Provence. His best royal connection was the fact that his aunt Teutberga had been married to Lothar II (the very woman that he had been so desperate to divorce), while he himself had served both Charles the Bald and then his son. In fact, the surviving Carolingians, although in the middle of their great mortality-fest, found sufficient energy and co-ordination more or less to stomp on this usurper. Odo, by contrast, prospered – up to a point – winning great prestige by sweeping the Vikings out of the Paris basin. In due course, a portion of his nobility decided that they preferred to support a Carolingian, Louis the Stammerer's posthumous son Charles the Simple, and, on Odo's death in 898, the entire kingdom came back into Carolingian hands, and would stay so for the best part of another century.[12]

So why all the hype about Odo? Why make all that fuss about February 888 when it proved to be just a blip? Well, in an obvious sense, it was just a blip: within a decade, the royal title reverted to the Carolingian line. But in another, it was anything but. Especially when you add Boso into the picture, the phenomenon becomes pretty extraordinary. For well over a century, Carolingian kings-cum-emperors had reigned untouched, but suddenly we find two aristocrats within the same decade seeing no reason why they shouldn't put themselves forward to be king, and other landowners who were entirely happy to support them. The clear blue water which the combined careers of Charles Martel, Pippin the Short and Charlemagne had managed to put between the Carolingians and what were originally their fellow aristocrats had all but disappeared. This brute fact did not go unnoticed. As one contemporary commentator, Regino of Prum, put it:

After Charles [the Fat's] death, the kingdoms . . . were loosened from their bodily structure into parts and now looked to no lord of hereditary descent, but each set out to create a king for itself out of its own guts. This event roused many impulses to war, not because Frankish princes of sufficient nobility, strength and wisdom to rule kingdoms were lacking, but because among themselves an equality of generosity, dignity, and power increased discord. No one so surpassed the others that they considered it fitting to submit themselves to follow his rule.[13]

Nor did the return of the Carolingians in the person of Charles the Simple materially change the situation. He was not by any means powerless (nor simple in a pejorative sense; it should probably be translated 'Charles the Straightforward'). But it is the case that the tenth-century Carolingian monarchs of West Francia were in a much less dominant position vis-à-vis their own nobility than Charlemagne and Louis the Pious had been. The gap in wealth between themselves and the greatest aristocratic families was nothing like so large, they controlled fewer monasteries and bishoprics, the effective geographical range of their power was confined to the Île-de-France and some close outliers, and elsewhere a quasi-monarchical power (including such old royal monopolies such as the right to hold courts and mint coins) was being wielded instead by the dominant aristocratic families of particular regions (although the patterns of intra-regional power were far from stable from one generation to the next).[14]

In short, the tenth-century Carolingian monarchs of West Francia look much more like their later Merovingian forebears than the dynasty of Carolingian godfathers who had dominated Europe for a hundred years. In their – relative – enfeeblement, they stand in stark contrast not only to Charlemagne, but also to the line of rulers who picked up the mantle of Louis the German and Arnulf of Carinthia in East Francia. There, dynastic accident meant that the Carolingian line again died out, in September 911 on the demise at age eighteen of Arnulf's only legitimate son, the himself childless Louis the Child.

But, despite a similar emergence within East Francia, just as in West Francia, of powerful regional nobilities from the mess of the ninth-century Carolingian political process, a powerful central monarchy persisted there alongside the dukes. Indeed, in the persons of what was originally the family line of the Dukes of Saxony, it would even regenerate empire when Otto I had himself crowned in Rome on 2 February 962. To understand why the Carolingian political process of the ninth century created these substantially different outcomes in East and West Francia, we need to think in a little more detail about how it intersected with the networks of loyal magnates which had made Charlemagne and Louis the Pious so powerful.

THE END OF TAXATION

When, in the later ninth and tenth centuries, we see Carolingian rulers struggling to exercise as much influence over the localities of their *regna* as Charlemagne or Louis the Pious had done, this is telling us that the levers of power at their disposal – gifts and fear – had become less potent. It has precisely the same meaning as it did when we compared Merovingian kings of the later seventh and early eighth centuries with their sixth-century predecessors. The phenomenon has nothing whatsoever to do with any degeneration in the Carolingian genetic stock, and everything to do with a structural shift in the relative quantities of resources being controlled at the centre and out in the localities.

As soon as you think about the political processes which unfolded in Charlemagne's empire in the ninth century in the light of this key factor, you can immediately see why, over time, control of various assets would have tended to pass out of royal hands. For one thing, dividing the empire between more than one heir immediately reduced the financial distance between the value of the stock of key assets held by any individual ruler (actual land, rights to draw revenues from ecclesiastical institutions or markets, valuable rights to appoint to important positions, lay and ecclesiastical, etc.), and that of those of their greatest magnates. In the Treaty of Verdun in 843, the royal fisc (the sum total of these assets) was divided between each of Louis the Pious' three sons. This immediately and dramatically narrowed the gap between any one of them and their greatest magnates. The eventual reallocation of Lothar's lands bought Louis the German and Charles the Bald considerable reinforcement, but they were also having to hand out lands to their children, and never again, except for that brief moment under Charles the Fat, would all the fisc of Charlemagne's entire empire fall to a single Carolingian. And not only did Charles the Fat not live long enough – that crucial five to ten years – to make it stick, but, by 885, there is every reason to think that the overall total value of the fisc had anyway undergone substantial reduction.

The reasons for thinking this are straightforward. By the 880s, we have magnates who clearly think of themselves, and were thought of by others, as essentially the peers of their Carolingian monarchs. Not only the famous Odo, but also Boso of Provence were considered ripe for royal promotion. Obviously, such individuals would take over the remaining royal fisc if successful in their bid for power, but their own personal wealth must have been more than a little monarch-like anyway. They also had their East Frankish equivalents in the region's various dukes who were pretty much immoveable from *c*.900 onwards, so that, there too, magnates were looking much more king-like than they had been a hundred years before: a clear sign of and in itself that substantial quantities of assets had been transferred.[15] Equally important, the political conditions of the ninth century are more than enough to explain why a substantial transfer *should* have occurred. Broadly speaking, the prevailing situation from the later 820s onwards was one of intense political rivalry on at least two levels: first between two or more (and often several) reigning monarchs, and then second between them and other potential royal wannabes, in the form, frequently, both of their own children and of collateral relatives. It does look as though Charles the Bald, at least, learned the lesson and tried – as it turned out unfortunately to ill effect – to limit the amount of political competition that he bequeathed to the next generation, but until the great Carolingian cull of the later 870s, the general political context was one of multiple Carolingians bidding for the support of the militarized landowning magnate class. Without their support, no bid for a throne stood any chance of success.

The price of magnate loyalty was not remotely fixed. If you were faced with a truly scary individual like Charlemagne after he had conquered the Lombards, then you were probably pretty grateful if he gave you anything at all. At the other end of the scale, a collateral pretender currently without a kingdom would have to promise the earth to win support for an attempted *coup d'état*, and half-installed monarchs facing several rivals would have to pay something in between to shore up the foundations of their rule. But the political narrative of the ninth century makes it obvious that the general Carolingian fear quotient was heading downwards, and correspondingly that the political price of sufficient loyal followers to avoid a lengthy monastic holiday was on the up. In these conditions, there is every reason to accept what the political narrative is telling us, that the building-blocks of power – land, revenues and rights over key appointments – were passing out of royal hands at a steady, and probably increasing rate.

Two additional factors hurried things along. First, the main foreign policy problem facing the Frankish world – and indeed its Anglo-Saxon counterpart north of the Channel – was Viking raiding. The chief military difficulty was Viking speed of movement. Vikings came by ship and often brought horses with them too, or captured them when they arrived, so they moved around with great speed. Countering fast-moving raids was extremely difficult in Carolingian conditions, when messages had first to be transmitted over considerable distances to a royal court, and orders then sent out to military forces which were often not already assembled, since part-time militarized landowners would normally be living on their home estates. One obvious strata-gem, therefore, was to devolve power to a trusted regional magnate in endangered territories (basically anywhere within range of a navig-able stretch of river), who would be much closer to the action and able to organize a swifter response. Charles the Bald, in particular, faced with the many rivers piercing his territories adopted this reason-able measure in systematic fashion. But one of his trustees was a certain Robert the Strong, who was given a key command on the Loire, and the Odo made king in 888 was Robert's son. A family of trusted subordinates in one generation might gather sufficient rewards from this service, therefore, to morph into potential usurpers in the next.

This much had been just as true in the early Merovingian era, where the Carolingians had started life as the Merovingians' most trusted supporters in Austrasia. In the ninth century, however, a second factor stacked the deck still further in the favour of local landowning magnates: castles. We're still talking prototype, largely wooden models here, not the great stone keeps whose gutted remains still dot much of the landscape of Western Europe. But, in the ninth century, elite home improvement was taking the form of fortification for the first time, and the habit spread fast. In part, it was another response to Viking mobility. If you couldn't hope to mobilize quickly enough to counter them with large numbers, an alternative approach was to use a smaller numbers of warriors more efficiently, by making it difficult for the Vikings to get their hands on anything worth stealing. Fortified centres could serve as more general refuges and could also be held by relatively few men against relatively many.

Charles the Bald, in particular, was very keen on a whole range of fortifications – not only standard-type strongpoints but also fortified bridges at key points on river systems. Once the habit had been picked up and generalized by the greater magnates, however, this made it more difficult to intimidate a rebellious subject, since a castle could be held against a king just as easily as against Vikings.[16]

Older generations of commentators, convinced – as everyone was in the era of nationalism – that central state power was inherently better than regional magnate power, saw this unfolding process as a great tragedy, and the Carolingian Empire as a whole, and West Francia in particular, as might-have-beens brutally cut short by the wicked plots of magnates determined to resist their rightful rulers. In this historiographical world, magnates and kings were usually portrayed locked in a death-struggle for control of the landscape and historical destiny, with France and Germany as the Promised Land to which all the better, centralizing trends would eventually lead. More recent writing, less obsessed with thinking of things as either 'good' (where they seem to move things on towards a modern world dominated by nation states) or 'bad' (where they don't), has pointed out that, most of the time, kings and landowning elites can be found co-operating and certainly cohabiting more or less happily, and, having experienced twentieth-century totalitarianism, we are also well aware that there is nothing inherently better in central as opposed to regional power. As a result, much of the heat has gone out of the issue and, instead of local magnates bitterly determined to throw off central power, we are happy with a world where most of the prominent individuals contesting power in the late ninth century were – like Odo or Boso – from families with impeccable records as Carolingian loyalists.

All this is fair enough, but any temptation to replace an old vision of magnates determined to undermine royal power with a new one in which loyalists just pick up the pieces of royal collapse should be resisted. Positing too clear a dichotomy between loyalty and rebellion in ninth-century conditions would be misleading. Being loyal to a dynasty never stopped anyone from profiting from their loyalty. By definition, those best placed to profit from a process whereby assets were passing out of central control would usually be loyalists, for they will have been in the right position to gain most from any process of transfer. In exactly the same fashion, the Carolingian line started out as the prime supporters of Merovingian rule in Austrasia. And, as early Carolingian history shows so well, being a loyalist at one moment never precluded more self-assertive activity at the next. The patterns of behaviour displayed by the line of Robert the Strong, therefore, are not remotely odd, and find their match in other magnate lines besides. What they actually do is mark out an excellent recipe for success: strong initial loyalty to the ruling dynasty bringing enough wealth and power for subsequent members of a magnate line then to make themselves independent of central control.[17] And, of course, should things go really well, you might even find yourself in a position to try to seize the throne itself.

Rather than worrying too much about magnate morals and the extent to which the beneficiaries from the erosion of central assets were loyalists or usurpers, there is a more interesting point to be made. The fact that the political processes of the ninth century had such a profound effect on the balance between centre and locality is actually telling us something important about the fragility of central power in early medieval conditions. Unless the transfer of power from one generation of the ruling dynasty to the next was very straight-forward, then the subsequent process of regime-building was always likely to transfer assets away from the centre. And ideal transfers of power were not that easy to arrange. The death of two half-brothers, a further brother's religious bent and the early death of another were required to make it easy for Charles Martel, Pippin and then Charle-magne to monopolize power from early on in their reigns, and two more sudden fraternal deaths were necessary to clear the path for Louis the Pious. The amount of luck involved in these four generations of unproblematic succession was staggering, and could not go on indefinitely. And once that luck gave out, a cycle of asset transfer was always going to set in to undermine the – or in fact any – dynasty's overall power. This had nothing to do with the capacity of individual members of the dynasty, or with the greed of particular magnates. It was the product of some key structural changes which meant that Carolingian kings and emperors had considerably fewer levers of power in their hands than any late Roman predecessor such as Justinian.

Both Carolingian and Roman emperors faced, it is worth emphasiz-ing, the same governmental problem. Trying to run geographically vast empires with communications technologies where pretty much everything moved at about forty kilometres a day meant that, in most respects, localities would run themselves. The central authority just didn't have the governmental capacity to involve itself intensely in local affairs. The trick in both the Roman and the Carolingian context, therefore, was how to devolve power in such a way that it did not allow unavoidable local autonomy to degenerate into a dangerous degree of local independence, at which point the empire would fragment. But if the problem was the same, the weaponry that Charlemagne and Louis the Pious could deploy was considerably less effective than that available 500 years before.

Most important, they had neither the legal-cum-political right nor the administrative capacity to draw systematic and substantial tax revenues from their empire's agricultural production, by far the largest sector of any pre-modern economy, employing upwards of 90 per cent of the total population. The Roman world was divided into city-based administrative units – called *civitates* (singular *civitas*) – which consisted both of an urban core and of a – sometimes very large – rural hinterland. Extensive records of productive capacity and ownership were kept in the relevant *civitas*, from which tax liabilities for the surrounding countryside were calculated, and officers appointed in the *civitas* were responsible for collecting and passing on the designated tax levies. These taxes could be taken in the form either of actual produce or of cash according to the requirements and orders of the imperial government. These – relatively – massive annual revenues were spent above all on supporting a large professional army, consisting of several hundred thousand soldiers. The best guess is that something like two-thirds of the annual tax take was spent on the army, the rest being devoted to prestige projects of various kinds and the maintenance of that – again relatively – massive central Roman bureaucracy which dwarfs anything we see in the Carolingian period, or for many a century afterwards.

This articulated, interdependent structure of systematic taxation, professional armies, and overarching bureaucratic apparatus placed some highly effective levers of power in the hands of Roman emperors. At worst, if all else failed, the professional army, independent of allegiance to any local community, could be turned loose on rebellious subjects to compel their adherence to the imperial system. Such a high level of dissent surfaced only with extreme rarity, however, because the other levers of power exercised such an effective pull on local loyalties. The need to survey and measure local agricultural production, in order to tax it effectively, meant that imperial officials were all over local society like a rash, at least once every fifteen years when the tax rates were reassessed. But the fact that these imperial officials tended to be larger landowners, often with established affiliations to the local society they were investigating, highlights another important dimension of the relationship: the vast central bureaucracy was not merely there to administer things, it was also a patronage-distribution machine. The kinds of benefits you got as an imperial bureaucrat – especially as a retired one, which is when you might be called upon to run a tax reassessment for your home community – made bureaucratic jobs both desirable in themselves and, at the same time, the path to local political pre-eminence: a clever little double act which tied locally important landowners tightly into the imperial centre. If you add to this the fact that the empire's legal system also defined and protected these landowners' property rights, you can easily see why the army was rarely called upon to keep even rich local landowners in line. The imperial system had far too much to offer them in terms of protection and reward, with just a little constraint being applied now and again to keep them honest.[18]

Most of the key elements in this Roman imperial balancing act disappeared in the aftermath of imperial collapse. The tax system did not survive the fall of the empire unscathed, especially in areas north of the Loire which saw extensive Frankish settlement, since it looks as though Merovingian kings never taxed their Frankish (as opposed to their Roman) subjects. But tax registers are mentioned occasionally elsewhere in sixth-century Gaul, and Frankish kings regularly fought each other for control of particular *civitates*. And when the kingdom was divided between a number of sons, sixth-century partitions often involved what look like geographically odd partitions, with individuals receiving not just discrete blocks of territory, but also clusters of *civitates* dispersed across the map (for an example, see Figure 14 and compare it to the nice straight lines of the ninth-century Carolingian partitions alongside. This makes most sense if individual *civitates* were still generating known annual tax incomes, making the purpose behind the geographically odd partitions to achieve a required balance in the annual revenues accruing to each of the parties. But by the later Merovingian and hence certainly the Carolingian periods, except perhaps in the form of limited residual dues (owed in cash, kind, or other services) attached to particular institutions, the Roman taxation structure had ceased to function. There was no attempt to tax agricultural production systematically, and the administrative structure which had made it all possible had disappeared. Royal revenues were now derived from a much more ad hoc mixture of landowning, customs tolls and an agreed percentage of judicial fines. The *civitas* had also been allowed to break up everywhere into a larger number of counties: a clear sign that its central function – raising taxation – had itself lapsed.

On the face of it, giving up systematic taxation rights was a ridiculous thing to do, but there were good short-term reasons for being so generous. As far as we can reconstruct it, three parallel processes made taxation rights an attractive asset for kings to give away. First, large-scale taxation was much less necessary to successor-state kings than it had been to their Roman imperial predecessors. The majority of Roman tax income was spent on maintaining a professional army. Merovingian armies (outside of semi-professional royal household forces) consisted of their greater and lesser landowners mobilized for individual campaigns, and this liability for military service was one of the key rights that kings enjoyed over their subject population. Second, all the more general evidence also indicates that the economy of the post-Roman West declined not only in overall output but also in complexity and frequency of exchange. This meant that, at the same time as taxation became less necessary, tax yields both declined overall and became increasingly difficult to turn into useful cash: as opposed to kilo after kilo of actual foodstuffs. Third, we can deduce that there was a huge desire on the part of one section of the kingdom's population for taxation rights to be granted away. The Merovingians' Frankish followers do not originally seem to have paid tax, and resisted all attempts to impose it with gusto – the odd lynching of tax officials is recorded in our sources – since they provided military service instead. But, from early in the sixth century at the latest, Roman landowners were also being called upon systematically to perform military service. There is a myth out there in some of the literature that fighting in the post-Roman West was done by incoming barbarians and their descendants, while surviving members of the old Roman elite hid themselves in the Church in disgust. There are some famous examples of such a response, but also of the descendants of incoming barbarians moving quickly into the Church too. And, when you go looking for it, there is an overwhelming body of evidence that the vast majority of the surviving Roman land-owning aristocracy and gentry morphed not into Christian clergy, but into the early medieval warrior elite. The sixth-century Merovingian Frankish army was built around contingents from *civitas* territories, before the *civitates* ceased to exist, and many of these had never seen a Frankish settler. These contingents were composed of local Roman landowners and a picked bunch of their largest and most aggressive retainers.

From early in the sixth century, therefore, Romans were fighting for their Frankish rulers alongside the descendants of Frankish settlers, but still had to pay taxes, whereas their new Frankish comrades did not. This must quickly have been perceived as unfair and, once it was, tax remissions will have become the favour of choice that Roman subjects wanted from their Merovingian rulers. There is no surviving documentation to allow us to follow the process in any detail. Only some ecclesiastical institutions have had a continuous existence and maintained archives from the early Middle Ages into more recent times, so the only surviving examples of Merovingian tax remission apply to monasteries and episcopal sees. I have no doubt, however, that the absence of extant remissions to lay landowners is merely reflecting the lack of any mechanism which might have preserved such records and has no greater significance than that. As the sixth century progressed, there became no easier way for a monarch to win a little political support than by granting a landowner of Roman descent the seemingly cheap favour of a little immunity from taxation, until, bit by bit, the whole tax structure eroded away. My own guess would be that these grants took the form of allowing the now tax-free landowner to form his own administrative unit free of the old *civitas*, so that this also explains how the old *civitas* network broke up into the pattern of much more numerous counties characteristic of the Carolingian period.[19]

This was a short-to-medium-term transformation with massive consequences for the future. In several critical respects, these changes made it significantly harder for rulers of geographically extensive entities in the early Middle Ages, such as the Carolingian Empire, to prevent local autonomy from cascading into independence. First, local elites were themselves now armed. This made it much more difficult (though certainly not impossible in individual instances) to constrain them *in extremis* than when Roman rulers had an entirely independent professional army at their disposal to turn on civilian local elites. Not only could armed local elites now put up more resistance, but there were also likely to be much more complex political problems involved in setting one set of armed landowners loose on another one. Second, the jewel in the crown of the local elites' financial assets – their landed estates – were not touched by systematic royal taxation, and, once the tax structure had eroded, early medieval rulers were much less rich than their late Roman counterparts. Not only did these rulers have less need of a bureaucracy, therefore, but they actually couldn't afford one, which further diminished the hold they might exercise on local elites. Since the late Roman bureaucracy was as much for distributing patronage as it was for actually administering things, its disappearance removed another magnate magnet from the ruler's armoury. Third, and not least, because the local elites ran their own courts and provided, through their own armed capacity, both their own legal structure and an enforcement mechanism, the central state mechanism was no longer the ultimate guarantee of elite status through the protection it provided for property rights.

Fundamentally, the early Middle Ages saw the emergence of a new 'smaller' type of state structure. With no state-run professional army, no large-scale systematic taxation of agriculture, and no developed central bureaucratic structures, the early medieval state swallowed up a much smaller percentage of GDP than had its Roman predecessor. As far as we can tell, this had nothing to do with right-wing ideologies and everything to do with a basic renegotiation of centre–local relations around the brute fact that landowning elites now owed their ruler actual military service, which put their own very physical bodies on the line. Equally important, all the changes conspired together (although I'm sure none of this was ever planned) to make it much more difficult for early medieval rulers to hold together large geographical areas over the longer term.[20]

There was also one further, critical difference in the *type* of economic assets that the ruler of a smaller early medieval state structure had at his disposal. Although late Roman emperors were landowners in their own right, like their Carolingian successors, they drew the majority of their much larger overall income from tax revenues. And tax revenues were entirely renewable. If you spent your entire tax income from year one in year one, you still received exactly the same income in year two, and so on ad infinitum. By contrast, most of the Carolingians' financial muscle came in the form of a fixed stock of capital assets, whether we're talking land or the various rights which might generate a revenue stream (to hold a market or court, or make an appointment to a desirable office, etc.). If, to win magnate support, you gave any of these items away in year one, that gift automatically reduced your income in year two. From this followed the fact that the Roman Empire could bumble along for centuries, however messy the succession process (and often it was extremely messy), because regime-building in the Roman world did not strip out the empire's central asset base. The Carolingians, on the other hand, required more or less untroubled successions to achieve the same outcome. And since genetic accident was only going to give you so many untroubled successions in a row, the central power of the Carolingians – or that of any imperial dynasty in early medieval conditions – was time-limited in a way that its Roman predecessor was not.

And yet, on occasion, you could still build up inter-regional, imperial-type authority in early medieval conditions. The Merovingians achieved it in the sixth century, the Carolingians in the eighth, and the Ottonians would manage the same feat in East Francia in the tenth. The reasons behind these exceptional moments, when the prevailing systemic obstacles to imperial or at least interregional authority were overcome, allow us to generate one final crucial perspective on the 'small' state of the early medieval West. This brings both Charlemagne's achievements and their limitations fully into focus.

THE FIRST REICH

It is possible to tell the story of what came subsequently to be known as the first Reich – though until there was a second Reich after the Franco-Prussian War, it was just 'the Reich' – in any number of ways, and in greater or lesser detail. An obvious path into it is the progression of its ruling dynasties and we need a little of that for scene-setting. It was a direct descendant of the East Frankish kingdom of Louis the German, although the Carolingian line was extinguished there in 911 when Arnulf's son Louis the Child died without issue. At that point the kingdom consisted of four duchies: Franconia, Saxony, Swabia and

Bavaria, each with their own ducal lines (Figure 15). Although it was never uncontested, the position of king passed from Louis the Child to Duke Conrad I of Franconia, whose wife was related to Louis' mother. He had to battle hard to establish his authority, however, and eventually died in 918 of wounds incurred in battle against the Duke of Bavaria: the fabulously named Arnulf the Bad. Conrad had a brother but was himself of the opinion that the man most likely to hold the monarchy together was the Duke of Saxony: Henry the Fowler (my old history teacher liked to indulge in a little bathroom humour at this point, but Henry just liked hunting). Henry first got the Franconians and Saxons to acclaim him king in 919, then constrained the Swabians and Bavarians into line. He also added a fifth duchy, Lorraine, to the kingdom before passing on the crown to his son Otto I. Otto prospered both in East Francia and beyond, even to the extent of conquering most of Italy, and this became the basis for his own imperial coronation on 2 February 962. Otto passed on the imperial mantle to eponymous sons and grandsons: Otto II and Otto III. But, on the latter's death in 1002, the imperial baton passed to the line of Otto's younger brother Henry, who had been installed as Duke of Bavaria, although the latest Henry (they were all called Henry to save confusion) was not crowned emperor until 1014. When he died in 1024, the Ottonian dynasty gave out entirely, and power passed to a succession of four king-emperors from the Salian line. Down the years, there followed a bewildering range of dynastic transmissions until Napoleon called time on the whole enterprise after the battle of Austerlitz in 1806, but we don't have to worry about anything beyond the mid-eleventh century. So the pattern of dynastic transmission within the East Frankish kingdom which became the Holy Roman Empire in 962 went from Carolingians to Conradines, to Ottonians, to Salians. And since the Ottonians clearly styled themselves as the direct descendants of Charlemagne, and their spin doctors invented the concept of *translatio imperii* – 'transfer of empire' – to explain a) that it was the direct continuation of the essence of Charlemagne's imperial authority, and b) that it was therefore God's will (where have we met this before?), you could be forgiven for supposing that the Holy Roman Empire of Otto the Great would be the next and final destination for this book.[21]

But as the same history teacher also liked to say, the Holy Roman Empire was neither Holy nor Roman. Behind the joke, there is an important sense in which these latest emperors, powerful and impressive as they were (and the Salians will play an important role in the final chapter), nonetheless do not stand in the direct line of attempted *Roman* imperial restorations examined in this book. Theoderic, Justinian and Charlemagne can be thought of as 'Roman' in one or more of three separate dimensions of meaning. Their empires can reasonably be called Roman either in terms of the character of the state they created (Theoderic and Justinian), or in the coincidence between the geographical extent of their power and the bulk of the old Western Empire (Theoderic and Charlemagne), or because the state they created was the overwhelming dominant force in the Christian European landscape of its time (Justinian and Charlemagne). Thanks to late Roman precedent and its Byzantine continuation, and as we saw in the course of Charlemagne's careful manoeuvrings towards it in the 790s, in early medieval Europe the imperial title had come to mean above all else 'supreme leader of Christendom'.

The Holy Roman Emperors do not quite pass muster as properly Roman on any of these counts. For one thing, the empire, even at its height under Otto I, comprised only East Francia and north and central Italy. The rich and extensive territories of West Francia were not brought under its wing, so that it never rivalled Charlemagne's creation in size. Moreover, as the empire was born, European Christendom was expanding rapidly. The *reconquista* was busy returning large parts of the Iberian peninsula to the Christian fold from the mid-eleventh century onwards, and the tenth century had seen the rise of the first Christian states in Poland, Bohemia, Hungary and western Russia (Figure 15). Otto and his successors were simply not in a position to echo the level of overarching dominance within the Christian and/or Roman landscapes achieved by Theoderic, Justinian and Charlemagne.[22]

But if, for that reason, there is no need to explore the history of the Ottonian Reich in its own right within the confines of this study, one particular feature of what was originally East Francia does demand our attention. What happened in East Francia in the later ninth and early tenth centuries, broadly speaking, was a kind of Carolingian Collapse Lite. The region saw much the same political process in action as the rest of the Carolingian world. Louis the German faced periodic rebellion from multiple offspring, aided and abetted by his half-brother's interference. It generated, likewise, exactly the same need for all pretenders to build solid bases of support by handing out the required levels of reward to the militarized landowning classes, with similar consequences. The transfer of assets, amongst other things, created the evident wealth and political security within their own domains of the ducal lines that were an established feature of East Frankish politics from the time of Arnulf of Carinthia at the very latest. But although the creation of four powerful dukedoms (or five, counting Lorraine) looks like a perfect setting for ultimate political fragmentation, as happened in West Francia, this was not the outcome. First Conrad, then Henry I and Otto had to battle away at times to prevent it, but that final political fragmentation did not occur in the Frankish east. Why not?

There are several elements to the answer. For one thing, East Francia was slightly less affected by the great Carolingian cull of the later ninth century, and Arnulf of Carinthia deliberately returned to the political rhythms of assembly and contact that had been established by his grandfather Louis the German. So, for the vast majority of the fifty-plus years between the Treaty of Verdun and Arnulf's death, East Frankish political life had operated in exactly the same way from the same centres of power. This generated a continuity of tradition which played a major role in shaping the mentalities of East Frankish magnates, who more naturally expected to operate together, for certain purposes at least, as a single unit. Such expectations played a major role, for instance, in their largely unanimous willingness to accept Louis the Child as king after Arnulf's death, at a time when non-Carolingian regional magnates of West Francia were either making themselves kings, or just ignoring royal authority as irrelevant.[23]

They also had strategic reasons to hang together. The first substantial Slavic-speaking polity to emerge in central Europe was so-called 'Great' Moravia, centred on modern Slovakia, where some astounding physical remains of the architecture of its capital at Mikulcice can still be seen. Moravia was a successor state to the Avar Empire which Charlemagne destroyed, and figures substantially in East Frankish annals from the mid-ninth century onwards as the main client state beyond its south-eastern borders. The history the annals tell – like that of any of the frontier clients of the old Roman Empire – saw alternating periods of war and peace, with Moravia being drawn ever closer into the Frankish orbit. Despite its best efforts, it even accepted – eventually – an East Frankish version of Christianity, expelling the Byzantine missionary Methodius who had originally operated there with his brother Cyril. But in the 890s the Moravian kingdom was destroyed by

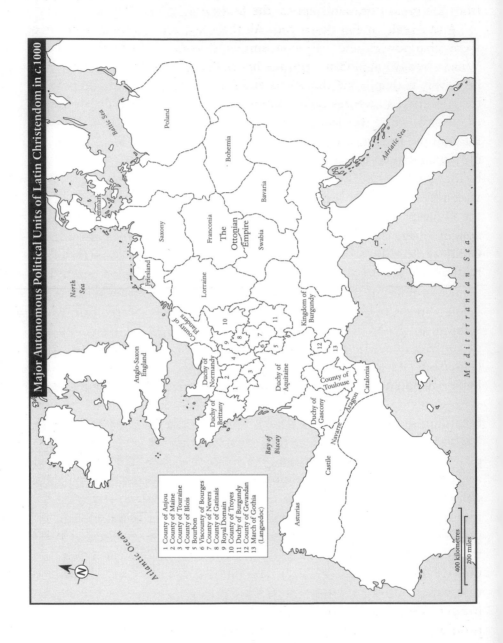

Major Autonomous Political Units of Latin Christendom in c.1000

1 County of Anjou
2 County of Maine
3 County of Touraine
4 County of Blois
5 Bourbon
6 Viscounty of Bourges
7 County of Nevers
8 County of Gatinais
9 Royal Domain
10 County of Troyes
11 Duchy of Burgundy
12 County of Gevandan
13 March of Gothia
(Languedoc)

Atlantic Ocean

North Sea

Baltic Sea

Denmark

Friesland

Anglo-Saxon England

Poland

Bohemia

Saxony

Franconia

The Ottonian Empire

Bavaria

Swabia

Lorraine

County of Flanders

Duchy of Normandy

Duchy of Brittany

Duchy of Aquitaine

Kingdom of Burgundy

Adriatic Sea

Mediterranean Sea

County of Toulouse

Catalonia

Duchy of Gascony

Bay of Biscay

Castle

Asturias

Navarre

Aragon

400 kilometres
200 miles

the latest wave of nomadic horsemen to penetrate into central Europe from the great Eurasian steppes: the Magyars.

And I really mean destroyed. All the great architectural structures were abandoned, and Moravia simply disappears from the annals. What's really significant about the Magyars for present purposes, however, is that – like the Huns and Avars before them (page 183) – their internal structures relied on large-scale downward redistributions of wealth from the leadership to smooth over potentially divisive internal political rivalries. As a result, the arrival of the Magyars could only spell danger for their new neighbours, and the early tenth-century history of Frankish Europe is marked by a new explosion of nomad violence. In 907, the Magyars inflicted a heavy defeat on the army of the Duke of Bavaria at Pressburg, and followed that up in 910 with an equally heavy defeat of the combined East Frankish army of Louis the Child at Augsburg. These victories presaged a decade and more of raiding which periodically disturbed the peace not only (if primarily) of East Francia, but ranged as far afield as Provence and northern Italy. Facing up to the Magyar threat required joint action, therefore, to stand any chance of success and a crucial factor in the rising prestige of the Saxon line was its ability – eventually – to provide effective leadership. As told by its own chroniclers, the story is that a truce Henry negotiated with the Magyars in 926 was critical to his eventual success, even though it cost him annual tribute payments. In the breathing space, a series of settlements were fortified as refuge centres for the rural population, with elements of the latter organized to provide them with effective garrisons, while the main East Frankish army was retrained and re-equipped as heavy armoured cavalry. This construction is surely hiding a degree of humiliation in the arrangements of 926, but the military reorganization was real enough and provided Henry with the wherewithal to inflict a first major defeat on the Magyars at Riade in 933 (which followed the unilateral ending of the tribute payments in 932). When the Magyars came off the reservation for the last time in 955 it further allowed Otto to inflict a massive defeat on them at the battle of the river Lech. This both prompted a major political restructuring among the Magyars, as they were forced to move towards a political economy which was not so dependent upon raiding, and propelled Otto on towards the imperial title.[24]

But none of this yet takes us quite to the heart of the matter, at least in terms of why Conrad should have thought, back in 918 before the Magyars had been defeated, that the Saxon was the best-placed ducal clan to maintain traditional East Frankish unity. When thinking about evolving patterns of power within any political landscape, it's usually a good idea to focus on economic resources. Power always has other components besides, but 'follow the money' – Deepthroat's famous advice to Woodward and Bernstein as they unravelled Watergate – usually works in historical analysis too, even if you're talking not just about cash (although there was some of it), but also land, jobs, and the bundle of varied rights which, as we've seen, often stood in for cash in early medieval contexts. Even more transparently in East Francia, since there is little sign of any central bureaucratic apparatus at all, the careful manipulation of these resources to create loyalty within the militarized landowning class underpinned the successful exercise of central power. The rulers of East Francia thus faced the same political problem as their Western peers. How could you generate the requisite loyalty in one generation without depleting the central stock of rewards available for regime-building in the next?

The Ottonian line of Saxon dukes did not manage to reinstitute large-scale taxation of agricultural production (if they had, they really would deserve to rank as a fourth 'Roman' imperial moment). But they did get their hands on two other sources of much more renewable wealth than the usual early medieval bundle of land, appointments and rights, which they could use to grease the wheels of magnate loyalty without bankrupting their own position. One was highly specific. From the 920s, the silver ores of the Harz Mountains were exploited with increasing intensity and to the particular profit of the Saxon line. There are no figures for the scale of production, but it funded the Ottonians silver coinage which rapidly became the predominant currency of tenth-century Europe. New mining settlements (of which there were many, all signalled by place names ending in -rode) grew up swiftly in the region, and the result was a flow of renewable income into the Ottonian coffers, much of which could be recycled towards the magnates without undermining the holdings of lands and rights which otherwise made the dynasty politically pre-eminent.[25]

The dynasty's other source of renewable wealth derived from regular expansionary warfare. In the Middle Ages in particular, but actually in most contexts, there is a key political distinction to be made between defensive and offensive warfare. The latter is usually much more popular, because the opportunities for economic benefit are often so much larger. Where you are fighting to protect your home-lands, there are few – legitimate at least – opportunities for collecting booty, but foreign opposition is always fair game. And if you are, strategically, in a position not just to conduct raiding, but steadily to expand your frontier line, this creates a whole stock of new positions for your magnates to hold, as well as bringing on stream a range of new lands that you can distribute to them without reducing your own stock of assets. In the case of East Francia, it was only the Saxon duchy in c.910 which had access to an open frontier. The other duchies either bordered other parts of Francia itself or the formidable Magyars, whereas the eastern border of Saxony, beyond the Elbe, opened out into Slavic-dominated territories. This West Slavic world was currently right in the middle of a process of demographic, economic and political development which would eventually so expand the borders of Euro-pean Christendom. In c.900, east of the Elbe, these processes had gone just far enough, however, to provide the armies of Henry I and his successors with a series of decent targets: areas with enough population density and general economic activity to make them worth the effort of conquest. The sources report extremely regular campaigns, and the dukes were quick to recycle the profits of conquest to secure the loyalty of their magnates. By the 950s, extensive marcher lands had been added to the duchy (Figure 15), and, within these regions, new positions and landed estates could be granted without it costing Otto a penny from the royal fisc.[26]

When you widen the scope to the early medieval West more generally, it becomes inescapable that there was a structural link between access to an open frontier of this kind, and periods when central as opposed to local power was in the ascendant. Not only did the fruits of expansion power the Ottonians to pre-eminence within East Francia, but they were also a crucial element in the rise of the Carolingians. It really is one of the most significant statistics of them all that Carolingian armies were in the field for eighty-five out of the ninety years from the accession of Charles Martel to 803/4. The vast majority of these campaigns were aggressive and expansionary, and the renewable wealth they liberated – in all its forms – made it possible for four generations of the dynasty to build their regimes without eroding the fixed assets of the royal fisc. The linkage works equally well for the Merovingian era – where the central authority of the dynasty was at its height during the generally expansionary sixth century – and even (if you're interested) to Anglo-Saxon England as well. There, the kingdoms which were originally the most wealthy and powerful were those benefiting from the profits of trading and other links with the continent, above all Kent. Its later fifth- and sixth-century cemeteries throw up a great deal of gold ornamentation and its kings were politically pre-eminent in the early seventh century when Bede's political narrative begins. As the seventh century progressed, however, political pre-eminence became increasingly the preserve of the 'outer' kingdoms of Wessex, Mercia and Northumbria, all of which shared borders with native sub-Romano-British kingdoms and were able to expand at their expense. This gave their kings booty to sell or recycle, not least slaves, and renewable stocks of land which they could use to attract further warriors to their train. Not long after 700, the residual wealth of Kent ceased to be a sufficient basis for political pre-eminence in the face of this military might. Instead, it became itself merely an attractive target for the predatory ambitions of the new powers in the land. In the small-state world of early medieval Europe, expansionary warfare replaced large-scale taxation as the source of renewable wealth that was necessary to maintaining a powerful central authority in anything but the very shortest of terms.

So intimate, indeed, was the link between controlling the fruits of expansion and maintaining central authority, that the inverse correlation works equally well. Whenever a previously powerful central authority ceased to benefit from the rewards of expansion, then its authority quickly eroded, because each subsequent generation was now having to fund regime-building from non-renewable assets. We have already seen this correlation at work with the ninth-century Carolingians, but it applies equally to the seventh-century Merovingians, and in Anglo-Saxon England too. There, once the Picts and northern British had organized themselves sufficiently to fend off further Northumbrian expansion in the later seventh century, the kingdom's eighth-century rulers paled into relative insignificance in the face of internal political instability. It also applies to the Ottonians. By the 980s, processes of development had gone far enough in the Slavic world to close off the open frontier. Via a mixture of rebellion on the part of previously subdued Slavs and outright resistance from new Slavic forces, where the kingdom of Poland plays a starring role, Ottonian expansion eastwards came to a grinding halt, and the later members of the dynasty and their Salian successors quickly found it much more difficult to exercise central authority than had Henry the Fowler or Otto I.[27]

All of which prompts one final question: if expansion was so crucial to the longer-term exercise of central authority, filling the massive gap in royal finance created by the end of taxation, why did later Carolingian monarchs allow it to end? Various suggestions have been put forward, including the thought that it was not felt to be legitimate to continue expansion beyond the area of old Merovingian hegemony at its height. But that is very unconvincing, not least because Charlemagne's rule actually went far beyond it in most directions. It has also been suggested that, after the imperial coronation, old age, the costs of the Saxon wars (which had taken twenty-plus years) and his interest in matters Christian between them deflected the royal eye from the ball of conquest. There is something to these other lines of thought, and the ageing Charlemagne was much more fixed in his new royal palace at Aachen, but they don't explain why expansion did not begin anew under his successors.

A more profitable route into the problem is to consider expansionary warfare in terms of the cost–benefit equations which governed it. Expansionary warfare would bring in profits, but also involved costs, not just in financial terms (food, weaponry, etc.), but also in personal terms since some of those participating would certainly die. If you think about it in this way, then the ideal profile of an area ripe for expansion is easy enough to construct: it needs to be economically developed enough to offer a satisfying level of reward both in terms of moveable booty and potential land-grabbing, but militarily not so well organized that too many of your expeditionary army, on average, are going to die winning access to the prize. There is also the further point that the costs – emotional as well as financial – increased with distance, since the stresses and strains all become much higher and you are cut off from your home and mainstream concerns for so much longer while on campaign to some distant land.

If you run your mind round the borders of the Carolingian Empire in the early ninth century, it becomes clear, I think, why expansion slowly ground to a halt. In the south, the territories of Muslim Spain were rich and highly desirable, but the peninsula was full of well-organized Islamic polities which fought expansion tooth and nail. Even apart from the famous defeat at Roncesvalles in the Pyrenees, extensive

Carolingian efforts succeeded only in expanding the frontier as far south as Barcelona. This slow progress contrasts massively, and revealingly, with, say, the conquest of the Lombards. The best bits of Italy, likewise, had already been swallowed up, and all that was left was either poor and mountainous or else still in those Byzantine hands which were not at all easy to prise open. In the Balkans, after the defeat of the Avars, further progress was blocked by a powerful mixture of the Bulgar and Byzantine empires and, anyway, the central Balkans were not the most attractive source of potential rewards that one might think of. The eastern frontier on the river Elbe, beyond Saxony, remained a possibility, and Louis the German did campaign effectively there, but that northern region was still not so economically developed as it would be a hundred years later when the Ottonians could exploit it to greater effect, while, further south, sufficiently solid Slavic structures were already emerging in Bohemia and Moravia to make expansion difficult. On every corner of the frontier, the cost–benefit equation was starting to deliver a negative answer, either because the enemy was too formidable (Spain), or because the likely benefits were not that great (the Balkans), or some combination of the two (southern Italy and the southern Elbe region).

The strategic situation was generally unripe for further expansion, but how did that generate a decision to stop mounting campaigns? It is inconceivable that Charlemagne or Louis the Pious sat down with a map, not least because they probably didn't have one, and went through the same kind of analysis that we have just done. The answer, I think, lies in the fact that the wars of expansion were actively fought by the politically important landowning class, who provided the bulk of the army. That the Carolingian express had reached the buffers of expansion would actually have become lived experience for them, taking the highly perceptible form of an increasing number of lives being lost for a decreasing level of benefit. And since these men were politically important, some of them having contact with their rulers in the regular cycle of assemblies, then the likeliest a priori model for how expansion actually came to a halt would be that the build-up of resistance to further campaigning on the ground eventually forced the rulers' hand. And when you go looking for it, there is just a little evidence that shows precisely this kind of process in action. It was Louis the Pious' determination to send Hugh of Tours and Matfrid of Orleans, two of Lothar's chief supporters, off to fight in Spain, for instance, which sparked off enough suspicion and outrage in Lothar to bring him into open revolt. In their view, and Lothar's too, the costs of being excluded from internal political manoeuvring had become more important than any benefits to be gained from participating in expansion warfare.

And this, to my mind, adds one more important layer to the analysis. The militarized magnates of the Carolingian world were actually working with a pair of simultaneous cost–benefit equations in their heads. On the one hand, they were calculating potential gains and losses from campaigning beyond the frontier, but, simultaneously, they were comparing the kind of answer they were getting from this with a similar calculation about the potential costs and benefits of political intrigue at home. Not only was the campaigning equation delivering a much more negative answer from c.800, but from the 810s, or certainly from the *divisio regni* of 817 at the latest, its internal political pair was looking much more positive. From then on, while there was currently still just the one ruler, stocks and shares in the futures market in political allegiance were rising steadily with three heirs looking for supporters, a trend which the arrival of Charles the Bald only accelerated. To my mind, therefore, political pressure from the military elite brought expansion to a halt, as it became less rewarding and the potential rewards of selling your loyalty grew internally. And the latter of course both offered rewards in a very local currency which our magnates highly prized, and meant that they would not have to go trekking off either across the Elbe or beyond the Pyrenees. The real story of the end of expansion, therefore, is not so much of the halting of violence altogether as of its refocusing from external to internal enemies, and this only emphasizes how dangerous to the power of the Carolingian monarchy the end of expansion actually was.[28]

THE CREATION OF EUROPE AND
THE END OF EMPIRE

Thinking about them in the round, the history of these three attempts at Roman imperial restoration prompts, I think, one conclusion above all. By the end of the first millennium, it was no longer possible to create imperial dominion across the European landscape on the same geographical scale that Rome had achieved. Rome had used a demographic and economic base in the Mediterranean to conquer all of western and southern Europe and broadly intimidate much of the north-central zone of secondary development besides. By the year 1000, the rise of Islam had fractured the unity of that power base, decoupling its southern shores from the rest, and turning the rump of the East Roman Empire into medieval Byzantium, as much of a successor state in its own way as any of the Western kingdoms.

But even if the Mediterranean had remained united, the region would no longer have provided sufficient resources to dominate western Eurasia on anything like the same scale. Around the birth of Christ, when Rome exploded to imperial dominion, there had been three distinct zones of development within northern Europe, and all three were operating less intensively in demographic, economic and political terms than the new empire's Mediterranean power base. By the year 1000, the gaps within northern Europe had narrowed dramatically and the overall strategic edge available in the earlier era to a Mediterranean-based state had disappeared. Population densities in what had been the western La Tene region a thousand years before, and in parts of the old north-central zone – in the heartlands of the Ottonian Reich as far east as the river Elbe at least – had by this point surpassed those of the Mediterranean, as the careers of Charlemagne and Otto I make so very clear. Western and north-central Europe were now the basis of states which could predate upon Italy and Rome, not vice versa. And while still lagging someway 'behind' as it were (not that anyone was racing), in the sense that its potential resources were as yet far from so fully mobilized, patterns of life in the third zone of northern and Eastern Europe had also been transformed out of all recognition. What had been the abode of small dispersed populations of simple Iron Age farmers – a world which was so cut off from the rest of Europe in the first half of the millennium that its archaeological remains show not the slightest signs of contact with Rome – now supported much larger populations, an increasingly diverse economy, and some robust political structures of its own.

All this amounted to a complete revolution in prevailing regional balances of strategic power, which was already so far advanced that, even if the north and east still lacked some of the complexity and intensity of agricultural and other economic activity visible in the west, its new dynasties still commanded power bases of sufficient size to fend off encroaching imperial domination from the west. In the later tenth and eleventh centuries, for instance, the Ottonian Reich became embroiled in complex diplomacy with the new state that the Piast dynasty was constructing in neighbouring Poland. Relations oscillated between friendship and competition, and the first Reich was undoubtedly the more powerful of the two. But when diplomacy gave way to conflict, the Reich did not find it possible simply to conquer the Piast state. Even though it was open to cultural influences from the Reich in the form of Christianity, the Polish kingdom was both too far away and too powerful to fall easily under its military subjugation. What we are really seeing by the end of the first millennium is that Europe – defined as a zone of more or less equal societies engaged in complex political, economic, and cultural interactions – was actually coming into existence. The old, massive disparities were a thing of the past, and, as a direct result, it was no longer possible to base a dominant empire on one corner of the European land mass which happened to have undergone a more precocious process of development than the rest.

Somewhat paradoxically, the evidence suggests that the past exercise of imperial dominion had played a fundamental role in stimulating these same extraordinary changes which now rendered empire impossible. What you see, again looking right across the first millennium, is broadly a two-stage process. The economic, social and political structures of the Germanic world went through a similar set of structural transformations on the fringes of the Roman world in its first 500 years, as the Slavic world did subsequently on the fringes of Francia in the 500 years which followed, with some extra imperial stimulation in their case being supplied by contacts with the Avars, Byzantium and, above all, Islam. In older traditions of writing about these kinds of subject, empires were usually portrayed as doing things to, or for, their less developed neighbours, bringing them such fruits of civilization as writing and Christianity. Having seen globalization at work, and moved in time beyond the great era of European imperialism, we are rightly less confident that empires always bring benefits to those with whom they come into contact. But trading with empires, picking up new farming techniques from them, receiving their diplomatic subsidies, copying their weaponry and ideologies, and organizing yourself to fend off the worst excesses of their domination, all pushed forward the sequential emergence of more developed economies and larger state structures in the Germanic and Slavic worlds in the two halves of the first millennium. The language of 'civilization' or 'gift' really doesn't capture the process. All empires operate in their peripheries over-whelmingly for their own benefit, and not everyone in the periphery comes out ahead in the long-term transformations which follow. Rather, particular groups in the periphery are able to take advantage of the opportunities opened up by the range of new contacts with an imperial neighbour, and this is precisely what we now call globaliza-tion. But out of that particular dance there does eventually emerge much greater overall economic strength in the periphery, bigger populations, and more robust political structures centred on those who benefited most. Over the long term – and we are talking centuries of contact – Roman and Frankish imperialism thus played a central if indirect role in constructing the peripheral powers which would eventually blunt their imperial spears. Instead of seeing peripheral populations as passive recipients of imperial civilization, the story is one of particular groups in the periphery exercising agency to profit from a new situation.[29] The aggregate strategic effect could not have been more profound.

As a direct result, a restored empire that captured the essence of the Roman original had become completely impossible by the year 1000. Not only had Islam broken apart ancient Mediterranean unity, and the balance of power in Western Europe shifted decisively north of the Alps, but, still more fundamentally, patterns of development were now much too equal across the broader European landscape. Thanks to this equalization of development, you might say, the scene was set for the thousand subsequent years of fruitless warfare which followed as Europe's dynasts intermittently struggled to achieve a level of overarching dominance that was in fact impossible. In that sense, it took the nightmare of two world wars in the twentieth century before the European Dream was finally called into existence to try to put a stop to the process of endless armed competition between powers that were always too equal for there to be an outright winner.

But if a traditional empire of military and economic dominance on the old Roman scale had become impossible by the year 1000, a new kind of empire was about to be reborn from the ashes of the Carolingian and Ottonian imperial projects. Emperors of the Roman type operating on a truly Roman scale were a thing of the past, and their centre could certainly no longer hold; yet a thousand years after the birth of Christ, a rough imperial beast of an entirely new kind was slouching forward to be born, this time not towards Bethlehem as Yeats imagined it, but towards the old imperial capital itself.

PART FOUR

SECOND COMING

7

CHARLES THE GREAT AND
LEO THE POPE

ST PETER'S IN ROME has the largest interior of any Christian Church on the planet. Sitting on the site of the original St Peter's constructed by the emperor Constantine in the fourth century AD, the current edifice was begun on 18 April 1506 and took over a hundred years to complete. Its dedication ceremony was finally held on 18 November 1626, the project having absorbed the energies and intellects of a Renaissance dream team that included Bramante, Michelangelo and Bernini. St Peter's is neither the mother church of the Roman Catholic communion, nor even the Pope's cathedral as Bishop of Rome. That honour belongs to the Lateran, where Pope Leo III originally erected his famous mosaic as part of his campaign to limit the damage done to his own position by Charlemagne's imperial coronation.

The extraordinary religious status of St Peter's stems entirely from the fact that its high altar stands over what the Christian community of Rome, since time immemorial, has considered the burial place of St Peter. And with some reason. He was executed in the Neronian persecution of AD 64 in the Circus of Nero which stood close by, and there is indeed a Roman cemetery of the right vintage containing early Christian burials under the basilica, some of which were explored in a decade of excavations from 1939. I wouldn't necessarily be as confident as was Pope Pius XII, in his famous radio broadcast of 23 December 1950, that the bones of St Peter had been found, but the downward trail had led the excavators to some fragments of bone folded in gold tissue and tinted with precious imperial purple in an area beneath the original Constantinian basilica which had been monumentalized in the late Roman period, and inaccessible since the ninth century. The excavators had at least found what late Roman and early medieval Roman Christians identified as Peter's last resting place. Which is enough to make St Peter's basilica a very special place indeed in any Christian language, but, above all, in that of Roman Catholicism.

For St Peter is the cornerstone of papal authority which binds together the Roman Catholic communion, as the great church itself reminds you. As soon as you enter its majestic doors, you are brought face to face with a very large, and very clear inscription (admittedly in Latin . . .) of the key verses from St Matthew's Gospel:

> You are Peter and upon this rock I will build my Church, and the gates of Hell shall not prevail against it. And to you I give the keys of the Kingdom of Heaven; and whatever you bind on earth shall be bound in Heaven, and whatever you loose on earth shall be loosed in Heaven.[1]

This is no accident. These words, Jesus' famous response when Peter correctly identified Him as 'the Christ, the Son of the living God', are the rock on which papal authority has itself been constructed. St Peter is considered the first Pope, the first Bishop of Rome, and to have passed on to his successors a unique religious authority – encapsulated in the right to bind and loose sins – which this passage can be read as indicating that Jesus himself had originally granted to St Peter. Filled out and refined over the years, papal authority within the Roman Catholic communion encompasses a number of key responsibilities. The Pope must ultimately define correct Christian theology, not necessarily by being an academic theologian himself (though he might be), but at least by instigating and controlling necessary debates and their outcomes. He must also make laws sometimes and define norms in others – again, of course, after taking the appropriate advice – which set out expected standards of religious practice and personal moral behaviour for both clergy and laity. He is responsible, too, for creating and sustaining the enforcement structures which ensure that these standards are adhered to. Last but not least, he exercises control over appointments at least to the top positions (bishop and upwards) within the Church.

Employed together, these powers allow the Roman Catholic Church to operate as a multinational religious corporation, bound together by one set of rules and a rule-making CEO in the person of the Pope himself. These papal powers, and their overall effect – a centralized Church body which functions as a unit across political boundaries – are indeed ancient features of the Christian landscape. They are not quite as ancient, however, as is usually imagined.

One of the most original poetic works to survive from the court of Charlemagne is an anonymous Virgilian epic which might have been penned by our old friend Einhard. It goes under the title given to it by its modern editor: *Karolus Magnus et Leo Papa*. As titles go, this is fair enough. The surviving fragment of (probably) its third book ends with the meeting of Charles and Leo at Paderborn, and it has long been supposed that there was a fourth book culminating in Christmas Day 800. But the poem originally contained much more besides. Two other books are entirely lost, and even the surviving fragment of book three contains a great deal more than the fateful meeting which led to the restoration of empire.

In the poem, Pope Leo is treated with the greatest sympathy and respect. The horrified poet recalls the appalling behaviour of the citizens of Rome towards 'the greatest pastor in the world', and pays due respect to the miracle of the Pope's recovery from his wounds:

> [Charlemagne] is amazed by the Pope's eyes which had been
> blinded,
> But to which sight had now returned,
> And he marvelled that a tongue mutilated with tongs now spoke.

But there is not the slightest doubt that the dominant figure in the poet's landscape is Charlemagne himself. Throughout the poem, Charlemagne is always placed in lofty positions, so that he physically dominates the action. When the Pope arrives, the Frankish army is drawn up at the bottom of a hill but Charlemagne himself is on the top, and descends to greet his guest. The word 'emperor' is dropped into the poem, likewise, even though its action is set in 799. This was indeed the contention, as we've seen, of Charlemagne and his court: God made Charlemagne emperor long before 800, and all Pope Leo did, as a Christmas present for the rest of humanity, was – eventually – recognize the fact. Of a piece with this, the poet's main focus, prior to the meeting, is on Charlemagne as the founder of a New Rome in the form of his palace complex at Aachen. This is central to the poet's choice of Virgilian epic because he took as his model Virgil's picture of Aeneas founding the first Rome. The image, however, is carefully adapted. The reader is left in absolutely no doubt that the new Rome is superior to the first (and this is a trope that is found more generally among the poets of Charlemagne's court).

Even more interesting is the general description of Charlemagne at work, with which the poem precedes its account of Aachen. It all begins as you might expect. Charlemagne is the great but compassionate victor of countless campaigns who is generosity itself to all his loyal followers. He also humbles the proud, raises up the weak (blah blah), but then it gets more interesting:

> He admonishes [the unjust] to learn justice by godly deeds,
> Bowing the heads of the impious, shackling them with stiff
> chains,
> And teaching them to fulfil the commands of God enthroned
> on high . . .
> Those who, barbarian-like, have long refused to be pious
> Are compelled from impiety to piety by a righteous fear.

And the reason he is able to do this is his superb intellect and devotion, which has allowed him alone to understand the mind of God:

> He alone has deserved to take possession of all approaches to
> learning,
> To penetrate its hidden paths and understand all its mysteries,
> For to him God reveals the universe's development from its
> beginnings.

The poet claims for Charlemagne a uniquely close relationship to the Almighty and provides him with a corresponding job description which tramples all over the preserve of the papacy as we now know it: not only compelling barbarians to become Christian, but defining correct Christian behaviour for all of his subjects. For all that Leo is treated with great respect, his religious authority pales into relative insignificance next to Charlemagne's hotline to the Almighty. Indeed, Charlemagne knew all about Leo's problems, long before any messenger came from Rome, precisely because God sent him news of it in a dream. In the picture painted by our poet, Charlemagne's relationship to God provides him with a political, moral and religious authority which transcends any possible rival, even the *apostolicus*, the Bishop of Rome.[2] Before dismissing this as the kind of thing a Carolingian court poet would say, we need to take a closer look at the inherited traditions of political and religious authority within which Charlemagne and Leo were operating.

EMPERORS AND PATRIARCHS

There was already a Christian community within the city of Rome in the time of the Acts of the Apostles. At this point, and as the new religion spread over subsequent generations, you have to envisage the broader Christian civilization, or ecumene as Christians themselves called it, taking the form of a slowly increasing number of essentially autonomous congregations dotted around the major cities of the Mediterranean (like frogs round a pond, as Socrates famously put it). These congregations ran themselves and were in only periodic contact with one another, not least because the Roman state unleashed occasional bouts of persecution against them. There was no formal, institutionalized hierarchy of religious authority either between the congregations, or even, at least to start with, within them, since the position of priests and bishops took time to formalize, and both general leadership and theological analysis were sometimes supplied by what we would now call members of the laity. But, from the haze which surrounds this earliest period of Christian history, we have the occasional moment of clarity which shows that the congregation of Rome, and particularly its leadership, occupied a position of special prestige thanks to its association with two of early Christianity's greatest leaders: Peter and Paul. This special prestige is already referred to in a famous letter of Ignatius of Antioch dating to the first decade or so of the second century, and could, on occasion, translate into an unusual degree of religious authority. From the same era, a famous letter survives from Pope Clement I in AD 96 to the congregation of Corinth, where he interferes in an intra-Corinthian dispute over the rights of priests. Or, a hundred years later, Pope Victor I acted much more generally to excommunicate any Christians (so-called Quartode-cimans) who insisted on celebrating Easter on the same date as the Jewish Passover. The congregation in Rome was itself also growing steadily and, already in 253, under Pope Cornelius, consisted, apart from its bishop, of no less than forty-six priests, seven deacons, seven sub-deacons, fifty-two exorcists, and assorted readers and doorkeepers. But because there was as yet no formalized hierarchical structure within Christianity as a whole, Rome's interference in the affairs of other communities was limited to the (very) occasional statement of general principle (such as Victor's excommunication), or particular moments when another congregation asked the Roman leadership for a ruling on a difficult issue. Precious few examples of such requests survive from before *c*. 300, and there is no hint that the surviving evidence preserves just the tip of some great melted iceberg.[3]

All of this changed with the conversion of the emperor Constantine in the early fourth century, and the Church's subsequent promotion to become the official religion of the Roman state. As this process unfolded, against the backdrop of an ever-increasing rate of conversion which multiplied the number of Christian congregations within the empire beyond measure, the Church acquired its first articulated authority structure. This formalized, for the first time, the role of the papacy within Christianity as a whole. Compared to later patterns of development, and even to what various popes liked to say about themselves at the time, the way these new structures actually operated comes as something of a surprise.

The importance of the Roman see within the new structure was formally acknowledged across the wider Christian world (which quickly became coterminous with the boundaries of the empire). One major effect of Constantine's conversion was to allow – indeed enable: he paid for it out of imperial funds – the tradition to grow up of Christian leaders from across the empire meeting together on an occasional basis in great ecumenical councils when there were serious issues to be settled. The very first of these met at Nicaea in 325, and its sixth canon (canons being the list of a council's decisions) recognized the special apostolic status which attached to the Bishop of Rome's see, because it had been founded by St Peter. In practice, this had several dimensions of importance. First – and most specifically – all bishops were no longer considered equal. Certain sees acquired metropolitan rank (effectively becoming archbishops, although that term was not yet in general use) with established rights to interfere in certain ways in the running of the subordinate sees of their province: specifically to call regular synods to maintain standards of belief and practice, and to confirm all episcopal elections. I use the word 'province' advisedly. With just the occasional exception, it was the capital cities of existing Roman imperial provinces which acquired metropolitan rank, and their areas of authority were generally coincident with provincial boundaries. More or less overnight, the administrative hierarchies of the Church came to mimic those of the imperial government. Within this extraordinary shake-up, the see of Rome acquired metropolitan rights over a substantial area around the city.[4]

Second – taking in a broader view now – Rome's traditional role as an occasional court of appeal for difficult Church matters acquired new importance. The form in which such rulings were customarily given changed in a highly significant manner. The straightforward letter-form of the early Christian period gave way in the time of Pope Innocent I (401–17) to the much more formal, and subsequently characteristic, papal decretal. The decretal was modelled on the imperial rescript, which was a specific type of letter used by emperors for centuries to give formal, fully reasoned answers on the bottom half of a letter, to a legal inquiry set out on the top. The emperor's answer had full legal force and often dictated subsequent legal practice for all analogous cases. Mimicking this particular letter form was a highly significant move, therefore, showing us a papacy which was determined that what had started out as little more than statements of opinion should now be viewed as legally binding rulings. The increasing frequency and wide geographical range of the decretals from a cluster of popes in the early decades of the fifth century is particularly impressive. Between them Innocent I, Zosimus I, Boniface I and Celestine I (covering the years 401–32) gave formal rulings to Christian congregations not only within Italy, but as far afield as Spain, Gaul and North Africa.[5]

Third, and widening the view still further, Rome's apostolic heritage meant that it had a prominent position to fill in the ongoing doctrinal disputes which are such a characteristic feature of late Roman Christianity, not least the so-called Arian dispute, which produced the variant form of Christianity adhered to by Theoderic. The basic reason why theological dispute was so prevalent in the years after Constantine's conversion offers a fascinating glimpse into the revolutionary effects of becoming a state religion. Up to the fourth century, there had been occasional doctrinal controversies, which led to a handful of splinter groups, such as the Quartodecimans, being effectively expelled

from the mainstream Christian tradition. Once Roman state persecution stopped, however, inter-congregational communication grew in
intensity, and it soon became clear that a great deal of Christian
doctrine had not yet been fully developed. Constantine's conversion
thus set loose – and also funded – what looks, from the perspective of
modern university life, like a 250-year research project to bring bishops
and other Christian intellectuals together on an irregular basis at a
mixture of smaller workshops and the occasional huge international
conference (the ecumenical councils) to fill in doctrinal gaps and tie up
any loose ends.

In broad terms, the theological subjects covered were, in chronological order: first, in what sense was Christ divine (the Arian dispute):
how should the position of the Holy Spirit within the Trinity be
understood; and, third, how exactly was the human and the divine
combined in the person of Christ (the Monophysite dispute). And, in
between, other more localized Church groups – with occasional help
from the outside – faced up to disciplinary issues such as whether
Christians who lapsed in the face of persecution could be fully
readmitted to the Church (the Donatist dispute in North Africa) and
could you have too much asceticism (the Priscillianist and Pelagian
controversies, among many others).[6]

Don't worry about the detail. The broad picture is what matters,
and that is straightforward. The relatively isolated and occasionally
persecuted congregations of the early Church had assumed they all
believed approximately the same things. When Constantine and his
successors put them in much closer contact with one another, it
rapidly became clear that they didn't, or at least hadn't thought about
some matters hard enough. The sequence of disputes marks an
unavoidable process by which sufficient i's were dotted and t's crossed
to bring an appropriate level of theological coherence to what had
now become the imperial religion. Rome's apostolic status meant that
its participation in this process was fundamental, and, in particular,
that any doctrinal formulation struggled to acquire the necessary aura
of legitimacy orthodoxy, if the Bishop of Rome failed to sign up to it.
Hence, in the time of Theoderic, as we saw in Chapter 2, the emperor
Zeno's Patriarch of Constantinople, Acacius, backed a compromise
solution to the Monophysite dispute which could just about work in
the Eastern Church, but Rome refused to accept it. In the end, Justin
and Justinian brought the East back into line with the papacy. Rome's

status meant that it functioned as a touchstone of orthodoxy in the developing world of late Roman Christianity.

Fourth, and finally, there was still time to tie up some ideological loose ends. This was necessary because a couple of distinct leaps of argument are required to turn Jesus' words in Matthew's Gospel into a justificatory charter for the powers of the papacy as they now stand. You had, first of all, to accept that the power granted to St Peter was transferable to his heirs, rather than a gift made to him as an individual. Then you had to make the case that Peter's heir was the current Bishop of Rome because he had been the first Bishop of Rome, even though there was nothing describing him as such in the Gospels or Acts of the Apostles, the key ancient texts of Christianity. But true believers have never allowed the absence of authentic documentation to stand in the way of something they believed to be correct, and, true to form, the gaps in the St Peter story were carefully filled in. At some point in our period, a key text was generated originally in Greek and then translated into Latin round about the year 400 by a Christian scholar monk by the name of Rufinus. Known as the *Clementine Recognitions*, this purported to be a letter of Pope Clement I to James, the brother of Jesus and leader of the Church in Jerusalem. In it, Clement told James how he had been converted and trained by St Peter, and how, lo and behold, Peter had eventually passed on his unique religious authority to Clement by virtue of naming him as his successor as Bishop of Rome. Both ideological gaps were filled with one textual stone. Clement was chosen as the subject of the forgery, presumably, because of that genuine early letter to the Corinthians which was already widely known. Just to make sure, Pope Leo I, a generation later, carefully demonstrated that all of this was entirely in accord with Roman law on inheritance, and the circle was fully closed. In the meantime, just in case one Apostle wasn't enough, Pope Damasus I had also got a local Roman synod to declare, in 382, that the Church of Rome was unlike any other Christian community because it had been founded by two Apostles, St Paul and St Peter, adding a further string to the bow of papal uniqueness.[7]

So far so good. In all of these areas, the papacy managed to exploit the exciting opportunities that opened up after Constantine's conversion to strengthen its claims to Christian religious authority. But the Roman Church was not the only Christian game in town, and if you broaden your gaze to consider overall patterns of Christian religious authority in the late Roman world, the position of the Bishop of Rome starts to look distinctly less impressive. Let's start specifically. The metropolitan powers the papacy acquired within the region of Rome, specifically over the same suburbicarian provinces which had long been subject to the administrative competence of Rome's urban prefect, were no more than those now exercised by the bishop of every other provincial capital. There was nothing at all unique here.[8]

The issuing of decretals, by contrast, was unique to popes, but the importance of this activity in building general papal power must not be overstated. For one thing, decretals – like imperial rescripts – could only be issued if someone asked the original question. At the height of the popularity of the imperial system, for instance, we know that emperors were turning out something like five rescripts a day. And even if, after the pattern of modern legal terms, you give emperors quite a bit of time off, they were still banging out several hundred a year. In the early sixth century, Dionysius Exiguus – the famous Denis the Little – whose collection is the ultimate source of most of our knowledge of papal decretal activity, could find only forty-one examples from the almost 200 years separating his own time from Constantine's conversion. This suggests that consulting the Pope had not yet become a regular activity in the Western Church. There was also a further problem. Producing an answer that you considered authoritative was one thing, and in their answers popes often stressed that their formally reasoned responses should command complete obedience. But they possessed no enforcement mechanism. If a Pope gave an answer that was not obeyed, there was nothing that he could do about it by himself. *In extremis*, imperial support was sometimes even needed, as in 445 when Leo I extracted an imperial ruling to support his own view in a quarrel with Bishop Hilary of Arles.[9]

Even that, however, is not the end of the bad news. Fellow late Roman Christians were happy enough to recognize that Rome was a very special place, but not that it was a unique one, since other early Christian communities had also been founded by Apostles. The sixth canon of Nicaea picked out the churches of Antioch and Alexandria as apostolic foundations, alongside Rome, and canon seven added Jerusalem to the list. These were joined in 381 by Constantinople which was declared (at a council unsurprisingly held in Constantinople) as the New Rome, which was henceforth to be viewed in every respect as equal to the Old Rome. By the 380s, therefore, the classic late Roman pattern had emerged, which consisted not of one see of unique prestige, but of five Christian patriarchates of equal pre-eminence. Consequently, Christian Orthodoxy was – ideally – to be defined as those things that all five patriarchs held to be true. In this context, the *Clementine Recognitions* and Damasus' emphasis on Rome's double-apostolic foundation were part of a fairly desperate attempt to put clear blue water between the see of Rome and a set of peers, who were perfectly happy to recognize it as an equal, but were not buying Rome's uniqueness.[10] And if it were not bad enough, the patriarchs were overshadowed by another source of Christian religious authority altogether: the emperor.

At this point it is worth recalling the checklist of functions which currently defines the papacy as the corporate head of the Roman Catholic communion: ultimate regulation of what constitutes orthodox belief; defining and enforcing standards of Christian practice for both clergy and laity; making Church law; and controlling senior Church appointments. If you analyse all the late Roman evidence against this checklist (and do not just focus on the papacy), then it quickly becomes apparent that the functioning head of the Christian Church in the late Roman period was in fact the emperor.

Let's start with doctrine. The 300 years or so following Constantine's conversion were an extraordinarily creative period in theological terms, when most of the key Christian teachings reached full definition. The papacy had some role in this process, but, in fact, a surprisingly marginal one. Decisions over correct doctrine were made at the great ecumenical councils, Nicaea in 325 followed at irregular intervals by Serdica, Constantinople and Chalcedon before the deposition of the last Western emperor in 476. These councils were all held in the East (even Serdica, modern Sofia, was in the eastern half of the Balkans), and most of the intellectual running in the big theological debates was being made in the East too, by Christian intellectuals working primarily in Greek. Apart from Chalcedon where Pope Leo I contributed a major document, known as the *Tome of Leo*, the Latinate papacy otherwise just sent a few observers and let Eastern churchmen get on with it. Many of the assumptions of Greek philosophy and science provided basic methodological tools for developing Christian doctrine.[11]

A still more fundamental role in the action, however, was played by the sequence of Christian emperors. We've already encountered the fact that emperors underwrote the mechanics of developing doctrine by providing free transport and board and lodging to hundreds of bishops at a time, as they were carted (literally) around the empire to the next theological shindig. A pagan historian of the fourth century, Ammianus Marcellinus, is particularly scathing on the frequency and cost of Church councils under the emperor Constantius II (337–51). Apart from the big four, there were many smaller councils besides, and some other equally large ones which came to what was eventually decided to be a 'wrong' answer so that they don't figure in standard lists of ecumenical councils, although that is in fact what they were. The emperor's role in all these councils was far greater than merely opening the imperial chequebook. It was always his decision whether and when to call the larger councils: without his say-so they simply didn't happen. Allied to this, emperors usually also set at least part of the agenda for discussion – which was only natural since most councils were called for a particular reason. They also applied vast pressure on the participants to achieve the outcome they wanted, and supplied the only enforcement mechanisms which were available to make conciliar decisions stick: by exiling deviant clergy, for instance, or confiscating Church buildings and wealth from whole sects that ended up being condemned.

Individuals varied greatly in the intensity of their interest in precise matters of doctrine, Constantius II and, later, Justinian, being known for their love of theological detail, but all emperors were interested in peace and unity within the Church, which is the other theme running alongside the purely intellectual element in late Roman doctrinal debate. All emperors were ready to get involved in the Church at least to that extent, therefore, and, in overall terms, the imperial will was more important even than conciliar debate, to the doctrinal outcomes which eventually emerged. Take, for instance, the so-called Arian debate on the right term to use to describe the relationship of the human and divine within the person of Christ. Nicaea came up with one definition in 325, but it took two generations for that definition to win final acceptance. In the meantime, other definitions entirely were supported as orthodox by the Roman state for lengthy periods. Debate only came to an end in the 380s when supporters of rival, non-Nicene definitions could no longer find any imperial support, and the state settled down to consistent enforcement of the Nicene position. The same pattern holds true in disciplinary matters. The big issue here came from North

Africa: the so-called Donatist dispute over the status of those Church leaders who had given way in the face of the Great Persecution which had preceded Constantine's conversion. While imperial will vacillated, which it did through much of the fourth century with different regimes adopting different policies, the dispute raged on. As soon, however, as imperial policy hardened behind one resolution of the dispute – deciding very firmly against the Donatists – and unfurled the full panoply of imperial enforcement behind that resolution, the dispute quickly declined to irritant status. It's not that all Donatists disappeared, any more than all non-Nicene strands of opinion had done either, but once the imperial will definitively backed a position, opponents' support tended to fall away so substantially that they quickly declined from a movement to a sect, at which point emperors ceased to care very much. Bishops and intellectuals may have done most of the thinking, but it was emperors who made doctrinal outcomes actually happen (or not), by calling councils, building the necessary coalitions at these councils to pass a particular view, and then enforcing that conciliar decision with due determination.[12]

The emperor's role in setting and enforcing general standards of practice for clergy and laity was also substantial. Papal decretals played some role here in the Latin West, but there were many more rules and regulations set out in the canons of different Church councils (where the emperor's role in at least the larger ones was primary), and also in direct imperial legislation. Book Sixteen of the *Theodosian Code* consists entirely of imperial legislation on religious matters made between the time of Constantine and c.435, and Justinian's *Code* collected a great deal more in the early 530s. The base line of canon law in the late Roman period was provided by a mixture of the conciliar decisions and imperial legislation, with papal decretals coming in a poor third in terms of the quantity of relevant and widely circulated rules for Christian clergy and laity. On enforcement, the empire's court structure was again important, but this was supplemented by one important novelty. From the time of Constantine onwards, bishops were empowered to hold courts and any Christian participant in a dispute might request that their case be transferred there. But, as matters developed, this court turned in practice into a kind of small-claims court which aimed at reconciliation and mediation rather than outright punishment. This obviously limited the kinds of cases that might be heard before it (certainly not, for instance, anything that might involve capital punishment since bishops were prohibited from shedding blood). And since episcopal courts had been licensed by imperial law in the first place, this again emphasizes imperial pre-eminence in the area of Church law.[13]

The same goes too, finally, for senior ecclesiastical appointments. Emperors cared not a jot who was bishop of the kind of tiny diocese you find, for instance, in and around the Pyrenees. But they cared very much about who was in charge of the great cities of the empire, and, above all, of its central and regional capitals. Interestingly, this did not really mean Rome. By the fourth century even the western half of the empire was being run from Milan or Trier, and later Ravenna, while the key cities of the East were Constantinople, Antioch and Alexandria. Rome remained a cultural capital, but, in the entire fourth century, emperors visited it at most on four occasions for about a month at a time. Papal elections, therefore, did not attract too much direct imperial interference, although when they led to violence, as in the election of Pope Damasus in 366, that was quite another matter. In the case of sees they cared about, emperors obtained and retained the right to control appointments.[14]

Without any doubt, the emperor was the functioning head of the Christian Church. Others, including popes, played a part, but the imperial role in the formulation of correct doctrine, in defining and enforcing expected standards of practice, and in selecting personnel was paramount. Nor was this domination purely de facto. Late Roman political theory – as we've seen adopted by Theoderic and inverted by Procopius – claimed that the emperor was directly appointed by God and carefully selected by Him to rule as His vicegerent on earth. These ideas came straight from non-Christian, Hellenistic visions of kingship, but the conversion of the empire to Christianity generated remarkably little change. The divinity in question was relabelled the Christian God and the divine purpose was recast as one of bringing the totality of mankind to Christianity, rather than creating perfectly rational *civilitas* for the few (page 56). But there was no reduction in the claim made about the closeness of the emperor's relationship to God. Everything to do with the emperor remained sacred – from his treasuries to his bedchamber – every imperial ceremonial from the greatest public occasion to the smallest, most intimate moments (such as the act of *proskynesis*: prostrating yourself in the imperial presence to show due respect) were orchestrated to ram home the point. The emperor was no ordinary mortal and, in public at least, was expected to maintain a superhuman impassivity as ceremonial moments unfolded around him. It's possible that Constantine took it all too far. His original burial arrangements entombed his remains in a great mausoleum (the Church of the Holy Apostles) in Constantinople, surrounded by altars to the twelve Apostles. It has often been said that he thought of himself as the thirteenth apostle. But the thirteenth individual usually found in the middle of the twelve apostles is Christ, so you do wonder who exactly Constantine thought himself to be. His son, Constantius II, quietly rearranged things to make a slightly more modest statement. But only slightly: Constantius and his successors, East and West, all the way to Justinian and beyond, were entirely consistent in their claim to have been picked out by God to rule with Him on earth.

Looking at how matters have unfolded in the many centuries following the late Roman period, and in particular at the more or less complete separation of Church and State which has been the norm in the Western political tradition for a couple of centuries, it is only natural to take notice of the past lines of thought which lead to this present. From the late Roman period, this means a voice such as that of Augustine of Hippo, who argued in *City of God* that no earthly state could ever be so perfectly reflective of the divine will as to last forever. God did make states rise and fall, Augustine argued, but for His purposes alone, and they would endure only for so long as they were able to serve His higher purpose which was systematically divorced from their own. Augustine had been thinking along these lines for some time, but an extra stimulus for him to put pen to paper in this way was the Gothic sack of Rome in August 410. Nor was he alone in directly challenging some of the central claims of Roman state ideology. Every time a churchman resisted an imperial attempt to impose a particular doctrinal settlement, they were implicitly and sometimes explicitly denying the emperor's right to order Church affairs, and, sometimes, that resistance was serious. Athanasius, Bishop of Alexandria, managed to make the province of Egypt pretty much ungovernable for a brief period in the 340s, for instance, because he was so opposed to the emperor Constantius' preference for non-Nicene theology. Or again, the whole Christian ascetic tradition which grew enormously in both numbers and influence from the mid-fourth century, was by implication denying the claims of imperial ideology. If the Roman emperor and the political structure he ruled reflected the divine will for humankind, then individuals should not drop out of it, and look to the salvation of their souls by imitating the self-denial and rejection of the world that was central to the examples of Christ, the Apostles, and many an Old Testament prophet. But we have numerous examples in Saints' Lives from this period of precisely this kind of rejection of public participation in the affairs of the Roman state, even among members of the elite. Put all this together, add a good dose of hindsight, and it's relatively easy to dismiss the claims of imperial ideology as so much hot air.[15]

To do so, however, would be a serious mistake. While you can trace lines of resistance to the emperor's religious authority in the writings of some churchmen, you can equally well find another line of acceptance in the writings of others. Almost at the moment of Constantine's conversion, for instance, Bishop Eusebius of Caesarea was ready to accept that it was no accident that Christ should have been born at the moment when Augustus – the first Roman emperor – was ruling in Rome. This showed, Eusebius argued, that God had foreordained, earlier persecutions notwithstanding, that the Roman state would become His vehicle for bringing humankind to Christianity. The Roman state did, in other words, have a role in the Divine Plan which was unlike that of any other. And, by extension, that made the emperor much more than merely another secular ruler. In the session of the fourth ecumenical council at Chalcedon on 25 October 451, likewise, 370 assembled bishops (some via agents, it's true) hailed the emperor Marcian as 'king and priest'. This cry was no break with tradition, just a specific formulation of a well-established line of thought. Or, again, this time at the fifth ecumenical council in Constantinople in May 553, 152 bishops, this time, were happy to declare that nothing should happen in Church matters without the emperor's explicit approval.[16]

For every dissenting clerical voice from the late Roman period, there are ten others which implicitly or explicitly accepted the emperor's claim to overarching religious authority. And, in fact, you need to be very careful with the dissenting voices anyway. It's not uncommon, when you look closely, to find the same individual violently objecting to imperial claims when the emperor was backing an alternative doctrinal position, but upholding them heartily when the emperor was onside. That's not to deny the existence of deep and principled dissent in some clerical quarters to the emperor's view of his religious authority, but the vast majority of Christian clergy and indeed upper-class laity – for the ascetics were only ever a small if noisy minority – essentially accepted that the emperor was chosen by God and should therefore exercise at least a watching brief over all Church matters. He might, and indeed should, let bishops do the detailed theology, but it was entirely in line with his job description to find the God-guided wisdom to choose between competing positions, and to ensure that his subjects – God's people – ended up following the paths of true belief and proper Christian piety. This left only a secondary role open to the papacy, especially in a world of five equal patriarchs, where most cutting-edge theology was being done in Greek.

KINGS AND BISHOPS

Most of the parameters within which the papacy had been operating since the conversion of Constantine were transformed out of all recognition in the period between the deposition of Romulus Augustulus and the coronation of Charlemagne. A unitary Western Empire gave way to a series of successor states, most of whom eventually became Nicene Christian at some point between the fifth and eighth centuries, even if their ruling elites had originally started out as something else. The political structures of this new world were far from stable, however, and within a 300-year period from AD 450, the papacy began by operating within the confines of a still-living Western Empire. It then spent sixty years under the rule of the successor states established by Odovacar and Theoderic, before finding itself part of the Eastern Empire run from Constantinople. This lasted for the best part of 150 years, until the eighth century when the papacy started to run Rome and its environs as an independent political unit, while having to fend off the unwelcome attentions both of Lombard kings and the independent Lombard Dukes of Spoleto and Benevento. Interesting times!

As with the late Roman period, if you approach these centuries with hindsight, it is possible to discern nascent chains of connection which would eventually help turn the papacy into the fully functional head of the Roman Catholic communion. From 494, early in the reign of Theoderic, there survives a famous letter from Pope Gelasius I to the emperor Anastasius. Known by its opening words *Duo sunt* ('There are two'), it proceeded to lay out the doctrine that there are two equal and separate authorities in the world: the holy power of bishops and the royal power of monarchs, and, of the two, the responsibilities of the priests are greater:

> There are two powers which for the most part control this world, the sacred authority of priests and the might of kings. Of these two the office of the priests is the greater in as much as they must give account even for kings to the Lord at the divine judgement . . . You must know therefore that you are dependent upon their decisions and they will not submit to your will.

God wills the powers to work in harmony, but they have separate spheres and should not interfere in each other's areas of competence. Gelasius composed this at the height of the Acacian schism and it challenged the claims of imperial state ideology that the emperor had the right to direct Church affairs. More specifically, it was an attack on the *Henotikon*, the imperial decree by which Zeno had tried to generate Church harmony in the East, but the particular point was framed within a more general statement of principle.

From pretty much the same intellectual context, we also have the important work of Dionysius Exiguus. His speciality was translating Greek into Latin, but it is his work on canon law that has a very particular significance for us here. The project came in two parts. First he retranslated (in two separate editions) the canons of the ecumenical councils from their original Greek. There had been earlier translations into Latin but they were not particularly accurate and sometimes even mixed up the canons (embarrassingly, a North African cleric had earlier appealed to Pope Zosimus (417–18) on the basis of what was one of the canons of Nicaea according to his translation, only to find that it was in fact a canon of Serdica). Part two (the *Collectio decretorum Pontificum Romanorum*) collected papal decretals from Popes Siricius I to Anastasius II (384–498). This text is the source of the vast majority of our knowledge of papal decretal activity in the late Roman period, but, also, it struck a blow for future papal importance by making a decent-sized collection of previous papal decisions available in a highly convenient form. The collection soon spread widely, and heightened Rome's profile as a source of authoritative rulings on Church matters.[17]

Other papal highlights from the period include Gregory I, the Great, whose writings were enormously influential, but who was also highly active administratively, reorganizing the running of papal estates to increase the revenue flow and revamping the central bureaucracy to make the whole enterprise more efficient. Famously, he also conducted virtually independent negotiations with the Lombards in the 590s, when they were bearing down on Rome and there was not an East Roman army in sight. This was followed up in the seventh century by some high-principled resistance to the attempts of East Roman emperors to short-cut the Christological debates left over from Chalcedon within their Eastern territories, by arguing that however many natures Christ may have had at different points (and Christians were banned from using the word 'Nature' at all) He had just the one will. Called Monothelitism (Greek for 'one will', you'll not be surprised to know), this doctrine implicitly rejected the teachings of the Council of Chalcedon to which Leo had contributed his famous tome, so the papacy – particularly Pope Martin I – was having none of it, whatever the cost (and the cost was high). Last but not least, the period also features the first evidence of serious papal interest in extending the boundaries of Christian Europe, with Gregory the Great again in the starring role. Famously remarking of some Anglo-Saxon slaves '*Non angli sed angeli*' ('They're not Angles, but angels'), he sent Augustine of Canterbury and an intrepid band of forty companions through Francia and north across the Channel in 597. Continued papal support for the project after Gregory's death was a bit sporadic, but did contribute one of the most extraordinary clerics ever to walk in England's green and pleasant land: Theodore of Tarsus. Born in Asia Minor and a refugee from the Persian and Arab successes there, he was suddenly plucked from a quiet Roman monastery at the age of sixty-six and sent off to be Archbishop of Canterbury. Undaunted by the terrible weather, he proceeded single-handedly to revolutionize the Anglo-Saxon Church before eventually passing away at the grand old age of eighty-eight: his earthly career was soon followed by one of the most deserved beatifications in history.[18]

If you string these papal highlights together, it's possible to fly the argument that the early Middle Ages saw some crucial steps towards the papacy as we know it. Dionysius highlighted the importance of papal authority to the developing body of canon law in the West. Popes Gelasius and Martin articulated exactly why emperors should keep their sticky hands off theology and proceeded to put theory into action, while Gregory the Great's teachings focused the minds of many a Western churchman on Rome, at the same time as he was revamping the papal bureaucracy into a much more serious outfit, increasing revenues, and starting the process which would see the papacy cast aside a Constantinopolitan orbit and go west to seek its future fortunes. But while the individual phenomena we have just reviewed are all real enough, any temptation to join up the dots to create an image of the papacy's conscious turn to the West in this period (as has sometimes been done, in fact, with Gregory in the lead role) must be resisted with might and main. Reality could hardly have been more different.

Above all, relations between the papacy and the emperor in Constantinople require closer evaluation. It's likely enough, I think, that the popes of the later fifth and early sixth centuries did 'enjoy' in a kind of way their freedom from close imperial control. Whether Gelasius would have been so bold in his letter to Anastasius had he been living in East Roman territory must be extremely doubtful. Certainly, there would have been substantial consequences, and, for nearly 200 years from the fall of Ravenna to Justinian's forces in summer 540, Rome found itself returned effectively to the rank of one of five equal patriarchs under overarching imperial supervision. Perhaps slightly annoying in itself to a papacy which had learned to live without the empire (although, as we saw in Chapter 2, Rome didn't move a muscle on the ending of the Acacian schism without consulting Theoderic first, so I'm not sure the situation was that different), being returned so forcefully to a Constantinopolitan orbit was periodically problematic because of the furore that still surrounded Chalcedon in the East. Some Eastern churchmen found its definition of Christ having been formed 'in two natures' impossible to accept without further comment. Hence the sequence of emperors who attempted to find compromise positions by adding something to Chalcedon, or taking something away from it, to make it acceptable to a critical mass of Eastern ecclesiastical opinion. But since Pope Leo's *Tome* was a central part of the record of the council (and about the only thing the West had ever contributed to ongoing Christological debate), Rome was consistently unwilling to accept any of the proffered compromises.

Despite this starting point, the pressure that emperors could bring to bear was so intense on occasions that particular popes could do nothing but buckle. Vigilius, for instance, was dragged off to Constan-

SCS
PE
TR
VS

☓ SCISSIMVS
DN
LE
O
PP

† DN CARVLO
R
E
G
I

BEATE·PETRE·DONAS
VITA·LEONI·PP·BICTO
RIA·CARVLO·REGI·DONAS

17. A copy of Pope Leo's famous mosaic, portraying both Charlemagne and the Pope as subordinate to Rome's founding apostle, St Peter. Charlemagne, by contrast, understood his imperial authority to have come directly from God Himself.

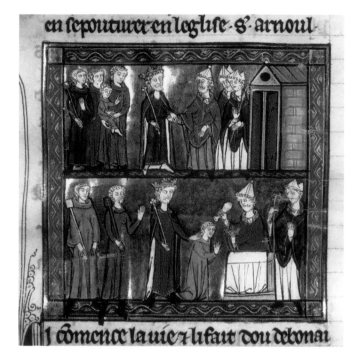

18. Coronation of Louis the Pious. The unexpected deaths of Charlemagne's older sons in the years before 813 left Louis as his father's sole heir. This he recognized in an imperial coronation ceremony to which the Pope was not even invited.

19. Charles the Bald portrayed in imperial style after Charlemagne from his great Gospel book.

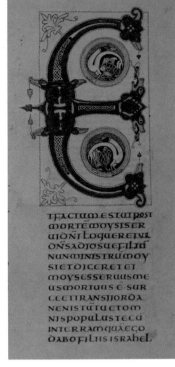

TFACTUM ESTUT POST
MORTE MOYSISER
UIONI LOQUERETUR
ONSADIOSUE FILIU
NUNMINISTRUMOY
SIETOICERETEI
MOYSESSERUUSME
USMORTUUS E SUR
CCETIRANSIIOROA
NENISTUTUETOM
NISPOPULUSTECU
INTERRAMQUAEGO
OABOFILIISISRAheL

20. Charles the Bald's Gospel
Book of Joshua: a beautiful
example of high-end book
production characteristic of
the Carolingian Renaissance.

21. Carolingian minuscule:
the highly efficient script
which the Carolingian
Renaissance normalized and
which was used to copy – in
their thousands – the texts
considered necessary to
correctio: the proper
understanding of the
Christian religion which
Charlemagne considered it
his duty to inculcate across
western Christendom.

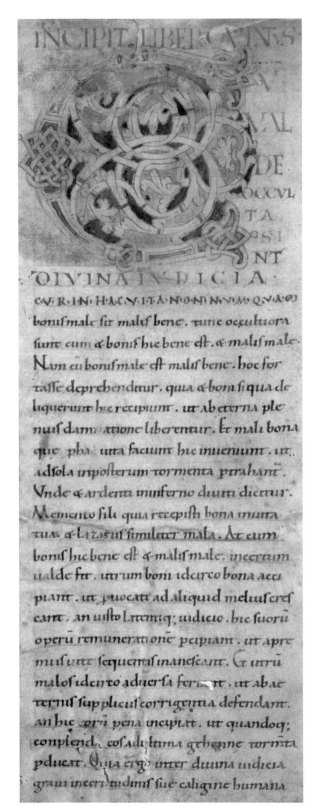

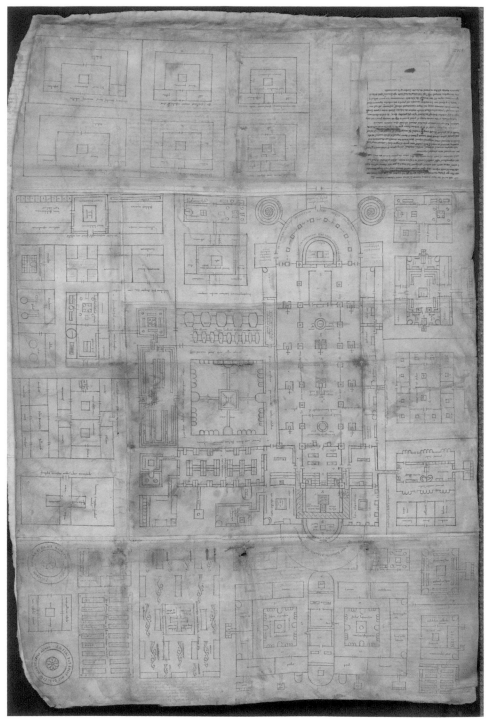

22. The Plan of St Gall: the great imperially sponsored monasteries (of which
St Gall was one) and the schools established in the households of Charlemagne's
archbishops and more important bishops pooled their resources to build up a shared
understanding of 'true' Christianity based on a common stock of religious texts.

23. The trial of Pope Formosus; when the Carolingian imperial structures through which it had begun to play a wider role in western Christendom collapsed, the ambitions of the papacy quickly narrowed into local, central Italian and largely material concerns.

24. Leo IX: the greatest of the barbarian Popes. Here, he is portrayed cutting the Patriarch of Constantinople down to size.

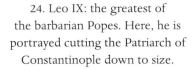

25. The death of Leo IX. Quickly and appropriately sanctified after his death, Leo's reign decisively shifted the papacy towards what would become its customary role as Latin Christendom's CEO.

26. An episode from the Investiture dispute. The Emperor Henry IV calls in Countess Matilda to mediate between himself and Pope Gregory VII. In reality, Gregory's career emphasizes that direct confrontation could never be the basis for a papal renewal of empire.

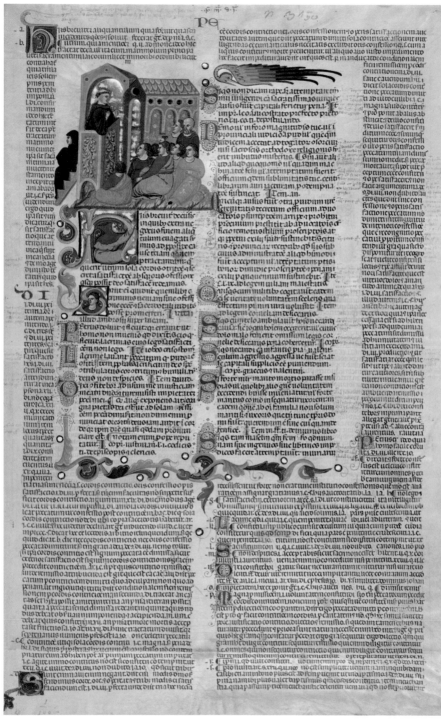

27. Gratian's *Decretum* in its classic form with the main text surrounded by the relevant sections of the *Glossa Ordinaria*. Consumer demand for authoritative legal guidance, not confrontation, is what really allowed popes to replace emperors as the recognized central authority of western Christendom.

28. The Church started under Constantine to commemorate the supposed remains of St Peter beneath. Possession of these relics and the claim they allowed Bishops of Rome to make – that they were the direct heirs of the unique authority that Christ had granted to Peter as Prince of the Apostles – formed the bedrock of the papacy's eventual claim first to rival and then surpass the long-established religious authority of emperors.

29. Pope Innocent III. His great reforming agenda set out in the Fourth Lateran Council of 1215 – the largest gathering of Christian leaders yet seen – both symbolized the emergence of the Papacy as the undisputed CEO of Latin Christendom, and set the high medieval Church forwards on a determined path of constraining its congregations into line with the precepts set out in the council's canons.

tinople in the late 540s and twice forced to accept a compromise which condemned one small corner of the text of Chalcedon. Called the Three Chapters, even this degree of compromise caused a storm across large parts of the Western Latinate Church which was used to an unflinching defence of Chalcedon. Nonetheless, two of Vigilius' successors as Pope felt the heat fiercely enough to accept the compromise he'd signed up to. When the 'one will' storm first broke in the seventh century, likewise, Pope Honorius I (625–38) signed up to the imperial position without demur. It was left to his successor Martin I to fight back by holding his own Lateran synod in 649, which condemned Monothelitism unreservedly. The comeuppance, however, was swift and decisive. He was abducted to Constantinople, tried, and exiled to the Crimea where he died (although things could have been worse: his chief abettor, Maximus Confessor, was condemned to lose his tongue and right hand so that he could no longer speak or write heresy). The weight of practical imperial authority was substantial, therefore, during the 'Byzantine' phase of the papacy, but – and this is the key point – there is no good evidence that, while it endured, popes were positively looking for any fundamental change in this basic situation.

Gregory the Great, for instance, had only engaged in independent negotiations with the Lombards because he had no choice, there being no imperial troops in the vicinity of Rome at that point. His correspondence makes it abundantly clear that his underlying aim, however, was to get Constantinople to make a serious commitment to the defence of his city by establishing a military command there: a ducate (so called because it would be commanded by a *dux*). This eventually happened, and, for all his broader interests, Gregory made no attempt whatsoever to break away from the Constantinopolitan orbit. And when, later on, the definitive loss of their Eastern provinces to the Arabs, where the bulk of anti-Chaledonian opinion was concentrated, made it possible for emperors to give up on their various attempts at compromise, the papacy welcomed them back into the orthodox fold with open arms. The year 681 was the *annus mirabilis*. It saw both a general peace between the empire and the Lombards, and the holding of a sixth ecumenical council in Constantinople which declared Monothelitism at an end. The papacy appeared ready at this point to remain a Byzantine Patriarchate for the foreseeable future.[19]

What really changed the situation was the deteriorating strategic position of the Byzantine Empire as its losses grew against the Arabs in the East. This had three main dimensions of effect, the first two necessary preconditions for the de-Byzantinization of Rome, the third its operative force. One precondition was straightforward. As Constantinople's tax revenues declined by maybe three-quarters in the face of these catastrophic losses (page 190), it was forced to scrimp and save on every front, with the result, especially after the reforms of Gregory the Great, that the papacy quickly emerged as the official body disposing of by far the largest annual income within the city of Rome. Over time (and it's hard to chart the process in great detail), the papal administration took over ever more of the public functions which kept the city operating: charity, food and water supplies, even the city's defences. Officially, the most important officer in the city was its imperial *dux*, and that had been true at the start of the seventh century, but two generations and one Arab invasion down the road, it was no longer the case.

To understand the new situation fully, however, it is necessary also to grasp a second structural change ushered in by all the defeats to the Arabs. Although the empire had lost such a large proportion of its revenue flow, the military threat had not declined. If anything, it actually increased as rampant Islam conquered and absorbed the resources of still more territories. Thus Constantinople still absolutely had to maintain large military forces on the basis of its now much-reduced tax base. To do so, it in part echoed the methods that Theoderic and his fellow kings of Western successor states had adopted when rewarding the militarized followings who had put them in power over the old Roman West. Across the empire, landed assets were distributed to Constantinople's armed forces as an important component of military pay. In fact, the empire preserved some of its tax structures besides, and there were periodic but valuable distributions of military pay on top of the land distribution, but the latter had important political consequences – especially within Italy. Right across Byzantine Italy, which was divided into a number of separate military commands (such as the exarchate around Ravenna, or the ducate Gregory the Great had managed to achieve for Rome), what started out as military garrisons quickly evolved into local landowning militias whose leading members now headed politically dominant networks of landowners in each of its subregions. Because they were similar in character now to the locally based armed militias of the Frankish kingdom, even if they had come into being by a different route, these networks naturally developed political agendas which were not so much imperial in view, but driven by their interests as local landowners. This happened everywhere from Naples, through the ducates of Perugia and the Pentapolis and even within the exarchate of Ravenna itself, but took a particular form in Rome because these landowners (called *proceres* and *possessores* in the Latin) also came to control papal elections. When exactly this happened is unclear, but it was a done deal by the mid-seventh century and, given that the papacy was the richest and most important public institution in their neighbourhood, you can see why this particular local Roman network would have looked to control it, as well as running the ducate.[20]

A bit like the Frankish world north of the Alps in the absence of expansion (page 287) the default setting of Byzantine Italy was thus tending towards local and centrifugal political agendas, since, shorn of much of its revenues, Constantinople had less to offer these landowning networks in positive terms, and lacked the independent military force to constrain them. Nonetheless, in 681, the overall situation of Byzantine Italy still looked solid enough. The new treaty with the Lombards and the full recognition of Chalcedon seemed to offer a peaceful path to an indefinite imperial future for Byzantine Italy in general and the city of Rome in particular. But then a third dimension of the Islamic factor hit home, and the potential for localism that the two previous developments had sown throughout Byzantine Italy reaped strange fruit indeed.

What happened was straightforward. The remission that Byzantium was currently enjoying from Islamic assault proved to be only short-lived, though, in fact, its ending was more than partly the fault of the emperor Justinian II. He tried to reverse some of the losses of the previous fifty years by reopening the Arab wars in the 690s, with entirely disastrous results. By the 710s, Islamic armies had not only defeated the attempted Byzantine counter-attack but were themselves on the warpath again, the high-water mark being a twelve-month siege of Constantinople in 717–18 which all but extinguished the empire forever. In fact, the city held out, but only just, and the crisis did not end with the failure of the siege. The emperor, Leo III (717–41), did what any ruler would be bound to do in such circumstances. In 722–3 he announced huge tax increases – reportedly doubling them – to try to find the funds to shore up his eastern front, and, shortly afterwards, announced the start of iconoclasm as he and his advisers sought to discover what it was that had made God so obviously angry (page 239).

The effects far within Byzantine Italy were electric. The tax rises generated huge resentment in all the militarized landowning networks. In Rome, the *proceres* and *possessores* used Pope Gregory II (715–31) to announce that they refused to pay, and went openly into revolt. And, because of the desperate situation of the empire as a whole, which had so few forces to spare, when push came to shove in 725 and the exarch approached Rome with everything he could muster, the Romans were able, from a mix of their own resources and a little help from outside, to find sufficient force to repel him. At this moment, more than in any other, the independent Republic of St Peter was born: the direct progenitor of the papal states which would finally be dismantled in the nineteenth century by a combination of the greater and lesser Napoleons.

It took a few years more for the situation to stabilize, and for everyone to realize that something irrevocable had occurred. In the late 720s, there was still one faction within Rome's landowning network, led by the then *dux*, Peter, that was ready to plot with Constantinople to remove Gregory II and restore a Byzantine allegiance. But the coup failed. Leo III's declaration of iconoclasm also greatly advanced the cause of local independence since it allowed Gregory to play the religious card in spades. He excommunicated the emperor and sent him another lecture on how emperors should not interfere in theology (like Gelasius before him, the current military-political situation obviously made it safe enough for him to do so). There were also losses. In 732–3, the emperor confiscated all the papal estates of southern Italy, Sicily and Illyricum that were still under imperial control, at an annual cost to the papacy, it is reported, of 350 pounds of gold in lost revenues. But, by the mid-730s, the dust had settled and a new pattern had emerged. The local, militarized landowners of the old Byzantine ducate of Rome had created and successfully sustained an independent Roman Republic under the overall leadership of the papacy, whose elections they controlled.[21] It was certainly a revolution, but it had nothing to do with a far-reaching vision to turn the papacy into the effective head of a Western Church. Rather, it was a process driven forward by some extremely local and hard-headed financial-cum-political agendas. Indeed, when you push the analysis further, the conclusion becomes inescapable that, taken together, these different developments of the early medieval period had actually *reduced* the broader influence exercised by the papacy over the Christian communities of the Latin West.

For one thing, as first the *dux* of Rome and then the central imperial authorities of Constantinople began to run out of money, and the papacy had taken over their functions, the religious component of the papal job description perforce declined. Organizing food and water supplies, charity, public building, then defence and, finally, politics and diplomacy for the area of the ducate was no small matter, even with an enlarged bureaucracy. Popes still found time for religious matters of course. Gregory II and Gregory III (715–41), who followed one after the other and guided the new state into existence, also famously provided extensive support for the Anglo-Saxon missionary Boniface. But the new state's political situation required constant attention. The great tax crisis of the 720s had generated a wave of localism right across Byzantine Italy as its strictures began to bite. Outside of Rome, the emperor managed to reassert his authority, but, as things turned out, only temporarily. At least in the north, ties between the local landowning networks and Constantinople suffered serious strain, and a sequence of Lombard kings – Liutprand, Ratchis and Aistulf – were quick to seize the opportunity to pick off bits and pieces of Byzantine territory. This piecemeal process culminated in Aistulf's definitive occupation of Ravenna and the Pentapolis in 751, which reduced Byzantine holdings in Italy to a limited body of territories in the south. In the meantime, the ducate of Perugia had attached itself to the Roman Republic, enlarging its power base, but the overall strategic context remained threatening. Instead of being protected by an imperial umbrella, a modest-sized republic was now responsible for its own defence in a fragmented Italy where its neighbours were the slightly larger independent Lombard duchies of Spoleto and Benevento, and the much larger Lombard kingdom of the north (Figure 13). Self-defence would eventually send popes north for Frankish support (Chapter 5), but the point for present purposes is simple. All of its immediate neighbours were relatively powerful and all had predatory intentions towards at least the fringes of St Peter's Republic. From the moment of its birth, popes had to spend a much greater proportion of their day worrying about armies, revenues and diplomatic relations.[22]

This was not the most fundamental way, however, in which Rome's general role had declined within developing Latin Christendom. Because we know that long-term papal development would later

involve an assertion of Rome's religious authority against the pretensions of medieval emperors, and because Roman emperors exercised
such a powerful religious authority themselves, it is easy to miss the
extent to which the late Roman papacy in fact depended on late
Roman structures for such broader role as it had managed to carve
out for itself within the Western Church in the period. Not only did
papal decretals echo the forms of Roman imperial law-making, but
their whole effectiveness relied on the existence of the imperial state.
Although all roads led to it, Rome was a hell of a long way from most
places, even in just the Roman West. The best recorded journey time
from England to Rome in pre-modern contexts was about six weeks.
This made the process of bringing an issue before the Pope not only
cumbersome but highly expensive, since you were going to have to
take several months off from your other activities. Because the Church
was a department of the Roman state, however, clerics had often been
able to use the imperial transport system – the *cursus publicus* – to
move around the empire. This didn't speed things up very much, but
it did massively reduce the cost of taking an appeal to Rome. And
then, although it didn't much like saying so, the effectiveness of papal
rulings actually depended on imperial backing for its legal teeth. In
445, Pope Leo I even went to the trouble of extracting an explicit
ruling from the emperor Valentinian III, which applied to the entirety
of the Western Empire (such as it still was): that 'nothing should be
done against or without the authority of the Roman Church'. The
authority structure which made Rome increasingly important for the
Western Church in the late Roman period was an imperial/papal
double act, which relied on the logistic and legal structures of the
empire actually to work.[23] Both of these disappeared with the collaps-
ing western Empire, and what we find instead is that the early
medieval Western Church developed new authority structures which
greatly reduced the role that any Pope might play.

Both de facto and *de jure* successor-state kings inherited within
their own areas of dominance the kinds of religious authority which
had previously belonged to Roman emperors; at least, once they
converted to Catholicism. The kings of the Franks (and hence everyone they conquered) were officially Catholic from the time of Clovis,
and the Visigoths from the Third Council of Toledo in 589. Anglo-
Saxon kings started to become good Catholic Christians from 597 and
had all converted by about 660. The Lombards were definitively

Nicene too, from some unknown point in the seventh century. All these kings quickly appropriated the old Roman imperial ideologies of power. They were all appointed by God, so they said, and all ruled by virtue of a special relationship with Him. Combining, as had late Roman emperors, Hellenistic kingship and Old Testament models, this made them a great deal more than merely secular rulers. They were God's chosen ones, there by divine appointment.[24] And, as had been the case for their late Roman predecessors, this empowered them ideologically to act as the effective heads of the Church within their own domains.

Taking the same checklist we have used before, there wasn't a whole lot of doctrinal activity going on in the West in these years. This was the era when the old late Roman structures of learning were busy giving way to their less intense (i.e. largely non-professional) early medieval successors, so that this is perhaps not surprising. But such doctrinal activity as there was shows the same pattern, whereby royal agendas now predominated in that crucial intersection between doctrine, councils and enforcement. The best examples come from the sixth-century Visigothic kingdom. King Liuvigild (568–86), who restored political unity to the kingdom after a series of Frankish defeats, tried the same trick on the religious front, attempting to ram home a doctrinal settlement which might work as a compromise between his kingdom's largely Arian Visigothic elite and the Hispano-Roman Nicene majority. The initiative failed, but it was a royal initiative after the classic late Roman pattern. In the next generation, likewise, it was Liuvigild's son Reccared (586–601) whose decisions and initiatives underlay the kingdom's formal adoption of Nicene Christianity at the Third Council of Toledo in 589. In Anglo-Saxon England at the synod of Whitby in 664, it was King Oswy's crucial intervention, as recounted by the venerable Bede, which made it certain that the Kingdom of Northumbria would follow the Roman rather than Irish method of calculating the date of Easter. Both sides having presented their cases, Oswy took the stage:

> Then the king concluded, 'And I also say unto you, that [St Peter] is the door-keeper, whom I will not contradict, but will, as far as I know and am able, in all things obey his decrees, lest, when I come to the gates of the kingdom of heaven, there should be none to open them, he being my adversary who is proved to have the keys.'

Certainly more than a walk-on part for the papacy here, since papal authority is what eventually swayed matters for the king, but, nonetheless, we have a king at a royally called synod, who, after listening to his clergy discuss the technicalities, took the crucial decision himself. This is a small-scale replica of the Roman imperial model of overarching religious authority.[25]

In the sphere of high Church appointments, too, the royal writ ran large. Our most vivid source, as for so many things early medieval, is the historical work of Gregory of Tours. It includes multiple anecdotes of the Frankish Church in action, which make it entirely clear that Frankish kings had the most important say over episcopal appointments within their domains. A host of factors might influence individual decisions, but when push came to shove it was up to the king to appoint, and a candidate without royal approval was lost. Gregory often complains about it, but also lets slip that he too had made sure of royal approval, in his case from King Sigibert, to trump the claims of a rival to his own see of Tours. But, then again, wasn't it Churchill who said that consistency is a mark of mediocrity? We lack equivalent narrative sources from the Catholic Visigothic kingdom, but, the odd counterexample notwithstanding, I'm confident that royal influence on episcopal appointments was just as marked there (as, fascinatingly, it remained after the Islamic conquest when the emirs and caliphs inherited the right to at least approve candidates before they were formally consecrated). In Anglo-Saxon England, likewise, it always proved problematic if a king was saddled with a bishop he didn't want for some reason, as Bede's detailed narrative in the *Ecclesiastical History of the English People* makes clear, and there too the royal will usually prevailed.[26]

The pattern really becomes clear, however, when we turn our attention to the setting of standards for clergy and laity and the operation of such structures as there were for enforcement. This had always been the second key job of Church councils in the late Roman period, beyond doctrinal questions, and in the post-Roman period it largely remained so. But, after 476, Western conciliar structures operated not across the Latin Church as a whole, but on a kingdom-by-kingdom basis.

Take, for example, the Christian Church of Frankish Gaul. Clovis called one council of the churchmen of his new kingdom at Orleans in 511, but subsequent activity was rather sporadic. The only concentrated Gallic activity we know about is the sequence of four reforming councils held by Bishop Caesarius of Arles between 524 and 529, but this was under the remit of Theoderic and Athalaric, who at that point held the dominant position in what is now Mediterranean France (page 80). Not until the early 580s, in fact, did Clovis' grandson Guntram acquire sufficient power and interest to initiate a sequence of reforming councils for the bishops of the Frankish kingdom, which set about, progressively, raising standards of religious behaviour and practice across the realm. That this rapidly became a self-conscious tradition is certain. An extraordinary manuscript originally from Lyons at the heart of Guntram's realm – but now divided between St Petersburg and Berlin – allows us to see that development unfold. What the bishops did in the twenty years or so after the First Council of Mâcon in 579 was to collect all the existing rulings they could find and then add to them from their own discussions, sometimes prompted by a particularly tricky case which had come before them. Over time, they both managed to find a few extra sets of old conciliar rulings and started, when making new decisions, deliberately to refer back to the rulings they had already collected or made. The work culminated in the production of a new, thematically arranged code of canon law, the *Vetus Gallica*, which rearranged all the existing materials in a way which made it much easier to find the current state of the law on any particular topic. What this shows us is a vibrant Frankish Church community taking determined responsibility for the progress of Christianity within its own area of jurisdiction.[27]

It's a fascinating vignette, and brings the early medieval Western Church to life in a way that gets completely lost if all you're concerned with is the development of the papacy. Several points jump out. The Frankish Church did not operate completely in isolation. Its bishops had a strong sense of belonging to a broader Christian tradition, in which the papacy had some role. In particular, one of its base texts of existing Christian tradition was the legal collection made by Dionysius Exiguus, both his Latin translation of the old Greek councils and his edition of papal decretals. At the same time, this Frankish community was totally dependent on the support of its king to function. Until Guntram had become interested, no kingdom-wide reforming tradition could get off the ground, and I suspect that, like his Roman imperial predecessors, Guntram was not only calling the councils but also paying expenses. When tackling new problems, likewise, the Frankish bishops were happy to depend upon their own intellectual resources and saw not the slightest need to refer anything to Rome. There is also no indication that any Roman observers were present either, or that anyone ever thought they might be. And when royal interest subsided again in the seventh century, perhaps an effect of the slow erosion of royal power in that period (page 216), the tradition ground to a halt. Only one more Church council is known from the entire seventh century.

The pattern is so similar in the corresponding evidence from the Visigothic and Anglo-Saxon kingdoms that there is no need to lay it out in detail. Once everyone had got over the shock of converting to Nicene Christianity at Toledo III, the new Visigothic kingdom eventually developed a tradition of functioning in some important ways through a sequence of kingdom-wide councils. These were always held at Toledo, but a more or less continuous sequence doesn't really begin until Toledo IV of 633, when, after a gap of nearly fifty years, the councils come (relatively) thick and fast. Unlike their Gallic counterparts of the later sixth century, these councils dealt with both secular and ecclesiastical business, although the bishops would go off by themselves to tackle purely religious matters. That feature aside, the pattern is identical. The councils were called by kings, and the developing collected body of ecclesiastical legislation that they generated (generally known as the *Hispana*) included copies of old councils and the collections of Dionysius Exiguus. They also had copies of many of the Merovingian Gallic councils (which had ground to a halt by the time that the Hispanic tradition really got under way). But if conscious of being part of a bigger Christian world, they nonetheless, just like their Frankish peers, set about dealing with any further issues entirely by themselves: from the resources of their own intellects and faiths. No outside experts were called in; no difficult matters were sent on to Rome for papal review.

In Anglo-Saxon England, a conciliar tradition began to find its feet under the so-called Mercian supremacy over southern Britain a century later. The Mercian kings called the councils, whose geographical scope coincided with the power of these kings, and, while conscious in the same ways of a wider Christian world, the English bishops generally got on with business by themselves. The only time outside experts were called in was when one of the kings, Offa, wanted something. He had conquered the old kingdom of Kent, where the archbishopric of

Canterbury lay, and was finding it problematic to have the supreme religious officer of the southern province of England, whose extent broadly coincided with the boundaries of his own kingdom, located far away (in British terms) from the heartlands of his kingdom. He wanted to divide the Church province in two, therefore, and create a second archbishopric at Lichfield in the heart of his kingdom. To smooth the wheels of papal approval, he invited two papal legates for a visit in 786. The recorded proceedings make fascinating reading. A great summit meeting was held at which everyone recorded their agreement to cutting-edge religious ideas such as it would be a good idea if children were always baptized. And then, a couple of parties later, and having signed the communiqué, the legates went home. It was entirely an exercise in PR, which dealt with nothing remotely tricky and set up no enforcement mechanisms to check on subsequent progress towards the various platitudinous targets that everyone had been so busily discussing. The king's special offer to the papacy thus cost him nothing, and it did the trick. Lichfield was duly made an archbishopric by Charlemagne's friend, Hadrian I, just a few months later in 787, although it was not destined to last. After Offa's death, Mercian supremacy was itself undermined, and, as you should be getting used to by now, Church matters bent with the political wind. Full primacy was restored to Canterbury in 803 by Pope Leo III, and thus matters have remained ever since.[28]

Even this episode just serves to emphasize the overarching point: everyone still accorded the Roman Church great prestige. Within the West, this status was unique since there were no other apostolic foundations. Nothing, likewise, interrupted the flow of pilgrims to monuments and martyria. Again, as the Holy Land became more inaccessible after the Islamic conquests, the traffic probably increased (although there's no complete survey). Rome – so full of martyrs and saints thanks to the pre-Constantinian persecuting empire – was also an increasing source of the valuable relics with which founders liked to empower the churches they constructed.[29] But, in the late Roman period, and particularly in the fifth century when, for a period under Valentinian III (425–55) and afterwards, emperors had gone back to Rome, the Pope had been able to function – to an extent – as the chief bishop of the Western Empire and a potential supreme arbiter on difficult Church matters. But all of that ground to a halt in the chaos of imperial collapse, and, when the dust had settled, the Western

Church emerged in kingdom-sized units which did not operate with reference to any overarching authority structure at all. In these circumstances, the early medieval, pre-Carolingian papacy gradually acquired a new and greater authority, combining both religious and secular functions, but was able to exercise it only within its own, limited political boundaries. With the disappearance of Western emperors, popes lost the support structure which had made it possible for them to exercise a broader function of religious leadership across Latin Christendom. Nor, despite some initial appearances to the contrary, did that function find any substantial restoration in the time of the Carolingians.

THE GODFATHER (PART 2)

In retrospect, the Carolingian era would be seen as a period when St Peter's successors took huge strides towards the pre-eminence they were to enjoy in the central and later Middle Ages. On the ideological front, the two great crowning moments of Pippin and Charlemagne would be used to show that the heir of St Peter had the right to act as political arbiter, an idea which nestled in cosily beside the claims of the *Donation of Constantine*. In reality, Pippin had had himself made king by the Franks first. But it was the story of the supposed letter and the Pope's definitive answer in Pippin's favour which would be remembered. Likewise, Leo III had had to be dragged to the altar to crown Charlemagne, but, again, because the papacy lasted so much longer than the Carolingians, the event went down in history as showing that the Pope was an essential component of any imperial coronation. This was not Charlemagne's view, as he demonstrated by crowning his own son by himself. But these ideological gains really came into play only in the longer term, and there were some more immediate ways in which Charlemagne and Louis the Pious increased the profile of the papacy in the minds and working lives of Western churchmen.

Not least, Charlemagne's generosity re-endowed the papacy on a truly epic scale, an excellent return on all the anxious letters and supporting documentation with which Pope Hadrian had bombarded the king in the later 770s. You can't put a figure on the increase in papal income, but it was clearly colossal. Its scale is strikingly reflected in the collection of more or less contemporary papal biographies, the *Liber Pontificalis*. Whereas their immediate predecessors such as Stephen II (752–7) or Paul I (757–67) were able to renovate respectively one of the great charitable hostels for pilgrims (*xenodochia*) and an admittedly major monastery, the new income allowed Hadrian I (772–95) and Leo III (795–816) to unleash an extraordinary wave of renovation, building and gift-giving aimed equally at the secular and religious infrastructures of the city.

Hadrian I, to judge by his investments, had a strong eye for urban planning. He is recorded as dropping a cool one hundred pounds weight of gold on a major restoration of the city's defences. He also put three of the city's ancient aqueducts – the Sabbatina, Virgo and Claudian – back into full working order, and commissioned a major restoration of the riverbank and porticos in front of St Peter's. Quite a set of achievements, but only a small selection from the record, which also included a grand new set of bronze doors for the main entrance to St Peter's. The biography of Leo III, on the other hand, is more or less completely taken over by the list of his donations, almost to the exclusion of anything else. Some of the omissions are deliberate. There is no mention in the *Liber Pontificalis* that he prostrated himself in front of Charlemagne after crowning him, or of the second rebellion against his authority on the part of some of the Roman nobility in 813. But some less charged events of importance, such as his second journey to Francia, also pass unmentioned. Instead, the biography largely consists of gifts made by Leo III to the various religious institutions of the city. In particular, under the year 807 the author inserted an unadorned list of donations, which begins:

> The Saviour our Lord's Church called Constantinian, fine silver
>   crown, 23 lb
> God's holy mother's basilica *ad praesepe*, pure silver crown,
>   13 lb 3 oz
> Her Church in Callistus' *titulus*, silver crown, 13 lb 3 oz
> Her deaconry called *Antiqua*, silver crown, 13 lb
> Her Church called *ad martyres*, silver crown, 12 lb 3 oz
> Her deaconry called Cosmedin, silver crown, 12 lb

It goes on to record, altogether, a total of one hundred and nineteen gifts of silver to different religious institutions around the city, and it has been calculated that the total comes to about a thousand pounds weight of precious metal gifts made in Leo's time. In later eighth- and early ninth-century Rome, the donation of Charlemagne was far more important than the *Donation of Constantine* and provided the means for a complete revamping of the Holy City in everything from its water supply to the splendour of its churches.[30]

Charlemagne's religious policies, too, made the papacy a stronger feature in the mindsets of most of the empire's clergy, because he saw Rome as a source of authentic Christian tradition. Particularly when he or his churchmen were in search of uncorrupted versions of key religious texts, Rome was their destination of choice. As early as 774, Charlemagne requested from Hadrian, and obtained, the most up-to-date collection of Church law to be had in Rome. Called the *Dionysio-Hadriana*, it was a slightly updated version of Dionysius Exiguus' double collection of canons and decretals. This was only the beginning. Charlemagne also obtained from Rome copies of their best texts of the Latin Bible, and good examples of the main service books in use there. He also imported singing masters from the city to teach Gallic churchmen how to perform the Mass in the Roman fashion. Not since the late Roman imperial period had there been so much toing and froing to Rome, in a process which clearly affirmed the centrality and authenticity of all things Roman when it came to identifying 'correct' Christianity.

Thanks to Charlemagne's attentions, the papacy was enriched, visited, courted and paid enormous respect, but all these gains came with a price tag. The emperor's respect for the papacy was genuine, but he was equally convinced, as we have seen, that he had his own hotline to the Almighty. No mere vassal of St Peter, he had no hesitation in making use of the papacy for his own purposes, as we saw in the run-up to the imperial coronation (page 244), for this too was God's will. Nor was Charlemagne afraid actually to disagree with the Pope – even on matters of doctrine. The example par excellence is the Council of Frankfurt. There and to the Pope's face (at least, to those of his legates) Charlemagne had his churchmen declare that Pope Hadrian's acceptance of Constantinople's new teaching on icons was in fact mistaken (page 240). A second, less charged example is provided by the famous *filioque* clause, an addition to what is commonly called the Nicene Creed but is actually the Creed of the Council of Constantinople of 381. This states that the Holy Spirit proceeds from 'the Father and the Son together' (*filioque* means 'and the Son') rather than just the Father. The Eastern Orthodox communion has never accepted the addition, which remains a sticking point in interfaith discussions. Both the phrase and the teaching which underlies it grew up in the early medieval West, and, in the late 790s Charlemagne and his churchmen formally adopted it as an article of their faith, spreading its use throughout the empire. He then started twisting the arm of Pope Leo. Caught between a rock and a hard place, because he well knew the storm the phrase would unleash in Eastern Christendom, which strongly resisted any changes to the wording of the traditional Creed, Leo eventually agreed that the underlying teaching was orthodox, but held that it was better not to go messing about with the creed, trying to stave off potential difficulties with Constantinople. It was not until 1014 that *filioque* was formally adopted within the city of Rome, but there is no doubt that Charlemagne felt perfectly entitled to use his own judgement to decide even on doctrinal orthodoxy.[31]

As such, we can place him firmly in a tradition which stretched back for the best part of half a millennium. From the time of Constantine onwards, overarching responsibility even for the identification of correct doctrine had been part of the Christian ruler's job description, and Charlemagne's attitude to Rome was nothing more than its direct continuation. Indeed, it would be extremely easy at this point to go through the same checklist we have used before, and come to the inescapable conclusion that Charlemagne was undoubtedly the head of the Church within his domains. He appointed all the leading churchmen, he called all the major councils and authorized most of the rest, and great tranches of legal directions on the practicalities of both clerical and lay piety were drawn up in his name.

But, while true enough, this procedure would also be a little dull and runs the risk of missing a much more important point about the Carolingian era. Of course Charlemagne was head of the Church (and Louis the Pious after him), again both de facto and *de jure* like their imperial Roman predecessors. It would also never even have occurred to most of their churchmen that the head of the Papal Republic, *apostolicus* as they acknowledged him to be, could possibly have aspired to anything remotely resembling the overarching religious authority

that it was the God-given duty of the king-emperor to wield. Fair
enough, but under Charlemagne's guidance something much more
interesting was happening. The sheer size of his empire, and the
economic resources Charlemagne had at his disposal, combined with
the collective ambition shown by both himself and his leading churchmen to unleash an extraordinary project of Christian reform, which
would transform the entire Western Church.

Its principles are articulated most completely in the preface to the
Admonitio Generalis (*General Admonition*) issued at Aachen on 23 March
789:

> How necessary it is not only to render unceasing thanks to His
> goodness with all our heart and voice but also to devote ourselves
> to His praise by the continuous practice of good works, that
> He Who has conferred such great honours on our realm may
> vouchsafe always to preserve us and it by His protection – for this
> reason it has pleased us to ask of your sagacity, O pastors of
> Christ's churches and leaders of his flock and brightest luminaries
> of the world, that you strive with vigilant care and sedulous
> admonition to lead the people of God to the pastures of eternal
> life and exert yourselves to bear the erring sheep back inside the
> walls of the ecclesiastical fortress on the shoulders of good
> example and exhortation, lest the wolf who lies in wait should
> find someone transgressing the sanctions of the canons or infring-
> ing the teachings of the fathers of the oecumenical councils –
> perish the thought! – and devour him.

God has given Charlemagne unprecedented victories that Christian
civilization might prevail in the world, and, to continue to deserve His
favour, the king (as he still was in 789) has a duty to make it happen.
This extraordinary text goes on for a total of eighty-two clauses
which range from general thoughts on living chastely to highly specific
ones about how services are to be conducted, but also takes in the
importance of using reliable weights and measures, and of judging
justly in court. For Charlemagne and his leading counsellors, secular
and ecclesiastical, there is no distinction between Church and State,
secular and sacred. Charlemagne's empire has been created to do
God's will, and this encompasses not only its religion but every other
dimension of its operations. Such a vision is absolutely in line with the
old Roman imperial ideologies, indeed it is no more than their main

consequence stated out loud, but the statement is an extraordinarily thorough exploration of the point. The principle was also maintained with total consistency throughout the reign, reoccurring – more succinctly – in a general characterization of Charlemagne's purpose in 812, drawn up by one of the leading ecclesiastical intellectuals of his court:

> For this is always dear to him: to exercise bishops in the search of the Holy Scriptures and prudent and sound doctrine, every cleric in discipline, philosophers in knowledge of things divine and human, monks in religion, all generally in sanctity, primates in counsel, judges in justice, soldiers in practice of aim, prelates in humility, subjects in obedience, all generally in prudence, justice, fortitude, temperance and concord.

Judges judging, soldiers practising their aim, and bishops studying the scriptures: all can be talked of in the same breath. The Carolingian programme recognized no fundamental distinction in kind between these activities. All had to be according to God's will in the empire that God had brought into existence.[32]

So, Charlemagne – like many a conqueror – had an exaggerated sense of his own importance, and enough intelligence to turn it into coherent statements of principle, which could be summed up in the Latin word *correctio*: the desire to correct prevailing ways of life according to a Christian model of perfection. Why should we pay much attention to all this preposterous nonsense about building God's society on earth? As the political narrative has already shown us, his own family could not maintain even a facade of fraternal love after his death, and there's little sign of any major outbreak of Christian values in ninth-century Francia as a whole. Nonetheless, Charlemagne's project had, and still has, enormous importance. The king and his churchmen didn't just proclaim the dream, they also tried to live it. And, thanks to his unprecedented run of conquests, Charlemagne had huge resources to devote to it himself, and more than enough leverage to make others sign up to the project as well. It allowed him, first of all, to assemble at his court an extraordinary weight of scholarly expertise, comprising the best he could find from every corner of Western Europe: Alcuin from York (which then had one of the best libraries in Western Christendom), Theodulf from Spain, and Peter of Pisa and Paul the Deacon from Italy, to name but a few of the superstars. This fluid assembly of scholars (individuals came and went over time) represented a unique gathering of intellectual talent that only a ruler with Charlemagne's wealth and reach could possibly have collected. And apart from writing him witty little praise poems, and bitching about each other, these men also signed up for the king-emperor's great project of Christian reform. Together with Charlemagne himself, and most of his leading secular and ecclesiastical advisers, they formed a team that was set to work to build the Christian society envisaged in the *Admonitio Generalis*. The result was a total transformation of the Church of Western, Latin Christendom.[33]

The first key step towards that dream was to entrench a much fuller and more accurate understanding of authentic Christian tradition and practice within the clergy of the empire. And the best, indeed only, means to that end was to increase the availability of the body of texts by which verified and verifiable Christian tradition – the guts of the religion – had been defined and transmitted across the centuries. We're talking the Bible here obviously, but the *Admonitio* also mentions Church law – the canons – and there was much else besides: everything from non-religious lawbooks to underwrite the new, more just era that was to come into being, to endless biblical commentaries. Christianity, it has often been said, is a religion of the book, and Charlemagne and his churchmen understood this completely. Charlemagne's project of *correctio* had to start with the books, therefore, and the reform councils of 812 (to which we'll return in a moment) were ready to be more specific about which ones. The key texts for building a Christian society were Gospels and Acts from the New Testament (because of the size of medieval manuscripts, complete Bibles – called *pandects* – with everything bound together under one cover were extremely rare at this date), liturgical books, patristic writings, the *Rule of Benedict* for monks, the *Cura Pastoralis* (*Pastoral Care*) of Pope Gregory the Great for bishops and priests, canon law, and secular law codes for lay officials.[34] Obtaining and distributing satisfactory copies of these key texts was far from straightforward in late eighth-century Francia. Books were certainly rare, and luxurious examples were extremely expensive – it took over 1,500 cows to provide the parchment for the Lindisfarne Gospels (Plate 21) – but the much bigger problem was arriving at an agreed 'correct' version of their texts.

Sometimes, with texts originally in Greek, this was because a number of separate Latin translations had been made in the past, the

Bible being the classic case in point. In the Roman imperial period, four separate Latin translations had been undertaken, and, by the late eighth century, their textual traditions had intermingled to such an extent that trying to sort out what any of them had originally said, and then which one of them might provide the best translation of any particular passage, was a complete nightmare.

But there was a still more fundamental problem. This stemmed from the fact that, with the disappearance of the civilian, highly literate culture of the late Roman elite, Latin had ceased to be taught by the professional language teachers, the grammarians, who had previously been found in most of the larger market towns of the empire. Collectively, these men had artificially prevented classical Latin, the spoken and written language of the Roman elite, from changing very much in the Roman period by producing complex rule books – the ancestors of the Latin grammars used to torture the young today – which defined the myriad endings of 'correct' (i.e. classical) Latin. But when these men went out of business with the transformation of elite life towards military rather than civilian careers (page 277), as they did north of the Alps before AD 500 and in Italy a generation or so later, the grammatical dam holding up normal processes of linguistic change was broken. The Pompeii graffiti show that, in less exalted circles, linguistic change had long been under way, and it soon spread into the elite. Everyday pronunciation, it seems, no longer distinguished between some of the sounds that had made separate case endings originally different from one another, and, because of this, pronunciation took much of the grammatical structure of classical Latin down with it. In the long term, this process turned Latin into its various Romance derivatives (such as French and Spanish) which can all be seen as Latin without most of the case endings, where word order within a sentence (like modern English) does much more of the work, since endings had lost their power to transmit meaning. Amongst the elite, this process happened gradually and more or less unconsciously from the fifth century onwards, and then worked its way into textual culture, affecting not only new compositions, but also attempts to copy older classical texts. The result was a complete dog's breakfast, with even educated clerics not necessarily realizing that their attempt at classical Latin was actually a mixture of Latin and Romance forms. As Charlemagne put it, in a famous capitulary *On the Study of Letters*:

> Numerous letters have been sent to us in recent years from
> various monasteries notifying us of the efforts made on our behalf
> in sacred and pious prayer by the brothers residing in them: and
> we have identified in most of these writings of theirs both correct
> sentiments and uncouth language. For what pious devotion dic-
> tated faithfully as regards matter, an uneducated tongue was
> unable, through neglect of learning, to express without fault.[35]

To stand any chance of success in his desire to restock the Western
Church with authentic copies of the key texts of Christianity, Charlemagne and his team had to combat this broader problem, and they
proceeded to do so with gusto. One strategy, as we've seen, was to
refer to the papacy, since you ought to be able to find authentic copies
of the key texts of Christian tradition in Rome if nowhere else. But
while Rome was of some help (*Admonitio Generalis* drew heavily for its
knowledge of Church law on the *Dionysio-Hadriana* that the Pope had
supplied), this proved an insufficient answer. Some of the books the
Pope supplied didn't really fit a Frankish context – this is true of the
Roman Massbook which lacked some of the readings that the Frankish
world required – and, more generally, even Roman Latin was found
to be not fully classical. For a proper solution, Charlemagne went back
to the drawing board, setting his scholars to work their way through
the key Christian texts and produce 'correct' versions, which would
then be distributed as such to the main religious centres of Charlemagne's Empire: the Cathedrals and major monasteries. Alcuin, for
instance, drew the short biblical straw and was given the Gospels and
the Psalms, critical texts not just for Christian understanding, but also
for the liturgy, since extracts from them provided many of the readings
used at all services.

But for all this to work properly, still more root-and-branch reform
was required. If the editing process was to have a lasting effect,
knowledge of 'correct' classical Latin needed to be spread much more
widely among Western Europe's churchmen. Otherwise, whenever a
text was copied, the old errors would simply creep back in. Absolutely
essential to Carolingian *correctio*, therefore, and operating hand in hand
with the editing initiatives, was a huge emphasis on learning 'accurate'
Latin, by which Charlemagne and his advisers meant their version of
the classical language. The best Latin grammarians he had were
unleashed on this task – notably Alcuin again and Peter of Pisa – and

they came up with a triple strategy. The old teaching texts produced by the professional Latin teachers of the late Roman period (particularly those of Donatus and Priscian) were dusted off, recopied and circulated widely. Second, they added some new teaching texts of their own, with Alcuin's work on how to pronounce the artificial language they were attempting to restore playing a starring role. In fact, because he was an Anglo-Saxon and had learned Latin entirely as a foreign language, this seems to have made Alcuin a better teacher of the new standards than some of his continental colleagues occupying that linguistic no-man's-land between Latin and Romance.[36] Third, the scholars started to copy and circulate substantial quantities of classical Roman texts in a strikingly wide variety of genres, from ancient astronomy to the love poetry of Catullus.

What we've come to now is the famous Carolingian Renaissance, and it's worth pausing a moment to explore its contours. Quite simply, it is thanks to the copying traditions established by Charlemagne's assembled scholars that the vast majority of surviving classical Latin literature comes down to us today. Anything that did not get copied in the later eighth and early ninth centuries (and there's plenty that we know to be missing) has simply not survived. Without Charlemagne's scholars, therefore, much of the ancient Roman cultural achievement would be entirely lost.

At the same time, 'Renaissance' – meaning, after the fourteenth-century original, a rebirth of interest in the classics *for their own sake* – isn't quite the right term for what went on. Charlemagne's scholars were interested in classical Latin texts for two main reasons: either because they could help teach you the language, including its rare grammatical oddities, or because they contained useful knowledge that any educated Christian might need to know. Potentially, this may have led them to ignore some classical texts that had limped as far as the late eighth century, but were then discarded because Carolingian Christian scholars did not find them useful. This really is the $64,000 question about the Carolingian Renaissance: how big was the Carolingian wasteparchment basket? Did they basically copy everything they found, or did they throw a lot away? It is impossible to answer with certainty. You might think that the survival of Catullus suggests that they copied more or less everything, but maybe Carolingian monks found some really fascinating grammatical points amongst all the sex. Whichever is more correct, and I do tend towards the 'copied most things' view, the broader cultural significance of Charlemagne's scholars is undeniable.[37]

That this proved to be the case is also telling us something else of importance. Charlemagne's scholars managed eventually to embed their corrected texts, and the knowledge of classical Latin which would guarantee their accurate reproduction, structurally within the Western Church. This too was part of the original design of the project. Charlemagne's scholars themselves, serious and industrious intellectuals as many of them were, were not that numerous: a few tens of individuals at most. Had *correctio* and its necessary cultural infrastructure just remained their project, its impact could only have been limited. No more than a dozen or so manuscripts now survive, for instance, that can with any plausibility be linked directly to Charlemagne's court.[38] But something like 9,000, many containing several works, survive from the Carolingian period as a whole (including the entirety of extant classical Latin literature). The scholars' efforts had the impact they did, in other words, because their values and products became part and parcel of a broader intellectual culture within the Western Church in the ninth century.

Two of the necessary tools for this outcome already existed, waiting to be employed to maximum effect. On the technical side, the first was a new type of bookhand: Carolingian minuscule, as it is called. Variants of this hand were coming into use before Charlemagne's time, and it was important because it was smaller and more cursive than older uncial hands (Plate 21). This meant both that it could be written faster and that you could get much more text on a page. In a world where manuscripts were hugely expensive in both parchment and copy-hours, this was a huge advance. True to form, Carolingian *correctio* identified one particular cursive minuscule as the best of all possible forms, and this script duly won out over all-comers. The vast majority of our 9,000 Carolingian manuscripts are written in it (although if you have the 'eye', which I do not, you can tell one scribe's handwriting from another).[39]

By itself, Carolingian minuscule would have speeded up book production and lowered costs, but *correctio* accelerated output in other ways too. As the Carolingian era dawned, religious institutions also had more money to spend. The wealth that Charlemagne liberated from his conquests provided some of this. He didn't found any monasteries as far as we can tell, but he did make huge numbers of donations to them, as he did to many cathedrals. All the metropolitan, archiepiscopal sees of his empire, for instance, came in for special dispensation in his will. More structurally, however, it was in the Carolingian era that the practice of tithing became firmly established within the Western Church. Charlemagne was not the innovator here; tithing already features in the reforming Church councils held by his father and uncle, Pippin and Carloman, and is the second of the tools sitting around awaiting full employment. Charlemagne, however, insisted that tithes be paid, and threw the weight of his legal authority behind the demand. As a result, fully 10 per cent of GDP (nearly as much as developed nations now spend on health care) notionally became available for religious purposes. In fact, the normal rules applied. Tithes belonged to religious institutions, but various members of the landowning class had rights over these institutions, including shares of their tithes, so nothing like 10 per cent of GDP was freed up in practice for religious purposes. Yet religious income certainly increased substantially, and further Carolingian reform measures ensured that some of the extra money was spent on teachers of Latin, and copying those texts which Charlemagne's scholars had identified as the crucial toolkit of Christianity.[40]

From the *Admonitio* onwards, huge emphasis was placed on the importance of cathedrals and monasteries having their own schools. It is a standard demand of Charlemagne's legislation, repeated on many occasions. Charlemagne and Louis the Pious also pushed through more specific reforms relating to the lifestyles of those living in these cathedral and monastic communities which piled on the pressure. The reform of clergy associated with cathedrals (cathedral canons) started before Charlemagne, but he redoubled the efforts to make it happen, and one of its key features was that it required schools, books, and a much greater commitment to Christian learning on the part of these communities.

The same is true of monasticism. Before the Carolingian period, there were monastic norms which always involved some kind of instruction in the faith, but the amount varied because most monasteries had their own specific rules which were individual adaptations from some of the best-known prototypes, such as the *Rule of Benedict* originally drawn up for the Italian monastery of Monte Cassino in the sixth century. Under Charlemagne and particularly Louis the Pious in this instance, the Carolingian monarchy demanded a much stricter observance of the Benedictine rule in its entirety, with no picking and mixing allowed. But it was not the original Benedictine rule. Louis threw his imperial weight behind a revised version which incorporated one highly significant change. The original rule had divided a monk's day into three equal parts: prayer, work (physical work, growing the monastery's food) and study. The revised version, drawn up by a second Benedict (just to avoid confusion) – Benedict of Aniane – promoted a two-part day divided between prayer and study. Physical work was now to be done by lay brethren who were not fully part of the community. The revision encompassed some other changes besides, but a greater emphasis on learning was again at the forefront.[41]

When it came to Christian reform, therefore, Charlemagne did not merely confine himself to pious platitudes. He and his scholars set about upping the level of Christian knowledge throughout the empire via an extraordinarily well-thought-out and thorough reform project. It dealt not just with superficial problems, such as a shortage of books, but looked to overhaul the cultural infrastructure of the Church completely, so that authentic Christian texts, and the knowledge to ensure that they would stay correct, was dispersed right across the empire. One conclusion is immediate. The Pope's role in all this was minimal. All the energy came from Charlemagne's court. He paid for it, and the scholars were working either at his command or with his approval. The image of overarching responsibility that we found at the beginning of the chapter in *Karolus Magnus et Leo Papa* precisely reflects reality. It was all as Charlemagne had set it out for the new Pope in his first ever letter to Leo III:

> It is our function – to the extent that divine goodness aids us – externally to defend Christ's holy church on every side by force of arms against the incursions of pagans and the devastations of infidels [and] internally to strengthen it in knowledge of the Catholic faith. It is yours, most holy father, to aid our struggle with hands raised to God, like Moses, to the end that, with you interceding and God guiding and granting, the Christian people should at all times and in all places enjoy victory over the enemies of its holy name and the name of our Lord Jesus Christ be glorified throughout the whole world.[42]

This is one of my favourite documents from the entire Middle Ages. The Pope is no more than Charlemagne's senior vice president for prayer, while he himself is the Church's CEO. While Hadrian and Leo were busy spending the money Charlemagne had given them glamming up Rome's religious attractions, Charlemagne was reforming the entirety of Western Christianity. The effort is impressive, and Charlemagne's position as the head of the Church is undeniable, but what did *correctio* actually achieve?

CHRISTIANITY IN OUR TIME?

What it clearly didn't do is fulfil Charlemagne's great dream of creating a Christian society. No one could seriously maintain that Charlemagne got anywhere near his aim of building a 'better' (or even a 'bigger') society worthy of God's support. Louis the Pious found the palace of Aachen full of whores, remember, and the administration of the empire of corruption, and there is nothing remotely Christian about the Carolingian political process of the ninth century. But Louis' criticisms appropriated the rhetoric of the dream, and to give both emperors and their churchmen their due, they all made serious efforts to translate Charlemagne's renewal of the empire's Christian infrastructure into higher levels of Christian devotion among both the clergy and laity.

Much of the effort was focused on the clergy, which only makes sense. If the clergy were not responding to *correctio*, there was not the slightest chance of it having any effect upon the laity. And once again, the measures adopted were not pious platitudes, but concrete and well directed. Early in Charlemagne's reign, hierarchy within the episcopate, some of which seems to have lapsed, was fully restored. The power of metropolitan bishops, as laid out at Nicaea, was reasserted in royal legislation, precisely so that the archbishops would be able to exercise leverage over any of their subordinate bishops who did not respond to *correctio* with enthusiasm. This was followed up with periodic enquiries, to check how much was being done, and then, towards the end of Charlemagne's reign, by a series of reform councils. We know that these were held in 813 at Arles, Châlons, Mainz, Rheims and Tours; there may also have been others. Their purpose was to reaffirm to all the clergy exactly what their contribution was to be to the creation of Charlemagne's Christian society.

The clergy, however, were only a means to the end of reaching the laity. This, too, was reaffirmed in the reform councils, where, for the first time, the principle was spelled out that priests must preach to their congregations in their native language, whatever that may be. This marked the culmination of a new emphasis on the importance of the sermon as key method of educating the laity, seen in statements from right across the reign, and, once more, the scholars provided concrete assistance. One old favourite, Pope Gregory the Great's *Forty Homilies on the Gospels* was corrected, copied and circulated, and some new collections were compiled. Paul the Deacon worked his way through existing sermons from the great Church fathers while Charlemagne celebrated the end result:

> Paul the Deacon . . . has read through the treatises and sermons of the various catholic fathers, culled all the best things and offered us two volumes of readings, suitable for each separate festival throughout the whole course of the year, and free from errors. Having examined the text of all these with our perceptive judgement, we confirm the said volumes by our authority and deliver them to your religiousness to be read in Christ's Churches.

This is a perfect snapshot of Carolingian *correctio*: define a 'correct' version of an important text, get the king-emperor to authorize it, and it alone, to be used throughout the empire. Right at the end of the reign, likewise, another large sermon collection was put together by Hrabanus Maurus.[43]

Other dimensions of lay piety and the provision of services for them were also addressed. Particularly interesting are the episcopal statutes which start to appear in Charlemagne's reign. This was only the start of a tradition which would flourish for centuries, but five of the extant statutes date from before the reform councils of 813. In them, a bishop laid out for the priests of his diocese exactly what they should be emphasizing in the religious experience they offered to their congregations, and there are some striking variations. At Liège, for instance, Bishop Gerbold felt able to do nothing more than emphasize the laity's basic duties of baptizing their children and paying their tithes: Christianity 101. At Orleans, further to the west, Bishop Theodulf was able to set out a much more ambitious programme including lay participation in the fasts and vigils of the liturgical year. This suggests that there was a great deal of variation in actual religiosity across different regions within Francia, but the really interesting thing is the fact of the statute itself. Whatever the current level of Christian piety, the statute form shows us bishops rolling up their sleeves and attempting to affect the religious experience of everyone within their diocese.

To my mind, this is the really interesting point. As with Charlemagne's reform of education and Christian learning, there is a fascinating, practical turn to every aspect of Carolingian *correctio*. Other imperial legislation insisted that the new service book, adapted from the Roman model that Hadrian sent north to Gaul, be used throughout the empire, and that all the laity had to learn the Creed and the Lord's Prayer. The programme surely didn't make people more Christian in the moral sense of the word that Charlemagne clearly had in mind in *Admonitio Generalis*, but it did manifestly affect general religious experience. Archbishops put pressure on the bishops, who, via reforming councils and their statutes, defined new religious standards for their priests to enact. The effort translated itself to the laity at least in terms – if slowly – of new ways of conducting Church services, but also in some new demands being placed upon them, and, as an absolute minimum, I feel reasonably confident that the Creed and the Lord's Prayer really were being taught right across the empire. All of this was only the start of an extremely long process and there were many limiting factors – clerical resistance, no doubt in some quarters, and continued shortages of books – but the important point is that the process began at all. Whatever its limits, Charlemagne used his religious authority to define a mass Christian piety which was to apply to everyone within his empire.[44] This was the first time that such a thoroughgoing programme had even been attempted, and the attempt is far more important than any failings. As Dr Johnson said of the dog walking on its hind legs, the point is not that the thing is being done badly, but that it is being done at all.

But alongside this more mixed record, there was one area where, at least in the long term, Charlemagne's efforts absolutely and unambiguously succeeded: his attempted overhaul of the intellectual infrastructure of the Western Church. In the end, all of the key elements of this part of the programme set in motion by Charlemagne and his intellectuals succeeded. Latin – their version of classical Latin – became the language of the Church right down to the modern era: a direct result of the Carolingian initiatives. As this also suggests by implication, the Carolingian emphasis on education and on copying texts also succeeded in changing the general culture of Western ecclesiastical life. Cathedral and monastic communities did become centres of education, and built up appropriate libraries which allowed them to teach, to preserve and disperse Christian knowledge, and to perform divine services according to the expected pattern. From the mid-ninth century, some monastic library catalogues start to survive, and the monks duly divided their collections to reflect those functions: service books, works of wider relevance to the community (monastic rules, canon law, hagiography), and finally the school books (grammar, rhetoric and history). A shared Latin Christian culture thus came to be maintained and nurtured in the 180 cathedrals and 700 great monasteries of the empire. Charlemagne's scholars had succeeded in pooling their expertise and making sure that the key texts of the Christian religious database could now be safely found in several hundred separate institutions.

But this, it needs to be stressed, was a longer-term outcome. What is less clear is how quickly the new learning, schools and books penetrated the old monasteries and cathedrals. From their special mention in Charlemagne's will, and the general way in which the *correctio* project operated, it's a fair bet that the cathedral communities of all his archbishops had quickly come into line. There are also some great, royally connected monasteries like Fulda, Reichenau and St Gall which seem to have adopted the new standards of Christian learning at a very early point. How quickly they spread to the lesser sees and smaller monasteries is much less clear, but from the emphasis still being put on the need for reform in the reign of Louis the Pious and afterwards, it seems best to assume not too fast a spread. Even so, many of Charlemagne's intellectuals were teachers, as were many of their pupils in turn, and the personal influence of this growing network of scholars, alongside the royal legislation, played a great part in winning widespread acceptance for the new standards of ecclesiastical culture. By the time of Charlemagne's grandsons, at least, we're certainly looking at several tens of institutions across the old empire where there is good evidence that the new Latin Church culture was flourishing (Figure 16). And as the new standards won a wider audience among the clergy they continued to affect the religious experience of the laity.[45]

You do wonder what Charlemagne thought about it all on his deathbed. Did he have a sense of success, or was he more conscious

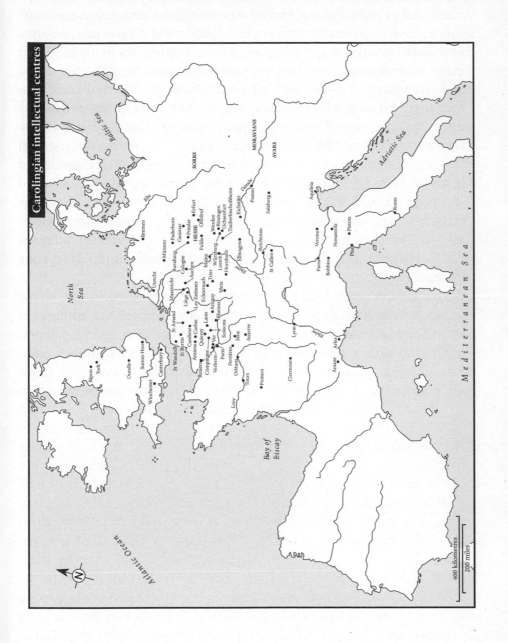

Carolingian intellectual centres

of the relatively small number – so far – of the centres where the new learning was yet flourishing, and of the fact that many Church services were still not being conducted as he would wish? The moral side of the project, from a more jaundiced modern perspective, looks completely hopeless, since even if you make people more devout they don't necessarily behave any better in moral terms, and perhaps Charlemagne, being a wily old bird, might have thought about that as well. But, in terms of historical importance at least, any flaws are massively outweighed by Charlemagne's extraordinary successes, even if it would still take a bit more time for these to become fully apparent. Above all, the ecclesiastical fragmentation which characterized the post-Roman period had been reversed by the emperor's exercise of an overarching and unchallenged religious authority. The entire empire now had one Christian culture, and Christianity had ceased to operate on a kingdom-by-kingdom basis (except in the British Isles). It is not remotely an exaggeration, in fact, to conclude that it was Charlemagne's reform project which first brought Latin Western Christendom into existence, since it defined and disseminated the common Latin Christian culture which would henceforth unite it. What happened to Western Christendom once the imperial power that had created it then ceased to exist, and how the process eventually gave birth to a second Roman Empire, is the subject of the final chapter.

8

HABEMUS PAPAM: PAPAL LIFT-OFF

ON 11 NOVEMBER 1215, there opened the largest council of Christian leaders the world had yet seen. Some 400 bishops and 800 abbots participated in person. Representatives were also there from all the cathedral clergy of the West, where the bishop himself was unavailable, along with another set of observers sent by the Eastern patriarchs. The assembled fathers of the Church then proceeded to lay down the most ambitious programme of total Christian reform ever seen: in the spirit of Carolingian *correctio*, but redefined now on an industrial scale.

One set of the council's canons hammered clerical corruption. Many practices were outlawed, including the appointing of underage relatives to Church positions, the selling of clerical offices, and open unchastity. The council also did its best to give these strictures teeth, with Canon 8 laying down that any formally registered complaint against a cleric had to be fully investigated, not just swept under the carpet. Monks too came in for their fair share of consideration, with Canon 12 requiring each archiepiscopal province to establish a supervisory body (called a chapter) to ensure that monastic discipline was being properly maintained within its boundaries (this idea generalized from precedents set in Denmark in 1205, and Rome in 1210).

Still greater emphasis, however, was laid on the mass of the lay population: both the responsibility of the clergy to provide parishioners with the best possible service, and the pious responsibilities of the laity in return. Amongst many highlights, Canon 21 decreed that all lay men and women should make their confession at least once a year, duly perform any penance that they were set, and take Holy Communion at Easter. Canon 10 concerned itself with preaching, the crucial mechanism by which the largely illiterate laity had always been taught about its religion, the council being particularly worried about arrangements in large dioceses where the bishop (responsible for preaching within Christianity since antiquity) might struggle to ensure suitable overall provision. Canon 11 demanded that each metropolitan archbishop teach the Holy Scriptures to priests and all other members of clerical orders who had any responsibility for lay congregations. Canons 19 and 20 turned their attention to Church buildings, requiring that consecrated bread and wine be kept in sanctified conditions within the church, and that churches themselves be treated as sacred places reserved only for religious services (this is the moment when villages started to need halls that were separate from their churches). Canons 50–2 even got around to marriage, demanding that it be solemnized in church as a fully paid up Christian sacrament, and redefining the incest prohibition from the almost-impossible-to-police seven degrees of kinship (under which rule, frankly, nearly everyone was too closely related to marry) to four.

Even this (which meant having less than one great-great-grand-parent in common) was a bit tricky both for the highly interconnected and relatively small upper class of Western Europe, and its relatively immobile village-dwelling peasantry. In nineteenth-century Lorraine, it has been estimated, nearly 50 per cent of peasant marriages contravened the limit, which was substantially wider than anything required to keep the gene pool healthy. Nor, more generally, was there a sudden outbreak of mass, intense Christian piety across Western Christendom in the immediate aftermath of the council. But that is not the point.

This extraordinary and ambitious council was being held in the Great Hall of the Lateran Palace in Rome, papal HQ since the fourth century. It was called and presided over by the reigning Pope, Innocent III, who not only dictated its agenda, but preached the opening sermon. Basing it on Luke 22:13, Innocent declared, 'I have earnestly desired to eat the Passover with you before I suffer, that is before I die.' His words were oddly premonitory since mortality would catch up with him the next summer on 16 July in Perugia, but his own death is not what the Pope had in mind. He used the Passover, commemorating the Israelites' flight out of Egypt, to introduce three other types of journey which were central to his conciliar agenda: the bodily journey to recover Jerusalem (since we are now in a world where crusades were a fact of life and Innocent was about to proclaim number five), the spiritual journey of the Church from corruption to reform, and the individual journey of each soul from earth to the glory of heaven.

But if Pope Innocent was contemplating several new journeys, one older one at least was complete. In the Fourth Lateran Council, we

finally encounter a papacy which was recognizably functioning as the
head of Western Christendom: calling councils of massed clergy,
dictating the agenda, setting standards of belief and practice for clergy
and laity alike, and attempting to have those standards enforced. And
here the contrast with Carolingian *correctio*, some 400 years before,
could not be more stark. Then, following well-established practice, the
emperor and his court had functioned as the mainspring of religious
reform. Innocent's pretensions to power ran further still. In 1201, in a
decretal discussing a current plethora of candidates for the throne of
the Holy Roman Empire, he had declared that it was the Pope's
business to look after the interests of the empire, because the empire
derived its origin and its final authority from the papacy. Nor was this
claimed authority limited just to the empire. In an equally famous
letter of 1198, he used an astronomical analogy to claim his authority
was actually superior to that of any of Europe's rulers:

> Now just as the moon derives its light from the sun and is indeed
> lower than it in quantity and quality, in position and in power, so
> too the royal power derives the splendour of its dignity from the
> pontifical authority.[1]

Not only did Innocent III claim total authority over the Western
Church, and demonstrate the reality of that claim in the extraordinary
gathering of churchmen who turned up in Rome for Lateran IV, but
he based that claim on the assertion that his authority was of a higher
order than any of the worldly rulers of Christendom. How had half a
millennium of imperial leadership of Christianity, based on its own
coherent ideologies, been overturned in the period between Charlemagne and Innocent III?

THE FORGING OF PAPAL AUTHORITY

As matters stood in the aftermath of Charlemagne's coronation, there
were two different kinds of obstacle standing between the papacy and
the level of Christian leadership that would be exercised by Innocent
III. First, there was an ideological deficit. Since the time of Gelasius,

the claim had been coming out of Rome that authority in religious matters was of such a different order that it could not legitimately be exercised by an emperor or king, and that the ecclesiastical sword should be wielded by the Pope as St Peter's successor. But this claim had not been recognized. The counterclaim of late Roman emperors, successor-state kings, and Carolingian rulers – that they had been appointed by God and hence should rule over matters both of Church and State in His name – had been accepted both in theory and practice by the vast majority of churchmen since Constantine's conversion.

Second, even if anyone wanted to recognize the papal alternative, the massive advantages in both wealth and practical influence enjoyed by emperors and kings presented a different kind of problem altogether. Throughout late antiquity and the early Middle Ages, emperors and kings were an overwhelming presence in the lives of the vast majority of especially senior Western churchmen, appointing bishops and the more important abbots, turning up from time to time in their localities, and calling them to assemblies, at which all the key ecclesiastical issues were discussed and new regulations passed. Thanks to Charlemagne in particular, the Church of Rome was now much wealthier, but even its new wealth paled into insignificance next to the revenues of the Carolingian monarchy; and there was, besides, that old problem which had made the city of Rome impractical as a centre of imperial authority in the late Roman period: now that the centre of West European gravity had moved north of the Alps, Rome was physically on the periphery in what was, given pre-modern speeds of movement, a highly inconvenient position. Rome remained, as one fourth-century commentator put it, a 'sacred precinct far from the highway'; i.e. a bit like Justiniana Prima, it was miles from bloody anywhere that mattered to most people, and making it the focal point every time a ruling was required, or a problem needed solving, was not a very practical prospect.[2]

In the middle decades of the ninth century, however a crucial step was taken towards solving at least the first of these problems. Everyone had long recognized that the see of Rome and its bishop, the Pope, could reasonably claim a very special kind of status within the Christian firmament, but faced with the potent combination of ideological justification and practical power that could be mobilized by kings and emperors, this had never amounted to much in the way of actual power and influence, as opposed to mere prestige. A bit like being a US vice president, you got to live somewhere nice and a lot of ceremonial fuss was made of you from time to time, but – the odd individual aside (Dick Cheney as Pope Gregory the Great comes to mind) you were largely irrelevant to the key operations of the Western Church. This was true in the Carolingian era, and it had been true back in the fourth century and earlier. If a documentary track record of leadership did not exist, however, it was always possible to invent one, and, in the mid-ninth century there started to circulate through Western Christendom a series of legal forgeries destined for a massive future.

The entire collection of four texts is known as *Pseudo-* (= false) *Isidore*, after the name which appears in the preface to the most important of them. It looks as though the intention was originally to attribute this part of the collection to Isidore of Seville, the great Spanish bishop, scholar and canon lawyer, but then someone with a greater sense of chronology noticed that some of the material dated from after his death, so the author morphed into an unidentifiable individual called Isidore Mercator. The texts comprise a collection of canons from Spanish and Gallic Church councils (the *Collectio Hispana Gallica Augustodunensis* if you'd like to be precise), a long letter from Pope Hadrian I (772–95) to Archbishop Angilram of Metz (the *Capitula Angilramni*), a continuation of the abbot Ansegius' collection of Carolingian capitularies which we encountered in Chapter 6 (*Benedictus Levita*) and finally *Pseudo-Isidore* proper: a mixed collection of rulings from a broader range of Church councils than the first of the texts (including all the old ecumenical councils) and a large collection of papal decretals. Encompassing ancient Church councils, their Gallic and Hispanic counterparts of the successor-state era, Carolingian materials and a mass of papal decretals, it added up to a more or less complete collection of Church law in all its various sources, as matters stood in the mid-ninth century.

The collection was throughout, however, a complex mixture of the genuine and the bogus, the one exception being the *Capitula Angilramni* which was a total fake. Many of the individual rulings in the *Collectio Hispana Gallica Augustodunensis* were genuine enough, but their Latin was systematically improved to come more into line with classicizing Carolingian norms, and this provided the necessary opportunity to 'adjust' some of the contents in accord with the purposes of the forger(s). About a quarter of the Carolingian material collected in *Benedictus Levita*, similarly, was genuine, but the remainder again consisted of forgeries.

The *pièce de résistance*, however, was *Pseudo-Isidore* itself which, like Gaul in the time of Julius Caesar, came in three parts. Two of the three were composed of largely genuine texts that were well known to a Latin ecclesiastical audience: a collection of Church council rulings from Nicaea down to the seventh century, and of papal decretals from the fourth century to the time of Gregory II (715–31). Much of this covered the same ground as the *Dionysio-Hadriana* collection which Pope Hadrian I had sent north to Charlemagne (page 332), and which had provided the starting point for subsequent Carolingian ecclesiastical legislation, but, again, there were some significant emendations. And to these familiar materials was then added a collection of earlier papal decretals running from the time of Pope Clement I at the end of the first century to Pope Miltiades (d.314). In the early sixth century, Dionysius Exiguus had been unable to find any fully formed decretals for his collection dating before the late fourth century, as we saw in the last chapter, and for a very good reason: there weren't any. Every one of these supposedly earlier decretals in *Pseudo-Isidore* was a complete fake. All told, the collection was a clever, high-grade fraud of the finest kind, combining its forgeries with a wide-ranging knowledge of real texts, an impressive control of different Latin styles, and a far from negligible understanding of the different eras of Christian history. Throughout, the genuine and familiar was carefully mobilized to make the unwary reader ready to accept the specious and forged.

As forgeries go, it was brilliantly successful, rapidly going viral across the monastic and cathedral *scriptoria* of Latin Christendom. Doubting voices were occasionally raised about particular texts, but over one hundred partial or complete manuscripts of *Pseudo-Isidore* survive from before the year 950, that is in the first hundred years of the collection's existence (this is a huge number of copies for this era), with thirty complete ones older even than the year 900.[3]

This success reflects, of course, the very cleverness of the forgery, but that is only part of the story. More fundamentally, the collection appeared at exactly the right moment to make such an impact. By the mid-ninth century, Carolingian *correctio* was in full swing, and Western churchmen were clear both that their practices ought to be governed by established Church law, and on what the main sources of that law actually were. From Charlemagne's *Admonitio Generalis* of 789 onwards, it had been hammered into them that correct Christian practice was defined by a combination of past rulings from ecumenical councils, major regional councils and papal decretals, as then updated, where appropriate, by the new rulings of the Carolingian capitularies. Getting hold of all the relevant texts, however, was far from straightforward. Even the most recent of them, the Carolingian capitularies, were being only haphazardly collected before the 840s, and access to the other texts remained partial. The manuscript evidence does not suggest that even every major ecclesiastical library would have had its own copy of all the main texts. Hence, at the time of its creation, there existed no other collection of Church law with anything like the same coverage of the necessary sources that *Pseudo-Isidore* appeared to offer. Everything you had ever heard of was included in one convenient collection, in excellent classicizing Carolingian Latin to boot. And any differences in detail between its readings and any other versions of duplicate texts you might happen to have, were easy to dismiss as copyists' errors, given the messy and patchy state of the available alternative manuscripts which still boasted more than one Latin translation of the ecumenical councils, for instance, and many partial collections of both papal letters and conciliar rulings. *Pseudo-Isidore*, in other words, appeared at a moment when Carolingian churchmen knew enough to know what materials they ought to drawing upon, but not yet enough to be able to see through its plausible forgeries.

But if an accident of timing played a crucial role in the collection's acceptance, you won't need me to tell you that much else about *Pseudo-Isidore*'s brilliant combination of genuine and fake was utterly deliberate. Such a learned, sophisticated, labour-intensive work of forgery would never have been undertaken without a very specific purpose in mind. What was it?

A first clue lies in its overall vision of the authority structures of late antique Christianity. Carolingian *correctio*, as we saw in the last chapter, placed much emphasis on the authority of archbishops over their bishops, making them, operating directly under the auspices of imperial authority, into the arm-twisters-in-chief of the reform process, responsible for levering the remainder of the clergy, including their suffragan bishops, into line. *Pseudo-Isidore* presented a significantly different view of what a legitimate Christian religious authority structure should look like. For one thing, its forgeries greatly boosted the vision of historical papal authority. As we saw in Chapter 5, some idea that the emperor Constantine had made a major concession of authority to Pope Sylvester was clearly already there in the eighth century, and was used by Hadrian I to 'encourage' Charlemagne to the utmost peaks of generosity after his conquest of the Lombard kingdom (page 235). But in *Pseudo-Isidore*, these ideas reached full maturity in the form of the *Donation of Constantine*, a fully worked-up forgery of what purported to be the emperor's original grant of the fourth century. This declared unambiguously that, on departing for Constantinople, the emperor granted full authority over the Western Church to Pope Sylvester.[4] This basic statement of principle was then reinforced by many practical examples of this supposed papal authority in action in the forged decretals. Equally important, beneath this papal umbrella, the power of archbishops was downplayed from two directions. Top down, the collection portrayed a late antique Church where papal grants of patriarchal status trumped the authority of metropolitan archbishops. Bottom up, the collection also championed the status of run-of-the-mill suffragan bishops against their metropolitan superiors, reducing an archbishop's rights to interfere in a bishop's running of his own diocese virtually to zero. Significantly, the collection also laid down strict rules which made it much more difficult to remove bishops from their sees than current, ninth-century practice would remotely have recognized.

Under Charlemagne and Louis the Pious, bishops were on the whole pretty expendable. Some kind of legal process had to be followed, but if you lost imperial favour, then your days in the job were soon numbered. *Pseudo-Isidore*, by contrast, asserted that without an episcopal confession of wrongdoing, it was necessary to assemble no less than seventy-two independent witnesses who were all willing to sign up to the charges being brought, before any proceedings could begin. And once a trial began, things got no easier for the prosecution. A bishop was allowed to reject the judge placed in charge of his case, even if that judge were his metropolitan archbishop, and lodge an appeal at any point in proceedings (before, during, or after the trial) to the higher authority of the Roman see. It was complete nonsense. None of this had ever been practised. But *Pseudo-Isidore* used outrageous forgery to conjure up a late antiquity where papal authority had dominated a coherent structure within which the other key players were not emperors and archbishops, but patriarchs appointed by papal dispensation and diocesan bishops.[5] For the first time, the collection translated the generally accepted but entirely vague concept that the Roman see was somehow special into a coherent vision of what that 'specialness' ought to mean in practice. A fake view of the past bridged the ideological deficit which had long relegated popes to a profoundly secondary position in the imperial wake. Finally, it is tempting to think, we are seeing the papacy on the move, seizing practical control of the authority structures of Western Christendom.

But while one strand of scholarship has long supposed the text of the *Donation of Constantine* to have been forged somewhere in the papal chancery, a second set of clues suggests otherwise. By the middle decades of the ninth century, the so-called Carolingian Renaissance meant that northern Frankish scholars were writing a much more classicizing form of Latin than their peers in the papal chancery, where the new standards had not yet taken root. *Pseudo-Isidore* is composed in impeccable Carolingian Latin, and this, together with some of the particular anachronisms it incorporates in individual forgeries such as the *Donation of Constantine* itself, strongly points the finger to northern Francia. The manuscript trail, likewise, is unmistakeable: the collection originated in the north and then disseminated outwards. So too, the first clear traces of its use. Sometime in 852/3, Archbishop Thietgaud of Trier claimed patriarchal primacy over his neighbour, the Archbishop of Rheims, on the grounds that he was archbishop of the old Roman province of Belgica I, where Rheims had been the capital of Belgica II. This was the first time that a vision of the late Roman past had been used to make a claim about the ninth century, and a clear sign of *Pseudo-Isidore* in action, even if the collection was not directly cited. The first direct citation of the text comes anyway from more or less the same time and place: synodal decrees published by Archbishop Hincmar of Rheims on 1 November 852. And from then on evidence for its implicit and explicit use, and even for its direct quotation, grows thick and fast, always starting in northern Francia and spreading outwards. The evidence is incontrovertible: *Pseudo-Isidore*'s fake vision of ancient papal authority was generated not in Rome but in northern Francia.[6] Why?

The smart money is now on the collection having grown up in stages, with some of it, at least, putting in a first appearance at the time of the quarrel between Louis the Pious and his sons in the early 830s. At a key moment, Abbot Wala of Corbie and Archbishop

Agobard of Lyons are recorded as presenting Pope Gregory IV with texts on the subject of papal authority, of which the Pope himself had no previous knowledge. The overwhelming likelihood is that the mystery documents were some part of the *Pseudo-Isidore* collection. Wala and Agobard were both close supporters of the rights of Louis' eldest son Lothar, and both were concerned that a rewriting of the projected succession settlement of 817 to include Charles the Bald might imperil the success of ecclesiastical reform by diminishing the prospects for continued, co-ordinated action. Gregory had come north in the summer of 833 to try to broker a peace settlement, at which point Lothar's party sought to employ him for their own purposes, serving up a heightened vision of papal authority to stiffen his sinews. Whether it was this which emboldened the Pope to go to Louis' camp to negotiate peace at the sons' explicit request, while they – successfully and secretly – attracted away all of the emperor's support, so that they could actually depose him, is unclear. But this overall pattern does accurately capture the general context in which we must place the creation of the text. *Pseudo-Isidore* was forged by a small group of well-connected Frankish churchmen for their own purposes, which included increasing the profile of papal authority not for its own sake, but only in so far as it suited themselves. And while they may have begun with the particular crisis of 833 in mind, their scope was or quickly became much wider. In particular, the collection's strong focus on making it much more difficult to get rid of bishops had its origins in a recent spate of depositions. Here again, though, the employment of papal authority was incidental rather than central to the design, and one of the attractions to the forgers of using a heightened vision of Roman authority in this way lay precisely in the fact of distance. Given that Rome was so far away and that the papacy was completely lacking in any effective levers of power in the Frankish context (at this point there were no papal courts, and no papal judges for instance), then it was extremely safe to use a vision of ancient papal authority to disturb the exercise of the combined and very present authority of the emperor and his archbishops. Bringing Rome into the picture did not so much increase practical papal power, as advance episcopal independence.[7]

But if such was the original purpose of the collection, its convenient scope and skilful forgery meant that it was seized upon by a series of other parties for their own purposes. In the 850s, as we have seen, the Archbishop of Trier took a fancy to reviving a supposedly ancient patriarchate (the point for himself being both higher status and increased revenues, since a successful assertion of superiority would have given him certain rights over Rheims' domains). In the 860s, likewise, the aggressively independent Bishop Hincmar of Laon, nephew and suffragan of Archbishop Hincmar of Rheims, used *Pseudo-Isidore* to try to insulate himself from his uncle's authority. In the end, neither of these gambits was successful, and the younger Hincmar's ended particularly nastily, costing him both his bishopric and his eyes.[8] But it was not the outcome of particular cases that mattered in the long term. What was really important was the fact that the employment of the conveniently full *Pseudo-Isidore* by a wide variety of Frankish churchmen, even if it was for their own purposes (and Hincmar the uncle was prone to using it too), both legitimated the collection as a Church law, and, bit by bit, started to integrate its vision of Christian authority – with the Pope at its head – into the consciousness of Western churchmen. It also eventually sowed the seeds of change within Rome itself.

Again, the individual agendas of a Frankish churchman provided the catalyst. In the early 860s, Hincmar of Rheims again found himself at loggerheads with another of his suffragans, this time Bishop Rothad of Soissons. The issue was whether the suffragan had the right (as asserted by *Pseudo-Isidore*: once more at the heart of the dispute) to deprive some clergy within his diocese of their livings. Hincmar said not, in accordance with what had been standard practice in the Carolingian Church, and eventually felt moved to depose Rothad from his see. At this point, invoking *Pseudo-Isidore*, Rothad appealed to Rome in the person of Pope Nicholas I (858–67). Nicholas' initial response was to refer the matter back to a provincial synod, as was again standard contemporary practice, and where the outcome, with Hincmar in the chair, was only too predictable. Rothad, however, was a resourceful individual who took to the road, which led, as of course they all do, direct to Rome, carrying with him a copy of *Pseudo-Isidore*. Nicholas' attitude then changed suddenly and drastically. On being confronted with its 'evidence' of ancient Christian practice, the Pope issued a new ruling on 24 December 862. Following the rules laid down in *Pseudo-Isidore*, he now required that Rothad's appeal should be heard in Rome, with himself in the chair.[9]

A weapon crafted in the north for other purposes entirely had found its way to Rome, into the hands of a Pope who was not afraid to use it. The results were explosive. Nicholas was no shy, retiring individual, and had not been afraid to involve himself widely in the affairs of the Western Church in any case, asserting his own authority ruthlessly in 860–1, prior to Rothad's arrival, over Archbishop John of Ravenna's attempts to remain independent. But the new ideological justifications and recommended procedures provided by *Pseudo-Isidore* elevated the scope of his ambitions to an entirely new level. As a result, the last five years of his reign were marked by a series of dramatic papal interventions in matters where his predecessors would never have dared to tread. The most significant was the attempted divorce of the emperor Lothar II from his childless wife Teutberga (page 266). Nicholas became involved, because, after much wrangling, Lothar persuaded a synod of his own churchmen at Aachen to sanction his remarriage to the fruitful concubine Waldrada in 862. Nicholas asserted his authority, however, by holding his own synod in the Lateran palace in October 863, which declared the rulings of the provincial synod invalid and even went so far as to excommunicate the two archbishops who had presided over it.

The route may have been convoluted, but it is the destination which counts. In the person of Pope Nicholas I armed with *Pseudo-Isidore*, we encounter a papacy that is finally beginning to correspond to its expected job description as the functioning head of the Western Church. Never mind that Nicholas did not win all his battles, he was at least trying to fight them, where his predecessors had mostly been willing to sit happily in Rome and receive periodic compliments. *Pseudo-Isidore* provided a model of how acknowledged papal prestige might translate into practical authority, and, in Nicholas' hands, the model was put into practice. The scent of revolution is there in his actions, and also in the responses of some of his contemporaries. Famously, the chronicler Regino of Prum caustically remarked that the Pope was trying 'to make himself the master of the whole world'. Certain elements even within Rome found Nicholas' newfangled pretensions a little hard to take: no cult was established in his memory. But there was no stepping back from the basic vigour of Nicholas' example. Pope Hadrian II (867–72) was every bit as assertive of papal rights to intervene in northern ecclesiastical affairs: in the later stages of the quarrel between the two Hincmars, for instance, or in lecturing the rulers of Brittany on how to run their Church's affairs.[10]

If you were taking stock of Western Christendom in the year 870, therefore, it would have been hard not to conclude that long-established patterns were on the move, that imperial authority over the Church was in the process of being replaced by that of the Bishop of Rome, or at least of being challenged properly for the first time. The journey was far from complete. But Charlemagne's behaviour in using the papacy for his own purposes had been mirrored in the next two political generations by a whole slew of Frankish churchmen, especially those wanting to escape – even if only for a particular moment – from the imperial/archiepiscopal authority structure that had underpinned *correctio*. Finding an outside authority to appeal to, when you don't like the ruling you're probably going to get closer to home, is a common human phenomenon. Years ago, I heard a wonderful paper which explored how the colonial courts of British Rhodesia found themselves swamped with divorce cases brought by women, because they tended to give judgements that were less automatically in favour of men than local village tribunals. When such appeals are made often enough, individual actions can relatively quickly change long-established patterns of authority. Pope Nicholas I is the last Bishop of Rome to have gone down in history with the formal epithet 'great' attached to his name, and this, you might think, is a reflection of his aggressive elevation of papal authority on to an entirely new level. He may or may not deserve his epithet; I don't feel remotely qualified to judge. What is entirely clear, however, is that, the ideological advances encoded into *Pseudo-Isidore* notwithstanding, Nicholas' apparent elevation of papal authority was almost entirely illusory.

PORNOCRACY

In January 897, Pope Stephen VII formally opened a synod in St John Lateran, archbasilica of the Roman Church. Little now remains of the actual building, the original begun in the time of Constantine himself, but the current structure stands on the same site. Stephen convened the synod to try the case of his predecessor, Pope Formosus (891–6), who was there in person – in a way. Formosus had died in April of the previous year, and Stephen had his putrescent corpse disinterred after eight months in the ground, clad in papal vestments, and put in the dock. The charges were that Formosus had broken canon law in being translated from his original see of Portus to become Bishop of Rome in 891 (the fifteenth canon of Nicaea banned such moves), perjury (at one point Formosus had been deposed as Bishop of Portus and sworn an oath that he would never operate as a bishop again), and exercising the functions of a bishop while a layman (since he had subsequently acted again as Bishop of Portus after taking the oath). Above all, Stephen accused Formosus of the cardinal sin of actively seeking the papal office, instead of letting the will of God work itself out: precisely the kind of charge that Charlemagne had been so desperate to avoid back in the 790s. According to one account, Stephen spent much of the trial, ranting back and forth at his predecessor's corpse on precisely this theme: 'When you were Bishop of Portus, why did you usurp the universal Roman See in such a spirit of ambition?'[11]

Formosus' defence, such as it was, was mounted by a junior and reportedly none too happy deacon, stood behind the corpse, who periodically muttered rather unenthusiastic denials. Subsequent revulsion means that the trial records – which probably were originally made – have not come down to us, but we do know (surprise, surprise) that Formosus was found guilty. His occupation of the papal throne was declared illegal, his name struck from the records, and all his formal acts as Pope were annulled. The corpse was accordingly stripped of its papal vestments, the three fingers of its right hand – those which Formosus had used when giving blessings – were cut off, and, after a brief sojourn in a cemetery reserved for strangers, the body was weighted down and chucked in the Tiber. None of this was remotely in keeping with the behaviour expected of an occupant of the papal throne, even at the end of the tenth century (nor would the Borgias pull off anything quite so scandalous), so it is perhaps not surprising that Stephen himself did not last very long. In August of the same year, he was removed from office and was dead by the end of the month, silenced by strangulation. A final comment on the proceedings was perhaps then passed by the Almighty, since, in the same year, a major earthquake devastated the scene of the trial, as one contemporary put it, 'from the altar to the doors'.

But if the trial of Formosus must stand as the most bizarre incident in the entirety of papal history, it was no isolated moment of violently vituperative rivalry. In the later ninth and tenth centuries, the grand ecclesiastical statesmanship of Pope Nicholas was replaced by a sequence of violent struggles for control of his see, which became the leitmotif of papal history for more than a hundred years. The antics of Pope Stephen belong to the absolute nadir: a period which saw no less than nine different individuals occupy the papal throne between 896 and 904. But the century and a half after the death of Nicholas' immediate successor, Hadrian II, was marked by so many, frequently violent, changes of papal regime, that it becomes downright impossible to catalogue a meaningful list of popes. There were often multiple contenders claiming the position simultaneously. It would all subsequently be restored to order by distinguishing between true popes and illegitimate antipopes, but this sometimes arbitrary process cannot hide the basic fact that periodic violent turbulence was utterly characteristic of the era. As many as one third of all the occupants of the papal throne between 872 and 1012 died in suspicious circumstances. And even if not all their fates are documented, we have a strong sense of what was going on. To the strangling of Formosus' accuser, we can add such highlights as the suffocation of John X (914–28), and the mutilation of the Greek antipope John XVI (997–8), who managed to survive the removal of his eyes, nose, lips, tongue, and hands. All the grandeur of the third quarter of the ninth century disappeared in a seemingly endless dogfight for control of the Roman see, the earlier part of which attracted the degrading label 'pornocracy' – rule of whores – from Liutprand of Cremona, the same commentator who reports the trial of Formosus with such horrified fascination. Liutprand was particularly exercised by the amount of influence being wielded over papal succession by female members of a dynasty of the local Roman nobility in the first half of the tenth century. These were the particular whores he had in mind. But closer analysis of this broader phenomenon of papal collapse suggests that pornocracy in a broader, less gender-specific sense, works extremely well as a label for the entire period.[12]

To understand what was going on, it is important to stop yourself from looking for a series of dots which, with hindsight, can be joined up to lead to the papacy as we know it, and consider the totality of the historical information available. If you do this for the Carolingian era, it quickly becomes clear that, even during the grander moments of the ninth century, papal politics had always been fiercely contentious, with a marked undercurrent of violence lurking not far from the surface. It was a violent rebellion threatening the eyes and tongue of Leo III, as we saw, which gave Charlemagne the leverage he needed to complete his imperial coronation, and Leo faced a second, much less famous episode of revolt towards the end of his reign besides. And Charlemagne's saving role in the 790s had to be reprised on several subsequent occasions, so that, in structural terms Carolingian emperors acted as a practical limit on violent internal divisions which were always threatening to blow the lid off political life in the Republic of St Peter. Pope Paschal I (817–24) was so unpopular among certain sections of the Roman populace, for instance, that they did not want him to be buried in St Peter's. To hold on to power, he had also to blind and decapitate, respectively, two of his most senior officials: the *primicerius* Theodore and the *nomenclator* Leo. A subsequent investigation at his father's instigation by Lothar, Louis the Pious' eldest son and emperor-designate, saw no need for any major Carolingian intervention on the matter, but did generate the *Constitutio Romana*. This laid down an agreed set of procedures for electing a Pope – including a cooling-off period while the emperor's approval was sought for the local candidate of choice – which were precisely designed to minimize the chances of future violence at election time.[13]

But the type of bitter internal division evident in the pontificate of Paschal never completely disappeared. His successor, Eugenius II (824–7), was a local Roman aristocrat, but he was a compromise candidate imposed by Lothar in the face of multiple contenders for the throne. Sergius II (844–7) likewise only achieved power by crushing a large group of opponents who had supported the candidacy of the archdeacon John. This struggle left many dead on the streets of Rome, but Sergius did at least refuse to sanction the execution of his defeated rival. And still the list goes on. Ragibert, envoy of Pope Leo IV (847–5), was killed en route to Francia. The Pope blamed and tried to have killed three of his fellow leading Romans: George, Hadrian and Peter. Even the great Nicholas failed to command universal support. His memory generated no cult, as we have seen, and his successor, Hadrian II, felt it necessary to order clerics assembled for a council at Troyes on 8 May 868, the year after Nicholas' death, to include his predecessor in their prayers at Mass. The implication is that, left to their own devices, they would not. Not that Hadrian himself fared any better. His reign is famous for the incident when his daughter was possibly raped and certainly kidnapped, along with her mother, by a certain Eleutherius, who then went on to have both of the women killed. It may all just have been personal – the sources don't tell us – but since Eleutherius was the brother of one Anastasius, who had been an imperially supported potential candidate for the papal throne since around the year 850, the smart money must surely be on there having been at least some element of business around the violence. Indeed, the whole sequence of violent papal mortalities gets under way with Hadrian himself, who was bludgeoned to death by his own retinue, when they got impatient at how long the poison they had given him was taking to work.[14]

The message from the ninth-century evidence as a whole is straightforward. The politics of the Papal Republic were always vicious and prone to division, but, while the Carolingian Empire remained strong enough to intervene, a degree of order was maintained, since rebellion against a duly elected (and hence imperially approved) Pope was likely to be punished at the point of a sword, while any overly scandalous gerrymandering at election time would prompt an intervention, and, likely enough, the imposition of a compromise candidate such as Eugenius II. It is no accident at all, therefore, that papal politics became dysfunctional at the precise moment they did. It was from the later 870s, with the deaths of Charles the Bald, Louis the German, Louis II and the great cull of their immediate successors, that political coherence was definitively lost to the Carolingian world (Chapter 6). As a direct result, the gloves could come off in Rome, and we quickly arrive in St John Lateran in January 897. But this only prompts a further question. Why was political life in the Republic of St Peter subject to such systemic division?

The treatment handed out to the putrefying carcass of Pope Formosus points us in the right direction. Stephen, you will remember, both annulled all of his predecessor's acts, and cut off those fingers with which he had performed the blessings which were an essential part of the ceremony by which any written papal ruling was formally enacted. One of these acts was decidedly personal. Stephen had been made a bishop by Formosus as Pope, so that annulling his acts freed Stephen from any imputation of having been translated from another see to the papal throne, in violation of the same fifteenth canon of Nicaea which was central to the charges against Formosus. Otherwise, however, we have no record of Formosus having engaged in anything very serious on the religious front, in terms either of making Church law or encouraging reform during his period in office, even though he had been a perfectly serious churchman in his time. His service on the papal mission to Bulgaria in the time of Nicholas seems to have been outstanding since the khan of the Bulgars is on record as wanting Formosus, and no one else, as his new archbishop.[15] Stephen's particular problem aside, the annulled acts in question were not primarily religious, but all the letters of appointment, grants of new gifts and confirmations of old gifts which Formosus had made during his six years in office. Just like a Carolingian emperor, a ninth-century Pope was the head of a state, the Republic of St Peter, and, aside from any religious functions, had decidedly secular roles to fill. Control of the papal throne also gave you final control over the direction of all the financial assets which fell within the republic's purview, and a considerable part of any reign had to be spent distributing patronage to repay favours and build the necessary body of support.

Thanks to Charlemagne and Louis the Pious, the stock of financial assets available to ninth-century popes really was huge. Between them, father and son endowed the Papal Republic with an enormous portfolio of landed estates, and a whole series of valuable rights in other parts of the Italian landscape: endless percentages of taxation, court and market toll revenues, not to mention countless other customary payments besides. It was this bonanza which allowed its first recipients – Hadrian I and Leo III – to refurbish the urban fabric of their city. In the longer term, however, all this wealth which kept on coming (Hadrian and Leo were spending the interest, not blowing the capital) proved to be a poisoned chalice, at least in terms of the papacy's capacity to provide religious leadership for the broader Western Church. Put simply, popes had a dual job description: enjoying a particular prestige within Latin Christianity while at the same time running the Republic of St Peter. Thanks to Charlemagne, the scale of papal wealth meant that so much local political calculation would be focused on the office that controlled the purse strings, that little time and energy was going to be left over for broader religious functions.

Even while the Carolingian Empire remained powerful, the struggle for control of the wealth periodically threatened to overwhelm the religious dimension of the office. The regime of Sergius III in the mid-840s, for instance, has gone down in history with a particularly bad reputation. The list of more or less contemporary papal biographies – the *Liber Pontificalis* – records that, in Sergius' time, his brother Benedict made a fortune by selling off estates and the right to hold particular offices. Before jumping to conclusions, however, it is important to note that Sergius' biography was written in the reign of his successor, and it was always an effective strategy to establish your own reputation at the expense of a now dead and hence silent predecessor. It was adopted by Pope Stephen V (885–91), who (according to the final surviving fragment we have from the *Liber Pontificalis*) ordered a public inventory to be undertaken to show that the looting of sacred vessels from Rome's churches had taken place before he entered office, and so too the reinstitution of an old custom whereby the clergy of St Peter's used to charge for their services.[16] Sergius III's regime may have been a bit more blatant than some in its moneymaking operations, but I strongly doubt that these were far outside the norm. The intense and entirely non-religious competition for control of the papal throne is otherwise inexplicable. Succession in particular was the focus of the action, since this was the moment when groups not benefiting from the current distribution of assets had their chance to support a candidate who would take more care of their interests in the future, any more than the sitting tenants would give up their benefits without a fight, so that it was only natural for competition to be fierce.

Behind the facade of asserted papal religious authority over Western Christendom, even in the glory days of Nicholas I, there was thus an underlying fragility. The fundamental issue inherent to the local politics of the Papal Republic – who was going to benefit from the asset flow – was always bubbling away. The divisions this generated were only remotely kept in check by at least the threat of imperial intervention, and as soon as the empire ceased to be a real force in central Italy, local politics won out, relegating the broader religious profile of the papal office to second place. Indeed, when you analyse the ninth-century evidence just a little more closely, a more general point emerges from all the detail.

In one sense, we have already encountered it in the particular guise of *Pseudo-Isidore*. It was the machinations of one group of imperial Frankish churchmen which created this text, and of a whole series of others which saw it cited, mobilized and copied as its imaginary vision of the Christian past was brought into play in a range of subsequent contexts that were unimaginable to its original creators. In all of this, individual popes, at least prior to Nicholas I, had never played, or even conceived of playing, the kind of role that the fraudulent texts accorded them. Ninth-century popes were the largely passive beneficiaries (if this be the right word) of the more active roles that imperial Frankish churchmen wanted to ascribe to them – for the latter's own purposes. Left to its own devices, the papacy's religious job description, even in the ninth century, revolved around such traditional concerns as sponsoring missionary work, and agreeing (or not) to the creation of new bishoprics and archbishoprics (again largely in the context of mission). Papal synods generally echoed the contemporary Carolingian concerns with *correctio*, and, even where they had something grander in mind, popes were careful not to tread on established imperial rights. Faced with a quarrel between two would-be Patriarchs of Aquileia – Bishop Andrew of Frejus and Venerius of Grado – Pope Sergius thought that the best response would be to call a general council of the Church. But calling such councils was a long-established right of emperors and Sergius duly approached Lothar for permission.[17] There is not the remotest sign in the first half of the ninth century, in other words, that popes had yet started to think that the particular status of the see of St Peter should translate into any general interference in high Church appointments, or the practical interrelationships of emperors, kings, archbishops and bishops living far beyond its own Italian domains.

And even when particular popes became more active in the third quarter of the century, this too was only possible within the evolving structures of the Carolingian *imperium*. Some of the moments that have gone down in history as great papal victories were entirely dependent on imperial support. In 860–1, Nicholas finally curtailed the independence of the Archbishop of Ravenna, forcing his would-be equal to come to Rome and bow in submission before him. At this point the Pope magnanimously forgave him, restoring John to full favour in return for a percentage of the Ravennate income. But, as even the *Liber Pontificalis* records, the key moment in this exchange came when the emperor (for his own reasons) refused any longer to support the archbishop's independence.[18] More generally, Nicholas was able to exercise such a greater degree of influence than his predecessors because he was operating in a brief window of opportunity provided by the division of the still functioning empire between different powerbrokers. In reality, the self-interested desires of Charles the Bald and Louis the German, their eyes firmly on inheriting his lands, did more to prevent the divorce of Lothar II than Nicholas' busy interference. And if there had only been one Carolingian ruler on the scene who wanted a divorce, it is unlikely that the Pope would have had any leverage in the matter at all. So too in the cases of Bishops Rothad of Soissons or Wulflad of Bourges: here again Nicholas was able in part to face down Archbishop Hincmar of Rheims. But he only managed to do so with the active consent of Charles the Bald, and it was a (temporary) difference of interest between the king and his archbishop which gave Nicholas this opportunity. The Pope was being used by the king to help browbeat the archbishop, and this was just a passing alliance.

Even in this era, moreover, if a Carolingian monarch truly set his heart on a particular religious outcome, the papacy lacked any truly substantive levers of power to shift his position. A classic case in point here is the Christian mission to Moravia, where Nicholas and several of his successors put their weight behind the famous Greek brothers, Cyril and Methodius. Many East Frankish churchmen were consistently hostile to them, but an alliance of papal support and imperial acquiescence kept the brothers and their successors in business for over twenty years between 862 and 885. When the (now royal) will changed after Methodius' death, however, Pope Stephen V (he of the 'it wasn't me who flogged off the vessels' fame) agreed, and the now deceased brothers' disciples were immediately expelled.[19] Papal success in the ninth century thus either directly depended on Carolingian imperial support, or came when it was possible to operate within some of the interstices which opened up as the previously monolithic imperial structure began to fragment. In neither case, however, was the papacy operating independently of the empire, and, once the empire really fell apart from the late 880s, it was impossible for it to maintain even the existing pattern of partial and occasional religious leadership. Not only was the empire no longer there to prompt papal interventions and give papal rulings any bite, but the whole papal office fell prey to the demands of local Roman political processes.

Of course, not everything in Rome collapsed into total chaos on the religious front. The trial of Formosus belongs to an initial period of shock, when the defining structures of the Carolingian period had disappeared, but before anything of even moderate stability had emerged to replace them. And although papal reigns in the later ninth, tenth and early eleventh centuries had a tendency to be quite short, nine popes in nine years is far out in left field even for this period. This degree of anarchy reflects the fact that all the interested parties were busy flexing their biceps to establish a new pecking order in a new world where all the old bets were off. But, from the middle of the first decade of the tenth century, the basic pattern of a new post-Carolingian order began to emerge. In the absence of any Carolingian check, the papacy became incorporated into the power structures of the local landed nobility of central Italy, and a dominant influence over it was generally exercised by whichever familial grouping had established its local political pre-eminence. Two such clans in particular largely swapped control over the papacy between them over much of the next 150 years.

First on the scene was the house of Theophylact. Its founder – called Theophylact, you will not be surprised to learn – was the Count of Tusculum, with large estates in the vicinity of Rome, and originally a loyal servant of the last of the spin-off Carolingian monarchs to show an interest in Roman affairs around the year 900: Louis the Blind, so-called because his Italian expedition cost him his eyesight. But, on the back of Louis' coat-tails, Theophylact extended his influence into the city of Rome itself, where he first emerges as commander of the republic's armies in 905. By 915, the rest of the Roman nobility had accepted his leadership, proclaiming him 'consul', and his first direct papal appointment – John X (914–28) – had been made in the previous year. Like the Carolingians themselves, there were many intrigues within this family as each new generation came to the fore, and many opportunities for other parties to assert themselves at the margins, but, broadly speaking, the clan held on to power over the next two generations in the persons first of all of his two daughters – Theodora the younger and the infamous Marozia – and then via Marozia's son Alberic II who held the honorific title of 'Duke and Senator of the Romans' between 933 and 954. Different members of the family (sometimes in competition with one another, and always in alliance with other members of the Roman nobility) were thus responsible for the vast majority of papal appointments between c.910 and 950. In the second half of the tenth century, the Crescentii, whose landed holdings were located in the Sabine hills to the south and east of the city, exercised a similar level of control, before, in the early eleventh century, pre-eminence returned to that branch of Theophylact's descendants who still controlled their original power base as Counts of Tusculum.[20]

In their domination of the papal office, these noble clans were certainly motivated by a desire to control the economic resources which, thanks to Charlemagne, were at the beck and call of the Roman Church. This did not mean, however, that all their appointments were made without regard for the religious dimensions of the job. Alberic II, for instance, was responsible for promoting Pope Leo VII (931–9), who had a long-established friendship with the great monastic reformer Odo of Cluny (on whom more in a moment), and even brought him to Rome to help reform the city's three ancient monasteries of St Paolo, St Lorenzo and St Agnese. The eleventh-century Counts of Tusculum, likewise, produced – literally – Benedict VIII (1012–24). Born 'Theophylact' he was not just an appointee of the dynasty, but actually a member of it. He was the son of Count Gregory, leader of the Tusculan clan from the later tenth century, and dominant within Rome from the early eleventh after leading the revolt which expelled the Crescentii. But despite being such an echt Roman noble, Benedict took the religious dimensions of his position extremely seriously, co-operating closely with the emperor Henry II (who would himself be canonized, so they made an excellent double act).

But, for every 'good' Pope in this period – i.e. one who took his broader religious duties seriously – it is easy to find another who showed relatively little interest. In addition to Leo VII, Alberic II was also responsible for appointing his own son as John XII (955–64). John took up the office at the uncanonical age of eighteen (bishops were meant to be at least thirty) and enjoyed the wealth and other perquisites of his position to the utmost, before dying of a stroke only nine years later, reputedly in bed with a married woman. In 1032, likewise, Gregory's son and successor at the head of the Tusculani, Alberic III, duly appointed one of his sons – also christened Theophylact like his uncle Benedict VIII – and the latest papal Tusculan further echoed his uncle by styling himself Benedict IX (1032–48/56). There, all resemblance ceased. The new Benedict showed not the slightest interest in anything religious and occupied himself with sex (reputedly in all possible forms), acquiring wealth, and plotting against the opposition whom his outrageous behaviour quickly generated within the city, to the extent – again reputedly – of organizing assassinations.

The uncertainty over his dates reflects the consequent turbulence of his reign. His first term in office came to an end when he was driven out of the city in 1044. He then forced his way back in the following year, before deciding to sell the job on to his godfather so that he could get married (the only Pope known to have sold his own position), but then reoccupied it again briefly before finally being deposed.[21]

All of this effectively illustrates the narrow limits of the position in which the papacy found itself once it was bereft of the structures of the Carolingian Empire. Even in the hands of higher-profile popes in the later ninth century, it had remained a reactive institution, dependent on emperors and imperial churchmen bringing matters to its attention and being willing to use their own authority structures – sometimes – to put its rulings into practice. When the empire disappeared, so too did the vast majority of the infrastructure which had allowed certain popes to stride forth on a wider stage. As a direct result, the Republic of St Peter collapsed into a series of always unedifying, and occasionally scandalous, struggles for control of the assets with which Charlemagne had endowed it.

The noble clans who came to the fore were certainly Christians, and not immune to the broader religious currents flowing around them. They or their appointees (often one and the same, given the Tusculani's tendency to keep the papal throne in the family) might sometimes be genuinely interested in the current preoccupations of Western Christendom as a whole. But, first and foremost, the papal office was a key element in the portfolio of assets by which these clans maintained their power in central Italy. As such, broader religious leadership was always going to come a poor second to local political function in the papal job description. The illusion that might be conjured up by an injudicious juxtaposition of the vision of the papal office in *Pseudo-Isidore* and its practical operation in the time of Pope Nicholas is completely dispelled by what happened afterwards. It was the Carolingian Empire in all its manifestations, and Frankish rulers and churchmen in all their different ways, which had made it possible for the papacy to exercise any kind of broader influence over the Western Church in the ninth century. Completely lacking its own independent levers of power, it relied utterly on Carolingian imperial structures for any broader role, and, when these disappeared, the office was reduced to the level of pawn in a very local political auction indeed. Sometimes literally sold off to the highest bidder, from the 890s the papal office became the whore – or maybe the milchcow if you're feeling charitable – of the nobility of central Italy: pornocracy indeed.

BARBARIAN POPES

But if the nobility of Rome had sufficient hold on the papacy to make it content – left to its own devices – to bumble along in the ceremonial role of Latin Christianity's vice president, with the bulk of its active job description centred on mediating a central Italian bunfight of major proportions, other constituencies within Western Christendom were far from satisified with this situation. The most obvious group with an interest in change was a sequence of imperial wannabes. Thanks to Charlemagne, there was a marked tendency for those who would be emperor to want to be crowned in Rome: the alternative Carolingian, do-it-yourself route pioneered for Louis the Pious, never managed to replace the symbolic power of Christmas Day 800. Thanks likewise to Carolingian example, it was also now a well-established principle that these emperors had a duty of care for the quality of religious life in Rome: the most important religious centre of the Latin West. In post-Carolingian Western Europe these two traditions periodically coincided to bring to Rome a north European ruler with his eyes on the imperial title, both to have himself crowned and to win extra brownie points by doing something about papal corruption.

It was these moments of imperial intervention, in fact, which underlay the rotating influence of the Tusculani and Crescentii. Otto I broke the first period of Tusculan domination, albeit as something of an afterthought. The excesses of John XII (937–64), son of the Tusculan count Alberic II, were already stirring up glimmers of internal Roman revolt by the early 960s. This made John willing to crown Otto emperor on 2 February 962, in search of some heavyweight political support, even though he knew that the imperial title would give Otto licence to intervene in Roman affairs. Once Otto had left again, John tried to minimize the damage by stirring up an alliance of Byzantines and Magyars against him, so Otto returned and replaced him with a new man, Leo VIII, a move which also eventually allowed – when the emperor's interest was dragged back north and Leo quickly died – the influence of the Crescentii to be asserted at the expense of the ousted Tusculani. The first Pope from that camp was John XIII (965–72), brother of the first Crescentius. In due course, the power of the Crescentii was broken partly by Otto III in the 990s and definitively by his cousin and successor Henry II in the second decade of the eleventh century. This eventually allowed the Tusculani to return, first in the person of Benedict VIII, brother of the then count.[22]

But Otto III and Henry II, at least, were not merely interested in having themselves crowned. They were also deeply committed to the cause of ecclesiastical reform. By the year 1000, the two really hot issues within the Western Church were simony and clerical marriage. Simony was the label given to the purchase of ecclesiastical office, named after Simon Magus recorded at Acts 8:9–24 as offering money to the Apostles Peter and John if they would pass on to him the power to confer the Holy Spirit by laying on of hands. Because many Church institutions (bishoprics, monasteries, and especially parish churches) were private property at this point, and since their founders (and the founders' heirs) retained rights over them, it was entirely normal in some places for a new occupant to pay financial compensation in return for taking up the post. Outright purchases were attracting general condemnation by the time of Otto III, but the issue posed more tricky questions of definition at the margins. If an appointee presented an owner with a gift upon appointment, was this simony? By extension, more radical reformers were also arguing that no layman – whether gifts were involved or not – should have any say over ecclesiastical appointments at all. But, then again, who was a layman? Kings and emperors did not think that they fell into that category. This broader agenda had its origins in the monastic reform movements of the ninth and tenth centuries, many reformers having come to the conclusion that lay interests, particularly in monastic wealth, were the main hindrance preventing many monasteries from signing up to the new standards of behaviour, learning and liturgy which had first come to the fore under Charlemagne and Louis the Pious (page 342). In the course of the tenth century, however, it had spread out from the monastic context to embrace the Church as a whole. The fulmination against clerical marriage had similar origins, reflecting, again, originally a monastic emphasis on the link between chastity and piety. It expanded first into demands and then expectations that the clergy attached to cathedrals ought to live communal, sex-free lives, and also give up private property, and then, with a bit of sacramental theory added, into the argument that no cleric could properly administer the sacraments if they were married or kept a concubine. As Peter Damian, one leading eleventh-century voice in favour of reform, put it, 'If you commit incest with your spiritual daughter, with what conscience do you dare to handle the mystery of the Lord's body?'[23]

Otto III and Henry II were ready and willing to tackle both of these issues, and saw a remodelled papacy as a vehicle which could assist them in their task. They held broadly the same view as Charlemagne, that it was their God-appointed duty to bring the Church to a more perfect form of Christian religiosity, but differed from him in according the papacy a more active role in the process. The partnership was nonetheless still to be formulated on the emperors' terms. Otto III in particular was uncompromising in his stance. He publicly repudiated the *Donation of Constantine* as a forgery, making it clear that he was and should be viewed as the senior partner in the alliance. Unimpressed by the standard of potential appointees he found in Rome (having originally been called in by Pope John XV as a counterweight to Crescentius the younger, son of the original), he also installed two northerners as his own papal appointees: first his cousin Bruno as Gregory V, and then, on Gregory's early (and mysterious) death in 999, Gerbert of Aurillac who became Sylvester II (999–1003). Bruno was a grandson of Otto I, of straightforwardly Saxon origins therefore, although his father had eventually been made Duke of Carinthia further to the south. Gerbert was from south-central France. Both were highly educated products of the post-Carolingian Church of northern Europe: Gregory, as Otto's chaplain, was a product of the cathedral schools of East Francia, while Gerbert, one of the greatest scholars of his day (famous for reintroducing the abacus and the armillary sphere to the West from his knowledge of Greek mathematics and science as preserved by the Arabs), was a monk trained in one of the most famous monasteries of the tenth century: Aurillac in the Haute Auvergne. Both were also committed to the same reform agenda, and Gerbert lasted long enough to make an impact. Henry II, for his part, was content to work with the Tusculan Benedict VIII, but Benedict was himself devoted to reform. Emperor and Pope jointly

presided over a reforming synod at Pavia in 1022, which beat the drum
once again against the twin abuses at the heart of the current reform
agenda.[24]

This new model of Christian leadership – with dominant emperor
acting alongside a much more active Pope – was necessary by the year
1000, where it had not been 200 years earlier, for one simple reason.
After his astonishing career of conquest, Charlemagne had brought
more or less the entirety of Western Christendom under his direct
control. Although they claimed the same title, however, the same was
no longer true of Charlemagne's Ottonian and Salian successors. In
Carolingian terms, the latter controlled East Francia, northern Italy
and a few additional bits and pieces. West Francia was outside of their
control, as were the very extensive, newly Christian lands in the
Iberian peninsula and east-central Europe, where, by the year 1000,
Bohemia, Poland and the Magyar kingdoms had all already converted
to Latin Christianity. Much of this expanded Western Christendom
was administered by churchmen who owed their allegiance to other
kings and princes, who would not take kindly to direct, purely imperial
interference in their lands. In these circumstances, the papacy made a
more neutral ally whose participation in the reform process helped
guard against suspicions that it might be a cover for interference of a
more political kind. With the papacy on board, reform could be
presented as an issue for the entirety of Western Christendom, heading
off any potential repeat of the situation between 500 and 700, where
Western Christendom in practice functioned in separate Church communities on a kingdom-by-kingdom basis (Chapter 7).

What made this imperial–papal alliance far more effective, and also
prevented any real possibility of a repeat of post-Roman fragmentation
in the post-Carolingian era, was that there was a second important
constituency pre-prepared for a more active papal involvement in the
running of the Western Church. Thanks to the structural transformations set in motion by Charlemagne and his successors, political
fragmentation had not been accompanied by religious-cum-cultural
disintegration, with the result that, even by the year 1000, many
Western senior Christian churchmen continued to speak with more or
less a single voice. Many of them were the products of the cathedrals
and their attached schools, whose basic pattern had been set in place
by Charlemagne and his advisers. Their libraries were now larger, and
new cathedrals had been established besides, as Christianity spread east

of the Rhine and the Elbe. Texts had continued to circulate among them, across political frontiers, and they continued to share essentially the same liturgical, homiletic, disciplinary and theological traditions. And because they shared broadly the same moral and intellectual formation, the products of these redoubtable institutions – which were also a prime recruiting ground for bishops and archbishops – tended to hold similar world views. Henry II got all his bishops, for instance, from the main cathedral schools of his realm, and other kings and rulers of the time usually did likewise.

A very similar world view was also to be found among the products of the other main source of Latin Christendom's leadership at the turn of the second millennium: the greater monasteries. The basic pattern of life in these institutions had been set in Carolingian times as well, at least in the imperial monasteries which had responded with enthusiasm to the monastic reform agendas of Benedict of Aniane and Louis the Pious. As a result, these communities, too, shared liturgical and intellectual traditions, and library holdings, which were very similar to their cathedral counterparts. Again, the post-Carolingian century had seen plenty of change, with Benedict of Aniane's model of reform spreading across a wide variety of houses in very different geographical and political contexts, and by an equally wide range of mechanisms. The most famous monastery of the age was Cluny in Burgundy, where the monks had essentially reformed themselves, but they did so after the established Carolingian, Benedictine pattern. Elsewhere, sometimes (as in Rome) with active Cluniac assistance, lay lords or bishops (or the Archbishop of Metz in the case of the famous monastery of Gorze in the Rhineland) had to buy into the principle first, but everywhere the same model of religious life, with a considerable overlap in intellectual terms to the culture of the cathedral schools, was spreading fast across the older and newer landscapes of Western Christendom. And even if there were differences in detail – such as at what point in the hierarchy was it necessary to draw the line against married clerics, and where did gift-giving become simony – the products of both leading monasteries and cathedrals were equally committed to the great reforming agenda of the year 1000.[25]

Not only was post-Carolingian political fragmentation not matched by a similar disintegration in the religious culture of Western Christendom, but one dimension of their shared culture pre-programmed both the monastic and cathedral-based components of this second constituency to accept, indeed expect, that the papacy should play a greater role in its religious leadership. Throughout the later ninth and tenth centuries, *Pseudo-Isidore* was busy being copied and read in the cathedrals and monasteries. The vast majority of all those early surviving manuscripts of the text belonged to the libraries in which Latin Christianity's leaders were being trained, so that *Pseudo-Isidore*'s vision of a papally run, more perfect Late Antique Christianity continued to spread down the generations. Indeed, when new handbooks of Church law were found to be necessary in the tenth century, such as those produced by Regino of Prum and Burchard of Worms, the new works naturally included many of the forged texts of *Pseudo-Isidore*. Even when the original collection was past its shelf life, therefore, it continued to work a powerful influence in favour of the idea that papal authority ought to be central to the running of Western Christendom.[26]

One reflection of the power of this idea is the fact that, even through the pornocratic era, Western ecclesiastical consumer demand required the papacy to fulfil at least some new functions. This process was not just a product of *Pseudo-Isidore*, but was also prompted by the higher profile adopted by some particular popes in the third quarter of the ninth century; albeit that this had been dependent on Carolingian imperial structures, and was itself more than partly a reflection of the collection's impact. Most famously, various reformed monastic houses started to put themselves under formal papal protection, asking for written charters to this effect. Cluny started the trend in 909 when the reforming monks obtained their original protective document, even though post-Carolingian Rome was then at its most chaotic worst. They then went on to obtain further confirmations of the fact of papal protection throughout the subsequent century, which included getting Pope Gregory V's name attached to a full and important inventory of the monastery's holdings put together in 998. As a highly influential study of Cluny's landowning has pointed out, these documents of papal protection had little practical value – the papacy had no effective leverage in tenth-century Burgundy, and for real protection the monastery relied on other mechanisms – but such documents advertised Cluny's status in a wider Christian world, and, as such, they had sufficient use for many other monasteries to follow suit. Between 896 and 1049, religious institutions, the vast majority of them monasteries (including most of the great reformed houses of the period), drew up

630 papal charters confirming rights of different kinds, with an over-whelming number referring to landed holdings. About one quarter are forgeries. Presumably, the institution didn't want to go to the bother and expense of obtaining a real document from Rome, and just fabricated their own.

Real or forged, however, the desire to obtain papal privileges, which were extremely rare before this period, is a clear sign of at least the greater symbolic role which now attached to the papacy in the minds of Western churchmen. They also eventually involved the papacy in the act of making saints. In Roman and early medieval Christianity, making a saint was entirely a matter for the local community in which she or he had operated. An interested party composed a *Life* as part of instituting a cult centre, and then the proposed saint either did or did not attract a following. In the last decade of the tenth century, for the first time ever, a local Christian community turned to Rome for extra validation in the proposed beatification of Bishop Ulrich of Augsburg. He had been a great voice in favour of reform in the Ottonian Church and Pope John XV was happy enough to confirm his sanctity at a Roman synod held in the Lateran on 31 January 993, the results being announced to the rest of the world in a formal bull. This innovation was followed up by the canonization of five missionary martyrs from the Baltic region within the next decade, and the whole new process quickly took off.[27]

In mobilizing the papacy as a more active ally in the cause of reform, Otto III and Henry II were sowing their seed on highly fertile ground. But as a solution to the problem of providing overarching religious authority for the unified cultural block that was Western Christendom, the papal–imperial alliance model was far from perfect. Because much of Western Christendom was under the control of other rulers, there would always be some suspicion in their minds that a papacy in alliance with the empire could not be trusted to act with proper impartiality. Equally important, although this was not visible at the great moments of imperial coronation, the tenth- and eleventh-century Holy Roman Empire was a somewhat ramshackle institution, whose rulers faced systemic instability particularly when they first came to power (just like their Carolingian counterparts: page 257). As a result, they were likely to have their attention diverted from Rome on a regular basis by a host of pressing concerns on their many frontiers. In practice, therefore, the empire could not be relied upon (any more than its Carolingian predecessor) to have the necessary capacity consistently to ensure that the nobility of central Italy did not divert the papacy back to the Romano-centric bunfight which was at the heart of all the great papal scandals of the post-Carolingian period. Immediately after the joint synod conducted by Henry II and Benedict VIII, for instance, Henry's successor just stood by and watched as Benedict IX, the previous Benedict's sexually voracious nephew who we met a few pages ago, used papal wealth as a vehicle for pleasure-seeking of an intensity which matched the worst excesses of the pornocracy. What the functional religious unity of Western Christendom really required, therefore, was a leadership structure which was actually independent of imperial rule; but, if this was to be the papacy, then some replacement mechanism had also to be found to keep it independent of the predatory pecuniary ambitions of the Italian nobility. The story of how this problem was resolved brings us face to face with the greatest barbarian Pope of them all: Bruno of Eguisheim-Dagsburg, who, upon accession, thankfully took the shorter name of Leo IX.

When this particular story began, it was not clear that anything out of the ordinary was unfolding. It opened with the tried and tested pattern of north European potentate taking an interest in Rome because he wanted the imperial title. This time it was Henry III, not a direct descendant of Henry II of Pavia fame, because that Henry and his wife had taken a vow of celibacy. Power had therefore passed from the direct Ottonian line to their Salian cousins, descended from a daughter of Otto I. Henry inherited power in the north on the death of his father in 1039, and having spent the customary period consolidating it, was ready by the mid-1040s to move in on the imperial title. At this point, he found himself confronted with three popes, all problematic in their different ways. The worst offender was Benedict IX, and while his godfather John Gratian (to whom he sold the office for 1,000 pounds of silver), renamed Gregory VI, was a well-regarded reformer, the current emphasis on simony meant that the manner of Gregory's election was enough to exclude him as a suitable master of ceremonies for Henry's projected coronation. The third Pope was Sylvester III, previously Bishop John of Sabina, who was clearly inserted into the chaos engendered by the antics of Benedict IX by party or parties unknown, but who is otherwise mysterious. Henry had no truck with any of them, promoting in their place one of his own churchmen, Suidger Bishop of Bamberg, who became Clement II, and who, on Christmas Day 1046, duly crowned Henry emperor. Henry III, like his earlier collaterally related namesake, was a convinced reformer, and it looked like Western Christendom was in for a repeat of the imperial–papal alliance motif. That matters turned out differently is thanks to a combination of the Italian climate, which had killed off both Clement and his immediate successor Damasus II (previously Bishop Poppo of Brixen, another of Henry's bishops) by the summer of 1048 (poor Poppo lasted only from 17 July to 9 August 1048: still only the seventh shortest papacy ever), and the astonishing energy of Henry's next appointee.

This was Bruno of Eguisheim-Dagsburg, aka Leo IX (1049–54). Nobly born, being a cousin of the Salian emperors themselves, he had been educated in the cathedral school of Toul, and, according to the contemporary *Life*, showed all the expected signs of burgeoning holiness there from an early age. This included a devotion to the shrines of the Holy See, which made him visit Rome on an almost annual basis. In a fascinating glimpse into the everyday life of a major tenth-century ecclesiastical institution, however, this did not make Bruno any pacific ascetic pushover. The *Life* equally celebrates, without the slightest blush, the care and skill shown by the young Bruno when he had to lead his bishop's contingent of knights off on campaign. In due course, he was elevated to the Bishopric of Toul in turn in 1026, and proved an ardent supporter both of the reforming causes against simony and clerical marriage, and of the reforming drive of the Cluniac monastic movement. None of this made him anything other than a standard aristocratic German bishop of his age. What picks him out is the clarity of his vision of the higher role that the papacy might play in the Western Church, and the energy and imagination he showed, during what was a relatively brief reign, in setting in motion a complete revolution in its workings to fit it for that position.

His clarity of purpose was there from the off. He was selected for the post by his imperial cousin, but refused to accept it (having shown, as the *Life* tells us, the requisite amount of hesitation) unless the clergy and people of Rome were fully willing to endorse him. He clearly had it in mind to be much more than another of those outside, imperial appointees who had consistently failed to alter the fundamentally local focus of the papal office since the collapse of the Carolingian Empire. A crucial and immediate strategy for effecting this change was to recruit the assistance of a series of like-minded churchmen from across Western Europe. Humbert was imported from the monastery of Moyenmoutier in Leo's own former diocese, and the list includes cathedral clergy (such as Frederic, brother of Godfrey Duke of Lorraine, from the cathedral chapter of Liège), as well as Italian clerics, most famously a certain Hildebrand (whom we will return to shortly) who had originally risen through the ranks in the entourage of John Gratian, and subsequently followed him out of Italy and into exile at Cluny. Leo was also in close touch with the prominent hermit leader and intellectual, originally from Ravenna and trained in northern Italy, Peter Damian. Leo thus flooded Rome with a coterie of reformers from across the rest of Western Christendom, some from inside the empire's borders, others from outside, representing all the main strands of contemporary Christianity: the cathedrals, the monasteries, and even the more radical wing, like Peter Damian, who found the monasteries too luxurious. These he promoted to senior positions within the Roman clergy, with the overall effect of breaking the close ties between the leadership of that body and the nobility of central Italy, and, in the process, refocusing the energies of the entire institution on to the project of reform.

Having filled the Lateran with international reformers, the greater part of Leo's energy for the remainder of his reign was devoted to advancing the reform agenda. Some of what he did was more or less normal. In 1049, he held a Lateran synod which once more, as at Pavia in 1022, condemned simony and clerical marriage. But this time the energy was so much greater. Leo declared that all clergy at the level of subdeacon and above should be celibate, drawing the line further down the clerical ladder than ever before. He also so intimidated the Bishop of Sutri with a direct, personal accusation that he had paid for his office, that the bishop dropped dead on the spot. Even more striking to contemporaries was the fact that Leo did not confine his activities merely to Rome and its environs, but swept outside the city, and outside even of Italy, to hold reforming synods in France and Germany as well: eleven or twelve of them in fact (it's not quite certain) in his five-year reign. While on tour, he summoned leading members of the regional clergy to synods where the reform agenda was put firmly on the table, and the Pope in person confronted any offenders among the churchmen present. Most famously, the translation (that is, the ceremonial re-burial in a new, customarily grander tomb) of the remains of St Remigius in 1049 was turned into a great reform council at Rheims where Leo asked the twenty assembled French bishops – point-blank – whether they had paid for their jobs and were thus guilty of simony. The Bishop of Langres refused to answer, at which point Leo excommunicated him, and, in a moment of high drama, the Archbishop of Besançon was suddenly struck dumb when trying to defend him (Langres was one of his suffragans). At this point, not surprisingly, five of the remainder confessed and were duly forgiven and reappointed to their posts. Only the Bishop of Nantes was actually deposed; he had succeeded his father, which was con-sidered utterly beyond the pale.

Suddenly, Western Christendom was confronted with a whole new papacy, literally ready to put the fear of God into offenders. Instead of sitting within Rome to receive ceremonial visits and write out grand charters of confirmation which meant absolutely nothing in practice, here was a Pope seizing the initiative in Church affairs. Leo exploded over the Alps and used his councils to place himself and the papacy at the epicentre of the current reforming agenda, and the shockwaves are visible in a whole slew of contemporary commentaries. One witness of the synod-cum-trial of Rheims still felt moved, many years later, to record the fear generated in him by the whole event. The senior vice president for prayer had become the self-appointed leader of Western Christendom in the hands of a visionary leader who could see the potential authority that might be constructed on the back of papal prestige.[28]

It is hardly coincidental, therefore, that the first direct citation of the *Donation of Constantine* in a papal letter was also made in Leo's reign. Its target was the Patriarch of Constantinople, and the issue was jurisdiction over parts of southern Italy. On the founding of the Papal Republic, Constantinople had withdrawn the sees of Sicily and southern Italy from Rome's purview. Leo wanted them back, and used the *Donation* to substantiate his claim to primacy over every other see of Christendom: East and West. When the Byzantines wouldn't play ball, Leo's mission, led by Humbert, now Cardinal Bishop of Silva Candida, had not the slightest hesitation issuing the bull of excommu-nication against the Patriarch of Constantinople which initiated the great schism between the Orthodox and Catholic communions. And it was Humbert who precisely formulated the new spirit which Leo had brought to the papacy in his disquisition to the Byzantines:

> All men have such reverence for the holder of the apostolic office of Rome that they prefer to receive the holy commandments and the traditions from the mouth of the head of the Church than from the Holy Scriptures and patristic writings. [Thus the Pope] makes almost the whole world run after God with delight and enthusiasm.

A long-standing claim to special prestige was now transformed into an active doctrine of papal primacy, and this was used to justify Leo's and his colleagues' seizure of the reins of Christian leadership.[29]

There had of course been moments of papal grandeur before – not least in the eras of Leo I and Nicholas the Great – and it was not immediately obvious that the revolution set in motion by Leo IX was destined permanently to change the nature of the papacy. After such magnificent beginnings, his reign petered out in a confrontation with intrusive Normans who were busy taking over much of Sicily and southern Italy (the reason why Leo had reopened the issue of jurisdictions with Constantinople). They first defeated the forces that the Pope could scrape together (true to form Henry was unavoidably detained in the north), and then captured the Pope himself. Although they treated Leo with due deference, they held him prisoner for the best part of a year and he died soon after his release. He was succeeded by two further northerners, Victor II (1055–7, the former Bishop of Eichstatt) and Stephen IX (1057–8, the Frederic of Lorraine imported to Rome by Leo IX). But, since Henry III had also died in the meantime, the Tusculani saw Stephen's death as the opportunity to return to business as usual. In 1058, they put forward their own man as Benedict X, to be followed after his death in 1061 by Honorius II.

This time, however, the clock could not be turned back. Leo's reign had created a coherent and self-confident leadership at the heart of the papacy which was not about to give up on the project that it had initiated. All the new blood that he had imported into the senior ranks of the Roman clergy was still there, and not to be sucked back so easily into the old norms of central Italian political manoeuvring. As a body, Leo's appointees were ready to carry forward the revolution into the next generation. A direct line from Leo continued after Stephen's death therefore in the pontificates of Nicholas II (1059–61, another imported northerner, born Gerard of Bourgogne near Arles) and Alexander II

(1061–73, previously the reforming Bishop Anselm of Lucca). In these two pontificates, crucial further steps were taken which entrenched and even extended the revolution. Most important, at Easter 1059, Nicholas brought 113 bishops from right across Christendom into Rome to a council which legitimated a crucial reform in papal election procedure. Henceforth, elections were to be conducted by the cardinal clergy alone, consisting of the seven cardinal bishops (of the seven old suburbicarian sees), the twenty-eight cardinal priests in charge of the city's major churches, and the eighteen cardinal deacons who ran what had originally been the centres from which charity was distributed. The emperor, should there be one, was to have no say. The papacy had made a unilateral declaration of independence: another crucial step forward. For all its fire and fury, Leo's great synod at Rheims had been attended by only twenty French bishops, while well over a hundred more stayed away. This is because the King of France, viewing Leo – not unfairly – as a creature of the empire, refused to allow the remainder to attend. To function as the true of head of Western Christendom, therefore, it was necessary, in the end, for the papacy to become independent of the empire.

As you might expect, the response to this in the north was hostile and the German-imperial party started to make its own anti-papal appointments. But the regime of the new ruler, Henry IV, who had become king in 1056 at the tender age of six, was in no position actually to intervene in Rome, and Nicholas made one further policy change which helped cement papal independence both in the face of the Holy Roman Empire, and of the Tusculani. In 1059, in a major volte-face, he concluded a crucial peace deal with the intrusive Normans. This recognized their conquests as fully legitimate in return for their military and political support. In the short term, this was exactly what the nascent papacy required: sufficient military clout to keep itself independent, while the broader dimensions of Leo's revolution took hold, both inside Rome and without.

Within Rome, the pontificate of Alexander II saw important steps in the reorganization of the papal bureaucracy to fit its operating systems for the job description the reformers had imposed upon the position. In particular, the formal registration of papal letters was readopted as an administrative practice. Alexander's registers don't survive, but those of his successor, Gregory VII, do. Registration involved making a second copy of every significant letter sent by a Pope to be kept in the papal archives, as a formal check on any decisions that had been given and to minimize opportunities for fraud (if it had been done consistently in the ancient past, ironically, the forged decretals of *Pseudo-Isidore* would have been impossible, at least without papal connivance). The practice mimicked the old late Roman imperial chancery, and had been followed in the deeper past at least for particular papal reigns, certainly that of Gregory I (some of whose registers still existed in crumbling papyrus in the ninth century) and again for some ninth-century popes (notably John VIII, 872–82). It may even have been completely standard late antique and early medieval papal practice, but it had certainly fallen into abeyance during the chaos of the pornocracy. Its readoption is a clear sign that the reformers understood that they were creating a new papacy, whose every word, thanks to the doctrine of papal primacy, might be of significance in the future, particularly in the matter of legal rulings, and therefore needed to be carefully recorded. Alexander's pontificate also saw the start of significant reorganizations of the financial bureaux (destined to be a running theme throughout the twelfth century) as the reformers sought to impose order on all the Roman revenue flows that survived both from ancient times and from the huge re-endowments of the Carolingian era. In the meantime, many papal estates had been leased out on exceedingly generous terms to different members of the central Italian nobility, and getting these back under papal control would be a major struggle.

Outside of Rome, both Nicholas and Alexander managed to maintain the traditions of Leo's proactive papacy, particularly in sending out papally appointed judges, so-called legates, to assert an active Roman voice, wherever possible. In the time of Nicholas, Peter Damian and the future Alexander II (then still Bishop of Lucca) successfully forced the Church of Milan to bend its appointment practices (which customarily involved substantial payments) to come more into line with reforming agendas. This involved the archbishop formally accepting papal authority, and he was one of the more unwilling attendees at Nicholas' great synod of 1059. Under Alexander, likewise, Peter Damian was again sent to judge a dispute between the monks of Cluny and the Bishop of Mâcon, in whose diocese the monastery was situated. Cluny, as we've seen, had long extracted charters of notional protection from Rome, but this time, the Roman axis had real meaning. Peter convened a council at Chalon-sur-Saône which ruled that the monastery should be completely independent of its bishop, to whom it would no longer owe any dues or duties whatsoever. Alexander sent out further legates besides, not least to England in 1070 at the invitation of William the Conqueror (whose expedition he had blessed in 1066) to help sort out the mess which was the Anglo-Saxon Church, and north into the empire to judge in a quarrel between the bishops of Bamberg and Constanz, and eventually to persuade Henry IV not to divorce his wife Bertha.[30]

Alexander was not himself a northerner, but his agenda and outlook had been forged by the sequence of northern popes which Henry III had initiated, and which ran the papacy through a twenty-year period of sustained revolution. By the end of it, the nature and practices of the papal office had changed out of all recognition. In the third quarter of the eleventh century, taken over by reformers from the north, the papacy was reinvented to become an active source of ecclesiastical authority, which energetically championed the reform agenda for Latin Christendom as a whole. It had also freed itself from dependence upon the imperial alliance which had been the rather unsatisfactory route by which some past popes had managed temporarily to achieve a higher profile, and asserted papal primacy explicitly on the back of the *Donation of Constantine*, if at this point only in the context of a quarrel with Constantinople. One of the least celebrated of the group, because he died so soon, Clement II also seems to have coined the specific term *papatus* – papacy – to describe the new institution they were creating. It was modelled on the term *episcopatus*, but designed to signal that the Pope occupied a hierarchical position that was straightforwardly above that of any bishop. By the time of Alexander's death, we are dealing with a papacy which was now at least attempting to act as the head of Western Christendom.

Perhaps the most striking feature of the story of papal development in the Carolingian era and afterwards, however, is that this newly transformed papacy was not at all the product of ambitions internal to the Roman Church itself. Rather, it was created by consumer demand, by reforming churchmen whose origins lay in lands that the ancient Romans would have regarded as utterly barbarian. In the mid-eleventh century, the northern barbarians swept into Rome and began to construct a new, ecclesiastical Roman Empire. They acted deliberately, and were entirely conscious of what they were doing. As Peter Damian put it:

Now the Roman Church, the see of the apostles, should imitate the ancient court of the Romans. Just as of old the earthly Senate strove to subdue the whole multitude of the peoples to the Roman Empire, so now the ministers of the apostolic see, the spiritual senators of the Church Universal, should make it their sole business by their laws to subdue the human race to God, the true emperor.[31]

But in 1173, this new Roman Empire was far from complete. The reformed papacy had at its disposal only extremely limited levers of power as it sought to extend the remit of its religious authority. Its practical ability to intervene in ecclesiastical matters was still largely limited to moments where its participation was invited, or areas which lacked strong central government. Where kings or emperors were powerful, its reach remained severely limited, and these men still held to the old teaching that they too were directly appointed by God. Establishing some real levers of power on the ground, which could be used actively to pursue its own agendas rather than having merely to respond, where possible, to the requirements of others, was the final obstacle in the path of the new Roman Empire of the papacy. It was to be solved by borrowing one of the key mechanisms by which the old Roman emperors had governed the largest and longest-lived state western Eurasia has ever known.

THE *HARMONY OF DISCORDANT CANONS*

A quick glance at the period after the death of Alexander II might lead you to think that the traditional Roman method employed to complete the papal empire was straightforward intimidation. This of course had been a trusty weapon in the hands of the founders of the first Roman Empire, even if, later on, the willingness of conquered provincial elites to buy into Roman values transformed the imperial structure, from particularly the second century AD onwards, into a much more consensual enterprise altogether. Alexander's successor was Gregory VII (1073–85), that Hildebrand who had originally served in the entourage of John Gratian. Gregory is famous for setting the reformed papacy on a new path of direct confrontation with the empire of Henry IV over the issue of simony, a policy which had all the subtlety of the charge of the Light Brigade at the battle of Balaclava.

In one sense, I do Gregory a disservice. He perceived the same problem in most of the other West European states of his age, and was savvy enough to realize that it was impossible to take them all on at once, so the kings of England and France he left well alone. He also tried persuasion for the first eighteen months of his reign. But when that got nowhere, he announced a shift of tack with a huge fanfare in January 1075 in the form of a papal letter which was widely distributed across the courts and major ecclesiastical institutions of Western Europe:

> I find hardly any bishops who conform to the law either in their appointment or in their way of life and who rule the Christian people in the love of Christ and not for worldly ambition. Among all the secular princes I know of none who place the honour of God before their own and righteousness before gain . . . Since there is no prince who troubles about such things, *we* must protect the lives of religious men.

The dig in the last line was aimed particularly against Henry IV, whose reform-minded father had kick-started the transformation of the papacy in the 1040s, and it was in imperial territory that Gregory chose to fight. His particular target was the see of Milan, the great imperial city in the north of Italy where simony – of a kind – was rife. Gregory's chosen weapon was to call on the wider population of the city to boycott all Church services offered by simoniac and married clergy. From there, the quarrel quickly spiralled out of control. By January 1076, Henry had decided that Gregory was impossible to live with and started manoeuvring to force his abdication. Gregory responded by excommunicating Henry at his Lenten synod of the same year. The Pope was being deliberately provocative, and knew that the internal troubles of the empire, where an alliance of German princes was in open revolt, were on his side. As a result, Henry decided to come to terms and publicly abased himself in January 1077, standing outside in the snow at the Tuscan castle of Countess Matilda of Canossa in which Gregory had taken refuge. He was readmitted to communion, but the issues between them had not been resolved. Gregory had now set his sights on preventing laymen, in which category he included kings and emperors, having any say at all in the appointment of bishops and other clergy, and what has come to be known as the Investiture Controversy (since much of the intellectual energy came to be focused on the ceremony by which bishops were invested with their office) got into full swing. By the spring of 1080, they were at loggerheads again, and Gregory both excommunicated Henry a second time, and recognized the leader of the German princely coalition, Rudolf of Swabia, as king in his place. On the basis of the *Donation of Constantine*, Gregory clearly understood himself to dispose of a higher order of authority than the emperor – since Constantine had passed imperial power on to Pope Sylvester upon departing for Constantinople – and hence felt free to depose any particular occupant of that post who failed to come up to scratch. At this point, the dimension of political authority was finally added to religious authority that had been attributed to Rome on the basis of the *Donation* in the ninth century. The papal claim to imperial power had finally found full articulation.[32]

But, in fact, in one key dimension Gregory's policies stood no chance whatsoever of success. When push came to shove, it was impossible for Henry (or indeed any of his peers in charge of France or England) to surrender all control over leading ecclesiastical appointments within their realms to Rome, for one straightforward reason: the bishoprics and major monasteries of medieval Europe were all funded from the revenues of large portfolios of landed estates. There was no other way to fund any major institution in this overwhelmingly agricultural world (the same had been true in the ancient world too). After centuries of endowment, encouraged by the tax breaks which often applied to Church donations, the different religious institutions of the later eleventh century controlled, under a variety of terms (i.e. the percentage of total revenues they received varied), vast tracts of the productive landscape of Western Europe: usually something between a quarter and a third of all the landed wealth of the realms in which they were situated. Naturally enough, since no state could afford to allow so much of its potential tax base to fall outside the system, these institutions were assessed on all this wealth for various payments and services by their local rulers. Many were economic dues of one sort or another – whether taken in cash or kind – but there were other duties besides. Abbots and bishops were sometimes entrusted with administrative and/or legal responsibilities for large sub-units of kingdoms, for instance, but not the least important of the duties, by any means, was the provision of knight service. This required bishoprics and monasteries to maintain a designated number of knights on a portion of their lands, whom the king could then draw upon when he needed to mobilize an army. Leo IX's *Life*, you'll remember, celebrates his leadership of precisely one of these contingents on campaign prior to ascending his episcopal throne. In England, where eleventh-century records are complete, the bishoprics and monasteries provided about a third of the entire military force that a king could mobilize, and there is no reason to think that the proportion would have been much different elsewhere. Because bishops and – to a considerable extent – major abbots were appointed by kings, moreover, there are strong hints in our sources that the military contingents from religious institutions were politically more reliable than the average. When a king was in trouble, therefore, he tended to turn to these knights rather than those of his secular magnates who might be too busy calculating to show up. Were the king's current troubles so serious that it was time to redirect their loyalties towards another leadership contender? Because the Church-controlled component was so large, and so politically important a part of the overall resources of a medieval kingdom, no king could ever afford to give up all his rights over leading ecclesiastical appointments.[33]

At the same time, lay piety was slowly but surely coming much more into line with at least some of the demands of the reform agenda, in particular over the issue of lay ownership of churches. Between 1028 and 1126, the monastery of Monte Cassino was gifted the ownership of no less than 193 churches, of which 186 were gifts from lay owners. Nor was this an isolated example. At Angers in the Loire valley, forty-four transfers of churches from lay ownership are recorded for the period 1050–1100, and another 102 in the subsequent half century.[34] At the same time as Gregory was trying to win an impossible battle, therefore, with a bit more thought he could have been claiming considerable success with a more sensible approach to the broader problem of lay involvement in the running of the Church, and not backed the reformed papacy into such a corner.

Overall, Gregory disastrously overplayed his hand, despite some eye-catching triumphs in the short term. The rebellion of the German princes did not in the end prove strong enough either to win outright, or to force major concessions on the religious front from Henry IV.

Henry also started appointing his own popes again, his choice being Clement III, while Gregory himself was eventually even driven out of Rome. He died in the castle of Salerno by the sea in 1085 under the protection of the Norman forces who had rescued him from Rome the previous year. At that point, he had been trapped by imperial forces in the Castel Sant'Angelo, and further damaged the Pope's reputation by taking the opportunity to sack the city at the same time. And all this in a truly hopeless cause after the empire had previously shown itself willing to accept the existence of an independent papacy.

The mess that Gregory had generated took the best part of forty years to sort out, the course of events marked by multiple blind alleys, half-victories, and changes of allegiance which show some resemblance to the convoluted struggles between Charlemagne's grandsons, not least in 1105 when Henry IV's son – yes, you've guessed it: Henry V – deposed his father, excommunicated once more at the hands this time of Pope Paschal II, on the grounds that a king who had been expelled from the Christian community could command no allegiance. Not only did Henry IV eventually bounce back, however, just before his death, but even Henry V was not about to surrender practical control over so such a large proportion of his kingdom's resources. But so much mutual condemnation and bitterly recriminatory rhetoric had been aired that it was not until 23 September 1122 (870 years to the day before the birth of one of my sons) that the Concordat of Worms finally generated the compromise which really should have been found much sooner. Henry V and Pope Callistus II finally agreed that kings and emperors could still take part in the ceremonial installation of bishops, but were only to invest them with a lance as the symbol of the secular duties which were part and parcel of such appointments, and not any more with the ring and staff which were symbols of their religious authority. But these regulations, of course, covered the public ceremonies which followed the much more private business of selecting the individual to be invested, and here kings and emperors continued by and large to get their way, even though they did from now on often refer that choice to Rome for rubber-stamping. The agreement was publicized at the first of a new type of Lateran Council, now recast as a general council of the whole Church (rather than – as before – a provincial council of the Roman Church), in March 1123, where 300 bishops and 600 abbots signed up to the deal.

Blushes saved all round, but the message was clear. The headlong charge led by Gregory VII had ended up in a dead end, costing the papacy far more than it gained. Not that everyone learned the lesson. Pseudo-Isidorean texts such as the *Donation of Constantine* encouraged papal overambition, and some Christians were always ready to support it. Bernard of Clairvaux, the great Cistercian intellectual, famously reinterpreted the old Gelasian doctrine of the two swords by arguing that both belonged to the Pope thanks to Constantine's donation. These kinds of arguments came to the fore when popes were faced with troublesome emperors, as they continued to be from time to time in the twelfth century. But emperors too had their own ideological self-justifications and could never afford, as we have seen, to give up a final say over key appointments. Direct confrontation tended, therefore, to generate only symbolic rather than fundamental change, as it did in the Investiture Controversy, or, again, in the quarrel between Henry II and Thomas Becket. After Becket's murder on 29 December 1170, Henry was forced to eat humble pie and accept many of the new papal rules for running the Church, but he retained, in fact, a final say over the key personnel in his episcopate.[35]

In reality, the final entrenchment of papal authority over Western Christendom came not through the series of high-profile confrontations which punctuated ecclesiastical life from Gregory VII onwards, but by other, much quieter means altogether. Some of these were more or less predictable given the patterns we have already observed. The Investiture Controversy did not prevent, for instance, continued institutional development within the papacy itself. Urban II (1088–99) was responsible for an overhaul of financial management. He imported the institution and practices of the so-called 'camera' from the great monastery of Cluny, which had developed effective techniques for keeping track of revenue flows and expenditures, which, thanks to the extensive network of daughter houses that it had built up, were comparable in diversity and complexity to those of the papacy itself. Under his successor, the former Cluniac monk Paschal II (1099–1118), the curia effectively came into being, even though the term was not yet in general use. He was responsible for creating a papal household which combined writing office, chapel and chancellery, and which became effectively the Pope's right arm: the bureaucratic organ that both controlled the flow of business into the papal in tray and was responsible for producing the appropriate responses for his out tray. More generally, as the reformed papacy generated further and different types of business, new letter forms were developed in response, and this period saw the final abandonment of the old formula book of prescribed letter types: the famous *Liber Diurnus* which had started life back in the fifth century. Slowly but surely the papal HQ was being turned into an administrative centre with real governmental capacity. A bureaucracy which had previously just written the odd charter for reforming monasteries, and kept vague track of assets passing into the hands of Italian nobles, was taking on new forms which would allow it to handle much larger amounts of more complex types of business, both legal and financial.

Outside of Rome, too, the period of dispute saw some broadening in the exercise of papal influence over Western Christendom as a whole. Many of its other rulers were happy enough to see Gregory causing so much trouble for the empire, and, as a result, accepted the presence of his legates – judges delegate – in their territories on a more permanent basis. Such legates had operated on an ad hoc basis in previous reigns but Gregory's pontificate is marked by much more systematic appointments: such as bishops Hugh of Die (later Archbishop of Lyons) in France, Amatus of Oleron in southern Gaul and Spain, and Anselm the Younger of Lucca in Lombardy. These permanent representatives increased the weight of papal presence outside Rome, and increased the amount of Church business over which the papacy could exercise some kind of influence. The legates' potential effectiveness still rested fundamentally, however, on the willingness of kings to accept their presence, and of higher clergy to bring cases to them, and, as such, the whole enterprise remained ad hoc.[36] Otherwise, Urban II at least continued Leo IX's tradition of taking the papacy himself outside Rome, most famously to the synod of Clermont in 1095 where he made the call to arms which generated the First Crusade. This was another example of the papacy putting itself at the head of current trends in Christianity, but cannot really be said to have extended papal control, since, famously, Urban's call was taken up in many different ways by many different people, and ended up generating something quite unlike what the Pope had in mind. He wanted a small number of well-equipped military professionals to take to the road; he did get this, but a whole lot else besides and the phenomenon as a whole was not his to control.[37] Although papal influence over the religious life of western Christendom certainly increased in the two generations after that of the barbarian Popes, therefore, this period

saw not the slightest sign of the emergence of any regular governmental mechanisms by which the papacy might systematically intrude
itself regularly into the detailed daily religious lives of the inhabitants
of Western Christendom, in the kind of way that Innocent III could
contemplate at the Fourth Lateran Council. Nor do we see the papacy
engaging in more than single-issue politics in religious affairs, rather
than taking a more comprehensive approach to the definition of best
ecclesiastical practice. The solution to this broader problem and the
key developments which made possible Innocent's more comprehensive approach to religious reform were to come about by an entirely
unexpected route.

To find it, we need to return to the subject of canon law. Here, the
post-Carolingian tenth century saw no sustained challenge to the dominance of *Pseudo-Isidore*; its forgeries being liberally incorporated into
the two major additional collections produced in that era (page 378).
The Investiture Controversy stimulated a renewed interest in the subject, however, as both sides sought to justify their positions in what
quickly became conflict of authority. Gregory VII and his successors, in
particular, encouraged the leading scholars among their supporters to
produce new collections of canons which would provide chapter and
verse in justification of the position on imperial sovereignty that they
were claiming; not surprisingly, Pseudo-Isidorean texts again provided
most of the ammunition. Apart from functioning as one of Gregory's
legates, Anselm the Younger of Lucca produced the first of these reforming collections in 1083, and others soon followed: that of Cardinal
Deusdedit in 1087, and the *Anonymous Collection in Seventy-Four Titles*
from the same decade. Thanks to *Pseudo-Isidore* and the *Donation of
Constantine* in particular, it was easy enough to bolster the reformers'
claims to papal superiority over the empire. What proved even more
significant in the long term, however, was the more general realization
that the existing texts of canon law were in fact almost completely
unmanageable. There were so many diverse sources – everything from
scripture to papal pronouncements with nearly a millennium's worth
of councils now in between – saying so many different things in so
many manuscript traditions, even without the purposeful distortions of
Pseudo-Isidore, that it was often impossible to make any sense of it, and
to know what one should, in practice, be doing. The greatest canonist
of this era was Ivo of Chartres, who had two attempts at the problem.
His first version was the *Decretum* which came out at an enormous

seventeen books. More popular was his shorter second effort, the *Panormia*, at a slightly more manageable eight. Ivo was perfectly well aware of the overall problem of inconsistency and had some thoughts on how it might be resolved which we will return to in a moment. But he didn't attempt any resolution himself, so, even with his helpful contributions, the user was still left with a mass of contradictory materials.[38]

Canon law was looking particularly messy in the later eleventh century, moreover, because, at exactly the same time as the papal reformers were scurrying back to it for ammunition, the great Justinianic texts of Roman Law were being rediscovered. This is an extraordinary story in its own right. All medieval (and hence modern) texts of Justinian's *Digest* descend from just the one sixth-century manuscript which was preserved at Pisa until 1406 when the victorious Florentines carried it home as booty. At Pisa, there is no sign that anyone had read it for 500 years although, somehow, it managed not to be thrown out. Then, in the second half of the eleventh century, a first copy was made from it (now lost), on which all medieval knowledge of the text depended. This first copying was done in three separate stages, and, throughout the Middle Ages, the resulting three chunks of text circulated as separate books in a five-volume set. The other two volumes were the first nine books of Justinian's *Code* and a catch-all final book containing the *Institutes*, the final three books of the *Code* (which had circulated separately from the first nine) and the imperial novels. Compared to the pared-down systematized version of old Roman law produced in the *Digest* by Tribonian and his fellow commissioners, the contradictory mass of texts which was canon law looked like a bad joke, and was generally disdained by the new Roman legal profession which grew up at Bologna from the last quarter of the eleventh century. As the study of Roman law developed at the hands of these professionals, however, its strategies and practices were quickly borrowed by the canon lawyers to turn their mass of disparate source material into a functioning system of written law.

The starting point for this extraordinary process, amazingly, was Justinian's claim in *Constitutio Tanta*:

> As for any contradiction occurring in this book, none such has any claim to a place in it, nor will any be found, if we consider fully the grounds of diversity; some special differential feature will be discovered, however obscure, which does away with the

imputation of inconsistency, puts a different complexion on the
matter and keeps it safe from the imputation of discrepancy.[39]

As we saw in Chapter 3, this was originally a piece of imperial bluster
designed to compensate for the fact that the *Digest* project had taken
huge short cuts. The Bologna law school, however, starting with Irnerius its famous founder, took the statement at face value, and dedicated
themselves – generation after generation – to demonstrating that there
were in fact no contradictions within the Justinianic legal corpus. To
do this, they worked their way through the texts one passage at a time,
and, whenever they hit an apparent contradiction, grabbed hold of
every argument they could find – discovering as Justinian would have
put in each case the 'special differential feature . . . which does away
with the imputation of inconsistency' – in an attempt to find some way
round it. The nature of the arguments they employed varied. The
lawyers always looked closely at the precise wording of the passage
under consideration, and sometimes solved problems by detailed grammatical or rhetorical analysis. What they also did, however, was compare each individual passage to every potentially analogous ruling
within the corpus, an approach which offered them another set of
potential explanations when grammar and rhetoric proved insufficient.
Some cases of seemingly contradictory rulings they resolved by deciding one or more of the contradictory texts should be categorized as
exceptions allowed only in precisely defined circumstances. They did
not, therefore, contradict the general rule which they identified in a
different law, and, very generally, the distinction between 'general' and
'particular' laws proved a highly fruitful avenue of approach. The
whole enterprise is a monument to the power of human ingenuity in
the face of a piece of wishful thinking.

The chosen method for presenting all these arguments was the
gloss. First came the Justinianic passage to be discussed, and then, in
the attendant gloss, a full explanation of its meaning and the preferred
resolution of any apparent contradiction. Over the course of the
twelfth century, detailed glosses were produced by many scholars,
with latecomers to the tradition commenting on the resolutions offered
by their predecessors, until the whole thing was threatening to spiral
out of control. Order was finally imposed by a legal hero called
Accursius who, between 1220 and 1240, collated over a hundred years'
worth of legal argument into a two-million-word text, the *Glossa*

Ordinaria, which quickly became the standard commentary upon the corpus, and the basic tool of all trainee and practising Roman lawyers. By the end, there were only 122 small contradictions left unresolved. A hundred years of highly inventive scholarship had almost proved Justinian correct.[40]

What had contemporary canon lawyers jumping up and down with excitement, while all this was unfolding, was the thought that the methods and principles of Roman legal studies offered them a way to resolve the difficulties of their own legal morass. This thought was presumably suggested and justified by the fact that there was considerable overlap between the two bodies of material because late Roman emperors in particular had often legislated on ecclesiastical matters. Already in the last decade of the eleventh century, Ivo of Chatres was aware of the potential. His two collections were composed of selections from the same old mass of material, but in the preface to the *Panormia* he outlined the principles – many of them based on the methods employed by the Bologna School in relation to Roman law – by which canonical conflict resolution might be attempted. He did not himself attempt – at least in writing – to put those principles into action, although he may have done orally in his teaching.

The great leap forward came two scholarly generations later with the publication in about 1140 of the *Concordantia disconcordantium Canonum* (*Harmony of Discordant Canons*, often just called *Decretum*) of the jurist Gratian, about whom more or less nothing is otherwise known. He was working at Bologna, alongside all those Roman lawyers therefore, but otherwise even the date of his work has to be arrived at by inference: it includes some of the provisions of the Second Lateran council of 1139, but they are not fully digested. What Gratian did, however, was follow Ivo of Chartres' advice and apply the principles he saw being employed by contemporary Roman lawyers to the problems of Church law. The Roman lawyers could structure their commentaries by working their way through Justinian's text from the beginning to the end. There was no agreed single text of canon law, however, so that, before he could even start, Gratian had first to generate a sequence of thematic headings under which he could then gather together all the relevant rulings from the vast mass of canonical texts. After that, following the methods of the Roman lawyers, he set about reducing the discordant clamour of his many texts to order with a series of discussions which attempted to employ consistent principles of analysis to come up with a correct answer on the issue being discussed.

It was an extraordinary labour of love, of scholarship, and of skill. Altogether he reduced to some kind of order a total of about 3,800 original rulings, patiently applying the same kind of principles that Ivo had outlined. Faced with a contradiction, you should always, both agreed, follow the best authority and here the input of *Pseudo-Isidore* is clear. Papal decretals rank highest, then rulings from ecumenical councils, then finally provincial synods. But Gratian invoked other principles deriving directly from Roman legal argumentation too. Invariable versus variable laws, and general versus particular laws were all categories of analysis that he found extremely helpful, and so too all the strictures on the importance of close textual analysis, whether of the actual language being used, or the original context of any decision.

Gratian's *Decretum* marked the start, not the end, of a revolution. The work he produced was so massively superior to anything that had previously been seen that, without ever being formally adopted, it immediately became the starting point for all future study, and this rattled along on similar lines to the contemporary school of Roman law. As with Roman law, the gloss was the weapon of choice and, since Gratian himself also worked by gloss, it is often hard to distinguish his original resolutions from those who continued his labours. And, again as with Roman law, a standard and utterly essential *über*-gloss – another *Glossa Ordinaria* – was the end result. In the case of Church law, 90 per cent of the work was done in the 1210s by Johannes Teutonicus, with a supplement being produced by Bartolomaius Brixiensis in the 1240s. Both of them studied and did the bulk of their work at Bologna, although Johannes eventually returned home north to become abbot of Halberstadt.[41] Gratian's *Decretum* and the full standard gloss that it generated did much to make canon law into a usable system, but, despite the fact that the influence of *Pseudo-Isidore* was entrenched throughout, we have still not yet got to the heart of the role Gratian played in systematizing papal authority across Western Christendom. To understand that, we need to take account of the second stage of development which followed on directly from the ground-breaking work of the Bologna canonists.

Gratian's *Decretum* immediately became not only the starting point for further academic study, but also quickly entrenched itself as the most important text yet available for settling practical Church disputes. By the third quarter of the twelfth century, a good knowledge of the text, and the developing tradition of Bolognese scholarship, was absolutely necessary to senior churchmen, and they were making sure either that they had that knowledge themselves (Thomas Becket, amongst many others, is know to have spent at least a year at Bologna), or were employing other clerics who did. As Bishop of London, Gilbert Foliot (1163–87) sent two of his nephews and a third unrelated cleric off to Bologna to acquire the necessary expertise, and the products of the Bologna schools were in high demand everywhere across Western Christendom by the second half of the twelfth century. But practical use in Church dispute combined very directly with continuing academic study first just at Bologna, but then more widely (Paris, in particular, shows up as an early centre of Church legal studies) to demonstrate that, in the case of canon law, a continued process of argument by gloss was not going to be sufficient to turn the original texts into a fully coherent legal system. With the Justinianic corpus it had done the trick, but, in that case, the Bolognese Roman lawyers were the indirect beneficiaries of hundreds of years of ancient Roman legal scholarship, and they had only the single source of law to deal with. The sources of canon law, by contrast, were so diverse, and Gratian's *Decretum* so much only a first step in the necessary process of academic legal consolidation, that glossing was never going to be sufficient. In very many places, the ecclesiastical *Glossa Ordinaria* produces either no answer at all to an observed problem, or only an unsatisfactory one.

What canon law required in addition, therefore, was a set of carefully targeted further rulings which would, on the one hand, fill in the obvious gaps identified by practice and study, and, on the other, make definitive decisions where the glosser's standard strategies had failed to deliver an answer. Given the reformed papacy's prominence in the life of Western Christendom by the twelfth century, and the recognition of the legal superiority of papally generated rulings that had been embedded into the developing legal tradition from *Pseudo-Isidore* onwards, there could only be one answer as to where such rulings might be found: Rome. In one key passage, indeed, Gratian himself had ensured that this was the only possible reflex:

> The holy Roman Church imparts right and authority to the sacred canons, but is not bound by them. For it has the right of establishing canons, since it is the head and hinge of all churches, from whose ruling no one may dissent.[42]

The process gathered sudden momentum in the mid-twelfth century. Pope Eugenius III (1145–53) issued twelve formal rulings – decretals – in the six or so years of his pontificate, Hadrian IV (1154–9) only eight in five years. But Pope Alexander III (1159–81) issued 713 in twenty-two. It took, in other words, about twenty years for the full implications of Gratian's *Decretum* to work their way through the ecclesiastical world of Western Christendom, but, once they did, new business came the papacy's way thick and fast. Many of these rulings were on small, everyday matters, only a relative few dealt with matters of great contention, and many (some contemporaries complained too many) consisted of automatic grants of favour which showed no sign of any real thought having gone into the process. But the overall effect of the flow of requests, and the answering flood of decretals, was to place the papacy practically now – as well as symbolically – at the heart of the operations of Latin Christendom. And once the flow of queries, requests for clarification, and questions began, it never halted. Very quickly, therefore, it became necessary to collect the answers that popes were giving in all their letters, since some of them were decisively changing the law. As was the case with the capitulary legislation of Charlemagne and his successors (page 254), it would seem that the need to collect all the new rulings was not immediately grasped, at least not at the top. The first attempts to collect the new papal decretal legislation seem to have been unauthorized, do-it-yourself initiatives, perhaps again by functioning lawyers (the spiritual descendants of those who had collected the legislation of late Roman emperors prior to the great moments of codification: page 120). Then in 1234 Pope Gregory IX authorized the publication of the *Liber Extra*. It was 'extra' because it contained material not in Gratian's *Decretum*. This work consisted of 1,971 decretal rulings organized in five books. A further supplement came in 1298 when Boniface VIII authorized the publication of *Sixtus*, so called because it was a sixth book of decretal legislation to go with the other five. Now the job was done: Gratian and its gloss, together with the six supplementary decretral volumes, would remain the standard sources of Western canon law all the way down to 1918.[43]

But our interest is only incidentally in this medieval resolution of the intellectual problems posed by the diversity and complexity of ancient canon law. What this unfolding process also did, in the century after the publication of Gratian's work (and this is where it becomes absolutely central to our purposes), was complete the transformation of the papacy into the fully functioning executive head of Western Christendom. By the time even of Alexander III, there was clearly only one place to go to resolve any outstanding ecclesiastical issue, and that was Rome. As a result, the decretal process killed two papal birds with one stone. First, any remaining ideological deficit was more than paid off. 500 years and more, where the divine appointment of monarchs – combined with their practical powers – had trumped the special status of the Roman see, were now a thing of the past. Papal authority in matters ecclesiastical was an unchallengeable fact.

Equally, if not actually much more important, since the barbarian popes had already largely won the ideological battle, the process eventually resolved the logistic problems which had always limited Rome's capacity to dictate detailed religious daily life. By 1200, precise Roman authority was now available in a form which could be easily transported into every area of Western Christendom. Previously, to know what a Pope thought, you had to travel to Rome or send him a letter and wait for a reply. From 1234, with the publication of the *Liber Extra* in particular, this was no longer the case. On the vast majority of matters, papal opinion was now available in written form which papally licensed judges could now use to settle thousands of cases in every part of the Latin Christian world. The growth of papally dominated canon law made it possible for the papal mountain to come to Muhammad, and religious life across broad tracts of Europe could for the first time march to the beat of a drum that was being thumped resoundingly in Rome.

Like Pope Innocent III at the Fourth Lateran Council, we are approaching the end of a journey. Thanks to the barbarian popes of the later eleventh century, the papacy had managed to make itself independent of the Holy Roman Empire, and thanks to Gratian and the decretalists, in the twelfth and early thirteenth, it was finally able to construct the practical levers of power which turned theoretical ideological superiority into a functioning ecclesiastical empire which could operate, despite pre-modern communications, over a vast territorial expanse. In all of this, two pre-eminent features of the story stand out. First, unlike its predecessor, this second Roman Empire was created without conscious Roman design, and, in fact, largely outside of Rome itself. Charlemagne's practical creation of Western Christendom – in the form of institutions of Christian devotion and learning which could guarantee the accurate replication of the essence of the religion across the generations, independent for the first time of the rise and fall of surrounding political structures – was the key first step on the road. All the significant subsequent developments, likewise, took place beyond the city's walls and on the initiatives of non-Roman parties. The post-Carolingian Church within Rome itself showed not the slightest sign of possessing the ability, or even of the desire, to transform its long-standing apostolic prestige into functioning papal power. Consumer demand in the north, faced with the inability of imperial structures to provide the necessary ecclesiastical unity, lies at the heart of this transformation. It was this demand, first of all, which forced a sequence of popes to take on more active roles, and then churchmen actually from the old barbarian north invaded Rome themselves to take hold of the office and refashion it after the new models that they themselves had created. The contrast with the old Roman Empire could not be stronger. Then, all the power and design had been situated within Rome itself. By 1100, echoing the demographic, economic and cultural changes of the intervening centuries, while Rome was again the vehicle of empire, all the power had shifted to the ex-barbarian north.

Second, in the history of the first Roman Empire, legal structures had played only a secondary role, and one that had had a broadly softening effect on the overall functioning of the empire. The original Roman Empire was created straightforwardly by force of arms, backed up by diplomatic bullying. The use of Roman law had subsequently and initially only slowly spread across its domains with the grants of citizenship which elevated the descendants of some of its conquered subjects into the status of fully enfranchised citizens. Operating alongside processes of Romanization, the wider effect of spreading Roman law, therefore, had been to turn a conquest state run out of Rome into a body of more or less equal communities. In the case of the papacy, however, it was the legal system – deriving its key methods, forms and much of its contents too from earlier Roman imperial models – which itself turned ideological superiority into actual imperial power. By 1200, a system of separate Church courts was coming into existence right across Western Europe, in which papally dominated canon law was applied by papally licensed judges, and any new or unclear situations were required to be referred to Rome for resolution. Where the spread of the old Roman Empire's civil law softened the impact of imperial power, the spread of the new Roman Empire's ecclesiastical law actually created it.

And if one journey ended in the time of Innocent III with the emergence of the papacy as fully fledged head of the Western Church, the latent power of the legal structures which had created it was about to initiate another. Between Charlemagne and Innocent III, consumer demand brought the papacy into being to provide the new CEO which the culturally united Church of Latin Europe now required, and which Europe's political structures could no longer deliver. It was an imperial structure, in other words, that was created if not by accident, then certainly by consensus. At the Fourth Lateran Council, however, Innocent set in motion the processes which would turn the passive into the active, and consensus into constraint. The machinery of an imperial structure that its consumers had initiated was about to be turned round upon them. Western Christendom would never be the same again.

EPILOGUE:

THE GODFATHER (PART 3)

The old Roman Empire of Julius Caesar, Augustus and their successors was a common or garden superpower of an entirely recognizable type. Its creators used a mixture of economic, military and demographic resources to project overwhelming force over a large body of surrounding territory, whose populations were then constrained – at javelin point if necessary – to become part of a new imperial order. At the centre of this new imperial construction was the city of Rome itself, and if, over time, the incorporated populations bought into the Roman imperial project by learning Latin and starting to wear togas, as pretty much everywhere they did, this does not for a moment hide the fact that the first Roman Empire was a conquest state run out of Rome for the benefit – initially – of Roman elites.

The medieval Roman Empire of the popes was a different kind of beast altogether. The power of the papacy is in fact an almost perfect example – the ideal-type to use some jargon – of the sociological category of ideological authority. Bishops of Rome were able to exercise power exactly and only because a sufficient body of influential opinion across the broader European landscape bought into a set of ideas which said that Popes *should* exercise such power. The idea set started from Jesus' words to St Peter in Matthew, but filled in all the gaps: that Peter had been the first Bishop of Rome; that his powers to bind and loose could be inherited by his successors; and that this pre-eminent religious authority could be turned into concrete rights to define doctrine, make law, and control top Church appointments. Because of these ideas, Bishops of Rome acquired wealth, legal rights, even soldiers, and could use them as additional means of projecting power. But in the papal case, these more usual constituents of imperial power were merely its secondary trappings. They extended but did not create papal power: that was the direct result of accepting the original set of ideological propositions.

The other overwhelming difference between the two Roman empires is the quite staggering degree to which the second was created outside of Rome itself. That's not to say that the history of the papacy doesn't throw up moments of quasi-imperial ambition as you chart the – extremely – slow process by which popes became Latin Christianity's CEOs. The late Roman popes who aped imperial rescripts to create the papal decretal were no shy retiring wallflowers, any more than was Pope Gelasius when he banged on about the two swords of authority at the height of the Acacian schism, or Nicholas I when he waded into the divorce case of Lothar II. But, a few moments of superlative forgery aside – particularly the *Clementine Recognitions* which filled in some crucial gaps in the Peter-to-papacy story – most of the key action actually happened outside of Rome itself, and beyond the direct control of the city's bishop and his key administrators.

Financially, it was Charlemagne who made the key move. His decision to endow the papal see so royally after his conquest of the Lombard kingdom marked a total watershed in the economic resources available to it. Poisoned chalice as this may have been in the shorter term, its longer-term benefit is incalculable. On the legal front, likewise, non-Roman Christians played a critical role at two different moments. It was Carolingian churchmen, first of all, who picked up some old ideas about Pope Sylvester and the emperor Constantine, and, via *Pseudo-Isidore* (which included the *Donation of Constantine* itself), turned them into a vision of a set of concrete rights enjoyed by the papacy of old over the Western Church. They produced this forgery entirely for their own purposes, but its long-term effects were enormous. Not least, and this is the crucial second stage of legal development, it was accepting this vision of the workings of ancient Christian organization which encouraged a flood of new requests into Rome from the middle of the twelfth century onwards. In response, the curia then generated the surge tide of new papal decretals, by which the papal domination of Western canon law became a concrete, irrevocable reality.

Politically too, even the ambition to turn the papacy into Western Christianity's proactive CEO was primarily located in Church circles outside of Rome itself. As late as the year 1000, the evidence suggests that Bishops of Rome were broadly content to enjoy pre-eminent prestige rather to exercise any kind of overarching control. Particular popes enjoyed being invited to the occasional reform summit meeting by emperors, and all were happy to sponsor missionary work and issue grand-looking charters which meant precious little in practice. But the main focus of the papal job description remained – religiously – to ensure that the city's shrines remained in excellent working order so that the pilgrims might keep flooding in, and – politically – to utilize the see's wealth effectively in orchestrating the play of ambitions among the landed aristocracy of central Italy. The whole idea that the papacy might be mobilized to function as the head of Latin Christianity was first conceived of in theoretical terms in the old barbarian north in the ninth century, although the forgers of *Pseudo-Isidore* had it far more in mind to emasculate emperors than empower popes. It was then turned into practical reality by the barbarian popes of the eleventh century, who first used an alliance with the empire's military dominance to take power in Rome, then reformed the papacy and shifted its operations in entirely new directions. The odd expression of properly Roman ambition notwithstanding, all the key ambitions which between them generated the second Roman Empire had their origins outside of the city.

As, of course, they pretty much had to have done, given the overall shape of Christianity's inherited authority structures. Because the religion first came to maturity as a mass world religion in the late Roman imperial context, the original overarching religious authority enjoyed by fourth- and fifth-century Roman emperors, and inherited in turn by the successor-state kings, was more or less unavoidable. Not only were emperors staggeringly rich and intimidatingly powerful, but the ancient ideological roots of monarchical authority in the classical world made them God's directly chosen representatives, and not mere secular rulers. In these circumstances, and especially as the new world religion was busy reinventing its administrative structures, rules and religious doctrines on the back of the emperor's authority, it was completely impossible that any alternative figure could emerge in this context as a serious rival to the emperor's rapidly developing role as the new mass religion's CEO. And, once this pattern had become firmly established, it proved extremely difficult to dislodge. Nearly 500 years after Constantine, Charlemagne saw himself as fulfilling God's will in launching *correctio*, and the vast majority of his churchmen were happy enough to agree. 200 years further on, reform-minded churchmen still had to win over pious political rulers, such as the Holy

Roman Emperors Henry III and Henry IV, to have any chance of putting their policies into action.

For the first 700 years of Christianity as a mass religion, the levers of religious power in the Latin West were located outside of Rome, and absolutely not in the hands of the papacy to pull. This could only change when the situation beyond Rome itself evolved – in two crucial ways. First, the long-term effect of Charlemagne's religious reforms generated a Latin Church with strong enough institutional roots in cathedrals and larger monasteries to form and maintain a continuous (though not unchanging) religious identity and reform programme, whatever the surrounding political situation. In contrast to what happened after the fall of the old Roman West, therefore, the collapse of Charlemagne's empire did not cause Western Christendom to fragment into its constituent parts. Second, as the Carolingian Empire broke apart and Latin Christendom itself expanded – thanks to *reconquista* in the Iberian peninsula and successful missionary work in the north and east – it became increasingly clear that no single ruler (even if they were called emperor) would ever again achieve a sufficient level of domination to act as the effective head of the Christian community which Charlemagne's institutions had brought into being. Latin churchmen therefore needed an alternative authority structure, insulated from the rise and fall of states, and it was this new requirement which fundamentally brought the second, Papal, Roman Empire into being: despite, rather than because of, anything that was happening within Rome itself.

Because of its particular nature, and the history which brought it into being, this new Roman Empire was in some ways much more limited than its predecessor. Lacking truly imperial levels of military and political force, it had always essentially to work in tandem with the prevailing political powers within its areas of religious jurisdiction. If the papacy pushed its luck too far, threatening the non-negotiable interests of these rulers, then the result was always messy, and, even if a face-saving form of words could eventually be found, popes did generally have to back off in practical terms. The investiture contest is a prime case in point, of course, and popes learned from it that they could not overplay their hands on top Church appointments, but the history of the medieval West throws up a number of analogies. During the Hundred Years War, for instance, John of Gaunt, then regent, effectively blackmailed the bishops of England into increasing their 'voluntary' contribution to his war effort by inviting more radical churchmen such as Wyclif to start contrasting current Church wealth with the poverty of Christ and His disciples. Likewise, if papal policy started to drift too closely into line with that of one of the two great powers of the high Middle Ages – the kings of France on the one hand, and the Holy Roman Emperors on the other – then the irritated party could fall back on the old strategy of electing their own Pope, and schism was no isolated occurrence in the centuries after Gregory VII.[1]

But, for the most part, head-on confrontations were avoided, and, such was the level of ideological force that the papacy could deploy, that the list of effected papal initiatives from the Middle Ages is quite extraordinary. Stalin once famously asked, when told that he should take account of the then Pope's views on a matter of policy, 'How many armoured divisions does the Pope possess?' But that was to miss the point of just how powerful a force ideology can be, although this was a fact of which he otherwise showed himself thoroughly well aware. And, on the whole, the really impressive point is just how much the medieval papacy could and did achieve, despite the particular constraints under which it was operating. The whole crusading movement, even if the precise course of many individual expeditions lay outside its direct control, owed its existence to the papacy, and the papal contribution to the shaping of medieval politics – not least by licensing or denying marriages among related royals in order to create particular alliances – was enormous. And that's not taking account of the role it played in dictating religious life in medieval Europe, on every level from the everyday world of lay piety, to the new standards of clerical sexual behaviour, to the great and truly nasty moments of internal persecution for heresy, such as the many and violent assaults launched on the so-called Cathars of south-western France.[2]

And of course, all empires do have their limits, so the basic fact that the medieval Papal Empire faced important constraints does not in itself deny its properly imperial status. Conventional empires, such as the first Roman Empire, the British Empire, or the current American Empire, typically come into existence when the imperial centre develops such a surplus of demographic and/or economic and/or technological resources that it is in a position to bring large tracts of territory into line either by conquest ('formal empire') or by intimidatory regimes of stick and carrot ('informal empire'). These kinds of empire will generally last only as long as the advantage in resources is maintained, plus maybe a couple of extra generations thanks to force of habit, before its disappearance is recognized, and they are overturned. It was precisely because a new equality in levels of development across the European landscape had made an old Roman-type empire imposs- ible by the end of the first millennium, that the new Papal Roman Empire came into existence, and the kinds of advantage that create more normal empires usually are time-limited, not least because the act of imperial projection tends anyway to erode them. This was cer- tainly the case with Europe in the first millennium, and is arguably the case now, where America and the West have encouraged massive economic expansion in Asia for their own purposes, but created in the process what is likely to become the next world economic superpower.

Seen against this background, the fact that the Papal Empire had to operate within strictly defined political limits looks much less of an issue, and there is another sense in which the ideological basis of its power made it significantly more powerful than its earlier Roman predecessor. Not, of course, that there isn't an ideological component to all empires. The old Roman Empire sold ideas of urban-based rational civilization so effectively, for instance, that conquered elites right across its territories, from Hadrian's Wall to the Euphrates, bought into these ideas, made themselves Romans, and acquired at least some political rights as a result, not least the right to be judged under Roman law. This whole process transformed the original Roman conquest state into something more of a community of communities, as well, of course, as generating the legal systems which would in due course allow the second Papal Roman Empire to come into being. But in ideological terms, the first Roman Empire never even tried to encompass the mass of the population, outside of the elite. The job of the peasantry, 90-plus per cent of the population, was merely to provide the tax revenues which funded all the serious work of empire and civilization.

Here the contrast with the Papal Roman Empire could not be more stark. The reform programme laid out by Innocent III at the Fourth Lateran Council in principle affected absolutely everyone. Some had more to do than others; the priesthood received a much more detailed to-do list than the laity, but the laity were not remotely ignored. Looking in broad terms at what happened subsequently, what's really fascinating to my eyes is both the outcome – the fact that the laity did largely come into line with Innocent's agenda in the years that followed – and the whole process which made it happen. In some ways, you could use the study of this process to stress, once again, the limits of papal power. Two generations after Innocent's death in the 1260s, for instance, it was still necessary to hold a meeting of all the clergy in the Worcester diocese in western England, in order to rehearse the Lateran agenda, and make clear for the clergy what it was that they should be doing. Fifty years after 1215, in other words, the Lateran agenda was far from second nature, even for the clergy. And from two further generations down the track, there survives a wonderfully vivid document which shows still how limited conformity could be amongst the English laity. Between 1292 and 1294, papally appointed inspectors worked their way round the local parishes of the Romney Marsh region of Kent in south-eastern England (then a poor and rather obscure area, though part of the Canterbury archdiocese), and made a list of all the abuses they found. It runs to many pages and is a wonderful teaching tool. Aside from recording a multiplicity of villages churches in which the proper service books were still not being provided, the Eucharist not being cared for, and priests either not doing their jobs or married, it also gives the lie to any idea that the medieval period was in any way more 'holy' – depending on how you might want to define holiness – than the present day. Because the Lateran agenda included making marriage a full-blown sacrament, sexual impropriety fell within the inspectors' remit, and there was a lot of it about, especially in the village of Woodbridge:

> Robert le Ster is noted for adultery committed with a certain Carter. He doth not appear. Wherefore we suspend him from entering the church.
>
> Juliana de Hornyngbroke is noted for adultery with Ralph de Pysinghe. The woman cited, does not appear, therefore suspended.
>
> John the Chaplain who was at Woodchurch in a former year is noted in connection with Joan the wife of William le Hert. The woman cited, does not appear, therefore suspended, subsequently cited again does not appear, therefore excommunicated.
>
> The same John [obviously a busy chap] is accused concerning the widow of le Spyle.

And so it goes on, for the best part of forty pages in the printed edition, cataloguing the many if not so varied failings of the would-be Christians of Romney Marsh.[3]

But rather than focusing on these very human failings, however amusing they might be (or not, depending on your point of view), there's a much more important point to make. Yes, the Lateran agenda was moving incredibly slowly (against modern expectations) across thirteenth-century Europe, but the more important point is that it was moving at all. And in fact, it continued to move. Certainly, people – including many clergy – continued to enjoy what was from the Church's official standpoint illicit sexual relations throughout the medieval period and beyond, but many of the other Lateran demands did eventually become absolutely standard practice. Clerical celibacy, regular attendance at Mass and confession, the separation of church buildings, the provision of proper service books and many other items: by the fifteenth century all of these were entirely accepted and uncontroversial items of standard Western European piety. Indeed, one of the fascinating historiographical trends of the last scholarly generation or so has been the gradual exposition of two facts. First, a handful of radicals aside, the reformation even in England was not powered by a groundswell of disgust at corrupt Church practices: the established patterns of Lateran piety were overwhelmingly accepted, and, by the fifteenth century, a comfortably familiar part of everyday existence. Second, by the same era, these standards were actually being enforced by the congregations themselves, among whom a new class of lay wardens had emerged so as to police the expected standards. It may have taken more than a century, but the papacy did eventually get the population of Latin Europe to buy into its ideologies of what being a good Christian actually meant.[4]

This, I think, is an extraordinary achievement in premodern conditions, where communication technologies were so limited, and it ought to make us pause for a moment to think about how it was done. The next entry from Woodbridge gives one clue:

> William son of William Lucas got Juliana Bructyn with child. The man appears and confesses and renounces his sin and is whipped three times round the church. It is afterwards granted that he should receive one discipline humbly in the procession because he appeared humbly, and the woman is excused because she lies in childbed.

It does mean what it says here: they would hit you or worse, if you didn't buy into the new standards of behaviour, as, on a much larger scale, the many Cathar, Jewish and other religious martyrs of the

European Middle Ages directly testify. And, in fact, that combination of discipline plus forgiveness is a particularly powerful one. Yes, you will be hit, but – so long as you weren't too awful – you can also be forgiven and readmitted. This is a highly satisfying resolution for most feelings of guilt.

Still more interesting to my mind, however, is one further question. The visitation of Romney Marsh was carried out by quite important churchmen who did not know the region. Any failings in the state of the church buildings or service books would have been easy enough to recognize, but how the hell did they know who'd been shagging whom, except in particular cases like that of William son of William Lucas who actually confessed? The answer, I think, must lie in one of the nastier sides of human nature, which there is no point in not recognizing, however much one might wish it were otherwise. If you introduce an intimidating outside authority into a small community, what often tends to follow is very well documented in any number of contexts. Existing local feuds and tensions tend to be played out on an entirely new level via a very nasty process of informing. A famous study of the medieval French village of Montaillou, accused of Cathar tendencies, showed that the inquisitors' capacity to operate was powered by exactly this mechanism, and this is surely what was also happening in the Romney Marsh. The information on the many and varied sexual peccadilloes of its village populations must have been provided by other members of the same villages. This is also precisely the same mechanism, of course, which allowed the security apparatuses of the old Eastern Bloc countries to work so effectively before the Berlin Wall came down in 1989. Only afterwards did it become so awfully apparent how much of the population – in the hope of gaining immediate favour for themselves or those they loved – had been willing to inform on their fellows.[5]

I'm not, I hasten to add, giving myself any airs and graces here. Thank God, I have never been put to this kind of test and don't know how I would react. What I do feel able to say, however, is that the post-Lateran Papal Empire, slowly but surely, was able to erect a kind of religious one-party state, which brought much of Latin Europe's population into line with the agenda that Innocent III had so triumphantly asserted. If you look at just fifteenth century sources, after the process had long been under way, compliance all looks very consensual, in the same way that the indoctrinated young of the new Soviet

Union on the whole were willing to fight the great patriotic war against Nazi Germany without thought for the appalling sacrifices required of them.[6] But the element of constraint, even if located in the past, is absolutely real in both cases nonetheless. The Papal Empire may have been created outside of Rome, and in a kind of way by consumer demand among a critical mass of Christian leaders and intellectuals in post-Carolingian Europe. And these men, like most of the old Bolsheviks, were certainly idealists with a real belief in the values they were attempting to uphold. But once the papacy had been reinvented to serve their wishes, it operated like a one-party state in demanding compliance with its vision of proper Christian piety. Limited as it certainly was in political and military terms, therefore, the papacy certainly created an empire nonetheless, and in some important ways a much more powerful and oppressive one than the first Romans had ever managed. The projection of their imperial values never got past the landowning elites, where their papal successors targeted the entirety of the population. And where the spread of Roman law in the first empire allowed consent to overturn constraint among the provinces of the empire, in the new Rome, consent to its legal authority was in fact the path to constraint, a constraint that was being exercised over the entirety of the constituent population. That, of course, may be one reason why the new Roman Empire has so far lasted approximately twice as long as its predecessor.

NOTES

Abbreviations

Acta synh. habit. Romae – *Acta Synhodorum habitarum Romae*

Anon. Val. – Anonymous Valesianus

Cod. Just. – *Codex Justinianus* (*Code of Justinian*), see *Corpus Iuris Civilis*

C. Th. – *Codex Theodosianus* (*Theodosian Code*)

Ep. Aust. – *Epistolae Austrasiacae*

H.E. – *Historia Ecclesiastica* (*Ecclesiastical History*).

ILS – *Inscriptiones Latinae Selectae*, see Dessau (1974)

Justinian *Nov.* – *Justinianus Novellae* (*Novels of the Emperor Justinian*), see *Corpus Iuris Civilis*

Lib. Pont. – *Liber Pontificalis* (*Book of the Pontiffs*)

MGH – Monumenta Germaniae Historica

Nov. Val. III – *Novels of the Emperor Valentinian III*, see *Codex Theodosianus*

PLRE – *Prosopography of the Later Roman Empire*

SH – Procopius, *Secret History*

PROLOGUE

1 How long the Roman Empire lasted depends, of course, on how you count. I'm dating its establishment here from the moment of its first major extra-Italian acquisition: the conquest of Sicily. The quotation is from Malchus fr. 14, trans. Blockley (1983), 410.

2 For a much fuller exploration of these crucial transformations, see Heather (2005), c. 3; (2009), cc. 2–3 with full guidance to the many and varied studies on which this picture is based.

3 This is a brief summary of the story I tried to tell in much more detail in *The Fall of Rome*: Heather (2005).

4 On the so-called Slavicization of Europe which redrew the map of central and

Eastern Europe, see Heather (2009), esp. cc. 7–8 with, again, full refs to the body of literature on which the picture is based.

1. GENS PURPURA

1 Cassiodorus, Variae 1.1, trans. Hodgkin (1886), 141–2. The best introduction to Hellenistic concepts of kingship and their (barely) Christianized continuation in the late Roman period is Dvornik (1966), with MacCormack (1981) on their regular acting out in imperial ceremonial.

2 Getica 52.271.

3 Gens purpura: e.g. Variae 4.1; 9.1; 10.1–4. The generations are numbered in Variae 9.25. A fuller Amal genealogy is laid out at Getica 14.79–81.

4 Jordanes gives his account of his usage of Cassiodorus' history at Getica Pref. 2–3. Momigliano (1955) famously argued that Jordanes was lying to cover up his closeness to Cassiodorus; Goffart (1988) argued the opposite. Both views have other advocates besides. I have laid out my own opinions in more detail in Heather (1991), c. 2 (1993). The two letters of Cassiodorus which pertain particularly to the debate are Variae 9.24–5.

5 The Thracian Goths have a large role to play in what follows. Goths under Hunnic domination: Priscus fr. 49. Crimea and Sea of Azov: Procopius, Wars 8. 4.9 ff.; Buildings 3.7.13.

6 Getica 48.246–52 unravelled in Heather (1989).

7 Valamer's 300 pounds of gold p.a.: Priscus fr. 37. The contrast between the visible wealth of the fourth-century Goth-dominated Cernjachov culture and the gold of the Hunnic era is staggering: compare, e.g., Heather (1996) c. 3 with Bierbrauer (1980) or Bona (1991). Heather (2009), c. 5 discussed the broader impact of the rise and fall of the Hunnic Empire in more detail and with full refs to current scholarship.

8 For more detail discussion of the Vandals and Visigoths, with full refs: Heather (2009), c. 4. Clovis: Gregory of Tours, Histories 2.40–2 with below, page 000.

9 On the politics of the city's creation, see Dagron (1974) with Heather and Moncur (2001) for the creation of the Senate and some of its subsequent political uses. Grig and Kelly (2012) contains some helpful additional contributions.

10 His body was never found, generating many romantic stories, not least the legend of the marble emperor who, a latter-day King Arthur, would awaken to retake Constantinople from the Turks: see further Nicol (1992).

11 Alföldi (1974); Mocsy (1974); Lengyel and Radan (1980) remain the best introduction, although much has been learned since; see e.g. Christie (1996); Whitby (2000).

12 Croke (2005) sparked off my train of thought on the young Theoderic's arrival. The best (and wonderfully brief) guide to the archaeological development of the city remains Mango (1985) with full refs.

13 Puzo (1969), 16.

14 Rosamund: Paul the Deacon, History of the Lombards 4.28. See Getica 52.271 for the division of opinion about sending Theoderic to Constantinople.

15 Braund (1984), esp. 9–31.

16 On Leo, Aspar, and the Isaurians, see e.g. Brooks (1893); Thompson (1946); Scott (1976); Stein (1949), c. 10, (1950), c. 1.

17 *Getica* 55.282 ff.; cf. *PLRE* 1, 905 for refs to Theodosius' Sarmatian triumph.

18 *Getica* 53.276; cf. Heather (2009), 246 ff. for a more detailed treatment of the post-Attilan fallout.

19 Pay: Malchus fr. 2. Theophanes AM 5931 suggests that some at least of the Thracian Goths had been established on imperial territory since the 420s. The text is not without problems, but does stack up with a chain of other evidence (Theoderic Strabo's relationship by marriage to Aspar, the fact that these Goths provided the garrison of Constantinople etc) which emphasizes how deeply embedded they were within the Constantinopolitan political establishment by the 470s: see in more detail Heather (1991), 251–63.

20 I have set out my own views on the identity debate as it relates to the so-called (by the Romans) 'barbarians' of late antiquity in fuller form in Heather (2008) with full refs. Alternative views can be found in e.g. various of the papers collected in Gillett (2002), and Halsall (2007), c. 2. See also Heather (2009), cc. 1 and 11 for the key intellectual linkage that operates in this period between conceptions of identity, and the reality or not of large-scale migration. The key evidence for the propensity of the Pannonian Goths actually to engage in farming is provided by Malchus fr. 18.3, p. 430.5 ff.; fr. 20, p. 438.55 ff.; fr. 20, p. 446.199 ff. with further discussion in Heather (1991), 242 ff. All subsequent page and line references to the surviving fragments of Malchus' history refer to the edition and translation of Blockley (1983).

21 Wagon train: Malchus fr. 20, p. 448, l. 245; cf. Heather (2009), 28 ff. with full refs on the migration habit.

22 Lots: *Getica* 56.283. Vithimer's son Vithimer may have received in Gaul two letters from Bishop Ruricius of Limoges: *Epp.* 2.61 and 63: trans. Mathisen (1999).

23 Advance on Thessalonica: *Getica* 56.287. Departure for Italy: *Getica* 57.289 ff.

24 The principle that only one group could be paid at a time is expressed at Malchus fr. 15, p. 420, ll. 10 ff.

25 Euboia: *Getica* 56.285–7. The text of Strabo's treaty with Leo can be found at Malchus fr. 2. p. 408. ll. 22 ff. Extensive quotations from Malchus' history were preserved by the tenth century. Byzantine Emperor Constantine VII Porphyry-ogenitus: see further Blockley (1981), c. 4. Brooks (1893) remains an excellent guide to the court politics within Constantinople, so long as you allow for the fact that he tended to see all Isaurians as natural allies, whereas the evidence is clear that there were distinct groups with their own potential inner rivalries.

26 For introductions to the burgeoning archaeology of Isauria: see e.g. Foss (1990); Mitchell (1993); Hill (1996).

27 A more detailed account of the rise and fall of Basiliscus can be found in e.g. Brooks (1893); Heather (1991), 272–8; Stein (1950), c. 1.

28 The sources for Armatus and his fall are listed at *PLRE* 2, 148. Strabo's 13,000 men: Malchus fr. 18.4. Theoderic the Amal at one point offered to campaign where the emperor wanted with 6,000 'of his best' men while leaving his non-combatants in the city of Dyrrhachium (Malchus fr. 20, p. 446.215 ff.) which required a garrison of 2,000 (Malchus fr. 20, p. 440.83 ff.). He wouldn't have

been taking any risks at this point, so we're again looking at *c*.10,000 combatants. Sideswapping: Malchus fr. 18. 1.

29 Malchus fr. 18.2.

30 Malchus fr. 20, p. 444.175 ff.

31 Malchus fr. 18.2, p. 428.30 ff.

32 Malchus frr. 18.3–4, 20. Some evidence of these Gothic assaults has emerged from archaeological investigation: Pallas (1977); Wiseman (1984) with refs.

33 Malchus fr. 20, p. 446.212 ff.

34 Malchus fr. 20, p. 446.226 ff.

35 Marcian's attempted coup in late 479 is the last incident recounted by Malchus: fr. 22. From 480, our main source becomes instead the surviving fragments of John of Antioch, which can be read in translation in Gordon (1966). The account of his death is taken from John of Antioch fr. 211.5; other sources as *PLRE* 2, 1076.

36 Recitach's murder of his uncles: John of Antioch fr. 211.5. His own death: John of Antioch fr. 214.3; cf. Heather (1991), 301 ff. for fuller discussion of the likely shift of allegiance among the bulk of the Thracian Goths.

37 See Brooks (1893) for a typically lively account.

38 Autumn, once the harvest had been gathered in but while the grass was still growing, was an excellent time to make such moves. The main source for his revolt and the move on Constantinople is John of Antioch fr. 214.4 ff.

39 The quotation is from John of Antioch fr. 214a. Good secondary accounts of the conquest of Italy can be found in Wolfram (1988), 278 ff.; Moorhead (1992), c. 1.

2. A PHILOSPHER IN PURPLE

1 Cassiodorus, *Variae* 9.24.

2 The letters are edited by Mommsen (1894a). Hodgkin (1886) is a sometimes highly abbreviated summary translation of the *Variae* collection; Barnish (1992) provides a fully annotated up-to-date translation of a selection of the letters. For an introduction to Cassiodorus and his career, see e.g. O'Donnell (1979); Barnish (1992), ix–liii; Heather (1993). Liberius certainly and arguably Symmachus and Boethius – all of whom we will return to later in the chapter – were all more important Roman advisers to Theoderic in the formative part of his reign than Cassiodorus.

3 Bjornlie (2009) is excellent on the context of the collection's creation, but – in my view implausibly – considers that the letters were substantially rewritten for a bureaucratic audience in Constantinople after 540. On the classicizing agenda of Theoderic's regime to which the letters' tone and contents were well suited, see Heather (1993). This is not to deny that Cassiodorus could and did play many tricks with the selection and arrangement of his chosen letters, as we shall see later in the chapter.

4 Kaster (1988), esp. 12–19 is excellent on the role ascribed to education; cf. Sorabji (1983), esp. cc. 13 and 20 for how these ideas intersected with the ancient view of the universe. The classic study of ancient political theory and the limited impact of Christianity is Dvornik (1966), esp. cc. 8, 10–12.

5 Mosaic decoration: MacCormack (1981), 236–9; cf. more generally on Theoderic's palaces: Johnson (1988); Ward-Perkins, 1984.

6 For an introduction to the Goths' non-Nicene Christianity, see Heather and Matthews (1991), cc. 4–7. Theoderic and the papacy: *Anon. Val.* 12.65 on the *adventus*, and Moorhead (1992), c. 4 on the disputed election. Synod: *Acta synh. habit. Romae*, I, p. 405. Ennodius: ed. Hartel, pp. 267–8; cf. id., *Life of Epiphanius* 97.35.

7 *Civilitas*: Barnish (1992), xxiv–xxv; cf. *Variae* 1.27; 2.24; 6.5; 8.33; 9.18. General importance of the law: e.g. *Variae* 2.7; 3.17 (cf. 18); 4.22; 5.40; 10.5. Actual cross-references to the *Theodosian Code* and other imperial laws are cited by Mommsen (1894a) at pp. 281–3. See too *Variae* 12.5 and 11.13 on *libertas*.

8 Panegyric: ed. Hartel, p. 264, 13 ff.; cf. *Variae* 3.13, 8.15, 8.31; with *Variae* 9.21 on grammarians' pay.

9 For fuller discussion of all these points, see Heather (1993); (1994a).

10 On the build-up of Church rights and property in the late Roman period, see Jones (1964), c. 22; Wood (2006), esp. c. 1. Vandal contrast: e.g. Courtois (1955), 289–310; Heather (2007); Merrills and Miles (2010), c. 7.

11 For the threat, see Ennodius, *Life of Epiphanius* 122–35. On the Italian aristocracy, see Barnish (1988); Schäfer (1991); Wickham (2005), 155–68.

12 For an introduction to Norman land grabbing, see e.g. Hooke (1998); Williams (1991); Baxter (2007), c. 7. Theoderic's loss of manpower to Strabo in *c.*477: above page 000.

13 Cassiodorus, *Variae* 2.15–16. Ennodius, *Ep.* 9.23. *PLRE* 2, 677–81 collects and discusses the other references to him in our sources.

14 Bierbraüer (1975), 23–39, based fundamentally on information which emerges incidentally from Procopius' narrative of the East Roman conquest.

15 Goffart (1980) – substantially restated in (2006), c. 6 – famously argued that no actual real estate changed hands and has won many followers. In my view, his argument is successful in bringing tax adjustments into the picture, and it is to Goffart that we owe a convincing identification of the Italian 'thirds'. But his insistence that no land changed hands stretches the argument beyond breaking point, and a necessary reaction has followed: see e.g. Barnish (1986); Wickham (1993); Halsall (2007), 442–7; and the papers collected in Riviere (2012).

16 Amory (1997) argued that Theoderic's army essentially disappeared into the landscape, and, like the accommodation argument of Goffart, it too has its admirers. Heather (1995) collects and discusses the evidence from the *Variae* relating to Gothic-army management, which is not insubstantial, including *Variae* 5.26–7 (calling in Goths from Picenum and Samnium to receive their donatives); 5.36 (a written discharge); 8.26 (subgroup in Riete choosing its own *prior*).

17 *Getica* 60: 313.

18 Good narratives can be found in James (1988), c. 3; Wood (1994), c. 4. The main points of controversy are detailed chronology, and the size of the entity based around Soissons: see further page 000.

19 *Variae* 3.1.2–3.

20 *Variae* 3.2.3–4.

21 *Variae* 3.5.2–5.

22 *Variae* 1.1.

23 An older strand of scholarship – e.g. Jones (1962) – tried to tie down Theoderic's exact constitutional position as ruler of Italy, but this is in the end a hopeless task. Prostko-Prostynski (1994), c. 1 and 131 ff. ably assembles and discusses the available evidence for the different rounds of negotiation, and it is his reconstruction that I broadly follow here. The one point I'm not completely sure about is whether Constantinople formally agreed to everything that Theoderic in practice did in such matters as statue placement and acclamation; as far as I can see, there is no way to be certain.

24 Amalafrida's wedding: Procopius, *Wars* 3.8.12. Letter exchange: Cassiodorus, *Variae* 5.43–4.

25 See further Wolfram (1988), 320 ff.

26 *Variae* 3.2.1 with 1.46.2–3 on the clocks. The excellent translation of a selection of Avitus' works in Shanzer and Wood (2002) has made important aspects of culture and politics of the Burgundian kingdom now much more accessible to a non-Latinate audience.

27 *Variae* 3.4.1–2; 2.41.2.

28 Conquest of Spain and centralization of the treasury: Procopius *Wars* 5.12.33 ff.; cf. *Variae* 5.35 and 39 for two snapshots of consolidated administration including Spain, presumably from 511 just before Cassiodorus left the post of quaestor.

29 *Life of Caesarius* 1.36–43 for the meeting, trans. in Klingshirn (1994b). The councils are discussed in more detail in Klingshirn (1994a), 124 ff.

30 *ILS* 827.

31 Eutharic appears in the *Getica* at 33:174–5. His roughness is commented upon at *Anon. Val.* 14.80. It is often assumed that Amalaric, Theoderic's grandson via his son-in-law the Visigothic king Alaric II, was destined to rule over Spain, but see below, page 000.

32 The literature on the background to the Acacian schism is inexhaustible, but see e.g. Allen (2000); Gray (2005); Millar (2006), c. 4.

33 For more detailed accounts with full refs, see Moorhead (1992), 194–200; cf. Noble (1993); Sotinel (2005).

34 On Cassiodorus' *Chronicle*, see O'Donnell (1979), 36–43. Justin's adoption of Eutharic is mentioned at *Variae* 8.1.3; cf. Claude (1989) on the significance of the act.

35 *Anon. Val.* 14.83 gives the diabolical explanation for the standard list of failures that have long been noted (it is also the source of the comment that Theoderic was about to launch a persecution of Catholics just before his death). See further e.g. Momigliano (1955); Moorhead (1992), c. 7.

36 Momigliano (1955). Its model of a Rome/Ravenna divide has remained hugely influential ever since: e.g. Moorhead (1992), c. 5.

37 *Variae* 6.6 provides a convenient job description for the post of *Magister Officiorum*. The sources for Boethius' career are collected and discussed at *PLRE* 2, 233–7.

38 Matthews (1975), cc. 1–2 is a superb treatment of *otium*: this ideal of rational, cultural, busyness on the part of the elite ties in tightly with the Graeco-Roman self-understanding of the cultural characteristics which made it an inherently superior human society: above, page 000.

39 Boethius: *Variae* 1.10; Gundobad: *Variae* 1.45; Clovis: *Variae* 2.40. Symmachus and Theoderic: *Variae* 1.23; 2.14; 4.6; 4.22; 4.51.

40 Marcellinus Comes ad a. 508. Croke (2001) is an excellent introduction to the chronicler and his connections.

41 *The Consolation of Philosophy* is available in translation in Stewart et al. (1918). Its evasive wording – deliberately evasive I suspect, as Boethius may still have been hoping for a positive eventual outcome when it was written – has been wrestled with by many historians, but, in the end, doesn't tell us what we'd like to know. See e.g. Chadwick (1981), esp. 56 ff. and c. 5, together with many of the essays in Gibson (1981).

42 *Gens purpura*: above, page 000. Theodahad: *Variae* 8.23; cf. 9.25.9. Ligurian disturbances: *Variae* 8.16. Tuluin, *Variae* 8.9–11; cf. *Variae* 8.3 for explicit acknowledgment that a non-Amal succession was thought about.

43 Split: Procopius, *Wars* 5.13.4 ff; cf. ibid. 5.12.50–4, and Jordanes, *Getica* 58.302 on Theudis' build up of power and independence in Spain.

44 For more detailed narrative reconstruction, see Wolfram (1988), pt 5, c. 10.

45 Non-adoption: *Variae* 8.1.3; cf. Moorhead (1992), c. 5 for a more detailed treatment of the problems of Theoderic's final years.

46 Barnish (1990) fully explores the evidence for ties between the two.

47 A certain Pitzas, for instance, surrendered to Belisarius with half the Goths settled in Samnium: Procopius, *Wars* 5.15.1–2 with Heather (1995) on the broader run of evidence for local, independent authority structures within the overall group. Amory (1997) tried to argue there was no solid group identity at all among Theoderic's following, based essentially on the case of one Gundilas who clearly did swap sides in the war according to immediate convenience (see esp. his App. 1, pp. 321–5). But this entirely fails to account for why the Byzantine war of conquest should have lasted for twenty years: Heather (2003).

48 The longer-term transformation of the Germanic world on the fringes of the imperium, and their strategic consequences, are treated in more detail in Heather (2009), esp. cc. 2 and 7 with full refs.

3. 'BY THE AUTHORITY OF GOD'

1 Justinian *Nov.* 11; cf. Bavant (2007) for a recent summary of findings.

2 'Autopsy' – literally witnessing something yourself – was considered the strongest guarantor of its veracity, so the ancient world liked historians who had been part of the events they described. The same conventions applied both to those working in Greek and Latin, although their stranglehold was not so strong as to prevent very different authorial voices from coming through. On the Greek tradition in late antiquity, see generally Blockley (1981), (1983), while Matthews (1989) looks at the main surviving Latin representative.

3 *Buildings* can be read in the English translation of Dewing (1940). The attack on its veracity was led by Croke and Crowe (1983), but see now e.g. Whitby (1986), (1988), c. 3; Curta (2001), c. 4.

4 *SH* 1.3: trans. Dewing (1935).

5 *SH* 8.22–33.

6 *SH* 9.10–30; *Cod. Just.* 5.4.23.1–4 records the relevant legal change, allowing former actresses to marry anyone of whatever rank.

7 The demoniacal character and alliances of the pair are laid clear at *SH* 12.14–32.

8 Averil Cameron (1985), c. 5 is excellent on the carefully drawn inversion of what Theodora should have been.

9 *SH* 8.12–22. The late fourth- and early fifth-century poetical satirist Claudian, who worked on behalf of the great Western *generalissimo* Stilicho, used sexuality to lampoon one of his employer's great East Roman enemies (Eutropius) and demonized the other (Rufinus): Alan Cameron (1970), cc. 4, 6. In reading the demonization of Justinian as an equally constructed piece of rhetorical artifice as the tarting up of Theodora, rather than as Procopius' genuine belief, my account is closer here to that of Kaldellis (2004), esp. 150–9, than Averil Cameron (1985), 56–9, but Kaldellis sees much less humorous intent here.

10 Kaldellis (2004), for the analysis, but reviews have been mixed and there are alternatives: e.g. Greatrex (2000). For myself, I have no doubt that Kaldellis adds many individually convincing insights to our understanding of Procopius the author, but suspect that his bigger picture is arguing for too politically precise a purpose behind Procopius' satire.

11 *Deo Auctore* 1: with above, page 000 on Theoderic's response to the importance of written law.

12 Athaulf: Orosius 7.43. Roman merchant turned Hun: Priscus fr. 11.2 (trans. Blockley (1983), pp. 269 ff.). The Preface to the Bavarian Code, trans. Rivers (1977), best captures the overall ideological significance of written law in the early Middle Ages, but it is very broadly present: see e.g. Heather (1994a).

13 Gaius' earlier textbook managed to survive by an extraordinary fluke in a single palimpsest MS (i.e. it could still be read underneath later material written in on top). Justinian's replacement can be read in the translation of Birks and McLeod (1987) and alongside Metzger (1988).

14 An excellent overview of the Justinianic project is Honoré (1978), esp. c. 7. On the work of Hermogenianus and Gregorianus, see Honoré (1994). Matthews (2000) and Sirks (2007) provide modern and in some ways contradictory accounts of the Theodosian project, but the disagreements focus on the reasons for slow progress, not the fact that it was so slow compared to its Justinianic successor.

15 *Deo Auctore* 4–5.

16 On the messy legal background which this reform needed to address, see Jones (1964) c. 14 (arguably a little pessimistic); Harries (1999), c. 1; Humfress (2007), pt 1.

17 On the deeper background, see Dodgeon and Lieu (1991); Heather (2005), cc. 1 and 3; Dignas and Winter (2007), 9–32.

18 The quotation is from Procopius, *Wars* 1.11.17–18; with further commentary and more detailed discussion of the backdrop in e.g. Greatrex (1998), c. 7; Greatrex and Lieu (2002), 79 ff.; Dignas and Winter (2007), 34–44.

19 On Constantius, Julian and the Persians, see Matthews (1989), c. 6.

20 The sources for Justin's coup are collected and discussed at *PLRE* 2, 650. The difference between taking the throne and really exercising power is a general theme among modern scholarship on late antiquity and the early Middle Ages. Its importance has been particularly stressed by Carolingian historians, where it has come to be reckoned that between five and ten years, and not an

inconsiderable amount of luck, was required to turn oneself into an effective ruler: see below, page 000.

21 *Const. Tanta* 12.

22 Fifty Decisions: Honoré (1978), 142–6. Suppression of rival schools: *Const. Omnem* 7.

23 *Const. Tanta* 13; 15.

24 For more detailed accounts, see Greatrex (1998), cc. 7–9; Greatrex and Lieu (2002), c. 6; Dignas and Winter (2007), 100–6.

25 Alan Cameron (1973), (1976) provides the best modern introduction to the circus factions. Our main sources for Nika are Procopius, *Wars* 1.24 and the *Chronicon Paschale* trans. Whitby and Whitby (1989), pp. 115 ff. For more detailed commentary, see e.g. Alan Cameron (1976); Greatrex (1997); Sarris (2011), 148–53.

26 As identified by Evans (1984). For Kaldellis (2004), 24 ff. this is an excellent example of the extremely clever, extremely subversive Procopius at work: cf. note 10 above.

27 The quotations are from respectively Justinian, *Nov.* 30.11.2 (AD 536), and *Cod. Just.* 1.27.1.1–2 (AD 534). Variations of the traditional vision of Justinian can be found in more academic commentators such as Jones (1964), 269 ff. and more popular studies: Norwich (1988), c. 10. But there have been doubters too: e.g. Moorhead (1994), 63 ff.

28 On the background, see Courtois (1955), pt 3, cc. 1–2; Heather (2007); Merrills and Miles (2010), c. 7.

29 On the rise of the Moors, see below, page 000. Gelimer's coup: Courtois (1955), 269 ff.; Merrills and Miles (2010), 74 ff.

30 The key source for the 'conversations' of 532 is translated in Brock (1981); cf. Gray (2005) for the broader context.

31 On these previous attacks, see further Heather (2005), 385–407.

32 Pudentius and Godas: Procopius, *Wars* 3.10–11.

33 Procopius, *Wars* 3.11.13–14.13 recounts the voyage, cf. *Wars* 3.14.1–5 for Procopius' scouting mission.

34 Procopius, *Wars* 3.14–21 for the campaign as far as the capture of Carthage.

35 Procopius, *Wars* 3.21–4.3.

36 Procopius, *Wars* 4.4–9; cf. *PLRE* 3, 192–3 for the many other sources which record the triumph.

37 *Const. Tanta* Pref.; cf. Honoré (1978), 170 ff. for a projected reconstruction of the working timetable.

38 The emergence of this new arm of the East Roman army still awaits comprehensive study, but Procopius' preface to the Gothic war (*Wars* 5) gives a stylized account of its undoubted importance, which is strongly supported by the battle narratives which follow. For some relevant secondary comment, see Thompson (1982), 77–81, 90–1; Elton (2007).

39 Our main source for Amalasuentha's reign is Procopius, *Wars* 5.2–4, with important supplementary material in Cassiorodus' *Variae*, esp. 9.8–9 (on Osuin). and 8.9–10 (Tuluin); cf. Wolfram (1988), pt 5, c. 9; Heather (1995) for further discussion.

40 The sources for Peter the Patrician are collected and discussed at *PLRE* 3, 994–8. Good news: *Wars* 5.3.30. Bad news: *SH* 24.22–3.

41 Procopius, *Wars* 5.3.30–7.25.

4. SAILING TO BYZANTIUM

1 *SH* 18.3–30 with footnote 1 on p. 213 of the Loeb translation.

2 Procopius, *Wars* 5.6–11 is our main source for Theodahad's reign. Modern secondary accounts of Justinian's conquest can be found in e.g. Wolfram (1988), pt 5, c. 10.; Heather (1996), c. 9; Moorhead (1994), c. 3; O'Donnell (2009), 257 ff. Thanks to Procopius, the events are well understood and there is no need to keep referring in what follows to this body of literature, and the greater one to which its footnotes give access.

3 Franks: *Wars* 5.11.28–9. Pitzas: *Wars* 5.15.1–2. Rome: *Wars* 5.14 to 6.6. Salona: *Wars* 5.16.8–18.

4 Picenum: *Wars* 6.7.28–34. Rimini: *Wars* 6.10. Garrisons: *Wars* 6.11.1–3. Belisarius: *Wars* 6.11–13.

5 Adriatic front: *Wars* 6.23–8. Urais: *Wars* 6.18 ff.

6 Abandonments: *Wars* 6.28.30–5. Negotiations: *Wars* 6.22.9–20.

7 *Wars* 6.29.1–3.

8 Gothic embassy: *Wars* 6.22.17–20. Armenians: *Wars* 2.3.31–57. Procopius' account of the invasion can be read at *Wars* 2.5–13. The destruction of Antioch is recorded at *Wars* 2.10.4–9, and the creation of new Antioch at 2.14. Secondary accounts: e.g. Greatrex and Lieu (2002), cc. 7–8; Greatrex (2005), 488 ff.; Dignas and Winter (2007), 37 ff. and 106 ff.; Sarris (2011), 153 ff.

9 Urais and Ildebadus: *Wars* 6.28.35; 29.39–41. Offers to Belisarius: *Wars* 6.30. The general's return to Constantinople is recounted at *Wars* 7.1.

10 *Wars* 7.1.25–2.13 with Goscinny and Uderzo (1963) on the Gothic disease.

11 For more detailed accounts of the rumbling on of the war with Persia, see the works cited in note 8. Heather (1996), 327–8 provides a full listing of the elements of the Roman army that Totila recruited at different moments, but note that the vast majority joined only on a contingent basis, usually because they had not been paid, and returned to an imperial allegiance once they had.

12 Totila's initial victories are described by Procopius at *Wars* 7.3–8.

13 Auximum: *Wars* 7.9–12. Rome: *Wars* 7.13–21.

14 Belisarius and Totila: *Wars* 7.21–37. The raiding fleet: *Wars* 7.35, 37–9, 8.22.

15 *Wars* 7.37.6–7; cf. 8.24.4.

16 *Wars* 8.23.

17 Totila's final campaign: *Wars* 8.26–32. Teias: *Wars* 8.33–5.

18 Three centres of resistance: Wars 8. 35. 37; *Wars* 8. 34. 19–20: Agathias, *Histories* 2.13–14); Butilinus' campaign and its failure is recounted by Agathias, *Histories* 2.1–14. The story of Widin is told by Paul the Deacon, *History of the Lombards* 2.2 with commentary at *PLRE* 3, 924.

19 Although this has never stopped people from trying. O'Donnell (2009), 289 quotes one recent attempt, more thoughtful than most, but even there the only

'real' figure is the report that Justinian inherited a reserve of 28 million solidi from Anastasius and Justin, whose status is unclear.

20 For a more detailed discussion of the problematic way in which new understandings of human group identity have been received into discussions of late antiquity, see Heather (2008). In the Italian case, the argument of Amory (1997) has convinced some that Theoderic's Gothic following was highly ephemeral in nature, but its evidential base is slight, and it has the overriding limitation of leaving entirely unexplained why many thousands of its members were willing to fight and die between 536 and 556, when, from at least 540, Justinian was willing to allow them to keep the lands they had received in the allocation process: cf. Heather (2003) for fuller argumentation. Much more convincing on the Vandals, than is Amory on the Goths, are Merrills and Miles (2010), esp. c. 4, who rightly stress that the rewards of the settlement process marked out Geiseric's followers as a new, and distinct military elite in North Africa, whose subsequent removal after the East Roman conquest was a similarly substantial historical phenomenon.

21 Heather (1996), esp. 273–5 and App. 1: Procopius uses three synonymous terms for this group: 'the best', the 'picked', and 'leading'. The narrative allows you to watch their destruction. On the destruction of the Vandal equivalent, see Merrills and Miles (2010), c. 9.

22 Wickham (2005), 728–39; cf. Wickham (2009), 140–7 for the evidence in more detail. Wickham's overall model in these works – see e.g. (2005), 708–17 – is that the economic complexity of the late Roman period was built around the structures and operations of the late Roman state. If so, then the disappearance of that state was bound to generate substantial simplification, even if the Gothic war hurried matters along. A less state-centred view is Ward Perkins (2005), who explains the complexity more in terms of the general conditions generated by the empire than the workings of its own political economy. In this model, the violence associated with the end of the empire and its aftermath has a more important causative role.

23 Courtois (1955), pt 3, c. 2 is the classic account; Rushworth (2004) and Merrills and Miles (2010), esp. 124–9 both with refs provide up-to-date supplements.

24 Pringle (1981) collects the evidence for fortification; cf. Merrills and Miles (2010), 241 ff. on religious reconstruction. Wickham (2005), 637–44 and 720–8 discusses the evidence for continued urban prosperity and economic complexity in post-conquest North Africa.

25 Curta (2001), c. 4 (mustering archaeological reinforcements) convincingly argues against the old tendency to dismiss the reality of Procopius' evidence for major Justinianic investment in the defences of the Balkans.

26 A good recent account of Justinian's tax reforms is Sarris (2011), 151–3; cf. SH 12 for some examples of great men's fortunes being destroyed.

27 Justinian, Nov. 148, discussed by Sarris (2011), 227–8.

28 There is an excellent recent literature in English on every aspect of the plague: Horden (2005); Stathakopoulos (2000); Sarris (2002). I generally follow Horden's guidance on matters of detail. On the continued prosperity of the eastern Mediterranean post-550, see Ward Perkins (2005); Holum (2005); Wickham

(2005), 443 ff. (on rural production), 626 ff. (on the cities), with 548–9 for his particular analysis of the effects of the plague as 'marginal'.

29 Cf. above, note 19, the guesswork quoted by O'Donnell (2009), 289 suggests that Justinian inherited a reserve of 28 million solidi, that the conquests cost about 36 million, and that Italy and North Africa brought in maybe 500,000 p.a. each: no figure is given for Sicily. Even using these figures, you would still have to reckon that the conquests did indeed pay for themselves in the medium to longer term.

30 Theophylact Simocatta 1.3.8–13; the apposite parallel is with Theoderic's rejection of the gifts by which the Vandal king Thrasamund attempted to buy himself back into favour in 511: above, page 000.

31 Menander fr. 5.1 trans. Blockley (1985), 49. Good introductions to Avar history are provided by Whitby (1988); Pohl (1988), (2003). For an introduction to Avar archaeology in English, see Daim (2003).

32 For some orientation on Eurasian nomads, see Lattimore (1940); Sinor (1977); Khazanov (1994).

33 Cutrigur raids: Procopius, *Wars* 2.4; Agathias, *Histories* 5.11 ff. Slav raids: *Buildings* 4.7.13 and 17f.; *Wars* 7.39–40. Curta (2001), cc. 5–6 (covering both Lombards and Gepids, and the Slavs) provides a good introduction into different aspects of the broader situation.

34 Menander fr. 5.1–2, trans. Blockley (1985), 50–1.

35 Justin's declaration: John of Ephesus, *H.E.* 6.24, trans. Smith (1860), 429; cf. Menander fr. 8, trans. Blockley (1985), 97.

36 For a fuller discussion of the Hunnic parallels, see Heather (2005), c. 8; (2009), c. 5. Sirmium: Menander fr. 12.5.

37 Menander fr. 11, trans. Blockley (1985), 429.

38 The story of Narses' invitation is told by Paul the Deacon, *History of the Lombards* 2.5, trans. Foulke (2003). For further discussion of their move into Italy, see e.g. Wickham (1981), 28 ff.; Jarnut (1983), c. 1; Christie (1995), c. 2; Pohl (2005), who puts the emphasis exclusively on Lombard predatoriness.

39 Whitby (1988), 156 ff. explores the effective East Roman counter-attack of the 590s. For a more detailed account of the Slavicization of the Balkans, see Heather (2009), c. 8, esp. 399–406.

40 The overall picture from the first set of excavations was famously pulled together by Foss (1977); cf. Foss (1996) for much greater detail. For a recent summary of subsequent material, see Wickham (2005), 626 ff. Ward Perkins (2000) and Wickham (2005), 609 ff. both emphasize the contrast provided by the continued prosperity of old Roman cities in Egypt and the Fertile Crescent that fell under Islamic, Umayyad rule.

41 Ottoman documents: Hendy (1985), 613–69; cf. more generally Haldon (1990) on the dramatic administrative, military and political adjustments required.

42 For good introductions to the general context of Roman–Persian conflict in late antiquity, see e.g. Whitby (1988), c. 7; Blockley (1992); Greatrex (2005). For the evolving situation later in Justinian's reign, see Dignas and Winter (2007), esp. 138 ff.; Sarris (2011), 153 ff.

43 Some of the diplomacy with the Western Turks is covered in extraordinary detail in the surviving fragments of Menander: esp. frr. 10 and 13. For more

detail and alternative views, particularly of Turkish motivation, see Dignas and Winter (2007), esp. 109–15; Sarris (2011), 226 ff.

44 The best account of Maurice's campaigns is Whitby (1988), cc. 9–11. See also Sarris (2011), 232 ff. for the 'Versailles moment'.

45 For more detailed narrative treatments, see e.g. Whitby (1988), c. 6; Sarris (2011), 236–42.

46 The *Chronicon Paschale*'s account of the siege of Constantinople can be read in the English translation of Whitby and Whitby (1989), 168 ff. The sources for the Persian wars of Phocas and Heraclius are brilliantly examined in Howard Johnston (2010). For more detailed narrative reconstruction, see e.g. Dignas and Winter (2007), 44 ff., 115 ff., and 148 ff.; Sarris (2011), 242–57.

47 On the third-century crisis and Roman recovery, see e.g. Dodgeon and Lieu (1991), pt 1; Potter (2004), cc. 6–7; Heather (2005), cc. 2–3.

48 For an introduction to the source problems, see esp. Crone and Cook (1972); Crone (1987).

49 The point emerges very clearly from Sartre (1982); cf. more generally on Arabia in late antiquity e.g. Donner (2005); Dignas and Winter (2007), c. 5. For parallels with the Germanic world, see Heather (2009), esp. cc. 2 and 11.

50 An excellent recent account in English (among many) is Kennedy (2007).

51 We will return to the history of Byzantine religious self-understanding in the next chapter via the iconoclast controversy.

52 For more detail on Justinian's Arab policy, and Maurice's reversal, see the works cited in notes 42 & 49.

5. CHRISTMAS DAY, 800

1 *Lib. Pont.* 98.23, trans. Davis (1992), 190–1. Einhard, *Life of Charlemagne* 28. Charlemagne is called *Pater Europae* in *Karolus Magnus et Leo Papa*, line 93 of the surviving fragment (the poem may also be by Einhard: see c. 7, note 2): trans. Godman, (1985), 203. It also sparked one rightly famous overview: Bullough (1985).

2 Priscus fr. 20.3 for Attila's attempt to interfere in a Frankish succession dispute of the 440s. The sources for Childeric's career are listed and discussed at *PLRE* 2, 285–6, his exile being recorded at Gregory of Tours, *Histories* 2.12; cf. Halsall (2007), 269–71, 303–6 for a broadly convincing attempt to place him in the context of Roman imperial unravelling. For a more detailed account of the grave, see Perin and Kazanski (1996).

3 On the swift unravelling of the final strands of empire after 468, see Heather (2005), 407–30.

4 Basina's dream is recounted at Fredegar 3.12. Good accounts of Clovis' conquests in English can be found in James (1988), 79–90; Wood (1994), 38–50. James argued that Clovis' first victim – Syagrius – controlled a much smaller entity than was traditionally believed, but this has not gone unchallenged: MacGeorge (2002), 111 ff. Gregory of Tours, *Histories* 2.40–2 records the hits, but see Heather (2009), 308–10 on the potential dating problem.

5 On the revised chronology and theological context of Clovis' conversion, see

Shanzer and Wood (2002), 362–73, with, above, c. 2 on the generally excellent relations that the non-Nicene Theoderic enjoyed with Catholic churchmen under his rule.

6 Good accounts of Frankish expansion subsequent to the removal of the Ostrogothic block, as well of the multiple civil wars and division of the kingdom, can be found in James (1988), 91–108 and c. 5; Wood (1994), 50–4 and c. 6. Theudebert's letter to Justinian: *Ep. Aust.* 20. Gold coins: Procopius, *Wars* 7.33. 5–6. The Merovingian court poet Venantius Fortunatus only uses 'Caesar' of a Frankish king on one occasion (6.1: Sigibert's marriage to Brunhild). Otherwise, he sticks to 'king' in the numerous poems he produced for a series of different Frankish kings.

7 Wickham (2009), cc. 4–6 provides a good general introduction to the post-Roman west. Nicene Visigothic kingdom: Collins (2004), c. 8, supplemented by the essays in Heather (1999) which provide an introduction in English to much recent Spanish-language scholarship on the Visigothic successor state. On the Lombards, see e.g. Wickham (1981), 28 ff; La Rocca (2005), esp. the essays of Pohl and Gaspari.

8 Einhard, *Life of Charlemagne*, c. 1; cf. Wallace-Hadrill (1982), 231 ff. for a high-quality example of the traditional mode of treating the later Merovingians.

9 Gerberding (1987), esp. c. 8.

10 On relations with the periphery: Wood (1994), c. 10.

11 The quotation is from Gibbon (1896–1900), c. 52. Fouracre (2000), 1–10 provides a brilliant survey and demolition combined of more traditional approaches to Charles Martel. Wood (1995) is an excellent case study in the tensions generated by the granting of lay tenancies to the 'wrong' laymen because of outside pressure imposed by a new overlord.

12 There are many good narratives in English, all of which deal with the issues raised by the fragmentary and biased nature of the surviving sources: e.g. Fouracre (2000), c. 3; Fouracre (2005); McKitterick (2008), 63 ff.; Costambeys et al. (2011), 41 ff.

13 More detailed narratives: Fouracre (2000), c. 4; McKitterick (2008), 63 ff.; Costambeys et al. (2011), 44–51. On the will of Abbo, see Geary (1985).

14 We will return to the importance of kings' providing rewards in the next chapter, but good introductions are: Bassett (1989); Reuter (1985), (1990). See further Fouracre (2000), esp. 175–84 on the origins of Charles' original success, although I would argue that Pippin's successes meant that matters were more strongly weighted in favour of whoever emerged as victorious from the power struggle within Austrasia than he would envisage.

15 More detailed guides to the events: e.g. McKitterick (1983), 33 ff.; Costambeys et al. (2011), 51 ff.; see also Fouracre (2005), esp. for similar suspicions about the appointment of the final Merovingian.

16 For further reading on Pippin's *coup d'état* (with full references to the massive scholarly literature), see, e.g., McKitterick (1983), c. 2; Fouracre (2005); McKitterick (2008), 71 ff.; Costambeys et al. (2011), 51 ff.

17 On Byzantine losses, see Mango (1977a); Whittow (1996), 82 ff. The works cited in note 11 also provide good accounts of eighth-century Lombard expansion.

18 Events in Italy: Noble (1984), 71 ff.; cf. the translations and excellent introduc-

tions to the relevant papal lives in Davis (1992), esp. nos. 92–95. Pippin and Francia: McKitterick (1983), 45–53; Costambeys et al. (2011), 57–65.

19 For fuller accounts of Charlemagne's manoeuvres, see e.g.: McKitterick (1983), 64 ff.; Nelson (1998); McKitterick (2008), 75 ff.; Costambeys et al. (2011), 65 ff.; cf. Nelson (2005), 28–31 for a fascinating account of the impact upon Charlemagne of his visit to Rome during the siege of Pavia. King (1987), 269–79 provides a translation of the letters to the Frankish kings of Pope Stephen from these years preserved in the *Codex Carolinus*. The Pope's anxiety in the face of the projected marriage alliance between Charlemagne and the Lombard royal family, and subsequent relief at its failure, is only too evident (Latin text: Gundlach (1892), nos. 44–8).

20 The letter is translated by King (1987), 286–8 (Latin text: Gundlach (1892), no. 60). In the sixth-century life of Sylvester in the *Liber Pontificalis*, trans. Davis (2000), 14, the cure and baptism are already there, but no mention of any great handover of power (on the date of the life, see Davis (2000), xlvi–xlvii). Many have – reasonably – thought that the appearance of the key linkage between cure, baptism and transfer of power in Hadrian's letter is a sign that the fully forged text of the *Constitutum* already existed: cf. Noble (1984), 134–7 with full refs to further reading. But as we shall see – below pages 000–000 – more recent research has shown that the actual document, as opposed to some of its key ideas, was produced later.

21 A good selection of Hadrian's run of letters to Charlemagne in these anxious years is translated by King (1987), 276 ff. (Latin text: Gundlach (1892), nos. 49 ff.). Their contents and context are superbly handled by Noble (1984), c. 5, whose overall conclusions about Charlemagne's gifts I summarize here.

22 Einhard, *Life of Charlemagne*, c. 13. For more detailed accounts of these later conquests, see e.g. McKitterick (1983), 59–72; Reuter (1985), (2005); McKitterick (2008), 103 ff.; Costambeys et al. (2011), 68 ff.

23 An excellent recent treatment is Story (2005a).

24 On the reflections of Charlemagne's intellectuals, see e.g. Godman (1987), c. 2; Collins (2005); McKitterick (2008), 114–18; Costambeys et al. (2011), 160–70.

25 A good introduction to iconoclasm is provided by Cormack (1985), esp. c. 3; Herrin (1987), c. 8; Whittow (1996), c. 6; Noble (2009), c. 2. On its ending, see in addition Mango (1977b).

26 See e.g. McKitterick (2008), 311 ff. and now in much more detail Noble (2009), c. 4.

27 This is a repeated emphasis in the papal letters of the *Codex Carolinus*: e.g. trans. King (1987), nos. 1, 2, 6, 8, 13, 17, 18, 26, 30, 35, 37 (Latin text Gundlach (1892), nos. 44, 45, 53, 50, 56, 60, 61, 72, 76, 82, 83).

28 Julian: Ammianus 15. 8. 17; cf. Matthews (1989), c. 6.

29 The sequence of events from the attack on Leo to the imperial coronation has to be unravelled from papal and Carolingian sources who, immediately after the event, started spinning the story in ways which best suited their own interpretation, a clear sign in itself that this was something which happened under duress for at least one of the parties. Good recent approaches are Noble (1984), 291 ff.; Collins (2005); McKitterick (2008), 88 ff.; Costambeys et al. (2011), 160 ff.

30 The supervisor in question is Professor John Matthews, now of Yale University: always to be distinguished from the other John Matthews who writes about King Arthur . . .

31 See e.g. McKitterick (2008), 96 ff.; Costambeys et al. (2011), 194 ff.

6. 'THE CENTRE CANNOT HOLD'

1 Einhard, *Life of Charlemagne* 22.

2 *Divisio Regnorum*: text Boretius (1883), no. 45, trans. King (1987), 251–6. For further discussion of the succession issue, see e.g. McKitterick (2008), 96–103; Costambeys et al. (2011), 194 ff.

3 The quotation is from Yeats, *The Second Coming*. *Ordinatio Imperii*: text Boretius (1883), no. 136, trans. Dutton (2004), 199–203; cf. both on Louis' own succession and the problems with his children, McKitterick (1983), c. 5; Nelson (1990); Collins (1990); Nelson (1992), c. 4; Goldberg (2006), pt. 1; de Jong (2009), c. 1, esp. 19–31, cc. 4–6; Costambeys et al. (2011), 196 ff.

4 There are many good accounts of the basic structure of the empire: e.g. Dunbabin (2000), c. 1; McKitterick (2008), cc. 3–4; Costambeys et al. (2011), c. 4. Tracing Carolingian failure to the bureaucratic limitations of its Empire is an argument particularly but not solely associated with F. L. Ganshof. See Ganshof (1971) for an excellent selection of his papers in English. On patterns of literacy in the early medieval west in general, and the Carolingian world in general, see McKitterick (1989), (1990).

5 On the profound significance attached to written law in Roman propaganda, see above, page 000. On developing patterns of law-making and collection under Carolingian rule: Nelson (1982); cf. McKitterick (1989), c. 2, (2008), 233 ff. For an alternative perspective, see also Wormald (1999), c. 2.1.

6 In addition to the literature cited in note 4, see also on military organization Reuter (1985), (1990); Halsall (2003), c. 4. See too Werner (1980), 191–211 on *missi*. Wulfad case: Nelson, (1986a), 53 ff.

7 Rule of thumb: Goldberg (2006), esp. introduction (1–11) and epilogue (335–46). On the frequency of campaigning: Reuter (1985). On Charlemagne's suppression of revolt: Nelson (2008); Costambeys et al. (2011), 65 ff.; cf. more generally Leyser (1979), pt 1 on the resentments that royal favour could arouse especially in aristocratic siblings not in receipt of it.

8 Engelbert: text Dummler (1884), 138–9; trans. Dutton (2004), 332–3. On the run up to the battle, see Nelson (1990); Goldberg (2006), c. 3; Costambeys et al. (2011), 379–88.

9 Charles the Bald's securing of power: Martindale (1981); Nelson (1992), cc. 5–6. On Louis the German: Goldberg (2006), cc. 4–5.

10 See generally Nelson (1992), cc. 7–8; Goldberg (2006), cc. 7–8; Costambeys et al. (2011), 388 ff. These works provide full references to the sources and further secondary reading. In addition, on Lothar II's divorce, see in particular Airlie (1998).

11 McKitterick (1983), c. 7; MacLean (2003), esp. cc. 5–6; Goldberg (2006), 335 ff.; Costambeys et al. (2011), 419 ff.

12 More detailed narratives of these developments are provided by e.g. McKitterick (1983), c. 10; Dunbabin (2000), cc. 3–4; MacLean (2003), cc. 3–4.

13 Regino of Prum, *Chronicle* 888; text Kurze (1890), 129; trans. Dutton (2004), 541.

14 Good introductions in English are Dunbabin (2000), cc. 4–5; MacLean (2003), cc. 3–4; cf. Hallam (1980) for a series of illuminating regional perspectives.

15 Odo and Boso: Hallam (1980), c. 1; Dunbabin (2000), cc. 3–5; MacLean (2003), c. 3. East Frankish duchies: Reuter (1991), cc. 4–5.

16 Dunbabin (2000), 37 ff. is excellent on the problems of defensive warfare for Carolingian-type armies and on the broader impact of fortification; cf. Halsall (2003), c. 10 and Hallam (1980), 13 ff. On Robert the Strong, see Nelson (1992), esp. 183 ff.

17 A similarly strategic mixture of loyalty and usurpation underlies, for instance, the emergence and subsequent growth of Flanders: Ganshof (1949). For a broader introduction and bibliographical orientation, see e.g. Werner (1979); Bourchard (1981); Poly and Bournazel (1991); Barthélemy (2009). Hallam (1980), c. 2 provides very necessary regional differentiation to fill out the general model.

18 See in more detail Heather (1994b) and (2005), cc. 1 and 3 with full refs.

19 The only exception to the pattern of administrative recasting was a religious one, in that dioceses of the early medieval, former Roman west often preserved the old *civitas* boundaries, even where these had ceased to be relevant for other purposes. I have explored the causes and consequences of this transformation in more detail in Heather (2000), (2010); cf. Halsall (2003), c. 3 for an excellent survey of the evidence for raising armies in post-Roman Europe.

20 The transformation of state structures is comprehensively discussed in Wickham (2005), esp. cc. 3 and 6 with full bibliography.

21 Good introductions to the empire's history in English are Leyser (1979); Reuter (1991).

22 A terrific introduction to the *reconquista* is provided by Fletcher (1989). For an introduction to the growth of Christian northern and Eastern Europe: Heather (2009), cc. 8–10.

23 Leyser (1979), cc. 7–8; Goldberg (2006), 335 ff.; Reuter (1991), c. 6.

24 On the Magyars and the history of the Reich, see esp. Leyser (1982a), (1982b); cf. more generally Macartney (1930); Bowlus (1995).

25 Reuter (1991), 94–102, 229–36.

26 Reuter (1991), esp. 77 ff.; cf. Heather (2009), c. 8 with refs for the deeper background.

27 Reuter (1985), (1990) develops the model in relation to Carolingian power; cf. Reuter (1991), 174–80, 253–64 on the collapse of the Ottonians' Slavic marches. On Anglo-Saxon England, see e.g. Bassett (1989); Charles Edwards (1979). Wickham (2005), 339 ff. provides a more general, comparative treatment.

28 Reuter (1990) set up the cost–benefit equation of expansion (which I largely follow here); cf. Depreux (1994) on Matfrid of Orleans. Halsall (2003), 89 ff; McKitterick (2008), 103 ff. esp. 135–6 have offered some critique and modification to Reuter's original accounts, which have influenced my vision of the pair of simultaneous cost–benefit equations.

29 Heather (2009), esp. cc. 2, 9–11 explores these processes and their consequences in more detail.

7. CHARLES THE GREAT AND LEO THE POPE

1 Matthew 16:18–19.
2 The text and a translation can be found conveniently together in Godman (1985), 197–207. Godman (1987), 82 ff. provides fuller discussion than his footnotes to the translation, including of the issue of Einhard's potential authorship.
3 Translations of *The Epistle of Clement* and the Ignatian letters can be found in Staniforth (1987). Victor: Eusebius, *Ecclesiastical History*. 5.24. For the early development of the Christian community in Rome in general, see Ullmann (1970), c. 1.
4 A fuller discussion can be found in Jones (1964), c. 22.
5 See further Ullmann (1970), 12 ff.; Jasper and Fuhrmann (2001), 7–22 with refs.
6 The literature that could and in some ways should be cited here is potentially limitless, but an excellent general introduction in English is Chadwick (1993) which can be supplemented by more detailed accounts of individual issues such as Hanson (1988) (the so-called Arian dispute); Burrus (1995) (Priscillianism); and Frend (1972) (the so-called Monophysite movement). The developing theological argument needs to be understood against the general spread of Christianity and transformation of its institutional structures surveyed in e.g. Jones (1964), c. 22; Herrin (1987), cc. 1–3; and Brown (1996), cc. 3–4.
7 This is all well discussed in Ullmann (1970), 13 ff. (cf. his fuller discussion in Ullmann, (1960)), usefully supplemented by Schatz (1990).
8 The suburbicarian sees originally subordinate to Rome's metropolitan authority were Albano, Tusculum, Palestrina, Sabina, Ostia, Portus and S. Rufina.
9 Decretal collections: Jasper and Fuhrmann (2001), 22 ff. with refs. Leo I left an extensive, separate letter collection, but only 17 of his missives made it into the decretal collections. Hilary: *Nov. Val. III* 17. For an introduction to the dispute which generated this ruling, see Mathisen (1989), c. 7. On the contrasting busyness of the imperial rescript system, see Heather (2005), 108–9 with refs.
10 Refs as above, note 6.
11 This conclusion emerges with great vigour from all the evidence; more detailed discussions can be found in the works cited in note 6. The canons of the first four ecumenical councils are translated in Bright (1892), and the proceedings of Constantinople (553) in Price (2009).
12 The imperial role in ongoing fourth-century Christian debate is examined in e.g. Barnes (1993); McLynn (1994). On the sixth century, see e.g. Gray (1979), (2005) with again Frend (1972). The standard outcome of losing out in a struggle for imperial validation in the fourth and early fifth centuries was not the complete eradication of the losing point of view, but its reduction to sect status, the fate suffered by so-called 'Arians' and Donatists.
13 A very brief introduction to developing Church (canon) law in this period is provided by Brundage (1995), c. 1; cf. on Church courts Jones (1964), c. 22; Harries (1999), c. 10; Humfress (2007), c. 7.
14 For an introduction to papal elections and their associated violence, see Curran (2000), esp. c. 4.

15 A good introduction to Augustine's thought is Brown (1967). On Athanasius, see Barnes (1993). The modern discussion of the ascetic movement is associated again with Peter Brown, see e.g. Brown (1970); (1981); Howard Johnston et al. (1999).

16 Dvornik (1966) remains seminal, usefully supplemented by MacCormack (1981) on the ideology's ceremonial manifestations.

17 Gelasius: see, e.g., Ullmann (1970), 31–5; Llewellyn (1971), 38–40; Richards (1979), c. 4; Duffy (2006), 49–53. Somerville and Brasington (1998), c. 2 provide both an introduction to the work of Dionysius, and translations of his various prefaces. On the influence of his decretal collection, see Jasper and Fuhrmann (2001), 22–8 with refs.

18 By far and away the best analysis of the pontificate of Gregory I is Markus (1997). For good introductions to the Monothelite Dispute and papal resistance, see Llewellyn (1971), c. 5; Herrin (1987), 207–18, 250–9. An excellent pathway into the Anglo-Saxon missions and Theodore of Tarsus is provided by Mayr-Harting (1972) pt 1; Campbell (1986), nos. 1 and 4.

19 Sotinel (2005) and the various papers in Chazelle and Cubitt (2007) offer good introductions to the Three Chapters Controversy. On Gregory and the Lombards, see Markus (1997), c. 7. AD 681: Noble (1984), 12–14.

20 Imperial restructuring in general: Haldon (1990). Consequences in Italy and in the vicinity of Rome in particular: Krautheimer (1980), c. 4; Brown (1984); Noble (1984), 2–11. The highly revealing papal biographies of the *Liber Pontificalis* for this crucial period are now available in the excellent translation of Davis (2000).

21 Noble (1984), c. 2 is by far the best account in English. Davis (1992) is an excellent translation of the relevant papal biographies.

22 The point emerges clearly from the well-crafted narrative of Noble (1984), cc. 2–4; cf. Llewellyn (1971), cc. 7–8; Duffy (2006), 86 ff.

23 *Nov. Val. III* 17; English trans. in Pharr (1952).

24 Reydellet (1981) is an excellent general survey; cf. Teillet (1984) specifically on the Visigothic kingdom, but incorporating much general material besides.

25 General accounts of the Visigothic Conversion to Catholicism in English are Thompson (1969), c. 4; Collins (2004), c. 2; cf. in more detail Hillgarth (1966); Fontaine (1967); Ripoll and Velázquez (1995). The quotation is from Bede, *Ecclesiastical History of the English People* 3.25 and further commentary is available in the works cited in note 18.

26 Gregory of Tours' *Histories* are translated by Thorpe (1974). The position of Spanish bishops under Umayyad rule emerges from John of Gorze's mission to Spain in the tenth century, trans. in Smith (1988).

27 The precocious initiatives of Caesarius can be explored in more detail through Klingshirn (1994a). Developing tradition from the 580s onwards: Turner (1903); Vessey (1993); cf. Mordek (1975) on the *Vetus Gallica*.

28 Vives (1963) provides a full edition and accompanying Spanish translation of the Visigothic councils; cf. Stocking (2000) for a recent study in English utilizing some of these materials. The best modern study of the Anglo-Saxon conciliar tradition is Cubitt (1995). The visit of the papal legates is translated in Whitelock (1996), no. 191, 170 ff.

29 For an introduction to Roman pilgrimage, see Llewellyn (1971), c. 6; Birch (1998).

30 Charlemagne's donations: above, page 000. The *vitae* of Hadrian I and Leo III are conveniently translated as nos. 97 and 98 in Davis (1992), who also provides excellent introductions to the lives, and what they omit. Secondary commentary on the building can be found in e.g. Llewellyn (1971), 242 ff; Krautheimer (1980), c. 5; Christie (2005).

31 End of iconoclasm: above, page 000. For further discussion of the *filioque*, see McKitterick (2008), 311–15.

32 The *Admonitio Generalis* is translated in King (1987), 209–20. It is followed there by further translations of much of Charlemagne's capitulary legislation. For further discussion of the general principles of reform, see e.g. de Jong (2005); McKitterick (2008), c. 5; Costambeys et al. (2011), c. 3;

33 The bibliography on Charlemagne's intellectuals is enormous, but, for a fuller introduction, see e.g. Godman (1987), c. 2; the highly useful collection of essays in McKitterick (1994a) esp. those of Law, Garrison and Rankin; the essays of Bullough and McKitterick in Story (2005). These can be supplemented by studies of individual thinkers such as Dutton (1998) (Einhard) and Bullough (2003) (Alcuin).

34 The essays collected under thematic headings in McKitterick (1994a) provide an excellent introduction to the portfolio of key texts.

35 *On the Study of Letters* (*De litteris colendis*) is translated in King (1987), 232–3. On the late Roman grammarian, see Kaster (1988), and on the subsequent evolution of Latin, Wright (1982), (1996); cf. Heather (1994a) on the underlying sociological transformations.

36 See further, among many possibilities, Law (1994); McKitterick (2005) with refs. The detailed individual studies collected in Bischoff (1994) shed intense, specific light.

37 On the general cultural significance of the Carolingian period for Latin literature as a whole, see Reynolds and Wilson (1991). Nelson (1977) is particularly good on the ideologically imposed limits of Carolingian intellectual activity. Otherwise, the works cited at note 33 are all extremely helpful.

38 An excellent recent reassessment of the issue is McKitterick (2008), 345 ff.

39 The best introduction to the history of script is Bischoff (1990); but see also Ganz (1989) and McKitterick (1994b).

40 Nelson (1987); Wood (2006), cc. 14–15.

41 On the cathedral schools and learning, see e.g. McKitterick (1994); Costambeys et al. (2011), 142 ff. Lawrence (2001), cc. 2–3 provides a good introduction to Carolingian monastic reform, and Cabaniss (1979) an English translation of Ardo's contemporary *Life* of Benedict of Aniane.

42 Trans. King (1987), 311–12.

43 Charlemagne's letter celebrating the work of Paul the Deacon is translated at King (1987), 208. On the reform project in general, see above all McKitterick (1977), c. 1 (bishops), and c. 3 (preaching). Helpful additional discussions include de Jong (2005); McKitterick (2008), 299–311; Costambeys et al. (2011), c. 3: all with further refs.

44 The evidence of key types of source material is gathered and analysed by McKitterick (1977), c. 2 (episcopal statutes), c. 4 (liturgical experience). My general conclusions echo those of other recent contributors (see previous note).

45 The point is well made in Costambeys et al. (2011), 142 ff., which summarizes the overall picture which has emerged from a century and a half of modern scholarship on the so-called Carolingian Renaissance, to which the works cited in notes 33, 36, 37 and 41 provide excellent points of entry.

8. *HABEMUS PAPAM*: PAPAL LIFT-OFF

1 The bibliography on Innocent III and the Fourth Lateran Council is immense, but a good introduction is provided by Morris (1989), c. 17, esp. 447–51; with fuller discussion in e.g. Tillmann (1980): a translation of the German original of 1954. An English version of the conciliar canons can be found in Rothwell (1975), 643–75. The new edition of Innocent's letters (Hageneder et al., 1965–), has so far reached the year 1208/9, but an excellent overall discussion of Innocent's views on papal authority is Hageneder (2000).

2 Themistius, *Orations* 6.83c–d; which is why the later Roman Empire had ended up being governed not from Rome but from political centres much closer to the key frontiers such as Trier, Constantinople, and Antioch: Heather (2005), c. 1.

3 A good introduction is Jasper and Fuhrmann (2001), 135 ff. with 154–5 and 184–6 on the MS dissemination.

4 I am convinced by Fried (2007), esp. c. 4, that only religious authority was meant to be ascribed to the Pope by the forgery at the moment it was produced. The extension of its wording into the realm of secular authority was a later development, as we shall see later in the chapter.

5 On the vision of the text, see generally Jasper and Fuhrmann (2001); Fried (2007), and Reynolds (1995).

6 Jasper and Fuhrmann (2001), esp. 173 ff.; Fried (2007), esp. 88 ff. with the App. A 115–28 (by Wolfram Brandes). By contrast, see Noble (1984), 134–7 with full refs for the alternative view that the *Donation of Constantine* at least was produced in eighth-century Rome.

7 On 833, see above, page 000, with refs and the particular comments of Jasper and Fuhrmann (2001), 173 ff.; Fried (2007), 88 ff.

8 A full treatment in English of the dispute between the two Hincmars is McKeon (1978); see now also Schieffer (2003).

9 Jasper and Fuhrmann (2001), 186–95.

10 Good accounts of the activities of both Nicholas and Hadrian with full refs can be found in the introductions to the translations of their lives in the *Liber Pontificalis*: Davis (1995), 189–202 (Nicholas), 249–58 (Hadrian). They are also discussed in all the standard general English-language treatments of the medieval papacy: e.g. Llewellyn (1971), c. 9; Ullmann (1972), c. 5; Duffy (1997), c. 4.

11 Liutprand, *Antapodosis*, I.30.

12 For general introductions to the period, see e.g. Ullmann (1970), 111 ff.; Llewellyn (1971), c. 10; Duffy (1997), 103 ff.

13 Noble (1984), 308–22; Davis (1995), 1–4.

14 See the introductions to, and actual biographies of, these Popes, with the lines of contention running through them, in Davis (1995).

15 *Liber Pontificalis* 107.68 ff., esp. 73–4 on the request that Formosus be made Archbishop. Nicholas refused – on the grounds of Nicaea 15 – because Formosus was already a bishop. See the introduction and footnotes of Davis (1995) for the complex webs of intrigue surrounding the mission.

16 *Liber Pontificalis* 104.40–3 (Sergius III); 112.6–11 (Stephen V).

17 Cf. Davis (1995), 72–3; Sergius' death probably ended this initiative.

18 *Liber Pontificalis* 107.21–35.

19 Fuller discussions of these incidents are available in Davis (1995), 189–202, 249–58 (introductions to the lives of Nicholas and Hadrian). See also on the divorce Airlie (1998); Nelson (1992), 215 ff.; Goldberg (2006), 292–5. And on Moravia: e.g. Dvornik (1970); Richter (1985); Goldberg (2006), 270–88.

20 General accounts in e.g. Llewellyn (1971), c. 10; Ullmann (1972), cc. 5 and 6; Duffy (1997), 103–9.

21 On Benedict IX, see Morris (1989), 82–4, drawing esp. on Herrmann (1973).

22 General accounts in e.g. Ullmann (1970), cc. 5 and 6; Llewellyn (1971), c. 10; Morris (1989), 18–33; Duffy (1997), 103–21.

23 Among many other good introductions to the origins and nature of the reform agenda in English, see Morris (1989), 28–33 and cc. 3–4 (the quotation from Peter Damian is from p. 103); Robinson (2004a), 1–12, or, in more detail, Cowdrey (1970).

24 Ullmann (1970), c. 6; McKitterick (1999); cf. Reuter (1982). For a more detailed study of Gerbert, see Riché (1987).

25 The relevant bibliography is enormous, but, for introductions, see Gibson (1975); Reuter (1982); Morris (1989), c. 3; McKitterick (1999); Wollasch (1999); Leonardi (1999); Cowdrey (2004).

26 On Burchard and Regino, see Austin (2009), esp. pt 1. Though cf. Jasper and Fuhrmann (2001), 184–6 (with full refs), Ullmann (1970), c. 7 is certainly overstating the situation to call this 'The Age of Pseudo-Isidore', since the text was so little used in practice.

27 Rosenwein (1989) on the property of Cluny, with, e.g., McKitterick (1999); Wood (2006) on more general patterns.

28 There are many excellent accounts of Leo IX, but good introductions in English can be found in Morris (1989), 79–89; Cowdrey (2004); Blumenthal (2004); and Robinson (2004a), 17–36. This work also incorporates a translation of the more or less contemporary *Life* of Leo, where his leadership of the knights is recounted at I.7. Among the usual suspects, see also Ullmann (1970), c. 6; Duffy (1997), 110 ff.

29 Morris (1989), 107–8; Fried (2007), esp. 16 ff.

30 On Nicholas and Alexander in general, see Morris (1989), 89–108; Cowdrey (2004); Blumenthal (2004); cf. in much more detail Schmidt (1977). On the return to registration, Cowdrey (2002), xi ff.

31 Letter 97, quoted in Cowdrey (2004), 260 f.

32 On Gregory's radical extension of the reform programme, see further Morris (1989), c. 5; Ullmann (1970), c. 7; Duffy (1997), 120 ff.; Robinson (2004b);

Blumenthal (2004). Gregory's letters are translated in Cowdrey (2002), and other contemporary materials relating to his pontificate in Robinson (2004a), 158 ff., which also provides a good introduction to his pontificate and these documents at 36 ff.

33 There is now an excellent general guide to processes of granting lands and other financial rights to ecclesiastical institutions in the Middle Ages: Wood (2006). For England, the evidence is comprehensive thanks to *Doomsday Book* and the *Cartae Baronum* of 1166: Douglas and Greenaway (1952), 903 ff. On the situation in Germany, Reuter (1982), and note in particular the *indiculus loricatorum*: when Otto II was in trouble after defeat in Italy in 981, it was exclusively to bishoprics and monasteries that he sent for reinforcements.

34 Morris (1989), 60–2.

35 For fuller accounts of the Investiture Controversy and subsequent confrontations, see e.g. Morris (1989), cc. 5, 7–8; Robinson (1990), (2004b), (2004d); Blumenthal (2004). The footnotes to these works and esp. Morris' bibliographical essays to each chapter provide excellent guidance to the (extensive) bibliography of more detailed and non-English-language studies available for this topic.

36 For further discussion of these developments inside and outside of Rome, see e.g. Morris (1989), esp. 164 ff. and c. 9; Robinson (2004c), (2004d); Blumenthal (2004).

37 The bibliography on crusading is immense, but for a more detailed introduction, see e.g. (in English) Riley-Smith (1986); Tyerman (2006).

38 For an introduction to these collections, see Robinson (1978); Brundage (1995), c. 2; Morris (1989), 126–33 drawing on more detailed studies such as Fuhrmann (1973) and Mordek (1985); cf. Austin (2009) on the deeper background. Some of the relevant material is still awaiting proper, scholarly editions, but the *Anonymous Collection in Seventy-Four Titles* has been both edited and translated: Gilchrist (1973), (1980).

39 *Const. Tanta* 13; 15 (see above page 000).

40 For an excellent introduction to the rediscovery of the *Digest*, see Stein (1999), 43–8 with full refs. Clarence Smith (1975) is an extremely helpful prosopographical guide to Roman and canon lawyers of the twelfth and thirteenth centuries.

41 Good introductions: e.g. Brundage (1995), c. 3; Stein (1999), 49 ff. The first part of Gratian's text is translated in Thompson and Gordley (1993), who also provide an extremely helpful introduction.

42 Gratian, *Decr.* C. IX. Q. 1 dictum post c. 16 (1011).

43 There are many possible treatments, but see, e.g., Morris (1989), 397–416; Brundage (1995), c. 3; Stein (1999), 49 ff.

EPILOGUE: THE GODFATHER (PART 3)

1 A highly readable introduction to the tendency for papal schism is Tuchman (1979).

2 On crusading in general, see Tyerman (2006), and on papal marriage strategies d'Avray (2005). Moore (1987) is a classic guide to the burgeoning persecution of heretics.

3 Trans. Rothwell (1975), no. 146, 705 ff.
4 See e.g. Duffy (2005); Burgess & Duffy (2006).
5 On Montaillou, see Le Roy Ladurie (1990).
6 On the ideological willingness of the Russian army to fight and die, see Merridale (2006).

Primary Sources

Acta Synhodorum habitarum Romae: text Mommsen (1894).
Admonitio Generalis: text Boretius (1883), no. 22; trans. King (1987), 209–20.
Agathias, *Histories*: text Keydell (1967); trans. Frendo (1975).
Ammianus Marcellinus: text and trans. Rolfe (1935–9).
Anonymous Valesianus: text and trans. Rolfe (1935–9), vol. 3.
Bavarian Code: text Krusch (1924); trans. Rivers (1977).
Bede, *Ecclesiastical History*: text and trans. Colgrave and Mynors (1969).
Boethius, *Consolation of Philosophy*: text and trans. Stewart et al. (1918).
Life of Caesarius: text Morin (2010); trans. Klingshirn (1994b).
Cassiodorus, *Variae*: text Mommsen (1894a); trans. Hodgkin (1886); Barnish (1992).
Chronicon Paschale: text Dindorf (1832); trans. Whitby and Whitby (1989).
Codex Carolinus: text Gundlach (1892); selected trans. King (1987).
Codex Theodosianus: text Mommsen and Kreuger (1905); trans. Pharr (1952).
Const. Omnem: see *Corpus Iuris Civilis*.
Const. Tanta: see *Corpus Iuris Civilis*.
Corpus Iuris Civilis:
    1. *Institutiones (Institutes)* and *Digesta (Digest)*: text Kruger and Mommsen (1928); trans. Birks and MacLeod (1987), Watson et al. (1998).
    2. *Codex Justinianus (Justinian's Code)*: text Kruger (1929); trans. Scott (1932).
    3. *Novellae (Novels)*: text Scholl and Kroll (1928); trans. Scott (1932).
Corripus, *Iohannis*: text Diggle and Goodyear (1970); trans. Shea (1998).
De litteris colendis: text Boretius (1883), no. 29; trans. King (1987), 232–3.
Deo Auctore: see *Corpus Iuris Civilis*.
Divisio Regnorum: text Boretius (1883), no. 45; trans. King (1987), 251–6.
Donation of Constantine: text and trans. Fried (2007).
Einhard, *Life of Charlemagne*: text Waitz (1911); trans. Dutton (1998).
Engelbert: text Dummler (1884), 138–9; trans. Dutton (2004).
Ennodius: text Hartel (1882).
Life of Epiphanius: trans. Deferrari (1952).
Epistolae Austrasiacae: text Gundlach (1902).
Eusebius, *Ecclesiastical History*: text Heinichen (1868–70); trans. McGiffert (1905).
Fredegar: text Krusch (1888).
Gregory of Tours, *Histories*: text Krusch and Levison (1951); trans. Thorpe (1974).
Inscriptiones Latinae Selectae: Dessau (1974).
John of Antioch: text Muller (1868/1870); trans. Gordon (1966).
John of Ephesus, *Ecclesiastical History*: trans. Smith (1860).
Jordanes, *Getica*: text Mommsen (1882); trans. Mierow (1915).

Justinian, *Novellae*: see *Corpus Iuris Civilis*.

Karolus Magnus et Leo Papa: text Beumann et al. (1966); trans. Godman (1985).

Liber Historiae Francorum: text and trans. Bachrach (1973).

Liber Pontificalis (*Book of the Pontiffs*): text Duchesne (1886–72); trans. Davies (1992) 1995, Davies (2000).

Liutprand, *Antapodosis*: text Dümmler (1877); trans. Wright (1993).

Malchus: text and trans. Blockley (1983).

Marcellinus Comes, *Chronicle*: text Mommsen (1894b).

Menander Protector: text and trans. Blockley (1985).

Ordinatio Imperii: text Boretius (1883), no. 136; trans. Dutton (2004),

Orosius, *Against the Pagans*: text Arnaud-Lindet (1990–1); trans. Deferrari (1964).

Parastaseis: text and trans. Cameron and Herrin (1984).

Paul the Deacon, *History of the Lombards*: text Bethmann and Waitz (1878); trans. Foulke (2003).

Priscus: text and trans. Blockley (1983).

Procopius, *Works*: text and trans. Dewing (1914–40).

Regino of Prum, *Chronicle*: text Kurze (1890); trans. Dutton (2004), 541.

Ruricius of Limoges: text Engelbrecht (1891); trans. Mathisen (1999).

Themistius, *Orations*: text Schenkl et al. (1965–74); trans. Heather and Moncur (2001).

Theodosian Code: see *Codex Theodosianus*.

Theophanes, *Chronographia*: text Niebuhr (1839–41); trans. Mango and Scott (1997).

Theophylact Simocatta, *History*: text de Boor and Wirth (1992); trans. Whitby and Whitby (1986).

Venantius Fortunatus, *Poems*: text Leo (1881); selected trans. George (1995).

BIBLIOGRAPHY

Airlie, S. (1998). 'Private Bodies and the Body Politic in the Divorce Case of Lothar II', *Past & Present* 161, 3–38.

Alföldi, G. (1974). *Noricum* (London).

Allen, P. (2000). 'The Definition and Enforcement of Orthodoxy', in Cameron et al. (2000), 811–34.

Amory, P. (1997). *People and Identity in Ostrogothic Italy, 489–554* (Cambridge).

Arnaud-Lindet, M.-P. (ed. and Fr. trans.) (1990–1). *Orose: Histoires contre les païens* (Paris).

Austin, G. (2009). *Shaping church law around the year 1000: the Decretum of Burchard of Worms* (Farnham).

Bachrach, B. S. (1973). *Liber historiae Francorum* (Lawrence, Kans.).

Barnes, T. D. (1993). *Athanasius and Constantius: theology and politics in the Constantinian Empire* (Cambridge, Mass.).

Barnish, S. J. B. (1986). 'Taxation, Land and Barbarian Settlement in the Western Empire', *Papers of the British School at Rome* 54, 170–95.

Barnish, S. J. B. (1988). 'Transformation and Survivial in the Western Senatorial Aristocracy, c. AD 400–700', *Papers of the British School at Rome* 56, 120–55.

Barnish, S. J. B. (1990). 'Cassiodorus, Boethius, Theodahad: Literature, Philosophy and Politics in Ostrogothic Italy', *Nottingham Medieval Studies* 34, 16–32.

Barnish, S. J. B. (1992). *Cassiodorus: Variae* (Liverpool).

Barthélemy, D. (2009). *The Serf, the Knight, and the Historian*, trans. G.R. Edwards (Ithaca).

Bassett, S. (ed.) (1989). *The Origins of Anglo-Saxon Kingdoms* (London).

Bavant, B (2007). 'Caricin Grad and the Changes in the Nature of Urbanism in the Central Balkans in the Sixth Century', in A. G. Poulter (ed.), *The Transition to Late Antiquity on the Danube and Beyond* (Oxford), 337–74.

Baxter, S. (2007). *The Earls of Mercia: Lordship and Power in Late Anglo-Saxon England* (Oxford).

Bethmann, L. and Waitz, G. (eds) (1878). *Pauli Historia Langobardum*, MGH Scriptores rerum Germanicarum (Hanover).

Beumann, H. et al. (1966). *Karolus Magnus et Leo Papa. Ein Paderborner Epos vom Jahre 799* (Paderborn).

Bierbrauer, V. (1975). *Die ostgotischen Grab- und Schatzfunde in Italien* (Spoleto).

Bierbrauer, V. (1980). 'Zur chronologischen, soziologischen und regionalen Gliederung des ostgermanischen Fundstoffs des 5. Jahrhunderts in Südosteuropa', in Wolfram, H. and Daim, V. (eds.), *Die Völker an der mittleren und unteren Donau im fünften und sechsten Jahrhundert*, Denkschriften der

Österreichischen Akademie der Wissenschaften, phil.-hist. Kl. 201 (Vienna), 131–42.

Birch, D. (1998). *Pilgrimage to Rome in the Middle Ages* (Woodbridge).

Birks, P. and McLeod, G. (1987). *Justinian's Institutes* (London).

Bischoff, B. (1990). *Latin Palaeography. Antiquity and the Middle Ages*, trans. D. Ganz and D. O. Cronin (Cambridge).

Bischoff, B. (1994). *Manuscripts and Libraries in the Age of Charlemagne* (Cambridge).

Bjornlie, S. (2009). 'What have Elephants to do with Sixth-Century Politics? A Reappraisal of the "Official" Governmental Dossier of Cassiodorus', *Journal of Late Antiquity* 2, 143–7.

Blockley, R. C. (1981). *The Fragmentary Classicising Historians of the Later Roman Empire: Eunapius, Olympiodorus, Priscus and Malchus*, vol. 1 (Liverpool).

Blockley, R. C. (1983). *The Fragmentary Classicising Historians of the Later Roman Empire: Eunapius, Olympiodorus, Priscus and Malchus*, vol. 2 (Liverpool).

Blockley, R. C. (1985). *The History of Menander the Guardsman* (Liverpool).

Blockley, R. C. (1992). *East Roman Foreign Policy: Formation and Conduct from Diocletian to Anastasius* (Leeds).

Blumenthal, U.-R. (2004). 'The Papacy 1024–1122', in Luscombe and Riley-Smith (2004b), 8–37.

Bona, I. (1991). *Das Hunnenreich* (Stuttgart).

Boretius, A. (1883). MGH Capitularia, Legum Sectio II, *Capitularia regum francorum* i (Hanover).

Bourchard, C. (1981). 'Origins of the French nobility: a reassessment', *American Historical Review* 86, 501–32.

Bowlus, C. (1995). *Franks, Moravians, and Magyars: The Struggle for the Middle Danube, 788–907* (Philadelphia).

Braund, D. C. (1984). *Rome and the Friendly King: The Character of Client Kingship* (London).

Bright, W. (1892). *The Canons of the First Four General Councils of Nicæa, Constantinople, Ephesus and Chalcedon*, 2nd ed. (Oxford).

Brock, S. (1981). 'The Conversations with the Syrian Orthodox under Justinian (532)', *Orientalia Christiana Periodica* 47, 87–121.

Brooks, E. R. (1893). 'The Emperor Zenon and the Isaurians', *English Historical Review* 8, 209–38.

Brown, P. R. L. (1967). *Augustine of Hippo: A Biography* (London).

Brown, P. (1970). 'The Rise and Function of the Holy Man in Late Antiquity', *Journal of Roman Studies* 61, 80–101.

Brown, P. R. L. (1981). *The Cult of the Saints: Its Rise and Function in Latin Christianity* (London).

Brown, P. (1996). *The Rise of Western Christendom: Triumph and Diversity, AD 200–1000* (Oxford).

Brown, T. S. (1984). *Gentlemen and Officers: Imperial Administration and Aristocratic Power in Byzantine Italy, AD 554–800* (London).

Brundage, J. A. (1995). *Medieval Canon Law* (London).

Bryer, A. and Herrin, J. (eds) (1977). *Iconoclasm* (Birmingham).

Bullough, D. (1970). '*Europae pater*: Charlemagne's Achievement in the light of recent Scholarship', *English Historical Review* 85, 59–105.

Bullough, D. (2003). *Alcuin: Achievement and Reputation* (Leiden).

Bullough, D. (2005). 'Charlemagne's "men of God": Alcuin, Hildebald, Arn', in Story (2005a), 136–50.

Burgess, C. and Duffy, E. (eds) (2006). *The Parish in Late Medieval England: Proceedings of the 2002 Harlaxton Symposium* (Donington).

Burrus, V. (1995). *The Making of a Heretic: Gender, Authority, and the Priscillianist Controversy* (Berkeley).

Bury, J. B. (1889). *History of the Later Roman Empire (AD 395 to 800)*, 2 vols (London).

Bury, J. B. (1923). *History of the Later Roman Empire from the Death of Theodosius to the Death of Justinian*, 2 vols (London).

Cabaniss, A. (1979). *The Emperor's Monk: Contemporary Life of Benedict of Aniane* (Ilfracombe).

Cameron, A. D. E. (Alan) (1970). *Claudian: Poetry and Propaganda at the Court of Honorius* (Oxford).

Cameron, A. D. E. (Alan) (1973). *Porphyrius the Charioteer* (Oxford).

Cameron, A. D. E. (Alan) (1976). *Circus Factions: Blues and Greens at Rome and Byzantium* (Oxford).

Cameron, A. M. (Averil) (1985). *Procopius and the Sixth Century* (London).

Cameron, A. M. (Averil) and Herrin, J. (1984). *Constantinople in the Early Eighth Century: The Parastaseis syntomoi chronikai: Introduction, Translation, and Commentary* (Leiden).

Cameron, A. M. (Averil) et al. (eds) (2000). *The Cambridge Ancient History*, 2nd ed., vol. 14 (Cambridge).

Campbell, J. (1986). *Essays in Anglo-Saxon History* (London).

Chadwick, H. (1981). *Boethius: The Consolations of Music, Logic, Theology and Philosophy* (Oxford).

Chadwick, H. (1993). *The Early Church*, rev. ed. (London).

Charles Edwards, T. M. (1979). 'The Distinction Between Land and Moveable Wealth in Anglo-Saxon England', in P. H. Sawyer (ed.), *English Medieval Settlement* (London), 97–104.

Chazelle, C. and Cubitt, C. (2007) (eds). *The Crisis of the Oikoumene: The Three Chapters and the Failed Quest for Unity in the Sixth-century Mediterranean* (Turnhout).

Christie, N. (1995). *The Lombards* (Oxford).

Christie, N. (1996). 'Towns and Peoples on the Middle Danube in Late Antiquity and the Early Middle Ages', in N. Christie and S. T. Loseby (eds), *Towns in Transition: Urban Evolution in Late Antiquity and the Early Middle Ages* (Aldershot), 71–98.

Christie, N. (2005). 'Charlemagne and the Renewal of Rome', in Story (2005a), 167–82.

Clarence Smith, J. A. (1975). *Medieval Law Teachers and Writers, Civilian and Canonist* (Ottowa).

Claude, D. (1989). 'Zur Begrundung familiarer Beziehungen zwischen dem Kaiser und barbarischen Herrschern', in E. K. Chrysos and A. Schwarcz (eds), *Das Reich und die Barbaren* (Vienna), 25–56.

Colgrave, B. and Mynors, R. A. B. (eds and trans.) (1969). *Bede's Ecclesiastical History of the English People* (Oxford).

Collins, R. (1990). 'Pippin I and the Kingdom of Aquitaine', in Godman and Collins (1990), 363–90.

Collins, R. (2004). *Visigothic Spain 409–711* (Oxford).

Collins, R. (2005). 'Charlemagne's Imperial Coronation and the Annals of Lorsch', in Story (2005a), 52–70.

Cormack, R. (1985). *Writing in Gold: Byzantine Society and its Icons* (London).

Costambeys, M. et al. (2011). *The Carolingian World* (Cambridge).

Courtois, C. (1955). *Les Vandales et l'Afrique* (Paris).

Cowdrey, H. E. J. (1970). *The Cluniacs and the Gregorian Reform* (Oxford).

Cowdrey, H. E. J. (2002). *The Register of Pope Gregory VII 1073–1085: An English Translation* (Oxford).

Cowdrey, H. E. J. (2004). 'The Structure of the Church 1024–73', in Luscombe and Riley-Smith (2004a), 229–267.

Croke, B. (2001). *Count Marcellinus and his Chronicle* (Oxford).

Croke, B. (2005). 'Justianian's Constantinople', in Maas (2005), 60–86.

Croke, B. and Crow, J. (1983). 'Procopius and Dara', *Journal of Roman Studies* 73, 143–59.

Crone, P. and Cook, M. (1977). *Hagarism: The Making of the Islamic world* (Cambridge).

Crone, P. (1987). *Meccan Trade and the Rise of Islam* (Oxford).

Cubitt, C. (1995). *Anglo-Saxon Church Councils c.650–c.850* (Leicester).

Curran, J. (2000). *Pagan City and Christian Capital: Rome in the Fourth Century* (Oxford).

Curta, F. (2001). *The Making of the Slavs: History and Archaeology of the Lower Danube Region, c.500–700* (Cambridge).

Dagron, G. (1974). *Naissance d'une capitale: Constantinople et ses institutions de 330 à 451* (Paris).

Daim, F. (2003). 'Avars and Avar Archaeology: An Introduction', in Goetz et al. (eds) (2003), 463–570.

Davies, W. and Fouracre, P. (1986). *The Settlement of Disputes in Early Medieval Europe* (Cambridge).

Davis, R. (1992). *The Lives of the Eighth-Century Popes (Liber Pontificalis)* (Liverpool).

Davis, R. (1995). *The Lives of the Ninth-Century Popes (Liber Pontificalis)* (Liverpool).

Davis, R. (2000). *The Book of Pontiffs (Liber Pontificalis). The ancient Biographies of the First Ninety Roman Bishops to* AD *715*, 2nd ed. (Liverpool).

d'Avray, D. (2005). *Medieval Marriage: Symbolism and Society* (Oxford).

De Boor, C. and Wirth, P. (eds) (1992). *Theophylacti Simocattae Historiae* (Stuttgart).

Deferrari, R. (1952). *Early Christian Biographies* (Washington DC).

Deferrari, R. (1964). *Orosius: Seven Books of History Against the Pagans* (Washington DC).

de Jong, M. (2009). *The Penitential State: Authority and Atonement in the Age of Louis the Pious, 814–840* (Cambridge).

Depreux, P. (1994). 'Le Comte Matfrid d'Orléans', *Bibliotheque de l'Ecole des Chartres* 152, 331–74.

Dessau, H. (1974). *Inscriptiones Latinae Selectae*, 4th ed. (Berlin).

Dewing, H. B. (1914–40). *The Works of Procopius* (London).

Diggle, J. and Goodyear, F. R. D. (eds) (1970). *Corippus Iohannis* (Cambridge).

Dignas, B. and Winter, E. (2007). *Rome and Persia in late antiquity: neighbours and rivals* (Cambridge).

Dindorf, L. (ed.) (1832). *Chronicon Paschale* (Bonn).

Dodgeon, M. H., and Lieu, S. N. C. (1991). *The Roman Eastern Frontier and the Persian Wars (AD 226–363): A Documentary History* (London).

Donner, F. M. (2005). 'The Background to Islam', in Maas (2005), 510–34.

Dooghe, D.-G. (2002). *Le Comté de Flandre et ses origines* (Wattignies)

Douglas, D. C. and Greenaway, G. W. (1952). *English historical documents, 1042–1189* (London).

Duchesne, L. (1886–82). *Le Liber Pontificalis, Texte, introduction et commentaire*, 2 vols (Paris).

Duffy, E. (2005). *Stripping of the Altars: Traditional Religion in England 1400–1580*, 2nd ed. (New Haven, Conn.).

Duffy, E. (2006). *Saints and Sinners: A History of the Popes*, 3rd ed. (London).

Dümmler, E. (1877). *Liudprandi episcopi Cremonensis Opera omnia* (Hanover).

Dümmler, E. (1884). MGH *Poetae Latini Aevi Carolini*, vol. 2 (Berlin).

Dunbabin, J. (2000). *France in the Making 843–1180*, 2nd ed. (Oxford).

Dutton, P. (1998). *Charlemagne's Courtier: The Complete Einhard* (Peterborough, Ontario).

Dutton, P. (2004). *Carolingian Civilization. A Reader* (Peterborough, Ontario).

Dvornik, F. (1966). *Early Christian and Byzantine Political Philosophy: Origins and Background*, The Dumbarton Oaks Center for Byzantine Studies (Washington DC).

Dvornik, F. (1970). *Byzantine Missions Among the Slavs: Saints Constantine-Cyril and Methodius* (New Brunswick, NJ).

Elton, H. (2007). 'Cavalry in Late Roman Warfare', in A. S. Lewin and P. Pellegrini (eds), *The Late Roman Army in the Near East from Diocletian to the Arab Conquest* (Oxford), 377–82.

Engelbrecht, A. (1891). *Fausti Reiensis Praeter sermones pseudo-eusebianos opera: accedunt Ruricii Epistulae* (Milan).

Evans, J. A. S. (1984). 'The "Nika" Rebellion and the Empress Theodora', *Byzantion* 54, 380–2.

Fletcher, R. A. (1989). *The Quest for El Cid* (London).

Fontaine, J. (1967). 'Conversion et Culture chez les Wisigoths d'Espagne', *Settimane di studi sull'Alto medioevo* 14, 87–147.

Foss, C. (1977). 'Archaeology and the Twenty Cities of Byzantine Asia', *American Journal of Archaeology* 81, 469–86.

Foss, C. (1990). *History and Archaeology of Byzantine Asia Minor* (Aldershot).

Foss, C. (1996). *Cities, Fortresses and Villages of Byzantine Asia Minor* (Aldershot).

Foulke, W. D. (2003). *History of the Lombards* (Philadelphia).

Fouracre, P. (1986). 'Placita and the Settlement of Disputes in Later Merovingian Francia', in Davies and Fouracre (1986), 23–44.

Fouracre, P. (2000) *The Age of Charles Martel* (Harlow).

Fouracre, P. (2005). 'The Long Shadow of the Merovingians', in Story (2005a), 5–21.

Frend, W. H. C. (1972). *The Rise of the Monophysite Movement: Chapters in the History of the Church in the Fifth and Sixth Centuries* (Cambridge).

Frendo, J. D. (trans.) (1975). *Agathias History* (Berlin).

Fried, J. (2007). *Donation of Constantine and Constitutum Constantini* (Berlin).

Fuhrmann, H. (1973). 'Das Reformpapsttum und die Rechtswissenschaft', *Vorträge und Forschungen* 17, 175–203.

Ganshof, F. L. (1949). *La Flandre sous les premiers comtes*, 3rd rev. ed. (Brussels).

Ganshof, F. L. (1971). *The Carolingians and the Frankish Monarchy* (London).

Ganz, D. (1989). 'The Preconditions for Caroline Minuscule', *Viator* 19, 23–44.

Geary, P. (1985). *Aristocracy in Provence: The Rhone Basin at the Dawn of the Carolingian Age* (Stuttgart).

George, J. (1995). *Venantius Fortunatus: Personal and Political Poems* (Liverpool).

Gerberding, R. (1987). *The Rise of the Carolingians and the Liber Historiae Francorum* (Oxford).

Gibbon, E. (1896–1900). *The Decline and Fall of the Roman Empire*, ed. J. B. Bury (London).

Gibson, M. T. (1975). *The Continuity of Learning c.850–c.1050* (Berkeley).

Gibson, M. T. (1981). *Boethius: His Life, Thought and Influence* (Oxford).

Gilchrist, J. (1973). *Diuersorum patrum sententie siue Collectio in LXXIV titulos digesta* (Vatican City).

Gilchrist, J. (1980). *The Collection in Seventy-Four Titles: A Canon Law Manual of the Gregorian Reform* (Toronto).

Gillet A. (ed.) (2002). *On Barbarian Identity: Critical Approaches to Ethnicity in the Early Middle Ages* (Turnhout).

Godman, P. (1985). *Poetry of the Carolingian Renaissance* (London).

Godman, P. (1987). *Poets and Emperors: Frankish Politics and Carolingian Poetry* (Oxford).

Godman, P. and Collins, R. (eds) (1990). *Charlemagne's Heir: New Perspectives on the Reign of Louis the Pious* (Oxford).

Goetz, H.-W. et al. (eds) (2003). *Regna and Gentes: The Relationship between Late Antique and Early Medieval Peoples and Kingdoms in the Transformation of the Roman World* (Leiden).

Goffart, W. (1980). *Barbarians and Romans AD 418–584: The Techniques of Accommodation* (Princeton).

Goffart, W. (1988). *The Narrators of Barbarian History (AD 550–800): Jordanes, Gregory of Tours, Bede, and Paul the Deacon* (Princeton).

Goffart. W. (2006). *Barbarian Tides: The Migration Age and the Later Roman Empire* (Philadelphia).

Goldberg, E. J. (2006). *Struggle for Empire: Kingship and Conflict under Louis the German 817–876* (Ithaca).

Gordon, D. C. (1966). *The Age of Attila* (Ann Arbor).

Goscinny and Uderzo (1963). *Astérix et les Goths* (Neuilly-sur-Seine).

Gray, P. (1979). *The Defence of Chalcedon in the East* (Leiden).

Gray, P. (2005). 'The Legacy of Chalcedon: Christological Problems and Their Significance', in Maas (2005), 215–38.

Greatrex, G. (1994). 'The Dates of Procopius' Works', *Byzantine and Modern Greek Studies* 18, 101–14.

Greatrex, G. (1997). 'The Nika Riot: A Reappraisal', *Journal of Hellenic Studies* 117, 60–86.

Greatrex, G. (1998). *Rome and Persia at War, 502–532* (Leeds).

Greatrex, G. (2000). 'Procopius the Outsider?', in D. S. Smythe (ed.), *Strangers to Themselves: The Byzantine Outsider* (Burlington, Vt.), 215–18.

Greatrex, G. and Lieu, S. (2002). *The Roman Eastern Frontier and the Persian Wars: A Narrative Sourcebook* (London).

Grig, L. and Kelly, G. (2012). *Two Romes: Rome and Constantinople in Late Antiquity* (Oxford Studies in Late Antiquity) (Oxford).

Gundlach, W. (ed.) (1892). Epistolae karolini aevi, MGH Epp. III, Epistolae merowingici et karolini aevi (Hanover).

Gundlach, W. (ed.) (1902). *Epistolae aevi merowingici collectae*, MGH Epp. III, Epistolae merowingici et karolini aevi (Hanover).

Hageneder, O. (2000). *Il sole e la luna: Papato, impero e regni nella teoria e nella prassi dei secoli XII e XIII* (Milan).

Hageneder, O. et al., (1965–). *Die Register Innocenz III* (Graz).

Haldon, J. F. (1990). *Byzantium in the Seventh Century: The Transformation of a Culture* (Cambridge).

Hallam, E. (1980). *Capetian France, 987–1328* (London).

Halsall, G. (2003). *Warfare and Society in the Barbarian West, 450–900* (London).

Halsall, G. (2007). *Barbarian Migrations and the Roman West 376–568* (Cambridge).

Hanson, R. P. C. (1988). *The Search for the Christian Doctrine of God* (Edinburgh).

Harries, J. (1999). *Law and Empire in Late Antiquity* (Cambridge).

Hartel, W. (1882). *Magni Felicis Ennodii Opera omnia* (Vienna).

Heather, P. J. (1989). 'Cassiodorus and the Rise of the Amals: Genealogy and the Goths under Hun Domination', *Journal of Roman Studies* 79, 103–28.

Heather, P. J. (1991). *Goths and Romans 332–489* (Oxford).

Heather, P. J. (1993). 'The Historical Culture of Ostrogothic Italy', in *Teoderico il grande e i Goti d'Italia*, Atti del XIII Congresso internazionale di studi sull'Alto Medioevo (Spoleto), 317–53.

Heather, P. J. (1994a). 'Literacy and Power in the Migration Period', in A. Bowman and G. Woolf (eds) (1994), *Literacy and Power in the Ancient World* (Cambridge), 177–97.

Heather, P. J. (1994b). 'New Men for New Constantines?: Creating an Imperial Elite in the Eastern Mediterranean', in P. Magdalino (ed.), *New Constantines: The Rhythm of Imperial Renewal in Byzantium, 4th–13th Centuries* (London), 11–33.

Heather, P. J. (1995). 'Theodoric King of the Goths', *Early Medieval Europe* 4.2, 145–73.

Heather, P. J. (1996). *The Goths* (Oxford).

Heather, P. J. (2000). 'State, Lordship and Community in the West (*c.* AD 400–600)', in Averil Cameron et al. (2000), 437–68.

Heather, P. (2003). 'Gens and regnum Among the Ostrogoths', in Goetz et al. (eds), 85–133.

Heather, P. (2005). *The Fall of Rome: A New History* (London).

Heather P. (2007). 'Goths in the Roman Balkans c.350–500, in A. Poulter (ed.), *The Transition to Late Antiquity on the Danube and Beyond* (Oxford), 163–90.

Heather, P. (2008). 'Ethnicity, Group Identity, and Social Status in the Migration Period', in I. Garipzanov et al. (eds), *Franks, Northmen, and Slavs: Identities and State Formation in Early Medieval Europe* (Turnhout), 17–50.

Heather, P. (2009). *Empires and Barbarians* (London).

Heather, P. (2010). 'Elite Militarisation and the Post-Roman West', in G. Bonamente and R. Lizzi Testa (eds), *Istituzioni, Carisimi et Esercizio del Potere (IV–VI secolo d.C.)* (Bari), 245–66.

Heather, P. (ed.) (1999). *The Visigoths from the Migration Period to the Seventh Century: An Ethnographic Perspective* (Woodbridge).

Heather, P. J. and Matthews, J. F. (1991). *The Goths in the Fourth Century*, Translated Texts for Historians (Liverpool).

Heather, P. J. and Moncur, D. (2001). *Politics, Philosophy, and Empire in the Fourth Century: Select Orations of Themistius*, Translated Texts for Historians (Liverpool).

Heinichen, F. A. (1868–70). *Eusebii Pamphili Scripta Historica* (Leipzig).

Hendy, M. F. (1985). *Studies in the Byzantine Monetary Economy, c.300–1450* (Cambridge).

Herrin, J. (1987). *The Formation of Christendom* (Oxford).

Herrmann, K. J. (1973). *Das Tuskulanerpapsttum (1012–1046): Benedikt VIII., Johannes XIX., Benedikt IX.* (Stuttgart).

Hillgarth, J. N. (1966). 'Coins and Chronicles: Propaganda in Sixth Century Spain', *Historia* 16, 482–508.

Hill, S. (1996). *The Early Byzantine Churches of Cilicia and Isauria* (Birmingham).

Hodgkin, T. (1886). *The Letters of Cassiodorus* (London).

Holum, K. (2005). 'The Classical City in the Sixth Century: Survival and Transformation', in Maas (2005), 87–112.

Honoré, A. M., (1978). *Tribonian* (London).

Honoré, A. (1994). *Emperors and Lawyers*, 2nd rev. ed. (Oxford).

Hooke, D. (1998). *The Landscape of Anglo-Saxon England* (London).

Horden, P. (2005). 'Mediterranean Plague in the Age of Justinian', in Maas (2005), 134–60.

Howard Johnston, J. (2010). *Witnesses to a World Crisis: Historians and Histories of the Middle East in the Seventh Century* (Oxford).

Howard Johnston, J. et al. (eds) (1999). *The Cult of Saints in Late Antiquity and the Middle Ages: Essays on the Contribution of Peter Brown* (Oxford).

Humfress, C. (2007). *Orthodoxy and the Courts in Late Antiquity* (Oxford).

James, E. F. (1988). *The Franks* (Oxford).

Jarnut, J. (1982). *Geschichte der Langobarden* (Stuttgart).

Jasper, D. and Fuhrmann, H. (2001). *Papal Letters in the Early Middle Ages* (Washington DC).

Johnson, M. J. (1988). 'Towards a History of Theoderic's Building Programme', *Dumbarton Oaks Papers* 42, 73–96.

Jones, A. H. M. (1962). 'The Constitutional Position of Odoacer and Theoderic', *Journal of Roman Studies* 52, 126–30.

Jones, A. H. M. (1964). *The Later Roman Empire: A Social Economic and Administrative Survey*, 3 vols (Oxford).

Kaldellis, A. (2004). *Procopius of Caesarea: Tyranny, History, and Philosophy at the End of Antiquity* (Philadelphia).

Kaster, R. A. (1988). *Guardians of Language: The Grammarian and Society in Late Antiquity* (Berkeley).

Kennedy, H. (2007). *The Great Arab Conquests: How the Spread of Islam Changed the World We Live in* (London).

Keydell, R. (1967). *Agathiae Myrinaei Historiarum libri quinque* (Berlin).

Khazanov, A. M. (1994). *Nomads and the Outside World*, 2nd ed. (Madison, Wis.).

King, P. D. (1987). *Charlemagne: Translated Sources* (Kendal).

Klingshirn, W. (1994a). *Caesarius of Arles: The Making of a Christian Community in Late Antique Gaul* (Cambridge).

Klingshirn, W. (1994b). *Caesarius of Arles: Life, Testament, Letters* (Liverpool).

Krautheimer R. (1980). *Rome: Profile of a City, 312–1308* (Princeton).

Kreuger, P. (ed.) (1877). *Corpus Iuris Civilis* (Berlin).

Kreuger, P. and Mommsen, Th. (1928). *Codex Theodosianus* (Berlin).

Krusch, B. (1888). *Fredegar Chronicorum libri IV cum continuationibus*, MGH scriptores rerum Merovingicarum 2 (Hanover).

Krusch, B. (1924). *Die Lex Bajuvariorum: Textgeschichte, Handschriftenkritik und Entstehung. Mit zwei Anhängen: Lex Alamannorum und Lex Ribuaria* (Berlin).

Krusch, B. and Levison, W. (eds) (1951). *Gregory of Tours Historiae*, MGH scriptores rerum Merovingicarum 1.1 (Berlin).

Kurze, F. (ed.) (1890). MGH SRG, *Reginonis abbatis Prumiensis Chronicon* (Hanover).

La Rocca, C. (ed.) (2005). *Italy in the Early Middle Ages: 476–1000* (Oxford).

Lattimore, O. (1940). *Inner Asian frontiers of China* (Oxford).

Law, V. (1994). 'The Study of Grammar', in McKitterick (1994a), 88–110.

Lawrence, C. H. (2001). *Medieval Monasticism: Forms of Religious Life in Western Europe in the Middle Ages*, 3rd ed. (Harlow).

Lengyel, A. and Radan, G. T. B. (eds) (1980). *The Archaeology of Roman Pannonia* (Budapest).

Leo, G. (1881). *Venantius Fortunatus, Opera Poetica*, MGH auctores antiquissimi 4.1 (Berlin).

Leonardi, C. (1999). 'Intellectual Life', in Reuter (1999), 186–211.

Le Roy Ladurie, E. (1990). *Montaillou: Cathars and Catholics in a French Village, 1294–1324* (Harmandsworth).

Leyser, K. (1979). *Rule and Conflict in an Early Medieval Society: Ottonian Saxony* (London).

Leyser, K. (1982). *Medieval Germany and Its Neighbours, 900–1250* (London).

Llewellyn, P. (1971). *Rome in the Dark Ages* (London).

Luscombe, D. and Riley-Smith, J. (eds) (2004a). *The New Cambridge Medieval History. Volume IV, c.1024–c.1198*, part 1 (Cambridge).

Luscombe, D. and Riley-Smith, J. (eds) (2004b). *The New Cambridge Medieval History. Volume IV, c.1024–c.1198*, part 2 (Cambridge).

Maas, M. (2005). *The Cambridge Companion to the Age of Justinian* (Cambridge).

Macartney, C. A. (1930). *The Magyars in the Ninth Century* (Cambridge).

MacCormack, S. A. (1981). *Art and Ceremony in Late Antiquity* (Los Angeles and Berkeley).

MacGeorge, P. (2002). *Late Roman Warlords* (Oxford).

McGiffert, A. S. (1905). *Eusebius: Church History, Life of Constantine the Great, and Oration in Praise of Constantine* (New York).

McKeon, P. R. (1978). *Hincmar of Laon and Carolingian Politics* (Urbana, Ill.).

McKitterick, R. (1977). *The Frankish Church and the Carolingian Reforms, 789–895* (London).

McKitterick, R. (1983). *The Frankish Kingdoms under the Carolingians, 751–987* (London).

McKitterick, R. (1989). *The Carolingians and the Written Word* (Cambridge).

McKitterick, R. (1990). *The Uses of Literacy in Early Mediaeval Europe* (Cambridge).

McKitterick, R. (ed.) (1994a). *Carolingian Culture: Emulation and Innovation* (Cambridge).

McKitterick R. (1994b). 'Script and Book Production', in McKitterick (1994a), 221–47.

McKitterick, R. (ed.) (1995). *The New Cambridge Medieval History, II: c.700–c.900* (Cambridge).

McKitterick, R. (1999). 'The Church', in Reuter (1999), 130–63.

McKitterick, R. (2005). 'The Carolingian Renaissance of Culture and Learning', in Story (2005a), 151–66.

McKitterick, R. (2008). *Charlemagne: The Formation of a European Identity* (Cambridge).

MacLean, S. (2003). *Kingship and Politics in the Late Ninth Century: Charles the Fat and the End of the Carolingian Empire* (Cambridge).

McLynn, N. (1994). *Ambrose of Milan* (Berkeley).

Mango, C. (1977a). 'Historical Introduction', in Bryer and Herrin (1977), 1–6.

Mango, C. (1977b). 'The Liquidation of Iconoclasm and the Patriarch Photius', in Bryer and Herrin (1977), 133–40.

Mango, C. (1985). *Le Développement urbain de Constantinople (IVe–VIIe siècles)*, Travaux et Mémoires, Monographies 2 (Paris).

Mango, C. and Scott, R. (trans.) (1997). *Chronographia, The Chronicle of Theophanes Confessor* (Oxford).

Markus, R. (1997). *Gregory the Great and his World* (Cambridge).

Martindale, J. (1981). 'Charles the Bald and the Government of the Kingdom of Aquitaine', in Gibson and Nelson, 115–38 (Oxford).

Mathisen, R. (1989). *Ecclesiastical Factionalism and Religious Controversy in Fifth-Century Gaul* (Washington DC).

Mathisen, R. (1999). *Ruricius of Limoges and Friends* (Liverpool).

Matthews, J. F. (1975). *Western Aristocracies and Imperial Court AD 364–425* (Oxford).

Matthews, J. F., 1989. *The Roman Empire of Ammianus* (London).

Matthews, J. F. (2000). *Laying Down the Law: A Study of the Theodosian Code* (New Haven).

Mayr-Harting, H. (1972). *The Coming of Christianity to Anglo-Saxon England* (London).

Merridale, C. (2006). *Ivan's War: the Red Army 1939–1945* (London).

Merrills, A. and Miles, D. (2010). *The Vandals* (Oxford).

Metzger, E. (ed.) (1988). *A Companion to Justinian's Institutes* (Ithaca).

Mierow, C. C. (1915). *Jordanes Getica* (New York).

Millar, F. (2006). *A Greek Roman Empire. Power and Belief under Theodosius II 408–450* (Berkeley).

Mitchell, S. (1993). *Anatolia. Land, Men and Gods in Asia Minor II. The Rise of the Church* (Oxford).

Mocsy, A.(1974). *Pannonia and Upper Moesia* (London).

Momigliano, A. (1955). 'Cassiodorus and the Italian Culture of His Time', *Proceedings of the British Academy* 41, 215–48.

Mommsen, Th. (ed.) (1882). *Jordanes Romana et Getica*, MGH auctores antiquissimi 5. 1 (Berlin).

Mommsen, Th. (ed.) (1894a). *Cassiodori . . . Variae: i. Epistulae Theodericianae variae.*

ii. *Acta synhodorum habitarum Romae*. iii. *Cassiodori Orationum reliquiae*, ed. L. Traube. MGH auctores antiquissimi 12 (Berlin).

Mommsen, Th. (ed.) (1894b). *Chronica Minora*, vol. 2, *auctores antiquissimi* (Berlin).

Moore, R. I. (1987). *The Formation of a Persecuting Society: Power and Deviance in Western Europe, 950–1250* (Oxford).

Moorhead, J. (1992). *Theoderic in Italy* (Oxford).

Moorhead, J. (1994). *Justinian* (London).

Mordek, H. (1975). *Kirchenrecht und Reform im Frankenreich: die collectio vetus Gallica: die älteste systematische Kanonessammlung des fränkischen Gallien: Studien und Edition* (Berlin).

Mordek, H. (1985). 'Kanonistik und gregorianische Reform', in K. Schmid (ed.), *Reich und Kirche vor dem Investiturstreit* (Sigmaringen), 65–82.

Morin, G. et al. (eds) (2010). *Vie de Césaire d'Arles* (Paris).

Morris, C. (1989). *The Papal Monarchy: The Western Church from 1050 to 1250* (Oxford).

Muller, C. (1868/1870). *Fragmenta Historicorum Graecorum*, vols 4 and 5 (Paris).

Nelson, J. (1977). 'On the Limits of the Carolingian Renaissance', *Studies in Church History*, 51–67 (reprinted as no. 2 in Nelson (1986b)).

Nelson, J. (1983), 'Legislation and Consensus in the Reign of Charles the Bald', in C. P. Wormald et al. (eds), *Ideal and Reality in Frankish and Anglo-Saxon Society: Studies presented to J. M. Wallace-Hadrill* (Oxford), 202–27 (reprinted as no. 5 in Nelson 1986b).

Nelson, J. (1986a). 'Dispute settlement in Carolingian West Francia', in Davies and Fouracre (1986), 45–64.

Nelson, J. (1986b). *Politics and Ritual in Early Medieval Europe* (London).

Nelson, J. (1987). 'Making Ends Meet: Wealth and Poverty in the Carolingian Church', *Studies in Church History* 24, 25–36.

Nelson, J. (1990). 'The Last Years of Louis the Pious', in Godman and Collins, 147–60.

Nelson, J. (1992), *Charles the Bald* (London).

Nelson, J. (1998). 'Making a Difference in Eighth-century Politics: The Daughters of Desiderius', in A. Murray (ed.), *After Rome's Fall* (Toronto), 171–90.

Nelson, J. (2005). 'Charlemagne the Man', in Story (2005a), 22–37.

Nelson, J. (2008). *Opposition to Charlemagne* (London).

Nicol, D. M. (1992). *The Immortal Emperor* (Cambridge).

Niebuhr, B. G. (ed.) (1839–41). *Theophanes Chronographia* (Bonn).

Noble, T. F. X. (1984). *The Republic of St Peter: The Birth of the Papal State, 680–825* (Philadelphia).

Noble, T. F. X. (1995). 'The Papacy in the Eighth and Ninth Centuries', in McKitterick (1995), 563–86.

Noble, T. F. X. (2009). *Images, Iconoclasm, and the Carolingians* (Philadelphia).

Norwich, J. J. (1988). *Byzantium: The Early Centuries* (London).

Obolensky, D. (1982). *The Byzantine Commonwealth: Eastern Europe, 500–1453* (New York).

O'Donnell, J. J. (1979). *Cassiodorus* (Berkeley).

O'Donnell, J. J. (2009). *The Ruin of the Roman Empire* (London).

Pallas, D. (1977). *Les Monuments paléochrétiens de Grèce découverts de 1959 à 1973* (Vatican City).

Perin, P. and Kazanski, M. (1996). 'Das Grab Childerichs I', in *Die Franken:*

Wegbereiter Europas: vor 1500 Jahren, König Chlodwig und seine Erben (Mainz), 173–82.

Pharr, C. (1952). *The Theodosian Code and Novels, and the Sirmondian Constitutions* (New York).

Pohl, W.(1988). *Die Awaren: ein Steppenvolk im Mitteleuropa, 567–822 n. Chr.* (Munich).

Pohl, W. (2003). 'A Non-Roman Empire in Central Europe: The Avars', in Goetz et al. (eds), 571–95.

Pohl. W. (2005). 'Invasions and Ethnic Identity', in La Rocca, 11–33.

Poly, J.-P. and Bournazel, E. (1991). *The Feudal Transformation, 900–1200* (New York).

Potter, D. (2004). *The Roman Empire at Bay: AD 180–395* (London).

Price, R. (2009). *The Acts of the Council of Constantinople of 553: with related texts on the Three Chapters Controversy* (Liverpool).

Pringle, D. (1981). *The Defence of Byzantine Africa from Justinian to the Arab Conquest* (Oxford).

PLRE = *The Prosopography of the later Roman Empire*, Jones, A. H. M. et al. (eds), 3 vols (Cambridge), 1971–92.

Prostko-Prostynski, J. (1994). *Utraeque Res Publicae: The Emperor Anastasius' Gothic Policy (491–518)* (Poznan).

Puzo, M. (1969). *The Godfather* (London).

Reuter, T. (1982). 'The "Imperial Church System" of the Ottonian and Salian Rulers: A Reconsideration', *Journal of Ecclesiastical History* 33, 347–74.

Reuter, T. (1985). 'Plunder and Tribute in the Carolingian Empire', in *Transactions of the Royal Historical Society*, 75–94.

Reuter, T. (1990). 'The End of Carolingian Military Expansion', in Godman and Collins, 391–407.

Reuter, T. (1991). *Germany in the Early Middle Ages c.800–1056* (London).

Reuter, T. (ed.) (2000). *The New Cambridge Medieval History*, vol. 3 (Cambridge),

Reuter, T. (2005). 'Charlemagne and the World beyond the Rhine', in Story (2005a), 183 94.

Reydellet, M. (1981). *La Royauté dans la littérature latine: de Sidoine Apollinaire à Isidore de Séville* (Rome).

Reynolds, L. D. and Wilson, N. G. (1991). *Scribes and scholars: a guide to the transmission of Greek and Latin literature*, 3rd ed. (Oxford).

Reynolds, R. E. (1995). 'The Organisation, Law, and Liturgy of the Western Church 700–900', in R. McKitterick (ed.), *The New Cambridge Medieval History*, vol. 2 (Cambridge), 587–621.

Richards, J. (1979). *The Popes and the Papacy in the Early Middle Ages, 476–752* (London).

Riché, P. (1987). *Gerbert d'Aurillac: le pape de l'an mille* (Paris).

Richter, M. (1985). 'Die politische Orientierung Mährens zur Zeit von Konstantin und Methodius', in H. Wolfram and A. Schwarcz (eds), *Die Bayern und ihre Nachbarn*, vol. 1 (Vienna), 281–92.

Riley-Smith, J. (1986). *The First Crusade and the Idea of Crusading* (London).

Ripoll, G. and Velázquez, I. (1995). *La Hispania visigoda: del rey Ataúlfo a don Rodrigo* (Madrid).

Rivers, T. J. (1977). *Laws of the Alamans and Bavarians* (Philadelphia).

Rivière, Y. de la (ed.) (2012). *Confiscations et l'histoire de l'Empire Romain* (Rome).

Robinson, I. S. (1978). *Authority and Resistance in the Investiture Contest. The Polemical Literature of the Eleventh Century* (Manchester).

Robinson, I. S. (1990). *The Papacy 1073–1198: Continuity and innovation* (Cambridge).

Robinson, I. S. (2004a). *The Papal Reform of the Eleventh Century: Lives of Pope Leo IX and Pope Gregory VII* (Manchester).

Robinson, I. S. (2004b). 'Reform and the Church 1073–1122', in Luscombe and Riley-Smith (2004a), 268–334.

Robinson, I. S. (2004c). 'Institutions of the Church 1073–1216', in Luscombe and Riley-Smith (2004a), 368–460.

Robinson, I. S. (2004d). 'The Papacy 1122–1198', in Luscombe and Riley-Smith (2004b), 317–83.

Rolfe, J. C. (ed.) (1935–9). *Ammianus Marcellinus* (London).

Rosenwein, B. (1989). *To be the Neighbor of Saint Peter: The Social Meaning of Cluny's Property, 909–1049* (Ithaca).

Rothwell, H. (ed.) (1975). *English Historical Documents 1189–1327* (London).

Rouche, M. (1979). *L'Aquitaine: des Wisigoths aux Arabes, 418–781; naissance d'une région* (Paris).

Rushworth, A. (2004). 'From Arzuges to Rustamids: State formation and regional identity in the Pre-Saharan Zone', in A. H. Merrills (ed.), *Vandals, Romans, and Berbers: New Perspectives on Late Antique North Africa* (Aldershot), 77–98.

Sarris, P. (2002). 'The Justinianic Plague: Origins and Effects', *Continuity and Change* 17, 169–82.

Sarris, P. (2011). *Empires of Faith: The Fall of Rome to the Rise of Islam, 500–700* (Oxford).

Sartre, M. (1982). 'Trois études sur l'Arabie romaine et byzantine', in *Revue d'études latines* (Brussels).

Schäfer, C. (1991). *Der weströmische Senat als Träger antiker Kontinuität unter den Ostgotenkönigen (490–540 n. Chr.)* (St Katharinen).

Schatz, K. (1990) *Papal Primacy from its Origins to the Present* (Collegeville, Minn.).

Schenkl, H. et al. (eds) (1965–74). *Themistii Orationes* (Leipzig).

Schieffer (2003). *Die Streitschriften Hinkmars von Reims und Hinkmars von Laon, 869–871* (Hanover).

Schmidt, T. (1977). *Alexander II. (1061–1073) und die römische Reformgruppe seiner Zeit* (Stuttgart).

Scholl, R. and Kroll, G. (eds) (1928). *Novellae* (Berlin).

Scott, L. R. (1976). 'Aspar and the Burden of Barbarian Heritage', *Byzantine Studies* 3, 59–69.

Scott, S. P. (trans.) (1932). *The Civil Law, Including the Twelve Tables: The Institutes of Gaius, the Rules of Ulpian, the Opinions of Paulus, the Enactments of Justinian, and the Constitutions of Leo* (Cincinnati).

Shanzer, D. and Wood, I. N. (trans.) (2002). *Avitus of Vienne: Letters and Selected Prose* (Liverpool).

Shea, G. W. (1998). *The Iohannis or De bellis libycis of Flavius Cresconius Corippus* (Lewiston, Me.).

Sinor, D. (1977). *Inner Asia and Its Contacts with Medieval Europe* (London).

Sirks, A. J. B. (2007). *The Theodosian Code: A Study* (Friedrichsdorf).

Smith, C. (1988). *Christians and Moors in Spain*, vol. 1 (Warminster).

Smith, R. P. (1860). *The Third Part of the Ecclesiastical History of John Bishop of Ephesus* (Oxford).

Somerville, R. and Brasington, B. C. (1998). *Prefaces to Canon Law Books in Latin Christianity: Selected Translations, 500–1245* (New Haven).

Sorabji, R. (1983). *Time, Creation and the Continuum: Theories in Antiquity and the Early Middle Ages* (London).

Sotinel, C. (2005). 'Emperors and Popes in the Sixth Century: The Western View', in Maas, 267–90.

Staniforth, M. (ed.) (1987). *Early Christian Writings* (Harmondsworth).

Stathakopoulos, D. (2000). 'The Justinianic Plague Revisited', *Byzantine and Modern Greek Studies* 24, 256–76.

Stein, E. (1949). *Histoire du Bas-Empire*, vol. 1 (Paris).

Stein, E. (1950). *Histoire du Bas-Empire*, vol. 2 (Paris).

Stein, P. (1999). *Roman Law in European History* (Cambridge).

Stewart, H. F. et al. (1918). *Boethius: Tractates, De Consolatione Philosophiae* (Cambridge, Mass.).

Stocking, R. (2000). *Bishops, Councils, and Consensus in the Visigothic Kingdom, 589–633* (Ann Arbor).

Story, J. (ed.) (2005a). *Charlemagne: Empire and Society* (Manchester).

Story, J. (2005b). 'Charlemagne and the Anglo-Saxons', in Story (2005a), 195–210.

Teillet, S. (1984). *Des Goths à la nation gothique: les origines de l'idée de nation en Occident du Ve au VIIe siècle* (Paris).

Thompson, A. and Gordley, J. (1993). *The Treatise on Laws: (Decretum DD 1–20)* (Washington DC).

Thompson, E. A. (1946). 'The Isaurians under Theodosius II', *Hermathena*, 18–31.

Thompson, E. A. (1969). *The Goths in Spain* (Oxford).

Thompson, E. A. (1982). *Romans and Barbarians: The Decline of the Western Empire* (Madison).

Thorpe, L. (1974), *Gregory of Tours: The History of the Franks* (London).

Tillmann, H. (1980). *Pope Innocent III* (Amsterdam).

Tuchman, B. (1979). *A Distant Mirror: The Calamitous 14th Century* (New York).

Turner, C. H. (1903). 'Chapters in the History of Latin MSS III: The Lyon-Petersburg MS of Councils', *Journal of Theological Studies* 4, 426–34.

Tyerman, C. (2006). *God's War: A New History of the Crusades* (London).

Ullmann, W. (1960). *The Medieval Papacy: St Thomas and Beyond* (London).

Ullmann, W. (1970). *Growth of Papal Government*, 3rd ed. (London).

Vessey, M. (1993), 'The Origins of the Collectio Sirmondiana', in *The Theodosian Code*, ed. I. N. Wood and J. Harries (London), 178–99.

Vives, J. (1963). *Concilios visigóticos e hispano-romanos* (Barcelona).

Waitz, G. (1911). *Einhardi Vita Karoli Magni*, 6th ed., MGH Scriptores rerum Germanicarum in usum scholarum (Hanover).

Wallace-Hadrill, J. M. (1982). *The Long-haired Kings* (Toronto).

Ward Perkins, B. (1984.). *From Classical Antiquity to the Middle Ages: Urban Public Building in Northern and Central Italy, AD 300–850* (Oxford).

Ward Perkins, B. (2005). *The Fall of Rome and the End of Civilization* (Oxford).

Watson, A. et al. (1998). *The Digest of Justinian* (Philadelphia).

Watt, J. A. (1999). 'The Papacy', in D. Abulafia (ed.), *The New Cambridge Medieval History*, vol. 5 (Cambridge), 107–63.

Werner, K. F. (1979). 'Kingdom and Principality in Twelfth Century France', in T. Reuter (ed.), *The Medieval Nobility: Studies on the Ruling Classes of France and Germany from the Sixth to the Twelfth Century* (Amsterdam), 243–90.

Werner, K. F. (1980). 'Missus-marchio-comes: entre l'administration centrale et l'administration locale de l'empire carolingien', in W. Paravicini and K. F. Werner (eds), *Histoire comparée de l'administration (IVe–XVIIIe siècle)*, Beihefte der Francia 9 (Munich), 191–239.

Whitby, L. M. (1985). 'Justinian's Bridge over the Sangarius and the Date of Procopius' *De aedeficiis*', *Journal of Hellenic Studies* 105, 129–48.

Whitby, L. M. (1986). 'Procopius and the Development of Roman Defences in Upper Mesopotamia, in H. Kennedy and P. Freeman (eds), *The Defence of the Roman and Byzantine Near East* (Oxford), 717–35.

Whitby, L. M. (1988). *The Emperor Maurice and his Historian: Theophylact Simocatta on Persian and Balkan Warfare* (Oxford).

Whitby, L. M. (2000). 'The Balkans and Greece, 420–602', in Cameron et al. (2000), 701–30.

Whitby, L. M., and Whitby, J. M. (1986). *The History of Theophylact Simocatta* (Oxford).

Whitby, L. M. and Whitby, J. M. (1989). *The Chronicon Paschale* (Liverpool).

Whitelock, D. (1996). *English Historical Documents, c.500–1042*, 2nd ed. (London).

Whittow, M. (1996). *The Making of Orthodox Byzantium, 600–1025* (London).

Wickham, C. J. (1981). *Early Medieval Italy: Central Power and Local Society, 400–1000* (London).

Wickham, C. J. (1993). 'La chute de Rome n'aura pas lieu. A propos d'un livre récent', *Le Moyen Age* 99, 107–26.

Wickham, C. J. (2005). *Framing the Early Middle Ages: Europe and the Mediterranean 400–800* (Oxford).

Wickham, C. J. (2009). *The Inheritance of Rome: A History of Europe from 400 to 1000* (London).

Williams, A. (1991). *The English and the Norman Conquest* (Woodbridge).

Wiseman, J. (1984). 'The City in Macedonia Secunda', in V. Popovic (ed.), *Villes et Peuplement dans l'Illyricum protobyzantin* (Rome), 289–313.

Wolfram, H. (1988). *History of the Goths*, trans. T. J. Dunlap (Berkeley).

Wollasch, J. (1999). 'Monasticism: the First Age of Reform', in Reuter (1999), 163–85.

Wood, I. N. (1994). *The Merovingian Kingdoms* (London).

Wood, I. N. (1995). 'Teutsind, Witlaic and the History of Merovingian Precaria', in W. Davies and P. Fouracre (eds), *Property and Power in the Early Middle Ages* (Cambridge), 31–52.

Wood, S. (2006). *The Proprietary Church in the Medieval West* (Oxford).

Wormald, P. (1999). *The Making of English Law: King Alfred to the Twelfth Century. Volume 1, Legislation and Its Limits* (Oxford).

Wright, F. A. (1993). *Liutprand of Cremona: The Embassy to Constantinople and Other Writings* (London).

Wright, R. (1982). *Late Latin and Early Romance in Spain and Carolingian France* (Liverpool).

Wright, R. (1996). *Latin and the Romance Languages in the Early Middle Ages* (Philadelphia).

ACKNOWLEDGEMENTS

It is a great pleasure to be able to acknowledge some of the debts – intellectual, practical, and personal – that I have incurred in writing this book. As always, the particular names that find mention here also have to stand in place of many others who should be mentioned but won't be: partly because a full list would be completely unmanageable and partly because the genesis of any lengthy book is in reality so convoluted that accurately reconstructing the debts which underlie it is in fact impossible.

I would like to thank, first, the Einstein Forum and Sander Evers, organizer of the current run of *Collectio Avellana* colloquia, for invitations to speak which have allowed me the chance to try out in more formal contexts versions of the arguments which underlie part four. The influence of my colleague and friend David d'Avray there is also profound. In part three, I am venturing into print on an area where I have only ever taught before, and my efforts are thoroughly dependent on a host of colleagues, from whom I have learned a great deal over the years, though I would particularly single out here Wendy Davies and Jinty Nelson with whom I have had the privilege of working directly alongside at different points in my career. Part one reflects my own long-standing obsessions with things Gothic, but my interests in Procopius and Justinian can be traced back directly to undergraduate days and particularly the combined influence of James Howard Johnston and Michael Whitby. My debt to these and a host of other scholars, whether they feature much in the footnotes or only in my head, is massive and my gratitude is entirely genuine.

I would also like to thank my agent, Felicity Bryan, and her team for all the encouragement they have given me through the writing process. Felicity's cheerful, never-say-die attitude, in particular, is always an enormous tonic. Equally important, my editor at Macmillan, Georgina Morley, has been patient and endlessly helpful throughout, not least when dealing with illustrations, and the rest of the production team – particularly Nicholas Blake, Tania Wilde, and my copy-editor David Milner – have both saved what follows from innumerable errors and brought it to completion with maximum efficiency and despatch. I really am enormously grateful.

Last, but resoundingly not least, it gives me great pleasure to thank Gail, William, and Nathaniel who have vicariously to share in the intense and lengthy process that is writing. I can only apologize for my many periods of fatigue and irritability, but I'm so happy that the project gave us an excellent excuse to share a wonderful trip to Istanbul. Tookie, Custance, Percy, Nottle and Bella – it could almost but not quite – go without saying more than paid for their keep by providing throughout an endless run of cheering distractions, and, in one case, an almost constant insistence on the importance of taking healthy exercise.

INDEX

Page numbers in *italics* refers to a figure

Abbo 223, 225
Abd ar-Rahman 218, 219
Acacian schism 84–6, 88, 107, 316, 318, 406
Acacius, Patriarch of Constantinople 84–5, 306
Accursius 397–8
Ad Decimum, battle of (533) 143–4, 147
Adaloald 214
Admonitio Generalis 334, 336, 338, 345, 355
Africa *see* North Africa; Vandal Africa
Agilulf, King 214
Agobard, Archbishop of Lyons 358
Aistulf 230–1, 323
Alamannia/Alamanni 70, 77, 166, 223
Alans 168 *see also* Vandal–Alans
Alaric II, King 70, 75, 78, 93
Alberic II 370, 371
Alboin, King 19, 185
Alcuin 338, 339
Alexander II, Pope 384–5, 386–7
Alexander III, Pope 401
Alexandria, church of 308
Aligern 166
Amal dynasty 5–9, *10* 208
Amalafrida (Theoderic's daughter) 94
Amalafrida (Theoderic's sister) 74, 139
Amalaric 93, 94
Amalasuentha 81, 82–3, 92, 150–1
Anastasius, Emperor 75, 79, 85, 110, 126, 316, 365
    Theoderic's letter to 3–4, 58, 60, 71, 72, 74, 78, 97
Anglo-Saxon England 324, 325, 326
    church councils 328–9
Ansegius 254
Anselm the Younger 395
Antioch 48
    capture of by Persians (540) 159–60
    church of 308
Aquitaine/Aquitanians 221, 222, 227, 231, 251
Arcadius, Emperor 123

archbishops 304, 343, 345, 349–50, 355–6
Ardaburius 22
Ariadne (Leo's daughter) 22, 34
Arian dispute 305, 306, 310
Arians/Arianism 58, 97, 212
Armatus 37–8, 49
Armenians 159
armies
    Carolingian 255–6
    East Roman 24, 147
    of Theoderic 63, 67–8, 99–101
Arminius xii
Arnulf the Bad 281
Arnulf of Carinthia 267, 269, 283
Aspar 21–2, 23, 25, 34
assemblies, annual 258
Athalaric 5, 86, 92, 93, 94, 95, 139, 149–50, 151
Athanaius, Bishop of Alexandria 313
Athaulf, King 118
Attila the Hun xiv, 6, 7, 14, 23, 140, 180, 199, 208
Audefleda 81
Augustine of Hippo: *City of God* 313
Austrasia/Austrasians 213, 216, 221, 222, 225, 229
Auximum 157, 163
Avars 179–88, 197, 238
    Balkan campaigns 187–8
    conquest of by Charlemagne 238
    relations with East Romans 183–4, 202
    rise and expansion 181, *182*, 186–7
    and siege of Constantinople (626) 195–6
    war against the Franks 184
Avitus, Bishop of Vienne 76

Bahram 193
Balkans 32, 172–3, 181, 196, 197, 290
    Bulgar attack on (539) 173
    Slavicization of large parts 187–8
Bartolomaius Brixiensis 399
Basiliscus, Emperor 36, 37–8
Basina 209, 211

Bavaria 238, 281, 285
Becket, Thomas 393, 400
Bede, Venerable 325, 326
Belisarius, General 108, 111, 178
    and conquest of Sicily 152
    and expedition against Vandal Africa 141,
        142, 144, 145
    and Italian war 155, 156–7, 158–9, 160, 163
    made consul-delegate 145
    and Nika revolt 133–4, 136, 141
Benedict of Aniane 377
Benedict VIII, Pope 371, 374, 375–6, 380
Benedict IX, Pope 371–2, 380
Benedict X, Pope 384
Benedictus Levita 353, 354
Benevento 237–8
Beremund 7, 83, 93
Bernard of Clairvaux 393
Bernard (Pippin of Italy's son) 261
Beroia (Aleppo) 159
Betrada 228
Bible 336, 337
    Book of Revelation 188
bishops 303, 304–5, 311–12, 327–8, 343, 356
Bittigur Huns 99
Black Death 175, 176
Boethius 87, 88–9, 90, 91–2, 96–7, 98
Bohemia 290
Bologna 399–400
Bologna law school 397, 398
Boniface 323
Book of Histories of the Franks 216
Boso of Provence 268, 271
Bulgars 187
Burgundians 70, 76, 80–1, 94–5, 97, 211
Busta Gallorum, battle of (552) 165
Butilinus 166
Byzacena 171
Byzantine expeditionary force (BEF) 141–2

Cadmus 41
Caesarea 108, 195
Caesarius, Bishop of Arles 80, 98, 327
Callinicum 131
Callistus II, Pope 392
canon law 395–404
Canstatt massacre (746) 227
Canterbury 329
Capitula Angilramni 353
capitularies 254, 355
Caricingrad 105–7, 106, 110
Carloman (son of Charles the Bald) 266, 267

Carloman (son of Charles Martel) 226, 227,
    229, 231, 232
Carloman (son of Louis the German) 266
Carolingian correctio 335–48, 351, 354, 355, 368
Carolingian minuscule 340
Carolingian Renaissance 339–40, 357
Carolingians/Carolingian Empire 215, 270
    army 255–6
    campaigns 287
    checking 256
    crowning of first monarch (Pippin) 227–9
    decline of influence of monarchs in West
        Francia 269, 270
    demise and reasons 249–50, 252, 408
    divisions of the 9th century 264–5
    emergence of local elites' independence
        278–9
    government of and bureaucracy 252–6
    halting of expansion and reasons 289–91
    intellectual centres 347
    and legal reform 253–4
    relations between elites and rulers 256–7,
        271–4
    replacement of Merovingians by 216–17
    rise of 220, 221
    sources of financial muscle 279–80
    succession battles and intra-familial disputes
        221, 225–9, 231–2, 259–67, 274
    taxation system 275, 276–7, 279, 289
    and Viking raiding 267, 273
    see also individual emperors
Carthage 143, 178
    Roman conquest (533) 144
    Vandal conquest of (439) 138, 170–1
Casilinum, battle of (554) 166
Cassiodorus 5, 30, 33, 52, 53–5, 64, 69, 78, 91,
        95, 169
    Chronicle 87
    lost history of 68, 69
    Variae 53–4, 55, 60–1, 64, 69, 70, 76, 90,
        158, 170
castles 272–3
Cathars 413
cathedral schools 375, 376–7, 377
cathedrals 346, 376–7, 408
Catholic Europe (1000) 284
Catholicism
    and Arians 97–8
    and kings 324–30
    Vandal hostility towards 138
    and Visigoths 324, 325, 328
Cavades 124, 125, 129, 131
cavalry, heavy armoured 219, 221

Chalcedon, Council of (451) 84, 197, 314, 317, 318, 319
chariot racing/charioteers 131–2
Charlemagne xvi, 231–59, 330–48, 403, 406, 407
    appearance and height 248
    birth 228
    conquest of Lombard kingdom 234–5, 237, 239, 241, 243
    conquest of the Saxons and Avars 238
    conquests and territories controlled 237–8
    and Constantinople 240
    crowned Emperor (800) 207–8, 242, 246–7, 299, 330, 332
    donations to monasteries and cathedrals 340–1
    grants of financial rights given to the papacy 236–7
    and iconoclasm 240, 332
    imperial ambitions 238–42, 243–6
    increasing availability and distribution of religious texts 336–41, 342
    and Latin 338–9
    and legal reform 253
    and Leo III 245–6, 302, 342–3
    On the Study of Letters 337–8
    and papacy 241–2, 330–1, 332–3, 352, 361
    portrayal of in Karolus Magnus et Leo Papa 301–3
    religious policies and reform 244, 252, 332–48, 408
    succession battle 231–2
    and succession issue 231–2, 248–9, 262
    and tithing 341
Charles the Bald 250, 254, 255, 260, 261, 262, 263, 266, 267, 270, 271, 358, 368–9, 369
Charles the Fat 266, 267, 270
Charles Martel ('the Hammer') 218–26, 229, 261
    and battle of Poitiers 218
    death and succession 225–6
    putting Church land into lay hands 219, 224
    reasons for success 224–5
    rise to power and expansion of control 221–4
Charles the Simple 249, 268, 269
Charles the Younger 248–9
Childebrand 221
Childeric 11, 70, 208–9
Childeric III 226
Chilperic II 222
Chosroes I 124, 125, 159, 164, 192, 202
Chosroes II 193, 194, 195, 196

Christianity 56, 58, 119, 303, 407
    doctrinal disputes 305–6, 310–11
    schism in 83–6 see also Acacian schism
Church councils 326
    Anglo-Saxon England 328–9
    Frankish 326–7
    Visigothic 328
Church of Hagia Sophia (Constantinople) 109, 135, 177
Church of the Holy Apostles (Constantinople) 15, 17
churches, lay ownership of 391
civitates 275, 276, 278
Clement I, Pope 303, 307
Clement II, Pope 381, 387
Clement III, Pope 392
Clementine Recognitions 307, 309, 406
clergy
    Charlemagne's reform of 343–4
    and reform councils 343–4
clerical marriage 374–5, 382
Clermont, synod of (1095) 394
Clovis 11, 35, 70, 71, 76–7, 78, 81–2, 97, 208, 209–12, 326
Cluny monastery (Burgundy) 377, 378, 381, 386–7, 393
Codex Carolinus 234, 241, 246
Collectio decretorum Pontificum Romanorum 316–17
Concordat of Worms 392
Conrad I of Franconia, Duke 281, 284
Constantine, Emperor 4, 12, 313
    conversion of to Christianity 304, 306, 314
    Donation of see Donation of Constantine
Constantine XI 14
Constantinople xi, xvi, 12–20, 29, 33, 95, 189–90, 238, 239–40
    ceremonial centre of 134
    and Charlemagne 240
    and Constantine 12
    and Constantius II 13
    declared the New Rome (381) 308
    decline in population in seventh century 190
    defence structures 13–14
    factors explaining political power 13
    fall of (1453) 14
    harbours 15
    Justin's rule 95
    Justinian's structures 109
    map 16
    monuments 15, 17

Constantinople (cont.)
    murder of Aspar and uprising by Thracian
        Goths 21–2, 23, 25, 34
    Nika riots (532) 132–6, 140, 145
    open-air reservoirs 15
    political struggles within 33–6, 48–9
    relations with papacy 318–24
    relations with Theoderic 72–4, 79, 83–7,
        95–6, 97–8
    return of Zeno to power 37–8
    scale and splendour of 14–15
    siege of (626) 195–6
    siege of (717–18) 321
    Strabo's assault on (481) 45
Constantinople, Council of (553) 314, 319
Constantius II, Emperor 13, 125, 310, 313
Constitutio Romana 364
Constitutio Tanta (533) 127, 128–9
Cornelius, Pope 304
Corsica 237
Crescentii clan 370–1, 373, 374
crusading movement 409
Cunimund 185
curia 393, 406
Cutrigurs 181, 183
Cyril and Methodius 369

Dagobert I 217
Dalmatia 75, 152
Damasus I, Pope 307, 312
Damasus II 381
Dara 131, 151, 192
Dara fortress 110
decretals see papal decretals
Denis the Little see Dionysius Exiguus
Desiderius, King 231–2, 234, 235
Digest 146, 396, 397
Dionysio-Hadriana 332, 338, 354
Dionysius Exiguus 316, 317, 327, 328, 354
Divisio Regnorum 248–9
doctrinal disputes 305–6, 310–11
Domesday Book 64
Domitian 114–15
Donation of Constantine 234–5, 236, 237, 241–2,
    246, 330, 356, 357, 375, 383, 393, 395
Donatist dispute 306, 311
donatives 65, 67
Drogo 222, 227, 228, 229

East Francia 255, 270, 280, 282–7, 376
    reasons for lack of political fragmentation
        283–4
East Roman Empire 81, 102, 196–7

army of 24, 147
and Avars 183–4, 202
collapse of economy 200
conquest of by Muslims 202, 230, 239,
    319–20, 321
impact of rise of Islam on 200
and Italy 91
loss of territories 108
map 130
peace treaty with Persians (591) 193
reconstruction of under Heraclius 196–7
taxation 321–2, 323
wars with Persia 123, 129–31, 136, 159–60,
    162, 163, 164, 190–3, 194–6, 202–3
see also Constantinople
ecclesiastical appointments 312, 390–3 see also
    Investiture Controversy
ecumenical councils 304, 309, 310, 316
Egypt 188, 313
    Persian invasion (621) 195
Einhard 207, 215, 216, 217, 242, 243, 248
Eleutherius 365
emperors 407
    and Christian doctrine 309–11
    closeness of relationship with God 312–13
    enforcing general standards of practice for
        clergy and laity 311
    as functioning head of Christian Church
        312
    religious authority of 312–15
    and senior ecclesiastical appointments 312
empire, end of 292–5
Engelbert 260
Ennodius 59–60, 66
Ephesus 188, 189, 190, 195
Epidamnus 40, 43
Epiphanius, Bishop of Milan 63
episcopal courts 311–12
episcopal statutes 344–5
Eraric 162
Euboia 34
Eudo, Duke of Aquitaine 218, 221, 222, 224
Eugenius II, Pope 364
Eugenius III, Pope 401
Euric, King 32
Europe, creation of 292–5
Eusebius of Caesarea, Bishop 56, 314
Eutharic 83, 86, 92, 93, 125, 149

Faenza, battle of (541–2) 162
filoque clause 332–3
First Crusade 394
foederati 24, 33, 34, 48, 63

Fontenoy, battle of 260, 262
Formosus, Pope
    trial of (897) 361–3, 365–6
Fourth Lateran Council (1215) 349–51, 395,
    402, 404, 410, 411–12
Franconia 280, 281
Frankfurt, Council of 240, 241, 332
Franks xiv, 70, 77, 97, 98, 101, 163
    Christian Church 326–8
    episcopal appointments and kings of 326
    in Gaul 70
    rise and expansion of 210 211–13
    war against the Avars 184
    see also Carolingians; Merovingians
Fredegar 209, 226
Frisians 221–2, 223

Gallic crisis (506–7) 70, 75–8
Gaul 69–70
    Christian Church of Frankish 326–7
    Pippin's focus on securing control of 231
Geiseric 139, 168
Gelasius I, Pope 316, 318, 406
Gelimer 139, 141, 142, 144, 145
Gensemund 7, 93
Gepids 50, 75, 181
    conflict with the Lombards 184–5, 186
Gerberga 232
Gerbold, Bishop 344
Germanus 164
Gesalic 78
Getica see Jordanes
Ghassanids 198
Gibbon, Edward 218–19
Glossa Ordinaria 397–8, 399, 400
Godas 141, 142
Godfather, The 18
Godomar 94
Goths/Gothic kingdom 6
    2,000th anniversary 68–80
    conquest of by East Roman forces 54, 55
    see also Ostrogoths; Pannonian Goths;
        Visigoths
grammarians 337, 338–9
Gratian 398, 398–9, 400–1
Greeks, ancient 118
Gregorianus 120
Gregory I (the Great), Pope 317, 318, 319, 386
    Forty Homilies on the Gospels 344
Gregory II, Pope 322, 323
Gregory III, Pope 323
Gregory IV, Pope 358
Gregory V, Pope 375

Gregory VI, Pope 380
Gregory VII, Pope (Hildebrand) 382, 388–92,
    394, 395
Gregory IX, Pope 401
Gregory of Tours, Bishop 11, 212, 215, 326
    Histories 211
Greuthungi 29
Grifo 226, 228–9
Grimoald 222
Gundobad 70–1, 76, 77
Guntram 327

Hadrian I, Pope 232, 234, 236–7, 240, 244, 329,
    331
Hadrian II, Pope 360, 364–5
Hadrian IV, Pope 401
Harmony of Discordant Canons 398–401
Henotikon 316
Henry the Fowler 281
Henry I, Emperor 284, 285, 287
Henry II, Emperor 371, 374, 375–6, 377, 380,
    393
Henry III, Emperor 380–1, 384
Henry IV, King 382, 385, 389–92
Henry V, King 392
Heraclius 196
Hermogenianus 120
Heruli 160
Hilarianus 32, 34
Hildebrand see Gregory VII, Pope
Hilderic, King 94, 97, 138–9
Hincmar, Archbishop of Rheims 357, 359, 369
Hincmar, Bishop of Laon 359
Hispana 328
Holy Roman Empire 281, 282, 379
Honorius I, Pope 319
Honorius II, Pope 384
Hormisdas IV, shah 193
Hormisdas, Pope 85
Hugh Capet 249
Hugh (Drogo's son) 222, 224
Humbert 383–4
Huneric 138–9
Hunimund 93
Hunnic Empire xiv, 6, 8, 199, 208
Hunoald 231
Huns xv–xvi
Hypatius 125, 133, 146

iconoclasm 239–40, 321–2, 332
Ignatius of Antioch 303
Ildebadus 160–2, 162
Illus, General 36, 37, 38, 41, 42, 48–9

Indulf 163, 166
Innocent I, Pope 305
Innocent III, Pope 350–1, 410, 413
Investiture Controversy 390, 393, 395, 408
Irene, Empress 240
Irnerius 397
Isauria/Isaurians 22, 25, 34, 36
Isidore Mercator 353
Isidore of Seville 353
Islam 188, 197, 294
   conquering of East Roman Empire 203, 320
   conquests 320
   and Muhammad 199
   rise of 197–9, 200, 201, 204, 292
   split between Sunni and Shia 198
   see also Muslims
Italian war 152–3, 154–66, 186
   battle of Busta Gallorum (552) 165
   battle of Faenza (541–2) 162
   destruction of Goths by Roman army
      164–6
   East Roman successes 157–8
   effects of 169–70, 172
   establishment of imperial control 166
   fall of Naples 155–6
   fall of Ravenna 158–9
   Gothic revolt and victories under Totila
      162–4
   losses for population 169
   map of conquest 161
   refusal of some Gothic leaders to surrender
      to East Romans 160
   rejection of Totila's approaches by Justinian
      164
   sieges of Rome during 156–7, 163
Italy 50, 149, 178–9, 230
   in 18th century 233
   conquest of by Justinian see Italian War
   East Roman rule 178
   invasion of by East Roman forces 65, 101
   and Lombards 178, 185–6, 230
   rule of by Theoderic see Theoderic
   succession battles after Theoderic's death
      149–51
Ivo of Chartres 395–6, 398

James (brother of Jesus) 307
Jerusalem 195, 308
Johannes Teutonicus 399
John of Gaunt 408
John I, Pope 87, 95
John X, Pope 363
John XII, Pope 371, 373–4

John XIII, Pope 374
John XVI, Pope 363
Jordanes 5, 19, 23, 29–30, 32, 46, 68–9
   Getica 5, 6, 68, 83
Julian, Emperor 15, 125–6, 243
jurisconsult writings 119, 121–2, 127, 128
Justin, Emperor 85, 86, 89, 95, 96, 107, 125, 126
Justin II, Emperor 175, 183, 186, 191–2, 201,
      203
Justinian I, Emperor xvi, 102, 105–79, 321
   accession to throne (527) 107, 117
   acquisition of Sicily (535) 137, 152
   and Avars 183, 187
   conquest of Italy see Italian War
   conquest of Vandal Africa (533) 108, 115,
      137, 138, 141–7, 148 177
   construction works 109–10
   death 177
   Deo Auctore 118, 121, 123
   foreign policy 181
   impact and costs of conquest strategy
      169–73, 176–9, 201
   insecurity underlying hold on power 126–7
   legacy of 107–8, 200–4
   marriage 112
   Nika riot against and crushing of 132–6,
      140, 145
   plague during reign of 175–6
   portrayal of in Anekdota 111–13, 114–15,
      155
   reform of Roman law 107, 117–23, 127–9,
      146, 396–7
   taxation policy 173–5, 186
   and wars of conquest in the West 137–8,
      142, 152, 166–7
   wars against Persia 124, 125, 131, 162, 163,
      164

Karolus Magnus et Leo Papa 301–3, 342–3
Kent (England) 288, 328–9, 411

Lakhmids 198
Lateran Council
   Fourth (1215) 349–51, 395, 402, 404, 410,
      411–12
   Second (1139) 398
Latin 337, 345, 357
   Charlemagne's emphasis on learning
      'accurate' 338–9
Laurentian schism 59
Lausanne, Treaty of (1923) 188
legates 386, 387, 394
Leo I, Emperor 22, 25, 33, 35

Leo I, Pope 84, 307, 308, 309, 324
Leo II, Emperor 22, 35
Leo III, Pope 244–6, 299, 301, 321–2, 331
    and Charlemagne 207–8, 242, 245–7, 299,
        302, 330, 332, 342–3
    declaration of iconoclasm 321–2
    donations made by 331–2
    relations with Constantinople 245–6, 302,
        342–3
Leo IV, Pope 364
Leo VII, Pope 371
Leo VIII, Pope 374
Leo IX, Pope 380–4, 391
Liber Diurnus 394
Liber Extra 401, 402
Liber Pontificalis 331, 367, 368
Liberius 65, 66, 67, 89, 91
Lindisfarne Gospels 336
Liutprand, King 230, 323, 363
Liuvigild, King 325
Lombards 178, 181, 214, 230, 319, 324–5
    conflict with the Gepids 184–5, 186
    conquest of by Charlemagne 234–5, 237,
        239, 241, 243
    Italian campaign 178, 185–6, 214, 230
    religious status 214
    and Rome 230–1, 232, 235, 317
Longinus (Zeno's brother) 37
Lorraine 281, 350
Lothar 250, 252, 261, 262, 263, 290–1, 358
Lothar II 263, 268, 360, 369, 406
Louis the Blind 370
Louis the Child 269, 280, 281, 283, 285
Louis the German 250, 251, 261, 262, 263, 266,
        270, 280, 282, 369
Louis Philippe 218
Louis the Pious 236, 248–9, 250–2, 257, 260,
        261, 274, 290–1, 341–2, 343
Louis II of Italy 266
Louis the Stammerer 266, 267, 268
Louis the Younger 263, 266

Magyars 285
Malchus 40–1, 44, 45–6
Marcellinus, Ammianus 310
Marcian, Emperor 17, 22, 84, 314
Marcian (grandson) 45
marriage, clerical 374–5, 382
Martin I, Pope 317, 319
Martyropolis 192
Matasuentha 164
Maurice, Emperor 192, 193, 194, 201, 202, 203
Maurontius 223

Menander 183
Mercian kings 328–9
Merovingians 9, 11, 18, 208–16, 271, 272, 280,
        287–8
    core components of kingdom 213
    hampering of pretensions to claim Western
        imperial title 213–14
    later 215–18
    political struggles 214
    replacement of by Carolingians 216–18
    rise of 208–13
    and taxation 276–8
Mesopotamia 190, 191, 192
Milan 389
missi 256
Momigliano, Arnaldo 88, 89, 91
monasteries 341–2, 346, 374, 377, 382, 408
    libraries 346
    under papal protection 378–9
Monophysite dispute 306
Monothelitism 317, 319
Montaillou (France) 413
Monte Cassino, monastery of 391
Moors 139, 145, 171
Moravia 283, 285, 369
Muhammad 198, 199, 201
Mundus 135, 136
Muslims 218, 239
    conquest of Christian territories by 188–9,
        190, 230
    conquest of East Roman territories 202,
        230, 239, 319–20, 321

Naissus (Niš) 32
Naples 155, 178
Narses, General 133, 136, 164–5, 166, 185
Nepos, Julius 43–4
Nestorius 84
Neustria/Neustrians 216, 221, 222, 223
New Testament 336
Nicaea, Council of (325) 58, 304, 309, 310
Nicene Creed 333
Nicholas I, Pope 359–60, 361, 364, 368
Nicholas II, Pope 384–5
Nika riot (532) 132–6, 140, 145
Nisibis 131, 192
nomads 180–1
Normans 384, 385
North Africa 170–2, 177–8
    confrontation with the Moors 171
    falls into Arab hands 178
    impact of Roman conquest of Vandals
        171–2, 177–8

North Africa (*cont.*)
    see also Vandal Africa
Numidia 171

Odo, King 249, 267–8
Odo of Cluny 371
Odovacar xiii, xvi–xvii, 38, 44, 50, 50–1, 66
Offa, King 238, 328–9
Onoulphus 38–9
Orange, Council of (529) 98
Ordinatio Imperii 250, 251
Orestes 43
Ostrogoths 6, 99
Osuine 150
Oswy, King 325
Otto I 269, 281, 282, 283, 285, 373–4
Otto II 281
Otto III 374, 375
Ottoman Empire 190
Ottonians 280, 280–91, 292, 293
    defeat of Magyars 285
    expansionary warfare 286–7
    halting of eastwards expansion 288–9
    silver coinage 286
    source of wealth 286–7

pagus, count of the 255, 256
Palestine 188, 195
Palmyra 197
Pannonia II 75
Pannonian Goths 6, 7, 18, 21, 23, 25, 168
    composition of groups moving 28
    and compromise (473) 34
    journey to Italy 50–1
    move from Euboia to Thracian Plain 37
    movement of on to East Roman soil under
        Theoderic 25–32, *31* 32–3, 105
    non-aggression pact with Thracian Goths
        41
    origins 99
    rivalry with Thracian Goths 33, 35, 37
    settlement in Euboia 34, 37
    split caused over move on to Eastern
        Roman soil 29–30, 32
    unification with Thracian Goths 47–8, 99
Panormia 396
papacy 304, 304–8, 315–16, 315–30
    administrative reforms of 393–4
    barbarian popes 373–88, 403
    and Charlemagne 241–2, 330–1, 332–3, 352,
        361
    Charlemagne's grant to 236–7

confrontation between Gregory VII and
        Henry IV over simony 389–90
    and doctrine 309
    and *Donation of Constantine* see *Donation of
        Constantine*
    fake vision of authority in *Pseudo-Isidore*
        353–67
    final entrenchment of authority over
        Western Christendom 393–4
    financial assets and wealth 366
    forging of authority 351–61
    formal protection of monasteries 378–9
    functions and responsibilities of popes 300,
        309, 323, 407
    and Gregory VII's reforms 388–92
    highlights 315–18
    impact of decline of empire on 372–3
    independence from Holy Roman Empire
        402
    internal divisions and violent struggles
        within 362–70, 372
    making saints 379
    in the medieval ages 409
    and Otto III 374, 375
    peace deal with Normans 385
    pornocratic era 361–73, 378
    reform in papal election procedure (1059)
        385
    reforms of Innocent III 350–1, 410
    reforms by Leo IX 381–4
    reforms by Nicholas II and Alexander II
        384–7
    relations with emperors/empire 318–24,
        368–9, 373–6, 379, 381, 388
    renovation and building in Rome 331
    strengthening of claims to Christian
        religious authority 304–8
    and Theophylact and Crescentii clans 370–1
    see also individual popes
papal decretals 305, 308, 311, 316, 324, 354,
        401, 402, 406
papal elections 312
papal letters, formal registration of 385–8
Paschal I, Pope 364
Paschal II, Pope 393
Paul, St 303
Paul the Deacon 335, 344
Pavia 51, 234
    synod (1022) 376
Persia/Persians 123–6, 188, 201
    capture of Antioch (540) 159–60
    'Eternal Peace' made with by Justinian (532)
        140

map *130*
peace treaty with Romans (591) 193, 194
succession disputes 193–4
wars against East Romans 123, 124, 125,
    129–31, 136, 159–60, 162, 163, 164,
    19–3, 194–6, 202–3
Western Turk attacks on 196
withdrawal from conquered Roman
    provinces 196
Perugia 323
Peter, St 298, 299–300, 303, 307, 405
Peter Damian 375, 382, 386–8
Peter the Patrician 151–2
Phocas 194
Piast dynasty 293
Picenum 156
Pippin the Hunchback 259
Pippin of Italy (son of Charlemagne) 221,
    248–9, 251
Pippin (son of Louis the Pious) 250
Pippin (the Short) (Charlemagne's father) 216,
    225, 227, 230–1, 261, 262–3, 330
Pius XII, Pope 299
plague, Justinianic 175–6, 180
Plectrude 221
Poitiers, battle of (732/733) 218–19
Poland 293
Pompeius 135, 146
primogeniture 18
Probus 132
Procopius 94, 108–17, 136, 142, 150, 154, 169,
    173–4, 213
   Anekdota 110–16, 151, 173
   Buildings 109–10, 113, 172
   Wars 108–9, 111, 133, 136, 141, 147
Proculus 124, 125
Protector, Menander 180
Pseudo-Isidore 353–68, 372, 378, 386, 395, 399,
    406, 407
Pudentius 141

Radbod, King 221–2
Ragnaris 166
Ravenna 51, 54, 58, 65, 78, 178
  fall of (540) 55, 158–9
Ravenna, Archbishop of 368
Reccared 325
Recitach 46–7
reform councils 336, 343–4
Regino of Prum 268–9, 360
religious texts: increasing availability and
    distribution of by Charlemagne 336–41,
    342

Republic of St Peter 230, 322, 364, 365, 366,
    372
Rheims, reform council at (1049) 383
Ridda wars 199
Rimini 157
Robert the Strong 272, 274
Roman Empire 56, 405, 410
  armies 24, 147
  division of into *civitates* 275
  taxation 275–6, 279
  see also East Roman Empire
Roman law 396, 403
  contemporary school of 399
  Justinian's reform of 107, 117–23, 127–9,
    146, 396–7
  rediscovery of Justinianic texts of 396–8
  Theoderic's commitment to 60, 63
Roman Massbook 339
Romanness 55–6
Rome 170, 178
  congregation of 303–4
  continuing psychological dominance 3
  foundation of 80
  independence of environs *see* Republic of St
    Peter
  and Lombards 230–1, 232, 235, 317
  reoccupation of by Romans (547) 163
  sieges of during Italian War 163, 171
  see also papacy
Romney Marsh (Kent) 411, 413
Romulus Augustulus, Emperor 38, 43–4, 69
Rosamund 19, 185
Rothad, Bishop of Soissons 359
royal fisc 270–1
Rufinus 307
Rugi 51, 64, 99, 100, 162
Rule of Benedict 341–2

St Peter's Church (Rome) 299–300
saints, making of by papacy 379
Salian dynasty 281, 282
Sardinia 141, 142
Sardis 188, 189, 190
Sarmatians 22–3, 25, 50
Sasanian dynasty 123
Savia 75
Saxons/Saxony 280, 286, 287
  conquest of by Charlemagne 238
Sciri 25, 39
Scupi (Skopje) 105
Senigallia medallion 81
Septimania 223, 231
Sergeric 94

Sergius II, Pope 364
Sergius III, Pope 366–7
Sicily 137, 177
    capture of by East Romans 152, 177
Sigibert, King 184, 186
Sigismund 94
Simocatta, Theophylact 179
simony 374, 377, 380, 382, 383, 389
Singidunum 22, 23, 25, 32
Sirmium 75, 184
Sixtus 401
slaves 66, 162, 169, 289, 317
Slavs xv, 181, 183, 187, 196, 197, 288
Spain 218, 238, 289
Spoleto 178, 185, 237–8, 323
Spoleto, Duke of 230
Staffordshire hoard 224
Stalin, J. 409
Stephen II, Pope 229, 230–1, 232, 236
Stephen V, Pope 367, 369
Stephen VII, Pope 361–2, 365–6
Stephen IX, Pope 384
Strabo 25, 34, 35, 38, 39, 40–1, 42, 44, 45–6, 47
Suetonius 243
Suevi 23, 25
Swabia 280
Syagrius 211
Sylvester I, Pope 234, 235, 237, 242, 246, 356
Sylvester II, Pope 375
Sylvester III, Pope 380
Symmachus 87, 88, 90, 91, 98
Syria 188

taxation 173–5, 186, 270–80, 321–2
    Carolingian 275, 276–7, 279, 289
    East Roman Empire 321–2, 323
    and Justinian's wars 176
    Merovingian 276–8
    Roman Empire 275–6, 279
    and wars 173
Teias 165
Tertry, battle of (687) 225
Tervingi 29
Teutberga 263, 268, 360
Teutoburg Forest, Battle of (AD 9) xii, 101
Tharsamund 74–5
Theodahad 92–3, 96, 150–2, 155
Theoderic xvi, 3–102, 168, 169, 208, 211, 212
    and Acacian schism 84–6, 88
    appointment as senior imperial general and
        consul designate 47
    army of 63, 67–8, 99–101
    betrayal of by Zeno and decision not to
        fight Thracian Goths/Strabo 40–2,
        47
    and Burgundians 80–1
    Cassiodorus's portrayal of as a 'philosopher
        wearing purple' 52–3
    childhood and early years 4–5, 14
    and Christianity 17, 58–9
    commitment to Roman law 60, 63
    death (526) 54, 87, 97
    and death of Eutharic 92–4
    diplomatic marriage alliances made 69
    downfall and roots to failure 87, 88–99
    elimination of Thracian Goths 47–8
    entry into Rome (500) 58, 59
    establishing legitimacy as potential leader
        22–3
    expansion of kingdom 75–9, 80, 81
    expedition against Sarmathians in
        Singidunum 22–3, 25, 32
    foreign policy 69–71
    and Gaul 69–71, 75–8
    genealogy and family history 5–9, 10
    Italian palaces 58
    journey to Italy with wagon trains and
        battles against Odovacar's army
        50–1, 75
    killing of Odovacar and becomes ruler of
        Italy 51, 52, 54
    kingship passes to after death of Thiudimer
        37
    last years 88–102
    letter to Anastasius 3–4, 58, 60, 71, 72, 74,
        78, 97
    moves Pannonian Goths on to East Roman
        soil as direct replacements of
        Thracians 25–30, 32–3
    recognition of choice of heir 86–7, 91
    relations with Catholic Church 59–60, 61–2,
        86, 87, 212
    relations with Constantinople 72–4, 79,
        83–7, 95–6, 97–8
    relations with Roman landowning elites
        62–3
    reward system and settlement process 64–7,
        100
    Roman education 20
    Romanness of 4, 21, 55, 56, 58–60, 61–8,
        68, 69, 72, 79
    seizure of Epidamnus (479) 43
    self-presentation of 58, 62, 71
    sent as hostage to Constantinople when

a child (461) 4–5, 9, 14, 17, 19–20, 58
and succession issue 81–3, 86, 92–3, 96, 97, 125
territorial extent and hegemony 97
and Thracian Goths 39–40
upbringing 17–18, 19
and Vandal Africa 74–5, 139
and Vandals 79
and Visigothic kingdom 75–7
Western Empire 57
and Zeno 37, 39, 46, 47, 48, 49–50, 72–3
Theodimund 30
Theodora, Empress 111, 112, 114, 133, 135–6
Theodore of Tarsus 317
Theodosian Code (438) 120–1, 311
Theodosius I, Emperor 15, 23, 120
Theodosius II, Emperor 123, 124
Theodulf, Bishop 344
Theophylact clan 370
Thessalonica 32, 34, 107
Theudebert 213
Theuderic IV 224
Theudis 93, 93–4
Theudoald 221, 222, 223, 225, 226
Thietgaud of Trier, Archbishop 357, 358–9
Thiudimer 6, 19, 21, 26, 30, 32, 36–7
Thorismund 93
Thracian Goths 22, 24, 34–5, 37, 38
    close relations with court 25
    death of Strabo and succession 46–7
    murder of Recitach by Theoderic 47
    non-aggression pact with Pannonian Goths 41
    origins 99
    privileged position of in East Roman polity 24–5
    revolt of after murder of Aspar 21–2, 24, 25, 34
    size of 39
    unification with Pannonian Goths 47–8, 99
Thrasamund, King 74–5, 78, 79, 94, 138
Thyatira 188
Tiflis 196
tithing 341
Toledo, Third Council of (589) 214, 325
Tome of Leo 309
Totila 162, 163–4, 165
Tournai 209
Tribonian 121, 128, 129, 132, 146, 396
Tricamarum, battle of (533) 144–5, 147
Troglita, John 171, 179
True Cross 195, 196

Tuluin 93, 94, 150
Tusculani 373, 374

Ulrich, Bishop of 379
Urais 157–8, 160
Urban II 393, 394
Utigurs 181, 183

Vadamerca 19
Valamer 6–7, 8–9, 11, 17–18, 19, 21, 23, 39, 208–9
Valentinian III 324
Valeria, Emperor 123
Vandal Africa 62, 138, 138–9, 168, 170–1
    conflict with Moorish groups 139
    conquest of by Justinian 108, 138, 141–6, 148 177
    expeditions against 140–1
    overthrow of Hilderic by Gelimer 139
    revolts against Gelimer 141
    and Theoderic 74–5, 139
Vandal–Alans xvi, 168–9 *see also* Vandal Africa
Vandals 9, 79, 95, 101, 138
Venetia 166
Verdun, Treaty of (843) 262, 270
Verina (Leo I's widow) 36
Verona 162
Versailles, Gallery of Battles 218
Vetus Gallica 327
Via Egnatia 43, 46
Victor I, Pope 303
Victor II, Pope 384
Vidimer 6, 19, 30, 37
Vigilius 318–19
Vikings 266, 267, 268, 272
Visigoths xvi, 6, 9, 73–4, 75–7, 101, 211–12, 214, 238, 324, 325
    and Catholicism 324, 325, 328
    and church councils 328
    and Gaul 69–70
Vitalian, General 85
Vitalianus 126
Vitalius 160
Vouille, battle of 70

Waifer, Duke 231
Wala of Crobie, Abbot 357–8
West Francia 268–9, 270, 282, 376
Western Roman Empire 100–1
    dismantling of xii, xvii, 9, 101
Western Turks 180, 180–1, 203
    alliance with East Romans 196
    attacks on Persians 196

Western Turks (*cont.*)
    attempts by Justin II to mobilize against the
        Persians 191–2
    growth in power 191–2
Whole Body of the Law, The 128
Widin, Count 166
William the Conqueror 387
Wittigis 54, 156, 157–9, 164, 213
Wulfad of Bourges, Bishop 256

Yazdegerd, shah-in-shah 123, 125
Yeats, W. B. 250

Zachariah, Pope 230
Zeno, Emperor xvi, 22, 34, 35–6, 37, 41–2,
    84
    advance on Constantinople and return to
        power 37–8
    betrayal of Theoderic 40–2, 47
    conflict with Strabo 45–6
    deal with Strabo and Thracian Goths 44,
        45
    and Illus 48, 48–9
    plot against 45
    and Theoderic 39, 47, 48, 49–50